Eriq Oliver Neale et al.

D0515233

Windows®
Small Business
Server 2008

UNLEASHED

SAMS | 800 East 96th Street, Indianapolis, Indiana 46240 USA

Windows® Small Business Server 2008 Unleashed

Copyright © 2009 by Pearson Education, Inc

All rights reserved. No part of this book shall be reproduced, stored in a retrieval system, or transmitted by any means, electronic, mechanical, photocopying, recording, or otherwise, without written permission from the publisher. No patent liability is assumed with respect to the use of the information contained herein. Although every precaution has been taken in the preparation of this book, the publisher and authors assume no responsibility for errors or omissions. Nor is any liability assumed for damages resulting from the use of the information contained herein.

ISBN-13: 978-0-672-32957-9
ISBN-10: 0-672-32957-3

Library of Congress Cataloging-in-Publication Data

Neale, Eriq Oliver.
  Windows Small business server 2008 unleashed/Eriq Oliver Neale, et al.
    p. cm.
  ISBN 978-0-672-32957-9
  1. Microsoft Small business server. 2. Client/server computing.
  3. Computer networks–Management. I. Title.
  QA76.9.C55N432 2008
  004.6–dc22

                            2008041644

Printed in the United States of America

First Printing December 2008

Trademarks

All terms mentioned in this book that are known to be trademarks or service marks have been appropriately capitalized. Sams Publishing cannot attest to the accuracy of this information. Use of a term in this book should not be regarded as affecting the validity of any trademark or service mark.

Warning and Disclaimer

Every effort has been made to make this book as complete and as accurate as possible, but no warranty or fitness is implied. The information provided is on an "as is" basis. The authors and the publisher shall have neither liability nor responsibility to any person or entity with respect to any loss or damages arising from the information contained in this book.

Bulk Sales

Sams Publishing offers excellent discounts on this book when ordered in quantity for bulk purchases or special sales. For more information, please contact

U.S. Corporate and Government Sales
1-800-382-3419
corpsales@pearsontechgroup.com

For sales outside of the U.S., please contact

International Sales
international@pearson.com

Associate Publisher
Greg Wiegand

Acquisitions Editor
Loretta Yates

Development Editor
Todd Brakke

Managing Editor
Kristy Hart

Project Editor
Betsy Harris

Copy Editor
Sarah Kearns

Indexer
Brad Herriman

Proofreader
Williams Wood
Publishing

Technical Editors
Joshua Jones
Jeff Middleton

Publishing Coordinator
Cindy Teeters

Book Designer
Gary Adair

Senior Compositor
Jake McFarland

Contents at a Glance

Table of Contents

About the Lead Author

Eriq Oliver Neale is the owner of EON Consulting (http://www.eonconsulting.net), a small business technology consulting practice in Denton, Texas, and a partner in Third Tier (http://www.thirdtier.net), an organization that provides escalation support for IT organizations around the globe. He is an internationally-recognized Small Business Server expert, and has been awarded the Most Valuable Professional designation for Small Business Server since 2005. Eriq was the lead author for *Microsoft Small Business Server 2003 Unleashed*, and his other writing credits include contributions to *The Internet Unleashed 1997*, *Windows 2000 Server System Administrator's Handbook*, *E-mail Virus Protection Handbook*, and several books in both the 2000 and 2003 series MCSE exam preparation series.

Eriq is a 20+-year veteran in the IT industry, getting his start with DOS 2.1 and Novell 1.1. Over the course of his career, he has worked with various operating platforms (Microsoft, Apple, Novell, UNIX, Linux, VAX, AS/400), and he has focused on providing integration solutions for differing platforms. He has worked for small organizations, as well as Fortune 500 companies. Eriq's introduction to the Small Business Server product line came in a one-year stint supporting the product for Microsoft Product Support and Services in Las Colinas, Texas. Since then, he has been focusing on providing solutions to make running and supporting SBS easier.

In addition to writing, Eriq maintains two blogs, one technical (http://simultaneouspancakes.com/Lessons) and one business-focused (http://msmvps.com/blogs/onq), and hosts a technology-focused weekly Internet radio program for small business owners (http://www.eoncall.com). He speaks regularly at industry conferences and user groups on a variety of SBS-related topics.

Eriq is a native Texan and makes his permanent residence in Denton. He is married, and he and his wife have a menagerie of animals for children. When not writing, blogging, or speaking about technology, he can be found attending baseball and women's college basketball games, writing and recording music, or reading mysteries.

About the Contributors

Amy Babinchak has officially been in IT since 1994 and unofficially for 10 years prior. Like many IT professionals, she started out helping people around the office and in the college dorm to build and use computers. Her knowledge grew from MS-DOS and the early PC applications into a full-time career, when she made the switch from professional environmentalist working from grant to grant into the world of enterprise IT support. In her career, she has supported MS-DOS, Windows 3.11, Novell, and Mac OS, all the way on up to the current versions. Having started her career in enterprise support, Amy noticed that many small businesses were languishing with poorly conceived networks and lack of consistent support. Excessive travel coerced her into opening her own business in 2000.

Amy is now the President of Harbor Computer Services (http://www.harborcomputerservices.net) to serve small businesses in the metro Detroit area and a Managing Partner in Third Tier (http://www.thirdtier.net), which provides escalation support services to IT organizations around the world. Harbor Computer Services has been recognized as a Small Business Specialist (SBSC). Amy actively participates in two local user groups and several online newsgroups. She has spoken at local and international conferences on SBS technical and security topics, including SMB Nation and SMB Summit. Amy is a Forefront MVP and has contributed her technical writing skills to *Microsoft SBS 2003 Unleashed* and various web sites. When these things don't keep her busy enough, she provides remote support services for small business consultants using ISA. Amy firmly believes in maintaining work-life balance and has designed her company around this concept. She practices what she preaches by spending as much time as possible on her sailboat, cruising northern Lake Huron.

Steve Banks is a speaker, author, and consultant focusing on the small business space and Windows Small Business Server. With more than 17 years in computer technology fields, he is also the founder of the Puget Sound Small Business Server User Group and president of Banks Consulting Northwest Inc. Steve has collaborated with Microsoft, Forbes, and Hewlett-Packard on white papers and case studies focusing on TechNet, Small Business Server 2000, and Windows Small Business Server 2003.

Timothy Truman Barrett is cleverly disguised as a mild-mannered geek. He actually is a happily married man with his lovely wife of 18 years, Dayna. They have two wonderful daughters, Stephanie and Lauren, who are also lovely. And Tim hates monkeys. A lot.

Obsessed with building things from Lincoln Logs and Tinker Toys almost from birth, Tim finally got his first computer at age 15—an old used TRS-80 Model I. It had no instructions or manuals, but by trial and error, he figured out how to make it work. He also learned BASIC and spent the entire summer bugging his mother and six siblings by constantly showing them all the "cool" stuff he could do with it.

After studying computer aided drafting (CAD) and physics at Louisville Technical Institute, he went to work in the healthcare industry and then moved into information technology. As a veritable jack-of-all-trades, Tim has worked with just about everything: sewing machines, table saws, X-ray machines, IBM mainframes, phone systems, servers, PCs, and the occasional backhoe.

At age 39, Tim is currently a Microsoft Certified Professional, a Microsoft Small Business Specialist, Microsoft SBS MVP, and the founder of the Kentucky Small Business Server User Group (KYSBSUG). His motto is, "No Geek Left Behind." He also has strong religious values as one of Jehovah's Witnesses.

Susan Bradley blogs at www.sbsdiva.com (http://www.sbsdiva.com) and writes on patch management issues for Brian Livingston's *Windows Secrets* newsletter. In addition to being one of the writers on this book and *Windows Small Business Server 2003 Unleashed* with Eriq Neale, she has been a contributing author to the *Windows Server 2008 Security Resource Kit*, and she has been a contributing author for Harry Brelsford's *SBS 2003 Best Practices* book.

Dean Calvert is owner and managing director of Adelaide-based Calvert Technologies (www.calvert.net.au), a Microsoft Gold Certified Partner, and South Australia's first Small Business Specialist. For more than 13 years, Calvert Technologies has been one of Adelaide's leading providers of IT solutions and services in the SMB market. Dean has presented at SMB Nation (Seattle and Redmond), Microsoft ANZ Partner Conference (Sunshine Coast), Microsoft Worldwide Partner Conference (Boston and Denver), and TechEd (Gold Coast and Sydney). He often works with Microsoft to present at partner and customer events throughout Australia. In October 2004 Dean became a Microsoft MVP (SBS) and was selected as Australia's first Small Business Specialist Community Partner Area Lead for the 2007–2008 year. Dean also facilitates the Adelaide SBS Users Group (www.sbsusers.net) which has been running since July 2003.

Dean is extremely fortunate to be the husband of Vivienne and father of Reece and Brittany, who regularly pull him away from his computer to show him what life really is all about.

Cris Hanna, BS, SBS-MVP, is the only remaining original SBS MVP, first recognized by Microsoft in 1997. Cris holds a Bachelor of Science in Computer Information Systems and in Management from Park University.

Cris is the owner and principal consultant of Computing Possibilities Unlimited in Belleville, IL and focuses on Small Business Customers and consumer support. With over 20 years experience in IT, ranging from enterprise to single users, you can typically find Cris regularly posting in the Microsoft Public Newsgroups specifically focused on Small Business Server.

Cris is the founder of the St. Louis area Small Business Solutions Group, made up of Microsoft Partners who focus on providing software and services to small business.

Kevin James is a solutions architect with more than 15 years of IT consulting experience in Microsoft technologies. He provides services and solutions to large international corporations and small business entities alike through organizations like Microsoft Consulting, HP Services, and his own consulting company. Kevin James is now in his second consecutive year as a Microsoft Small Business Server Most Valuable Professional award recipient.

Jeff Middleton is well recognized worldwide in the Microsoft Small Business Server (SBS) community, known as a speaker, author, advisor, and technical community leader. Microsoft has awarded him each year since 1999 with the prestigious Small Business Server Most Valuable Professional recognition.

Based upon 20 years of experience as a consultant and system integrator in small business and vertical market applications, he's operated his own business located in New Orleans since 1990. Jeff's name is now synonymous with Swing Migration, the worldwide SMB consultant's choice of methodology for SBS Server replacement. He founded SBSmigration.com in 2004, providing a technical mentor and training product as a project consultant to consultants. His work is both published and cited in books and trade journals.

As an expert in disaster recovery, domain migration, and a full-range of topics on the SBS and Windows platforms, Jeff travels constantly as a popular speaker. He has presented at conferences internationally including the Microsoft Partner Program, Tech Ed, SMBTN, ITA, and SMB Nation, as well as lending his support in person as a guest speaker to more than 50 local IT Pro groups of all sizes in North America, Australia, and Europe. Starting in 2007, he launched the SBSmigration.com IT Pro Conference held annually during May in New Orleans, offering a unique discussion forum for experts in SMB business and technology.

David Shackelford works for himself as an instructor and gun-for-hire for Exchange, Windows Server, and SBS-related projects. He plans deployments and migrations, conducts audits, and troubleshoots Exchange and SBS problems around the world, all remotely from his office in Olympia, WA. He is associated with CoopLink Ltd, a Microsoft Gold Partner, where he serves as the network architect and project planner. David actively participates on the technical forums at Tek-Tips.com and other random places where Exchange and SBS are being discussed, and he authored a TrainSignal video course on Exchange 2007. He has been awarded the Microsoft MVP award for his contributions to the Exchange community every year since 2004, and keeps a close involvement with the SBS production cycle and program group.

Kevin Weilbacher, SBS-MVP, is a small business consultant in the Tampa, Florida area, and is involved with the Tampa Bay SBS User group. He has worked with the Microsoft SBS Server product for eight years, and was first selected as a Microsoft SBS MVP in 2004. He has managed IT departments in the automobile, healthcare, and financial industries, and speaks on the topics of SBS and small business issues, especially security and compliance, at both the local and national levels.

Dedication

This book is dedicated to the small business IT professionals around the world. Whether you are a single-person firm or part of a larger organization, a relative newcomer to the profession or a seasoned veteran of the industry, the SBS 2008 product, and thus this book, would not be possible without you. Your efforts are helping keep small businesses alive, and hopefully this book will help do the same for you.

Acknowledgments

Anyone who has spent any amount of time working with SBS has come to know the community that exists in support of the product. This community extends well beyond the reach of Microsoft and is championed by the SBS MVPs (Most Valuable Professionals). This book is for the SBS community, by the SBS community. The individuals who have contributed to this book are consultants, MVPs, and former PSS (Product Support Service) engineers who share one key trait—they are evangelists for the Small Business Server product and want everyone who works with this product to be successful with it.

Work on this book was a massive undertaking, dating all the way back to November 2006. Most of the contributors to the book have been working with SBS 2008 since the first test builds were made available outside the development team. Since that first load, we have seen the product undergo some significant changes, and as a result, the book did as well. Writing against a moving target, a product that was essentially still being developed as we were going back and editing our first drafts of the chapters, is not an easy task. As such, there are a number of people who the contributors would like to acknowledge and thank for their assistance with this project.

Eriq Neale would like to start by thanking those who collaborated on this book for their contributions and efforts:

- ▶ Amy Babinchak and Susan Bradley, who jumped in on the project in its early stages and took on the lion's share of the chapters. Both picked up different topics from their contributions to the *SBS 2003 Unleashed* book and pushed their individual envelopes to learn the material well enough to present it in book form. I can't thank them enough for taking on the load that I simply could not commit to this time around.

- Tim Barrett for reprising his role in the 2008 book. I know the last year has had some significant challenges for you, and I greatly appreciate your commitment to the project.

- Jeff Middleton for his insight, guidance, and technical review of the material. Jeff worked with me as I was formulating the direction I wanted the book to take, and he helped to keep me on track as we went through the development of the book. Jeff's understanding of the product and the community has helped to keep this book focused on the correct goals. Thank you for your counsel and your honesty!

- Dean Calvert, Cris Hanna, Kevin James, David Shackelford, and Kevin Weilbacher for jumping on board late in the production cycle. Each of these individuals were willing to come into the process mid-cycle without the benefit of the conference calls and mailing list discussions that helped to shape the form of the book. Their readiness and enthusiasm are appreciated more than they will ever know.

I also worked with a number of people at Microsoft while developing the book, and several of those individuals deserve special recognition:

- Dean Paron, Microsoft Program Manager for SBS 2008, for taking a great deal of time out of his incredibly busy schedule to answer questions the best he could at the times I asked them. Dean was willing to work with us to gain better access to some of the resources behind the product so we could come out with the best book possible about the software. Thank you for being so understanding of our deadlines while juggling your own!

- Terri Schmidt, Microsoft Content Publishing Manager, for working with me on the overall outline and content flow of the book. By sharing the approach that MS was taking with their own documentation, Terri allowed us the opportunity to try to "fill in the gaps" for those areas that would not get covered in the initial documentation that Microsoft is developing for the product.

- Chris Almida, Microsoft Program Manager, for working with me on the migration process. Chris was willing to work with me at all times of day and weekend to troubleshoot and clear up aspects of the process that turned into the Advanced Setup chapter. He went above and beyond in being accessible for assistance.

- Becky Ochs, Microsoft Program Manager, for her insight and assistance with the answer file and other setup issues. The Advanced Setup chapter really came as a result of extended discussions with Becky.

- Sean Daniel, Microsoft Program Manager, for all his assistance in the SBS 2008 beta newsgroups and other offline assistance. Sean was instrumental in helping direct resources as we were debugging the initial releases of the software and helped us keep on our toes as components changed during the development.

- Damian Leibaschoff, Chris Puckett, and James Frederickson, Microsoft Customer Service and Support Engineers, for answering technical questions on a regular basis throughout the testing process.

I could not wrap up the listing of Microsoft resources without a specific mention of Kevin Beares, Microsoft Community Lead, for all the assistance he provided through the process. Kevin worked with me countless times as I was asking for dates, access to software, and access to resources to try to make the writing process easier and more focused for the author team. Kevin helped make sure we had introductions to appropriate resources within the team, and generally spent a lot of time working with me when I'm sure he would rather have been dealing with other issues. Kevin is a huge asset to the SBS community, and we are all better off for his efforts!

I need to thank Loretta Yates, our Acquisitions Editor, for all her time and patience over the last two years as we took this project from a nice idea into a finished product. Loretta stuck with us through shifts in the product release schedule, changes in the author team, and all the other things that make her job a challenge. She never had a negative word for us about the project and was very supportive as we went through numerous transitions over the last year.

I also have to thank my peers in the MVP community, whether they carry the SBS designation or another award group. This is an incredibly insightful and passionate group of people, and I would not be where I am today without the interaction I've been fortunate to have with them. I am continually in awe of what you do individually and as a group. You guys (and gals) rock!

Finally, I want to thank my amazing wife, Anna, for all the sacrifices she made while I was working on this project. I spent several months straight working late nights and weekends to get this project done, and without her understanding and support, I would have called it quits a long time ago. Now that we have this behind us, hopefully we can get back to something resembling a normal life, whatever that means. Thank you for putting up with me through all of this, I could never have done it without you!

David Shackelford would like to thank his wife, Heather, for putting up with the cash flow problems that every authoring project creates (these are always labors of love), and to the other Exchange MVPs for graciously clarifying several subjects for him.

Susan Bradley would like to send kudos to Eriq Neale who once again pulled this off. In addition she would like to thank all the great SBS 2008 beta testers that spent their time and energy on beta testing. She would like to say a special thanks to Kevin James and the rest of the SBS MVPs who do the hard work of keeping an eye on SBS boxes around the world.

We Want to Hear from You!

As the reader of this book, *you* are our most important critic and commentator. We value your opinion and want to know what we're doing right, what we could do better, what areas you'd like to see us publish in, and any other words of wisdom you're willing to pass our way.

You can email or write me directly to let me know what you did or didn't like about this book—as well as what we can do to make our books stronger.

Please note that I cannot help you with technical problems related to the topic of this book, and that due to the high volume of mail I receive, I might not be able to reply to every message.

When you write, please be sure to include this book's title and author as well as your name and phone or e-mail address. I will carefully review your comments and share them with the author and editors who worked on the book.

E-mail: feedback@samspublishing.com

Mail: Greg Wiegand
            Associate Publisher
            Sams Publishing
            800 East 96th Street
            Indianapolis, IN 46240 USA

Reader Services

Visit our web site and register this book at informit.com/register for convenient access to any updates, downloads, or errata that might be available for this book.

Foreword

By Jeff Middleton

It's my pleasure to offer this brief introduction to *Small Business Server 2008 Unleashed*, an introduction that provides some helpful perspective about four topics: SBS 2008, this book, the team of authors, and the extensive worldwide community of IT professionals who use SBS. I think you will see the connection and opportunity for you very quickly.

Microsoft Small Business Server 2008 takes over the flagship designation of an extremely popular server brand. SBS is an efficient product concept that Microsoft has now refined over several releases in the last 11 years. Based upon the integration and value established in the SBS 2003 release five years ago, the SBS suite has effectively defined the standard of "designed for SMB" for a server products bundle. As you may already know, or otherwise will learn from this book, SBS 2008 introduces a second server configuration bundle for the first time, establishing a one-server standard edition and two-server premium edition. This provides a clear signal that Microsoft considers SBS 2008 to be a gateway to larger-scale deployments, as well as recognizing that even small SMB operations are a candidate for more than just a single server solution.

If you are new to the SBS platform, you will find that it is designed as a niche market product. It establishes a foundation for complementary products, and attracts alignment of services and service providers who know and quite literally love the product. The history of SBS has been periodically plagued by disconnected criticisms that "SBS is too limited," or "SBS is overkill," or "SBS has too many constraints." I say "disconnected" because a loyal community of successful, skilled, and enthusiastic advocates continue to demonstrate the value by example. It is a powerful tool that enables you to deliver a specific value: optimizing the management of a robust set of tools for a small business.

SBS provides a sweet spot wherein the scale, flexibility, and ingenuity of design are most deeply enriched. I routinely describe "it's not the number of seats that matters, it's how you leverage the overall business with it." SBS servers make an ideal catalyst for a small business, a focal point as a technology platform, plus a shrewd productivity growth asset as well. Naturally, a business may, over time, evolve out of the center of the ideal fit, scale, or return on value and gravitate toward the edges. SBS then becomes either a step-stone gateway or an integral building block to extend. It's your choice. You can enrich your investment with an SBS best by being informed about what an SBS server can do well and how to optimize it. Approaching this product without the benefit of enjoying the advice of experience contained in this book makes little sense, and that leads me to highlight the leverage offered both directly within this book and the perspective you will gain.

As your advisors and guides into SBS 2008, the author team is quite in tune and experienced with the SBS product line, both past and present. The writing team's efforts focus upon what you are most likely to need for the central value of the product based on their experiences. There's a depth of coverage for the essential elements across the feature set, plus valuable perspective as orientation to topics and issues best addressed in a specialized application or technology reference dedicated to that subject.

Returning as lead author for this edition of *SBS Unleashed*, Eriq Neale is notable for his perspective currently as an independent SBS consultant, as well as a former member of the Microsoft Product Support Services (now CSS) SBS team. Take a further glance across the author team credits, and you may notice the Microsoft award recognition of Most Valuable Professionals (MVPs). This tells you two things: They are independent and experienced voices who don't work for Microsoft, yet they do obtain a depth of engagement with the product teams. As a full disclosure, I too participated on a technical edit team for this title, and I can count each and every one of the authors as a friend and my respected colleague.

I can attest firsthand that the author team presents a wealth of experience. It's born of their individual hard work with SMB solutions, SBS product applications, and also of professional investments in this industry. They are acknowledged leaders in the SMB community, an example of only a fraction of so many more professionals who are exchanging ideas on the Web, collaborating at conferences worldwide, via blogs and newsgroups, and even dedicated to professional development groups meeting in their local cities. You will find that the work of these authors, once introduced here, resonates and melds into a global set of resources of continuing value. I know from my personal experience the enrichment that comes from joining in these conversations. It's an essential resource to me.

Over the years in my career, I have known too many people—and some time back, even myself included—who struggled in SMB consulting work simply for lack of guidance by an experienced peer or mentor. There's a wealth of information, education, partnerships, and even channel opportunities that orbit this product. I have now come to know so many more people, literally thousands of successful professionals, who are engaged in using, deploying, managing, or selling products that bind with SBS. They gained an understanding of the product, and then generally have one more thing in common: They remain well informed because they reached out and explored the connected space.

I encourage you to tap into this global perspective. Begin a journey as you digest the value in this book as your starting point, but continue to explore beyond just mousing around inside the SBS product itself. With little effort, you will likely find a continuing dialog with all of us, and many more who share a passion for SBS and the small business world in SMB. Treat this book and the authors listed as a valuable jazz collection that you can explore even further if you trace the musicians and music. It may surprise you to find out you are just a step away from a problem resolution, just following the footsteps of a peer on the same trail. So much time spent on search engines is lost to the wrong keywords. Search for the people, not just the product, find the nexus of communication in SMB and SBS topics, and then jump into the conversation!

When offered the opportunity to work as a technical editor for this book, my agreement was instantaneous. The simple reason is that I have looked forward year after year to reading and learning for myself what these folks have to say. What a pleasure it is to have their thoughts as a reference as the new journey begins with SBS 2008!

Introduction

Whether you have been working with the Small Business Server product line for years or are seeing an SBS server for the first time, you will find that Small Business Server 2008 is not like many other Microsoft products. Like its predecessors, SBS 2008 combines core Microsoft technologies such as Exchange, SharePoint, and IIS, all on the same box, but SBS 2008 goes beyond just providing the glue that allows those tools to interact seamlessly. And that is where the learning curve comes in.

This book has been written to help the reader shorten the learning curve for SBS 2008. Readers who have never touched a Small Business Server before may be mystified by all the wizards and consoles and tools that are not found on "standard" Microsoft server products. Readers who have a solid working knowledge of previous SBS versions will recognize many of the elements of previous versions in SBS 2008, but those elements have changed drastically in this edition. To that end, the contributors for this book have worked to present SBS 2008 in such a way that the qualified consultant can quickly learn about the product as he or she first starts to work with it, as well as using the book as a reference guide for ongoing support of SBS 2008 after initial installation.

Whether SBS 2008 will be a big seller when it hits the streets in Fall 2008 or not remains to be seen. Regardless of how many units Microsoft sells in the first six months of the product life, the author team believes that any consultant who plans to provide support for SBS 2008 should start becoming comfortable with the product sooner rather than later. To help make that goal a reality, the contributors have worked to bring this book to print as close to the release of the product as possible.

One element that is not included in this book is a discussion of the use of virtualization technology in and around an SBS 2008 installation. This was a conscious decision on the part of the development team for several reasons. Most importantly, the virtualization story provided by Microsoft was not announced until after the product was released to manufacturing, and the author team did not feel that there was enough time to fully develop content related to virtualization, given the very short amount of time between RTM and the release of the book. Rather than present an incomplete, or worse, incorrect, story related to virtualization, the team opted to wait for the best practices of virtualization to develop in the industry. That said, there will be content related to virtualization in and around SBS 2008 posted to the book's web site as the process and understanding matures. Quite honestly, the story surrounding virtualization and SBS may not even be fully complete by the time this book hits the shelves.

With changes in the licensing model and enforcement, the inclusion of multiple server OS licenses in the Premium Edition, the ability to split the bundled SQL software on a separate server, and the updates to the core technologies, there is much to learn about SBS 2008. The contributors hope that the material you find in the remaining pages of this book will help you quickly improve your ability to support the SBS 2008 product and grow your practice at the same time.

Book Overview

- ▶ Part 1, "Introduction and Setup," details the history of the product and how to plan for and install an SBS 2008 server.

- ▶ Part 2, "Managing Network and Web Configuration," focuses on the networking technologies of SBS, including DHCP, DNS, IIS, remote access, and VPN, as well as discussing SharePoint and Companyweb.

- ▶ Part 3, "Managing E-Mail," focuses on the e-mail features of SBS at the client and server level and covers Exchange disaster recovery issues as well.

- ▶ Part 4, "Managing Client Connectivity," details the management of clients in the SBS network and covers incorporating Macintosh clients and setting up Terminal Services.

- ▶ Part 5, "Managing Security and System Health," takes an in-depth look at the maintenance side of SBS, including the monitoring and reporting tools, backups, group policy, and keeping systems up to date with security patches.

- ▶ Part 6, "Beyond SBS 2008," covers two of the newer technologies incorporated into SBS 2008, IPv6 and PowerShell, as well as covering advanced topics for setup.

PART 1

Introduction and Setup

IN THIS PART

Welcome to Small Business Server 2008

Midway through 2008, Microsoft announced the release of the latest edition to the Small Business Server family, SBS 2008. The product continues in the tradition of earlier versions of Small Business Server, combining many of Microsoft's premier technologies in an installation that can run on a single server, allowing small businesses with limited budgets to have access to the same technologies that larger businesses use to run their operations. Incorporating Windows Server 2008, Exchange Server 2007, Windows SharePoint Services 3.0, and Windows Server Update Service 3.0, SBS 2008 provides a solid technology foundation for businesses of 5–75 employees around the world.

In addition to the businesses that have been looking forward to the release of SBS 2008, IT professionals around the globe have been anxiously awaiting the release as well. Thousands of technology consultants have built businesses around deploying and supporting Small Business Server products, and they are looking forward to the opportunities awaiting them with new installations and migrations in the coming months and years. This book is geared toward those IT professionals who are new to the SBS 2008 product, but come from backgrounds supporting previous versions of SBS or any of the core technologies in larger environments.

History of the SBS Product

SBS 2008, known by its code name Cougar through its years in the development process, is the latest release of an all-in-one product that, quite frankly, breaks many of the "rules" that Microsoft has established for the products that comprise SBS. Traditionally, Microsoft's best practice has been to have a separate server for each of the key technologies in SBS. In other words, Exchange should not be installed on the main Domain Controller server, and ISA should not be installed on a Domain Controller at all. But the product has been successfully sidestepping those rules for over ten years, combining messaging, directory services, and security tools into a single, affordable solution for small businesses. To understand how the product got to where it is today, a brief history of the development of the product follows.

BackOffice Small Business Server 4.0

In 1997, Microsoft adopted a BackOffice Products suite family name, which was established and better known for a three-server license suite called BackOffice Server 4.0. The family name designated an aggressively priced product bundle combining Enterprise class server applications as a "solution" built on top of Windows NT Server 4.0. Whereas "full" BackOffice (as the three-server suite was known then) was a modestly integrated bundle of CDs, SBS 4.0 was a very ambitious product concept that fully integrated the same diverse suite of products all into one server. By combining Windows NT, Exchange Server 5.0, SQL Server 6.5, Proxy Server 1.0, and Internet Information Server 3.0 onto a single box, Microsoft hoped to challenge Novell for an entry-level server marketplace that, perhaps, had not yet even been born. Shared modem and fax services and a POP3 connector for Exchange were introduced with the product as well, a signal that small business customers needed familiar problems solved as part of the solution suite.

SBS 4.0, as it came to be known, was limited to a maximum of 25 users, and had some initial deployment issues. Only Windows 95 and NT clients could connect (not Windows 98), and many of the wizards that handled management of the server would routinely crash. But the release of SBS 4.0a (effectively SBS 4.0 SP1) addressed many of these issues by including Internet Explorer 4.01 for both the server and the clients, and the management tools were updated to work with the added functionality in IE 4.01.

For the first time, small businesses were able to use the same tools that larger companies used for messaging, security, and application support. Outlook 97 enabled employees to have their e-mail, calendar, and contacts stored in a central, protected location, and users could easily share calendar and contact information through the Exchange server. Proxy Server helped increase Internet performance by caching Internet traffic on the server for commonly-accessed web sites. SQL Server 6.5 allowed businesses to look at using a wider variety of line-of-business applications that relied on SQL as a back end, because they did not have to take on the cost of a separate SQL Server license with the product.

The BackOffice product family also introduced the unified Client Access License (CAL) concept that continues with the SBS product today. Instead of purchasing a separate CAL for each of the Windows, Exchange, SQL, and Proxy Server components, SBS customers purchased a single CAL per seat. The unified CAL allows access to each of the technologies in the SBS deployment, and the CAL was (and remains in current versions) priced at a lower cost than purchasing each of the other CALs individually. For this reason, SBS is established as the longest-standing product from Microsoft with a technology enforced CAL license manager.

BackOffice Small Business Server 4.5

Microsoft released SBS 4.5 in May of 1999. Still based on Windows NT 4, SBS 4.5 included significant updates to the other technologies bundled with the previous version. Exchange 5.5, IIS 4.0, Proxy Server 2.0, and SQL Server 7.0 rounded out the component updates. For the client side, SBS 4.5 bundled Internet Explorer 5.0 and Outlook 2000, and included FrontPage 2000 as a tool to modify the web content hosted on the SBS server. Another significant change was the increase of users from 25 to 50.

Recognizing that the communications landscape was changing, the Internet Connection Wizard in SBS 4.5 added support for routers and direct Internet connections in addition to modem support. Proxy Server 2.0 offered some control and protection from the Internet, now that many SBS servers would be connected to the Internet full-time instead of connecting as needed.

New management services were added to enhance the ability of the server to e-mail or fax system status information to designated recipients. The ability to select different locations for shared folder paths was also introduced in this version.

The growth and maturity of the product gave the marketplace reason to embrace the product line for use in small businesses and an anticipation of future versions to see what new functionality would be added.

Microsoft Small Business Server 2000

Released in February of 2001, SBS 2000 was a significant departure from its SBS predecessors. In more than just the change of the name (shedding the cumbersome BackOffice label), Microsoft stopped development of the "full-BackOffice Suite" following BackOffice 2000 because SBS 2000 was successfully able to define an identity uniquely and specifically oriented to the small business marketplace and technology goals.

Based on Windows 2000, which introduced Active Directory to the SBS product line, the entire component product line was updated to include the current technologies of the time. With SBS 2000, Microsoft developed the model that future builds of SBS would follow. Once the core operating system was released, the SBS team followed the OS release by about six months, making sure that the available technologies all worked together, in harmony, on the same box. SBS 2000 included Exchange 2000, IIS 5.0, SQL Server 2000, and the new ISA Server 2000. Client tools included IE 5.0, Outlook 2000, and FrontPage 2000, the same as SBS 4.5. The maximum number of users remained the same.

System status information collection and reporting also significantly improved in SBS 2000. Health Monitor was better able to collect and report status information, giving system administrators a better way to keep tabs on the health of a server.

Another significant introduction to the product line with SBS 2000 was the ability to run Terminal Server in Application Mode on the SBS 2000 server itself. This enabled users to remotely connect to the network and run applications on the server just like they would on their workstations.

Many in the community started to question the overall security of the server with SBS 2000, given the ability for "normal" users to log in on the server via Terminal Services, and that the server could be directly connected to the Internet, even with ISA 2000 acting as the gateway. Some of these security concerns would start to become factors in the development of future versions of SBS.

Microsoft Small Business Server 2003

Released in October of 2003, SBS 2003 gained worldwide notoriety almost immediately. Built on Windows Server 2003, SBS 2003 also included Exchange 2003, IIS 6.0, and Windows SharePoint Services 2.0. Client technologies included Internet Explorer 6.0 and Outlook 2003. A new web technology, the Remote Web Workplace, was introduced with SBS 2003, not available in any other Microsoft product, and continues to be one of the most sought-after technologies from Microsoft. The maximum user limit was raised to 75 from 50, meaning that SBS could be used in even larger organizations, particularly if you consider agile use of a combined mix of "per seat" and "per device" licensing, which SBS 2003 adopted.

SBS 2003 also introduced editions of the product, now available in Standard and Premium Editions. SBS 2003 Premium included all the technologies in Standard, plus SQL 2000, ISA 2000, and FrontPage 2003. The price for Premium Edition remained very close to the historical pricing. Yet a key factor in the dramatic adoption of SBS 2003 was the significantly lower price, placing the Standard Edition at half the cost of Premium Edition, and well below the price of just Windows 2003 Server itself.

Despite all the improvements in the product, several aspects of the product generated discord in the SBS reseller community. Many VARs and product users were upset about the split of the product into two editions, especially because they were going to be paying significantly more to keep all the same functionality that they had with SBS 2000. For security reasons, SBS 2003 also removed the Terminal Server in Application Mode functionality, intending for that functionality to be replaced by the Remote Web Workplace's ability to connect to workstations inside the network from offsite. SBS 2003 had also hoped to ship with updated versions of both SQL and ISA, but product delays kept both of those updates out of the initial release. ISA 2004 was later included as a no-cost upgrade for owners of the Premium Edition when SBS 2003 Service Pack 1 was released in July of 2005. SQL 2005 Workgroup Edition was included as part of the Premium Edition of SBS 2003 R2, which was released in July of 2006.

Still, SBS 2003 was very well received by the small business community, and product sales reflected that. The security improvements in the underlying technologies made SBS 2003 a very stable product, which was needed, given the five-year gap until the next major release of SBS. The product contained greatly improved management tools, aimed at giving the business owner, who might not have a technical background, the ability to perform basic ongoing maintenance on the server. Partnering with OEM vendors, the "15-minute" install was developed and marketed for the product, again appealing to the do-it-yourself business owner who could buy a server from a vendor with SBS 2003 pre-loaded and have a working network after answering a few simple questions during the scripted setup process.

Essential Server Solution Family

On February 20, 2008, Microsoft announced the Essential Server Solution family of products, which includes Small Business Server 2008. The other product announced in the family was the return of a "big brother" to SBS, Essential Business Server 2008. Unlike the birth of SBS as a scaled-down "baby-BackOffice" server, EBS 2008 is building upon the concepts proven in the evolution of SBS, extended and adapted for the demands of a medium-sized business. EBS 2008 is a three- or four-server solution that can be managed and maintained using a similar set of deployment and administration wizards, similar to the SBS product. EBS 2008 splits the Exchange 2007 services onto a dedicated server, and includes an Edge server that runs a special version of ISA to provide protection from the Internet. EBS also has Standard and Premium Editions, with the Premium Edition including the ability to run SQL Server 2008 on a fourth server on the network. EBS therefore provides a suite of applications bundled with the related Windows 2008 Server licenses for the designated number of servers.

The basic framework of SBS 2008 was also released on that date, including the move of SBS from the traditional single-server solution to an optional two-server license implementation with the Premium Edition. Table 1.1 details the differences between SBS 2008 Standard and Premium Editions.

TABLE 1.1   SBS 2008 Editions

Component	Standard	Premium
Windows Server 2008	✓	✓
Exchange Server 2007	✓	✓
Windows SharePoint Services 3.0	✓	✓
Forefront Security for Exchange	✓	✓
Windows Live OneCare for Server	✓	✓
Second copy of Windows Server 2008		✓
SQL 2008 Standard Edition		✓

Features of SBS 2008

Like its predecessors, SBS 2008 is built on the current Windows Server operating system (2008), and includes many of the components of its older siblings. The following sections detail the tools and technologies that SBS 2008 includes.

Communication

Undoubtedly, one of the biggest selling points in the history of SBS has been the inclusion of Exchange Server, and SBS 2008 is no different. Exchange Server 2007 SP1 not only gives SBS 2008 enterprise-quality e-mail and shared contacts and calendaring, but the built-in and pre-configured Office Outlook Web Access also gives remote users secure access to their mailbox on the server. SBS 2008 is pre-configured to support Windows Mobile 5 and 6 devices.

Small businesses that have large amounts of mail data to store will welcome the larger storage capacities provided with Exchange Server 2007. With the ability to store mail on multiple mail stores and with a complete removal of store size restrictions, heavy e-mail users have only to worry about storage and backup capacity and not about artificial limits imposed for sales and licensing reasons.

The POP3 Connector for Exchange lives on in SBS 2008, giving businesses the opportunity to transition their hosted e-mail solution to SBS 2008 in a controlled manner. That said, the POP3 Connector for Exchange is still intended to be a transitional tool and not a permanent solution. With that goal in mind, SBS 2008 includes tools to make it easier to enable direct e-mail delivery to the server instead of pulling messages into Exchange from an externally-hosted POP3 server.

New connection tools make it easier to set up Internet connectivity for both incoming and outgoing connections. Businesses can now use these tools to easily register their own public domain names and manage public DNS records so the SBS server is easily accessible from across the Internet for e-mail delivery and remote access.

Changes from SBS 2003—Outlook Client Licenses

SBS 2008 is the first version of SBS that does not include a license for the Outlook mail client with the SBS Client Access License. This is not due to a change in the SBS approach to licensing, but a change in Exchange Server 2007 licensing.

Previous versions of Exchange included the Outlook license in the Exchange CAL. However, because many employees were purchasing Office licenses for their systems, which come with a license for Outlook, they were really paying twice for the same Outlook license—once in Office, and once in the Exchange CAL.

So, Exchange Server 2007 has removed the Outlook license from the CAL to avoid this perceived "double billing" for Outlook. It is now expected that those users running Office already have Outlook (or Entourage in Mac Office) to connect to Exchange, and those who don't will find that the improved Office Outlook Web Access interface gives most users the same functionality as the Outlook client.

SBS 2008 also still includes the Shared Fax service. The service enables businesses to connect a fax modem to the SBS server and store incoming faxes in a folder on the server, in SharePoint, or in Exchange. Workstations can also connect to the shared fax printer and send faxes directly from applications on the workstation.

Collaboration

The inclusion of SharePoint Services 2.0 in SBS 2003 significantly increased the product's value as a true collaboration tool, and SBS 2008 continues that tradition. SBS 2008 includes SharePoint Services 3.0, along with the customized initial installation known as

Companyweb. With the increased functionality in WSS 3.0, users running Office 2007 can access files in the SharePoint document libraries from within the Open and Save dialogs, as though the documents were stored on the local disk or on a network file share. But SharePoint includes many more features, including a number of new web parts that make it a solid foundation for shared workflow access for both internal and external users.

System administrators can still create and protect shared folders on the server, making use of the native Windows Server 2008 sharing and security tools. SBS 2008 creates a new Public shared folder, where administrators can place documents and make them available for all users of the network, local or remote.

A new design for the Remote Web Workplace also makes it easier for remote users, through a web browser, to access data on the server, including files stored on shares on the server. Administrators will appreciate the new restrictions that can be placed on users so that they can see only specific workstations to connect to through the Remote Web Workplace.

Protection

Security continues to be an issue that businesses of all sizes struggle to manage, but small businesses probably struggle more than their larger counterparts. SBS 2008 continues the move toward better security with a number of improved and new features.

Protecting user data remains a critical function, and SBS 2008 provides several avenues to protect workstation and user data. Through Group Policy, local folders on the workstation can be redirected and saved on the server. SBS 2003 was able to redirect the My Documents folder, and SBS 2008 is able to redirect the Desktop and Start Menu folders to the server as well.

Server backup in SBS 2008 differs from earlier versions, thanks to changes in Windows Server 2008. The native backup tools no longer support backing up to tape, and the ntbackup tool can only be used to restore from tape in SBS 2008. That said, the native tools now use imaging technology to aid in faster recovery of the server in case of a disaster. Still, it's likely that IT professionals will continue to use third-party backup solutions for the server, especially where backing up to tape is a business requirement.

SBS 2003 included a self-signed SSL certificate to help protect access to the web services at a time when purchasing third-party SSL certificates was still cost-prohibitive. SBS 2008 also provides a self-signed certificate, but it is initially generated as a root cert for a Certificate Authority that runs by default on SBS 2008. This enables administrators to create new self-signed certs for additional services without having to add those new certs to the trusted certificate list if the root certificate is already installed. But because there are instances where a self-signed certificate is just not sufficient, SBS 2008 provides a way to more easily manage the certificate request process; this makes it easier and more cost-effective to acquire and install a trusted certificate from third-party vendors. This allows Internet Explorer 7 to connect to the secured sites hosted on the SBS server without the confusing security warnings the browser displays when a self-signed certificate is used, even when the certificate has been installed correctly in the workstation's certificate store.

SBS 2008 now includes two malware protection tools to help guard the server and the mail system from unwanted problems. The Exchange server can be protected with the included one-year trial of Forefront Security for Exchange service that is pre-installed with SBS 2008. Because the Forefront subscription only provides protection for Exchange, an included one-year trial subscription for Windows Live OneCare for Server helps to protect the server file system. Both of these trials can be extended at the end of the initial trial period, or they can be removed and replaced with third-party solutions.

Changes from SBS 2003—Where Is ISA?

SBS 2008 does not include ISA in either edition of the product, and this change from previous versions has already caused a significant uproar in the community. But the architectural changes in Windows Server 2008, along with concerns about physically having a domain controller directly connected to the Internet—ISA or not—have removed ISA from the SBS 2008 product offering. A version of ISA is included in the Essential Business Server 2008 suite, just not in SBS 2008.

Essentially, SBS 2008 is out of the firewall business altogether, since Routing and Remote Access Services (RRAS) no longer functions in Windows 2008. So, businesses that had been running SBS as a firewall, with or without ISA, will have to adopt the new model of having a separate device sitting on the edge, either a business-class firewall/router device or some other edge solution.

Microsoft has a solution for those customers who purchased SBS 2003 with Software Assurance. As posted on the official SBS blog (http://blogs.technet.com/sbs/archive/2008/06/30/software-assurance-entitlement-for-sbs-2003-customers-upgrading-to-sbs-2008.aspx), customers who have a current Software Assurance subscription for their SBS 2003 server will receive a license for ISA 2006 and a separate license for Windows Server 2003 on which to run ISA 2006 (because ISA 2006 does not run on Windows Server 2008). These products can be run on a separate box at the edge of the network, and Microsoft has written a whitepaper (http://go.microsoft.com/fwlink/?LinkID=122167) on how to configure this ISA 2006 server for use in front of an SBS 2008 installation.

Expansion

As businesses attempt to expand by "thinking outside the box," SBS 2008 can help them by growing outside the box, literally. SBS 2008 Premium not only includes SQL 2008 Standard Edition, but it also includes a second copy of Windows Server 2008 to run on a second server. Although the idea behind the second server addresses giving SQL 2008 a separate box to run on for resource-heavy line-of-business applications based on SQL, the second server license can be used for any of a number of purposes. The second server could be a Terminal Server, a second domain controller, or even an edge server that could run ISA (when a version of ISA releases that will run on Windows Server 2008). The bottom line is that SBS 2008 Premium adds a second server license and effectively turns SBS 2008 Premium into a multi-server suite and not just a standalone server.

> **NOTE**
>
> As with previous versions of SBS, even with a second server in the SBS network, the core SBS technologies must be run on the primary SBS box. The SBS 2008 license prohibits splitting Exchange, Companyweb, and the other core SBS technologies off onto the second server.

Limitations of SBS 2008

SBS 2008, like its predecessors, is a limited product, given its price point and other factors. Those who have worked with previous versions of SBS are used to the limitations of the product, but those who are looking at SBS for the first time might not be aware of what the restrictions are or why they are in place.

> **What the SBS 2008 Limitations Are *Not***
>
> Many people who are not very familiar with the SBS product line have developed the misunderstanding about what the actual limitations of the product are. There has been a perception that SBS is built on watered-down versions of the core products. For example, the Exchange Server that is included with SBS is not "real" Exchange Server, or that the underlying Windows Server operating system is not "real" Windows Server.
>
> This has not been the case with previous SBS versions, and is definitely not the case with SBS 2008. The Exchange 2007 that bundles with SBS is the same Exchange 2007 Standard Edition that "regular" Windows networks can use. Windows Server 2008 that runs underneath SBS 2008 is the same Windows Server 2008 that was released in early 2008.
>
> As the next sections of the chapter indicate, there are some restrictions that have been placed on SBS 2008 that have it behave slightly differently than non-SBS versions of the components, but these restrictions have been placed on top of the core components that make up SBS. Microsoft did not build special versions of Exchange, Windows, SharePoint, and so on to include in SBS. The SBS development team took the standard tools and made adjustments to the deployment of these tools to meet with the restrictions needed for the product, but they did not go through and rewrite the core components to remove functionality in order to bundle them with SBS 2008.

Hardware Limitations

For the first time in the lifecycle of SBS, there are specific hardware requirements that are different for SBS than there would be for a regular Windows Server implementation. Historically, SBS has had the same general core hardware requirements as the version of

Windows Server that it was built on. Yes, SBS needed more RAM and more disk space at minimum than the published specs for Windows Server, but processor and other hardware minimums matched the core OS.

Not so in SBS 2008. Because of the requirements of Exchange 2007, SBS 2008 must run on a 64-bit platform despite the fact that Windows Server 2008 is capable of running on either 32-bit or 64-bit hardware. This is a fairly significant change in the product, and it means that, in many cases, existing SBS 2003 server deployments will not be able to run SBS 2008 on the current hardware, unless 64-bit–compliant hardware was purchased within a couple of years prior to the release of SBS 2008.

Software Limitations

Table 1.2 details some of the limitations SBS 2008 has with its core components.

TABLE 1.2   SBS 2008 Software Restrictions

Category	Restriction
Operating System	
Users/Devices	A maximum of 75 user and device licenses can be installed.
Active Directory	SBS 2008 must be the root of the Active Directory forest.
Active Directory	SBS 2008 cannot have any Active Directory Domain Trusts with other domains or forests.

Support for SBS 2008

Given its "kitchen sink" nature, SBS is and has been a difficult product to support. Not that the product is unwieldy or cantankerous, but there are so many differing technologies squeezed into a single server that it becomes difficult for a single person to know all the pieces in enough detail to be self-sufficient in supporting the product. When a box is up and running smoothly, not much regular maintenance is needed, which is by design. When things go wrong, however, even the top-notch support professionals can find themselves out of their league fairly quickly, given the right circumstances. ·

Fortunately, there are a number of resources that the support professional can turn to when he or she gets into one of these situations. The following are a few of the resources that the top-tier support professional should be familiar with.

Community Support

One of the greatest resources for SBS support is the worldwide SBS community. Thousands of support professionals who ply their craft in supporting small businesses have built one of the strongest user support communities for any Microsoft product. Through mailing lists, blogs, newsgroups, webcasts, radio programs, electronic discussion forums, and so on, these individuals give their knowledge and experience back to the community for the benefit of all.

One manifestation of this community spirit is in the large number of SBS user groups that exist around the world. Many large metropolitan areas have a user group, or maybe more than one, and some smaller areas do as well. Some groups have strong affiliations with Microsoft, some have affiliations with other professional organizations or vendors, and others are entirely self-sustaining.

As you move forward into the world of SBS 2008, look in your local area for an SBS user group, if you do not already belong to one. If there is not a group in your area, look to start one. Contact user group leaders to help you get information on how to start a group, or use one of the online group resources to get started. You can also start a blog and document some of the solutions you have run across as you get familiar with SBS 2008 in your client space. Join a mailing list and participate in the discussions, especially if you have expertise in a topic being discussed. By participating in the larger community, you might build contacts and relationships with others who may be able to help you out should you find yourself in a real jam.

Best Practice—Get Involved in the Community

Many small business technology consultants who have already made the effort to get involved in the community—either through a local user group or through participation in mailing lists, discussion groups, and so on—have found the benefits of being a part of the community. Reading their blogs or hearing them talk in other venues, you can get an idea of how powerful and useful community involvement can be.

The appendix provides a number of resources related to SBS 2008, including a section on community resources. If you are not already participating in the community, look to these resources to find ways of getting involved in local community activities or even starting your own!

Online Support

A number of web sites around the globe offer documentation or forums geared toward the SBS product space. Some even offer support for other support professionals. If you find that you are unable to locate a resolution to an issue you may be facing in the mailing lists or blogs space, joining one of these online support forums may help put you in touch with someone who has resolved your issue, or something similar. Some of these sites might have a subscription fee to access some of their content, but many offer free registration or open access to their services. In general, gaining access to these forums and resources before you need them is best.

The public SBS newsgroups also make an excellent support resource. Found at news://connectnews.microsoft.com/microsoft.connect.windows.server.sbs08, these forums are monitored by a large number of individuals, including Most Valuable Professionals (MVPs), who share their time and expertise to answer questions posted to the group. Microsoft employees monitor these groups as well, and some Microsoft support professionals respond to posts in the newsgroups.

Official Product Support

Of course, Microsoft also provides support for the SBS 2008 product, and there are a number of avenues for the support professional to get support from Microsoft. In addition to the traditional call for support line, Microsoft also has a web-based support offering that has a lower cost than phone support and can be used for less-critical support needs. Support professionals who are either Microsoft partners or work for a Microsoft partner can get access to the Partner newsgroups as well.

Summary

Although SBS 2008 is almost completely new under the hood, it follows in the tradition of its predecessors by bringing a complete set of business productivity tools at a competitive price for small businesses. Many of the IT professionals who are familiar with previous versions of SBS should have little trouble adapting to the new product, although there will be a significant learning curve for some of the updated and new technologies in SBS 2008. And now that the introductions are out of the way, it's time to start getting ready for SBS 2008!

CHAPTER 2

Planning for the SBS 2008 Deployment

Deploying Small Business Server 2008 into a client network is more involved than simply installing the software on a server and plugging it into the network. As such, when planning for an SBS 2008 installation, hardware requirements are not the only factors that need to be addressed. Merely running the SBS 2008 installation process and providing the correct network settings will not guarantee a successful deployment for a business.

There are two general categories of people who install SBS 2008—those who install it for their own use, and those who install on behalf of others. No matter which category you fall into, there are a number of preparatory steps you need to take prior to inserting the installation media and powering on the new server. This chapter covers the basic hardware guidelines for running an effective SBS 2008 server, as well as the other factors that need to be addressed prior to implementation.

Knowing the Client Base

Unfortunately, there are no hard and fast rules that you can use to determine what resources you need to implement an SBS 2008 server. The implementation needs depend on how the system will be used. An SBS 2008 server for a 20-person company that primarily uses the system for e-mail and file and print services may be configured very differently from a 10-person company that has high-volume line-of-business applications with a large SQL database that integrates with Exchange.

Getting to know the business needs and the day-to-day manner in which the employees operate will help you better plan the implementation of the SBS 2008 network. The following are some basic questions you will likely need to be answered. A more detailed examination of other aspects of the installation follows. Questions that should be asked before attempting an SBS installation include the following:

▸ How many users are in the organization?

▸ How many devices are in the organization?

▸ What is the geographic layout of the organization (one site, multiple sites, and so on)?

▸ What desktop technologies are being used (Windows XP, Windows 2000, Windows 98, Mac OS X, Mac OS 9, Linux, and so on)?

▸ What is the connection to the Internet?

▸ Does the organization have an existing domain name for the web?

▸ Does the organization have an existing e-mail domain name and provider?

▸ Does the organization have users who want to work remotely, either from home or while traveling for business?

▸ Does the organization want to restrict or track access to external web sites?

▸ How many printers are in the organization? How many of them need to be shared?

▸ Does the organization have a fax machine? Will the organization be using the fax services of SBS?

▸ Does the organization have or need a Terminal Server?

Understanding How the Server Will Be Used

With previous versions of SBS, everything was on one box, so the determination of how to build and configure that box was fairly straightforward. As long as you provided enough CPU power, RAM, and disk space to accommodate the business needs, you would be in pretty good shape.

With the second server option in SBS 2008 Premium, this planning gets a little more complex. In some cases, installing everything on one box may still be feasible, even if SQL is needed for a line-of-business application. In some cases, the ability to split SQL off to its own server gives greater performance for the database and the application that relies on it. In some cases, the business might have a need for deploying Terminal Services on the second server and not use SQL at all. The end result of this more complex set of possibilities is that the approach to determining appropriate resources levels becomes more complex as well.

As a result, this book can offer only general guidelines for the various configuration options for your SBS server. The information contained in this chapter focuses on the core components of SBS, Server 2008, Exchange 2007, SharePoint Services 3.0, WSUS 3.0, and so on, and not on any third-party applications or resources. If tools other than the core

SBS components will be installed on the main SBS server, you need to work with the vendor to determine the appropriate resources required to support those additions on the main server.

Planning for Correct Licensing

As with previous versions of SBS, SBS 2008 has some basic restrictions for how the server can be used in a network. The basic license for SBS requires that the core components reside on the SBS server. This means that Exchange, IIS, and SharePoint have to remain on the SBS server. Even though the Premium Edition provides a second server operating system, the SBS license prevents the core components from being installed on the second server. SQL is the exception to this rule, as the SQL software bundled with the Premium Edition can be installed on either server.

One common misunderstanding about the SBS product space relates to using more than one server in an SBS network. SBS has always allowed for additional servers to be present in the SBS network, even as Domain Controllers. The only restrictions about additional servers is that the SBS server must have all the core components installed on it, and the SBS server must hold the master roles for Active Directory. As long as those items are met, the SBS network can have as many additional member servers and Domain Controllers as is reasonable for a small network. Many consultants have installed additional servers in SBS networks to keep line-of-business applications off the SBS server, and the inclusion of the second server OS license in the Premium Edition of SBS 2008 recognizes the practicality of this approach.

Access to the SBS 2008 server is granted through a Client Access License, or CAL. Microsoft has used the concept of CALs for many years to govern access to software resources, and the SBS product line has followed in this design. The SBS product uses a different type of CAL from other Windows Server products, however, because it encompasses a number of technologies. For instance, in a "traditional" server setup running Windows Server 2008 and Exchange Server 2007, each user accessing the network would need a Server 2008 CAL and an Exchange 2007 CAL to be properly licensed to access the file and print services on the server, as well as the mail services in Exchange. The SBS CAL, however, covers access to all the bundled technologies, so separate CAL purchases are not needed.

Microsoft has changed one aspect of CAL purchases with SBS 2008 that will be welcomed by sites needing more than five CALs. SBS 2008 still has the initial five CALs bundled with the product, but additional CALs can be purchased singly instead of in 5- or 20-CAL packs, as with previous versions. So, those sites needing 17 CALs total can purchase an additional 12 CALs instead of an additional 15 to meet their CAL requirements.

Standard Versus Premium CALs

One other important difference in SBS 2008 from previous versions of SBS is that there are separate CALs for the Standard and Premium products, specifically in relation to SQL. In SBS 2003, a single SBS CAL covered access to both the Standard and Premium products, meaning that you were essentially buying the license for the premium technologies even if you did not have the Premium version of SBS 2003 in production.

Microsoft has addressed this concern by splitting the CALs along the SQL lines and lowering the cost of the Standard CAL. There is a potential for confusion in the way that Premium CALs have been positioned. If SBS 2008 Premium is deployed in a network, you do not necessarily need to purchase Premium CALs for all users and devices in the network. You only need to purchase a Premium CAL for a user or device that will be accessing the SQL resources. Table 2.1 breaks down the four CAL types with SBS 2008.

TABLE 2.1   SBS 2008 Client Access Licenses

CAL Type	Description
Standard User CAL	Allows a single person to access resources of the SBS server from any device.
Standard Device CAL	Allows a single device to access resources of the SBS server for any number of people.
Premium User CAL	Allows a single person to access SQL resources of SBS 2008 Premium from any device.
Premium Device CAL	Allows a single device to access SQL resources of SBS 2008 Premium for any number of people.

As an example, suppose you have 20 users on your SBS 2008 Premium network. You have the SBS 2008 SQL server installed, and 8 of those users need to access the SQL resources. In this instance, you would need 12 Standard User CALs and 8 Premium User CALs. If you allocate the five included CALs from SBS 2008 as Premium CALs, you would need to purchase only three Premium CALs and 12 Standard CALs.

In another example, you have purchased SBS 2008 Premium to get the second server license and will not be installing or using SQL. In this instance, you would not need to purchase any Premium CALs.

In short, you need to provide a Premium CAL for every person who will be using SQL on the network, and all other users can make use of Standard CALs.

When to Use User CALs

For the majority of SBS 2008 installation, User CALs are the proper CAL to use. A User CAL is assigned to a person, and authorizes that person to access any of the network resources managed by the SBS 2008 server from any device. If an employee has a workstation in the office, a cell phone/PDA that accesses his or her mailbox, and a workstation at home used to get into Outlook Web Access or the Remote Web Workplace, a single User CAL assigned to that person covers his or her access from all of those devices and locations. If that person were not covered by a User CAL, each device that person used to access the server would need to have a Device CAL assigned to it. In this example, that would mean three Device CALs would be needed: one for the PC at the office, one for the cell phone/PDA, and one for the workstation at home. If that person attempted to use Outlook Web Access from another device—say, a kiosk at a trade show or a relative's home computer—that person would be accessing the server without a valid license.

When to Use Device CALs

A Device CAL makes sense when there is a single resource that is shared by multiple people. The most common example of when to use a Device CAL is for a facility that runs work in shifts, and each computer may have two or more people who use that resource during their shift. If, for example, a facility has 30 workstations on a plant floor and the facility runs three shifts, there would potentially be 90 people accessing the server from those resources. Acquiring 90 User CALs for these people would go beyond the licensing limit for SBS. However, only 30 Device CALs would be needed to cover these devices, keeping well within the SBS licensing restrictions.

However, each person accessing those workstations would not be allowed, from a licensing perspective, to access the SBS resources from another workstation that is not covered by a Device CAL. This means that the people accessing the workstations in this example would not be able to use Outlook Web Access from home and still be covered by adequate licenses. For some facilities dealing with shift work, this might be a reasonable approach. But for people who are regularly accessing SBS resources from a number of devices, the Device CAL approach can become very limiting very quickly.

Changes from SBS 2003—Licensing Enforcement

One significant difference in SBS 2008 from previous editions is that no licensing enforcement engine runs on the server. As with Windows Server 2008, the standard paper license enforcement is all that is needed for SBS 2008. No tools in the software track current license usage, maximum license usage, or whether User or Device CALs are being used.

By removing the licensing enforcement engine from the product, it is less painful for system administrators to deal with licensing issues (that is, no need to install license codes on the server, so no worrying about backing up license data in case of disaster or data corruption, no users prevented from logging into the server because there are not enough licenses installed, and so on). On the other hand, it does allow for more abuse of licensing, and no one is sure at this point how that will play out over the life of the product. It will still be important for the consultant and the business to keep track of the licensing paperwork to be able to document appropriate licensing for the server and network should the business be audited.

When to Use Terminal Server CALs

Because the second server license in SBS 2008 Premium could be used to set up a dedicated Terminal Server on the SBS 2008 network, a word about Terminal Server CALs is warranted. The SBS 2008 CAL does not cover access to Terminal Services on the second server. If you choose to implement the second server as a Terminal Server, or if you bring in another server licensed outside of the SBS 2008 product license to run as a Terminal Server, you need to acquire Terminal Server CALs for the users who access the server.

For a Terminal Server based on Windows Server 2008, there are two types of CALs that are supported for providing access to the Terminal Server—User and Device. As with the SBS CAL, using a Terminal Server User CAL will likely be the most commonly-chosen CAL type for the majority of Terminal Server implementations. As with the SBS User CAL, the Terminal Server User CAL enables a user to access the Terminal Server from any device. A Terminal Server Device CAL allows only that specific device to access the Terminal Server. As with earlier versions of Terminal Server implementations, Device CALs are tracked in the Terminal Server Licensing Server, but User CALs are not.

The bottom line for anyone wanting to add a Terminal Server to the SBS 2008 network is that you need to purchase and install appropriate Terminal Server CALs in order to meet Microsoft licensing requirements.

Planning the Hardware

Once you have an understanding of how the server will be used in the environment, you can begin determining the specifications for the hardware that will be used in the box. As mentioned earlier, the requirements of any third-party applications that might be installed and run from the server are beyond the scope of what can be addressed in this book. However, the following sections discuss the limitations of the hardware that can be used in the server and provide some guidance as to the minimum specifications needed in general cases.

Processor

SBS 2008 is built on Windows Server 2008 Standard Edition, and inherits the hardware requirements for that OS. Server 2008 can run on one to four processors. With current processors having one to four cores, you could build a server with up to 16 cores, as long as you are comfortable with the pricing. Server 2008 requires a minimum 1.4GHz processor speed for 64-bit processors, but a minimum 2GHz processor is recommended.

The second server license that comes with SBS 2008 Premium can be installed as the 32-bit or 64-bit version of Windows Server 2008. The only difference between the two is that the minimum listed CPU speed for the 32-bit version of Server 2008 is 1GHz. Still, a minimum of 2GHz for the 32-bit version of Server 2008 is recommended.

Memory

The SBS 2008 server can use between 3 and 32GB of RAM. The recommended minimum RAM for the SBS 2008 server is 4GB, and if any third-party applications will be installed on the box, installing more than 4GB of RAM on the SBS server is highly recommended.

If the second server license from the Premium Edition is used, both the 32-bit and the 64-bit versions of Server 2008 require a minimum of 512MB of RAM, but 2GB of RAM is the minimum recommended amount for the second server. Again, the actual use of the second server license determines how much RAM will really be needed on the system.

Related Hardware

Because the SBS 2008 installation media (both Standard and Premium Editions) are on DVD discs, all servers in the network need a DVD reader to be able to install the software. Having a writeable removable media drive is not required, and if you choose to try to use a writeable drive in the system, make sure any writing software you install is compatible with Server 2008.

A video card and monitor capable of displaying an 800×600 resolution is required. Most of the software tools in SBS 2008 can be run in this resolution, but a 1024×768 resolution or higher is recommended. You could also select a video card that is capable of handling the Aero interface, but that is not required.

At least one USB 2.0 interface is needed on the server. This is to connect the external disk drive for backup, if the built-in backup utility will be used on the server. Additionally, a FireWire (IEEE1394) interface could be used to connect an external hard drive for backup as well.

Planning the Network

After you have the licensing counts established, you can focus on the network implementation. This aspect of the installation covers a number of networking issues, from connecting to the Internet to internal IP address schemes to internal and external domain names. Each piece of this puzzle has a significant impact on the way the server is set up, and because some networking changes are difficult to impossible to change down the line, it's best to spend some quality time in this area to make sure that you can get it right the first time.

Changes in Network Options from Previous Versions

All previous versions of SBS supported the ability to use the SBS server as an edge device and a network router, but that is no longer the case with SBS 2008. Due to changes in the underlying network architecture with Server 2008, SBS 2008 can no longer be used in a two-NIC configuration where the SBS server sits between the internal network and the external network.

This change has caused a bit of an uproar in the SBS community because of the related changes. ISA is no longer included with the SBS product, the first time in any release of SBS. The previous best practice of using SBS as a router between the internal and external networks, even if it was not an edge device, no longer applies. Consultants who had built their practice on the security provided by using the SBS server in this way have to rework their own approach to network security.

This change simplifies the network layout in many ways, but it also makes it more complex in others. The following sections outline the standard network configuration for the SBS 2008 network, as well as the best practice recommendations for network implementation.

Connection to the Internet

SBS 2008, in its single-NIC configuration, expects that it will access the Internet in the same way that the other workstations on the network will—through a firewall/router at the edge of the network. Historically, this has often been through a consumer-class DSL or cable modem or other consumer-class router device. And for those who used the SBS server as a router (with or without ISA), this might have been a reasonable approach. But now that SBS 2008 is a node on the network just like any other workstation, those who are implementing

SBS 2008 networks should give serious consideration to a business-class device at the edge, especially one that can control outbound traffic as well as inbound traffic.

There are a number of business-class firewall devices on the market as standalone hardware devices. Those who are comfortable with ISA as a solution can still implement an ISA solution, but it must be on a separate computer. Regardless of which approach is chosen, be sure to budget appropriately for the edge device, as a business-class firewall is not going to be found in the sub-$100 range of consumer-class devices. There are a number of business-class devices ranging in price from $300–$1000, with some devices having basic inbound firewall features and others offering Active Directory–integrated outbound filtering, for example. The choice of which firewall to use will likely be heavily based on personal preference or brand loyalty, but the general consensus is that a consumer-class device does not provide the level of protection most businesses want or need.

Using ISA in the SBS 2008 Network

At the time of publication, the ability to run ISA on an edge device in the SBS 2008 network has some key limitations. The current version of ISA, ISA 2006, cannot be run on Windows Server 2008. That means that the second server license included in SBS 2008 Premium cannot be used as the OS for the computer running ISA. A separate Windows Server 2003 license would be needed to run on the ISA device.

Microsoft will have a whitepaper (http://go.microsoft.com/fwlink/?LinkID=122167) on configuring ISA on a separate server as an edge device for the SBS 2008 network. Because there will be no wizard integration for the configuration of ISA, the ISA configuration must be performed manually. For those who want to use ISA as the edge device, refer to the Microsoft whitepaper on the topic.

IP Address Ranges

SBS 2008 expects that the IP address for the network will be a private, non-routable IP address range. During installation, SBS 2008 will look in several 192.168.x. subnet range locations (based on common defaults) for the firewall device and configure the network accordingly. However, this does not limit the SBS 2008 network to only use the 192.168.x.x address ranges for the local network. If other private address ranges are used, they must be configured manually. See Chapter 3, "Installing and Configuring SBS 2008," for more information about configuring the network settings on the server.

Best Practice—Selecting the Internal Network Address Range

If you have the option and the ability to adjust the internal network address range when installing SBS 2008, you should select an address range that is not a "default" address range. Many recent firewall devices use a 192.168.0.x or 192.168.1.x address range for the internal network connection. If a user wants to connect into the network via VPN, and his or her home router also has the same internal subnet, the VPN connection will not work correctly (for more information about setting up a VPN connection using SBS 2008 tools, see Chapter 6, "Remote Web Workplace and Other Remote Access Solutions"). Moving the internal subnet away from these router defaults will help avoid VPN access problems down the road.

VPN access can also be an issue for the IT consultant who has many different networks that he or she supports. Even if the consultant has a different internal network range than a client site, if he or she needs to connect to more than one client site at a time, and those two client sites have the same IP network address range, communicating with the client sites will be problematic.

To avoid these issues, select a unique internal network address range for each SBS 2008 installation, where possible. When installing into an existing peer-to-peer network, or when setting up a network for a new business, this can be done when first setting up the firewall. When installing into an existing network, especially one with an existing server, the change may be more difficult to make. If there are a large number of devices with static IP addresses, you might opt not to make the change for that site.

DHCP Configuration

Many small networks use DHCP to allocate IP addresses to network resources, and this is the expected practice with SBS 2008 as well. SBS 2008 wants to install a DHCP server as part of the Windows services, but the DHCP service will shut itself down if it detects another DHCP server (provided by the firewall, for example) on the network to avoid DHCP confusion and the possibility of assigning duplicate IP addresses to network devices.

Best Practice—Use SBS as the DHCP Server for the Network

In cases where an SBS 2008 server is being introduced to an existing network, there might already be a functioning DHCP server on the LAN. Any devices that are providing DHCP services should have the DHCP function disabled so that the SBS 2008 server is the only device that provides dynamic network configuration information to the workstations.

The reasoning behind this is simple. When the SBS 2008 server is configured using the setup wizards, the proper network configuration information is put into the DHCP server settings and provided to the clients. When the SBS 2008 server is not allowed to serve DHCP, it falls on the network administrator to manually configure the DHCP server settings on the device. Chapter 4, "DNS, DHCP, and Active Directory Integration," covers the default DHCP settings for an SBS 2008 network in greater detail. However, when planning a new SBS 2008 implementation, the plan should include making use of the SBS 2008 server's DHCP services in place of any other DHCP services on the internal network.

DHCP can also be used to assign "static" IP addresses for network devices that need to have a consistent IP address, such as a network printer. The DHCP service on the SBS 2008 server can be used to create IP address reservations for these devices to ensure that they receive the same IP address every time they are restarted. Again, more information about this process can be found in Chapter 4.

Public and Private Domain Names

The argument over whether to use a public domain name (that is, smallbizco.net) as the internal network name for an Active Directory network is a passionate one for most parties. Those who believe a public name should not be used internally will generally not be swayed to think otherwise. Those who believe that the public name should be used internally will generally not budge from their position, either.

Microsoft's recommendation, and the way the wizards are built, is to use a private, non-routable domain name for the internal network, and once again Microsoft has chosen the .local namespace as the default for SBS 2008. The installation process does have options for choosing a different internal domain name (see Chapter 21, "Advanced Installation Options"), which can be a public domain name or a different private domain name. There is not any reason that one has to be chosen over the other, but those who go with a standard installation end up with a .local internal domain name.

The only caveat to using a public domain name for the internal domain name is that the DNS records for any public services, such as the company's web site, have to be manually maintained in the SBS 2008 DNS configuration. If the web host changes to a different public IP address, someone has to update the DNS records for the www site in the SBS 2008 DNS configuration to match the new IP address. For those who do not want to manage DNS at this level, or who are unsure how to do so, a private domain name should be used internally.

> **NOTE**
>
> The `.local` and `.lan` top-level domains (TLDs) are not reserved domains. That means those domains could be put into service at some point in the future and become routable domains. Four reserved domains are identified in RFC 2606 (http://www.ietf.org/rfc/rfc2606.txt) for testing: `.test`, `.example`, `.invalid`, and `.localhost`. Although it's unlikely that the domains `.local` and `.lan` would be used as live top-level domains in the near future, a systems administrator who wanted to be absolutely certain that his internal domain would never be publicly routed could use one of the four reserved domains. Doing so would present a special set of challenges, because the `.localhost` name has special functions for referring back to the local machine, and the other names do not imply permanence.

Planning the Storage Layout

Determining the appropriate storage layout for the SBS 2008 server is probably the most complex process in the planning stage. So much of the storage requirement depends on the data needs for the site implementing the new server that it is difficult to make a generalized recommendation for what an appropriate storage layout should look like. The remaining sections in this portion of the chapter cover terminology and some baseline recommendations for bare minimum storage requirements. Depending on the level of usage expected on your server implementations, these baseline recommendations may be insufficient for a final deployment.

Changes in Storage from Previous Versions

Because SBS 2008 is built on updated versions of the included components, there are a number of differences in the way the product handles storage needs. The amount of overall storage capacity needed in SBS 2008 is higher than SBS 2003. Where SBS 2003 could originally fit in a 12GB C: partition, SBS 2008 requires a 60GB C: partition. Exchange 2007 now allows for stores of larger than 75GB and can have multiple stores instead of one, which has implications for total storage capacity as well as disk performance. The following sections cover possible approaches to designing storage for an SBS 2008 server given these and other factors.

Multiple Partitions Versus Multiple Spindles

Finding the ideal storage layout is a giant puzzle with a number of key pieces. In the end, the layout implemented is the result of a number of compromises with these pieces.

Ideally, some suggest that an optimum SBS installation would have three *spindles*, or separate drive mechanisms. One spindle would contain the OS and key applications, one would contain the Exchange log files, and one would contain the Exchange mail databases. This layout would be optimized for performance because the type of disk access needed to read and process the Exchange log files (sequential) is different from the disk access needed to process the Exchange databases (random). User data could be stored on the spindle with the Exchange logs because most user data would be read and written sequentially, and any system-wide databases would be stored on the spindle with the Exchange databases because they would use a similar type of drive access.

The cost of such a layout, however, would keep a small business from implementing it. To achieve any level of fault tolerance, you would need to at least mirror each of the spindles, a total of six drives. If performance were truly the primary consideration, the two non-OS spindles would likely be a RAID 5 or RAID 50 array, jumping up the number of disk drives to at least eight.

Although SBS 2008 will install and run on a single spindle with multiple partitions, if disk performance is a concern for the operation, the server should be built with a minimum of two spindles—one for the OS and one for the remaining data. At a minimum, both spindles need to be mirrored, but a mirrored OS spindle and a RAID 5 (or similar) array for the data.

If a single spindle is all that can be used in the server, the space in the disk should be partitioned into at least two partitions. The C: partition should contain only the operating system and key applications. Dynamic data should be kept off the C: partition to protect against accidental filling of the disk. Should the C: partition get completely full, the server could crash unexpectedly and cause data problems in addition to downtime. As discussed in Chapter 3, "Installing and Configuring SBS 2008," the default installation places all data and applications on the C: partition, even if multiple partitions or drives are available during setup. Only after setup can you move dynamic data off the C: drive and onto other storage areas of the server.

Minimum Partition/Spindle Sizes

The SBS 2008 installation routine requires a C: partition of at least 60GB before it will perform the installation. This is a far cry from the 12GB C: partition that OEM installs of SBS 2003 regularly used. But a 60GB C: partition still may not be large enough, depending on your server configuration. The following sections provide some baseline suggestions for how to devise minimum partition sizes for your server. These sections assume a two-disk or two-partition installation of SBS 2008.

Sizing the OS Partition

One of the significant challenges in supporting existing SBS 2003 installations is maintaining a server with a very small C: partition. When SBS 2003 was originally released, a 12GB C: drive seemed like it would be large enough. When SBS 2003 SP1 was released, a 20GB C: partition seemed like an appropriate recommendation. With SBS 2003 R2, a 30GB or larger C: partition was recommended. The same progression may well happen over the lifespan of SBS 2008, so when reviewing these minimums, understand that they might not be appropriate in a few years; you should try to have as large a C: partition as reasonably possible.

As for the minimums, SBS 2008 installs and uses about 24GB of disk space on the C: drive after all the dynamic data has been moved to other partitions. The remaining space can be used by new applications, OS log files, and swap file storage.

When planning the size of the C: partition, the swap file is probably the single biggest factor to consider; this has not been the case in previous versions of SBS. Microsoft recommends a swap file of 1.5 times the size of physical RAM installed in the server. Because the 64-bit OS can access 32GB of RAM, this could be significantly more storage than IT consultants have been accustomed to using.

To help gauge how much disk space could be used by the basic installation, plus swap file and memory dump free space, Table 2.2 lists the recommended sizes for swap file and minimum total disk space for C: based on the amount of RAM installed in the system.

TABLE 2.2   OS Partition Size Minimums

Installed RAM	Recommended Swap File	Minimum Partition Size
4GB	6GB	60GB (6GB swap file, 24GB for OS and applications, plus 30GB free space)
8GB	12GB	60GB (12GB swap file, 24GB for OS and applications, plus 24GB free space)
16GB	24GB	68GB (24GB swap file, 24GB for OS and applications, plus 20GB free space)
32GB	48GB	92GB (48GB swap file, 24GB for OS and applications, plus 20GB free space)

If you expect the usage of space on C: to grow more than 20GB in the life of the server, you would need to adjust the initial partition size accordingly. This also highlights the importance of understanding how your RAM needs in the server might increase over the life of the server. If you initially install the server with the minimum 4GB of RAM, and then discover in a year that you really need to have 16GB for the server plus new applications, the 60GB minimum C: partition might not have enough space to handle the increased swap file size and the other applications. Although you can move all or part of the swap file to a different partition, you will not get a crash dump file generated if the swap file is not stored on the C: partition. This is an important consideration because a crash dump can be used by support professionals to help determine the cause of a system crash if the cause is not evident from the crash code itself. If a crash dump is not created on a system failure, it eliminates one possible tool for identifying and resolving the issue.

Sizing the Data Partition

If trying to determine an appropriate size for the OS partition was a bit vague, coming up with an appropriate minimum size for the data partition is even more nebulous. The guidance for partition size in this section is based upon having sufficient free space on the data partition to perform a repair of the Exchange databases, should such a repair be needed. In general, Exchange needs 1.2 times the size of the database file in free space to perform the repair (specifics of the Exchange database repair process are detailed in Chapter 10, "Exchange Disaster Recovery"). If you have a 60GB mail database, you need around 72GB of free space available on the server to be able to repair the database.

Obviously, trying to figure out how large your mail databases could get over the next few years, and then allocating space not only for the database but the repair space, is going to require a bit of guesswork. The bottom line is that you need to allocate as much disk space as you can for future growth.

Fault Tolerance

Fault tolerance defines a system's capability to recover from a failure of hardware or software in such a way as to minimize the impact on the system. In most computer systems, hard disk drives are the first components to fail because they have the most moving parts and are accessed constantly while the system is powered on. Knowing this, most server systems are built with some form of fault tolerance for the disk system to minimize the impact when a disk drive fails.

SBS servers can achieve fault tolerance for the disk subsystems using either hardware or software solutions. Hardware solutions rely on specialized disk controllers to handle the management of the fault tolerance implementation selected. These controllers are more expensive than standard disk controllers. Hardware fault tolerant solutions provide either a mirrored solution—where two disks of the same size act as one—or a *RAID (redundant array of inexpensive disks)* solution—where three or more disks function as a single drive.

See the next section, "RAID Types," for a more detailed explanation of RAID arrays and their functions.

Hardware Versus Software Fault Tolerance

Microsoft servers can implement mirrored and RAID-like solutions via software, avoiding the expense of a specialized disk controller card. Through Disk Manager, partitions of the same size can be mirrored by the operating system or combined into a RAID.

Although more expensive, hardware-based fault-tolerance solutions are preferred over the software solutions for one reason—performance. Although the software implementations Microsoft provides for mirroring and RAID are less expensive from a hardware standpoint, the amount of overhead involved in managing the mirror or RAID has a significant impact on server performance.

Traditionally, SCSI or Serial-Attached SCSI (SAS) RAID controllers are the devices of choice for fault-tolerance solutions for the disk subsystem. Over the last few years, many servers have been built using Serial-ATA (SATA) drives attached to RAID controllers for a lower-cost solution than SAS. The lower cost does come with a price, however. SAS drives have a greater data throughput than SATA drives, so for servers where disk I/O is going to be critical, SAS should be chosen over SATA.

RAID Types

RAID—which stands for redundant array of inexpensive disks or redundant array of individual disks, depending on whom you ask—is a specification for combining multiple disk units of the same size into a single logical unit for the purpose of improving read/write performance, providing fault tolerance, or both. Although there are a number of RAID specifications, only a few are actually used in practice. Table 2.3 lists the most commonly used types of RAID and describes their functions, advantages, and disadvantages. The number of disks needed for each RAID type is listed as the total available disk space for each type. (The values are based on 80GB drives used as individual elements in the array.)

One other advantage of a RAID configuration is that most RAID controllers can accommodate a *hot spare*—an extra disk drive on the controller that automatically becomes active if one of the other members of the array fails. Plus, when combined with a hot-swappable drive technology, the failed drive can be removed and replaced without bringing down the server. The upside is obvious because the system automatically rebuilds the necessary information on the newly activated disk if one fails and reduces the time the server spends without fault tolerance due to the failed drive. The downside is the overhead associated with rebuilding data onto the newly added drive, and that can be observed by end users during the rebuilding process. Use of a hot spare is more commonly found with RAID 5 implementations but can be used with a mirrored configuration as well.

TABLE 2.3   Commonly Used RAID Types

RAID Level	Format	Number of Disks	Array Size	Description
0	Striping	2 or more	80GB * # of disks used	Technically not a RAID type because it provides no redundancy, RAID 0 arrays stripe the data written to the array equally across each disk in the array. This results in an increase in disk read/write performance, but if one of the devices in the array fails, the entire array fails.
1	Mirroring	2	80GB	RAID 1 arrays are disk mirrors. The data written to one disk is also written to the other. There is no read/write performance gain in a RAID 1 array, but if one of the devices fails, the other device kicks in, and no data is lost.
5	Striping with Parity	3 or more	160GB with three disks, 240GB with four disks, 320GB with five ((n-1)*# of disks)	RAID 5 arrays combine fault tolerance with improved read/write performance. When data is written to a RAID 5 array, a portion of the data is written to all but one member of the array. Parity information is written to the remaining member. If one member of the array fails, the remaining members have sufficient information to rebuild data on the array when read. RAID 5 is more efficient with disk space than RAID 1 but can cost more because more disks are needed than in a RAID 1 array.
6	Striping with Dual Parity	4 or more	160GB with four disks, 240GB with five disks, 320GB with six ((n-2)*# of disks)	RAID 6 arrays combine fault tolerance similar to RAID 5, but has enhanced performance in that a RAID 6 array can handle the loss of two members of the array and continue functioning. Two sets of parity information are written to the disks in addition to the data. RAID 6 makes sense for larger element arrays where the chance of individual element failure is increased. Performance during failure and rebuild with RAID 6 is significantly slower because the controller has to perform two parity calculations.

2

TABLE 2.3   Commonly Used RAID Types

RAID Level	Format	Number of Disks	Array Size	Description
10 (a.k.a. 1+0)	Striping with mirroring	4 or more (in multiples of 2)	160GB with four disks, 240GB with six disks, 320GB with eight disks	RAID 10 is really a RAID 0 (striped) array made up of RAID 1 (mirrored) elements. Two pairs of mirrored disks are connected, and data is striped across the pairs. Offers some read/write performance improvement over a RAID 1 array and adds fault tolerance to a RAID 0 array. There is a greater amount of overhead in processing this type of array and is costlier to implement because a minimum of four disks are needed. One element in each mirror can be lost with no data loss, but fault tolerance is effectively lost across the entire array with the loss of only one disk.
50 (a.k.a. 5+0)	Striping with parity sets	6 or more	320GB with six disks, 480GB with eight disks	RAID 50 is really a RAID 0 (striped) array made up of RAID 5 (parity) elements. Two or more sets of RAID 5 arrays are set up in a striped configuration. This configuration offers better read/write performance than RAID 10, but is much costlier in terms of disks needed at a minimum and the controller to manage the array. One element in each parity set can be lost with no loss of data, but fault tolerance is effectively lost across the entire array with the loss of only one disk.

Backup Technologies

One of the most significant changes to backup in SBS 2008 actually comes from a change in Server 2008—no tape drive support in the native backup tools. The backup tools in Server 2008 make use of an imaging technology that writes backup data to hard disk rather than tape, and SBS 2008 inherits that change. Now, this does not mean that you cannot use a tape drive to do backups in SBS 2008; it simply means that the native tools will not write to the tape drive. If you want to use tape technology, you need to use a third-party solution for that.

Making the correct decision about which backup technology to use is important during the planning stage. External USB storage drives have become popular in the last few years, but those devices are far from the only option when looking into SBS 2008. Most name-brand OEM server manufacturers include multiple USB ports on their server configurations, but a few are beginning to include other ports on the server as well. Some servers can be configured with a Firewire (IEEE1394) interface, and others have started including eSATA connectors. Although each of these technologies has their own individual advantages when compared with the others, they all have a similar challenge when dealing with SBS 2008—how to safely disconnect the external drive from the server to rotate the backup media.

In addition, you need to have an external backup disk that is at least as large as the combined capacity available on the server to successfully back up the server. If there is going to be a large amount of data churn on the system, you may want to look at backup devices that have double or triple the capacity of the internal storage to ensure that there is room for incremental backup files during the backup process.

For a complete discussion about backup technologies and how to use the native tools, see Chapter 17, "Managing Server and Workstation Security," and Chapter 18, "Backup and Disaster Recovery."

Summary

Now that you've looked at all the options you need to consider for the design of the server and the network, you should be ready to prepare a proposal that outlines how the installation should look. Be sure to include the technical as well as the business justifications for the choices made in the proposal.

Best Practice Summary

▶ **Determining the Number and Type of CALs Needed**—Purchase a sufficient number of User CALs to cover all the employees in the organization. Only look at Device CALs in a shift-work environment where employees are sharing terminals.

▶ **Selecting the Internal Network Address Range**—The internal address range for the SBS 2008 network should not be one of the commonly-used address ranges used by routers and firewalls (that is, 192.168.0.x, 192.168.1.x). The internal address should be unique so users and support staff can make incoming VPN connections, if needed.

▶ **Use SBS as the DHCP Server for the Network**—To ensure that workstations and other network devices have the correct settings to allow them to communicate efficiently with the SBS server, use the DHCP services on the SBS server instead of the DHCP services on the firewall or other device.

Installing and Configuring SBS 2008

IT professionals who have gone through the installation process with Windows Server 2008 and Windows Vista will be familiar in general with the installation process for SBS 2008. For those who have not, a bit of explanation is in order before detailing the installation process.

Windows Vista was the first of the new breed of Microsoft operating systems that uses the image-based installation. Unlike the previous versions of setup, which copied core files to the hard drive in order to boot into a setup environment, the new setup architecture drops an image of the complete OS onto the hard drive with a basic configuration and then handles hardware configuration after the core OS boots.

There are essentially three installation stories for SBS 2008: new installation into a network with no server, installation into an existing Active Directory network, and migration from an existing SBS 2003 installation. This chapter covers basic installation and configuration of a new SBS 2008 server. Microsoft provides a white paper for the process of migrating an SBS 2003 network to an SBS 2008 installation (http://technet.microsoft.com/en-us/library/cc546034.aspx), and that process has a number of specialized steps, so the reader is encouraged to review that paper for migration needs. Additionally, the Swing Migration method has been updated for SBS 2008 and can be found at http://www.sbsmigration.com. Finally, Chapter 21, "Advanced Installation Options," details the process for installing SBS 2008 into an existing Active Directory Network that does not have an SBS server.

To OEM or Not to OEM

At the time of publication, the author team has not had access to any OEM builds of SBS 2008 from the major manufacturers, so a definitive stance on the effectiveness of an OEM installation of SBS cannot be made yet. Based on previous experiences, however, there is still a general recommendation to perform a full installation of SBS, even if an OEM version is pre-installed on a server by the manufacturer.

Microsoft's OEM partners will still be placing their own configuration options on the server to allow for the pre-install build to be modified with the customer-specified settings following initial startup. Until these modifications are known and tested, the IT service providers are encouraged to perform the installation on their own, allowing them to select appropriate partition sizes and other setup configurations that will not be available with the OEM install. This will give the installer a known state for the server following installation.

Preparing for SBS 2008 Installation

Despite the new image-based installation technology Microsoft uses to streamline the installation process, there are still a number of tasks to complete prior to plugging in the server and turning it on. Some steps relate to information needed for the setup process itself, while some steps involve making sure the existing network is configured properly prior to installation. This section of the chapter covers the basic information needed to prepare for the installation process.

Collecting Information for the Setup Process

The following list identifies information that will be needed during the setup process for the SBS server. Collect this information prior to performing the setup, and make sure that all network resources can be accessed as needed:

- ▶ Company name and address information
- ▶ Internal IP network range (see the next section)
- ▶ Server name and internal domain name
- ▶ Name for server administrator account
- ▶ Drivers for disk controller (if needed)
- ▶ Drivers for network interface card (if needed)
- ▶ USB key or external disk for storage of hardware drivers (if needed)
- ▶ Public DNS information
- ▶ Credentials to log in to DNS management system

Configuring the Internal Network

SBS 2008 assumes that it will be installed in a private network with a 24-bit subnet mask (255.255.255.0). This means that SBS 2008 only works as designed when the network address falls in the 192.168.x.x private range.

If the existing network has an internal address range in one of the other private network ranges, the internal network needs to be reconfigured to use a 24-bit subnet mask. Although this does mean that you can use a 10.x.x.x or a 172.16.x.x-172.31.x.x address space, the wizards only work correctly if the 24-bit subnet mask is used. SBS 2008 also assumes that the hardware firewall used as the Internet gateway will have an address ending in .1, so the firewall should be set for an address of 192.168.x.1.

Any devices on the existing network that have static IP addresses assigned, such as networked printers, need to be manually configured for the new network subnet (if the network address range needs to change) and should be configured to point to the SBS server IP address for DNS. Alternately, a DHCP reservation for these devices can be set up on the SBS server, so that the device not only gets the same network address each time it comes online, but so that it gets the correct network settings for the internal network.

Best Practice—Selecting the Internal Network Address Range

Small business IT consultants who manage a number of SBS networks should configure the internal network for each site to have unique network address ranges. Keeping these network ranges different can help in a number of ways. One, it can help identify which site is being accessed, especially if there are multiple connections to different client sites. Two, if you need to connect into a client site via VPN, you will encounter difficulty routing traffic to the client site if the machine you connect from has an address in the same range as the remote network.

Because many firewall devices default to a small set of private IP address ranges for the internal network (192.168.0.x, 192.168.1.x, 192.168.168.x, and so on), you will likely need to change the internal IP range on the firewall and make sure all the local devices on the internal network can still communicate correctly before starting with the SBS server installation. Any devices on the network that have static IP addresses, such as network printers, will need to be changed manually, and proper operation should be confirmed before continuing.

Even though the installation examples in this book use an internal address of 192.168.1.x, that address range should be avoided for production installations.

Disabling DHCP on the Network

The last step prior to installing SBS 2008 is to disable any DHCP servers that may exist on the network. This includes the DHCP services in the firewall or any other devices on the network. SBS 2008 expects to provide DHCP services to the network, so if it detects a DHCP server on the network during installation, the installation process will appear to complete normally, but when you first launch the SBS Management Console, you'll see an error listed under Other Errors, which indicates that the DHCP service failed to start.

Installing SBS 2008

The next part of the process is to load the SBS 2008 software on the server. To accomplish this, you need the installation media and the server needs to be connected to the network, specifically to the hardware firewall. The firewall does not need to have an active connection to the Internet, but the SBS server must be able to locate the firewall on the internal network in order to complete setup successfully. Once you have the media ready and the server connected to the network, you can continue with the process.

Collect the Initial Setup Data

Follow these steps to complete the first phase of installation:

1. Boot from the installation DVD. If prompted, press any key to boot from DVD.
2. The setup process goes through the initial Windows load from DVD, and then switches into GUI setup mode. Select the appropriate installation language, time and currency values, and keyboard type, and then click Next.
3. In the Windows Server 2008 setup screen, click Install Now.
4. Enter the product key from the installation media. If you do not want Activation to happen automatically at the end of installation, turn off the Automatically Activate Windows When I'm Online checkbox. Click Next.

Best Practice—Do Not Automatically Activate Windows

Even though the installation default is to automatically activate Windows once the server gets connected to the Internet, best practice is to disable this checkbox during installation. SBS 2008 will run for 30 days before activation is required, and you may want to verify that the server is built properly and ready to be put into production before activating the software.

In addition, it is still considered a best practice to go through three complete installs of SBS 2008 in a test environment before building your first production server using the software. Telling setup not to automatically activate the software when it connects to the Internet will help avoid any problems with activation during this process.

---

5. Agree to the license terms by selecting the "I Accept the License Terms" checkbox; then click Next.
6. Click Custom (advanced) to perform a clean install on the server.

Prepare the Disk Infrastructure

There are many different ways to configure the disk layout for SBS 2008, as discussed in Chapter 2, "Planning for the SBS 2008 Deployment." For the purposes of example, the following steps prepare a single disk array by creating two disk partitions and formatting them for use in the server. The reader can interpret from these instructions how to configure other disk options for his or her own configuration needs:

1. The Where Do You Want to Install Windows screen displays the available disk media, as shown in Figure 3.1.

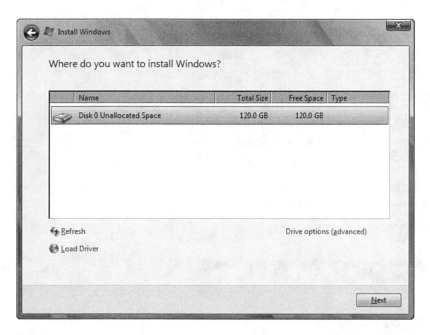

FIGURE 3.1   Available storage for installation.

If you need to load drivers for the disk controller, click Load Driver and follow the instructions to locate and load the appropriate driver for the server (see Figure 3.2).

2. To partition the drive, select the drive from the list; then click Drive Options. From the expanded selection list, click New (see Figure 3.3).

3. Enter the desired size of the partition and click Apply.

NOTE

The SBS 2008 setup process expects a minimum partition size of 60GB for the installation. Setup will complete on a partition smaller than 60GB, but will generate warnings about doing so. The minimum partition size for installation is 40GB. Even if multiple partitions will be used, the C: partition should be at least 60GB in size.

4. Create the remaining desired partitions by selecting the Unallocated Space on the drive and clicking New.

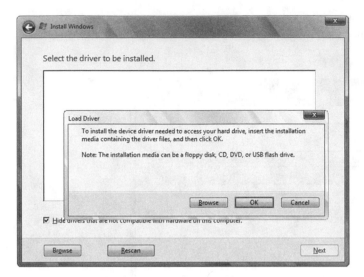

FIGURE 3.2   Loading hard disk drivers.

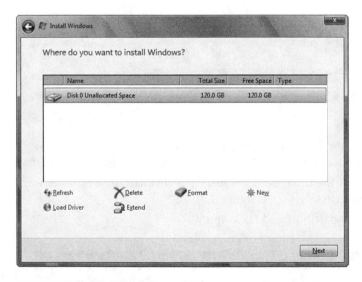

FIGURE 3.3   Creating new partitions.

5. After creating the desired partitions, select the one where SBS 2008 should install; then click Next (see Figure 3.4).

Complete Setup

The next phase of setup finishes loading the installation image of SBS on the selected disk partition and prompts for input for basic network and Active Directory configuration information:

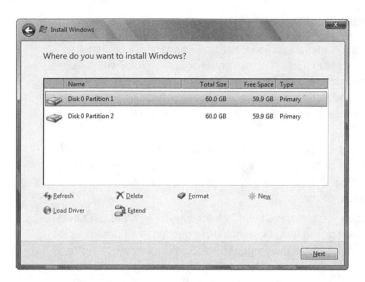

FIGURE 3.4   Verifying proper partitions.

1. Setup starts copying and expanding files on the disk and will go through at least one restart during the process.

2. Setup will reach the Completing Installation screen and then reboot.

3. Now that the core Windows 2008 operating system has been installed, the SBS portion of the setup launches (see Figure 3.5). Click Next to continue with the installation.

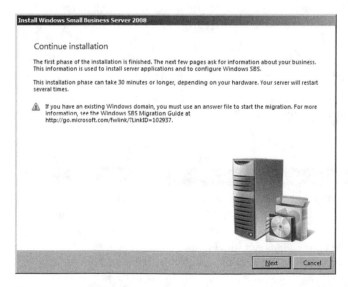

FIGURE 3.5   Continuing setup.

Installing Additional Hardware Drivers

This is the point in the installation where additional hardware drivers can be installed that will be needed to complete setup. Even though Windows Server 2008 contains drivers for a large range of hardware, any devices, specifically network interface cards, that were designed and released after the release of Windows Server 2008 may not be correctly recognized during setup. If the network adapter is not recognized by setup, the installation process will fail.

At this point of the installation, the Windows Server 2008 operating system can recognize USB disk devices connected to the server, so you can put the hardware drivers on a USB device (flash drive, external disk, and so on) and attach that device to the server to make the files available to the server.

To install hardware drivers, when you see the Continue Installation page, press Shift-F10 to bring up a command prompt. From that command prompt, you can use a number of tools to load hardware drivers. You can open an Explorer window by typing `start .` and pressing Enter. You can open the Device Management console by typing `devmgmt.msc` and pressing Enter. You can also navigate directly to the path where the install files are located in the command prompt and run the installer from there, if the drivers are bundled in an installer package.

If the driver installer requires a restart, it is safe to restart the server at this point, because the setup routine will come back to this point of the process when the server comes back online. After installing the drivers, check in the Device Management console to ensure that the device is showing properly. Once the devices are showing as properly installed, you may continue with the installation process.

---

4. In the Verify Clock and Time Zone Settings page of the setup wizard, click Open Date and Time to verify the clock and time zone settings link to open the Date and Time control panel.

5. Select the appropriate time zone for the server; then adjust the time to match local time. Close the control panel when completed, and click Next in the wizard to continue setup.

6. In the Get Important Updates window, click the Do Not Get the Most Recent Installation Updates button.

Best Practice—Do Not Get Installation Updates

At the time of this writing, the best practice for installation is to skip checking for installation updates and continuing with installation. In this release of SBS, the update process does not only look for updates to the installer, but it downloads and installs all available critical updates. To ensure a consistent installation process, the recommendation is to skip updating during setup; then install updates as soon as installation completes.

It is possible that after publication, some issue is identified that impacts the installation process (for example, the SharePoint installation error from SBS 2003 that surfaced a couple of months after the product released: http://www.microsoft.com/windowsserver2003/sbs/techinfo/sharePointinstall.mspx) and Microsoft releases an update to address that issue. At that point, the recommendation may change to check for updates during install, and an update will be released to the errata site for this book, at http://www.informit.com/store/product.aspx?isbn=0672329573.

7. In the Company Information window, enter the appropriate information and click Next when complete. Although most of this information is optional, be sure to select the appropriate value for the Country/Region field, shown in Figure 3.6, as that will impact other tools on the system.

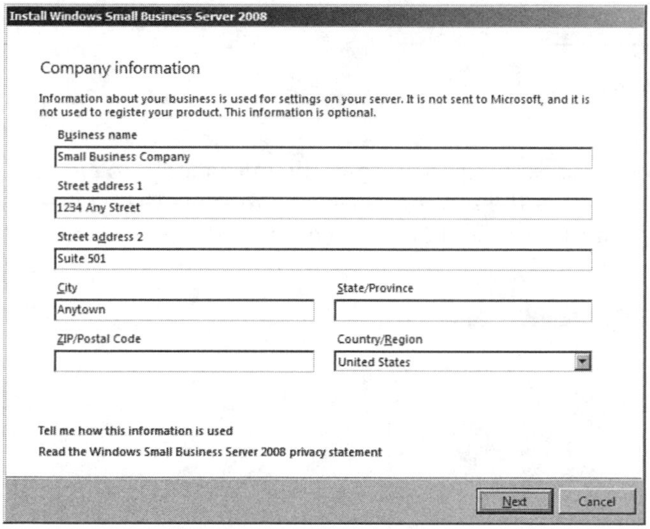

FIGURE 3.6   Entering company information.

8. In the Personalize Your Server and Your Network page, enter the name for the server and the internal domain name (see Figure 3.7). Click Next when finished.

NOTE

The internal domain name entered in this page is equivalent to the NetBIOS domain name from Windows 2003. The suffix ".local" will be added to the name entered into this field. If you want to use an internal domain name other than .local, you need to prepare an answer file and run setup with the answer file present, as described in Chapter 21.

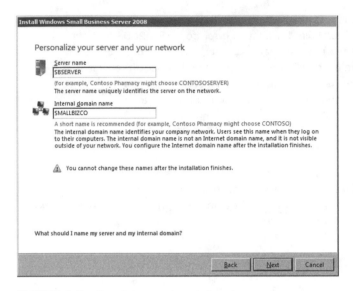

FIGURE 3.7 . Entering server and domain name.

9. In the Add a Network Administrator Account page, enter the information to create the account you will use to administer the server (see Figure 3.8). Note that you cannot name this account Administrator. Click Next when finished.

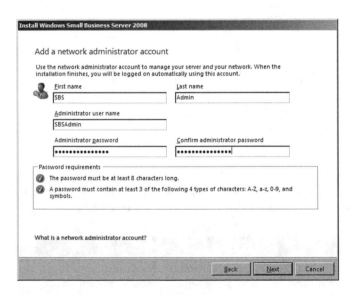

FIGURE 3.8   Entering administrator account information.

10. In the Install Security Services page, you can choose to install Windows Live OneCare for Server and Microsoft Forefront Security for Exchange Server. The

options to install both products are selected by default, but you can turn off the checkboxes for either product at this point and skip the installation of these tools during setup. If you want to install these products later, see Chapter 21 for instructions. Click Next when ready to continue.

11. Review the setup information in the That Is All the Information Needed page. Click Next when ready, or click Back to make changes if needed.

CAUTION

Once you click Next in this page, you will not be able to change any of the information that is listed on this page.

12. Setup starts installing the SBS components and configuring Active Directory based on the collected information. This process can take up to an hour to complete, and the server will reboot at least twice during this process.

When setup completes, you see the Successful Installation window and you will be logged in with the network administrator account you created earlier. When you click the Start Using Your Server button, you will be ready to start the configuration of the server.

Performing the Initial Configuration of SBS 2008

Now that the core operating system and the SBS components have been installed, you can start configuring the server for daily use. The remainder of this chapter gives basic configuration information and steps.

Run the Connect to the Internet Wizard

The Connect to the Internet Wizard performs one task and one task only—configure the SBS server to be able to connect through the firewall to the Internet. It does this by identifying the internal network configuration the firewall uses and then modifying the settings on the network interface on the server to communicate to and through the firewall. At the end of the wizard, the TCP/IP settings for the network interface are properly configured for the local network and should not need to be modified further.

Changes from SBS 2003—Configuring Network Connections

Readers who work with SBS 2003 will be familiar with the granddaddy of all wizards, the Configure E-mail and Internet Connection Wizard (CEICW). This one wizard managed a large number of tasks in a single, somewhat convoluted, process. When run with the proper information, the CEICW would correctly establish a large number of network settings on the server. When something went wrong with network or Internet access configurations, running this wizard could resolve many problems with no further work needed.

Alas, the CEICW is no longer with us in SBS 2008, and this is not necessarily a bad thing. The functions of the CEICW have been split into a couple of different wizards. Table 3.1 lists the components of the CEICW and where/how they are handled in SBS 2008.

TABLE 3.1   SBS 2003 CEICW Functions in SBS 2008

Configuration Group in SBS 2003	Wizard in SBS 2008
Connection Type (Network Configuration)	Connect to the Internet Wizard.
Firewall Configuration	Deprecated—Since SBS 2008 no longer routes traffic through the server, and it no longer can act as a basic firewall, these features are not available.
Web Services Configuration	Set Up Internet Address Wizard.
Internet E-mail Configuration	Set Up Internet Address Wizard.
E-mail Smarthost Configuration	Configure a Smarthost for Internet E-mail Wizard.

By separating the network configuration into a separate wizard, SBS 2008 allows administrators to have more granular control over server environment. Rather than having to select "Do not change connection type" in the CEICW to make sure you only modified e-mail settings, changing e-mail settings in SBS 2008 is relegated to the Set Up Internet Address Wizard (covered later in the chapter), and you do not have to modify or risk modifying the network interface card settings to change the e-mail domain.

Follow these steps to run the Connect to the Internet Wizard:

1. Go to the Home tab in the Windows SBS Console.

2. Under Getting Started Tasks, click on the Connect to the Internet link.

3. Read the information in the Before You Begin page to make sure you have the information needed to connect to the Internet; then click Next.

4. The Connect to the Internet Wizard starts the process of detecting the existing network. This can take some time, depending on how the network is configured.

5. Once the wizard detects your router, the Detecting the Router and Configuring Your Network page shows the IP address of the router (see Figure 3.9). This address should

match the address you configured in the router earlier in the chapter. The IP address that will be assigned to the SBS server is also displayed. Click Next to continue.

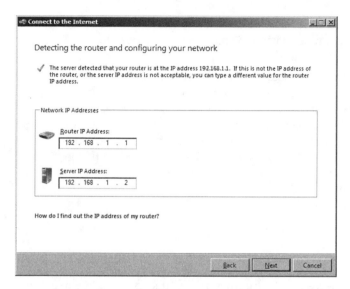

FIGURE 3.9   Confirming the network address information.

NOTE

If the wizard is unable to detect the address on the router, you are prompted to enter the IP address for the server and the IP address of the router. Note that a subnet mask of 255.255.255.0 is assumed for these connections.

6. When you see the Your Network Is Now Connected to the Internet page, click Finish to close the wizard.

The server is now configured for proper Internet communication. The server network card is assigned an IP address, the proper subnet mask and default gateway are configured, and the DNS settings for the NIC point to the IP address of the SBS 2008 server per recommendations. Click on the checkbox next to the Connect to the Internet Wizard to mark the task as complete.

Best Practice—Run DHCP Services on SBS

Because of the relationship between Active Directory and DNS (covered in detail in Chapter 4, "DNS, DHCP, and Active Directory Integration"), it has long been a best practice to let the SBS server provide DHCP services to the internal network. To help reinforce this approach, the Connect to the Internet Wizard will not complete if it detects a DHCP server elsewhere on the internal network.

The Connect to the Internet Wizard checks for DHCP servers on the internal network as part of the process, and when it does detect one, it presents a dialog box with two options: Postpone and Continue.

Clicking the Postpone button stops the Connect to the Internet Wizard and leaves the server in a disconnected state. The wizard simply will not allow the process to complete if it detects a DHCP server elsewhere on the network.

To this end, the wizard is really forcing the issue of DHCP. In SBS 2003, the server would not install DHCP services if it detected a DHCP device on the network during setup, and it would complete the Configure E-mail and Internet Connection Wizard process if another DHCP server was seen on the network. With SBS 2008, in order to complete the Connect to the Internet Wizard, you must at least temporarily disable DHCP on the network to allow the wizard to complete. The SBS server should be the only device handing out DHCP to the network, but if there are reasons to have other DHCP devices on the network, those needs can be accommodated. See Chapter 4 for more information.

Install Security Updates

Now that the server has been connected to the Internet, the next step should be installing security updates. This ensures that any known threats at the time of installation are patched before making any services on the server available to the rest of the network.

To check for an install update, select the Windows Update icon from the Start Menu. In the Windows Update screen, click on the Check online for updates from Microsoft Update link and install any updates marked as important or critical. As covered in Chapter 17, "Managing Server and Workstation Security," Windows Update in SBS 2008 is handled like Server 2008 and Vista. If you attempt to open the Windows Update web site (http://update.microsoft.com/microsoftupdate), the Windows Update interface redirects you to the built-in Windows Update interface and lets you interact from there.

Run the Set Up Internet Address Wizard

The Set Up Internet Address Wizard handles a large number of Internet addressing functions for the SBS server. This includes configuring the web sites in IIS and the mail domain for Exchange. It also configures internal DNS records and, if selected, external DNS records as well. Ideally, the Set Up Internet Address Wizard would be run once during initial server setup and never again. However, if the public domain name used by the server changes, the Set Up Internet Address Wizard will handle transitioning the SBS Internet services to the new domain name.

The wizard also attempts to configure the hardware firewall to allow the proper inbound access to the server. If the router supports Universal Plug and Play (UPnP) and UPnP is enabled, the wizard communicates with the router and sets up the proper inbound access. If the firewall does not support UPnP, or UPnP is disabled, the wizard returns a warning on the Internet router component at the end.

Best Practice—Do Not Enable UPnP

Many IT professionals consider enabling UPnP on a firewall a security risk. The UPnP protocol does not require any authentication, so any device on the internal network could send UPnP requests to the firewall and reconfigure the settings at any point. While allowing the Internet Address Management Wizard to connect to the firewall and configure the settings is a convenience and will help the do-it-yourself installer get the server up on the network, the best practice from a security perspective is to disable UPnP on the firewall and configure the inbound access settings manually.

If UPnP is not enabled on the firewall, the Internet Address Management Wizard will report a failure at the end of the process. You can click the View Warning Details link and see that the wizard was unable to configure the port forwarding (see Figure 3.10). The details page lists the ports that SBS 2008 expects to be forwarded in the firewall. The wizard will complete all other tasks successfully even if UPnP is not enabled, so this warning can be safely ignored.

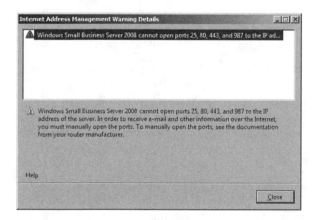

FIGURE 3.10   UPnP configuration warning.

If you choose not to use UPnP, you will need to set up the appropriate access from the outside. To allow the basic features of SBS to communicate correctly, you will need to open the following ports at a minimum:

▶ **Port 25**—Inbound SMTP (Simple Mail Transport Protocol) for e-mail.

▶ **Port 443**—HTTPS for inbound access to Outlook Web Access and Remote Web Workplace.

▶ **Port 987**—Inbound access to SharePoint.

SBS 2008 provides several options for setting up the Internet address for the server. The three scenarios covered in this chapter are the following:

▶ Establishing a new domain name using one of the registration partners.

▶ Using an existing domain name and managing that domain through one of the registration partners.

▶ Using an existing domain name and managing the public DNS settings yourself.

The SBS team has partnered with a number of domain registration providers around the globe to assist with the management of public DNS settings for SBS 2008. This list will continue to grow as new providers are selected for the program. The Set Up Internet Address Wizard will check for available providers based on the location selected in the Company Information window, as well as on the Top Level Domain (TLD, for example, .com, .net, .eu, and so on) entered in the wizard. The wizard polls Microsoft for this information as the wizard is run, so the list is up-to-date on every launch. Internet connectivity is needed for this to happen, so make sure you run the Set Up Internet Address Wizard after establishing network connectivity to the server and running the Connect to the Internet Wizard.

The process starts the same for each of the scenarios. From the Home tab of the Windows SBS Console, click the Set Up Internet Address link and make sure you have all the information listed in the first page of the wizard available: the name of the Internet domain, the name of the domain provider, and the logon information for the domain provider.

Establishing a New Domain Name

Follow these steps to set up a new domain name with one of the domain partners:

1. In the Do You Want to Register a New Domain Name page, select I Want to Purchase a New Domain Name and click Next.

NOTE

If you have not selected a Country/Region in the Company Information screen, you receive an error that prompts you to complete this information so that the wizard can select the appropriate domain registration partner for your area.

---

2. Enter the domain name you want to register and select the appropriate extension from the drop-down list and click Next (see Figure 3.11). Not all domain extensions are available in all areas and for all partners, so you may not see the domain extension you want in the list.

3. Select one of the domain name providers from the list. Microsoft is continually working to add new partners, so you may see the list change over time. Click Next to continue.

4. If the domain you've selected is available from the provider, the domain will be listed in the next page of the wizard (see Figure 3.12). Click Register Now to open a web page to the provider's site and complete the registration process. Once the registration process has completed, click Next in the wizard to continue.

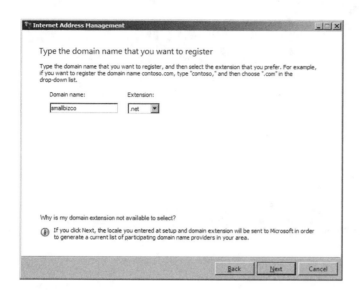

FIGURE 3.11   Selecting a new public domain name.

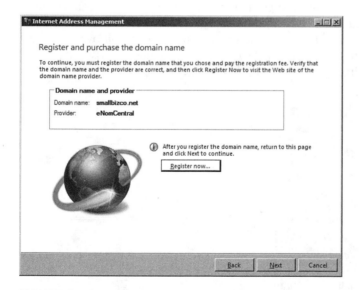

FIGURE 3.12   Completing domain registration with the registrar.

5. In the Store Your Domain Name Information page, enter the credentials you created (or already had) from the domain provider in the appropriate fields (see Figure 3.13). This allows the server to automatically connect with the domain provider and manage the domain through them.

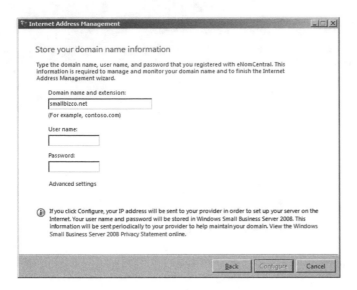

FIGURE 3.13   Storing domain name information.

6. Clicking the Advanced Settings link brings up a window where you can change the default domain name (see Figure 3.14). By default, SBS uses remote.domain.com, but the Advanced Settings window enables you to change the name or remove the name altogether (although it is not recommended to remove the name and associate the server with just the domain). Click OK to accept any changes.

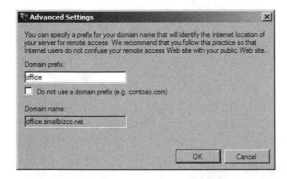

FIGURE 3.14   Changing the default server name.

7. Click Configure to complete the Internet Address Management Wizard. When the wizard completes the process, the Congratulations page displays the status of the wizard. Any errors that occurred during the process will be listed in this page.

Using an Existing Domain Name with One of the Domain Partners

If a public domain already exists, you can transfer management of the domain to one of the registration partners so that SBS can manage the public domain records through the partner. If you created the domain through one of the partners, no transfer would be necessary. Follow these instructions to set up the Internet address using an existing domain with one of the registration partners:

1. In the Do You Want to Register a New Domain Name page, click the I Already Have a Domain Name I Want to Use radio button and click Next.

2. In the How Do You Want to Manage Your Domain Name page, click the I Want the Server to Manage the Domain Name for Me radio button and click Next.

3. Enter the domain name and extension that you want to use and click Next.

4. Select the desired domain name provider from the list and click Next.

NOTE

If the provider you want to use is not listed, you will need to select one of the providers listed and transfer your domain to that provider. Note that it can take 7–10 days for a domain transfer to complete, so you may need to plan ahead for this process.

5. In the Store Your Domain Name Information screen, enter the username and password for the domain partner, along with the domain name, and click Configure.

Using an Existing Domain Name and Managing the Public DNS Settings Yourself

If you already have a public domain registered and your domain registration partner is not in the list, or you do not want to have the partner manage the public DNS records, you can select the appropriate settings in the wizard so that the server will not attempt to manage the public domain settings for you. Follow these steps to complete this configuration option:

1. In the Do You Want to Register a New Domain Name page, click the I Already Have a Domain Name I Want to Use radio button and click Next.

2. In the How Do You Want to Manage Your Domain Name page, click the I Want the Server to Manage the Domain Name for Me radio button and click Next.

3. Enter the domain name and extension that you want to use. If you want your public URL to start with a name other than Remote, click the Advanced Settings link and enter the desired name in the Advanced Settings page.

4. Click Configure to finish the wizard.

DNS Records Configured by the Set Up Internet Address Wizard

Management of public DNS records by wizards is new to the SBS product line. In all previous versions of SBS, management of public DNS records had to be handled outside of the SBS environment, and this caused a great deal of confusion for many business owners who attempted to set up and manage their own SBS networks. Management of these records by the wizards is an effort by the SBS development team to help ease the challenge for the business owner who is self-managing an SBS server.

But management of public DNS is not the only change in the way SBS deals with DNS both internally and externally. Chapter 4 details how the Set Up Internet Address Wizard creates an internal DNS zone that matches the public DNS name of the server so laptops that are used both internally and externally can use the public name for the server and resolve that name to the best IP address to use, depending on where the laptop is connected at the time. The new Autodiscover feature of Outlook 2007 also relies on a special DNS record being created in the domain to help Outlook figure out how to automatically connect to the Exchange server, no matter where Outlook is connecting from.

Table 3.2 lists the public DNS records created and managed by the wizards when automatic management is selected in the Set Up Internet Address Wizard. For those choosing to manage DNS through other means, the table provides the information needed to create these records.

TABLE 3.2   Public DNS Records Managed by SBS 2008

DNS Record	Record Type	Record Contents	Description
remote.domain.com	A	Public IP address of the SBS server	This record points the public name of the SBS server to the IP address of the firewall at the installation site. This can be either a static IP or a dynamic IP, depending on the management service used to control the records.
domain.com	MX	remote.domain.com	This record identifies the host that handles e-mail services for the domain domain.com. The value of the record should always be a name and not a numeric address, and the name used should be an A (host) record and not a CNAME (alias) record.
_autodiscover._tcp.domain.com	SRV	0 0 443 remote.domain.com	This special service (SRV) record is used by Outlook 2007 to attempt to automatically locate and configure access to the Exchange server. This record requires a very different format than other records and should only be manually created with a full understanding of the options for the record. See RFC 2782 (http://www.faqs.org/rfcs/rfc2782.html) for a full description of the SRV record format, and KB940881 (http://support.microsoft.com/kb/940881) for information on the way the Autodiscover record is used by Outlook.

Complete Other Setup Tasks

Once the server has been connected to the Internet and the Internet addresses have been established, the server is essentially ready to go. This section of this chapter identifies a few other configuration steps you may need to complete before allowing users full access to the server.

Move Data Folders

Due to the imaging technology used for the setup process, all data and data locations for the server are located on the C: partition of the server, even when multiple partitions/disks are available. As discussed in Chapter 18, "Backup and Disaster Recovery," all data features should be moved off of C: and onto the other disks/partitions that are available. Fortunately, the SBS development team provided a number of wizards to make the process of moving the data easy.

To find the Move Data Wizards, click on the Backup and Server Storage tab of the Windows SBS Console; then select the Server Storage tab. In the Tasks pane, shown in Figure 3.15, you will find the associated Move Data Wizards.

Table 3.3 identifies and describes each of the Move Data Wizards.

TABLE 3.3   Move Data Wizards in SBS 2008

Wizard	Description
Move Exchange Server Data	Moves the Exchange messages stores from C:\Program Files\Microsoft\Exchange\Mailbox\First Storage Group and Second Storage Group to the same folder path on the destination drive. Mail services are unavailable during the move.
Move Windows SharePoint Services Data	Moves the SharePoint databases from C:\Windows\SYSMSI\SSEE\MSSQL.2005\MSSQL\DATA folder to the same path on the destination drive.
Move Users' Shared Data	Moves the users' shared data paths from C:\Users\Shares to the same path on the destination drive.
Move Users' Redirected Documents Data	Moves the users' redirected data path from C:\Users\FolderRedirections to the same path on the destination drive.
Move Windows Update Repository Data	Moves the Windows Update repository for WSUS from C:\WSUS to the same path on the destination drive.

Each of the Move Data Wizards prompts you about collecting a backup of the server prior to moving the data. When these wizards are run at initial setup, backing up the data can be skipped, as there is very little data in each of the identified storage locations. In addition, the Move Data Wizards do not enable you to specify the path where the data will exist on the new partition. This not only allows the SBS tools to keep track of where the data is, but also enables support personnel to find these folders in the expected locations.

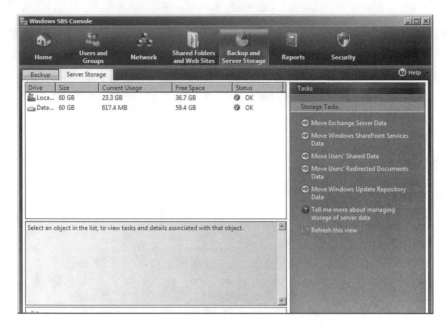

FIGURE 3.15   Finding the Move Data Wizards.

Install/Configure Security Software

At this point in the setup process, it is recommended that you install or configure the security software that will be used on the server. If you plan to use the Windows Live OneCare or the Forefront Security for Exchange trials that install with SBS 2008, you need to configure those tools at this point. Refer to Chapter 17, "Managing Server and Workstation Security," for information on configuring Windows Live OneCare for the server. Refer to Chapter 8, "Exchange Management," for information on configuring Forefront Security for Exchange.

If you already have a security suite that you will be using instead of one or both of these tools, you need to uninstall them prior to installing your own third-party solution. Both Windows Live OneCare and Forefront Security for Exchange can be uninstalled from the Programs and Features node in the Control Panel.

Add Users

After you have completed the previous steps in the installation and configuration process, you can begin to add users to the domain and start the workstation configuration process. More detailed information about managing users and workstations can be found in Chapter 12, "User and Computer Management," and Chapter 13, "Macintosh Integration." To add user accounts, select the Users and Groups tab from the Windows SBS Console and run the Add User Wizard from there.

Troubleshooting SBS 2008 Installation Issues

Thanks to the streamlined installation process, there are fewer places for problems to occur during initial setup and configuration. However, there will still be issues encountered that may impact the setup process. This section covers the items that could cause difficulties during installation and configuration, and is broken down into those two categories. Should other setup problems be encountered following the initial release of the software, this troubleshooting section will be updated at the errata site for the book.

Log Files

The best way to troubleshoot setup and initial configuration errors is looking through the various log files. Fortunately, the SBS 2008 development team made the effort to centralize as many of the log files in a single location on the server, making them easier to find. The default location for the SBS log files is C:\Program Files\Windows Small Business Server\Logs. Table 3.4 identifies and describes some of the log files related to the setup and configuration process.

TABLE 3.4   SBS 2008 Setup/Configuration Log Files

Wizard	Description
SBSSetup.log	Contains information from the SBS portion of the setup. Does not include data from the core Windows Server 2008 setup.
DCPromo*.log	Contains information from the domain controller promotion process triggered during SBS setup. Filename contains the date and time the promotion occurred.
GPOTask.log	Contains information from the process that creates the SBS-specific group policy objects during setup.
CTIW.log	Contains information from the Connect to the Internet Wizard process.
DPCW.log	Contains information from the Set Up Internet Address Wizard.
MoveData.log	Contains information from the Move Data Wizards.

Setup Issues

The image-based setup process leaves very few areas for installation trouble to occur. The following items identify the potential problem areas and workarounds for them should they be encountered during setup.

Incorrect/Incompatible Drivers

As SBS 2008 becomes a more mature product, the installation DVD will not contain all the drivers needed for hardware that is developed and released to market after the release of the product. In that case, the setup routine may not correctly recognize drivers for key hardware components and impact setup.

As mentioned earlier in the chapter, Setup provides an option to load disk drivers in the Where Do You Want to Install Windows screen. Only disk drivers can be loaded at this point, as this interface is a basic setup program that does not provide a full Windows interface to hardware and the OS. Not all disk drivers will be compatible with SBS 2008, either. Some XP/Vista/Server 2003 drivers will work for the setup process, but a 64-bit Server 2008 driver is highly recommended for use with the server installation. If an incompatible driver is loaded during setup, the initial load may appear to go through and then fail to come back up after the first reboot.

The other critical hardware device needed for setup and initial configuration is the network card driver. In order for setup to complete, it must be connected to a network, even if that network is just a switch that is not connected to anything else. If setup cannot detect a network card, it will stop the installation process and prompt you to install a driver for the network card. This prompt, shown in Figure 3.16, gives you the option to open the Device Manager to install the drivers. You can also, at this point, press Shift-F10 to open a command prompt, as described earlier in the chapter.

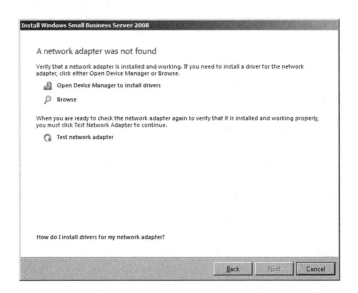

FIGURE 3.16   Installing network card drivers.

Cannot Access USB Devices

The use of USB is more and more prevalent than in recent years, and the use of USB devices during setup is no exception. Because floppy disk drives are quickly going the way of the dinosaur, the new setup tools for SBS 2008 look for external data on USB devices instead of on floppy disk—disk drivers attempt to load from USB, answer files are looked for on USB devices, and so on. But if the setup process cannot locate a USB device because either the USB device is not recognized by the setup tool, or the USB interface is malfunctioning, there is another option for making information available to the setup routine.

Setup will instead look for resources on the root of any recognizable disk volume attached to the server. So, if the server has multiple CD/DVD drives, the information needed for setup (drivers, answer files, and so on) could be burned to CD media and placed in the secondary drive during setup (unfortunately, the installation DVD cannot be removed during setup to put a CD with driver information in the drive). Alternately, a formatted IDE or SATA drive with driver or configuration information could be installed into the server prior to setup and accessed as a data location during setup (just not as an install location).

Known Installation Issues

At the time of publication, there are three known installation issues with the released version of SBS 2008. Information about these items has been documented on the official SBS blog (http://blogs.technet.com/sbs/archive/2008/08/26/known-post-installation-event-errors-in-sbs-2008-and-how-to-resolve-them.aspx), but they are identified here for clarity as well. Should other installation issues arise after the release of the book, those issues and their resolutions will be posted to the book site, http://www.informit.com/title/ 9780672329579.

▶ **DCOM Event 10016**—After a successful installation, you will see several 10016 errors from DCOM in the event logs. These are related to Windows SharePoint Services 3.0 and can be resolved by following the instructions in KB 920783 (http://support.microsoft.com/kb/920783).

▶ **MSExchange Search event 4625**—This error appears every few minutes in the event logs following a successful installation. This issue is scheduled to be resolved with the release of Exchange 2007 Rollup 4, which may be available by the time you read this. If you install all updates following installation, as recommended in this chapter, this update should automatically get installed when it becomes available and you may not see this issue.

▶ **DCOM Event 10009**—Following a successful installation, you will see multiple 10009 events from DCOM in the event logs. This issue occurs when workstations cannot correctly communicate with the server because firewall or other configuration issues are preventing the workstation and the server from communicating properly. If the workstations are in the same logical subnet as the server and are using the Windows firewall service only, you should not see these errors. If you do see these errors, there may be a third-party firewall running on the workstation or the workstation does not have the SBS Group Policy Objects applied correctly. The SBS blog post on this issue has steps to try to resolve the errors, and that site will be kept up to date on resolutions for this issue.

Summary

The setup process for SBS 2008 is significantly streamlined over previous versions of SBS. This improved process cuts down on the time and labor involved in doing an install of

SBS, and also reduces the number of things that can go wrong during installation. The initial configuration of the server is key to proper operation down the road, so the setup process should be carefully observed and managed.

Best Practice Summary

▶ **Selecting the Internal Network Address Range**—Prior to installing SBS 2008, the internal address range should be set in one of the 192.168.x.x address ranges. The Connect to the Internet Wizard is expecting to find the router in one of these ranges. The internal address range should also be different at each client site if you manage a number of SBS networks for small businesses.

▶ **Do Not Automatically Activate Windows**—Even though SBS 2008 will attempt to automatically activate following installation, you should select the option during setup to skip automatic activation. This will give you the opportunity to make sure the server is set up the way you want before activating the software. This will also allow you to go through the recommended three installations as tests before performing a production install.

▶ **Do Not Get Installation Updates**—Because of the way the update engine in setup is designed, selecting to install updates during installation will bring down all available updates, not just setup-related updates, and could cause problems during installation, or at the very least result in inconsistent install cores among different servers. Security updates should be installed manually as soon as installation completes, but should not be done as part of setup.

▶ **Do Not Enable UPnP**—Even though the Set Up Internet Address Wizard will configure a UPnP-enabled firewall with the correct incoming ports, UPnP should not be enabled on firewall devices for security reasons. Any device that attempts to configure the firewall using UPnP would be able to alter the firewall without anyone's knowledge. If you do want to use UPnP to configure the firewall, enable UPnP immediately before running the Set Up Internet Address Wizard and disable UPnP immediately afterward.

PART 2

Managing Network and Web Configuration

IN THIS PART

DNS, DHCP, and Active Directory Integration

Without DNS, DHCP, and Active Directory, there is no network domain. Computers don't authenticate or communicate, and the networking world as we know it comes to an abrupt halt. DNS, DHCP, and their integration with Active Directory provide the road map for data flow. Without them, users get the dreaded "unable to locate a domain controller" login error or a "401 Site not Found" when trying to view a web site. Without a properly configured DNS, e-mail doesn't end up at your server and users won't be able to send e-mail out. Any of these symptoms result in an unhappy computer user and potential business lost. Clearly, such symptoms must be remediated quickly. SBS 2008 helps set up your DNS and DHCP structure. Additional wizards can assist in quickly identifying and repairing a data flow problem.

Being able to follow a packet through the network, understand where data is supposed to flow, and identify where the road block has occurred are some of the most important skills an IT professional can possess.

Understanding the Role of DNS and DHCP

DNS provides name resolution for IP addresses. It makes it possible for humans to use names rather than IP addresses to identify neighbors on the network and web sites on the Internet. When you enter the name of a web site, the computer sends the name to a DNS server, which responds with the IP address. After the computer has the address, it can then send messages directly to the remote host's IP address. If the DNS server does not have an entry in its database for the remote host, it will send the client the address of a DNS server that is more likely to have information about that remote host, or it can query the other DNS server itself. This process repeats until either the client computer receives the IP address or the request fails.

Active Directory is integrated into DNS. The relationship runs deep into the proper function of Active Directory. The Active Directory zones are configured automatically when an Active Directory integrated zone is set up. The installation process of SBS 2008 creates an Active Directory integrated zone, as shown in Figure 4.1. A whole variety of server service records can be included in this zone; however, for most small business networks, the default records are sufficient and do need not be altered or added to.

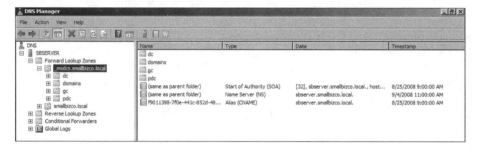

FIGURE 4.1   DNS Active Directory Integration can be seen in the _msdcs.SMALLBIZCO.local Forward Lookup Zone.

DHCP allows SBS to lease IP addresses to computers and other devices that are enabled as DHCP clients. The DHCP server automatically provides valid IP addresses and the additional configuration parameters configured as DHCP options to devices that allow them to connect to other network resources. DHCP options may include the addresses of your router, time server, DNS servers, and so on. The options necessary for the proper configuration of your client PCs are included by default.

DNS and DHCP cooperate with each other to provide an orderly and consistent network. The SBS 2008 implementation of DNS allows for records to be automatically updated by computers that receive an IP address from the DHCP server.

Native Tools

DNS and DHCP are configured during setup. There are several tasks that you need to complete from the Getting Started section of the home page that determine your DNS settings. These are Connect to the Internet, Setup Your Internet Address, and Configure Internet E-mail. After running these configuration tools, you use the Windows 2008 native DNS Manager to make any customizations that your environment may require. In DNS Manager, notice that during the setup process, several records have been configured:

Companyweb, connect, SBSConnectComputer, SharePointSMTPServer, Sites, and a record for the name of your server, which, in our case, is server. Collectively, these DNS records represent all the available web applications that the server is hosting. The default records on your server should look very similar to those highlighted in Figure 4.2.

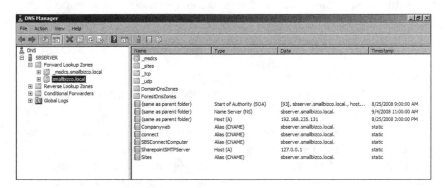

FIGURE 4.2   All the default DNS records are configured in the SMALLBIZCO.local Forward Lookup Zone.

The layout of DNS Manager has not changed substantially from previous versions, but its capabilities have. In the small business environment, one of the biggest changes you will notice is the capacity to host records in both IPv4 and IPv6. For example, an IPv4 host record is an A record. The IPv6 version is an AAAA record. Similarly, other types of DNS records have new names in IPv6. The function of each IPv6 record is identical to the IPv4 version; only the naming convention has changed. The transition from IPv4 to IPv6 is likely to occur during the lifespan of your SBS 2008 server, so understanding how it works is important. For a more detailed look at IPv6, see Chapter 19, "IPv6 Overview."

DHCP is initially configured when your server sets up the network connection to your router. If it detects the router, and your router is configured to serve DHCP addresses, DHCP will not be enabled on your server, and you will receive an alert during installation. At this time, you should stop and disable any other DHCP servers on your network. If it detects the router, but the router is not serving DHCP addresses, DHCP will be enabled and installation will continue. If during setup, a router is not detected, DHCP will be enabled on your server.

The layout of the DHCP MMC has not changed substantially from previous versions but, like DNS, it is now IPv6 capable. Setting up and configuring DHCP for IPv6 is beyond the scope of this chapter. However, more information on IPv6 can be found in Chapter 19.

Best Practice—Use the Wizards to Create DNS and DHCP Initial Configuration

SBS includes a great set of wizards that the development team spent untold hours scripting. The use of these wizards results in a standards-based installation of your SBS server and should be used whenever you are configuring one of the included components of SBS. These wizards will save you hours of setup and configuration time.

Native tools should only be used to configure items outside the scope of the wizard—for example, configuring access to your ISP-hosted web site.

DNS Server Status Window

The DNS Server status window provides a handy glimpse into alerts and system status of your DNS server.

To view the DNS Server status, open Server Manager, expand Roles, and click on DNS Server. In the right pane, you see the DNS Server status page. This page is made up of three sections: Events, System Services, and Resources and Support. Unlike previous versions of SBS that provided a static view, this window provides an active view of DNS. Expanding each category exposes a window in which you can click and manipulate items. For example, expanding the System Services item exposes a small window showing the DNS Server service. A right-click on the service brings up the standard service options of Start, Stop, Pause, Resume, and Restart, as shown in Figure 4.3.

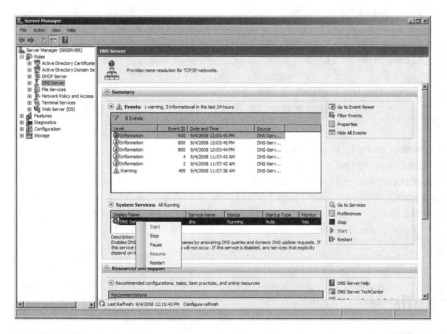

FIGURE 4.3   The DNS Server status page is interactive, allowing the administrator not only a glimpse into DNS, but also the ability to act upon the findings immediately.

DHCP Server Status Window

The DHCP Server status window behaves in exactly the same manner as the DNS Server status window described in the previous section. Because it provides access to events, services and troubleshooting articles, this is a useful tool for monitoring and troubleshooting DHCP.

> **TIP**
>
> Don't ignore the Resource and Support section of the DNS and DHCP Server status window. The development team has saved a great deal of legwork for administrators looking to expand their knowledge on the topics by providing direct links to TechNet and support documents, along with a brief description of the feature and why you may want to implement it.

Preparations and Caveats

There are a couple of issues that you need to be aware of when configuring DNS.

DNS Naming Convention .local

The standard naming convention for single forest AD domains is to use a private name scheme like .local. This can sometimes cause a problem with mobile devices, like laptops that move from the .local internal network to the .net external network. Fortunately, configuration of a split DNS has been built-in to handle these requests. The split DNS configuration in SBS 2008 is discussed later in this chapter.

DNS and DHCP When No Router Is Present

DNS and DHCP will not be configured correctly if SBS 2008 is unable to detect a gateway at the time of installation. The automatic install assumes that this server will be live on your local network at installation and it will have a connection to the Internet gateway. If this condition is not true, installation will continue; however, you will receive errors on the home page of the SBS Console. Click View Installation Issues to see the list of errors. After you have the server connected to the gateway, run the Fix My Network Wizard to configure DNS and DHCP. This wizard is located in the Windows SBS Console, under Network, on the Tasks pane of the Connectivity tab.

The Fix My Network Wizard looks at 70–80 server settings, as shown in Figure 4.4, and configures them to their defaults.

Default Configuration of DNS and DHCP

DNS and DHCP are configured by default on your server and on all DHCP clients. Knowing what the default configuration looks like lets you know if your system is configured correctly. The following tables can be used for this reference point. Table 4.1 lists the DHCP server default configuration settings. Table 4.2 lists the DNS server default configuration.

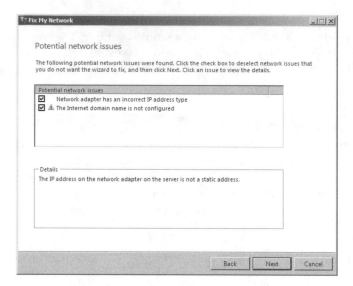

FIGURE 4.4   The Fix My Network Wizard checks between 70–80 configuration settings on your server.

TABLE 4.1   DHCP Server Default Configuration

DHCP Settings	Default Value
Scope	192.168.
Reservations	None
Scope Options	003 Router 192.168.
	006 DNS Servers 192.168.
	015 DNS Domain Name SMALLBIZCO.local
Server Options	None

TABLE 4.2   DNS Server Default Configuration

DNS Server Properties	Default Value
Interfaces	Only the following IP addresses. Both IPv4 and IPv6 address of the NIC are selected.
Forwarders	None.
Advanced	Enable Round Robin, enable netmask ordering, secure cache against pollution are selected.
Root Hints	Root servers are populated with IPv4 addresses.
Debug Logging	Nothing selected.
Event Logging	All events radio button selected.
Monitoring	Nothing is selected.

Table 4.2   DNS Server Default Configuration

DNS Server Properties	Default Value
Security	Thirteen service and user groups are listed, each with unique permissions too numerous to list.

One of the most common troubleshooting tools used by SBS support professionals is the command `ipconfig /all`. This command displays the IP addressing settings for the network card. Running this command on both the server and a connected workstation should produce the default settings shown in Figure 4.5 and Figure 4.6.

FIGURE 4.5   If you have configured your SBS 2008 with all default settings, the output of the `ipconfig /all` command looks exactly as shown here.

Best Practice—Use the `ipconfig /all` Command Liberally

The `ipconfig /all` command is one of the most useful tools the network administrator has at hand. It should be applied liberally. If you suspect a networking problem, first check to see if your server and workstation have the correct network settings. Verifying these settings should be the first troubleshooting step that you apply. Compare the settings of your server and workstation with the figures in this book to determine if your network is configured correctly.

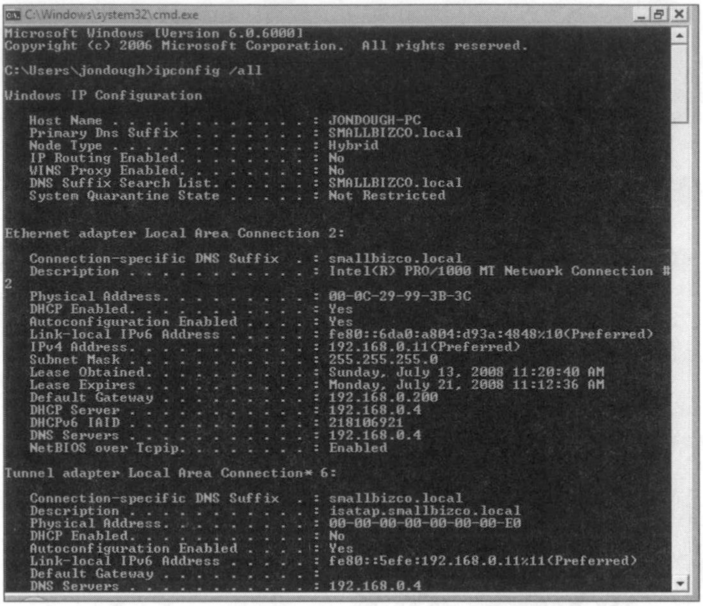

FIGURE 4.6   If you have configured your workstations with all default settings, the output of the `ipconfig /all` command looks exactly as shown here.

NOTE

If your `ipconfig /all` returns an IP address for the local machines of 169.254.X.X, your computer has not been successful at receiving an IP address from your DHCP server. The DHCP service might not be running. Microsoft built in this address scheme as the default fallback so that the computer would continue to boot normally and services would start. This address is known as automatic private IP addressing (APIPA).

Securing DNS and DHCP

The implementation of DNS and DHCP are, by default, configured with most of the security you will need. However, depending on your environment, you might want to implement additional security measures.

Securing DNS

The DNS configuration in SBS 2008 is configured with the same default settings as any Windows 2008 server. There are a few choices that the administrator should make to maintain the security of your DNS. All modifications to DNS are done using the native DNS Management tool.

The first choice that should be made is to use forwarders. A *forwarder* is a DNS server that resolves names that your internal DNS server is not aware of. Once the forwarder is selected, you should configure your firewall to allow only DNS traffic to flow to this DNS server. This prevents a rogue DNS server from diverting traffic from your internal network to a compromised DNS server.

The actual firewall rule configuration procedure depends upon the brand of firewall you choose for your network. The rule in plain English will look like the following:

```
Rule Name: Primary DNS
From Internal Network, Port 53 (DNS), to <IP address of primary DNS>
Rule Name: Secondary DNS
From Internal Network, Port 53 (DNS), to <IP address of secondary DNS>
```

By restricting the DNS server that is used to resolve addresses to a known good and trusted server, this configuration protects your network from being unwittingly directed to use a compromised DNS server.

> **NOTE**
>
> DNS poisoning, or pollution, is one of the most common DNS security problems. It occurs when a compromised computer inserts bad records into a DNS server. A bad record could cause an unsuspecting user to be redirected to a web site infected with malware or virus. Microsoft DNS enables detection of DNS cache pollution by default. In addition, the DNS server can only be updated by computers that are members of the Active Directory. Therefore, external attacks of your DNS server are unlikely to be successful.

Securing DHCP

In the default configuration of SBS 2008, there can only be one DHCP server per subnet on your network. In an SBS 2008 network, this can either be a router or your SBS 2008 server. In most cases, the DHCP server included with SBS 2008 allows for more advanced settings and will be the one that is used. This is the preferred configuration.

Microsoft DHCP is secure by default, and only an Active Directory-registered device is allowed to provide DHCP addresses to domain members. Even so, you still need to take care to turn off any other DHCP servers on your network. See the "Troubleshooting" section of this chapter if you are having difficulty locating other DHCP servers on your network.

> **When to Use a Second DHCP Server**
>
> There are several scenarios where you may want to set up a second DHCP server, as follows:
>
> ▶ You would like redundancy.
> ▶ You have a branch office.
> ▶ You have multiple subnets.

Regardless of whether you are managing a branch office with a server, you have multiple servers and a single office, or you have multiple subnets, you might want to configure multiple DHCP servers. It all boils down to redundancy. Multiple DHCP servers can happily coexist on the network, provided they are not attempting to serve the same address range.

Microsoft has a well-documented procedure for configuring multiple DHCP servers using the 80/20 rule. That rules states that on your main DHCP server, you should configure the scope to serve 80% of the addresses and exclude 20% of the scope; on your secondary DHCP server, you configure the reverse.

There are a couple of gotchas to look out for when configuring multiple DHCP servers.

> ▶ If your DHCP servers are separated by a router, you need to enable DHCP relay. You want to delay that relay to be sure to give the local server time to reply to a DHCP request.

> ▶ You need to create a complete set of DHCP reservations on both servers. In the event that one server goes down, the remaining server can assign the appropriate address to your printers and other machines with DHCP reservations.

> ▶ If the scope you are configuring is for a branch office or another subnet, you need to configure Server Option 249 and specify the subnetmask and router address. Otherwise, responses will not route properly.

Configuring multiple DHCP servers, which is not a difficult process, is an excellent tool to add redundancy to a small business network.

New in SBS 2008

Once you have set up your server, you'll notice that it has a completely new look for the administrator. In this next section, we look at one new tool, the Fix My Network Wizard, and the new split DNS configuration.

Understanding the Fix My Network Wizard

The Fix My Network Wizard is a new feature of SBS 2008. It runs 70–80 checks on the configuration of the server. The wizard checks to see if your server has had configuration changes that would interfere with the proper functioning of the server and its default applications. For the purpose of this chapter, we'll focus on the DNS and DHCP checks and configuration settings the wizard is implementing.

To start the Fix My Network Wizard, from the Windows SBS Console, move to the Networking navigation tab, and then the Connectivity tab. In the righthand pane, click Fix My Network, as shown in Figure 4.7. The Fix My Network Wizard will launch.

First, the wizard checks to see that all the services for DNS and DHCP are installed and started and that the startup type is set to automatic.

During the DNS inspection and repair phase, it inspects DNS for the existence of forward and reverse DNS zones and queries for the A and AAAA record of the server. It also checks that records exist for Companyweb, connect, Sites, SharePointSMTPServer, server, and SBSConnectComputer.

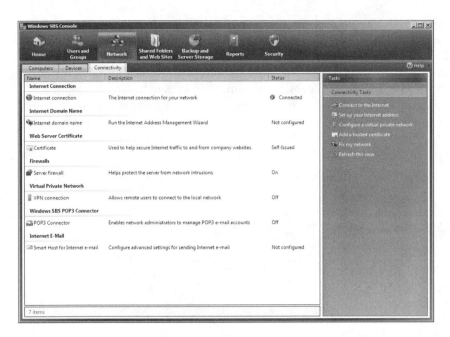

FIGURE 4.7   The Fix My Network Wizard is launched from the Windows SBS Console. It will check that your server conforms to best practices.

During the DHCP inspection and repair phase, it makes similar checks, looking for an authorized server, that the scope is configured, the server is excluded, and that bindings are valid. If you have chosen to not configure DHCP on your SBS 2008 server and chose "disable DHCP" in the advanced SBS Console, this step is skipped.

The Fix My Network Wizard attempts to configure each item it encounters with the default installation settings. In the case where services have to be installed or started, the wizard may need to run several times before it completes successfully. In addition, your server may require rebooting.

CAUTION

Be aware that when you run the Fix My Network Wizard, it resets all settings to known good default values. If you have made customizations to your configuration, you need to reset those after the wizard completes.

After the wizard has completed its initial checks, you are presented with a list of items that need correcting. After you complete the wizard, all the settings are set to known good default values.

Understanding Split DNS

Now that low-cost, high-bandwidth Internet solutions are available nearly everywhere, as is the availability of wireless networks, the roaming laptop is a common addition to small business networks. Having a workstation roam in and out of your network poses a number of issues, one of which is how will it identify the same resources by their public and private names? For this, SBS uses a DNS configuration known as split DNS. With split DNS, the roaming machines do not have to alter their configuration as they move in and out of your local network. They will be able to resolve resource names by their public .com name, even when they are physically within your .local network.

SBS 2008 creates a split DNS. The default configuration of split DNS can be seen in Figure 4.8.

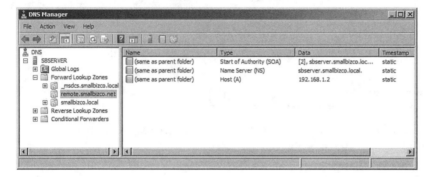

FIGURE 4.8   A split DNS configuration requires two Forward Lookup Zones: one for your internal domain, and another for your external domain.

You will notice two zones: One is called smallbizco.local, and the other is called remote.smallbizco.net. For each zone, the DNS server assumes that it is the authority for that zone—that is, no other DNS server will have information about the resources included in the network. By making the second zone match the public name of the SBS server (remote.smallbizco.net, in this case) and pointing that zone to the internal IP address of the SBS server, any workstation or other device that looks up the public name remote.smallbizco.net will return the proper IP address, no matter where the device is located. When querying the DNS name from the Internet, the device gets the public IP address for the server. When querying the DNS name from the internal network, it gets the internal IP address for the SBS server. This configuration will also not impact the lookups of any other DNS records in the public domain. For instance, any queries to www.smallbizco.net always return the public IP for that server.

Why Should I Use .local for My Internal Domain?

Controversy sometimes rages over whether you should configure a private domain for your internal network (smallbizco.local) or use the public domain name (smallbizco.net). Microsoft's official stance is that a private internal network is more secure than a publicly named internal network because it provides for a clear separation between the two networks.

The only exception to this rule is for enterprise networks that require Active Directory federation. Because this situation is not normally seen in small business networks, an SBS network is configured with a private internal domain name.

There are a couple of advantages to using a private domain name:

1. As the authority for the internal domain, access to internal resources is not dependent upon any third party.

2. Public DNS servers require zone transfer to stay up to date, whereas private DNS servers do not. They can operate in isolation, keeping your internal network hidden from the outside world and safe from rogue entries.

Adding DNS Records

You can create DNS records for internal devices, such as printers, that have static IP addresses and may not automatically register with DNS on the server. If you have a shared printer for the Accounting department that is named Accounting, you can create a DNS record for the printer so it can be accessed by name on the network and not by IP.

Creating and Testing a New Host Record

Follow these instructions to create and test a new host record:

1. Open the DNS Management console.

2. Expand Forward Lookup Zones.

3. Right-click on the internal domain name and select New Host (A or AAAA).

4. In the New Host dialog box, type Accounting in the Name field.

5. Enter the IP address of the printer in the IP Address field. Your entries will look like those in Figure 4.9.

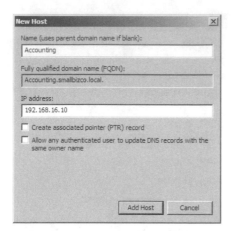

FIGURE 4.9   Creating a new Host DNS entry.

6. Click Add Host.

7. Click OK; then click Done.

8. Test the name resolution by opening a command prompt, typing `ping accounting`, and then pressing Enter.

Creating and Testing a New Alias

Although DNS was developed to prevent computer users from having to remember long IP number schemes, cnames were invented because IT staff have a tendency to make server names complex or obscure, and there was a need to create an alias that everyone could remember. In DNS, an alias is called a cname. A new cname can be created for any local resource. Follow these instructions to create a new cname record in the DNS Management Console:

1. Right-click on the internal domain name under Forward Lookup Zones and choose New Alias (CNAME).

2. In the New Alias dialog box, type SBS in the Alias Name field.

3. In the Fully Qualified Domain Name field, enter the fully-qualified domain name for the server. Click OK.

4. Test the name resolution by opening a browser window and typing SBS. You should be taken to the default web site.

Reserving IP Addresses in DHCP Server

One of the things that bothers some administrators about DHCP is that they don't know which devices have what IP address. Every network has some need for certain devices to have a specific IP address. This is most often used to specify an IP address for shared printers, wireless access point, or server. In addition to simply knowing what IP address the device has, administrators also find that IP address reservations can aid in helping you remember how the network is configured.

By using DHCP as a standard in your network and not configuring any device with a static IP address, you have only one place to look for IP addressing information in your network—that is, in the DHCP management console.

Follow these steps to create a DHCP reservation:

1. Open Server Manager.

2. Expand Role, DHCP Server, the internal server name, IPv4, and Scope. Figure 4.10 shows what the screen looks like after you have drilled down to the Scope.

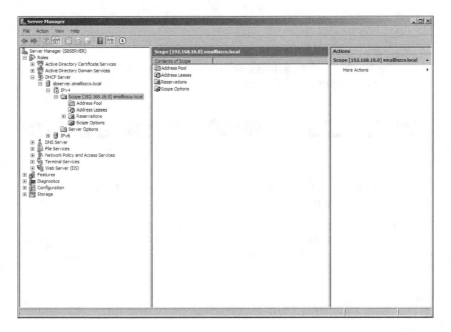

FIGURE 4.10   Server Manager is where most advanced configuration takes place, including DHCP and DNS configuration.

3. Select and right-click on Reservations and choose New Reservation. The New Reservation configuration window opens.

4. In the Reservation name field, enter a description name for the device, like Accounting Printer.

5. In the IP address field, enter the IP address that you would like to reserve for the printer. For organizational purposes, you should keep your reservations in the exclusion range.

6. In the MAC address field, enter the MAC address for the device (see Figure 4.11).

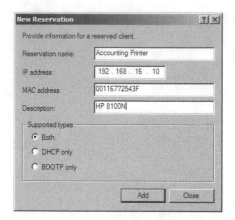

FIGURE 4.11   The New Reservation configuration window requires that you know the MAC address of the device you want to reserve an IP address for.

TIP

To find the MAC address of a printer, have the printer print out a configuration page. This will be an item in the printer menu.

To find the MAC address of a computer, type `ipconfig /all`. In this command, the MAC address is represented as the physical address for the network card.

You can also find the MAC address of these devices by running `arp -a` in a command prompt on the server. The MAC address is listed following the IP address for the device. If the device does not show in the list, ping the device; then run `arp -a` again.

---

7. In the description field, you can add any additional information you would like to record. Click Add.

8. When you are finished reserving addresses for devices, click the Close button.

Troubleshooting

Knowledge on how to troubleshoot DNS and DHCP is a staple for every administrator. SBS 2008 networks are not unique in their DNS and DHCP troubleshooting skills requirements. Some of the most common tools can help us expose the trouble area in the flow of our data packets.

Event Log Errors

DNS and DHCP will both put events into the event log. The event log can be used to troubleshoot why your DNS or DHCP server is not working. Fortunately for administrators, the event descriptions continue to get better and more descriptive with each new version.

DHCP

When your server starts up, you will notice several DHCP entries in the event logs. This is because during startup, DHCP checks for a static IP address, checks that it is authorized in Active Directory, and checks the integrity of its database, among other things. These event log entries will always be of source DHCP-Server. If your DHCP server stops working or fails to start, check the event log first and sort by Source. The DHCP events are quite descriptive and should provide you with enough information to begin your troubleshooting process. Table 4.3 provides a sample of the type of event errors that you might see.

TABLE 4.3   Common DHCP Events

Event ID	Interpretation
1005	Server found in our domain. This indicates that another DHCP is present and has registered with Active Directory.
1144	This computer has at least one dynamically assigned IP address. For reliable DHCP server operation, you should use only static IP addresses. DHCP requires that your server be configured with a static IP address.

DNS

When your server starts up, you will notice several DNS entries in the event logs. During startup, DNS checks that it can read the Active Directory zones for which it is authoritative, that services have started, that it can write to specific registry keys, and that the root-hints are present and working, among other things. These event log entries will always be of source DNS-Server-Service. If your DNS server stops working or fails to start, check the event log first and sort by Source. Most DNS server errors occur at the time the services are started. Table 4.4 provides a sample of the type of event errors that you might see.

TABLE 4.4   Common DNS Events

Event ID	Interpretation
4	The DNS server has finished the background loading of zones. All zones are now available for DNS updates and zone transfers, as allowed by their individual zone configuration. This event is new in Server 2008 and is a feature of DNS that allows faster startup of the service.
706	The DNS server does not have a cache or other database entry for root name servers.

Dcdiag

Dcdiag is a tool that can perform Active Directory integration tests for DNS. Dcdiag has a switch for testing your DNS configuration. From a command prompt, type **dcdiag /test:DNS** to run the DNS-specific tests.

First, dcdiag checks the Active Directory integration; then it runs specific tests on configuration and function of DNS. Notice that when you run this command, the dcdiag warns you that it has not found AAAA records in the domain. This is because the default installation of SBS 2008 does not configure IPv6 records. This warning can be safely ignored. Other errors that can be safely ignored are the resolution of some root hint servers. Root hint servers are not always up, so it is normal for dcdiag to find one or two that do not respond. It then flags them as invalid.

Unfortunately, because the IPv6 records are not present, the summary of the dcdiag tests indicates that smallbizco.local has failed the DNS tests. This result can be safely ignored if you have read through the result details and determined that everything else passed.

Ping

Ping is an excellent informational tool. A DNS server should respond to a ping request. If you suspect a problem with your ISP's DNS server, ping the IP address. It should quickly reply. If not, call the ISP and report the problem, and consider changing to another DNS server.

To use the Ping command, open a command prompt and type **ping <public DNS IP address>**. If the ping is successful and the server is responding, the output should look like this:

```
Pinging 4.2.2.2 with 32 byte of data:
Reply from 4.2.2.2: bytes=32 time=27ms TTL=52
Reply from 4.2.2.2: bytes=32 time=27ms TTL=52
Reply from 4.2.2.2: bytes=32 time=29ms TTL=52
Reply from 4.2.2.2: bytes=32 time=39ms TTL=52
Ping statistics for 4.2.2.2:
      Packet: Sent = 4, Received = 4, Lost = 0 (0% loss),
Approximate round trip times in milli-seconds:
      Minimum = 27ms, Maximum =39ms, Average = 30ms
If the DNS server is not responding the output from Ping will look like this:
Pinging 4.2.2.2 with 32 byte of data:
Request timed out.
Request timed out.
Request timed out.
Request timed out.

Ping statistics for 4.2.2.2:
      Packet: Sent = 4, Received = 0, Lost = 4 (100% loss),
```

If the ping response is Destination Host Unreachable, this means that the route to the server is incorrect or not functioning.

You may also ping a host name. For example, the command ping yahoo.com returns the IP address of the web site, but the pings fail because the web site is configured to not respond to ping requests. This does, however, let you know if your DNS is able to resolve the name to an IP address.

NSLookup

Like Ping, NSLookup is a tool to troubleshoot whether or not there is a route to your destination. Unlike Ping, NSLookup can tell you whether or not the destination you are reaching is the correct one.

NSLookup is an interactive application. It is used for troubleshooting DNS resolution. To use NSLookup, open a command prompt and type **nslookup** to start the application. It immediately returns the name of the local DNS server and its IP address:

```
Default Server:  server.smallbizco.local
Address:   192.168.0.2
```

To test whether your server is able to resolve addresses, type in the name of a web site that you know no one in the office has visited. This will tell you whether or not the forwarder that your local server is using to resolve web site addresses is working:

```
www.thirdtier.net
```

If everything is working, the response is immediate and the server returns the name and IP address of the web site:

```
Name: www.thirdtier.net
IP Address: 68.178.232.99
```

To test the responsiveness of the DNS server, type in the request several times. If there is a delay, the response will be as follows:

```
DNS request timed out.
    timeout was 2 seconds.
```

This indicates that the forwarding server is not responding in a timely manner. In general, if the DNS server is not responding quickly and consistently to requests, the best course of action is to change DNS servers. There are several publicly available DNS servers from Open DNS. Your ISP should also have more than one DNS server for you to use.

Can't Resolve a Host or Web Site Name

If users are having difficulty resolving a name to an IP address, ping the web site URL to get its IP address. Type the IP address into the address bar of your browser and see if the web site comes up. If it does, you have shown that there is a problem with DNS resolution to that site. The problem is most likely that the administrator for the web site has not updated the DNS records or, if this problem affects name resolution to all web sites, that your DNS or your ISP's DNS is not functioning.

ISP's DNS Server Is Down

The primary forwarder for your DNS server is mostly likely the DNS server maintained by your ISP. These DNS servers do occasionally go down or change IP addresses. Users notice that they are unable to resolve some web site addresses or that it takes a little longer for web sites to "come up." Administrators might notice that e-mail sits in the queues or gets returned. These are common signs that something is up with your ISP's DNS server. All too often, the solution that IT administrators choose is to forego using DNS forwarders and instead rely upon the DNS root servers. DNS root servers should not be used as your primary DNS resolution for Internet accesses. The root hint servers are often under heavy load, resulting in a longer time to name resolution. For the same reason, it is best to forward to a DNS server that is closest to you.

Your ISP should provide you with two DNS servers to use as forwarders. If you suspect a problem with your ISP's DNS server, contact them and ask for the current DNS server IP addresses. If the addresses they give you match what you have entered as forwarders, report a problem with their DNS servers.

DNS Returns a Bad Location

Both the DNS server and the workstation maintain a DNS cache. The purpose of the cache is to prevent undue load on the network by keeping commonly requested resources at hand. However, if the location of a resource has changed recently, a DNS query might return the old location. In this case, you need to flush the cache.

To flush the cache on the workstation, open a command prompt, type `ipconfig /flushdns`, and press Enter.

To flush the cache of the DNS server, open the DNS mmc, right-click on the server, and select Empty Cache. Note that there is no confirmation that the DNS cache has flushed.

Curse of the Hosts File

The common hosts file has been located in the \windows\system32\drivers\etc folder since Windows networking began. In a last-ditch effort to find the location of a resource, your computer will look in the hosts file. Many times, an administrator created a hosts file on a PC for some reason in the distant past and has forgotten about it. If you find that your requests are being diverted to another location, be sure to check the hosts file and remove or correct any entries therein. In today's modern network, there is rarely a reason to have any entries in the hosts file.

There's a Rogue DHCP Server

If another DHCP server appears on your network, your DHCP server will shut down and stop serving addresses. Your computers will receive an IP address from this rogue DHCP server and will have difficulty contacting network resources. The rogue DHCP server must be shut down. SBS 2008 should be the only DHCP server on your network.

If you do not know if there are other DHCP servers on your network, the DHCPLOC tool can be used to find them. The DHCPLOC tool provides you with the IP address of all DHCP servers on the network. This tool can be found in the \support\tools folder on the server installation DVD.

Summary

This chapter covered the default configuration of DNS and DHCP in SBS 2008. Most administrators will find that the default configuration suits the needs of their small business, but when the need arises to make a change or resolve a problem, this chapter also covers these topics. Securing DNS, adding additional records, and troubleshooting both DNS and DHCP using common tools round out the chapter.

Best Practice Summary

▶ Use the wizards to create DNS and DHCP initial configuration. Use native tools when configuring unique settings only. Using the wizards saves administrators from manual configuration of standard settings. Native tools should only be used when you are creating custom settings beyond the scope of the wizard.

▶ Use the `ipconfig /all` command liberally. Running this command and comparing the results against known good network settings is the first troubleshooting step that should be taken if you suspect a networking problem.

▶ Run the Fix My Network Wizard to get your server back to its original settings, after first documenting any customizations that you have made.

CHAPTER 5

Internet Information Services 7.0

Internet Information Services (IIS) has been a key part of the foundation of Small Business Server since its introduction as a software suite. In SBS 2008 we are now on revision 7 of Microsoft's web site platform. For SBS, these web sites make up key features for both administrators and information workers alike. From remote access to communication, it is all tied to the web sites under the hood in SBS 2008.

IIS 7.0 is the integration glue of SBS 2008. It is where the information worker in the field enters the server from within Remote Web Workplace and where the owner of the firm can check e-mail remotely without having Outlook 2007 on his or her computer. Next to Active Directory and Exchange it is probably the third pillar upon which SBS 2008 is built. Without it, it just would not be an SBS 2008 server.

IIS 7.0 is dependable and secure and only needs a few best practices and rules of thumb to ensure that the server is sound, secure, and healthy. The guidelines and recommendations in this chapter will ensure that administrators and information workers of the firm are as productive as they can be with SBS 2008.

The Web Sites Under the Hood

The Internet is a powerful tool in today's technology-driven world, and the web sites under the hood in Small Business Server 2008 are the pillars and foundation blocks for many of the key features of the server. These web sites provide key business functions for the small businesses that use the server. These roles include e-mail, remote access, sharing technologies, and even a billboard for new business.

External-Facing Web Sites Included with SBS 2008

Let's take a moment to introduce you to the external facing web sites that are the business building blocks of SBS 2008:

▶ **Remote Web Workplace (RWW)**—This is often the backbone of remote access to the desktops. The web site leverages the technology of Terminal Services Gateway to provide remote access from the web back to the desktops. Visualize Remote Desktop pushed over an SSL web site and you have RWW. The only port you need to open through the firewall for full functionality is 443. Those of you who used this technology in the Small Business Server 2003 platform might recall that RWW in that version needed both port 443 and 4125 open; in the SBS 2008 era, only the SSL port 443 is needed.

▶ **Outlook Web Access (OWA)**—This web site provides web-based e-mail over an SSL connection. Whereas in earlier versions, OWA was a poor replacement for Outlook, in the new version provided by Exchange 2007, that is no longer true. Out of the box, once the Set Up Your Internet Wizard is configured, it also ensures the site is ready to be synchronized to Windows Mobile phones and iPhones.

▶ **SharePoint**—Updated to version 3 of Windows SharePoint Services, this is a web-based shared file location for the internal domain. SharePoint provides an easy way to share files, set up a wiki, have an internal blog for the firm needs, have surveys, provide an internal help desk, and have an internal repository for faxes, among other things. Windows Small Business Server 2008 has provided a preconfigured site with certain items predeployed.

Internal Web Sites Included with SBS 2008

Several key web sites are included in SBS 2008 that provide servicing function to the network. Some of them are products unto themselves, such as Windows Software Update Services; some are unique only to the SBS 2008 platform. These sites include:

▶ **Windows Software Update Services (WSUS)**—If you think of your own internal version of Microsoft updates for all the computers and servers in your network, that describes what WSUS is in a nutshell. The WSUS service synchronizes with Microsoft and then all the workstations and servers pick up their patches from the central patching server.

▶ **SBS Client deployment**—When you go to each workstation and type in http://connect and use the web site offered to connect each workstation to the domain, you are utilizing the SBS Client deployment web site.

▶ **Default web site**—In past versions of Windows Small Business Server, the default web site was where most of the web sites were located. In SBS 2008, however, the default web site has only a few duties, one of which is to have several key sites that the workstations access for their security patch synchronizations.

Additional Web Sites That Can Be Combined with SBS 2008

In addition to the web sites that I have listed thus far, there are additional web properties that are designed to augment the server's capabilities:

▶ **Office Live Small Business**—Included in the Windows Small Business Server console is the ability to provide a connection between the Server and external web sites hosted by Microsoft's Office Live Small Business. These hosted web sites offer a simple but functional SharePoint-like web site that is easy to set up and configure. You can use these external sites as client-facing web sites to provide collaboration between you and your clients without exposing your server to unnecessary risks.

▶ **Microsoft Online Services**—Microsoft also has an additional Software as a Service (SaaS) offering called Microsoft Online Services, which provides more enterprise-class offerings. Although these are not designed to be as integrated as the Office Live Small Business offerings, if you are looking for a means to provide external, collaborative web platforms between the users inside the domain and the clients they service outside the domain, these SaaS offerings should be carefully investigated as possible ways to provide collaboration while reducing risk to the Small Business Server. Currently, Microsoft Online Services offer Hosted Exchange, Hosted SharePoint, and Office Live Meeting, a collaborative meeting site.

▶ **Other SaaS services**—Don't limit yourself to merely looking at the Microsoft designed platforms. The SaaS marketplace is full of offerings that can be designed to fit into the small business solution.

Protecting the Server

Similar to doctors who promise to do no harm to their patients, when you approach Internet Information Services in Windows Small Business Server, your first task is to do no harm to the myriad web sites that are default to the Small Business Server network. The primary function of IIS 7.0 on Small Business Server is to be a remote access portal for the network as well as the underlying patch management control web site. The default web sites in the server are designed to co-exist with one another. Furthermore, the fundamental changes in IIS 7.0 make it more conducive to having multiple web sites that can be run securely and separately from each other—what might be described as being in separate "sandboxes" from one another. However, before we begin to discuss the structure and changes in IIS 7.0, let's first discuss some foundational issues regarding web site hosting on your domain controller.

IIS in the Windows Server 2000 era was vulnerable to remote attacks if unpatched. In the Windows Server 2003 era, this risk was mitigated through the use of integration of security features, as well as ensuring that the server remained patched. In the Windows Server 2008 era, the means for mitgation are the same: Limit the number and type of external web sites that you use the server for and maintain vigilance in patching.

Windows Small Business Server 2008 is intended to have internal-only web sites hosted on the server and utilize hosted/third-party solutions for external-facing web sites. Office Live

Small Business or other third-party hosted solutions are the preferred means to provide an external-facing web site.

Default SBS Web Sites

If you've used prior versions of Windows Small Business Server, your first hint that things are a little different in this version comes early on in a brand new console, as you can see in Figure 5.1. Notice that the tab called Shared Folders and Web Sites allows you easy access to the status information for any web sites that are currently running. The green checks notify you that all the sites are operating as they should.

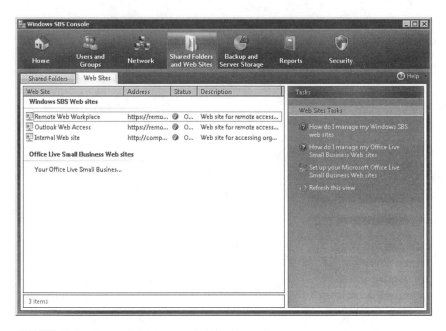

FIGURE 5.1   Shared Folders and Web Sites view.

The console hides a bigger technical change between earlier versions of SBS and the current SBS 2008. The major change between Internet Information Service 6.0 (included in SBS 2003) and 7.0 (included in SBS 2008) is the .NET integration. ASP.NET and the .NET framework have been integrated by placing the ASP.NET runtime extensibility model into the core server.

Just like in the previous version of SBS, you have three default web sites. The first is Remote Web Workplace, a remote access portal that allows access to the server and desktops to individuals with the appropriate permissions. Then there is Outlook Web Access, a web-based version of the Outlook e-mail platform that enables you to send, receive, and access e-mail. And finally, there is the web site that the server calls the "Internal web site," which is, in reality, merely SharePoint 3.0 with some preinstalled customizations so that the site is ready to go. If you set up Office Live Small Business integration, this is also showcased in this console view.

Changes from SBS 2003—Remote Web Workplace Changes

Two of the biggest changes between this version of SBS and prior versions is the manner in which Remote Access is configured and accessed. No longer do you need to allow access through port 4125. The new Terminal Services Gateway feature of Windows Server 2008 is now utilized by SBS 2008 to allow the remote desktop feature of each workstation to be published through an SSL web page. It no longer requires the additional opening of port 4125 as the "control" port.

SBS 2008 now uses traditional server Public Key Infrastructure, with Active Directory Certificate Services and the Role Service of Certification Authority installed. The end result of this is that machines that need remote access must have installed this Enterprise Certificate in order to have full access to the computers back at the office. Although they will be able to obtain access to Outlook Web Access and the internal company site, they will not be able to connect to the desktop of the chosen system without this certificate installed. For more detailed information on the changes in the Remote Web Workplace, Chapter 6, "Remote Web Workplace and Other Remote Access Solutions," discusses it in more detail.

Integration with SharePoint

SBS 2008 includes a web portal called SharePoint. As in prior versions, SharePoint is integrated with SBS 2008, and is intended to be the internal "bulletin board" site for the company. Chapter 7, "SharePoint and Companyweb," details the changes that have occurred in this version of SharePoint. From inside the SBS Console, you can easily enable or disable the web site and adjust permissions as needed. From this portal, you can also easily modify the name and description of the internal web site:

1. Click on the SBS Console and approve the User Account Control prompt.
2. Click on Shared Folders and Web Sites on the navigational bar and then on Internal Web Site.
3. Click on Internal Web Properties and, on the General Information tab, change the name of the web site under Site Title, as shown in Figure 5.2.

From inside the network, you access the internal SharePoint merely by typing in http://companyweb. Externally, it is intended that you access it via the remote web workplace portal by going through https://remote.yourdomainname.com and then by clicking on Internal Web Site.

Configuring the Default SBS Web Sites

If there is any lesson to be learned from past versions of Windows Small Business Server, it's that, more often than not, if you let the system set up all that it requires, it also takes care of the rest. Thus, for the three main default SBS web sites, the server has done the configuration work for you. SharePoint and Windows Software Update Services are preconfigured.

When you open the new IIS 7.0 console, you notice a few things. First, note that you have both an administration console for IIS 6.0, as well as one for IIS 7.0. This is very helpful

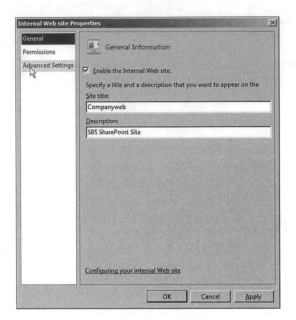

FIGURE 5.2   Changing the default site title.

should you have applications that need to run on the older IIS 6.0 platform. To launch the new IIS console, click Start, All Programs, Administrative Tools. You see that you have an IIS 6.0 Manager and an IIS 7.0 Manager.

The IIS 6.0 Manager looks like our old friend IIS 6 (see Figure 5.3). Click Start, All Programs, Administrative Tools, and then on Internet Information Services 6.0. Click the resulting User account control prompt, and you see the familiar IIS Manager. For Windows Small Business Server 2008, the only site under the IIS 6.0 console is a disabled FTP console tree. While file transfer protocol (FTP) can be enabled on the server, you should, as with all external public web access to the server, consider carefully all the alternatives available to you before enabling file transfer protocol. There are many easier ways to set up file transfer programs, including Microsoft's Sky Drive, to transfer files.

Now, click Start, All Programs, Administrative Tools, and then click Internet Informational Services 7.0 to launch the new console. Click the resulting User account control prompt, and you see the new IIS manager that shows you the connected web sites. In the middle task pane, you see the task view grouped by ASP.NET, IIS, and Management (see Figure 5.4).

Don't be overwhelmed by the options available. For most servers that you administer, the basics are installed by the server itself and any applications that you install. On the right side of the console, you see that the ability to restart IIS services is now an easy-to-click button. This is notable because in past versions of IIS you had to right click and select Stop and Start or drop to a command line and type in IISRESET. Now the resetting of the IIS is built into the console.

By default, the server is set to only allow and accept connections from accounts with Windows credentials. Adjusting any web site to allow anonymous connections from

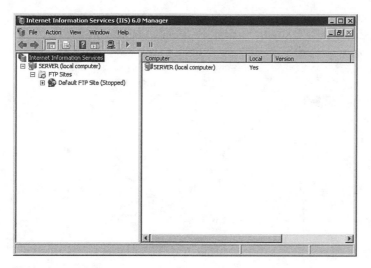

FIGURE 5.3   IIS 6.0 manager.

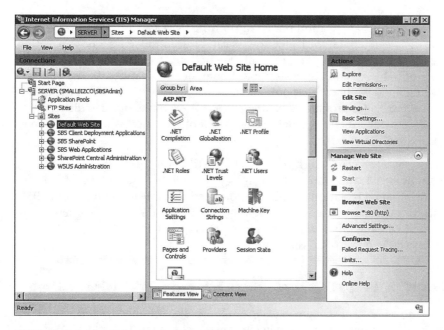

FIGURE 5.4   IIS 7.0 new task-based console.

external sources reduces the security of not only the web site, but the server as a whole. If third-party applications that install web sites are installed on the server, review their requirements for permissions and ensure that they don't remove this setting.

Note that the server ships with six web sites enabled, as shown in Figure 5.5. During the installation you are not able to choose to not install specific options. Thus, after you have deployed the server, if for whatever reason you want to turn off certain web functions, it's recommended to leave the web sites as is and set them to be disabled rather than attempt to uninstall any of the web sites that are default to the SBS Server.

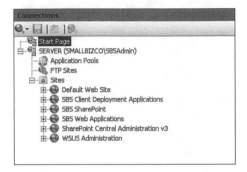

FIGURE 5.5   SBS default web sites.

The server also ships with 13 application pools, all running .NET version 2.0 with various support of Classic or Integrated ASP.NET pipeline, as can be seen in Figure 5.6. Application pools are unique to .NET applications and typically are tied to a web site. In past versions of SBS the number of web sites and application pools matched in quantity. In the SBS 2008 version, the additional application pools allow for more isolation between the different functions the SBS web sites provide. Exchange 2007, for example, has five different application pools to provide functions ranging from Outlook Web Access to Autodiscover, which is used for Outlook Anywhere.

Web sites can select the .NET Framework version when setting up a web site. If the site chooses .NET Framework 1.1, the Managed pipeline option will be disabled. Managed pipeline mode is determined based on the application needs. In Integrated mode, the IIS processes requests for managed content with the integrated IIS and ASP.NET request-processing pipeline. In Classic mode, IIS processes requests for managed content with separate IIS and ASP.NET request-processing pipelines.

> **CAUTION**
>
> Check with your web application vendors regarding which version they need and document this setting. If the web site cannot run in Integrated mode, it must be installed in Classic mode.

In comparison to Windows Small Business Server 2003, Windows Small Business Server 2008 does not put its web sites or application pools in the default sites, and thus their settings should not interfere with the default settings of the server. The 13 default application pools and their settings are listed in Table 5.1. Historically, past lines of business applications, and even .NET patches, have potentially changed these settings; thus, it's wise to keep this table handy or set up a virtual server to confirm the default settings:

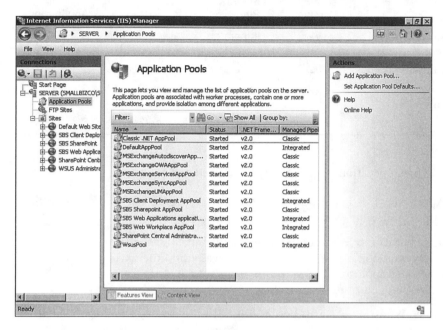

FIGURE 5.6   Thirteen application pools.

TABLE 5.1   Default Application Pool Settings

Name	.NET Framework Version	Managed Pipe	Identity	Applications
Classic .NET AppPool	V2.0	Classic	NetworkService	0
Default AppPool	V2.0	Integrated	NetworkService	1
MSExchangeAutodiscover AppPool	V2.0	Classic	LocalSystem	3
MSExchangeOWAAppPool	V2.0	Classic	LocalSystem	6
MSExchangeServicesAppPool	V2.0	Classic	LocalSystem	2
MSExchangeSyncAppPool	V2.0	Classic	LocalSystem	1
MSExchangeUMAppPool	V2.0	Classic	LocalSystem	2
SBS Client Deployment AppPool	V2.0	Integrated	NetworkService	1
SBS SharePoint AppPool	V2.0	Classic	NetworkService	3

TABLE 5.1 Default Application Pool Settings

Name	.NET Framework Version	Managed Pipe	Identity	Applications
SBS Web Applications Application Pool	V2.0	Integrated	NetworkService	5
SBS Web Workplace AppPool	V2.0	Integrated	NetworkService	1
SharePoint Central Administration v3	V2.0	Classic	NetworkService	3
WSUSPool	V2.0	Integrated	NetworkService	8

Each of the following application pools has a specific need and function.

▶ **Default App Pool**—This application pool is linked to the Default web site and the system path is located at %SystemDrive%\inetpub\wwwroot.

▶ **MSExchangeAutoDiscoverAppPool**—This pool is linked to the /Autodiscover web site that allows Outlook 2007 clients to automatically find the Exchange server settings. The three applications tied to this app pool are /Autodiscover, /Autodiscover/bin, and /Autodiscover/help.

▶ **MSExchangeOWAAppPool**—This pool is linked to the various Exchange-related web sites including /Exadmin, /Exchange, /Exchweb, /owa, and /Public.

▶ **MSExchangeServicesAppPool**—This pool is linked to the various web sites including /EWS and /EWS/bin. This pool is used for Exchange 2007's web services components.

▶ **MSExchangeSyncAppPool**—This pool is linked to the Microsoft Server-ActiveSync application.

▶ **MSExchangeUMAppPool**—This pool is linked to the /UnifiedMessaging and /UnifiedMessaging/bin web sites.

▶ **SBS Client Deployment AppPool**—This pool is linked to the root application.

▶ **SBSSharePointAppPool**—This pool is linked to /_layouts/images, /_layouts/inc, and the root application.

▶ **SBS Web Applications application pool**—This pool is linked to /BPService, /FileCopy, /Rpc, /RpcWithCert, /WebHelp, and the root application.

▶ **SBS Web Workplace AppPool**—This pool is linked to /Remote, which is the Remote Web Workplace portal.

▶ **SharePoint Central Administration v3 Application Pool**—This pool is linked to /_layouts/images, /_layouts/inc, and the root application.

▶ **WsusPool application pool**—This pool is linked to /ApiRemoting30, /ClientWebService, /DssAuthWebService, /Inventory, /ReportingWebService, /ServerSyncWeb, /SimpleAuthWeb, and the root application.

CAUTION

If suddenly after the installation of a third party application your web sites stop functioning, begin by confirming that the application pool settings are as they should be. Third-party antivirus programs have been known to change an IIS application pool from version 2.0 of .NET back to 1.1 without indicating that it is doing so. If suddenly you get a message similar to "'C:\WINDOWS\Microsoft.NET\Framework\v2.0.50727\asp-net_filter.dll' could not be loaded due to a configuration problem. The current configuration only supports loading images built for a AMD64 processor architecture," that is a tell-tale sign that the application has changed settings.

The function and purpose of each of the application pools included in SBS 2008 range from providing Exchange functions to patching functions. None of them should be removed, but if you do not need the application that they support, merely disable the application pool; do not remove it.

If you have installed antivirus, this might also impact the number of pools and the number of web sites installed. Antivirus suites typically add another web site so that it can be managed and monitored at the server. Thus, you might have an additional application pool on your server that was not previously listed.

For the web sites themselves, there are six web sites enabled on the SBS server. These sites are listed in Table 5.2.

TABLE 5.2   SBS Web Sites

Name	Binding
Default web site	*:80 (http)
SBS Client Application Deployment	*.:80:connect
SBS SharePoint	Companyweb on *:80 (http), *:987 (https)
SBS Web Applications	Sites on *:80 (http), *:443(https), remote.yourdomain.com
SharePoint Central Administration	:(various port chosen at random on setup) (http)
WSUS Administration	:8530 (http),:8531(https)

Settings for the Default Web Site

When a web site fails to load properly, one of the first items to examine is the permissions of the web site. If these settings are changed, not only does it impact the security of the web site, but it could impact operations of the firm also. If you change the permissions on the Outlook Web Access web site such that users no longer have read and execute rights, you will not be able to access web based e-mail. Conversely, if you change the settings for all web sites to allow anonymous users to have full control for a web site, you might adversely affect the security of the domain controller. Review the settings shown in Table 5.3 for the default web site and ensure that they are as shown here.

TABLE 5.3   Permissions for Default Web Site

Allow Permission	Creator Owner	System	Administrators	Users	IIS_Users	Trusted Installer
Full Control		✓	✓			✓
Modify		✓	✓			✓
Read & Execute		✓	✓	✓	✓	✓
List Folder Contents		✓	✓	✓	✓	✓
Read		✓	✓	✓	✓	✓
Write		✓	✓			✓
Special Permissions	✓					

The default web site is used only for the self-update web site location used for the Windows Software Update Services. Unlike previous versions of SBS, OWA is not a web site underneath the default web site and is therefore less likely to be impacted by the installation of third-party software that may want to change settings.

Settings for the SBS SharePoint Site and for the SharePoint Central Administration v3

In SBS 2003, SharePoint version 2 was preinstalled and named "Companyweb" and provided an internal collaboration web site. In SBS 2008, Companyweb has been updated to version 3 of SharePoint and serves the same purpose. It can also provide additional connectivity to externally hosted applications and services through a connection to Office Live Small Business Services. Table 5.4 lists the default permissions settings needed for a fully functional SBS SharePoint web site. One troubleshooting step that you might find useful is to review the permissions of the web site listed in Table 5.4.

TABLE 5.4   Default Settings for SBS SharePoint (Companyweb)

Allow Permission	System	Network Service	WSS_Admin_WPG	WSS_WPG	Administrators
Full Control	✓	✓	✓		✓
Modify	✓	✓	✓		✓
Read & Execute	✓	✓	✓	✓	✓
List Folder Contents	✓	✓	✓	✓	✓

TABLE 5.4   Default Settings for SBS SharePoint (Companyweb)

Allow Permission	System	Network Service	WSS_Admin_WPG	WSS_WPG	Administrators
Read	✓	✓	✓	✓	✓
Write	✓	✓	✓		✓
Special Permissions					

Both the SBS SharePoint site and the SharePoint Central Administration v3 site have the same permission settings. Therefore, if you need to review the permissions for either SBS SharePoint or the permissions for the Central Administration portal, you can use this table. The Central Administration web site is used by SharePoint administrators to set up, configure, and add additional SharePoint sites as you see fit. If SharePoint or the SharePoint administrator's web site is not working, review the permissions on the web site to see if something has accidentally been reset.

Settings for the SBS Web Applications and Windows Server Client Deployment Applications

When you open up the IIS console, note that the bulk of the web sites used in the day-to-day operation of e-mail used by the firm are located under this site location, named the SBS Web Application web site. Exchange, OWA, and Remote access are all located under this location. The SBS Client Deployment Applications web site holds the location for application deployment. If OWA suddenly no longer functions, one troubleshooting solution might be to review the permissions of the SBS Web Applications web site listed in Table 5.5.

TABLE 5.5   Default Permissions for SBS Web Applications

Allow Permission	Creator Owner	System	Administrators	Users	Trusted Installer
Full Control		✓	✓		
Modify		✓	✓		
Read & Execute		✓	✓	✓	
List Folder Contents		✓	✓	✓	✓
Read		✓	✓	✓	
Write		✓	✓		
Special Permissions	✓				

Both the SBS Web Applications and the SBS Client Deployment Applications have the same permission settings. Thus, use Table 5.5 as your guide for reviewing the permissions for the SBS Client Deployment Applications web site also.

Settings for the WSUS Administrator Web Site

Windows Software Update Services 3.0 is the final default web site of SBS 2008. The WSUS server uses it to store and deploy software patches and updates to the server. The default permissions for the WSUS Administrator web site are listed in Table 5.6.

TABLE 5.6   Default Permissions for WSUS Administrator Web Site

Allow Permission	Authenticated Users	System	Network Service	Administrators	Users
Full Control		✓		✓	
Modify		✓		✓	
Read & Execute	✓	✓	✓	✓	✓
List Folder Contents	✓	✓	✓	✓	✓
Read	✓	✓	✓	✓	✓
Write		✓		✓	
Special Permissions					

This web site uses port 8530 for http and port 8531 for https connections to the WSUS web site. More on the settings for WSUS are included in Chapter 17, "Managing Server and Workstation Security."

Changes from SBS 2003—So Where's My SharePoint on Port 444 and /ConnectComputer?

If you've used SBS in the past, you might notice two changes in the setup documentation. The first change is the port that SharePoint used for external secured access. In the past, SharePoint used port 444, but now that external access port is port 987. The SBS development team found that too many companies (including Microsoft) already used that port for other applications. The second noticeable change is the internal web site that you are directed to go to on the client workstations to begin the process of joining the domain and moving the local profile to a domain profile is now merely http://connect. No longer do you need to memorize the server name to use in a web site address—http://connect is the only name you need to remember.

Protecting Web Site Configuration

With the advent of Windows Server 2008 image-based deployment, it is more important, not less, to have a good backup. If you want to provide a value-add to the business and ensure that you have multiple ways to restore a web site, having a backup of the IIS metadata is a valuable recovery tool. Whereas Microsoft support engineers have been known to dig into Shadow File Copy and retrieve an IIS metadata file in a worst-case scenario, you can make your disaster recovery options more flexible by having a few more recovery techniques ready to go.

Backup and Recovery of Metadata Information

Like with any server, making backups of the entire server is wise. Making a backup of the IIS configuration before you begin working on a web site is very wise. Having multiple backups of the IIS configuration and even considering having one on removable media is extremely wise.

With an IISMetabase backup, you can reset the web site file and folder permissions as they were. Without an IISMetabase backup, you are possibly looking at a full recovery of the server from the image based backup. Merely obtaining the IISmetabase.xml file from the backup may not be good enough. As when you go to re-import the XML file into IIS, if the file was not exported out using the proper backup command, it may not be in the file structure to be imported into IIS.

In general, the goal for IIS backup is to provide the following options for recovery:

- ▶ **Recover the IIS configuration using the IIS configuration backup**—This is a process where you export out the IIS configuration and then if necessary import it back into the IIS console.

- ▶ **Recover a corrupted IIS install by reinstalling IIS and then recovering a prior IIS configuration**—In an SBS 2008 server, given the wizard deployment, the chances that IIS will be corrupted during install are lessened; however, you might be directed by Microsoft support personnel to reinstall IIS due to a third-party deployment that impacted your web sites.

- ▶ **Recover the server and web site by recovering the web from archives**—You may be directed by support personnel to use Shadow File Copies to roll back to a prior web version.

- ▶ **Perform a partial system restore to retrieve missing or corrupted data**—You may need to utilize the SBS backup to recover specific web sites.

The unique configuration of the Small Business Server 2008 server means that you need to take special precautions due to the fact that Exchange and WSUS services are impacted. For a Small Business Server configuration, the option to remove and then reinstall IIS is actually not recommended. Due to the interconnection between IIS and Exchange, you should not remove one without seriously considering the impact of the other.

There are two types of backups that the system can make, as follows:

▶ The file applicationHost.config is backed up automatically and stored under %SystemDrive%\InetPub\History by default as part of the normal processes on the server

▶ Manual backups can be made of the server's current configuration and running state and stored at %SystemRoot%\System32\InetServ\Backup.

Administrator backups include the following files:

▶ **ApplicationHost.config**—The current configuration and running state of the server, including applications, application pools, and virtual directories.

▶ **Administration.config**—The current configuration for delegation and management.

▶ **Mbschema.xml**—The schema for the IIS6 metabase.

▶ **Metabase.xml**—The IIS6 metabase file.

▶ **Redirection.config**—Redirection information.

The Appcmd Command

Many of the functions and features of IIS7 can be controlled by one command, called Appcmd.exe. It administers sites and, among other tasks, does backup of sites. The commands and options that it can do at a high level are listed in Table 5.7.

TABLE 5.7   **Appcmd.exe** Command Options

Options	Task
SITE	Administration of virtual sites
APP	Administration of applications
VDIR	Administration of virtual directories
APPPOOL	Administration of application pools
CONFIG	Administration of general configuration sections
WP	Administration of worker processes
REQUEST	Administration of HTTP requests
MODULE	Administration of server modules
BACKUP	Administration of server configuration backups
TRACE	Working with failed request trace logs

Backing Up the Web Site Configuration

To back up the IIS configuration, you normally use one of the command line included in this section. The following command backs up the IIS configuration to the default location:

```
appcmd add backup "backupname"
```

This command restores the IIS configuration:

```
appcmd restore backup "backupname"
```

To perform the backup using Appcmd, from an elevated command prompt (right-click command and select Runas Administrator), type the following:

```
cd \windows\system32\inetsrv
```

Now type the following:

```
appcmd add backup yourbackupname
```

As you can see in Figure 5.7, the command completes successfully.

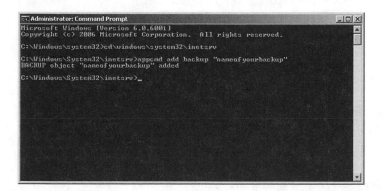

FIGURE 5.7   Command to back up metadata.

However, there are additional ways that a backup can be made. One methodology includes a third-party dll that adds a GUI interface to enable a backup, as described in the following steps:

1. Download the IIS7BackupRestore.dll from http://www.iis.net/downloads/default.aspx?tabid=34&g=6&i=1552.

2. Right-click the downloaded files and select Properties.

3. Click the Unblock button to allow the externally obtained file to be opened on a server (see Figure 5.8). (Anytime you download files from the Internet, the Server blocks your access until you adjust the security setting.)

4. For temporary purposes *only*, open the Security Center and temporarily disable the User Account Control in order to copy the IIS7BackupRestore.dll to the c:\Windows\Assembly folder. This is a special .net folder and is a system-protected folder, which is why UAC needs to be temporarily disabled to copy this file. It is extremely important that UAC is not permanently disabled, as this also disables the

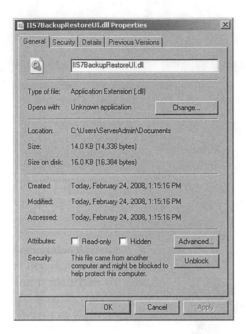

FIGURE 5.8   Unblock the file.

protected mode setting for Internet Explorer 7 (among many other things) and significantly weakens protection on the server.

5. Copy the DLL to the \windows\system32\inetsrv folder by clicking on the Administrative permission prompt and clicking Continue when prompted to do so.

6. Type the command **Copy IIS7BackupRestoreUI.dll c:\Windows\Assembly**, ensuring that you are still in an elevated command prompt window.

7. Under the File menu, browse for the file windows\System32\InetSrv\config\Administration.config. (You need to click on a UAC permission prompt to obtain permissions.)

8. Open the file in Notepad.

9. Search for the <moduleProviders> section and add the following:
```
<add name="IIS7BackupRestoreUI"
    type="IIS7BackupRestoreUI.MyModuleProvider, IIS7BackupRestoreUI,
    Version=1.0.0.0, Culture=neutral,
    PublicKeyToken=db9daa3d2ea5f6fd" />
```

10. Search for the <modules> section and add the following:
```
<add name="IIS7BackupRestoreUI" />
```

11. Open Inetmgr, and you see the module listed in your IIS 7 Manager, as shown in Figure 5.9.

FIGURE 5.9   GUI add-on to backup metadata.

NOTE

Windows Small Business Server 2008, by default, disables the built-in Administrator account and enables a second Administrator account. This, by default, enables User Account Control (UAC). You might find that documents and instructions on the web do not work as is stated because the UAC is enabled. Because of this, you should always launch applications and command lines with "Run as Administrator" invoked. This does not disable UAC, but is merely the means to elevate applications to the proper permission level that they need. Only as a *very* last resort should you disable UAC; once you have performed your task, re-enable it *immediately*.

Using System State Backup

The native backup system in Server 2008 is an image-based backup and is meant to do a backup of the entire system. A smaller backup, called System State Backup, backs up the IIS metabase, registry, COM+ catalog, and other key elements of a server, but with a much smaller size and a much shorter duration. In this case, it's command line to the rescue again:

```
wbadmin start systemstatebackup
wbadmin start systemstaterecovery
wbadmin delete systemstatebackup
```

Example of the use of the command line for System State is as follows:

```
wbadmin start systemstaterecovery -backupTarget:f :
```

You can configure this easily as a schedule task as well. Just build a batch file that includes that command. Then, go into the Windows 2008 task schedule and build a rule that runs that batch file once a week at a scheduled time.

Backup and Recovery of Web Sites

When working with any IIS server that shares space with Exchange 2007, you must remember that you need to remove both Exchange and the IIS and reinstall both of them. This should only be considered as a final last-resort step when all other troubleshooting steps have failed. In fact, I'd highly recommend that you take all other troubleshooting steps and ensure that you call technical support when you do so. The job is not for the faint of heart and could have some repercussions. In general, this step of totally removing IIS and Exchange and reinstalling them is considered an ultimate last resort. The number of prerequisites for the integration of Exchange include the following:

- ▶ Active Directory Management Services
- ▶ Active Directory Application Mode
- ▶ PowerShell
- ▶ Media player components (if unified messaging is fully installed)

Typically, you can repair permissions on web sites, roll back to a backup configuration, or any number of options that do not include uninstalling and reinstalling these two key components of the server. *Always* ensure that you have a good, tested backup of the server at all times.

Configuring Additional Web Sites

Your first step when considering adding more web sites to the SBS Server is finding out if the system can handle the load, function, and risk that an additional web site can bring. For many small firms, most additional web sites are automatically installed by antivirus or line-of-business vendors on the server itself. In addition, most small businesses merely add additional SharePoint sites to their system; thus, it's not adding an application pool or web services to the system. Third-party applications that are not designed to share sites and pools with other systems might not perform well on the same server that is running the Small Business Server functions. Thus, you need to determine if the server should be used for additional web sites in the first place. If there is the necessary overhead and the site will not be adding risk to the server, it's very easy to set one up.

The Risks of Adding Additional External Web Sites

For many, the issue of hosting external web sites on top of and in addition to the default web sites included in Small Business Server doesn't seem like it increases the risk to the domain controller. The server is already connected to the Internet, having open ports to the Internet already.

Given that it already has IIS installed, how can adding an additional web site open to the world be any riskier than what is already there? Consider, however, that if you install a web application that doesn't properly sanitize input, or control variables or any number of improper coding techniques, users could unknowingly introduce web-based risks on a domain controller that they were not anticipating.

With the advent of Windows Server 2008 Web Edition and external web hosting through Windows Live Services, consider carefully the proposition of adding additional web sites to be used for external access on the server. Given that the default web sites of the server have gone through a secure development lifecycle process, they have been reviewed to minimize issues. Third-party applications or home-grown web sites might not be built with the concerns of ensuring that cross-site scripting issues are addressed and minimized. Thus, be aware of the issues of supportability, security, and risk on the domain controller as you add third-party web sites when setting up additional server(s).

In the era of virtualization and SaaS (Software as a Service), using alternative platforms, servers and solutions to provide web platforms that are meant to be public facing is the wiser choice to make. Furthermore, with external hosted solutions, there might be alternatives that make better sense from a risk perspective.

Finally SBS 2008 Premium provides an additional Server license that can be used for your needs. Consider placing line-of-business web applications on this second box. It isolates them from the main SBS box and reduces the risk to the business web sites running there.

If there is the necessary overhead and the site will not be adding risk from potential exposure to SQL injection attacks and poor coding to the server, it's easy to add one. It's always wise to add a new site to a new application pool. This allows for easy troubleshooting and ensures that you can manually stop the pool should the web site that you've added cause issues on the server.

To add a web site, go to Sites, right-click on Add Web Site, and follow the wizard:

1. In the Site name, add the name of the web site you want to add.
2. Select the application pool that you previously built.
3. Place the location of the file on your system. One recommendation has been to place it in a folder location with appropriate permissions. On the default c:\inetpub\wwwroot location, IIS_IUSERS users only have read and execute, list

folder contents, and read writes. If the application needs permissions greater than that to service web pages, you might leave the server at risk.

4. Choose the host name to make it easier for local workstations to resolve to the site.

5. In order to complete the web site so that you can resolve to it from the workstations, go to Administrative Tools, and then to DNS. Expand the Server settings and click on Forward Lookup Zones.

6. Right-click the internal name of the server and click to add a new Alias (CNAME).

7. Enter the alias name and the fully qualified domain name for the target host. This should be the same setting that you find for the web sites called Companyweb and Connect.

Note that adding an external facing web site that would need SSL for security purposes adds a great deal of complexity. You might need to publish the site on another port because it cannot reside or be bound to port 443—that location is already reserved and used by the Remote Web Workplace.

If you add a web site using the Add Web Site Wizard, it builds a new application pool by default. If the application did not build an application pool when it installed and the application requires a separate pool, click Application pool, and then click Add Pool to open the Add Application Pool dialog (see Figure 5.10). Choose the default settings or choose nonmanaged code from the .NET Framework version drop-down option and Integrated or Classic Managed pipeline from the Managed Pipeline Mode option. For older applications, you might need to set the Managed Pipeline Mode as Classic, which sets up the system to run as IIS 6.0 settings rather than IIS 7.0. You might need to test to determine which setting works for your needs, as shown in Figure 5.10.

FIGURE 5.10   Adding a new pool to the server's web applications.

Managing SSL Certificates in IIS

SBS 2008 ships with a wizard that deploys a self-signed certificate for secured external web access. For many years this was considered appropriate and provided good security and functionality. As our needs for remote access have increased, as mobile phone choices have expanded, and finally as web browsers have included security messages to our end users, self-signed certificates are no longer "good enough" for the typical SBS 2008 deployment.

Although the default self-signed certificate process included in SBS 2008 should be utilized to set up the server, it should be considered as a proof of concept that the server's security system works. After you've run the Set Up Your Internet Wizard address, you will have a fully functional SSL-protected web site to be used for remote access. However, the self-signed certification that the wizard provided needs to be carefully added to Internet Explorer in order for the end user not to see a warning about the certificate being self signed. This does not mean that the SSL protection of the web site is at risk—merely that the certificate is not able to be confirmed as being from the site that it purports to be.

Understanding the Default Certificates

The Set Up Your Internet Wizard, by default, sets up a self-signed certificate. Self signed means that the server itself is the one that generated the certificate, and that there is no external verification from any other source, other than the server itself, that it is a valid certificate. The certificate must be then manually added to each remote mobile phone device to allow it to synchronize with the server. Any change to the self-signed certificate has to be redeployed to each phone and remote user that needs access to the server.

Deciding When to Use a Third-Party Certificate

It might seem to be cheaper up front to use self-signed certificates, but you will soon find that external third-party certificates provide less hassle in the long run. You will have an easier time setting up mobile phones and, most important, fewer questions from confused end users about the ominous red warning from Internet Explorer 7 that their RWW web site should not be trusted.

For many firms, the self-signed certificate provided by the Set Up Your Internet Wizard is just fine as a temporary means of securing the server. For many in the SBS 2003 era, the self-signed cert worked perfectly. With the advent, however, of newer mobile phones, and a need for better security, you might reconsider the use of the self-signed certificate and instead purchase an external third party. This third-party certificate vendor should be one that sets up an external trusted verification structure, such that there is a location on the Internet that has performed a verification of the certificate that the cert is indeed coming from the server it purports to be coming from.

> **NOTE**
>
> Mobile phones also rely on SSL certificates for their remote access for synchronizing to the server. One trick to determine the best certificate provider is to look at your mobile phones. Are they the PocketPC variety that are more lenient toward certificates? Are they the Smart Phone variety that have a few select root certificates already on the device? You need to see if you can add your vendor's certificate bundle to it if the external provider is not already installed as a root certificate. Review the trusted certificate list in the device and consider purchasing a certificate from one of these vendors.

For some industries, this self-signed certificate is not appropriate given the regulations. The Payment Card Industry Standards actually strongly suggest that a third-party external certificate is obtained and installed. Some automated scanning tools that base their recommendations on the PCI/DSS standards even go further to state that if you do not have a third-party certificate, your server will not be PCI/PSS compliant without it.

Working with Third-Party Certificates

The one decision you need to make early on is the impact of the Office Live solutions in the certificate you request. If you decide that you do want to have the ability to integrate your server with Office Live initiatives, you must run the wizard and name your remote access http://remote.domain.com. This leaves you with a decision to make. There are two types of certificates you can purchase. The first is a specific certificate that matches exactly that web site name. This will be the least expensive certificate but might be more restrictive if you attempt to or need additional SSL-accessible web sites. If you need to be more flexible in your needs for a certificate, you need to purchase the more expensive wild-card version that allows for subdomains in front of the main domain name.

The alternative is that you choose to make your domain name via the wizard to be http://www.domain.com. This blocks you from using any Office Live Integration, so ensure that this is a limitation that you can live with.

NOTE

Why do so many security best practices and PCI-DSS checklists recommend a third-party certificate? Well, there are several reasons. The first is for anti-spoofing reasons. A third party holds part of your security certificate in their repository so that someone can verify that the web site they are connecting to really is the web site to which they intend to connect. The second is to train your clients and users with proper security warnings. When you use Internet Explorer 7, Firefox, or Safari, when any site that contains a self-signed certificate is encountered, the end user receives severe warnings. If you train your employees to ignore what their security notifications are trying to teach them, they will be unable to make proper and wise decisions. Installing a third-party certificate removes these confusing warnings and allows your end users to be assured that they are connected to the web site to which they intended.

Requesting and Installing a Third-Party Certificate with the Add a Trusted Certificate Wizard

Windows Small Business Server 2008 has added a new Add a Trusted Certificate option to the Home tab on the SBS console. This wizard performs steps similar to those that you perform manually, except that it does it correctly, dependably, and consistently between servers. The first step it does is to run the wizard process that performs the certificate request process on the IIS web site. You submit this CER request to the certificate provider and then wait for the purchased certificate to be processed. After it is approved and the approved certificate is received, then the second part of the wizard is run to insert the certificate into the IIS7 web site and bind it to the appropriate web site.

The certificate name is normally remote.domain.com. You do not need a wildcard certificate or a SAN cert in order to properly set up the Exchange 2007 auto-discover settings. You need to fill in the name of your firm, the city, the state, and the country. These are prefilled if you already entered these values in your server setup. Copy the resulting trusted certificate request or save the file, and then go to your SSL certificate provider and purchase the certificate. After you have received the approved certificate, return back to the wizard, browse to the saved location, and the wizard adds the certificate appropriately. Vendors of SSL certificates include Thawte, Verisign, Cybertrust, Entrust, GlobalSign, Equifax, and Godaddy. Typically all you need is the least expensive SSL certificate from these vendors. The SBS 2008 server has been configured in OWA not to mandate a wildcard certificate for synchronization purposes. However, if you host multiple web sites on your server you may need to have a wild card certificate. Given that it's not recommended to host external public facing web sites on your SBS 2008 box, the chances that you will need an expensive wildcard certificate is very rare.

The first part of the wizard places a log file in the c:\Program Files\Windows Small Business Server\Logs subdirectory. By looking at the file, you can attempt to see what the wizard is doing:

```
[3840] 080823.155052.8420: General: Initializing...C:\Program Files\Windows Small
➥Business Server\Bin\TrustedCert.exe
[3840] 080823.155054.9042: CoreNet: No Pending request distinguished name found in
➥NetworkConfig
[3840] 080823.155056.8258: CoreNet: 5 certificate in all.
[3840] 080823.155056.8258: CoreNet: Closing Store
[3840] 080823.155057.1538: CoreNet: Getting root cert
[3840] 080823.155058.5755: CoreNet: CA ConfigString:
➥SERVER.smallbizco.local\smallbizco-SERVER-CA
[3840] 080823.155058.9036: CoreNet: CA ConfigString:
➥SERVER.smallbizco.local\smallbizco-SERVER-CA
[3840] 080823.155058.9192: CoreNet: Converting to bytes
[3840] 080823.155058.9192: CoreNet: Self-issued Cert found:
➥0CC0BE5DB5E35CB6684A18354BA56A85FA824925
[3840] 080823.155103.3092: WizardChainEngine Next Clicked: Going to page {0}.:
➥Networking.Wizards.TCIWizard.TrustedFindPage
[3840] 080823.155103.3248: CoreNet: Choose use the new certificate.
[3840] 080823.155109.2770: WizardChainEngine Next Clicked: Going to page {0}.:
➥Networking.Wizards.TCIWizard.ConfirmRequestDataPage
[3840] 080823.155121.4470: WizardChainEngine Next Clicked: Going to page {0}.:
➥Networking.Wizards.TCIWizard.GenerateRequestPage
[3840] 080823.155121.4782: CoreNet: Retrieving Domain Name Max Length from
➥NetworkConfig
```

5

```
[3840] 080823.155121.7126: CoreNet: Retrieving Domain Config Service URL
➥fromNetworkConfig
[3840] 080823.155121.7126: CoreNet: No domain NetworkConfig service URL is defined
➥in NetworkConfig
[3840] 080823.155121.7282: CoreNet: Retrieving Domain Provider Homepage URL
➥fromNetworkConfig
[3840] 080823.155121.7282: CoreNet: No domain provider homepage URL is defined
➥inNetworkConfig
[3840] 080823.155121.7282: CoreNet: Retrieving Domain Provider Name from
➥NetworkConfig
[3840] 080823.155121.7282: CoreNet: No domain provider name is defined in
➥NetworkConfig
[3840] 080823.155121.7282: CoreNet: Retrieving Domain Provider Logo from
➥NetworkConfig
[3840] 080823.155121.7282: CoreNet: Domain Provider Logo found.
[3840] 080823.155121.7282: CoreNet: No domain provider logo is defined in
➥NetworkConfig
[3840] 080823.155121.7751: CoreNet: Getting provider service data 1.
[3840] 080823.155121.7751: CoreNet: Getting provider service data 2.
[6456] 080823.155121.8219: CoreNet: Generate request using information data.
[6456] 080823.155121.8376: CoreNet: CN to validate:
➥CN=remote.smallbizco.net,O=Smallbizco, OU=Smallbizco, L=Denton, S=Texas, C=US
[6456] 080823.155121.9313: CoreNet: Returning CN of
➥CN=remote.smallbizco.net,O=Smallbizco, OU=Smallbizco, L=Denton, S=Texas, C=US
[3840] 080823.155131.8985: WizardChainEngine Next Clicked: Going to page {0}.:
➥Networking.Wizards.TCIWizard.RequestInProcessPage
```

In plain English, the steps that this wizard goes through to insert and install a third-party certificate are the standard steps one normally goes through to request and install a certificate on an IIS web site.

Manually Requesting and Installing a Third-Party Certificate

Although all of the steps presented in this section are done for you with the Trusted Certificate Wizard, you might find that understanding what the wizard is doing helps you debug better, should something go wrong in the process. Thus, read though the instructions to get a better understanding but use the Trusted Certificate Wizard to request and install a third-party certificate because it will properly place the certificate on all the web sites that SBS uses for external access.

You begin the Certificate Signing Request process by running a wizard that prepares the request. The CSR file is a Base-64–encoded PKCS#10 message that includes the information needed to identify the person or company applying for the certificate. The request includes the public key.

Launch the IIS manager to begin the process.

1. Click Start, Administrative Tools, Internet Information Services (IIS) Manager 7.0.

2. Click Continue to approve the User Account Control prompt.

3. Click the server name in the Recent Connections pane in the middle.

4. In the management pane view, ensure that the Group By field is set to Category. Now scroll to the Security section and click Server Certificates.

5. If you have previously run the wizard to connect to the Internet, there are already several certificates on the web site. One of these certificates is for remote.domain.com, as can be seen in Figure 5.11.

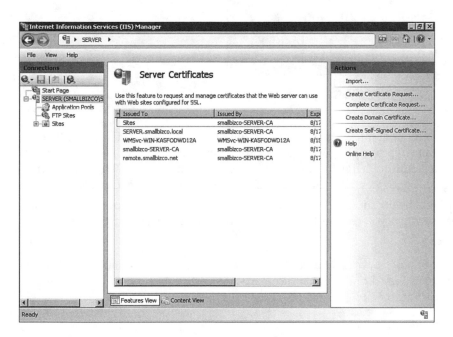

FIGURE 5.11   The server certificates.

6. Select the existing certificate, right-click that selection, and select Export. Save the certificate to a location and provide a password. In case you need to roll back and use the self-signed certificate, you need access to this. Ensure that the password is appropriate and consider taking the normal precautions for protecting firm secrets as your policy deems appropriate.

7. Click the certificate labeled remote.domain.com again and click Create Certificate Request.

8. Enter the Common Name, Organization, Organizational Unit, City/Locality, State/Province, and Country/Region (see Figure 5.12). Click Next to continue.

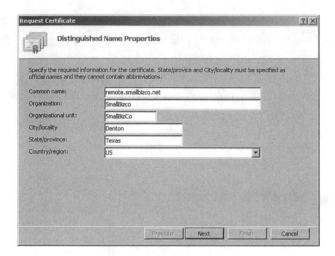

FIGURE 5.12   Entering the common name to begin the wizard.

9. Choose the Cryptographic Service Provider and Bit Length. The defaults of Microsoft RSA Schannel Cryptographic Provider and 1024-bit length in this case are sufficient. Choosing a certificate length stronger than this might impact the performance of your remote access. Staying with the default values is appropriate. Click Next.

10. Make a file name for the certificate request and place the file in a location that you can later use when you request the certificate from the External certificate site.

11. Click Finish.

At this point in the process we have used the certificate wizard in IIS to build a certificate request file. This file is used to request a third-party SSL certificate from a vendor that specializes in certificates.

Requesting the Certificate from the Vendor
The next step in the process is to request the third-party SSL certificate from your chosen vendor. There are many good vendors.

1. Determine your third-party certificate provider and purchase a certificate. Vendors include Thawte, Verisign, Cybertrust, Entrust, GlobalSign, Equifax, and Godaddy.

2. As was stated earlier, depending on your needs, you might need to choose a wild card certificate. This more expensive certificate enables you to have domains that are subdomains of your master domain.

3. Browse to the provider's site and begin the request certification process. This typically involves purchasing a certificate; it also might mean that you send them a driver's license or other means of identification.

4. In the Third-Party Certificate Requestor Information screen, copy and paste the contents of the Certificate Signing Request that the IIS wizard generated. The request looks something like this:

```
---BEGIN NEW CERTIFICATE REQUEST---
MIIDazCCAtQCAQAwdDELMAkGA1UEBhMCVVMxCzAJBgNVBAgMAkNBMQ8wDQYDVQQH
DAZGcmVzbm8xFDASBgNVBAoMC1NCU2RpdmEubmV0MRQwEgYDVQQLDAtDZXJ0aWZp
Y2F0ZTEbMBkGA1UEAwwScmVtb3RlLnNic2RpdmEubmV0MIGfMA0GCSqGSIb3DQEB
AQUAA4GNADCBiQKBgQCrsWLVD18LISmZ6F46rWx5qSBKvtGkQJ2WWVsnPVJ9E4D2
3qbov6rNliAfiEuRpmycK6t/4ykLlI883ENmQ0w3hpl9wJM72yiTi4Y+Wy1NAiul
zKkjTVwV6+1Uak3ykPUhh/2jvSiPDSoWa3qdFRMZHgL+ESzhWs2DoQjD0ygoiwID
AQABoIIBtTAaBgorBgEAYI3DQIDMQwWCjYuMC42MDAxLjIIwUQYJKwYBBAGCNxUU
MUQwQgIBBQweU0VSVkVVSTkFNRS5ET01BSU5OQU1FLmludGVybmFsDBBET01BSU5O
QU1FXN1c2FuDAtJbmV0TWdyLmV4ZTByBgorBgEAYI3DQICMWQwYgIBAR5aAE0A
aQBjAHIAbwBzAG8AZgB0ACAAUgBTAEEAIABTAEMAaABhG4AbgBlAGwAIABDAHIA
eQBwAHQAbwBnAHIAYQBwAGgAaQBjACAAUAByAG8AdgBpAGQAZQByAwEAMIHPBgkq
hkiG9w0BCQ4xgcEwgb4wDgYDVR0PAQH/BAQDAgTwMBMGA1UdJQQMMAoGCCsGAQUF
BwMBMHgGCSqGSIb3DQEJDwRrMGkwDgYIKoZIhvcNAwICAgCAMA4GCCqGSIb3DQME
AgIAgDALBglghkgBZQMEASowCwYJYIZIAWUDBAEtMAsGCWCGSAFlAwQBAjALBglg
hkgBZQMEAQUwBwYFKw4DAgcwCgYIKoZIhvcNAwcwHQYDVR0OBBYEFFPev0Fn6rLS
ohzVVdjDRT6g0yjKMA0GCSqGSIb3DQEBBQUAA4GBABhw2/bhe5aKIC8GGKRKzJ0S
3qXtW/uicuzH6GE+6v8xYtMm/SuZitALWxSBJBfF2idmdFDpOapAPb5QommSW43h
v5JcSHoO71HhocXp1ytSR4jWITmEGFlBB53HATWZwgp4Z0IOs1x04xOyWMbmqrmY
iinVq1RqcxdF/4mPnPyU
---END NEW CERTIFICATE REQUEST---
```

5. Specify that the server software being requested on behalf is Microsoft IIS.

6. The domain administrator gets several messages from the Cert authority that need to be approved.

7. You typically get an e-mail with a link to a certificate download.

This step of the process involves requesting the certificate from the SSL vendor. You place the certificate request file containing the needed information included in the certificate on the vendor's SSL purchase portal, and it sends you the necessary certificate file.

Installing the Intermediary Certificate (If Needed)

Some SSL vendors such as Godaddy.com require you to install two certificates. One of these certificates is called an intermediary certificate.

1. Depending on the certificate provider, you might need to install an intermediary certificate. If you do, download the package to a location on the server.

2. Click Start, Run. Then type in **MMC** and press Enter.

3. Click Continue on the User Account Control prompt that appears.

4. In the MMC console that appears, click File, Add/Remove Snap-In.

5. Click Certificates and then Add in the middle of the window.

6. Click the My User Account radio button, and then click the Finish button.

7. On the right side you should see Certificates-Current User.

8. Click the OK button at the bottom of the screen.

9. Expand the Certificates-Current User, and expand Intermediate Certificate Authorities.

10. Right-click Intermediate Certificate Authorities and click on Tasks and then select Import.

11. Click Next and browse to the location on your server where you have saved the Intermediate Certificate Authority PKCS #7 Certificate file. Change the file type to All Files to find the exact file.

12. Click Next, ensure that Place All Certificates in the Following Store selection window has Intermediate Certification Authorities selected, and click Finish.

13. Click OK when it indicates that the import was successful.

14. Click on the certificates and ensure that the intermediate certificate is in place.

15. Close the MMC.

These steps import the intermediary certificate into the proper location on the certificate store on the server. This step is only needed by some SSL vendors.

Installing the Cert on the IIS Web Site

The next step is to insert the certificate back into the web site that we want to ensure will have Secure Sockets Layer (SSL) access to external users. You go back to the IIS wizard that began the SSL certificate request process and complete the certificate request process in this step.

1. Go back to the Internet Information Services (IIS) Manager and right-click on the certificate that you are replacing with the third-party certificate.

2. Click on Complete Certificate Request and browse to the location of the file you downloaded from the third-party certificate provider. You might need to change the file type to *.* to browse to the proper file.

3. Enter the friendly name of the certificate and click OK.

4. The certificate is now installed in addition to the self-signed certificate.

In this step you have now inserted the SSL certificate back to the web site on the server.

Change the Bindings to Reflect the New Certificate

The final step is to change the IIS web site to bind or connect the SSL certificate to the proper web site you intend to secure for external users.

1. Expand the Sites tree.

2. Find the web site section titled SBS Web Applications and click Bindings.

3. On the Site Bindings section, click Type Https and click Edit.

4. In the section titled SSL certificate, scroll down and choose the third-party certificate that you installed from the vendor.

5. Click View to confirm that you are installing the external certificate that you intended.

Your remote access is now secured with an external SSL certificate, as shown in Figure 5.13.

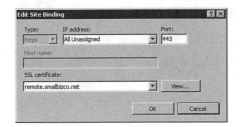

FIGURE 5.13   Editing the bindings of the secure web site.

If you believe that your external secured access is not working properly, review the binding tab in IIS to see if the wizard properly bound the SSL certificate to the web site.

Disabling SSLv2

Some industries might find that doing an external compliance scan for the Payment Card Industry on a SBS 2008 box indicates that the server is running SSL v2. When this happens, it's usually recommended to adjust the compliance scan to only run SSLv3. You need to review if external access will be impacted by this change. In general, most browsers today already support SSLv3.

The historical guidance for adjusting SSL to only support SSLv3 or TLSv1 is included in Microsoft Knowledge Base Article KB 187498, "How to Disable SSLv2 on IIS," located at http://support.microsoft.com/default.aspx?scid=kb;en-us;187498. This guidance is also included in Microsoft Knowledge Base Article KB 245030, "How to Restrict the Use of Certain Cryptographic Algorithms and Protocols in Schannel.dll," located at http://support.microsoft.com/default.aspx?scid=kb;en-us;245030.

To limit the web server to use only SSLv3, perform the following steps:

1. Click Start, Run, and in the open box type in **Regedit**.
2. Click Continue to approve the UAC prompt that occurs.
3. Under HKEY_LOCAL_MACHINE, navigate to SYSTEM\CurrentControlSet\Control\SecurityProviders\SCHANNEL.
4. Under the Protocols, find SSL 2.0. There is a Client key, but no Server key.
5. Right-click SSL 2.0 and select New Key.
6. Type **Server** and press Enter.
7. Click Server, right-click in the pane on the right side, and select New, DWORD (32-bit) Value.
8. Type **Enabled**, press Enter, and ensure that the data value is 0x0.
9. Reboot the server.

As you can see, setting up secure and trusted web connections is quite easy and effective to do.

Integrating External Web Publishing

When choosing to set up remote access using the wizard, you might have noted that if you choose to set up your remote access using merely www.domain.com, you are warned that you might lose functionality with external Office Live Small Business web hosting. Your domain will be externally hosted through the Office Live Services, but remote access will be redirected to remote.domain.com.

The Office Live Small Business platform also includes locations to share files with external users, as well as a place to transfer Office Accounting files. To add an Office Live Small Business web site to your network, browse to the SBS console and click on the Home tab. Choose the Office Live Small Business Wizard and click to begin the process. A web site launches to enter in the selection of the Office Live Small Business site you want. The name of the resulting collaboration site is http://domaincom.officelive.com; thus, decide on your domain and consider the impact when setting up the server.

Setting up an Office Live Small Business web site can provide you with external client collaboration tools without having to worry about server licenses, external access by nonemployees, and other issues (see Figure 5.14).

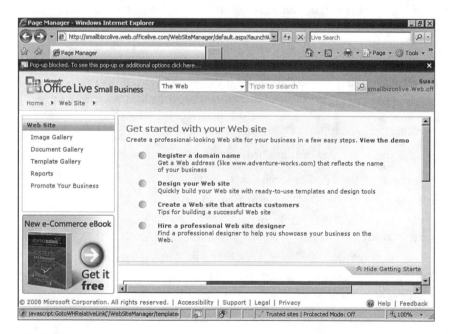

FIGURE 5.14   Setting up an Office Live Small Business site.

Office Live Small Business

In order to set up Office Live Small Business, you need a LiveID (the old Passport) that does not have any other Office Live Small Business accounts hooked to it. Thus, you want to use a separate LiveID per client, or have the client walk over to the server at this time and enter the credentials to set up the Office Live Small Business web site. You cannot have more than one domain hooked to a LiveID.

Troubleshooting IIS

For most of the time, typing `iisreset` at the command line or merely rebooting the server is enough to correct issues. But sometimes you get additional errors. In the next two sections, I address how to handle Service Unavailable and Server Not Found error messages.

Service Unavailable

The Service Unavailable error is evidenced by an "HTTP Error 503. The service is unavailable"; the error is generated by the Web Admin Service (WAS). When WAS fails to create a worker process, this error occurs. It could be caused by the following:

▶ Invalid application pool configuration

▶ Failure to create the process due to incorrect pool settings

▶ Bad IIS configurations that cause the worker process to fail

▶ Process crash due to an error in the logic of the application

To get rid of this error, you can take several troubleshooting steps, as follows:

1. Check if the application pool is running or stopped:

   a. Launch the IIS 7 console and review the application pools to see if one is stopped.

   b. Determine if it can be manually restarted.

2. Check event logs:

   a. Click Start, Control Panel. Open Administration Tools and select the Event Viewer. (Approve the UAC prompt that appears.)

   b. Navigate to the application event log.

   c. Review for errors from the IIS-W3SVC-WP source.

3. Fix the cause:

   a. If Web Admin Service failed to start the worker process:

      i. Check the configuration file.

      ii. Check the application pool identity. (Is there a wrong name or account password?)

      iii. Are the worker processes out of resources?

    b. IIS initialization failed:

        i. Check the configuration file.

        ii. Module DLL failed to load.

    c. Application crash:

        i. Module causing the problem.

        ii. The application causes the process to terminate abruptly.

4. Restart the pool:

    a. Launch the IIS 7 console and review the application pools to see if one is stopped.

    b. Determine if it can be manually restarted.

Many times merely not panicking, reviewing if the service is running, and restarting it will solve the issue. Double-check the basics when troubleshooting.

Server Not Found

The Server Not Found error is evidenced by a Cannot Find Server or DNS error. The issues might be caused on the client site, might be due to DNS resolution issues or network connectivity, or it could be an issue on your server. To see if it's a problem on your server:

1. Make sure that you can ping the server:

    a. From an elevated command line (click Start, find the command line icon on the start menu, right-click, and choose Run as Administrator), type `ping` *www.yourdomain.com.*

    b. If you do not get a response back, the issue might be with DNS or network connectivity.

2. Make sure the IIS service is started:

    a. From an elevated command line (click Start, find the Command line icon on the start menu, right-click, and choose Run as Administrator), type `net start w3svc`.

    b. You should get a response that the web site has started. If it does not respond that the service started, review the event log for possible additional issues.

3. Ensure that the web site is listening to requests:

    a. From an elevated command line (click Start, find the Command line icon on the Start menu, right-click, and choose Run as Administrator), type the following: `%windir%\system32\inetsrv\AppCmd.exe list sites`

    b. If the web site you are working with is not listed, you know that it's not running and listening as it should.

    c. Review the event viewer in the system event logs under window logs for "WAS" as the event source:

        i. Site might not contain a root application.

        ii. It is missing a single valid binding.

        iii. The binding is invalid or conflicts with another binding.

  4. After you make the corrections, restart the web server.

Summary

Small Business Server's integrated and automated processes make setting up the needed web sites for an active, mobile firm easy to do. Remote access and patch management depend on web sites running on the Small Business Server 2008 box. Internet Information Services is the backbone on which many business solutions are built. The key to a healthy and well-protected SBS box is to understand that not everything truly needs to go on a single box. With virtualization, SaaS, and—most important—the ability to cheaply obtain a second Windows Server with the SBS 2008 Premium offering, it is not wise to place third-party web based applications on the main SBS 2008 server.

The integrated nature of SBS also provides additional backup and recovery needs given its tight integration with Exchange. Native backup features provide the administrator the capability to back up the IIS configurations and assure full recovery.

The advantage of SBS 2008 is clearly that, after installation, it is fully configured with Outlook Web Access, SharePoint, and WSUS with appropriate and proper permissions. Unlike standard Windows Server 2008, there is no need to add roles or functions to the server; it has been set up appropriately for the needs and opportunities for a small firm.

Internet Information Services 7 is a rock-solid foundation upon which SBS 2008 has built business tools for a small firm.

Best Practice Summary

▶ **Don't host an external-facing web site on a Windows Small Business Server 2008 system**—External web hosting is easy and inexpensive and ensures that the risk from nonauthenticated users is outsourced to an external vendor.

▶ **Purchase a third-party external certificate for the web site access**—You will find that you can easily deploy mobile phones and provide a better experience for remote users.

▶ **Ensure that you have a backup routine that backs up the server, web sites, and contents**—At a minimum, review Chapter 19, "IPv6 Overview," and at least use the built in SBS backup technology to back up the server. Manually performing IISmetabase backups and System State backups provide you with additional restoration options should you need them.

▶ **Resources** (Microsoft's IIS development team web site, blog, and code repository) are located at http://www.iis.net/default.aspx?tabid=1

CHAPTER 6

Remote Web Workplace and Other Remote Access Solutions

As high-speed Internet solutions become more and more widely available, the ability for even the smallest of businesses to have a mobile workforce has become an affordable reality instead of a pipe dream. But having a high-speed connection is only one part of the equation—there must still be something in the office to connect with remotely for a mobile workforce to be effective.

SBS 2008 continues the SBS tradition of offering affordable remote accessibility services for small businesses. In addition to remote access to e-mail and the ability to remotely control a Windows workstation in the office across the Internet, SBS 2008 provides additional remote data access functionality with the ability to access files on the server through a secure web interface.

This chapter focuses on remote connection technologies provided through the Remote Web Workplace interface, Virtual Private Network (VPN) connectivity, and the Remote Desktop Protocol (RDP). Chapter 9, "Exchange 2007 Client Connectivity," covers remote access to e-mail and accessing server files through the web as that functionality is provided through the Outlook Web Access interface.

Understanding the Role of Remote Accessibility Solutions in SBS 2008

The ability to access company data or line of business applications from remote locations is becoming increasingly important to small businesses, as is the ability to remotely manage servers for IT support professionals. SBS 2008 provides a number of technologies that can be used to meet these needs. Each has their own benefits and drawbacks, so there is not a "one size fits all" solution that will address every need. The following sections introduce the remote access technologies supported in SBS 2008 and the reasons why one solution may be preferred over another for specific situations.

Remote Web Workplace

The Remote Web Workplace (RWW) was introduced with SBS 2003 and became one of the biggest-selling points of the product. In fact, the technology was so well received that large enterprises asked Microsoft on a regular basis how to get the RWW technology for their Windows networks. To date, the RWW technology has moved outside of the SBS realm, but is still not available as a separate installable technology for Windows-based systems. The Remote Web Workplace has been included in the Windows Home Server product as well as Essential Business Server. Each implementation has their own variations, but the core functionality, remotely controlling a PC on the internal network through a web interface, is common across all implementations.

Figure 6.1 shows the default Remote Web Workplace menu as preconfigured by the SBS 2008 installation process. The main functions are accessible in the three large buttons at the top of the page, and the lesser-used functions are displayed off to the side and below.

FIGURE 6.1   Remote Web Workplace main menu.

In SBS 2008, the Remote Web Workplace interface provides a number of different features depending on the level of access of the user who logs into the interface. Figure 6.1 shows the menu as it appears to the domain administrator account. As discussed in Chapter 12, "User and Computer Management," there are three default security roles for user accounts, and each of those roles has access to different features within the RWW interface. Table 6.1 introduces the functions in RWW and which of the default security roles have access to those functions. Each of the functions is described in more detail in the following sections.

TABLE 6.1   Security Role Access to RWW Functions

Function	Network Administrator	Standard User with Administration Links	Standard User
Check E-Mail	✓	✓	✓
Connect to a Computer	✓	✓	✓
Connect to Server	✓	✓	
Internal Web Site	✓	✓	✓
Change Password	✓	✓	✓
Organization Links	✓	✓	✓
Administration Links	✓	✓	
Help	✓	✓	✓

Check E-Mail

Clicking the Check E-Mail button opens a new browser window to the Outlook Web Access interface. The user is automatically logged in with the credentials used to access RWW. Note that if you click the Log Off button in the OWA interface, you will be logged out of RWW as well. For more information about the features of OWA, including how to access file shares on the server through the web interface, see Chapter 9.

Connect to a Computer

Clicking on the Connect to a Computer button displays a list (if applicable) of the computers that the user is allowed to connect to remotely. Only Windows XP Professional and Windows Vista Business and Ultimate workstation allow remote connections. If the user account is not configured to remotely connect to a workstation, the button will be visible, but no workstations will appear in the list.

By default, the Connect to a Computer tools will not connect to an internal workstation unless the remote workstation trusts the SSL certificate installed on the server. For SBS 2008 installations that use the default self-generated certificate, this can cause problems. Users wanting to access workstations through RWW must install the self-signed certificate from the SBS server, and they will not be able to access that certificate information from the server remotely.

NOTE

The remote computer connection feature of Remote Web Workplace still relies on an ActiveX control to make the connection from external workstations to internal resources, which means that the remote connectivity functions are only possible within Internet Explorer. This means that Macintosh workstations or users who run Firefox or other non-IE browsers cannot take advantage of this feature. This is an unfortunate limitation of a service that adds significant value to the SBS product.

An alternate connection method for Macintosh workstations is discussed in the VPN section later in this chapter.

Internal Web Site

Clicking the Internal Web Site button opens a new window to the Companyweb SharePoint site. The user will be prompted to enter his or her username and password again. Changing users in SharePoint does not impact access to the RWW menu. For more information about using SharePoint and the Companyweb implementation, see Chapter 7, "SharePoint and Companyweb."

Change Password

Clicking on the Change Password link opens a new window where the user can modify his or her password. For security, the user must enter the old password as well as the new password twice.

Connect to Server

As noted in Table 6.1, only users with the Network Administrator or the Standard User with Administrative Links roles will be able to see this link. Clicking this link opens a full-screen Remote Desktop session to the server, allowing the user to manage the server across the Internet.

View Help

Opens a link to the web-based help documentation for SBS 2008.

Organizational Links

This list of web links can be customized in the Windows SBS Console and can be used to provide employees with a collection of web sites useful for their job or for the business. This could be set to include a link to a support portal for the IT service provider, a link to a commonly-used business resource, and so on.

Administrative Links

This selection of links is visible only to administrators who log in, or to users with the Standard User with Administrative Links role. This collection of links could include links to vendor support sites or other references for administration or support needs.

Shortcomings of Remote Web Workplace

The Remote Web Workplace interface is designed for use with Internet Explorer, and as such is not fully usable in other browser platforms. This was the case with the original RWW in SBS 2003, and although support for other browsers is improved with SBS 2008, there are still some features that cannot be accessed from this interface.

The key tool of RWW, connecting to workstations or the server, is delivered through an ActiveX control, which can only be used in Internet Explorer on Windows. The 2008 edition of RWW is better able to detect non-IE browsers and will not display the Connect to a Computer or the Connect to Server items in the menu. Figure 6.2 shows how the RWW interface changes when accessed using the Google Chrome browser. Even though the domain administrator is logged in to the RWW interface, neither the Connect to a Computer or Connect to Server items are visible. The remaining links and buttons in the menu, however, work as expected.

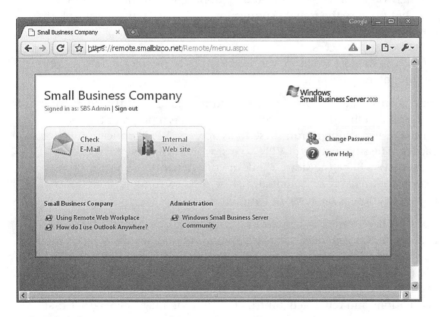

FIGURE 6.2   RWW menu as seen in a non-IE browser.

The biggest challenge administrators will face in managing access to Remote Web Workplace is getting the self-generated certificate installed on the remote workstation so that users can connect to their workstations on the internal network. See the "Managing the Remote Web Workplace Interface" section later in the chapter for a deeper discussion on this issue.

VPN

A Virtual Private Network is a network implementation that allows a remote network device to interact with local network resources as though it were directly connected to the local network as well. VPN technology has been in use for a number of years, and previous editions of SBS supported VPN access to the network. SBS 2008 can act as a VPN endpoint so that a remote workstation can authenticate using an SBS network user account to determine if VPN access should be allowed for the incoming connection.

Whether to allow VPN access into a network or not can be a hotly contested issue. Many security consultants recommend against using VPN to provide access to internal network resources, especially if the remote workstation is either unknown or not managed by the company. However, there are times when VPN access is the only, if not the best, way to provide access.

One specific example is for remote Macintosh workstations wanting to remotely control PCs on the internal network. Normally, this would be done through the Remote Web Workplace interface, but because the remote connection tool is an ActiveX control, that solution is not available for the Macintosh platform. One way of providing Mac users the ability to use Remote Desktop to access an internal PC is to set up a VPN connection on the Mac, and then use the Remote Desktop Connection tool to remotely control a PC once the Mac is on the internal network.

There are also times when VPN access absolutely should not be used. If the business is running a client server-based line of business application or has a program that accesses a database stored on the server, trying to run these tools across a VPN connection is not a recommended practice. The slow nature of VPN access, where you have to assume that your best data transfer rate will be the slowest link in your network connection, can cause these programs to not work reliably or potentially cause data corruption if data cannot be written back to the application or database fast enough.

Still, when VPN access is determined to be needed for a particular situation, the VPN solution provided with SBS 2008 is generally sufficient enough to manage the VPN connection and authentication process where needed. Now that an SBS 2008 network is based on a server with a single network card and a hardware firewall at the edge of the network, some consultants may choose to implement a hardware firewall solution that has its own VPN software and configurations and rely solely on the firewall to manage VPN rather than passing the VPN requests through the firewall for the SBS server to manage. The choice of how to implement a VPN solution has so many factors that guidance on that topic is beyond the scope of this book.

RDP

Using the Remote Desktop Protocol to connect to remote workstations and servers has become an accepted method for delivering remote support over the last few years. However, there are some limitations and security concerns surrounding the use of RDP to access servers.

First, it is important to understand that the Remote Desktop Protocol itself is not a cause for concern. RDP is the underlying technology used to enable remote users to access their internal workstations through the Remote Web Workplace tools. The connection between the RDP client and a machine hosting Remote Desktop services is encrypted, so no user credentials are passed in clear text between the client and server. However, advertising an open RDP service to the Internet with a common account and a weak password will leave a system vulnerable to compromise. This is but one of the long list of reasons behind the decision in SBS 2008 to disable the default Administrator account and force the creation of a new administrator-equivalent account—people trying to hack services using the Administrator account name are thwarted right away. This doesn't mean that the determined hackers won't find a way to guess what the other account names might be, so it's still important to have a very secure password on the account used for administration.

Second, Windows Server 2008 has changed the way remote administration is handled when making an RDP connection to a server, and SBS 2008 adopts this model. In previous versions, there were essentially three remote connections that could be made—the two remote connections supported by the terminal server service running in Remote Administration mode on the server, and the console session, which could also be accessed and controlled remotely. Windows Server 2008 still maintains the two connection limit for remote administration, but there are some significant behavioral changes to note. By default, only one connection can be made with a single username. Thus, if one administrator is logged onto the server with an account named SBSAdmin, and a second person attempts to log onto the server remotely with the same username, the second person will take over the session of the first person, and the first person will lose his or her session. The remote connection window will remain open, but the second person will have control of the session.

One way to have two individuals with simultaneous remote logins on the server is to set up two administrator-equivalent accounts. The other is to modify the Restrict Users to One Session setting in Terminal Service Configuration. Additionally, the notion of the "console" session (also known as Session 0) has gone away. All connections to the server, even logging in directly on the console, are essentially remote sessions. This means that if you have an active session on the server console, and remote into the server using the same username that is logged in on the console, the remote connection will take over the console session, and the display at the console will become locked.

One other item to note is that the Windows SBS Console can only have one active instance on an SBS server. If you have two active administration sessions on the server, only one of those sessions can have the SBS Console application open.

SBS 2008 introduces another way to get RDP access to the server console, and that is through the TS Gateway service that is pre-configured on the SBS server. Using TS Gateway enables you to make the Remote Desktop connection tunneled through HTTPS instead of accessing port 3389 directly. This eliminates the need of "VPN first, then RDP" that had been a commonly-recommended solution for people to get RDP access to the server. But because TS Gateway sits on top of IIS, if there is a problem with IIS, or if the IIS service gets restarted during a TS Gateway connection, the RDP via TS Gateway solution may not always work.

Terminal Services Gateway Service

The Terminal Services Gateway service, or TS Gateway, is new to Windows Server 2008. This service is one element of the Terminal Service role for Server 2008 that allows extended remote connectivity through an authenticated connection. The Connect to Computer service of the Remote Web Workplace uses the TS Gateway service to redirect incoming RDP connections to workstations on the internal network instead of the Remote Desktop Proxy that came with SBS 2003.

TS Gateway is preinstalled and preconfigured with SBS 2008, so no manual configuration is needed to enable the functionality. Unfortunately, use of the TS Gateway service is limited to the Windows RDP client. A further discussion of how the TS Gateway service can be used appears later in the chapter.

Managing and Using Remote Web Workplace

In a default installation of SBS 2008, all users in the network have access to log into the Remote Web Workplace interface, but not all the features may be available to them. The following two sections cover how to configure the RWW interface for the users, as well as how to access the features of RWW.

Managing the Remote Web Workplace Interface

Management of the various aspects of the Remote Web Workplace interface is performed in several areas of the SBS server. The majority of management tools are in the Windows SBS Console under the Shared Folders and Web Sites tab, but other tools can be found in the Users and Groups tab and the Network tab. The following sections of the chapter walk you through configuring and managing the Remote Web Workplace interface.

Configuring Access to RWW

By default, the SBS 2008 setup enables access to Remote Web Workplace and assigns users the ability to log into the interface. Although most people who deploy SBS 2008 will want to make use of the RWW interface, there might be those who want to disable the interface altogether. This can be done easily in the Windows SBS Console. The Web Sites sub-tab of the Shared Folders and Web Sites tab lists all the Windows SBS Web Sites, including the Remote Web Workplace. To disable RWW entirely, click the Remote Web Workplace site in the list; then click the Disable This Site link in the Tasks list. This will mark the site as Offline in IIS, and users will be unable to load the login page when accessing the site. Specifically, trying to open the RWW URL when the site is disabled will display a Service Unavailable HTTP Error 503 in the web browser. To enable the site if it has been disabled, click the Enable This Site link in the Tasks list.

Unlike with SBS 2003, individual users can be denied permission to access the RWW interface. Individual user access can be controlled either in the user object properties or in the

Shared Folders and Web Sites tab. Ultimately, access is governed by membership in the Windows SBS Remote Web Workplace Users security group in Active Directory, so access can be managed simply by opening Active Directory Users and Computers and changing the membership of the Windows SBS Remote Web Workplace Users group.

To review or manage access to all RWW users through the Shared Folders and Web Sites tab, follow these steps:

1. In the Windows SBS Console, select the Shared Folder and Web Sites tab; then select the Web Sites sub-tab.

2. Select the Remote Web Workplace site; then click Manage Permissions under the Tasks list.

3. In the Remote Web Workplace Properties page, review the users who are currently allowed to access the Remote Web Workplace interface (see Figure 6.3).

FIGURE 6.3   Managing permissions to the RWW interface.

4. If you need to make changes to this list, click the Modify button.

5. In the Change Group Membership window, add or remove the desired objects and click OK when finished.

Configuring the RWW Home Page

Another significant difference between the implementations of the Remote Web Workplace in SBS 2003 and SBS 2008 is how much the main user interface can be customized. In SBS 2003, there were two views for the RWW menu: the normal user view and an administrator view. Many of the elements in each view were present, but the administrator view had additional elements present and a different element layout.

In SBS 2008, the RWW menu has one view for all users, but additional administration elements can be made visible depending on the user role assigned to the user object. Many of the other elements visible on the RWW home page can also be modified.

These settings can be accessed through the Remote Web Workplace Properties page from the Shared Folders and Web Sites tab of the Windows SBS Console. To open the Properties page, select the Remote Web Workplace web site from the Web Sites sub-tab and click View Site Properties from the Tasks list.

The first two items in the Properties page have already been covered. The General item presents another way to enable or disable the entire RWW site on the SBS 2008 box, the same as using the Disable This Site or Enable This Site item in the Tasks list. The Permissions item lists the users who have access to the RWW interface.

Home Page Links   The Home Page Links item, shown in Figure 6.4, lists the items that can appear on the RWW menu. Each of these items can be enabled or disabled globally. So, if you wanted to prevent all users from being able to change their password through the RWW interface, you would turn off the Change Password checkbox, and that element would not be visible in the home page.

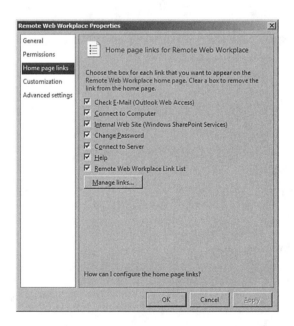

FIGURE 6.4   Remote Web Workplace home page links.

The Remote Web Workplace Link List object refers to the Organizational links and the Administration links visible in the RWW home page, as seen in Figures 6.1 and 6.2. These links are customizable and can be managed by clicking the Manage Links button.

The Remote Web Workplace Link List Properties page controls whether the list of links are visible (Organization links, Administration links, or both), who has access to view the link lists, as well as modifying the links themselves.

The Permissions item enables you to specify which users can access which set of lists. Access to the lists is controlled through two security groups: Members of the Windows SBS Link Users security group can view the Organization links, and members of the Windows SBS Admin Tools Group security group can view the Administration links. You can modify the membership of both groups through this page, or you can use the standard AD tools for modifying group membership.

The Organization Links and the Administration Links items list all the links present for that list. In this interface, you can change the order in which the links appear and add or remove links as necessary.

The Customization item enables you to change the titles of the Administration Links section and the Organizational Links section. By default, the title of the Organizational Links is the name of the business entered during setup.

Customization and Advanced Settings   The last two items in the Remote Web Workplace Properties page are the Customization and Advanced Settings items. The Customization item alters how the main login page and the home page appear. The Organization Name, shown in Figure 6.5, is set to be the business name entered during the server setup, but can be modified in this text field.

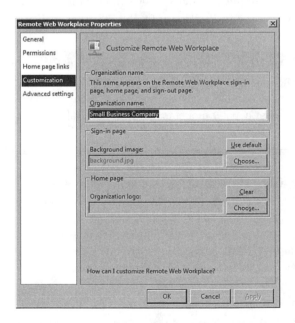

FIGURE 6.5   Customize Remote Web Workplace settings.

You can change the background image to use in the sign-in page for Remote Web Workplace. The default background image for the sign-in page is a 760 by 500 pixel image named background.jpg, and it is stored in the C:\Program Files\Windows Small Business Server\Bin\webapp\Remote\images folder on the server. If you want to create a custom image for your sign-in page, place the image in the same folder as background.jpg and then select that image in the customized settings.

The customized settings also let you upload a logo file to be displayed in the home page for RWW. This logo file is limited to a 48 by 48 pixel image in the display, and it will appear in the upper-left corner of the home page when selected. The logo file must also be placed in the images folder under the RWW folder on the server to be selected in this portion of the interface.

Finally, if you click the Advanced item in the Remote Web Workplace Properties page, you will get a shortcut to open the IIS 7 management console. The page warns that only experienced users should attempt to adjust settings for RWW in IIS, and that is the case. Only in certain circumstances should you modify any of the settings for RWW in IIS, otherwise you should leave the configuration alone.

Configuring Users Access to Computers

Chapter 12 discusses how to assign users to workstations on the network, as well as how to assign access to the Remote Web Workplace. These settings can be modified from the user account properties, discussed in the "Modifying Remote Access Permissions" section, or from the computer object properties, discussed in the "Modifying Access to Computers" section. These settings are used to build the computer list that will be displayed to the user in the RWW menu when they want to connect to a computer inside the network.

Changes from SBS 2003—Connecting to Computers

Several aspects of the implementation of Remote Web Workplace in SBS 2003 generated a flurry of requests to Microsoft, and many of those requests resulted in feature changes for RWW in SBS 2008. Two of the most popular requests dealt with controlling access to computers for users.

One request was to keep certain users from being able to access remote workstations via RWW at all. This request has been implemented in SBS 2008 as access to the entire RWW interface can be controlled on a per-user level, as can the ability for a user to even see the Connect to a Computer item in the RWW home page.

Another request was to restrict which computers a user could see as available in the Connect to Computer interface. In SBS 2003, all workstations on the internal network running XP or Vista showed in the menu. In SBS 2008, a user can be granted permission to connect to only one workstation. Alternately, users could be given access to several workstations, but have one show as the default in the RWW menu.

With these changes in SBS 2008, system administrators have a much more granular level of control over remote access for users.

Using the Remote Web Workplace Interface

The real beauty of the Remote Web Workplace interface is its simplicity. The only real training needed for most users of the interface is to get them to remember (or bookmark) the public URL. Fortunately, even the URL is easier in SBS 2008. Unlike SBS 2003, where you had to enter https://server.domain.com/remote, with SBS 2008, users only have to remember https://remote.domain.com, and nothing else. If you have port 80 open in the firewall to the SBS server, you don't even have to have them remember the https portion. Once they've landed on the home page, accessing their e-mail and the internal web site is very straightforward.

The primary reason many people will be using the RWW interface, however, is to gain access to their workstations at the office, and there are a few tricks to that process that can trip up even seasoned system administrators.

Using the Connect to a Computer Feature

With a default SBS 2008 setup, when a workstation is connected to the network, the primary user of the workstation is automatically granted remote access to that workstation. So when that user logs into the RWW interface, the Connect to a Computer item on the main menu enables them to access that workstation remotely. If the user has been given access to more than one workstation, the first time the user selects the Connect to a Computer item, he or she is prompted to select a workstation to connect to, as shown in Figure 6.6. In addition, the user can select one of the workstations from the list as the default workstation by clicking the Make This My Default Computer checkbox when the desired computer is highlighted.

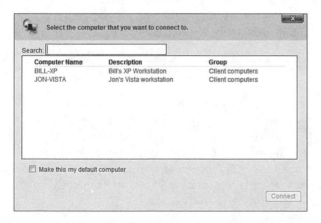

FIGURE 6.6   Selecting a computer from the Connect to a Computer list.

If the user does select one of the workstations as the default, the next time he or she logs into the RWW interface and clicks the Connect to a Computer item, the user is automatically connected to the workstation. Users can always click the Show List link at the bottom of the Connect to a Computer item to see a list of all the workstations to which he or she has access.

Before the user will be able to complete a connection to the workstation, however, the workstation the user is connecting from must recognize the SSL certificate on the SBS server. If you have purchased and installed a third-party certificate on the SBS server, no further interaction is needed on behalf of the user and the connection will complete. If you are using the self-generated certificate from the SBS default setup, however, the user must install the certificate on the remote workstation before the connection back to the SBS network will complete. This is a restriction of the TS Gateway service that SBS 2008 uses to manage the incoming remote connections.

Changes from SBS 2003—TS Gateway

When the Remote Web Workplace was originally designed for SBS 2003, the SBS development team devised a novel way to get around the problem of the Remote Desktop Protocol being a one-to-one connection. A service running on the SBS server would listen on port 4125 when a remote connection was made through the Remote Web Workplace, and that service would take the incoming RDP traffic from the external workstation and route it to port 3389 on the workstation on the internal network. This was known as Remote Desktop Proxy, and it took a while for SBS implementers to catch on that port 4125 needed to be opened in the firewall.

With the new TS Gateway service in Windows Server 2008, there is no longer a need for the Remote Desktop Proxy on port 4125. All Remote Desktop traffic from the Remote Web Workplace is tunneled through the HTTPS protocol on port 443.

By using the TS Gateway service for remote desktop access, SBS 2008 uses standard tools for this function (a theme echoed throughout the SBS 2008 product), and one less port has to be configured in the firewall, making the network configuration less complex as well.

For security reasons, there is not a way to install the SSL certificate on the remote workstation through the RWW interface. The user must be given the SSL certificate installer to run on the external workstation in order to have the certificate installed correctly. This can present a challenge if the user is traveling and wants to access his or her computer from another workstation. As discussed in Chapter 5, "Internet Information Services 7.0," installing a third-party SSL cert on the server resolves a number of remote connectivity issues, and using the Connect to a Computer feature is another way.

When the user initiates the connection to the remote computer, a small browser window appears, verifying with the user that the connection is trusted. In this window, shown in Figure 6.7, the user also has the option to disable clipboard synchronization and printer sharing between the two computers, if desired. The default settings allow synchronization of the clipboard so information put in the clipboard on the remote workstation can be copied and pasted to the external workstation.

FIGURE 6.7   Remote Desktop Connection Verification window.

When the user clicks Connect in that prompt, another window appears, prompting the user to enter his or her username and password again. This prompt is the authentication against the TS Gateway service running on the SBS server.

NOTE

When connecting with a Windows XP workstation, you will need to enter the username as domain\username. On Vista, as shown in Figure 6.7, the domain information is already present.

After the user authenticates against the TS Gateway service, the connection to the remote workstation will appear. The connection comes across in full screen mode and using the full desktop experience, meaning that the full desktop, including background, animations, and transitions, as well as all audio, are sent across the Internet to the external workstation. Although this will give the user the full look and feel of their desktop at the office, it does significantly slow down the remote connection. At this time, there is not a way to modify those settings on the fly. If this is a problem for the external user, the section "Using Remote Desktop" at the end of the chapter offers a couple of alternate solutions to getting more control over the remote access connection.

When logging into RWW as a network administrator or a standard user with administration links, the Connect to Computer item will display a list of all the workstations on the network. This enables an administrator to connect to any available system on the internal network.

> **NOTE**
>
> When logging into RWW with administrator access, the Connect to Computer item will list ALL the computers on the internal network, even if the computer cannot be remotely connected. If you join Macintosh workstations to Active Directory (discussed in Chapter 13, "Macintosh Integration"), those computers will show in the list for connection, even though they do not support inbound RDP connections.

Using the Connect to Server Feature

As with the Connect to Computer link, the Connect to Server link uses TS Gateway to make an RDP connection to the server over HTTPS. Like Connect to Computer, Connect to Server connects at full screen with the full environment. Unlike Connect to Computer, there is no list of servers available (this link connects directly to the SBS server, even if there are other servers available on the network), and, of course, the link is only visible to administrator users.

From a management point of view, the forced full screen and full bandwidth configuration is problematic, especially because there is no way to modify those settings on the fly. See the "Using Remote Desktop" section at the end of the chapter for an alternate solution for connecting to the server through the RWW interface.

Managing and Using VPN

Configuring VPN connections to the SBS 2008 network is a fairly straightforward process. There are no special tools needed on the client side, and the server configuration is handled through a single wizard. The trickiest part of ensuring proper VPN communication deals with configuring the hardware firewall at the edge of the network.

Managing VPN

Management of the VPN configuration is performed in three areas of the SBS server. The Configure a Virtual Private Network wizard is used to set up or disable VPN services on the SBS server, individual users must have VPN permissions granted, and the Routing and Remote Access console is used to monitor or modify connection-specific VPN settings.

Configure a Virtual Private Network

The Configure a Virtual Private Network wizard is located in the Network tab of the Windows SBS Console under the Connectivity sub-tab. In the sub-tab, you can see the current status of VPN on the server, which will be On or Off. This status is changed through the wizard.

Opening the wizard gives you two choices: Allow Users to Connect to the Server by Using a VPN and Do Not Allow Users to Connect to the Server by Using a VPN. The wizard then performs two tasks. It configures the Routing and Remote Access service to either accept VPN authentication requests or not, and it attempts to configure the external firewall to allow the correct inbound ports through the firewall to the SBS server.

> **NOTE**
>
> The Configure a Virtual Private Network wizard attempts to connect to the hardware firewall using the UPnP protocol to configure the firewall ports correctly. If you are following the recommended Best Practice of keeping UPnP disabled on your firewall, the Configure a Virtual Private Network wizard will show an error at the end of the wizard because it was not able to connect to the firewall and make the configuration changes. In that case, you will need to modify the firewall settings yourself.

There are two network configurations that are needed in the firewall for VPN connections to be forwarded correctly to the SBS server for authentication and management:

▶ **PPTP (Point to Point Tunneling Protocol)**—PPTP uses port 1723 for its communication between the remote VPN client and the VPN server. A standard port forward of port 1723 from the firewall to the SBS server is sufficient to allow a PPTP connection to be initiated.

▶ **PPTP Passthrough**—PPTP Passthrough is a user-friendly term that specifically refers to the proper way to handle GRE (Generic Route Encapsulation) Protocol 47 in a firewall. GRE Protocol 47 is not a port-forward type of protocol. It is used in conjunction with PPTP traffic to establish the VPN tunnel between the VPN client and the VPN server. Microsoft KB 241251 (http://support.microsoft.com/kb/241251) discusses this packet type in more detail. However, if your firewall is not configured for PPTP Passthrough, you will never be able to establish a VPN tunnel with your SBS server. Most modern firewalls have standard configurations for PPTP Passthrough, but some older and less-expensive firewalls have been known to cause problems with VPN connections.

By default, the Configure a Virtual Private Network wizard creates five VPN ports that can be accessed by remote users. Each user connection uses one of these ports. If there are five active VPN connections, and a sixth workstation attempts to connect, the connection will be refused. See the "Use Routing and Remote Access" section later in the chapter to see how to change this behavior.

Configure VPN Access for Users

When VPN access is enabled on an SBS server, accounts with the Network Administrator role are the only accounts that are allowed to access VPN. For other users to access VPN, individual permissions must be assigned.

Access to the SBS VPN network is controlled through the Windows SBS Virtual Private Network Users security group. Membership in that group can be edited directly from the Active Directory Users and Computers console, or you can edit the properties of the individual user account in the Windows SBS Console and toggle the User Can Access Virtual Private Network checkbox under the Remote Access item.

Additionally, you can view the membership of the Windows SBS Virtual Private Network Users security group from the Virtual Private Networking properties. You can access this item by selecting the VPN Connection item in the Network, Connectivity sub-tab in the Windows SBS Console and clicking the View Virtual Private Network Properties task.

Use Routing and Remote Access

The Routing and Remote Access (RRAS) service manages the VPN connections on the SBS 2008 server, and that service can be managed with the Routing and Remote Access console. The RRAS console can be found from the Start menu under the Administrative Tools folder, and it can also be opened from a command prompt or Start, Run as rrasmgmt.msc.

When you open the RRAS console, you can tell immediately if VPN access has been enabled on the server or not. If it has, the server icon in the navigation tree will have a green arrow pointing up. If not, the server icon will have a red arrow pointing down. If VPN has not been configured, you will not be able to access any of the settings for the server from the RRAS console. When VPN has been enabled, you will be able to modify a number of settings related to the VPN configuration.

Figure 6.8 shows the RRAS console expanded and the Ports item selected. Here you can see the five default PPTP ports. In the figure, you can also see that one of the ports is active.

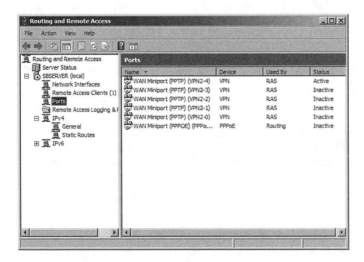

FIGURE 6.8   VPN ports from the RRAS console.

You can get detailed information about the active VPN connection by right-clicking on the connection and selecting Status. In Figure 6.9, you can see who the authenticated user is (in this case, the sbsadmin account is connected), how much traffic has passed across the connection, the internal IP addresses assigned to the connection, and any errors that may have occurred during the session.

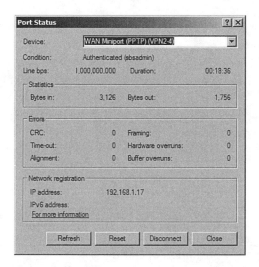

FIGURE 6.9   VPN port status from the RRAS console.

The buttons along the bottom of the status window enable you to take several actions with the connection:

- ▶ **Refresh**—Updates the status window to show the most current statistics.

- ▶ **Reset**—Resets the traffic statistics back to zero but maintains the connection.

- ▶ **Disconnect**—Forcibly drops the VPN connection without prompting.

If you need more than five VPN ports active for your network, you must modify the VPN port settings in the RRAS console. Follow these steps to add to the number of ports used for PPTP VPN connections:

1. In the Routing and Remote Access console, right-click the Ports item from the navigation tree and select Properties.

2. In the Ports Properties page, select WAN Miniport (PPTP) and click Configure.

3. In the Configure Device—WAN Miniport (PPTP) page (see Figure 6.10), adjust the Maximum Ports value to be the maximum number of VPN connections that you will need.

FIGURE 6.10   Configure the number of VPN ports in RRAS.

4. Click OK; then click OK to close the Ports Properties page.

The RRAS console will now reflect the number of available PPTP ports.

Using VPN

Once the server and firewall are properly configured to accept incoming VPN connections, configuring the workstation to establish a VPN connection is a fairly straightforward process. You can use the native VPN tools with your workstation operating system (Windows, Macintosh, UNIX/Linux, and so on) to create the connection. The only information you will need in order to make the connection is the public name or IP address of the SBS network (that is, remote.domain.com) and the user credentials for an account that is authorized to access the VPN connection.

Changes from SBS 2003—Connection Manager

In SBS 2003, running the Configure Remote Access wizard built a package called the Connection Manager and made that package available for download from the RWW home page. When the package was installed on an XP workstation, it built a VPN connectoid that could be used to connect the workstation back to the SBS network.

SBS 2008 no longer provides a Connection Manager package. The user must configure the VPN connector manually on the remote workstation. For information about creating a VPN connector on the workstation, refer to the Help system for the operating system of that workstation. Fortunately, all desktop operating systems support creating a PPTP VPN connector, so no special tools are needed to accomplish this.

Once the VPN connection has been established from the workstation to the SBS 2008 network, the workstation will have an IP assigned for the SBS network. Depending on how the VPN connection was made, the connection may route all Internet traffic across the VPN connection, or the workstation may simply look to the VPN network for SBS resources.

Managing and Using Remote Desktop

Though the Remote Desktop tools can be used internally to connect to and control other workstations on the local network, this section of the chapter focuses on using Remote Desktop to connect to the SBS 2008 server for the purposes of remote administration. Using the Connect to Server link in the Remote Web Workplace interface does make a remote connection to the SBS server, but that connection uses the TS Gateway method to connect (which means you cannot control certain aspects of the connection, such as screen size and speed settings) and is dependent upon IIS (if IIS is not running, you cannot access the RWW interface, and if IIS gets reset during your remote connection, that connection is lost). For these reasons, many IT professionals allow Remote Desktop connectivity directly to the SBS server from the Internet.

> **NOTE**
>
> One common concern raised about opening port 3389 to the Internet is that doing so is a potential security risk. For a thorough discussion of the security implications and recommendations related to this, please see the "Securing Remote Access Solutions" section later in the chapter.

Managing Remote Desktop

In a default SBS 2008 installation, the SBS 2008 server is preconfigured for Remote Administration mode, meaning that it can support up to two simultaneous remote connections to the server. This allows any workstation in the local network to connect to the server on port 3389 using a Remote Desktop Connection tool. The server setup process, specifically the Connect to the Internet and Fix My Network wizards, does not attempt to configure the external firewall to forward port 3389 from the firewall to the SBS server. If you want to allow access to the server desktop using Remote Desktop from outside the network, you need to manually configure the router to forward port 3389.

Should you choose to allow access to the server via Remote Desktop from the Internet, there are several tools on the server to help you manage those connections. These tools can be found from Start, Administrative Tools, Terminal Services. The following sections discuss the various ways these tools can be used to control and manage access to the server via Remote Desktop.

Terminal Services Configuration

The Terminal Services Configuration console enables you to control the way Remote Desktop can be used to access the server. There are two nodes in the navigation tree of the console. The Licensing Diagnosis node is grayed out since the Terminal Services role is not installed on the SBS 2008 server, and access to the SBS box does not use Terminal Server licenses.

The Terminal Server Configuration node displays the existing connections for the server and the settings that can be configured for the server (see Figure 6.11).

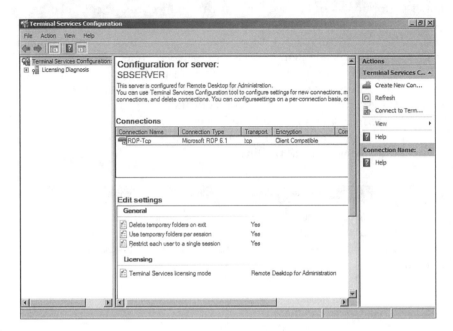

FIGURE 6.11   Terminal Services Configuration console.

The setting that probably will be the most commonly changed item in SBS 2008 deployments is the Restrict Each User to a Single Session setting. By default, this setting is enabled, but it can be changed in the Terminal Services Configuration console to allow two simultaneous logons to the server from the same account. To change this setting, double-click one of the items under General to open the Properties window. In the Properties window, disable the Restrict Each User to a Single Session checkbox and click OK.

The other settings available in this console govern how temporary files are handled in remote sessions. By default, a set of temporary folders is created for each session at the time of the connection, and those folders are cleaned up when the remote session closes. This is recommended to keep the environments for each remote session clean, especially if multiple logons for the same account are allowed.

The Licensing settings are unavailable on the SBS server as the server is running in Remote Desktop for Administration mode, so no license tracking is needed.

The default RDP connection is listed in the Connections section of the console. Double-clicking on the RDP-Tcp session opens the properties for the connection. This Properties page has a number of tabs that control various aspects of the connection. These tabs are detailed in the following sections.

General   The General tab contains settings for security, encryption, and Network Level Authentication, as shown in Figure 6.12.

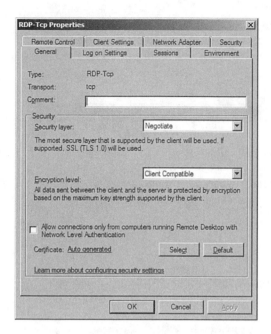

FIGURE 6.12   General settings for the RDP-Tcp connection.

The Security Layer setting has three options:

▶ **RDP Security Layer**—This setting establishes a connection between the client and the server using the default RDP encryption package. This allows older RDP clients to access the connection.

▶ **SSL (TLS 1.0)**—This setting establishes an SSL connection using TLS 1.0 between the client and the server and is the most secure method for establishing a connection between systems. Only the newest RDP clients support this type of connection.

▶ **Negotiate**—This default setting allows the RDP session to negotiate which security layer will be used. If the client can support the SSL connection, it will be used. Otherwise, the connection will default back to default RDP encryption.

The Encryption Level setting has four options:

▶ **Low**—This setting establishes the encrypted communication using the maximum encryption key strength supported by the client tool. This applies only to data sent from the client to the server.

▶ **Client Compatible**—This default setting establishes two-way encryption between the client and server using the maximum encryption key strength supported by the client.

▶ **High**—This setting establishes two-way encryption between the client and server using the maximum encryption key strength supported on the server. If the client cannot support the key strength of the server, the connection is refused.

▶ **FIPS Compliant**—This setting establishes two-way encryption between the client and server using Federal Information Processing Standard 140-1 encryption methods. This is the highest level of encryption available and is supported by the fewest RDP clients.

NOTE

FIPS Compliant encryption is supported in the Windows Remote Desktop Client version 5.2 and later, and in the Macintosh Remote Desktop Client version 2.0 and later. Not all third-party RDP clients support FIPS Compliant connections. The default Connect to Server link in the RWW home page also does not support FIPS connections, so be careful about enabling FIPS if you plan to use the Connect to Server link to access the SBS console remotely.

The Allow Connections Only From Computers Running Remote Desktop with Network Level Authentication is disabled by default, allowing RDP connections from all RDP clients. If you enable this setting, only operating systems that support Network Level Authentication (NLA) will be able to make a connection to the SBS server. This excludes workstations running Windows XP and earlier and connections coming from Server 2003 or earlier operating systems. NLA connections are supported from Vista workstations, 2008 servers, and Macintosh workstations running OS 10.4 and later.

The last item that can be configured in this tab is the SSL certificate used for the connection. By default, this uses the same SSL certificate that is configured in the setup wizards and should not be modified.

Log On Settings   The Log On Settings tab contains two items. A radio button enables you to choose between allowing the connection to log in with the credentials supplied in the client or forcing a logon with a specific account. Although the latter option may be useful in certain types of environments, it is definitely not advised for access to the SBS server.

The Always Prompt for Password checkbox, when enabled, forces the connection to present the traditional logon screen after the initial connection is made instead of accepting the credentials presented in the RDP client. Enabling this feature forces the connecting user to enter the password twice, which does not provide a significant level of additional protection.

Sessions   The Sessions tab enables you to override the settings for handling disconnected sessions and session limits that are configured in the user account object. Again, this page is primarily used for configuring Terminal Servers, not for managing remote administration, so these settings do not need to be modified.

Environment   The Environment tab controls the ability to launch an application upon connection to the session. The default setting, Run Initial Program Specified by the User Profile and Remote Desktop Connection or Client, automatically opens an application that is specified for launch in the user object's profile or in the settings for the Remote Desktop client. For Remote Administration, this setting should be left at default or set to Do Not Allow an Initial Program to be Launched; Always Show Desktop so that no application can be set to launch at connection time.

Remote Control   The settings in the Remote Control tab govern how one remote connection can share control with another. The default setting, Use Remote Control With Default User Settings, allows one remote connection to be controlled by another after the user accepts a request for control. For an SBS server, you should consider selecting the Use Remote Control with the Following Settings, and then deselecting the Request User's Permission checkbox and selecting the Interact with the Session button, as shown in Figure 6.13. This is discussed in more detail in the "Using Remote Desktop" section later in the chapter.

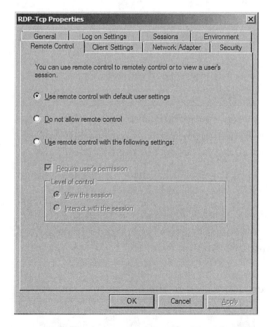

FIGURE 6.13   Recommended Remote Control settings for the RDP-Tcp connection.

Client Settings   In the Client Settings tab, you can force certain environmental settings for the remote connections. As shown in Figure 6.14, you can choose to force the client to connect at a specific color depth setting, selecting from five different options. A lower color depth transmits less display information across to the remote client, making the connection faster, which can be a benefit when connecting over a slow link. Because the RWW Connect to Server link does not have the option to select the color depth for the remote connection, you may choose to override the default settings here and select a lower color depth. By default, SBS 2008 configures the connection to force a 16-bit color depth.

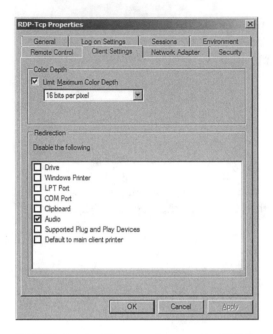

FIGURE 6.14   Client settings for the RDP-Tcp connection.

In the Redirection section, you can disable certain types of resources from being shared in the session. By default, audio information is not transmitted from the server to the remote client. The other options that can be disabled for all connections are the following:

▶ **Drive**—When selected, prevents the sharing of the local disk drive from the client to the server.

▶ **Windows Printer**—When selected, prevents Windows printer objects on the client workstation from appearing as shared printers on the server. This would prevent the remote connection from being able to print information from the server to a printer connected to the remote client.

▶ **LPT Port**—When selected, prevents printers connected to the LPT port of the workstation from appearing as shared printers on the server.

▶ **COM Port**—When selected, prevents any devices connected to the COM port of the workstation from appearing as a shared device on the server.

▶ **Clipboard**—When selected, prevents information from being transmitted between the server and client via the clipboard.

▶ **Supported Plug and Play Devices**—When selected, prevents certain devices on the remote workstation from showing as shared devices on the server.

▶ **Default to Main Client Printer**—When selected, and if remote printing is allowed, prevents the default printer for the remote session from mapping to the default printer on the remote workstation, instead keeping the default printer selection for the server session intact.

Network Adapter   This tab identifies which network adapter the connection settings apply to and specifies how many remote connections are allowed. In a Remote Administration configuration, these settings do not need to be changed. If desired, the maximum number of connections could be reduced from two to one, but the maximum number cannot be increased to more than two for remote administration.

Security   The Security tab lists the security groups that have permission to access the connection, as shown in Figure 6.15. When selecting this tab, you will receive a pop-up warning that recommends that you use the Remote Desktop Users group to determine who has access to the server. If you make any changes to the security settings in this tab, it could lead to greater troubleshooting challenges should problems arise later. As the pop-up recommends, the settings in this tab should be left alone.

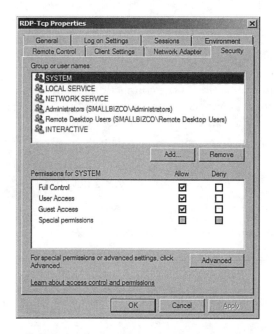

FIGURE 6.15   Security settings for the RDP-Tcp connection.

Terminal Services Manager

The Terminal Services Manager console enables you to monitor and manage active RDP connections to the server. When the Terminal Services Manager console is open, any active connections appear in the main console window, as shown in Figure 6.16.

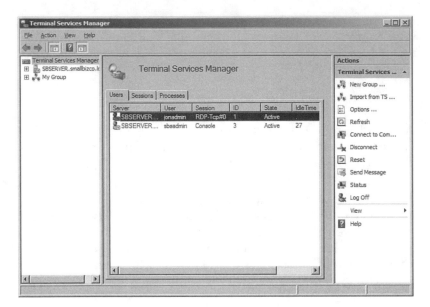

FIGURE 6.16   Active connections in Terminal Services Manager.

Although it is difficult to tell from the grayscale figure, the person icon for each connection has either a green up arrow or a red down arrow, indicating which connection is "your" connection. In this figure, the sbsadmin connection is the connection for the currently logged-on account, whereas the jonadmin connection belongs to the other session. The display also gives other information about the status of the connection:

▶ **Session**—Gives the RDP session number, or displays "Disconnected" if the session has been dropped remotely.

▶ **ID**—Displays the unique ID for the session. Each new session is given a new ID.

▶ **State**—Indicates the current state of the session, either Active or Disconnected.

▶ **Idle Time**—Indicates how long the active connection has been idle.

▶ **LogOn Time**—Indicates when the connection was made.

You can interact with the sessions through the Terminal Services Manager console as well. Right-clicking on a session enables you to choose one of several actions to take, depending on the state of the remote session. These items also appear as Actions in the right column of the display when a session is selected:

▶ **Connect**—Enables you to connect to (take over) the remote session. This can only be done if you also have a remote connection to the server. This option will not be visible if you open the Terminal Services Manager directly from the server console. You must also enter the password for the account before you can take over the session. You cannot connect to your own session.

▶ **Disconnect**—Enables you to disconnect an active session without losing the session information. You will be prompted to confirm that you want to disconnect the remote session, and the user with the remote session will receive a message that his or her connection was dropped through an administration tool. You can disconnect your own session.

▶ **Send Message**—Enables you to send a message, via pop-up window, to the session. You can send a message to your own session.

▶ **Remote Control**—Enables you to share control with the other session so that both parties can see the screen and use keyboard and mouse in the session. In order to complete a remote control, both connections must be remote connections (the console session cannot control or be controlled). Needless to say, you cannot remote control your own session.

▶ **Reset**—Enables you to forcibly disconnect the session. A reset drops the connection and kills all processes that were active in the session. You can reset your own session. This is the harsh version of the Log Off option.

▶ **Status**—Enables you to view detailed information about the status of the remote session. A sample status window is shown in Figure 6.17. From the status window, you see the name of the user, the name of the workstation making the connection, the address of the workstation (if available), the version of the RDP client being used, the color depth, resolution, and encryption level, as well as network traffic data.

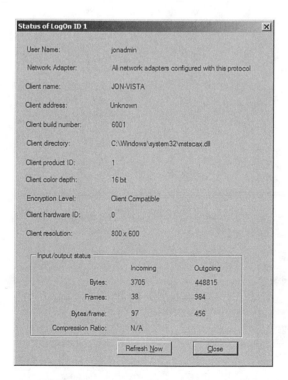

FIGURE 6.17   Active connection status in Terminal Services Manager.

▶ **Log Off**—Enables you to politely disconnect the session. All open applications are sent exit commands, and the session waits until the applications have closed before dropping the session. You can Log Off your own session. This is the polite version of the Reset option.

The Terminal Services Manager console can be used to monitor and interact with sessions on terminal servers in the network, not just the remote administration connections on the SBS 2008 server.

TS Gateway Manager

The TS Gateway Manager can be used to modify settings for the TS Gateway services on the SBS server. In general, these settings should not be modified, as that would impact the ability to connect to workstations and the server through the RWW interface.

Connection Authorization Policies   SBS 2008 creates a single Connection Authorization Policy (CAP) during setup. This policy is named General Connection Authorization Policy, and it identifies the users who are allowed to connect to the TS Gateway service on the SBS box. By default, the Domain Users security group is listed in the Requirements tab (shown in Figure 6.18), meaning that any domain user is allowed to access the TS Gateway. In addition, all devices are enabled for redirection by default in the Device Redirection tab (not shown).

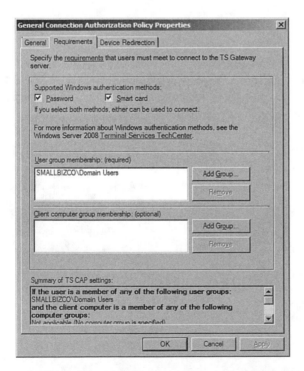

FIGURE 6.18   General Connection Authorization Policy requirements.

Resource Authorization Policies   SBS 2008 configures two Resource Authorization Policies during setup. One policy enables access to domain controllers (in this case, the SBS server, but it would also cover access to other domain controllers in the network), and the other enables access to domain computers (which would include a members server or a terminal server).

Both policies list the Domain Users security group in the User Groups tab of the policy. This does not mean that any user would be able to log onto all machines; this just allows any user to authenticate against the TS Gateway to get redirected to the destination machine, and the destination machine ultimately controls whether the requesting user has access to the computer or not. Both policies also specify port 3389, the Remote Desktop port, as the only allowed port for access through the TS Gateway.

The distinction between the two policies is that one identifies domain controllers as the allowed computer group, and the other identifies domain computers. If you wanted to be more restrictive about who could authenticate against the TS Gateway to connect to a domain controller, you could modify the user group for that policy and remove the Domain Users group and add in a different security group.

Monitoring TS Gateway Sessions   You can view and manage the TS Gateway connection in the Monitoring node of the console. Figure 6.19 shows active TS Gateway connections. You can tell from this display which user has authenticated against the gateway, which machine the user has connected to, and the protocol and port used for the connection. The display will also show the date and time the connection was made, the duration of the connection, the idle time on the connection, the IP address of the connecting computer, and the amount of data sent and received through the gateway.

From this interface, you could disconnect one of the connections, or disconnect the user. In this example, if you selected Disconnect This User, both of the sessions would be dropped. If you wanted to drop just one of the connections instead, you would highlight that connection and select Disconnect This Session.

You can view or adjust the properties of the TS Gateway service by right-clicking on the server name and selecting Properties. The Properties page has several tabs to configure the settings. The default values for an SBS 2008 installation are listed in Table 6.2.

TABLE 6.2   Default Settings for TS Gateway

Tab	Setting	Value
General	Maximum Connections	Allows the maximum supported simultaneous connections
SSL Certificate	Select an Existing Certificate for SSL Encryption	Uses the default cert created during setup or a third-party cert added with the Add a Trusted Certificate wizard
TS CAP Store	Request Clients to Send a Statement of Health	Enabled
	NPS Server Selection	Local NPS Server

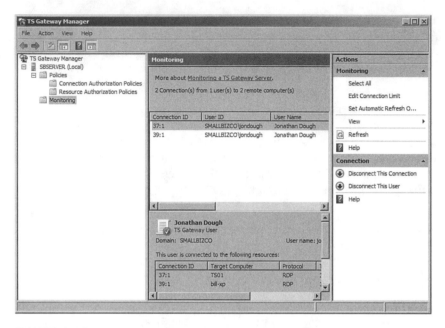

FIGURE 6.19   Active connections in TS Gateway Manager.

TABLE 6.2   Default Settings for TS Gateway

Tab	Setting	Value
Server Farm	TS Gateway Server Farm Member	[none]
Auditing	Successful User Disconnection from the Resource	Enabled
	Failed User Connection to the Resource	Enabled
	Failed Connection Authorization	Enabled
	Failed Resource Authorization	Enabled
	Successful User Connection to the Resource	Enabled
	Successful Connection Authorization	Enabled
	Successful Resource Authorization	Enabled
SSL Bridging	Use HTTPS-HTTP Bridging (Terminate SSL Requests and Initiate New HTTP Requests)	Disabled

Using Remote Desktop

Many system administrators are already familiar with using Remote Desktop to remotely manage a server session, and if you are in this category, you might be tempted to skip this section. However, this chapter has alluded to an alternate solution for connecting to the server via the Connect to Server link in Remote Web Workplace, and that solution is outlined in this section. Plus, this section covers using Remote Desktop on the server to offer or receive support with another individual or organization.

Traditional Remote Desktop

The traditional method for connecting to a server via Remote Desktop is to open port 3389 through the firewall to the server, and then running a Remote Desktop client outside the network and connecting to the public IP of the network. Several support organizations might request access to the server using this method, as it requires little special configuration and, when done properly, is still secure.

There are several third-party Remote Desktop clients for a variety of platforms, and unless you have configured the RDP-Tcp connector to require a higher level of encryption, those tools may connect to an SBS 2008 server. To take full advantage of the built-in security of the Remote Desktop protocol, you should use the RDP client from Microsoft for XP, Vista, or Macintosh.

The single biggest advantage of using the Remote Desktop client versus the Connect to Server link in RWW is the ability to customize the connection. With the Remote Desktop Client, you can specify the screen size for the connection, and you can modify the performance settings.

Figure 6.20 shows the different performance options available in the Windows Remote desktop client. You can select from one of the preconfigured connection speeds (Modem (28.8Kbps), Modem (56KBps), Broadband (128Kbps–1.5Mbps), or LAN (10Mbps or higher)) or select a custom option. The slower the connection speed selected from the list, the fewer visual elements are transmitted across the remote connection.

Many support professionals prefer the slower connection settings because it ends up improving the responsiveness of the remote system over an Internet connection. Many of the visual elements of the server desktop are not needed to successfully and efficiently navigate the server console while connected remotely, so these elements can be disabled without loss of functionality.

Remote Desktop via TS Gateway

Configuring a Remote Desktop session to use the TS Gateway of the SBS server is a straightforward process. There are essentially only two changes that need to be made to the traditional RDP configuration.

First, the computer name entered into the RDP client will be the internal name of the workstation or server that you want to connect to. Normally, you would put the public DNS name or IP address of the network connection and let the firewall forward your port 3389 traffic to the server, but in this case, you want to enter the name of the destination workstation.

Second, you need to enter the information for the TS Gateway. This is done in the Advanced tab of the RDP client under Connect from Anywhere. Clicking the Settings button opens the Gateway Server Settings window, shown in Figure 6.21.

FIGURE 6.20   Performance selections in the Remote Desktop Connection Client.

FIGURE 6.21   Gateway Server Settings in the Remote Desktop Connection Client.

To build your own connection to the network from offsite, you would need to select the Use These TS Gateway Server Settings radio button, and then enter the public DNS name of the SBS server.

When you initiate the connection from the client, the client first looks for the TS Gateway server and, if it locates it, attempts to authenticate against the service. If the authentication is successful, the client asks the TS Gateway to forward the connection to the machine listed in the configuration, and the TS Gateway will then attempt to route the connection to the destination computer. Once that connection is established and authenticated, the remote desktop session starts, and you are able to access the remote machine.

> **NOTE**
>
> At this time, only the Windows Remote Desktop Client allows for a TS Gateway connection. The Macintosh RDP client does not yet have support for using TS Gateway. It is possible that future releases of the Macintosh RDP client will have this functionality, but at the time of the release of this book, that functionality is not present.

Sharing Console Sessions via RDP

As discussed in the Remote Control section earlier in the chapter, it is possible for one connection on the server console to remotely control another. This ability, often referred to as "shadowing a session," is routinely used by support organizations to troubleshoot problems on a server. Even though there are a number of third-party troubleshooting tools available that use a web-sharing method for sharing a server session, the default security for Internet Explorer on the SBS 2008 server will not allow many of these tools to run. Although the IE security settings can be changed, some organizations prefer using the native tools to get the most responsive access to the server possible during a troubleshooting session.

To enter into a remote control session, both connections to the server must be remote connections. A remote connection cannot control a console session, and vice versa. So in order to achieve this, you would need to either enable multiple server logon for the same account, or create a separate admin account on the network. This latter method is preferred because the account can be created and deleted easily, and the support technician never has to have the primary administration account and password.

After both remote sessions are live, one session would open the Terminal Services Manager console and initiate a Remote Control session with the other session. The default sharing configuration prompts the session that is receiving the remote control request and gives that user the ability to accept or reject the connection. This behavior can be changed in the Remote Control tab of the RDP-Tcp connection properties discussed previously.

Once the remote session has been initiated, both users see the same desktop and have control of the mouse and keyboard. To end the session, the controlling session can press the session end key (Control-Tab by default in Server 2008) or the controlled session can simply log out.

Working with screen sizes and color depth can be a factor in initiating a successful remote control session. If the controlling session has a smaller screen size than the session being controlled, the controlling session will have scroll bars in the RDP window, and the user may have to scroll around quite a bit during the session. Best practice is to try to match the RDP screen size on both systems prior to initiating a remote control session. Color depth can also be a factor, but that is primarily dealing with the Macintosh RDP client, which uses a 15-bit color depth by default. Unless the controlled session is running with a 15-bit or less color depth, the Mac RDP client is unable to establish a session. The reverse does not hold true, however.

Building .RDP Files

The Microsoft Remote Desktop clients enable you to save session configuration files so that you can open a connection to a remote system by double-clicking on the configuration file. These files are plain text files and can be edited within Notepad or other text editor as needed. The following listing shows the contents of a file named sbs.rdp that connects to a server named SBServer at a screen resolution of 1024×768 through a TS Gateway at remote.smallbizco.net:

```
screen mode id:i:1
desktopwidth:i:1024
desktopheight:i:768
session bpp:i:16
full address:s:sbserver
compression:i:1
keyboardhook:i:2
audiomode:i:0
redirectprinters:i:0
redirectcomports:i:0
redirectsmartcards:i:1
redirectclipboard:i:1
redirectposdevices:i:0
displayconnectionbar:i:1
autoreconnection enabled:i:1
authentication level:i:0
prompt for credentials:i:0
negotiate security layer:i:1
remoteapplicationmode:i:0
alternate shell:s:
shell working directory:s:
disable wallpaper:i:1
disable full window drag:i:1
allow desktop composition:i:0
allow font smoothing:i:0
disable menu anims:i:1
disable themes:i:0
disable cursor setting:i:0
bitmapcachepersistenable:i:1
gatewayhostname:s:remote.smallbizco.net
gatewayusagemethod:i:2
gatewaycredentialssource:i:4
gatewayprofileusagemethod:i:1
```

```
promptcredentialonce:i:1
drivestoredirect:s:
```

> **NOTE**
>
> For a full description of all the options in the RDP session file, see MS KB 885187 (http://support.microsoft.com/kb/885187).

The `desktopwidth` and `desktopheight` items set the screen size for the connection, and `session bpp` indicates the video bit depth. The internal server name is specified in `full address`, and the TS gateway address is found in `gatewayhostname`.

> **TIP**
>
> For the power user who wants to generate and maintain a number of RDP files for various systems, a really helpful blog post describing a way to handle this programmatically can be found at http://blogs.msdn.com/powershell/archive/2008/09/14/rdp-file-generation-use-of-here-strings.aspx.

Again, these RDP files can only be used with the Windows RDP client. The Macintosh RDP 2.0 client saves its RDP files in an XML format that is not interchangeable with the Windows RDP client.

> **Best Practice—Add RDP Files to RWW Links**
>
> Because the Remote Web Workplace links for Connect to Computer and Connect to Server cannot be modified, if you want or need to have a connection with a smaller screen size or better performance, you can create a custom RDP file that connects to the device through the TS Gateway and then publish that RDP file through the Remote Web Workplace home page in the home page links. Follow these steps to publish an RDP file through RWW:
>
> 1. Build an RDP file for the connection you want to make active through the TS Gateway. Test the file to ensure the settings work correctly from outside the network.
> 2. Create a directory on the server that is accessible through the web to store these RDP files. As an example, you could create a folder named RDP under the Remote Web Workplace folder on the server, in `C:\Program Files\Windows Small Business Server\Bin\webapp\Remote`.
> 3. Go into the IIS Management Console and drill down to the location where you placed the new folder (see Figure 6.22 for this example of placing an RDP folder beneath the Remote folder).

FIGURE 6.22   Location of the RDP folder in the IIS Management Console.

4. Add a MIME type to that folder of application/x-rdp with a file extension of .rdp (see Figure 6.23).

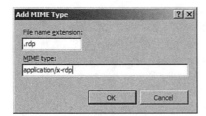

FIGURE 6.23   Adding the RDP MIME type.

5. Close the IIS Management Console.

6. Copy the RDP file(s) into the RDP folder.

7. Edit the home page links in RWW from Windows SBS Console, Shared Folders and Web Sites, Web Sites, Remote Web Workplace, View Site Properties, Home Page Links, and Manage Links.

8. To add a link to the Administration links, enter the link description and the URL path to the RDP file (in this case, https://remote.smallbizco.net/Remote/RDP/smallbizco.rdp), as shown in Figure 6.24.

9. Close the Remote Web Workplace properties.

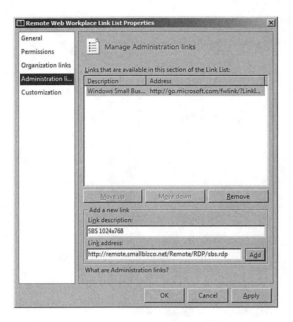

FIGURE 6.24   Adding the RDP file to the link list.

When you next connect to RWW, you will see the new link that points to the RDP file (see Figure 6.25). When you click the link, the RDP file will start to download. You can click Open to automatically launch the RDP client. Next, you will get a window stating that the published cannot be verified, and you can click Connect to continue. Finally, you will be prompted to enter your username and password. You will need to enter the username as domain\username, as the connection will otherwise assume the local domain for the workstation you're connecting from. After that, you get connected to the remote computer and have access based on the settings you entered into the RDP file.

You can repeat this process for as many connection configurations as you need. If you want to create connections like this for users to connect to their workstations, you would place those RDP files in the Organization Links list rather than the Administration Links list.

Securing Remote Access Solutions

As useful and empowering as remote access is, it does come with its own set of security concerns: having user account information leaked to unknown parties, opening ports to the server to allow for potential password cracking, and so on. The following sections cover a few suggestions for addressing some of these security concerns.

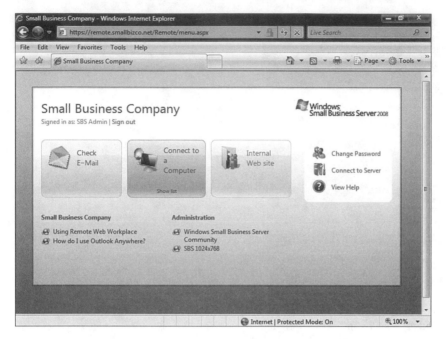

FIGURE 6.25   The RDP link contained in the Administration links.

Network Security

One concern commonly associated with remote access, specifically RDP, is that allowing inbound RDP access increases the threat of account compromise because yet another authentication avenue is open. If you are concerned about this possibility, here are some steps you could take to reduce the risk associated with opening port 3389:

▸ **Restrict inbound access to port 3389 to a specific set of IP addresses in the firewall**—This requires use of a firewall device that supports this function, but if you only allow inbound access to port 3389 from the IP address of your remote office or a known support entity, you reduce the risk of a drive-by scan of that port.

▸ **Increase the level of encryption on RDP sessions**—In the RDP-Tcp connector, raise the level of encryption to High or FIPS Compliant. Understand that if you do this, you could break the Connect to Server functionality in RWW.

▸ **Restrict RDP access only through TS Gateway**—Simply do not open port 3389 to the Internet and require access to the server to be handled through TS Gateway. This is already set up in the SBS server, so no additional configuration needs to be done, but if there is a problem with IIS, you might not be able to get in.

▸ **Use a third-party remote control solution to provide remote access to the server**—This keeps the ports open from the Internet to the server to a minimum, but you are relying on a service to run on the server and communications with the third party to be in good shape for you to have reliable access.

Password Security

Protecting passwords is increasingly important as the business of identity theft continues to grow. As users travel, they risk compromising their account passwords when using unknown or unmanaged systems, such as kiosks or other personal computers. Many malware threats attempt to install keyloggers on systems to be able to capture usernames and passwords and transmit those back to someone who will validate the information and then sell it to another party for other nefarious purposes.

Users should be required to keep secure, complex passwords, especially users who might attempt to access the network from other locations. Passwords should be changed on a regular basis.

Best Practice—Use Two-Factor Authentication to Secure Remote Passwords

Two-factor authentication has not historically been a common technology in the small business space, mostly because of cost. However, multiple solutions are now available that are both affordable for the segment and easy to implement.

Two-factor authentication increases the security of a connection by adding an element to the traditional username and password. Similar to a bank ATM card, two-factor authentication systems require two elements: something you have, and something you know. With an ATM card, you must have both the card and the PIN in order to get access to cash from your account. If a thief stole your card, that would not be enough for them to get access to your account. This is the same if the thief only got your PIN.

For computer access, two-factor authentication comes in the form of a token that generates a one-time password (OTP) and a system that ties that token to a user PIN. Both the PIN and the OTP from the token are needed to validate access for a specific user in these systems.

Solutions are available today for SBS, such as AuthAnvil (http://www.authanvil.com), that add two-factor authentication to the Remote Web Workplace as well as the workstation login. Figure 6.26 shows the RWW login screen for a server with a two-factor authentication solution installed. In order to gain access, the user must enter the user name, password, and the access token, which is a combination of the PIN and the OTP from the token, in order to get access into the Remote Web Workplace. Even if the user were logging in from a workstation that had a keylogger in place, the OTP would not be valid on a subsequent access attempt.

For additional security, a two-factor authentication solution can be installed that requires the use of a one-time password at the login prompt on the server console. You could create a special admin user account in the network and give only that account permission to access the server via RDP; then install a two-factor authentication system to require that account to enter username, password, and OTP in order to log onto the server console. Given the affordable nature of current two-factor authentication solutions, there is really no reason not to implement one of these solutions for your network.

6

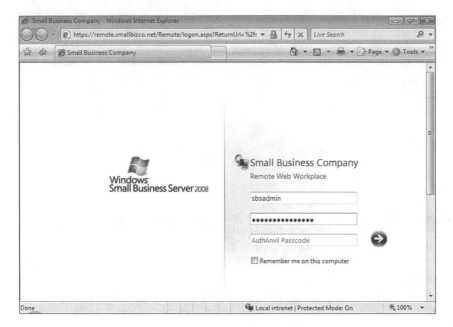

FIGURE 6.26   Two-factor authentication solution for the Remote Web Workplace.

Troubleshooting Remote Access Solutions

Even though the SBS setup configures workable remote access solutions out of the box, there are times when users will encounter issues gaining access to network resources remotely. This section offers a few common problems and solutions.

RWW Access Issues

The following are some access issues you might encounter with users trying to gain access to the Remote Web Workplace:

▶ **RDP Client 6.0 not installed on the workstation**—This applies primarily to older XP workstations that have not installed the RDP 6.0 client (KB 925876). The user might get an error, when trying to connect to a workstation, that the RDP 6.0 client is not installed, or might get a message that the Terminal Services Client ActiveX Control is not available.

▶ **Windows XP SP3 installed**—When Windows XP SP3 is installed on a workstation, it disables the Terminal Services Client ActiveX control by default. If you get a message that the control is disabled or not available, go into the Manage Add-Ons area of Internet Explorer and enable the control.

▶ **HTTP error 503, Service Unavailable**—This error indicates that the Remote Web Workplace site has been disabled, or there is a problem in the IIS configuration for RWW. Either enable the site in the Windows SBS Console, or look in the IIS configuration and see why the site is not working properly.

VPN Access Issues

The following are some access issues you might encounter with users trying to gain access to network resources via VPN:

► **Error 800**—Unfortunately, there are a number of causes that could lead to authentication errors. Some include problems with a NAT router (some NAT routers simply do not handle inbound or outbound VPN connections well at all), firewall configuration (port 1723 must be forwarded to the SBS server in the firewall protecting the SBS network), and ISP restrictions (some ISPs and other locations like hotels and public access sites block outbound VPN connections). It could also result from the firewall having VPN enabled on the device itself.

► **Error 721**—An error 721 from a Windows VPN client is almost always the remote firewall not allowing GRE protocol 47 (VPN Passthrough) into the network. Either figure out how to enable VPN Passthrough or switch firewalls to troubleshoot.

► **VPN connection, but cannot access resources on the remote network**—This issue will likely appear more often with SBS 2008 installations now that the SBS server setup does not attempt to configure the SBS LAN as 192.168.16.x. If the local network and the remote VPN network are on the same subnet (that is, 192.168.1.x), there is no way for the remote workstation to route traffic across the VPN tunnel, because the workstation thinks that this is a local subnet that does not need to be routed. The best practice is to set up the SBS network with a subnet other than 192.168.0.x or 192.168.1.x to help avoid these issues.

RDP Access Issues

The following are some common issues that could impact a user's ability to access network resources via RDP:

► **Cannot make an NLA connection from XP/2003**—The RDP client running on XP and earlier workstations or 2003 and earlier servers do not support NLA. If NLA is required on the RDP-Tcp connection, these downlevel clients will not be able to connect.

► **Cannot connect to the server, a Vista workstation, or another 2008-based server via RDP**—The Remote Desktop Client 6.0 or later is required to connect to computers running Vista and Server 2008.

► **Cannot locate settings for TS Gateway in the RDP client**—TS Gateway settings are only supported in RDP client 6.0 and later. Beta versions of the Mac RDP client version 2.0 do not support TS Gateway.

Summary

This chapter has covered the powerful and complex world of remote access to the SBS network. SBS 2008 continues the trend of increasing network resource availability to remote users through a number of tools: Outlook Web Access and Exchange ActiveSync, Outlook Anywhere, SharePoint, and through the Remote Web Workplace and TS Gateway services. Some of the services have been streamlined so the SBS 2008 server requires fewer open ports to the Internet than its predecessors. But SBS 2008 also provides a greater level of control over who can access these services. Users can be allowed to see all or only some of the RWW elements, and they can be blocked from accessing RWW at all. They can be assigned access to a single workstation to connect to remotely instead of being able to see all the workstations in the domain as in SBS 2003.

All in all, SBS 2008 provides small businesses a way to empower a more mobile workforce at an affordable price, while maintaining security for the users and their data.

Best Practice Summary

▶ **Add RDP Files to RWW Links**—Because you can no longer customize your remote computer connection settings on the fly in SBS 2008, you can take advantage of the TS Gateway services to build static RDP files to connect to internal resources and publish those RDP files in the Remote Web Workplace links sections.

▶ **Use Two-Factor Authentication to Secure Remote Passwords**—Several two-factor authentication solutions are available (and affordable!) for the small business market that allow for greater password security for remote users. Install and use a two-factor authentication solution for controlling/monitoring administrative access to the server or to control user access into RWW.

CHAPTER 7

SharePoint and Companyweb

When Windows Small Business Server 2003 originally launched in October of 2003, a pre-configured implementation of Windows SharePoint Services (WSS) 2.0 was unveiled to the world as the SBS Companyweb. It was thought by many to be the wave of the future in document collaboration, but it fought a tough battle with end users and IT staff alike as they attempted to adjust to it after years of using the company-shared folders of Windows Small Business Server 4.5 and 2000. Five years later, Companyweb returns in Small Business Server 2008, this time running on the much-improved, .NET Framework 3.0–based Windows SharePoint Services 3.0, Service Pack 1.

Part of the core feature set of SBS 2008, Companyweb provides SBS 2008 users with a wide array of tools for storing faxes and archived distribution group e-mails, sharing contacts, calendars, links, announcements, documents, and photos all within a familiar, easy-to-use, and easy-to-customize Web-based interface.

This chapter discusses the role SharePoint plays in SBS 2008 and covers the default settings, along with suggestions for customization, data protection, and troubleshooting.

SBS Companyweb Trivia—SBS Making History

A little-known fact that was shared with the author by John Harris, a long-time Small Business Server consultant, and a Small Business Server Technology Adoption Program (TAP) participant in both Small Business Server 2003 and Small Business Server 2008, is that one of his customers, which was one of the SBS 2003 Technology Adoption Program sites, was the test site for much of what was used in SBS 2003's Companyweb. The site had one of the first, if not the first, SharePoint deployments outside the corporate walls of Microsoft. SBS development team members were onsite to research how the small business performed tasks throughout their workday and studied how to incorporate those tasks into what became the SBS Companyweb. As Susan Bradley stated back in 2006 on her blog (http://msmvps.com/blogs/bradley/archive/2006/08/03/106676.aspx), "Keep a look out for those pesky SBS cockroaches! The idea behind the 'cockroach' is that we're little...indestructible...and EVERYWHERE YOU TURN AROUND." Well put, Susan. Even in the early adoption of SharePoint, SBSers were there, making an impact on a product that would change how all sizes of organizations and business, from small to large, the world over, would share and use their teams' documents and files.

Understanding the Role of SharePoint and Companyweb in SBS 2008

The two primary roles of SharePoint are document sharing and document management. A common joke among the IT community is that Microsoft solutions tend to mature at version three. Windows SharePoint Services 3.0 seems to follow this pattern. Small Business Server 2008's Companyweb uses Windows SharePoint Services 3.0, SP1, and is built on .NET Framework 3.0—nothing like a v3 product written on a v3 release of .NET.

Although Windows SharePoint Services 2.0 in SBS 2003 lacked in some critical backup and recovery areas compared to file sharing using NTFS (WSS 2.0 had complicated backup/restore story and no recycle bin) and in document management (search available only with SBS Premium Edition after updating to SQL database, and restore of single items involving restoration of an entire site and then copying items over), WSS 3.0 has made great improvements. This chapter covers some of the improvements in detail.

Companyweb's Components

To start our discussion of Companyweb's components, here are some Windows SharePoint Services terms to be familiar with:

- At a top level, you have what is referred to as a "farm." The farm consists of all SharePoint installations on a domain. Installations within the farm share data with the others via common database servers.

- Sites that share a server, IP address, and port number are collectively called a "SharePoint application," or "web application."

▶ Within a SharePoint web application, the group of sites contained in it is referred to as a "site collection."

▶ Individual sites are called both "web" and "site" interchangeably.

What's "In the Box" with SharePoint?

Small Business Server 2008 users who take advantage of Companyweb have an incredible productivity tool for use within their organizations. Companyweb enables SBS users to create team workspaces, calendars, document libraries, blogs, wikis, and group team sites for departments and projects. Security can be set at the site level, document level, and item level. End users are given the option to define their own e-mail-enabled alerts for changes to site collections and when changes to documents within a collection are made. Users are able to use both optional and required document checkout and can view document revisions and restore from past versions of documents. Version 3.0 of Windows SharePoint Services includes a Recycle Bin (new from WSS 2.0 in SBS 2003), providing end user recovery of data and an improved backup and recovery model for the administrator.

To access Companyweb from inside the SBS network, the address is http://companyweb. Externally, it can be accessed from within the Remote Web Workplace shown in Figure 7.1, or by browsing directly to https://FQDN:987 (https://your Remote Web Workplace address with the addition of the port number, 987). Using our example of remote.smallbizco.net address, this would be https://remote.smallbizco.net:987.

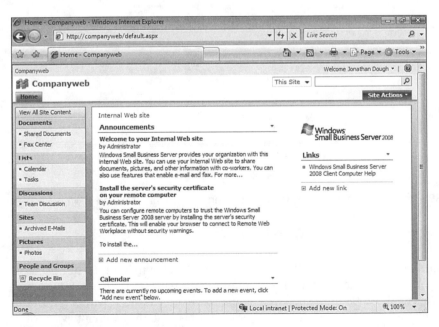

FIGURE 7.1   Default Companyweb home page.

The mobile edition of Companyweb is available internally at http://companyweb/m or externally at https://remote.smallbizco.net:987/m.

Best Practice—Use a Commercial SSL Certificate

Do yourself a huge favor and use a commercially available SSL certificate like Dotster or GoDaddy and don't go with the SBS-created server certificate. If you do not go with a third party public certificate, your Windows Mobile devices will not load the /m page if you don't first download the certificate installer package (the certificate installer package is available at \\SBSSERVER\public\downloads on our example SBS Server), launch it on your PC, and install the cert to your Windows Mobile 6 device (see Figures 7.2 and 7.3). With a third-party certificate users can use the mobile SharePoint site without the extra hassle and across any Wireless Application Protocol (WAP) browser, regardless of device platform. In addition, you'll be taken care of for your regular SharePoint site and Outlook Anywhere's use of SSL.

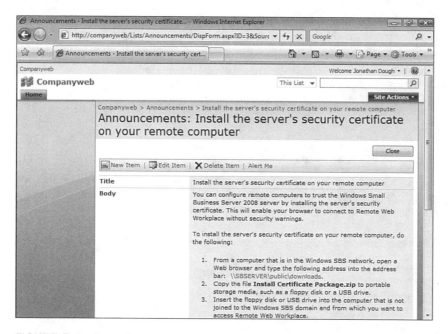

FIGURE 7.2   SBS Self-assignedCertificate Installation Announcement Help Screen in Companyweb.

Wikis and Blogs

During early training on Small Business Server 2008's final Release to Manufacturing (RTM) product, some individuals had no intention of migrating from their Small Business Server 2003 Servers to SBS 2008 until they were going to be forced into it with a hardware refresh. This wasn't because of any faults of SBS 2008, but because they weren't aware of any compelling reasons to goad them into a change. By the end of the week, one partici-

FIGURE 7.3   SBS Self-assignedCertificate Installation to a windows Mobile Device.

pant had not only been sold on migrating his network, he was encouraging the rest of the group to seriously consider migrating their own networks and to start blogging about their top ten lists of reasons why each individual was going to switch, so that others could be encouraged to migrate their SBS 2003 networks sooner. What caused the shift in his reasoning to stay on 2003 or move to 2008? Wikis and blogs.

If you are new to the term wiki, it is a Hawaiian term for quick. Wikis allow users to freely and quickly enter and edit informative text within a Web browser, whether they are the original author or not. In comparison to a blog, which is a one-to-many style of information transfer, wikis are a collaborative experience with all users having full editing rights to the wiki. If you have accessed your SBS 2003 Companyweb from offsite and wished you had a copy of Word on the computer you are accessing it from rather than having to use an application like Notepad, a wiki is for you. With quick editing available through your Web browser, it is a great way to document best practices and workflow while working in a project and allowing others to contribute quickly and easily.

Creating a Wiki Site   There are two types of wiki content supported in SharePoint 3.0: a full wiki site or wiki pages within an existing site. Follow these instructions to create a full wiki site within SharePoint. Because these steps create a new site, you need to access Companyweb with an account that has administrative permissions in SharePoint to complete the process.

1. From any page in your Companyweb, click Site Actions then select Create.
2. In the Create page, select Sites and Workspaces (see Figure 7.4).
3. On the New SharePoint Site page, enter a title for your new site, a URL name, and select the Wiki Site template (Figure 7.5).
4. Under Permissions and Navigation keep the default settings (Figure 7.6). Click Create at the bottom of the page to complete.

Once the site creation process has completed, the new Wiki site will be displayed. The default page gives you guidance and an introduction on how to use the site (Figure 7.7).

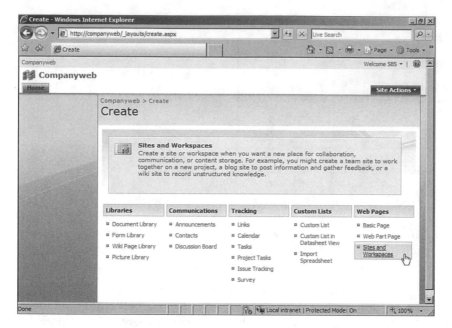

FIGURE 7.4   Creating a new site.

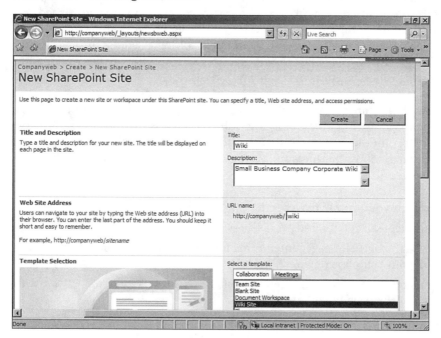

FIGURE 7.5   Name and URL of your new wiki.

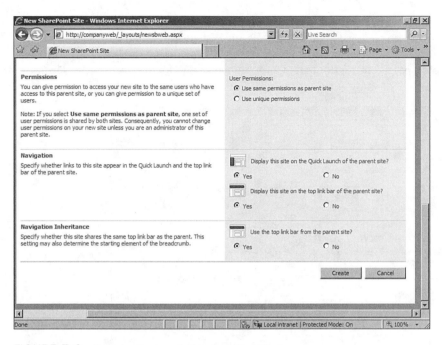

FIGURE 7.6   Permissions and placement settings.

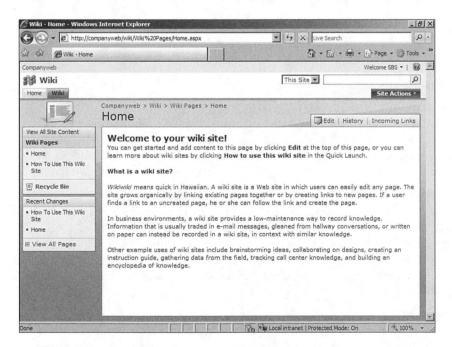

FIGURE 7.7   Wiki home page.

Creating a Blog   Following the same directions except for choosing the blog site template from the SharePoint site page gets your blog page up and running. Figure 7.8 shows a sample blog. You can also see that a link to an RSS feed is available in SharePoint on the left side of the blog page. Throughout the Companyweb you are able to use RSS, Outlook integration, and e-mail alerting for notification of new content within the site.

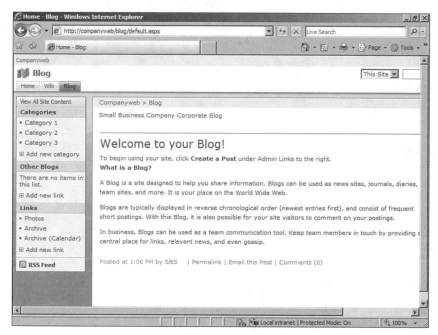

FIGURE 7.8   Sample Blog page.

Other New Features

In addition to new wikis and blog sites, WSS 3 SP1 has added the mobility access mentioned earlier, an end user Recycle Bin, and e-mail-enabled folders and archiving. With the inclusion of additional Microsoft tools like Microsoft Search Server 2008 Express (http://www.microsoft.com/enterprisesearch/serverproducts/searchserverexpress/default. aspx), life just keeps getting better.

▶ **Recycle Bin**—A sure-to-be-favorite improvement from an administration perspective over WSS 2.0 is the SharePoint Recycle Bin. If you have ever had an end user call you in a panic after they have just deleted an entire list in their SBS 2003 Companyweb, you will enjoy having the new site level dumpster, more commonly referred to as the Recycle Bin, giving you an extra level of data prevention coverage in your Companyweb.

With the Recycle Bin in place, users can toss in (and in turn, are able to retrieve before emptying, or having an admin retrieve within 30 days if they have emptied it) documents, folders, lists, list items, attachments, Web parts, forms folders, subscriptions (if not in another item when deleting), personalization, and Web discussions.

▶ **E-mail-enabled SharePoint libraries**—To enable this feature with any of your document libraries, while inside the library, go to Settings and then Incoming E-mail

Settings. Here you will be able to set default settings to allow attachments to be saved to the list, decide whether or not to save the original .eml file, set up meeting notifications, and decide whether to accept mail from any sender, based on list permissions.

▶ **E-mail Archiving**—With security groups (read this as NO distribution groups due to distribution groups not having security settings to interact with the archive library), while you are configuring your security group in the SBS Console, or editing at a later time, you can enable this feature.

Behind the Scenes—Archive Library

Behind the scenes, when enabled, a new document library is created in the EmailArchive sub-site. SBS creates a hidden mail contact with a prefix of "dl-." For example, if you create an accounting security group and enable e-mail distribution and archiving, a new "dl-accounting" hidden contact is created. The contact has an e-mail address of "dl-accounting@companyweb" that matches the address given to an auto-created SharePoint library.

Understanding the Default Settings of SharePoint and Companyweb

The Windows Small Business Server team has done a great job behind the scenes integrating the Companyweb web site into SBS 2008. One visible change over their Small Business Server 2003 implementation of Windows SharePoint Services 2.0 is the concerted effort to move all SBS sites in IIS over to custom SBS sites, leaving the Default Web Site to be just that, the Default Web Site. SBS SharePoint and SharePoint Central Administration v3 are shown in Internet Information Services 7 in Figure 7.9.

Companyweb Port Settings

For a full review of Internet Information Services in SBS 2008, refer to Chapter 5, "Internet Information Services 7.0." To reiterate one quick point, the SBS SharePoint Companyweb web site is served internally on port 80 (http) and externally on port 987 (https). Those of you familiar with Small Business Server 2003 will recognize the change from port 444 used for Companyweb in SBS 2003.

Companyweb Mobile Settings

The mobile Companyweb site is a convenient addition, given the growing number of Internet-capable Windows mobile devices. The default mobile web page presents a simplified mobile-friendly version of Companyweb. On any web-enabled cellular phone or mobile device capable of WAP browsing, a text based Web page is rendered in the device's Web browser and uses the text layout as shown in the following:

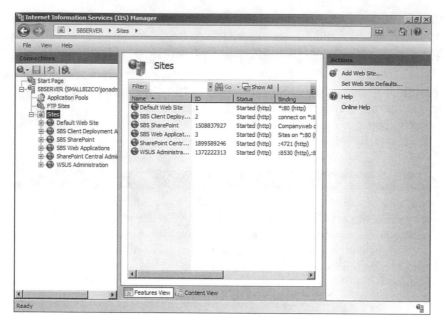

FIGURE 7.9   SBS IIS 7 custom sites.

```
Companyweb Mobile Lists:
Example URL:
https://remote.smallbizco.net:987/_layouts/mobile/mbllists.aspx
Lists
+Announcements
+Calendar
+Tasks
Document Libraries
+Fax Center
+Shared Documents
Picture Libraries
```

SharePoint Default URL Mappings

The default mappings for Companyweb can be viewed and modified by going to SharePoint Central Admin, accessing the SharePoint 3.0 Central Administration page (Start menu, All Programs, SharePoint 3.0 Central Administration), and going to the Operations tab and selecting the Alternative Access Mappings link under Global Configuration (Figure 7.10). From here you can customize your company's URLs to access SharePoint if desired.

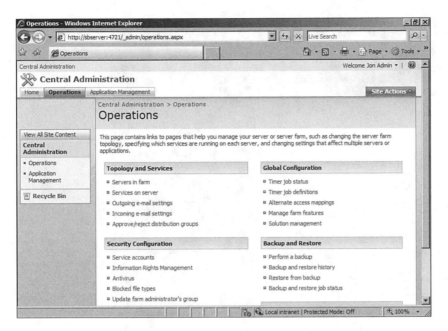

FIGURE 7.10   SBS 2008 Companyweb Central Administration Operations Page.

Default Program and Data File Locations

Chapter 3, "Installing and Configuring SBS 2008," discusses the image-based installation of Small Business Server 2008 and how all application and data is installed to the C:\ drive. Specific to WSS/Companyweb, the locations for the Companyweb data files is by default in the C:\Windows\SYSMSI\SSEE\MSSQL.2005\MSSQL\DATA folder, even when multiple partitions/disks are available. As a best practice, all data features should be moved off C: and onto the other disks/partitions that are available. (See Chapter 18, "Backup and Disaster Recovery," for an in-depth discussion of this.)

To locate the Move Data Wizards, click the Backup and Server Storage tab of the Windows SBS Console; then select the Server Storage tab. In the Tasks pane, shown in Figure 7.11, you will find the Move Windows SharePoint Services Data task as the second task listed.

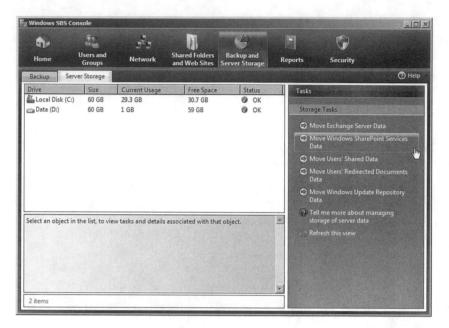

FIGURE 7.11   Windows SharePoint Services Data task location.

Best Practice—Selecting the Windows SharePoint Services Data Folder Location

For consistency in deployments, take the original default location and only change the drive letter of the data folder original location. For example, if you are moving your data to the E:\ drive, take C:\Windows\SYSMSI\SSEE\MSSQL.2005\MSSQL\DATA and move to E:\Windows\SYSMSI\SSEE\MSSQL.2005\MSSQL\DATA. This will give you a consistency with the original deployment that will be helpful when other administrators are assisting you, when you are referencing Microsoft documentation as you maintain your server, and especially when you are administrating multiple Small Business Servers. The Move Windows SharePoint Services Data task will do just this: change the drive letter only and duplicate the path.

Customizing SharePoint and Companyweb

The Small Business Server Development team has done a tremendous amount of work integrating SharePoint into SBS 2008. Out of the box, the site is fully functional and a great productivity tool. This chapter now discusses how to migrate other SharePoint sites, such as the WSS 2.0 site on SBS 2003, over to your SBS 2008 Server, and how to customize the Companyweb site using Microsoft.

Merging Data from an Existing WSS 3.0 Site into Companyweb

For those who have been running Windows SharePoint Services 3.0, either on your exist-ing Small Business Server 2003 server in a side-by-side installation with your original WSS 2.0 site, or on an additional server and want to bring your existing WSS 3.0 site into your new SBS 2008 WSS 3.0 site, you can use STSADM to merge the data from the source server to your SBS 2008 destination server.

STSADM -O EXPORT

STSADM is the command line tool that provides access to the complete set of WSS opera-tions. It is great to use with scripts and batch files. When using it, you need to be on the Small Business Server running it under an administrative account.

You can use STSADM with the EXPORT option to back up a WSS site and restore it, with all security intact, to another WSS instance or even to a separate WSS/MOSS server.

There is no need to download STSADM.EXE; it is already on your server, located here:

```
%PROGRAMFILES%\common files\microsoft shared\web server extensions\12\bin
```

To make a backup of the source database with STSADM, do the following:

1. Login to the server that had the files that you need to copy.
2. Create a directory on your hard drive named "spbackup" on a drive that has enough storage space for the backup files.
3. If the source database is on a Windows 2003 server, from the Start menu, right-click Command Prompt and select Run As Administrator.
4. At the command line, enter the following:

   ```
   cd C:\Program Files\Common Files\Microsoft Shared\web server
   ➥extensions\12\BIN
   ```

5. Type the following at the command prompt, replacing *d:\spbackup\backup* with the path and the filename for your backup file:

   ```
   stsadm.exe -o export -url http://(Your Site) -includeusersecurity
   ➥-filename d:\spbackup\backup -haltonfatalerror -versions 2 -
   ```

   This command starts the backup of your sites, so be prepared. It may take a few minutes, depending on the size of the site.

When the backup has successfully completed, your next step is to move the spbackup folder onto the new server. After this is done, you should login to the new server and repeat steps 3–4. Then, when you are ready, type the following command to import the sites onto the new SharePoint site:

```
stsadm.exe -o import -url https://(Your Site) -includeusersecurity
➥-filename d:\spbackup
```

7

The way Microsoft designed their product around import/exportability allows an administrator to move around more than merely content. The deployment object model also allows metadata like workflows, versioning data, and user roles to be moved.

For additional data export/import using Microsoft.SharePoint.Deployment API object model see the following link for a batch file that can be edited to export and import sites from one place to another in a collection or between collections:

>   http://msdn2.microsoft.com/en-us/library/aa979099.aspx

Installing the SharePoint Sample Application Solutions

A great resource for customization of your SharePoint site is the Microsoft Application Templates for Windows SharePoint Services 3.0 web page at http://technet.microsoft.com/en-us/windowsserver/sharepoint/bb407286.aspx. There are out-of-the-box application templates designed to meet the needs of specific business processes and tasks. Currently, there are 40 of these templates available in English, 20 of which are also offered in multiple languages. These templates are listed in Table 7.1.

TABLE 7.1   Microsoft Application Templates for Windows SharePoint Services 3.0

Site Admin Templates	Server Admin Templates
Board of Directors	Absence Request and Vacation Schedule Management
Business Performance Reporting	Budgeting and Tracking Multiple Projects
Case Management for Government Agencies	Bug Database
Classroom Management	Call Center
Clinical Trial Initiation and Management	Change Request Management
Competitive Analysis Site	Compliance Process Support Site
Discussion Database	Contacts Management
Disputed Invoice Management	Document Library and Review
Employee Activities Site	Event Planning
Employee Self-Service Benefits	Expense Reimbursement and Approval
Employee Training Scheduling and Materials	Help Desk
Equity Research	Inventory Tracking
Integrated Marketing Campaign Tracking	IT Team Workspace
Manufacturing Process Management	Job Requisition and Interview Management
New Store Opening	Knowledge Base
Product and Marketing Requirements Planning	Lending Library
Request for Proposal	Physical Asset Tracking and Management
Sports League	Project Tracking Workspace

TABLE 7.1   Microsoft Application Templates for Windows SharePoint Services 3.0

Site Admin Templates	Server Admin Templates
Team Work Site	Room and Equipment Reservations
Timecard Management	Sales Lead Pipeline

The following steps are compliments of Dustin Miller (http://www.sharepointblogs.com/dustin/archive/2007/02/23/having-problems-installing-the-latest-20-sample-sharepoint-applications.aspx) to help you install the sample applications.

> **NOTE**
>
> These steps assume that you downloaded the package that contains all the server admin templates, because there is a required WSP, applicationtemplatecore.wsp, which seems to be missing from some of the individual downloads.

1. Download the full ApplicationTemplates package from the Microsoft SharePoint web site.

2. Extract it to the c:\program files\common files\microsoft shared\web server extensions\12\bin directory.

3. From the command line on the server, logged on as an admin, navigate to the directory where you just extracted the templates and enter the following commands:

```
stsadm -o addsolution -FILENAME applicationtemplatecore.wsp
➥stsadm -o deploysolution -immediate -allowgacdeployment -name
➥applicationtemplatecore.wsp
```

   Note that these should be done first because they are dependencies, although you could probably get away with skipping ahead to Step 4 and coming back to Step 2 when it becomes necessary (at Step 6).

4. Open your browser to Central Administration, click the Operations tab, and then click Solution Management on the right, under Global Configuration.

5. Verify that the `applicationtemplatecore.wsp` solution is marked as "Deployed." If it's not, wait ten more seconds or so, and refresh again to see if it's finished. Once it's "Deployed," move on.

6. Return to the command prompt and type the following command exactly as it is displayed here. It looks weird, but that's because it's built to repeat itself multiple times, once for each sample application:

```
for %f in (*.wsp) do stsadm -o addsolution -filename %f
```

7. You'll see an error when it tries to add the applicationcoretemplate.wsp solution (since it's already there)—ignore it. Once it's done, enter the following command:

```
for %f in (*.wsp) do stsadm -o deploysolution -allowgacdeployment
➥-immediate -name %f
```

8. This step can take anywhere from a minute on fast hardware to ten or more minutes on slower boxes. When you come back, go back to your browser and refresh the Solution Management page. Once the timers are finished running—you might have to refresh a few times over a few minutes to verify this—you may find some solutions that didn't deploy, or that had an error deploying. You can re-run the command line in step 6 if you want (you'll just get quick errors on the ones that are already deployed; it's safe to ignore them), or manually deploy the solutions using your browser.

Developing a Data Protection Plan for SharePoint and Companyweb

SharePoint's native backup has been greatly improved over what was used in WSS 2.0, but you still need to carefully plan out your data protection and disaster recovery plans and how these plans fit into the scope of your entire Small Business Server data protection plan. Small Business Server's built-in backup is SQL aware and therefore will give you good image based backups as described below, but also consider in your planning third party products that can be used in concert with, or as a replacement for, the native SBS backup.

The Recycle Bin

The Recycle Bin has two levels: a library level and a site level. Before you reach for the most recent backup image off a USB drive or NAS device, give the dumpster a try first.

When end users delete items from lists, they are placed in their Recycle Bin and can be retrieved before emptying the bin. If the end user has emptied their Recycle Bin and it has been less than 30 days, the item should be retrievable from the Site Collection Recycle Bin. Log onto the server with an administrative account and access http://companyweb and follow these steps:

1. Under the Site Actions pull down menu, select Site Settings.
2. Select Recycle Bin from the Site Collection Administration list.
3. Select your view on the left side of the page. Options are End User Recycle Bin items and Deleted from End User Recycle Bin.
4. Restore items, or in the case of the Deleted from End User Recycle Bin, restore or permanently delete. All items over 30 days old are automatically deleted.

> **CAUTION**
>
> End users cannot restore items they have deleted. If they are accustomed to Outlook's Recover Deleted Items feature, users may be expecting to perform restores themselves. In addition, early testing by the author has shown that the Site Collection Administration List is only available for use by an administrative account when logged into http://companyweb directly from the server. External access to the https site from an administrative account does not have the Site Collection Administration List as an option.

Backup and Restore with Native SharePoint Backup

If you remember what was involved to back up SharePoint in SBS 2003, you'll be happy to hear that the cryptic command-line entries have been replaced with a GUI (but don't worry; they are still there for other tasks). Here, you'll find the steps you'll need to walk through a backup and restore the operation using SharePoint's native backup.

Follow these steps to run a native SharePoint backup:

1. Launch SharePoint 3.0 Central Administration.
2. Elevate at the UAC prompt.
3. Select the Operations tab.
4. Select Perform a Backup from the Backup and Restore task list.
5. Put a check in the checkbox next to Farm and then select Continue to Backup Operations as shown in Figure 7.12.
6. Ensure that Farm is selected for backup content under the Backup the Following Component drop-down menu, and Full is selected under Type of Backup as shown in Figure 7.13.
7. Under Backup location, enter a backup location.

> **CAUTION**
>
> Only existing folders can be selected here, so ensure that you have created the folder before choosing your backup location, or you will get the following error below your Backup location entry:
>
> Directory "incorrect file path" does not exist or the SQL Server service account and the "user" service account do not have permission to read or write to the backup folder. Specify a different directory.

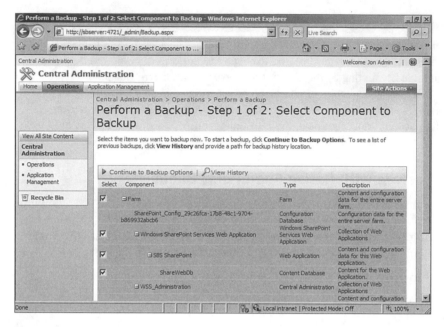

FIGURE 7.12   SharePoint Backup Screen 1 of 2.

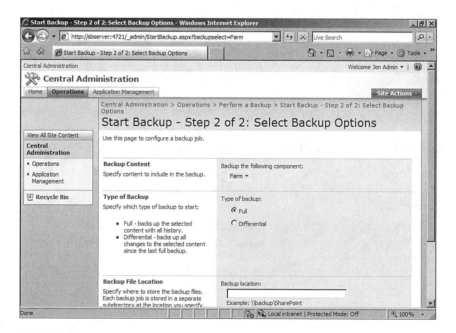

FIGURE 7.13   SharePoint Backup Screen 2 of 2.

When you have a backup of SharePoint, you can use the following steps to run a native SharePoint restore:

1. Launch SharePoint 3.0 Central Administration.

2. Elevate at the UAC prompt.

3. Select the Operations tab.

4. Select Restore from Backup from the Backup and Restore task list.

5. Enter the path of the backup location as shown in Figure 7.14.

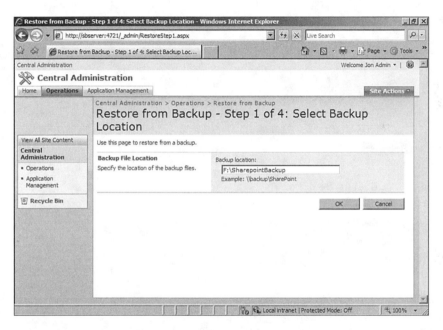

FIGURE 7.14   SharePoint Restore Step 1 of 4.

6. Select the backup set you wish to restore from and click Continue Restore Process, as shown in Figure 7.15.

7. Ensure that Farm is selected under the Restore the Following Content drop-down menu (see Figure 7.16), and Same Configuration is selected under Type of Restore for a full restore; click Continue Restore Process.

8. The restore process generates an alert that all selected components will be overwritten (Figure 7.17). Click OK to continue with the restore process.

Backup and Restore with Small Business Server Backup

In addition to the native backup and restore processes provided within SharePoint, the SBS 2008 native backup tool gives you another avenue to protect the data within the SharePoint interface. The process of using the native SBS 2008 backup is discussed in detail in Chapter 18, but you can use the following steps to restore Companyweb from an existing Small Business Server 2008 backup:

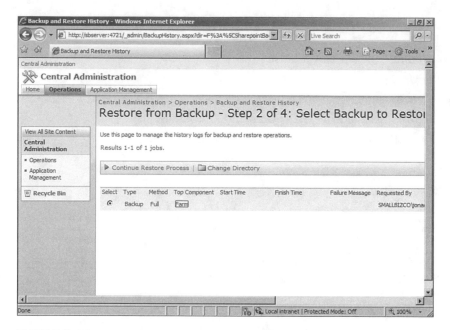

FIGURE 7.15   SharePoint Restore Step 2 of 4.

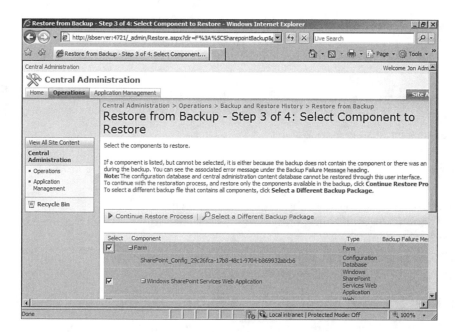

FIGURE 7.16   SharePoint Restore Step 3 of 4.

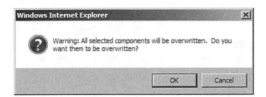

FIGURE 7.17   SharePoint Restore Step 4 of 4.

1. Stop the Windows Internal Database (MICROSOFT##SSEE) service.
2. Copy the existing SharePoint database files to a different location on the server.
3. Open the Windows SBS Console.
4. Select the Backup and Server Storage tab.
5. Select the Restore Server Data from Backup backup task.
6. Click the Recover... action.
7. Select This Server and click Next.
8. Choose the appropriate date and time and click Next
9. Select Applications and click Next.
10. Select Windows SharePoint Services and click Next.
11. Select Recover to Original Location and click Next.
12. Click Recover.
13. Start the Windows Internal Database (MICROSOFT##SSEE) service.

Troubleshooting SharePoint and Companyweb

Providing an in-depth discussion of troubleshooting SharePoint issues is beyond the scope of this book, but several common issues appear in the SBS implementation of SharePoint that are worth noting for the reader.

Event ID Error Message 10016 Is Logged in the System Log After You Install Windows SharePoint Services 3.0

When you view the system log after installing Windows SharePoint Services 3.0 and come across event ID 10016 error message logged one or more times, Microsoft Knowledge Base Article 920783 (http://support.microsoft.com/kb/920783) should get you back on track. The following is a sample of the event and the workaround from the KB article:

```
Type: Error
Source: DCOM
Category: None
```

```
Event ID: 10016
Description:
The application-specific permissions settings do not grant Local Activation permis-
sion for the COM Server application with CLSID {CLSID} to the user DomainName\User-
Name SID {SID}. This security permission can be modified using the Component
Services administration tool.
```

You can safely ignore the event ID error messages 10017 or 10016 that are logged in the system log. If you want to prevent the event ID error messages from being logged in the system log, use the Component Services snap-in to enable the Local Activation permission to the IIS Wamreg Admin Service for the domain user account that you specified as the Windows SharePoint Services 3.0 service account. To do this, follow these steps:

1. Click Start, Run and type **dcomcnfg** in the Open box, and then click OK.
2. Expand Component Services, Computers, My Computer, and then click DCOM Config.
3. Right-click IIS WAMREG admin Service and then click Properties.
4. Click the Security tab.
5. Under Launch and Activation Permissions, click Edit.
6. In the Launch Permission dialog box, click Add.
7. In the Select Users, Computers, or Groups dialog box, type the domain user account that you specified as the Windows SharePoint Services 3.0 service account, click Check Names, and then click OK.
8. In the Permissions for UserName list, click to select the Allow checkbox that is next to Local Activation, and then click OK two times.

Migration

Per Microsoft's Windows Small Business Server 2008 Release Documentation, there are several important items to be aware of when migrating from Windows Server 2003 or Windows Server 2008 to SBS 2008.

The first is that an Alias (CNAME) resource record is not created for the http://companyweb web site. To resolve this issue, run the Fix My Network Wizard:

1. From the server running Windows SBS 2008, open the Windows SBS Console.
2. On the navigation bar, click Network, and then click Connectivity.
3. In the task pane, click Fix My Network.
4. Follow the instructions in the wizard. You can click each potential problem that the wizard lists to get more information about the problem.

The Release Documentation goes on to point out that if the problem persists after you run the Fix My Network Wizard, clear the list of DNS addresses that are stored on the computer (server or Vista client) by following these steps:

1. Open a command prompt using administrator privileges.

2. Enter the following command:

```
ipconfig /flushdns
```

To clear the list of DNS addresses that are stored on a client computer that is running Windows XP, follow these steps:

1. Click Start, All Programs, Accessories, right-click Command Prompt, and then click Run As.

2. In the Run As dialog box, select The Following User (the first option in the Run As dialog box).

3. Ensure that the User Name text box displays Administrator, type the password for the local administrator account, and then click OK.

4. At the command prompt, type **ipconfig /flushdns**, and then press Enter.

The second item is a post-installation issue with the Windows SharePoint Services Timer process. According to the article, if you set the clock on Windows SBS 2008 to be earlier than the current time, the Windows SharePoint Services Timer process (owstimer.exe) consumes more than 50 percent of the available CPU. To release the CPU resources, you must restart the Windows SharePoint Services Timer process. Be sure to check http://go.microsoft.com/fwlink/?LinkId=115883 for future updates to this information.

Summary

In this author's opinion, it looks as if this version of Windows SharePoint Services and the resulting Companyweb presented by the Microsoft SBS team is the final nail in the coffin for NTFS shares and the traditional shared folder structures Small Business Server networks have grown up on. Mobile access to lists from Windows Mobile Devices, the addition of the recycle bin (versus WSS 2.0 in SBS 2003), mail-enabled security group, simplified backup and restore, and the prefab solutions available freely from Microsoft's web site are just some of the great reasons to consider a paradigm shift in your SBS shared data infrastructure over to WSS and Companyweb.

Best Practice Summary

▶ **Use a Commercial SSL Certificate**—Do yourself a huge favor and use a commercially available SSL certificate like Dotster or GoDaddy, and don't go with the SBS-created server certificate. If you do not go with a third party public certificate, your Windows Mobile devices will not load the /m page if you don't first download the certificate installer package (the certificate installer package is available at \\SBSSERVER\public\downloads on our example SBS Server), launch it on your PC, and install the cert to your Windows Mobile 6 Device. With a third-party certificate, users can use the mobile SharePoint site without the extra hassle and across any

Wireless Application Protocol (WAP) browser, regardless of device platform. In addition, you'll be taken care of for your regular SharePoint site and Outlook Anywhere's use of SSL.

▶ **Selecting the Windows SharePoint Services Data Folder Location**—For consistency in deployments, take the original default location and only change the drive letter of the data folder original location. For example, if you are moving your data to the E:\ drive, then take C:\Windows\SYSMSI\SSEE\MSSQL.2005\MSSQL\DATA and move to E:\Windows\SYSMSI\SSEE\MSSQL.2005\MSSQL\DATA. This gives you a consistency with the original deployment that is helpful when other administrators are assisting you, when you are referencing Microsoft documentation as you maintain your server, and especially when you are administrating multiple Small Business Servers. The Move Windows SharePoint Services Data task will do just this: change the drive letter only and duplicate the path.

PART 3

Managing E-Mail

IN THIS PART

CHAPTER 8

Exchange Management

SBS 2008 installs with Exchange Server 2007 Standard and offers a significant improvement over the previous version of Exchange. Aside from the performance bonus that a 64-bit messaging application provides, and the benefit of no longer having a mailbox database size cap, SBS 2008 leverages Exchange 2007 to dramatically improve the remote worker experience in the following ways:

▶ Outlook Web Access now allows users access to file shares and SharePoint libraries via remote web browser, reducing the need for a VPN.

▶ Users with Outlook 2007 can configure RPC-over-HTTPS (now called Outlook Anywhere) by merely providing their e-mail address and password, eliminating configuration procedure that was not end-user friendly.

▶ It allows users to restore deleted items, create signatures, open Office docs (even without Office installed locally), and view message headers from within OWA.

▶ It provides the means for users with delegated access to other mailboxes to open them from within their own OWA session without having to provide separate credentials.

In addition to the remote-work improvements, new features in Exchange Management reduce the likelihood of losing messaging data:

▶ A feature called Local Continuous Replication allows you to easily maintain a continuously updated copy of your production Exchange databases on a separate internal or external disk, and that copy can be brought into production in the event of a problem with the original database.

▶ Many database maintenance and recovery procedures that previously required complex command-line tools are now wizard-driven and detailed in their output, making recovery much less expensive and uncertainty-ridden.

This is the first version of Exchange on which customizations of mail flow that were only available via third-party products or specialized programming are now in the hands of an average SBS admin. Exchange 2007's Transport Rules provide a foundation to meet several common needs that were previously unaddressed:

▶ Rules can be applied to control the flow of information in and out of the company on a per mailbox basis or on the basis of message content, making it easier to enforce legal compliance.

▶ Rules can be used to create organization-wide disclaimers and similar appended notices.

▶ Rules can be used to audit mailboxes or redirect mail to particular users, based on information in a given message.

On the level of improvements to business processes, Exchange 2007 introduced several features that streamline the collaboration and scheduling environment:

▶ There are now room and equipment objects that can be scheduled and whose calendars can be viewed by all users, simplifying resource scheduling in busy offices.

▶ Out-of-office (OOF) messages can be configured to provide separate messages for internal and external recipients, and the OOF period can be scheduled ahead of time, giving the user much more control over automated communication.

▶ Increased synergy between Exchange and SharePoint allow inbound messages to distribution lists to be stored and managed in SharePoint libraries and to be accessed completely from Outlook, giving customer-facing business teams much more collaborative power with which to address customer needs.

On the mail hygiene front, Exchange 2007 offers a significant advancement in how it protects the organization from spam, beginning with a good default filter configuration and providing extensive options for tweaking at multiple levels if an administrator desires. Microsoft ForeFront for Exchange is also provided on a trial basis to meet the need for messaging-specific antivirus.

The last stop on this summary tool of new features is the new command-line tool, the Exchange Management Shell (EMS), which allows administrators to get customized information about Exchange objects and easily conduct bulk operations that would be extremely tedious in the GUI. In fact, a few administrative tasks can only be accomplished using the EMS, so it is not a tool that can be ignored for long. The EMS uses PowerShell, a scripting language native to Windows 2008, to accomplish these tasks.

> **TIP**
>
> There is significant coverage of PowerShell and how to utilize it to enhance your administrative powers in Chapter 20, "PowerShell," but we begin to use the Exchange-specific implementation of it in this chapter. If you need deeper coverage on PowerShell before using the scripts provided in this chapter, refer to Chapter 20 to get the basics, but those with any command-line experience should not be daunted by the minor PowerShell operations used in this chapter.

As you can see, there are many reasons to be excited about Exchange 2007's presence on SBS 2008, and this chapter guides you through the configuration of Exchange and advises you on the best practices for the most common maintenance and management tasks.

Default Mail Configuration

During setup, Exchange features are configured using the Connect to Internet, and Set Up Your Internet Address Wizards. Between the Exchange Server defaults and the changes that the wizards make, the following are the settings a newly configured server will have:

▶ **Deleted Item and Mailbox Retention**—By default, deleted messages are kept for 30 days, and deleted mailboxes are retained for 30 days.

▶ **Mailbox Limits**—The default mailbox size cap is 2.3GB. The users are warned when their mailboxes reach 1.9GB, and sending is prohibited when the size reaches 2GB. When a mailbox reaches the cap, it will no longer store new incoming mail, but will bounce the mail with an error message.

▶ **Circular Logging**—Enabled by default, it will be disabled after the Backup Configuration Wizard is run. Until the Backup Configuration Wizard is run, logs will automatically be deleted over time to save disk space. A normal backup automatically purges transaction logs so that circular logging is not needed.

▶ **Idle User Sessions**—Outlook Web Access sessions time out after 20 minutes.

▶ **SMTP Connector**—By default, the server is set up to route mail to the Internet using DNS. To configure the server to use a smart host, run the Configure a Smart Host for Internet E-Mail Wizard.

▶ **E-Mail Address Policy**—During setup, the Set Up Your Internet Address Wizard should have been run and all e-mail addresses should be configured to use your public Internet domain name.

▶ **POP3 Connector**—By default, the POP3 Connector used to download e-mail from an ISP is not set up. In many scenarios, using the POP3 Connector is not necessary for inbound and outbound mailflow. To configure the POP3 Connector, go to the Network tab in the SBS Manager and choose POP3 Connector under the Connectivity tab there.

8

▶ **Exchange Features Enabled per User**—By default, every feature is enabled for every user. That includes Outlook Web Access, Outlook Anywhere, Exchange ActiveSync, MAPI (standard Outlook access method), POP3, and IMAP. The latter two are enabled, but the actual server services that they would depend on are not enabled by default.

▶ **Transport Rules**—These enable you to apply "special handling" to specific types and classes of messages that are entering or leaving your server. That might include appending disclaimers, adding a cc: to another address, blocking certain messages, and a variety of other actions. By default, there are no rules in place after the initial setup.

▶ **Online Defrag**—Exchange automatically runs an online mail and public folder database defrag every night. That process rearranges database pages in the databases in order to create larger blocks of contiguous empty space. By default, online defrag runs between 1 a.m. and 5 a.m. nightly. Normally, you want to configure your backup schedule not to be happening at the same time, because on online backup of Exchange stops any online defrag process that is running.

Mail Hygiene

E-mail has quickly become one of the most popular ways that people communicate with each other. With it, you can instantly send pictures, send attachments, or give someone information that just a decade ago would have required a phone call or fax, or would have taken days to receive.

Both viruses and spam have become a significant problem for mail system administrators. Some problems stem from receiving spam and virus-infected attachments, and some from the measures other companies have taken to curtail the flow of spam into their networks. The next two sections discuss each of these scenarios in more detail.

A number of third-party solutions have come and gone over the years to help combat spam and viruses. Unfortunately, many of those work only on messages after they have been received by Exchange and processed into the message store. As the volume of received messages increases, this approach becomes inefficient. It is best to stop messages before they are processed. Exchange 2007 improves on the groundwork that Exchange 2003 laid in this regard and provides a multi-layer filter to minimize both the amount of spam that reaches the mailboxes and the amount of processing needed to protect those mailboxes. To see the filtering agents, load the Exchange Management Console and look at the Anti-Spam tab in the Organization, Hub Transport section of the interface. Figure 8.1 shows the list of agents.

These are the technologies used in the Exchange 2007 anti-spam filters and agents, in order:

▶ **Connection Filtering**—Blocks servers attempting to connect by checking a connecting server's IP address against IP Allow and Block lists. These lists include both locally configured lists of IPs and lists maintained by third parties, otherwise known

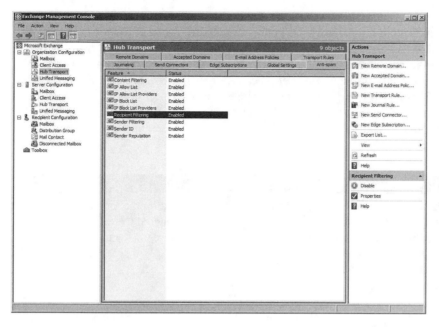

FIGURE 8.1   The anti-spam agents and filters display.

as Real-time Blackhole Lists, or RBLs. This is the first agent involved in evaluating an incoming connection.

For more information about RBLs, see http://en.wikipedia.org/wiki/DNSBL. You can also go to http://stats.dnsbl.com/ and http://en.wikipedia.org/wiki/Comparison_of_DNS_blacklists for information about which RBLs to implement.

▶ **Sender Filtering**—The next agent to handle an incoming message checks the e-mail address of the sender against a list of e-mail addresses and source domains that has been configured. The agent is configured to reject any message whose sender matches one of the list entries, but there is an option to configure it to merely stamp the message with metadata that tracks the fact that it was sent by a blocked sender. This will raise the Spam Confidence Level (or SCL) value of the message, and may cause it to be quarantined or deleted later by the Content Filter. By default, messages from blank senders are blocked.

▶ **Recipient Filtering**—This agent checks the message's intended recipient against a list of recipients who are barred from receiving mail and rejects the message if it finds a match. It also rejects addresses that do not exist in the Global Address List. Note that this agent only acts on inbound mail. You cannot specify addresses in this list in order to block outbound mail generated by internal users from going to them.

▶ **SenderID**—Using a DNS query to ascertain the identity of a remote mail server, this agent protects against spoofed originating domains and phishing scams. Sender ID attempts to verify that each incoming e-mail actually originated from the domain from which it claims to have been sent. To do this, it queries the DNS servers for the remote domain looking for a Sender Policy Framework (normally known as SPF) record, which lists the names of servers authorized to send mail for that domain. Although many mail servers have SPF records set up, many more do not, as it has not been universally implemented yet. Because of this, the default setting for Sender ID is to stamp it with the query result for the purpose of later determining SCL and then allowing it through. To manually check the SPF record of a remote domain like microsoft.com, open up a command prompt and type **nslookup -q=TXT microsoft.com.**

TIP

It is a good idea to create an SPF record to protect your domain's reputation, and it's not difficult. A good resource for learning how to set up an SPF record for your domain can be found at http://www.microsoft.com/mscorp/safety/content/technologies/senderid/wizard/.

▶ **Content Filtering**—Exchange 2007 improved the Internet Mail Filter that came with Exchange 2003. With the content filter agent, each message is evaluated based on its textual content and then assigned an SCL rating based on what it finds. If the message has been stamped with information by earlier agents in the pipeline, that metadata plays into the rating assigned. This rating is stamped on the message as additional metadata.

The content filter is updated at regular intervals to keep up with the evolving tactics of spammers.

The content filter agent also determines what happens to messages whose SCL ratings are high. Messages with an SCL as high as 9 are almost assuredly spam, whereas messages with a value of 4 or 5 might be legitimate. Most legitimate messages have an SCL of 0 or 1. By default, SBS 2008 is configured to reject messages with an SCL rating of 7 or higher.

▶ **Sender Reputation**—This is actually Microsoft's own version of a blacklist. Microsoft maintains a database of known spam-sending IP addresses, and the SBS 2008 Server regularly downloads an updated list to apply against inbound connections. Normally this is only available to Exchange Enterprise customers, but it has been included in SBS 2008.

The native Exchange 2007 anti-spam features include three kinds of regularly updated definition files, as follows:

▶ Content Filter

▶ Spam Signatures

▶ Sender/IP Reputation

If your server is not configured for Automatic Updates, these files will be included in the list of available downloads at the Windows Update site for you to manually download and install. SBS 2008 relies on the Microsoft Exchange Anti-Spam Update Service.

All Exchange 2007 anti-spam features function in the context of a transport pipeline, in which each piece of mail has to progress through different layers of analysis and processing. Because these technologies are applied in a synchronous fashion, one after the other, the order in which the filters are applied is important for efficiency reasons. Because some filters require higher levels of processing than others, they are arranged in such a way as to eliminate as much spam as possible before it gets to those "expensive" filters and drains system resources.

A good example is the difference between connection filtering and content filtering. Connection filtering drops a conversation with a remote mail-host before even accepting the spam from it. Therefore, no time has to be spent processing it. If it's possible to block a spamming server's communication before it can feed your server a few hundred mail items, it's worth doing. Once messages arrive at the content-filtering stage, the contents of each e-mail have to be examined by the server to determine the likelihood of their being spam, and that's potentially process-expensive.

Preventing the Reverse NDR Attack

A reverse NDR attack occurs when a spammer or other malicious individual sends a flood of e-mail messages to a server with bad recipient addresses and bad return addresses. In normal Exchange operations, these messages are received by the SMTP server and passed on to Exchange for processing. Only when Exchange attempts to put the message in the message store does the process recognize that the addresses are invalid. At that point, Exchange generates an NDR and sends it back to the faked sender.

This is where the invalid return address comes into play. When Exchange attempts to deliver the NDR back to the sender, it gets hung in the outgoing mail queue while Exchange goes through its normal process of attempting to send the message. By default, Exchange attempts delivery for 48 hours before deleting the message. When thousands upon thousands of these undeliverable NDRs begin filing up the queue, however, not only does the Exchange/SMTP process slow down, but it can slow down the entire server. In addition, server disk space is used up quickly for the storage of these messages that can never be delivered.

The best way to prevent an NDR attack is to simply refuse delivery of messages with invalid mail addresses at the SMTP server level so that no NDR is generated within Exchange. If Exchange is not configured this way, the pain inflicted by a reverse NDR attack can be sudden and severe. By default, SBS 2008 uses recipient filtering to block these messages, but disabling that filter could make you vulnerable to this sort of attack.

8

Configuring Recipient Filtering

To check the recipient-filtering configuration, do the following:

1. Open up the Advanced Management Console and go to the Exchange section.
2. Expand it and then expand the Organization Configuration section.
3. Select Hub Transport from the list and go to the Anti-Spam tab.
4. Open up Recipient Filtering and go to the Blocked Recipients tab (see Figure 8.2).

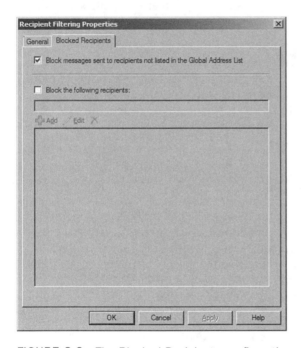

FIGURE 8.2   The Blocked Recipients configuration set to prevent NDR attacks.

Notice that by default, Block Messages to Recipients Not Listed in the Global Address List is selected. That configuration allows the server to immediately reject any e-mail that is addressed to a non-existent recipient on the server.

SMTP Tarpitting

In the past, if a mail server administrator was using recipient filtering as described previously, spammers would use this as a way to obtain valid e-mail addresses by running scripts against the server's SMTP service, looking for valid addresses. The spammer would use the immediate rejection as a sign that the address was not valid and would continue to try names until it got to addresses that did not trigger a rejection. These valid addresses were then sold to other spammers and bulk mailers. Fortunately, SMTP tarpitting is a measure that was created to combat this practice.

This anti-spam feature intentionally slows down the response speed of the Exchange server's 5.1.1 user unknown reply to a remote mail server. This delay forces any spamming server using a dictionary of possible names to spend more time communicating with the server, and most spamming servers will switch to another target rather than continue to wait to verify whether its names are active. This feature makes it "too expensive" for spammers to use directory harvesting techniques against the server.

By default, the tarpitting timeout is set to five seconds, and there is usually no need to change it. If you did need to change it to troubleshoot a problem with connection delays, you would do so with these PowerShell cmdlets. A cmdlet is a very short but powerful script that is accessible using the Exchange Management Console.

> **TIP**
>
> To utilize a PowerShell cmdlet, open the Exchange Management Console by locating it in the Start menu, within the Microsoft Exchange Server 2007 folder. Once the EMS window opens to display a command line, you can use the cmdlets outlined in the following text. Note that the "pipe" character is frequently used in PowerShell scripts and can by created using the Shift+backslash key.

First, get the name of the Receive Connectors and display their settings:

```
Get-ReceiveConnector | select name,tarpitinterval
```

Then use this command, using the name of the connector, usually "Default *Servername*":

```
set-ReceiveConnector "Receive Connector Name" -tarpitinterval 00:00:05
```

The preceding command sets the interval to 5 seconds, but you could remove tarpitting by setting it to 00:00:00 or raise it to 10 seconds by setting it to 00:00:10.

Hosted Anti-Spam Solutions

A significant trend in spam management is to use a third party to filter the mail prior to delivery to your server. Typically, this involves changing your public MX record to direct mail to the hosted anti-spam service and configuring their server as your smart host for your own outbound. The service processes the mail through several types of anti-virus engines and then uses a variety of methods to sift legitimate mail out of the inbound stream and deliver it to your server. Microsoft Exchange Hosted Services provides an offering of this type, and some other well-established vendors of this service are MXLogic, Postini, MessageLabs, Symantec, and Exchange Defender.

The advantages of using a hosted anti-spam solution are significant, and include the following:

▸ No physical installation required, and thus no potentially problematic conflicts on the software or local networking level.

▶ Bandwidth is preserved because spam traffic never touches the private Internet connection.

▶ Most hosted solutions also provide several days of queuing in the event that your Internet connection or server go offline, and the queued mail is accessible via web interface.

▶ Consistently current spam and anti-virus definition updates and RBLs that are continuously optimized by experts.

▶ Redundancy is a standard feature of hosted services, which is not something that a small business can duplicate at the same level, due to cost.

Getting Your Mail Delivered

With the focus on spam, addressing, and local mailboxes, it's sometimes easy to forget that it is just as important to make sure that outbound mail is being properly routed and delivered. This next section focuses on how to ensure that your server is a reliable platform for outbound mail delivery.

How Mail Gets Delivered

Exchange can use two methods to send e-mail to other mail servers. These are commonly referred to as smart host delivery and DNS delivery.

By default, SBS 2008 uses smart host to send Internet e-mail. A *smart host* is a "middleman" e-mail server that forwards/sends e-mail for your domain's e-mail server on its behalf. When a smart host is in place, Exchange takes outgoing mail and sends it to another mail server that you specify (the smart host). The smart host then sends your e-mail to the destination mail server. This feature makes it appear that e-mail from your domain is originating from the smart host server. Most client-side POP3 accounts function this way for sending mail, and using a smart host on your server puts your server in a similar position.

If the SBS server is not configured to use a smart host, it will use DNS to find the MX records for the recipient domains and attempt to deliver mail directly. So, for example, if you use Outlook to send an e-mail to john@newcompany.com, your server will query DNS to find the MX records for newcompany.com. Let's assume the MX query returns with the name mail01.newcompany.com as the mail server. Your server will then connect to mail01.newcompany.com on TCP port 25 to deliver the outbound e-mail.

Ensuring Delivery

Given the number of new and often aggressive anti-spam technologies that are being deployed by organizations across the spectrum, another important consideration for any mail admin is how to ensure that mail originating from your server is not misconstrued as spam. To that end, we will now look at a number of configurations that will raise the likelihood of your mail being accepted. Some of these configurations are required, while others are just recommended.

Reverse DNS Record

If you are not using a smart host, one of the most important things on your checklist should be getting an RDNS record created. When a recipient server gets an e-mail from your server, it will usually check the name of your server (as specified in the Send Connector settings) against the IP address of your server and then do a DNS reverse lookup to see what name is associated with your IP address. If the name returned by the query does not match the name that your server provided, it might decide to refuse your server's connection, depending on how the recipient server has been configured.

Setting up an RDNS record is not something you do at your own external DNS management console. This is a record that exists at your ISP, and your ISP is usually responsible for creating it after you request it. Normally, you would give them the hostname of your mail server and the public IP address that it is listening on. Some ISPs enable you to configure it yourself in their console.

Dynamic IP Lists

Many large ISPs that provide both business and residential broadband have their IP address blocks marked as "dynamic," and assume that their customers will be using a smart host for outbound mail delivery. If you are not using a smart host, and your static IP happens to be in one of these "dynamic" blocks, you may have trouble with your mail being blocked by ISPs like AOL. If this is your situation, you get an error like this one:

```
554- The IP address you are using to connect to AOL is a dynamic (residential) IP
address. AOL will not accept future e-mail transactions from this IP address until
your ISP removes this IP address from its list of dynamic IP addresses.
```

Your chances of having your ISP do this for you may be low, and if you already have a static IP, you will probably have to get a new static IP in a different block of addresses. Your best solution at this point is to work with a smart host.

Blacklists

Blacklists or RBLs (Real-Time Black Lists) are lists of IP addresses that have been known to send out spam. The most likely reason for an SBS 2008 server to end up on a blacklist is if you aren't using a smart host and someone in your organization sent out a lot of unsolicited mail through the server. It's common to have someone send out a marketing campaign without checking with the mail administrator first, but doing so could put your server on a blacklist or cause your smart host to stop relaying mail for your server. Best practice is to not use the SBS server for marketing campaigns and for bulk newsletters. Instead, use a service designed to handle that kind of communication, like Constant Contact.

If your server's IP does get put on a blacklist, you can usually request it to be removed from the blacklist. Each blacklist has its own procedure for being removed. Some automatically remove your IP after 12 hours; others let you manually remove the address via a web interface.

Routing Mail Directly Versus Using a Smart Host

When choosing whether to route mail directly through DNS or through a smart host, there are multiple factors worth considering. The benefits of routing through DNS include the following:

▶ Not having a "middleman" usually reduces troubleshooting complexity.

▶ No reliance on a third-party e-mail server to ensure mail delivery.

▶ Increased control over how mail to different destinations is handled.

That said, using a smart host does have a lot of perks, including the following:

▶ No need to configure an RDNS record.

▶ Less hassle with remote anti-spam measures.

▶ Greatly reduced likelihood of being affected by blacklists.

▶ Queues are offloaded to the smart host and don't consume local resources.

▶ It's the best way to handle mail if your network has a dynamic IP.

All in all, the benefits of using a smart host are higher than the benefits for routing directly. Using a smart host offloads some of the need for mail and DNS expertise and puts some of the responsibility for proper mail delivery in the hands of your ISP or other smart host provider. Depending on who that provider is, this may be a great arrangement, but care should be taken not to leave this important responsibility in the hands of a business entity that you cannot count on.

SPF Records

How often have you gotten an error message response from a server regarding an e-mail that you never sent? It's a common occurrence, and it usually is caused by someone forging your address as the reply address on a spam message. There is a system in place called Sender Policy Framework (SPF) to prevent this sort of spoofing of addresses, but adoption is still growing. Using the system involves creating an SPF record in your DNS zone file.

An SPF record is a DNS record that publishes information about which mail servers are authorized to send out mail with your domain name on the return address. Having an SPF record provides a domain with additional protection against spammers, because it makes it more difficult for them to spoof your domain name on spam they send out. Many anti-spam filters use SPF to see if the server that sent a message was authorized to do so, and depending on how the filter is configured, it may drop the message if there was an SPF record in place and the sending server was not on the authorized list. Because many domains do not have SPF records, passing this test is not a requirement to get mail delivered, but having an SPF record does cut down on the amount of bounce-back spam that will come to your domain. Because the anti-spam filters on many mail servers (including Exchange 2007) use SPF information to help calculate SCL values, having an SPF record improves the prospects of your domain's mail avoiding the junk mail folder at other domains!

Creating the SPF record can be tricky, but Microsoft has built an online wizard that simplifies the process. As long as you have the ability to create records in your DNS zone, you can use this wizard to generate the contents of the SPF record. For more information, see http://www.microsoft.com/mscorp/safety/content/technologies/senderid/wizard/.

The Windows SBS POP3 Connector

Many small businesses still use and rely on their ISPs to handle the maintenance and flow of their e-mail every day. This job could be as small as managing a single e-mail box to handling many individual e-mail accounts for all the company's employees. The Windows SBS POP3 Connector, usually referred to as just POP3 Connector, gives small businesses the capability to download and distribute POP3 e-mail into individual mailboxes automatically, usually on a temporary basis when first migrating mail handling from the ISP over to the SBS server.

When to Use The POP3 Connector

Microsoft's clear position on the POP3 Connector is that it's a transitional tool for easing the transition of mail during the initial SBS setup period, during which the mail delivery method is switching between POP3 mail delivery to direct SMTP delivery. It is not intended to be a long-term solution for mail delivery. Microsoft's removal of support for global mailboxes in this version of the POP3 Connector makes it less useful for long-term POP3 delivery scenarios and re-emphasizes that moving away from use of the POP3 Connector should be a best-practice in most scenarios. That being said, there are still some situations in which long-term use of this tool may be the only workable solution.

The POP3 Connector supports the following:

> **Individual user mailboxes for POP3 accounts**—Enable you to download mail for a single user from a remote POP3 server and then deliver this mail to a valid mailbox on the Exchange server.

> **Scheduling**—You can schedule mail retrieval in 15-minute increments. The user interface also includes a Retrieve Now button to allow for immediate retrieval of e-mail for testing purposes.

How Does the POP3 Connector Work?

The POP3 Connector performs a set of tasks to pull mail from the POP3 server and store messages in the correct local mailbox. The process is as follows:

1. The POP3 Connector service initiates a connection to the remote POP3 server.
2. The service then connects and logs on to the remote POP3 server.
3. E-mail is retrieved and then placed into the SMTP receive queue, just as if it had arrived from a standard SMTP connection from an external server.

4. In the SMTP receive queue, any anti-spam filters and transport rules are applied to the message.

5. The message is moved from the receive queue to the submission queue, and then to the delivery queue.

6. After arriving in the delivery queue, the mail is delivered to the destination mailbox.

Because the downloaded messages are first put into the general SMTP receive queue, they will be screened for spam just like mail being sent to the server by conventional means. This is different than SBS 2003, in which download messages bypassed the Internet Mail Filter.

Limitations of the POP3 Connector

One of the main complaints about the POP3 Connector is that it does not offer as many features as other third-party POP3 solutions. Some of the downsides of the POP3 Connector include the following:

▶ POP3 enables you to schedule e-mail downloads in 15-minute increments, but unfortunately the minimum is 15 minutes.

▶ Setting up new e-mail accounts requires quite a bit more work: building the local Exchange mailbox and setting up an account on the connector, not to mention building the remote POP3 account in the first place.

▶ SBS 2008's implementation of the POP3 Connector does not support global accounts. There has to be a 1:1 relationship between e-mail in a remote mailbox and destination mailboxes on the local server.

Setting Up the POP3 Connector

To set up the POP3 Connector to download mail from an external mail-hosting system, use the Windows SBS Console and go to the Network tab, looking under the Connectivity sub-tab. In that list is the POP3 Connector, which can be opened and configured. There are two sections of the POP3 Connector configurator: Mail Accounts and Scheduling.

Mail Accounts

In the Mail Accounts section, there is the option to add and delete mail accounts. Normally, an admin would set up an account for each external POP3 mailbox from which she wants to download mail. So, if a single local user has four external mail accounts that need to be downloaded from, she would set up each of those four accounts separately.

To set up an account, click the Add button, and you get the configuration screen shown in Figure 8.3.

What you enter on this screen will be the same information you would use if you were setting up a POP3 client in Outlook or other mail client software, except that you do not need to specify an SMTP server address.

The section at the bottom specifies where the downloaded mail should be routed. Mail can be routed to either a mailbox or a distribution list.

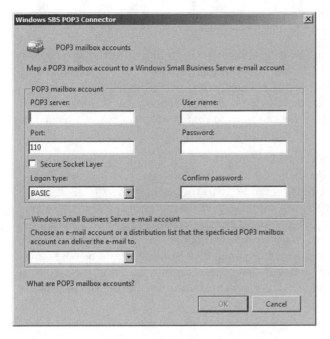

FIGURE 8.3   Enter the information needed to connect and authenticate with the remote POP3 server.

Routing Mail from a Global Account

Some Internet Service Providers (ISPs) collect all incoming e-mail for a mail domain and store the information in one POP3 account. In other words, any e-mail destined for any account at smallbizco.net would be stored in a single account on the ISP's mail server instead of individual mailboxes for each account. If you connected to this account with Outlook or Outlook Express, you would see that the messages downloaded would have different "to:" addresses, but they would all be in the same mail domain.

Although the POP3 Connector in SBS 2003 supported downloading mail from a global account and routing the mail to individual mailboxes, the version of the POP3 Connector in SBS 2008 does not offer that functionality, and if the POP3 Connector was used to download mail from a global account, all the mail could only be downloaded to a single local mailbox, and any subsequent distribution would have to be done via other means. To get a functionality close to what SBS 2003's POP3 Connector had, the best option is to look to a third-party POP3 downloader.

Scheduling

On the Scheduling tab, you configure how often the server downloads mail from the external POP3 accounts. The minimum configurable interval is 15 minutes. If that time-frame is not acceptable for an organization, remember that using the POP3 Connector is not intended to be a good long-term solution, and the arrangement should be changed to allow mail to be routed directly to the SBS 2008 Server.

Some admins have found a way to use POP3 and have a shorter download interval by configuring all the Outlook clients with both Exchange accounts and POP3 accounts and setting a shorter interval on the desktop client. The clients are configured to save their mail on the server, so all mail does ultimately end up in their Exchange mailbox. This can work, but the configuration has to be done carefully so that Outlook does not leave copies of mail on the POP3 server; otherwise, the result is duplicate messages.

A significant downside of this method is that having the client download the e-mails bypasses the filtering pipeline that Exchange 2007 uses to block spam and viruses, and when the Outlook client saves those messages directly to the Exchange mail database, those filters are not applied. This is also a good reason why a policy against having users configure their Outlook clients with other external e-mail accounts might be a good idea. If you do allow users to download mail from external accounts via their Outlook client, limiting the external accounts to big players like Gmail and Hotmail would be wise—those networks already run some anti-virus and anti-spam filters against mail that they allow into the hosted inbox, and that provides a layer of defense before entering the business network.

Receiving Mail for Multiple Domains

A frequently asked question in SBS newsgroups is how to set up Exchange so that it can receive and distribute inbound mail for more than one domain. The setup wizard only provides for a single public domain, which leads people to believe that the server can only accept mail for a single domain, but it is not difficult to set up additional domains.

Because SBS 2008 uses Exchange 2007 Standard for mail, the same features that are available in Exchange 2007 are also available for SBS 2008, and the method for setting up multiple domains is also the same.

Adding Additional E-Mail Domains

To set up additional domains on the server, you will not be using any SBS wizards, but will be working with the Exchange Management Console:

1. Open up the Advanced Management Console and go to the Exchange section.

2. Expand it and then expand the Organization Configuration section.

3. Select the Hub Transport section, and then select the Accepted Domains pane on the right (see Figure 8.4). You will see the existing domains for which the server is configured to accept mail. By default, there will be two: your internal domain name and the external one that you set up initially.

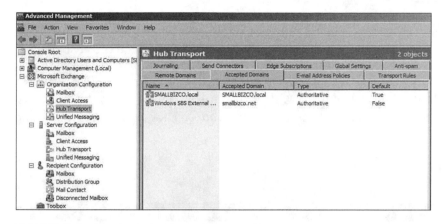

FIGURE 8.4   The Accepted Domains list shows you what domain names "live" on your server.

4. Next, select New Accepted Domain from the list of options on the right. This kicks off the New Accepted Domain Wizard (see Figure 8.5).

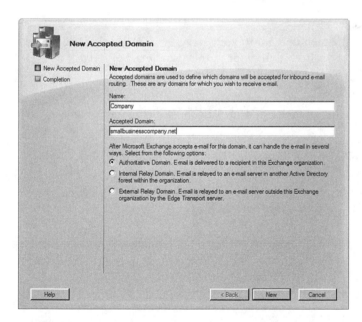

FIGURE 8.5   The New Accepted Domain Wizard helps you configure the server to receive mail for a new domain.

5. Enter a descriptive name for the entry, and then the domain name that you want to be handled on this server.

6. Next, we look at the radio buttons. If this server is the only place that mail for your new domain will be delivered, leave the default Authoritative Domain selected. This will normally be the case. If some of the mail for this domain is taken care of by a separate server, maybe at a corporate office, you'd select the third option, External Relay Domain. That way, if a local user sends an e-mail to someone in that domain who is not hosted on the local server, the e-mail will be routed to the outside world.

7. When you have verified that the information is correct, click New, and Finish on the next page.

8. From the main console page, you see your new domain added to the Accepted domains list.

> **NOTE**
>
> Remember that for you to receive mail for the new domain, public DNS needs to be modified so that the MX record for the domain directs mail to the SBS 2008 box. For more information about that process, revisit Chapter 3, "Installing and Configuring SBS 2008."

Adding Additional E-mail Addresses

Once you've added an additional e-mail domain to your server, you might want to have your mailboxes have e-mail addresses from both your public domains. So, Jonathan Dough might want to have both jon.dough@smallbizco.net and jon.dough@smallbizcompany.net addresses.

To do this, you will do the following in the same Hub Transport configuration area as previous:

1. Go to the E-Mail Address Policies tab and select New E-Mail Address Policy from the Actions pane on the right.

2. On the Intro page, enter a name for the policy and specify the type of recipients (see Figure 8.6). Usually, Users with Exchange Mailboxes is the proper selection. Click Next.

3. On the Conditions page, let's assume that you want new domain addresses for all users, so we won't configure anything there, but if you were sharing the server with other business entities, this is where you would differentiate between one group's users and another's, and only apply the new address to a subset of users. Click Next.

4. On the E-Mail Addresses page, click Add.

5. On the SMTP E-Mail Address page, pick the appropriate type of address formatting, and then choose the Select Accepted Domain radio button (see Figure 8.7).

6. Next, browse the list of accepted domains and select the domain that you want to use for this policy.

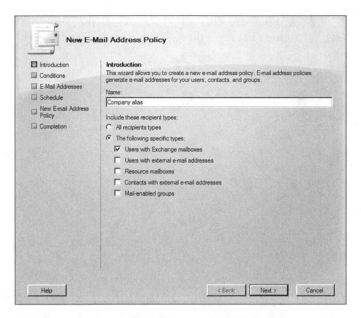

FIGURE 8.6   Every address policy has a name and at least one selected recipient type.

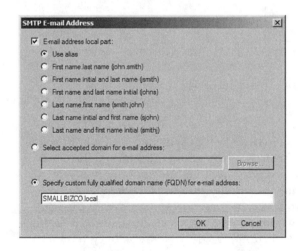

FIGURE 8.7   Configure the formatting of the addresses that the policy will generate.

7. Skip through the Schedule step (it should be set to Immediately) by clicking Next, continue to New, and Finish.

Now if you go into the Recipients, Mailbox configuration pane, you can open up a mailbox user's properties and check the E-Mail Addresses tab to verify that the new policy has been applied properly (see Figure 8.8). What you find is that the new policy you created has added the additional e-mail address to the mailbox, and it has become the default reply address.

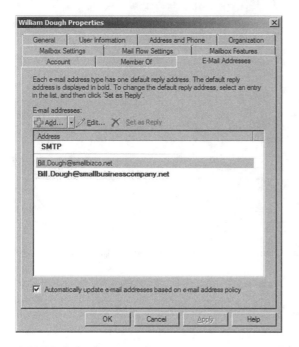

FIGURE 8.8   Check to make sure that a new address policy has created the intended addresses for your users.

The default reply address is dictated by the e-mail address policies and the order in which they are set up (see Figure 8.9). Whichever policy has top priority determines the default reply address. Because any new policy that is created becomes the top-priority policy, it causes the default reply address to match it. If you desire to make a different e-mail address policy the default one, you need to select the target policy and choose Change Priority from the Actions pane on the right. Once you set a new policy as the top-priority policy, choose Apply in the Actions pane, and an Apply E-Mail Address Policy Wizard runs to update the default reply addresses of your domain users.

Controlling E-Mail Addresses at the Mailbox Level

There may be need to create additional e-mail addresses for a particular user. Common reasons to create additional addresses include the following:

▶ To cover common misspellings of the user's e-mail address. Jonathan Dough might, for example, have an additional Jonothan.Dough@smallbizco.net address.

▶ To add additional addresses in the event of a name change, such as after a marriage.

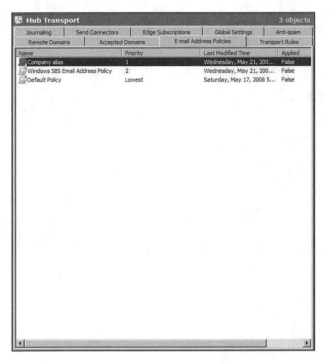

FIGURE 8.9   The policy with the priority of 1 will be the one that takes precedence over the others with higher numbers.

▶ To route mail that was previously delivered to a mailbox that has been deleted. If Harold Dough, who previously handled accounting, left the company, one option would be to add Harold.Dough@smallbizco.net as an additional address for the new accountant for the sake of continuity with clients. Normally, it is a better idea to leave the old mailbox intact and edit the Mail Flow settings in Harold's mailbox to have mail forwarded to the new accountant.

To add an additional e-mail address for a particular user, pull up that user's properties and go to the E-Mail Addresses tab. From there, you can create additional SMTP addresses. Note that any address you create needs to be one for a domain that is defined in the Accepted Domains list; otherwise, the e-mail will not come to the user's mailbox.

Additionally, some situations require that a particular user's e-mail address be different than the default address policy dictates. For example, if it was necessary to create a distinct user account called Customer Service, the system may try and make the default e-mail address cservice@smallbizco.net. To keep the default address policy from applying to this mailbox, you need to open properties on the mailbox and go to the E-Mail Addresses tab. Once there, change the e-mail address to what you desire it to be and then uncheck the box at the bottom of the window, labeled Automatically Update E-Mail Addresses Based on E-Mail Address Policy (see Figure 8.10).

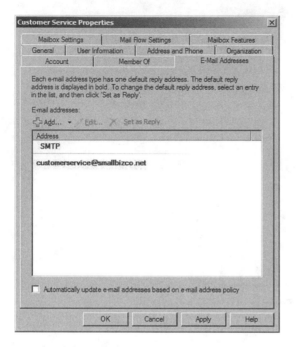

FIGURE 8.10   Uncheck the Automatically Update box in order to prevent a policy from applying to a particular mailbox.

Routing Mail for a Non-Authoritative Zone

Dealing with split delivery is not as uncommon in the small business environment as you might think. Many small businesses rely on split delivery mail solutions, especially when the POP3 Connector is being used. One common scenario would be when a corporate office receives all mail from the Internet, and then a branch office with an SBS 2008 Server downloads the mail using a POP3 Connector. Outbound mail could be routed through the corporate server or routed directly out via the Internet, but the important consideration is that not all company.com addresses are homed on the local server. Because of that, it is important to route any non-local @company.com addresses to the corporate server.

Simply put, a split delivery mail system is a mail setup where not all the accounts for an e-mail domain exist on a single mail server—in this case, the SBS server. The initial Configure Internet E-mail Wizard cannot handle a split delivery mail domain during Exchange configuration, so if this scenario applies to you, you need to configure the setup manually.

The problem arises when Exchange is told that it is the authoritative server for the split delivery mail domain. When a user on the SBS network attempts to send e-mail to an account that does not reside on the SBS server, Exchange will immediately return the message as undeliverable because it cannot find that mail address in Active Directory.

The best solution for this situation is to configure Exchange so that it is not the authoritative server for the domain. To change this configuration, follow these steps:

1. In Exchange Management Console, open the Organization Configuration section and select the Hub Transport object.

2. Select the Accepted Domains tab and double-click Windows SBS External Domain in the center pane.

3. If the public MX record for your domain routes mail to your server, select Internal Relay Domain. If the public DNS MX record for your domain routes mail to another server that is the primary handler of mail for your domain, select External Relay Domain. Read further to ensure you are making the right decision.

Internal Relay Domain Configuration

If you chose Internal Relay Domain, you also need to create a new Send Connector on your server to route domain mail whose mailboxes are not local. The Send Connector ensures that after local messages are delivered locally, any mail that needs to go to the other mail server can get there.

To create a Send Connector, do the following:

1. In the Exchange Management Console, expand the Organization Configuration container and select Hub Transport.

2. Select the Send Connectors tab.

3. Select New Send Connector from the Actions pane to start the New Send Connector Wizard.

4. Name the connector and select Custom from the Intended Use list. Proceed to the next page of the wizard.

5. Add a new address space. Type your own public domain name in there (see Figure 8.11).

6. Click Next to proceed to the Network Settings screen. Select Route Mail Through the Following Smart Hosts.

7. Enter the IP address of the host that you will route mail through (see Figure 8.12). This would be the mail server at another office where mailboxes using your public domain name are located. Continue to the next page of the wizard.

8. Set your authentication method (see Figure 8.13). Normally, None or Basic is going to be used, and you would configure the server to authenticate using an account that exists on the smart host server. None is an option because normally a mail server will always accept mail whose recipient address matches an accepted domain there.

9. Click Next and move past the Source Server page to finish the wizard.

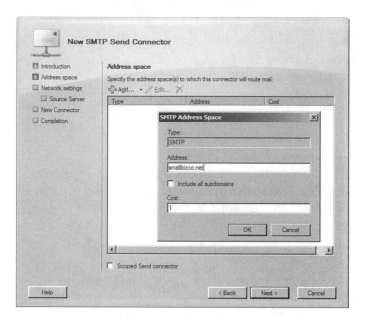

FIGURE 8.11   Enter your domain name as an address space for the connector to route.

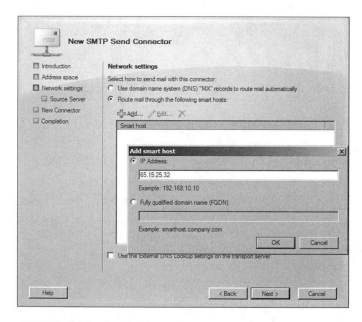

FIGURE 8.12   Configure the IP address of your smart host.

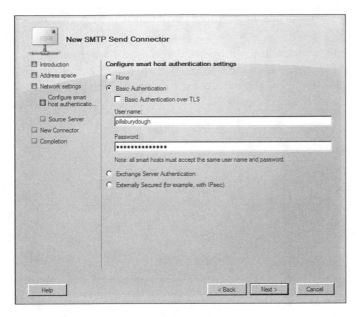

New SMTP Send Connector

Introduction | Configure smart host authentication settings
Address space
Network settings | ○ None
Configure smart | ● Basic Authentication
host authenticatio... | □ Basic Authentication over TLS
Source Server | User name:
New Connector | pillsburydough
Completion | Password:
•••••••••••••
Note: all smart hosts must accept the same user name and password.
○ Exchange Server Authentication
○ Externally Secured (for example, with IPsec).

Help   < Back   Next >   Cancel

FIGURE 8.13   Configure authentication if your smart host requires it.

External Relay Domain Configuration

If you chose External Relay Domain, your server will use DNS or your existing smarthost and send messages out to the Internet to be routed to the server that is the primary public server for your domain name.

Cohosting Multiple Organizations on a Single Server

It's not difficult to host mail for multiple organizations on a single Small Business Server 2008 if you go about it in an organized fashion. One of the most useful tools you have with this task is Active Directory Users and Computers. That tool enables you to select multiple users from a list and assign them all a particular common property, like a company name. Doing that, a condition can then be set in the e-mail address policies so the policy only applies to the users who have that particular property value. In the following example, you assign several of the users on the domain to be employees of Betty's Flowers so that you can then give them their own unique e-mail addresses. Do the following to prepare a set of users to be assigned an e-mail address policy as a group:

1. Open the SBS Advanced Management console and expand the Active Directory Users and Computers object.

2. Expand the domain object named after your domain name. In this case, it is smallbizco.local.

3. Expand the MyBusiness organizational unit, then the Users organizational unit, and finally the SBS Users organizational unit.

4. Use Shift+Click to select all the users that belong to a particular company that uses the server.

5. Once they are all selected, right-click and get Properties. You see a properties dialogue that represents all the users who were selected. Go to the Organization tab, check the Company checkbox, and type the name of the company (see Figure 8.14). Click OK to finish.

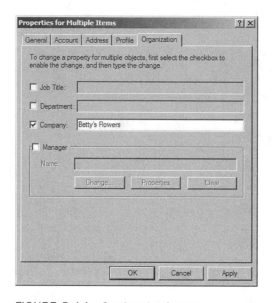

FIGURE 8.14　Setting the Company property in the Active Directory for multiple users.

6. Look at the process outlined in the "Adding Additional E-Mail Addresses" section. On the Conditions screen in the New E-Mail Address Policy Wizard in Step 3, you specify Recipient Is in a Company to create a policy that only applied to members of a particular organization that was homed on the server (see Figure 8.15).

Make sure that any selective e-mail address policies you create are higher (closer to zero!) priority than the built-in policies. If the Windows SBS E-Mail Address Policy is higher priority, it dictates the default e-mail address for all the mailboxes. Once you add a new policy, the Windows SBS E-Mail Address Policy should be set at a priority of 2, and the new policy you create should have a priority of 1.

If you have set up an E-Mail Address Policy, but it doesn't seem to have caused new addresses to be generated for your target user accounts, select the policy you created and click Apply in the Actions pane at the E-Mail Address Policy area to reapply the policy. Any mailboxes that meet the conditions that you set will have the policy reapplied to it.

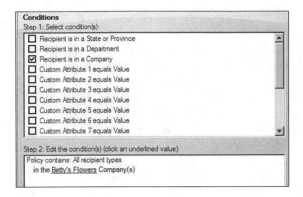

FIGURE 8.15   Set the condition based on criteria that you've already established in the Active Directory.

Getting Information About Mailboxes

Server administrators frequently need to check on resource utilization, and in the realm of e-mail, knowing how large your user mailboxes are and how many items are in them is a valuable bit of data. Unfortunately, these numbers are not exposed in the GUI, so we have to access them using PowerShell.

To use a PowerShell cmdlet to retrieve mailbox information, open the Exchange Management Shell. You can find it in the All Programs menu, under Microsoft Exchange Server 2007. Once the Exchange Management Shell command-line interface opens, you will be able to use commands like these:

▶ To get information about a particular mailbox, use this command:

```
Get-MailboxStatistics Bill.Dough
```

▶ To dump all available information about all mailboxes, use the following command:

```
Get-MailboxStatistics | list
```

▶ To show only the size and item count in each mailbox, use this command:

```
Get-MailboxStatistics | list DisplayName,TotalItemSize,ItemCount
```

▶ A more complex command to list the sizes in descending order would look like this:

```
Get-MailboxStatistics -server SBSERVER | select DisplayName,@{n="Size
➡(MB)";e={$_.TotalItemSize.value.ToMB()}} | sort Size -desc | ft -auto
```

For most readers, this reinforces the fact that although simple scripts are usually able to provide the information you need, there will also be the ones you copy and paste from the Internet, editing the variables for your context.

Managing Limits

Normally when a server is purchased, projections are made regarding the number of users and the size of their mailboxes, and the hardware is chosen accordingly. In a perfect world, there could be a four-year cycle between each round of hardware upgrades that perfectly matched the rate of resource growth on an organization's server. Unfortunately, not all users are created equal when it comes to the rate of mailbox space consumption, and not all business plans take into account the changes that an organization will undergo with regard to the number of employees and the manner in which information is exchanged with internal and external contacts. Because of this uncertainty, the ability to set limits on the sizes of mailboxes can be an important administration tool to help users keep a lid on their own mailbox growth.

In the previous version of SBS, the default mailbox size cap was 200MB. As mentioned at the beginning of this chapter, the size limit for an SBS 2008 mailbox is 2.3GB. Limits can be set on any individual mailbox, or limits can be imposed by setting a mailbox to accept the default values that have been configured on the mailbox database. By default, all mailboxes defer to the settings on the mailbox database. You may find that the default limits do not match your environment, so in the following section, you look at how to modify the default settings on the mailbox database and how to change limits on an individual mailbox. You also look at how to use PowerShell to enforce limits on all mailboxes programmatically.

With the GUI

To modify the universal default limits, open the Exchange Management Console and follow these steps:

1. On the left pane, expand the Server object and select the Mailbox container.
2. Under the First Storage Group in the center pane, select Mailbox Database and open up the properties on it.
3. Click the Limits tab (see Figure 8.16, which shows the default settings).
4. Change the settings appropriately and click Apply to finish.

Also listed in the Limits tab is the deleted items retention period, which is 30 days by default. Any of the settings on this page can be changed as needed for your particular environment. If the network has only five or six users and the volume of e-mail sent and received by the user base is low, you might be able to remove the limits on the mailbox database and enable the users to store more e-mail on the server than the limits would otherwise allow. On the other hand, you need to keep a closer eye on the total size of the mailbox database if you remove the limits; this is not because the mailbox database has a maximum size, because it doesn't (functionally, not theoretically), but because a larger database increases backup and restore times. You might not actually have sufficient physical storage to adequately protect your server against a ballooning database.

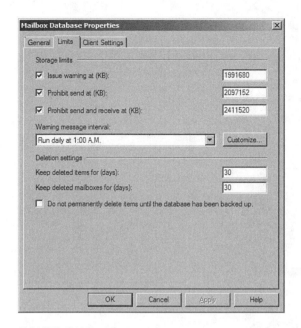

FIGURE 8.16   The limits you set on the mailbox database apply to any users who do not have their own settings.

NOTE

Although there is a high theoretical size limit on how large a mailbox database can grow, Microsoft has put a soft cap on the mailbox database size. That cap is 250GB. Normally, when you keep your databases smaller by distributing them among multiple storage groups, you won't need to exceed 80GB, and that is a good rule to observe, but an extreme condition may arise that requires you to lift that cap. To raise the cap, make the registry change detailed in this article: http://technet.microsoft.com/en-us/library/aa997432.aspx.

Although the settings on the mailbox database determine the default limits for all the users, the limits can be modified on a per-mailbox basis by going into the properties of a mailbox and setting the limits there. This can be done in two places: the SBS Console or the Exchange Management Console. The SBS Console exposes a simpler set of settings. To see them, open up the properties of a user and go to the E-Mail settings. You see something like Figure 8.17.

As you can see, within the SBS Console, you can enforce quotas or turn them off, and you can set the max mailbox size.

You can also access these properties using the Exchange Management Console by expanding the Recipients container and getting properties on a mailbox. If you go to the Mail Settings tab and open up Mail Quotas, you see the dialog shown in Figure 8.18.

To set unique settings for a particular mailbox, uncheck the Use Mailbox Database Defaults checkbox. If you want to remove all limits, leave the other boxes beneath unchecked; otherwise, populate them with the limits you want to set.

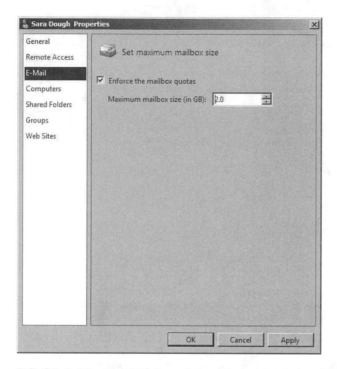

FIGURE 8.17   The SBS Console provides a simple interface to change mailbox size limits.

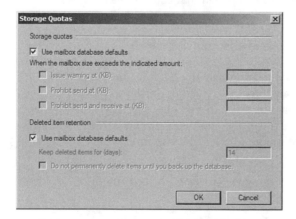

FIGURE 8.18   When a mailbox is configured to inherit the mailbox default limits, it looks like this.

Setting Limits with PowerShell

Using PowerShell, it would be easy to enforce the limits on all the mailboxes on the server. Perhaps you want to ensure that all mailboxes are set to accept the mailbox database defaults. How long would it take to check each mailbox and change the setting if it wasn't the desired one? If you have quite a few users, a simple script would make that time-consuming operation quite simple.

Let's look first at how easy it is to display the quotas of all the mailboxes on the server using the Exchange Management Shell. The following script retrieves all mailbox properties and then displays the name property and any property with the word "quota" in it:

```
Get-mailbox | ft name,*quota*
```

You can see the results of running this script in Figure 8.19.

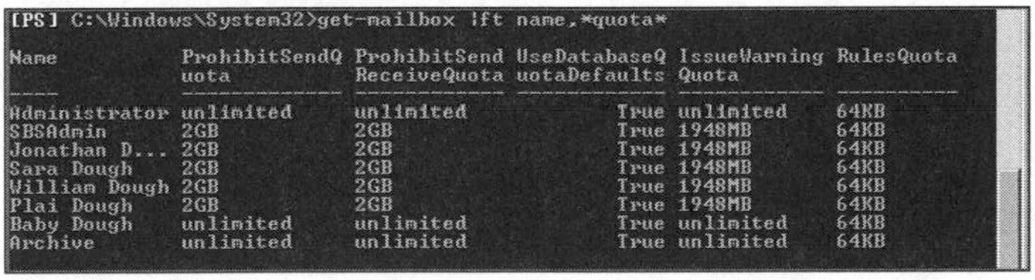

FIGURE 8.19   This commandlet displays the quota settings for each mailbox on the server.

The following script enforces the default mailbox database settings for all mailboxes:

```
Get-mailbox | set-mailbox –usedatabasequotadefaults $True
```

When you run this command, you will be shown what effect the command has on each mailbox that it is applied to as shown in Figure 8.20.

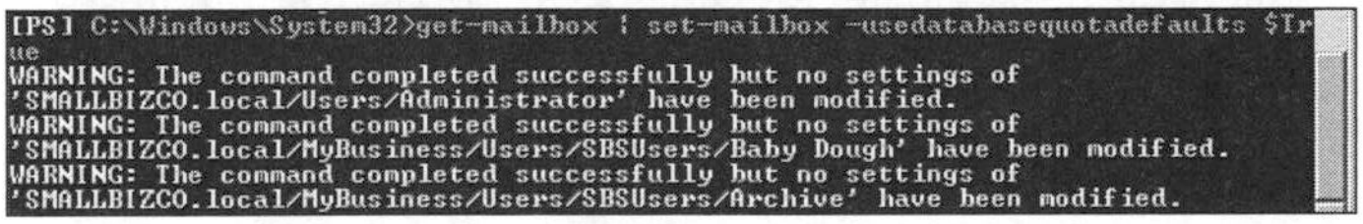

FIGURE 8.20   The setting is applied to each mailbox, but only causes changes to certain ones.

To configure the archive mailbox to have a unique set of limits, you might use a script like this one:

```
Get-mailbox archive | set-mailbox -usedatabasequotadefaults $false
➥-prohibitsendquota 2000mb –prohibitsendreceivequota 2gb –issuewarningquota 1900mb
```

Note how we are able to use megabyte and gigabyte designations and not just kilobytes, which the Exchange Management Console requires. That's one thing that makes it a little easier to work with PowerShell, rather than having to convert everything when using the Exchange Console when configuring specific limits. The SBS Console makes it easy too, by allowing you to set limits in half gigabyte increments.

Using Transport Rules

Transport rules make accessible functionality that in previous versions of Exchange were only available to developers and providers of third-party products. Transport rules can be used to modify inbound and outbound messages and perform additional routing and handling operations on them if they meet certain criteria. They run on the Hub Transport server and are applied to messages in transit, affecting messages on their way to and from user mailboxes.

One of the more useful things you can do with transport rules is to add disclaimer text to all outbound e-mails. In many industries, legal departments require some sort of disclaimers to be used to limit liability. Here is how you would set that up on Small Business Server 2008.

Setting Up Disclaimers with Transport Rules

When you are setting up a disclaimer, keep your eyes open and notice the wealth of options you have for creating transport rules to perform all sorts of functions. Both conditions and actions provide ample resources for an enterprising admin. Let's get started on the disclaimer:

1. Open up the Exchange Management Console.
2. Expand the Organization Configuration section and select the Hub Transport container.
3. From the middle pane, select the Transport Rules tab to display any existing rules.
4. In the right-hand Actions pane, select New Transport Rule.
5. On the Introduction page of the New Transport Rule Wizard, give the disclaimer rule a name, such as "Company Disclaimer," and go to the next page of the wizard.
6. On the Conditions page, select from users inside or outside the organization, and go to the next screen.
7. On the Actions page, select Append Disclaimer Text Using Font, Size, Color, with Separator and Fallback to Action if Unable to Apply (see Figure 8.21).
8. In the editing area, click disclaimer text, and in the pop-up window, type the message that you would like to have appended to each message sent from your organization. Click OK when finished and then Next to the next screen.
9. Click Finish to complete the rule.

Now each outgoing message sent from a user in your organization will include an appended disclaimer.

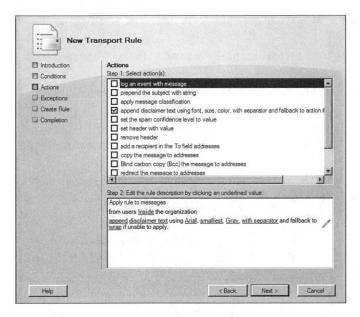

FIGURE 8.21   Configure the options for the disclaimer text.

Another need some organizations have is to make copies of e-mail going to a specific mailbox and have it forwarded to a different box. This could be done by setting the delivery options on the mailbox to forward copies of all messages to another user's mailbox, or a transport rule could be created to do the same thing, but with the advantage of being able to set specific conditions on the forwarding. Perhaps one user is managing an external e-mail alias like info@smallbizco.com: A transport rule could be configured to forward all e-mails that were sent to that alias to that person's manager as well, and an exclusion could be added to keep test messages from being forwarded. The following section shows how you would go about setting that up.

To Create Copies of E-Mails

The process of setting up forwarding is different from setting up a disclaimer only in the actions and conditions chosen, and it illustrates the fact that Transport Rules open up a whole new field for simple customization of your messaging environment. Follow these steps to set up Transport Rule–based message forwarding:

1. Open up the Exchange Management Console.

2. Expand the Organization Configuration section and select the Hub Transport container.

3. From the middle pane, select the Transport Rules tab to display any existing rules.

4. In the right Actions pane, select New Transport Rule.

5. On the Introduction page of the New Transport Rule Wizard, give the disclaimer rule a name, such as "Copying Inquiry E-Mails," and go to the next page of the wizard.

6. On the Conditions page, select when the message header contains text patterns.

7. In the lower section, click the message header link, type **To** in the text field, and click OK.

8. Next, click text patterns and type **info@smallbizco.com** and click OK. Proceed to the next page of the wizard.

9. On the Action page, select Blind Carbon Copy the Message to Addresses. Click addresses and add any local mailboxes that you would want copies of these messages sent to. Select William Dough in your example. Go to the next page of the wizard.

10. On the Exceptions page, select Except when the text-specific words appear in the subject.

11. In the area below, select specific words and add the word "test" to the list of specific words. Click OK and click next to move on.

12. Click New to finish creating the rule.

Now that you've created the rule, any inbound messages sent to info@smallbizco.com should be modified, adding a bcc: field to send the message to William Dough. If the word "test" is in the subject line, the rule will not add a bcc: field to the message.

These two exercises should have given you a taste of the potential of transport rules, but they only scratch the surface of what's possible. There is a lot of room for using carefully crafted and tested rules to customize your environment in ways that Small Business Server 2003 admins could only dream of.

Archiving Mail

The need to retain mail in a central repository can be driven by several different business needs. Some organizations need certain kinds of mail archived in order to accurately track sales or support activity for a team. Other organizations might need to archive mail for legal reasons or to comply with federal guidelines for maintaining records. Still other businesses might see archiving as a failsafe in case a user deletes messages that may be needed later on. Depending on which type of business needs exist, there are several options available for the SBS 2008 administrator to meet these needs. In this section, we will explore archiving mail to SharePoint, archiving via the Exchange 2007 journaling feature, and integrating third-party archiving products to provide more robust archiving solutions.

Using SharePoint Libraries

Organizations frequently have a customer support e-mail alias that they use to handle all public queries to a company support unit. Similar aliases usually exist for sales, information, marketing, and so on. Although one option is to have these e-mails go to a distribution list, another option is to also (or only) have them land in a SharePoint library or a public folder, where everyone in a particular unit or department can process them. This is usually a better option than just a distribution list, because it's easier to tell whether a particular message has been replied to or has yet to be handled when it is in a common area for others to notate and organize.

To have incoming e-mails go to a SharePoint library, follow this procedure:

1. In the main SBS Console, go to the Users and Groups tab and select the Groups sub-tab.

2. Click the Add a New Group link on the right Task pane to start the wizard.

3. On the Add a New Group page, specify a group name and select Security Group as the type of group you want to create.

4. Check the Enable This Security Group to Receive E-Mail box.

5. On the next screen, specify an e-mail address that the group will use, and make sure both E-Mail Delivery Options checkboxes are selected (see Figure 8.22).

FIGURE 8.22   Give the security group an e-mail address and configure it to archive to SharePoint.

6. On the next screen, you select members of the group. Any member of this group will receive copies of the e-mails that are sent to the group's public address. Once you select the users, you can finish the wizard.

Depending on how your workflow is arranged, you might not want to have anyone be members of this group, but have everyone in the unit who owns this group go only to the SharePoint library to handle messages so that every item response can be tracked. If users reply to incoming messages from their own mailboxes without going to the SharePoint library to mark an item as responded to, other users in the group may not know that a message has been handled already. Alternately, if everyone sends a cc: message to the group address, the SharePoint library will also have an archive of all responses to the incoming messages.

Using Exchange Journaling

If your business need is to archive all company mail for either recovery or legal compliance reasons, you want to be using the journaling feature of Exchange 2007. The journaling features that come licensed with SBS 2007 don't have a lot of granularity: You cannot choose to capture mail from a subset of mailboxes, only on the entire mailbox database. Advanced journaling features that can be licensed separately are described later in this section.

Creating the Journaling Mailbox

To set this up, you use the Exchange Management Console to create a mailbox to be used for journaling. Let's name this Archive. The reason you create it in the Exchange console is because you aren't creating a user who needs a home folder, SharePoint permissions, or any of the other things that a user created in the SBS Console receives. Creating this account in the EMC reduces the "overhead" that this account requires:

1. Open the Exchange Management Console and go to the Recipients container in the left pane.

2. Choose the New Mailbox task in the right Task pane.

3. When the wizard comes up, walk through it, choosing to create a new User mailbox.

4. On the User Information Screen, name the user (see Figure 8.23).

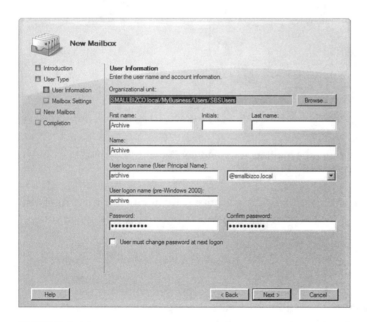

FIGURE 8.23   Create a new mailbox for the journaling account using the Exchange Management Console.

5. On the Mailbox Settings page, browse for a Mailbox Database and select your server's database from the list (see Figure 8.24).

6. Click Next and New to finish the mailbox creation process.

The new user you created will not show up in the SBS Console right away due to the way the Users view is generated; to administer that account immediately, go into the Recipients container of the Exchange Management Console, and access the properties of the new account.

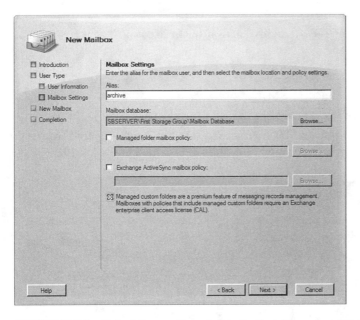

FIGURE 8.24   Select the mailbox database that the new mailbox will use.

It is usually a good idea to hide the Archive mailbox from the Global Address List. To do that, access the properties of the Archive account using the Exchange Management Console as mentioned previously, and look at the General tab. Check the Hide from Exchange Address Lists checkbox and apply the settings.

In addition to hiding the mailbox from address lists, you also need to go into the Mailbox Settings, Storage Quotas area of the archive mailbox properties and remove any limits on this mailbox. Uncheck the Use Mailbox Database Defaults checkbox and make sure that the three checkboxes below it are unchecked (see Figure 8.25).

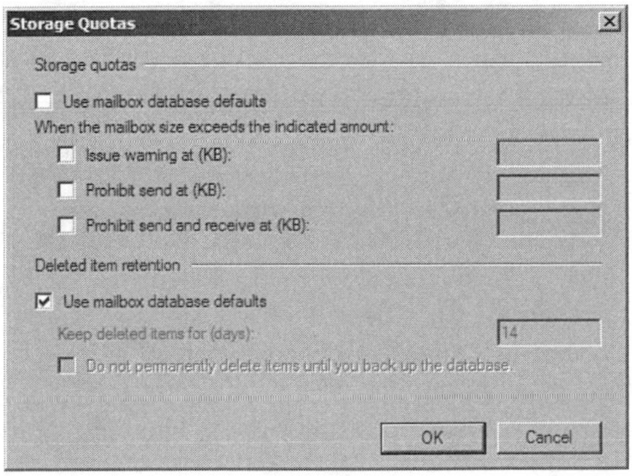

FIGURE 8.25   Choosing to bypass the Mailbox Database default limits.

Enabling Journaling

The next step is to configure the server to archive mail into the account that was set up, as follows:

1. Open the Exchange Management Console.

2. Under the Server container, select the Mailbox object.

3. Get properties on the Mailbox Database in the First Storage Group.

4. Check the Journaling checkbox and click Browse to select a journaling account (see Figure 8.26). Choose the Archive account from the list provided and click OK.

FIGURE 8.26   Choosing a journaling account.

That's it! Now a copy of every inbound, outbound, or internal e-mail will be bcc'd to this journaling mailbox. To view the mail in the journaling mailbox, connect to the mailbox with an Outlook client or using Outlook Web Access.

Single Instance Storage and Journaling

One valid concern admins have is with how much storage journaling could take up. Maintaining, for example, a copy of every attachment that has been e-mailed will take up a lot of space. For the last couple of versions of Exchange, a technology called Single Instance Storage (SIS) has saved a great deal of space in the mailbox database by only maintaining a single copy of every attachment, regardless of how many users in the company received the message containing the attachment.

In an archiving context, this means that it doesn't take the archiving service any additional space to archive an attachment unless the e-mails containing the attachment have been deleted from any non-archive mailboxes that contained them. It is only then, when the archiving mailbox is the only place in which a message containing the attachment exists, that more space is used to archive that attachment.

One implication of this is that having users delete messages with large attachments will not save you space in the database if you are also maintaining a populated journaling mailbox. If you are now wondering how to handle the space problems that journaling can create, check out the upcoming section, "Using Third-Party Products," to learn about some products that pick up where Exchange journaling leaves off.

Advanced Journaling

If you want more versatility with regards to what is captured, you may need to purchase Exchange Enterprise Client Access Licenses. If you own those, you can use Enterprise journaling features. There is no interface for entering the licenses, so licensing is a legal, not a technical, requirement. Companies using Enterprise features of Exchange 2007 need to keep Enterprise CALs on file to meet licensing requirements.

Enterprise journaling is configured differently than basic journaling, and uses journaling rules to control what types of messages are captured and where those captured messages are forwarded. It would be possible, for example, to capture all mail sent to a person who was having health issues and have it forwarded to his supervisor to make sure nothing fell through the cracks. It could be used to capture all outbound e-mail of an employee who handles sensitive contracts and have it sent to the mailbox of a compliance officer in order to ensure that all communications by that employee met policy guidelines. It would be wise to make sure that any journaling methods used are covered by a corporate privacy policy that employees are familiar with.

To set up Advanced Journaling, follow these steps:

1. Open the Exchange Management Console.
2. Under the Organization Configuration container, select the Hub Transport object. One of the configuration tab areas is Journaling. Select the Journaling tab.
3. On the right Task pane, select New Journal Rule.
4. Name the journaling rule and select a destination mailbox for journaling to send messages to.
5. Choose the scope of this journaling rule: global, internal, or external only.
6. You can narrow down the scope of the journaling rule by selecting a particular mailbox to filter. Pick a name for the Journal messages for recipient field to do this. If you do not select a mailbox, journaling will be turned on for all mailboxes in the organization, and will only be narrowed by the configured scope of the rule.
7. Finally, you can choose to enable or disable this rule. Naturally, if you want it to work, it needs to be enabled.

Using Third-Party Products

Third-party products solve several problems that plague organizations that use only Exchange journaling. Let's outline some of those problems.

Although the journaling features of Exchange 2007 do actually capture all mail and allow it to be accessed via normal means (that is, Outlook or OWA), a journaling mailbox is a cumbersome thing to index, search, and export. Even if you were to try and dump it all to a .pst file and give it to some lawyers to look through, you'd run up against the 2GB .pst size limit, and journaling mailboxes get much, much larger than that.

Beyond that, your mail archive is still on your mail server, making your mail database larger and that much more cumbersome to back up and restore. If you would like to maintain your mail archive on a separate partition or on a separate server, and by doing so keep your mailbox database at a reasonable size, simple journaling is not a complete solution.

Third-party archiving products are built to handle those issues. Archiving is often (but not always) conducted on a separate server, and archives can be rotated every month or quarter to keep your archive stores a manageable size. These products generally have an export function coupled with advanced search techniques to make it easy to export very specific sets of messages to portable media when needed.

Most of the third-party archiving products on the market require you to set up basic journaling on your server, as was initially described in this section. Once that journaling account has been set up and mail is being routed to it, the archiving application will usually connect to that mailbox with MAPI or IMAP to move mail into its own database. Archiving databases are usually SQL-driven, but some vendors provide file-based non-SQL options.

It is usually a good idea to configure anti-virus exclusion for directories used for archiving and indexing of mail. On-access anti-virus has been responsible for slow indexing and for causing the sizes of indexes to bloat. Some vendors who have designed archiving products for use with SBS 2008 are Exclaimer, GFI, and Sunbelt Software.

Troubleshooting Exchange Management Issues

Exchange is a complex product, and the SBS implementation of Exchange makes it a bit more so. One chapter in a book cannot begin to cover all the troubleshooting possibilities for Exchange. The remainder of this chapter instead covers some of the commonly-encountered issues with Exchange related to topics covered in the chapter.

Troubleshooting Outbound Mail Delivery

When it comes to troubleshooting tools, some slick new tools provide a lot of previously unavailable guidance for inexperienced administrators and some trustworthy older tools for everyone to use.

Using the Mail Flow Troubleshooter Tool

SBS 2008 comes with a troubleshooting wizard that helps administrators by pairing symptoms with possible causes for mail disruptions. At each point, the wizard provides links that take an admin directly to the tool or console that they may need to resolve the issue.

To launch the Exchange Mail Flow Troubleshooter, do the following:

1. Open the Exchange Management Console.

2. Click the Toolbox object in the left pane.

3. Run the Exchange Mail Flow Troubleshooter tool from the options in the center pane.

Additional Troubleshooting Tools

In addition to the Mail Flow Troubleshooter tool, many outbound mail delivery issues can be identified with just a couple of basic tools: the Queue Viewer and `telnet`. When you suspect outbound mail delivery problems, open the Queue Viewer and look at the outbound SMTP queues. To open the Queue Viewer, go into the Exchange Management Console and select the toolbox at the bottom of the left pane. Run the Queue Viewer from the list in the center pane.

When you have mail configured to route through DNS, you will see a queue for each mail domain where Exchange has recently attempted delivery. The status of the queue is listed in the Status column, shown in Figure 8.27. If the status is anything other than Ready, you need to identify and resolve the problem before Exchange will be able to deliver mail.

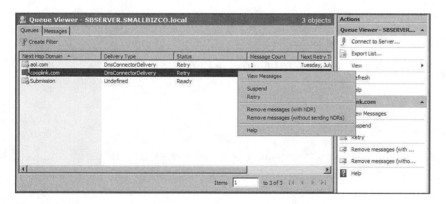

FIGURE 8.27   The Queue Viewer displays the status of each outbound mail queue.

When you look at the problem mail queue, the Last Error field gives you an indication of the problem (see Figure 8.28). If you can't read the entire error, just mouse-over it, and a pop-up shows you the full text of the error.

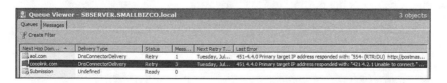

FIGURE 8.28   The Last Error field of the Queue Viewer gives information about why delivery has failed.

In Figure 8.29, the queue for delivery to aol.com is in a Retry state, meaning that Exchange will make another attempt to deliver mail to aol.com. The Last Error field indicates that the last connection attempt failed because of an SMTP protocol error. In most cases, this is likely not a protocol error, but a delivery refusal.

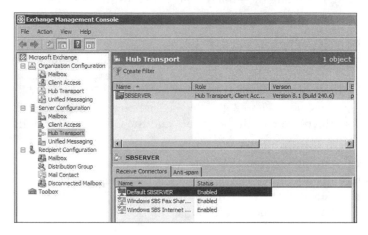

FIGURE 8.29   Select the Default receive connector.

You can narrow down the cause in one of two ways from here. First, you can enable SMTP logging and review the information collected in the log file. Logging is handled separately for inbound and outbound SMTP traffic.

Configuring Inbound SMTP Logging

Follow these instructions to enable inbound SMTP logging:

1. In Exchange Management Console, expand Server and select the Hub Transport object.
2. In the center pane, you see several receive connectors. Select the one titled Default *[servername]*, as shown in Figure 8.29.
3. Right-click that connector and click Properties.
4. On the General tab, set the Protocol logging level to Verbose (see Figure 8.30).
5. Click Apply to save the changes.

Configuring Outbound SMTP Logging

Follow these instructions to enable outbound SMTP logging:

1. In Exchange Management Console, expand Organization Configuration and select the Hub Transport object.
2. In the center pane, select the Send Connector tab. You see a connector titled Windows SBS Internet Send *[servername]*, as shown in Figure 8.31.
3. Right-click that connector and click Properties.
4. On the General tab, set the Protocol logging level to Verbose (see Figure 8.32).
5. Click Apply to save the changes.

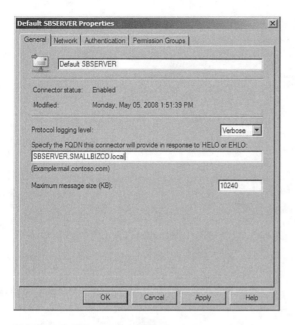

FIGURE 8.30   Setting the protocol logging level to Verbose on the receive connector.

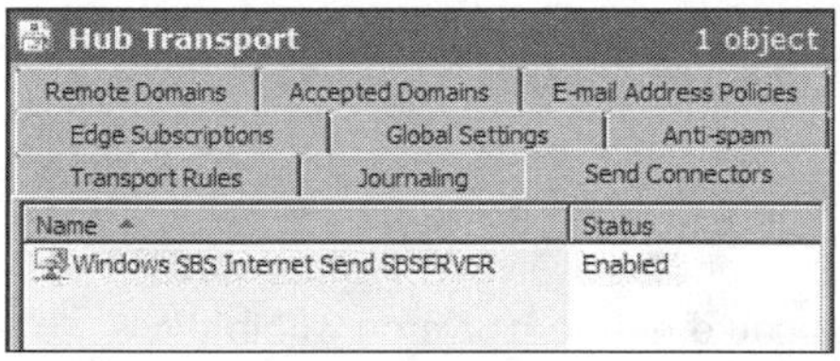

FIGURE 8.31   Select the Windows SBS Internet Send connector.

Now that you have outbound SMTP logging enabled, you can force Exchange to make another connection attempt and record the transaction in the logs. You can do this by right-clicking the connector in the Queues listing and selecting Force Connection.

Next, you can review the information in the SMTP log file. Browse to the folder where the log files are stored (C:\Program Files\Microsoft\Exchange Server\TransportRoles\Logs\ProtocolLog by default), open the smtpreceive folder, and open the most recent log file. The following listing displays a typical response you might get from a refused connection:

```
year-mo-da 15:22:20 hostserverIP OutboundConnectionResponse SMTPSVC1 SBS - 25 -
➡- 554-+(RTR:BB)++http://postmaster.info.aol.com/errors/554rtrbb.html
year-mo-da 15:22:20 hostserverIP OutboundConnectionResponse SMTPSVC1 SBS - 25 -
➡- 554-+AOL+does+not+accept+e-mail+transactions+from+dynamic+or+residential
```

In this example, you can see that AOL responds to the connection attempt with a notice that it does not accept connections from IPs that are registered as residential or dynamic by ISPs. AOL even provides a URL in the error that gives you more information about why they refused the connection.

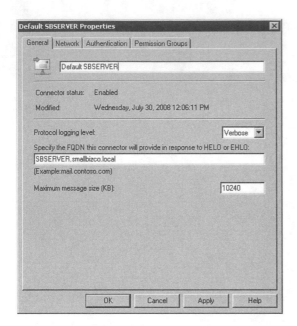

FIGURE 8.32   Setting the protocol logging level to Verbose on the Send Connector.

NOTE

Some mail hosts handle refusing mail in different ways. AOL refuses to accept the connection, but in such a way that no NDR is generated. The Exchange SMTP queue will continue to attempt delivery to AOL until the delivery timeout is received, at which point it generates its own NDR, indicating that the message could not be delivered within the time configured on the server. Other ISPs refuse the connection in such a way that an NDR is generated immediately and tells the sender exactly why the mail has been rejected. It is generally easier to troubleshoot delivery failures when these NDRs are generated, because they generally indicate which blacklist or other spam-blocking tool they used to refuse your request.

Another way to investigate mail delivery problems is to make a manual SMTP connection to see what is happening. This can be useful for those occasions when no information about the connection problem is listed in the SMTP logs. You will use the `telnet` tool to connect to the mail server and attempt mail delivery to see how the remote system responds.

Before you can `telnet` to the mail server, you will need to know where the mail server is. Use `nslookup` to find the address or name of the mail server. Follow these steps to find a remote mail server using nslookup:

1. In a command prompt window, type **nslookup** and hit Enter.
2. At the nslookup prompt, type **set type=mx** and hit Enter.
3. Type the mail domain and hit Enter.

Nslookup returns the mail exchanger record(s) for the mail domain. Once you have noted the name or address of the remote mail server, type **exit** and hit Enter to quit `nslookup`. Now you can use `telnet` to attempt a manual message delivery by following these steps:

1. At the command prompt, type **telnet[*name of mail sever*]25** and hit Enter.

2. If you receive a 220 response from the mail server, type **ehlo[*your mail domain*]** and hit Enter.

3. If you receive a number of 250 responses, type **mail from:[*your return e-mail address*]** and hit Enter.

4. If you receive a 250 response, type **rcpt to:[*address of recipient*]** and hit Enter.

5. If you receive a 250 response here, you will be able to send a message to that user successfully, so you can type **quit** and then hit Enter to close the `telnet` session.

If you get anything other than a 220 response on the initial connection or a 250 response after any of the other steps, review the SMTP server responses and continue troubleshooting from there. For some responses, it will be obvious what the problem is. For instance, if you don't have the correct server address for a mail domain, you may get a `550 5.7.1 Unable to relay` error. Other errors may not be as obvious, but you can at least look up the errors on the Internet and see what may be causing the problems.

Best Practice—Avoid BackPressure Related Outages

No, this isn't about back pain; it's about making sure that Exchange can do its job. Because the mail queues are stored on the C:\ drive, Exchange regularly checks to make sure that there is at least 4GB available there at all times. If there is less than 5GB, Exchange disables the Transport service, and it has to be manually restarted. The recommendation is to keep plenty of free space on your install drive at all times to prevent this from happening. If you cannot keep at least 4GB free, you can edit the `EdgeTransport.exe.config` file, which is located in the \bin folder of the Exchange installation directory, to resolve the issue. The parameter `EnableResourceMonitor` needs to be set to `False` to keep Exchange from shutting down the Transport service in low-space situations. Once you've made that file change, restart the Exchange Transport service.

∞

Troubleshooting the Content Filter

One indicator that there may be a problem with the configuration of the IMF is users reporting that they are not getting messages they are expecting. The first place to look for trouble is the SMTP receive log file. The following two samples from the SMTP receive log file show two different mail delivery sessions:

```
year-mo-da 16:05:10 [remoteIP] - SMTPSVC1 SBS [externalIP] 0 EHLO - - 250 0
year-mo-da 16:05:14 [remoteIP] - SMTPSVC1 SBS [externalIP] 0 MAIL -
➡+from:+user@remotedomain.net 250
year-mo-da 16:05:18 [remoteIP] - SMTPSVC1 SBS [externalIP] 0 RCPT -
➡+to:+jondough@smallbizco.net 250 0 0 17 0 SMTP -
```

```
year-mo-da 16:05:36 [remoteIP] - SMTPSVC1 SBS [externalIP] 0 DATA -
➥<SBS8FCc6OiA86YmJueD00000002@smallbizco.net> 250
year-mo-da 16:05:41 [remoteIP] - SMTPSVC1 SBS [externalIP] 0 QUIT - - 240

year-mo-da 16:06:11 [remoteIP] - SMTPSVC1 SBS [externalIP] 0 EHLO - - 250
year-mo-da 16:06:21 [remoteIP] - SMTPSVC1 SBS [externalIP] 0 MAIL -
➥+from:+spam@spam.net 250
year-mo-da 16:06:31 [remoteIP] - SMTPSVC1 SBS [externalIP] 0 RCPT -
➥+to:+jondough@smallbizco.net 250
year-mo-da 16:07:32 [remoteIP] - SMTPSVC1 SBS [externalIP] 0 QUIT - - 240
```

The difference between these two sessions in the log is the DATA response line in the first listing. This line indicates that the message was accepted for delivery and queued into the Exchange process. The second listing has no DATA line, which means that no message was queued for delivery in Exchange. This typically means that the message was blocked by the content filters.

If a user complains that he or she is not receiving messages from a particular person, you can search through the SMTP logs for that e-mail address and see if a connection attempt has even been made. If it has and you see the e-mail address listed in one of the MAIL lines in the log, you see a corresponding DATA line once the message has been queued for delivery.

One option to identify if the anti-spam filters have been blocking messages that it should not have is to set the content filter action to do nothing.

To configure the content filter settings, do the following:

1. In the Organization Configuration section of the Exchange Management Console, select the Hub Transport container.
2. In the center pane, select the Anti-Spam tab.
3. Get properties on the Content Filter item (see Figure 8.33).

By default, the content filter is configured to reject messages with an SCL value greater than 7. The lower the SCL level is, the more likely that valid e-mail will be accidentally blocked. Unchecking the Reject box will allow any messages that would be blocked to pass through to the client, where they may be dumped into the Junk Mail folder for the client. Once an e-mail arrives at the client, the SCL level for a particular message can be determined by looking at the message header. To check the SCL in the message header in Outlook 2007, open a message, and on the Options group, click Message Options or the tiny icon in the lower right of the Options group. If you examine the header details you might see an anti-spam stamp that looks like this:

```
X-MS-Exchange-Organization-SCL:8
```

The number at the end will depend on the SCL that was assigned to the message by the various filters that examined it. There are other types of anti-spam stamps that you might see in a message header. For more information about them, go to http://technet.microsoft.com/en-us/library/aa996878(EXCHG.80).aspx.

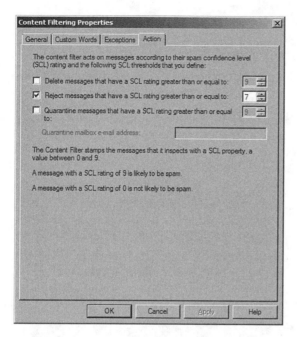

FIGURE 8.33   Configure the content filter actions and SCL levels.

Alternately, you can configure the content filter to quarantine e-mails to a quarantine account. You don't have to specifically create a quarantine account, however. You could, for example, just use the Administrator mailbox because it would be easy to log into it via OWA and check for items that shouldn't have been quarantined. Because the SBS 2008 version of OWA enables you to look at message headers, OWA is a good client to use to see how the SCL levels and anti-spam stamps on incoming junk mail are being assigned. If you set the content filter to quarantine, don't forget to monitor the mailbox, the size of the mailbox could balloon during a spam attack on your server.

Troubleshooting POP3 Connector

Troubleshooting issues with the POP3 Connector is a similar process to troubleshooting outbound mail delivery. Setting up and reviewing the extended logging with the POP3 Connector and using telnet to test connectivity are your primary tools for determining why the POP3 Connector failed to download mail or why mail that is downloaded may fail to be delivered to a user's mailbox.

The best place to look for information about what's happening with your POP3 Connector processes is in the POP3 Connector log, which can be found at C:\Program Files\Windows Small Business Server\logs\pop3connector. From that log, you can tell whether there were authentication errors, how many e-mails were downloaded, and whether any were blocked by the content filter, among other things.

Any serious errors that are generated in the process of the POP3 Connector retrieving mail should be logged in the Application log, but if you want to log more information to the POP3 Connector log and to the App log, you can do the following:

1. Open up a command line and navigate to C:\Program Files\Windows Small Business Server\bin.

2. Enter the command **pop3connector.exe -logVerbose.**

This should log more information both to the App log and to the POP3Connector log. To change the logging level back to the default, you can issue the command pop3connector.exe -lognormal from the same command-line location.

Once you've set up more verbose logging, you can force connection attempts by clicking the Retrieve Now button in the Scheduling tab of the POP3 Connector console. After the connection attempt has had time to complete, you can open the Event Viewer and go through the messages related to the POP3 Connector. Fortunately, when logging is set to verbose for the POP3 Connector, you can view each step of the entire process to see where problems are actually occurring. Unfortunately, there is so much information stored in the logs, it may take a long time to sort through the data to find the information you need.

CAUTION

Do not forget to set logging back to normal when you have finished your troubleshooting session. Otherwise, your event logs will fill up very quickly and may cause you to overlook other problems on the server.

Alternately, you can use telnet to verify access credentials and message availability on the remote POP3 server, assuming that the POP3 server listens on port 110 and doesn't require an SSL connection like many now do. Follow these steps to connect to the server and see how many messages are waiting:

1. At a command prompt, type **telnet[remote mail server]110** and press Enter.

2. At the +OK prompt, type **user[pop3username]** and press Enter.

3. At the +OK prompt, type **pass[pop3password]** and press Enter.

4. At the +OK prompt, type **list** and press Enter. This shows the number of messages waiting for download and the size of each message.

This process verifies several pieces of the POP3 puzzle. First, if the username and password are not correct, you get an -ERR response after the password entry line. Second, you can see if there are messages waiting to be downloaded. This can be helpful if you suspect mail delivery problems at the other side. You can simply keep repeating the list command to get the current count and size of the messages and watch for changes to indicate when new messages have arrived.

> **CAUTION**
>
> You can also use Windows Mail, Outlook Express, or another POP mail client to verify the user name and password on the remote server. Be sure that when you build a profile in a mail client for testing purposes, you configure the profile to leave the messages on the POP3 server when checking mail. Otherwise, those messages will be deleted from the server and the POP3 Connector will not be able to download and deliver them.

One scenario in particular that can cause much grief for an SBS administrator is when a user has his or her POP3 mail account configured for use in Outlook or Windows Mail. If more than one POP3 client is pulling mail from the POP3 server, irregular mail delivery is practically guaranteed. When a new SBS server is installed in an environment where users had been relying solely on POP3 for mail delivery, you should make sure that all users remove the POP3 account configuration from their mail clients in order for the POP3 Connector to work correctly.

If there are other external POP3 accounts (perhaps ones that use a separate domain name) that need to be downloaded to a local mailbox, it's a good idea to do it with the POP3 Connector so that proper spam filtering can be done. Users downloading mail directly to their client and storing it on the server will be able to check for mail more often than every 15 minutes, which seems desirable, but will not get the benefit of having those messages go through the server's anti-spam filters.

One last step to verify that a message on the POP3 server will get delivered correctly is to issue the `retr` command in the POP3 `telnet` session to view the contents of the message without deleting it from the server. Simply type **`retr[message#]`** after authenticating to the POP3 server, and the server will send the entire contents of the message. At that point, you can look through the headers for the TO: and CC: fields for a valid address for your server. If an address within your domain space is not listed in the TO: or CC: fields, the message will download to the server but not get delivered, unless you specify a mailbox to receive delivery of all undeliverable messages.

Summary

This chapter covered some of the main management aspects of the Exchange and POP3 Connector services included with SBS 2008. Most of the main settings of Exchange are configured through the initial setup wizards, but some features, such as mail delivery to multiple domains and setting up a disclaimer or a journaling account, require manual setup by the system administrator. The chapter also addressed other issues related to the prevention of spam and virus attacks on the server and gave troubleshooting steps for several processes related to mail delivery and processing. With this information, an SBS system administrator should be better prepared to handle the day-to-day management of Exchange and its related components.

Best Practice Summary

▶ **Route Outbound E-Mail Through a Smart Host**—To protect against current and future problems that could impact your server's ability to deliver mail to other servers reliably, you should configure your server to send all outbound e-mail through your ISP's SMTP server.

▶ **Use the POP3 Connector as a Transitional Tool, not as a Mail Solution**—If you must use the POP3 Connector at all, use it only to transition mail services away from POP3 toward full SMTP.

▶ **Use the Content Filter Wisely**—Check the SCL values of messages received by the Outlook client and use the filter actions to determine the ideal SCL values to set.

▶ **Avoid BackPressure Related Outages**—Avoid an untimely shutdown of your Transport service by always maintaining well over 4GB of free space on your C: drive. Use monitoring reports to alert you of a disk space situation that could stop mail delivery.

CHAPTER 9

Exchange 2007 Client Connectivity

Proper communication is key to the success of any business, regardless of size. As the modern workforce becomes increasingly more mobile, the need to have accurate and timely business information anywhere, at any time, on a variety of devices, becomes necessary. Because Exchange 2007 is the engine that drives that communication in Small Business Server 2008, there are numerous ways to connect employees to that information repository, giving them "anytime/anywhere" access to make them more efficient and productive.

This chapter discusses the various clients available that can leverage the data stored in Exchange 2007, namely Microsoft Office Outlook, Outlook Anywhere, Outlook Web Access (OWA), and Windows Mobile devices.

> **NOTE**
>
> Outlook Mobile Access (OMA) has been deprecated from Exchange 2007 and is therefore not included in SBS 2008.

This chapter also covers available methods for connecting these clients to the Exchange server, and finally, troubleshoots connectivity issues. For information regarding the Macintosh Exchange client Entourage, see Chapter 13, "Macintosh Integration."

Choosing the Right Exchange Client

Due to the variety of worker roles, infrastructure limitations, and budgetary considerations, unfortunately, there is no silver bullet solution for an Exchange client for all users. Although it is true that the majority of organizations will deploy Outlook 2007 in Cached Exchange Mode (the default recommended solution), some organizations will use a mix of clients and configurations to best fit individual users or teams of users.

By way of example, it is more common to see Windows Mobile devices in the hands of sales or service staff than in use by workers who never leave the office. Also, it may make more sense from a security and licensing standpoint to use Outlook Web Access 2007 and a Device CAL in a warehouse where a machine is shared by multiple factory workers. Remote workers prefer the ease of Outlook 2007 via Outlook Anywhere over setting up a VPN, and some users may utilize multiple Exchange clients, depending upon their location and circumstances.

The key takeaway is that numerous factors merit consideration and should be weighed carefully when evaluating and planning your organization's Exchange client needs, some of which are detailed later in the chapter. Keep in mind that this list is not all-inclusive or in any sequential order, because each organization is different:

- ▶ Mobility and offline capability
- ▶ Network connectivity and bandwidth
- ▶ Security inside and outside the office
- ▶ Preference and experience of the IT staff or consultant
- ▶ End-user training and ongoing support
- ▶ Data storage on the server and on the device
- ▶ Any recurring monthly or annual fees
- ▶ Regulatory requirements or considerations
- ▶ Managing patching and updates on various systems
- ▶ Licensing and hardware costs

It can be overwhelming with all the options available, and if you do not understand some important limitations, you might find yourself halfway down the deployment path, only to find a hidden limitation that won't allow you to achieve the desired result. Table 9.1 details some of the key bandwidth and connectivity considerations for Exchange 2007 clients.

TABLE 9.1   Exchange Client Bandwidth and Connectivity Considerations

Exchange Client— Client Mode	Bandwidth Required	Offline Access to Mailbox	Works on Exchange LAN	Works Remotely
Outlook 2007—Cached Exchange Mode (default)	Uses least bandwidth	Yes	Yes	Yes, via VPN
Outlook 2007—Cached Exchange Mode with Outlook Anywhere	Uses 19% more than cached mode	Yes	No	Yes, does not require VPN
Outlook 2007—Online Mode	Uses 108% more than cached mode	No	Yes, via LAN	Yes, via VPN
Outlook Web Access 2007	Uses 365% more than cached mode	No	Yes, via web browser	Yes, via web browser
Mobile Devices via Exchange Active Sync	Depends on amount of information being cached	Yes	Yes, for devices with Wi-Fi	Yes, via cellular network or Wi-Fi

For more information regarding calculating client network traffic on Exchange 2007, check out the Microsoft TechNet article, "Outlook Anywhere Scalability with Outlook 2007, Outlook 2003, and Exchange 2007" (http://technet.microsoft.com/en-us/ library/cc540453(EXCHG.80).aspx).

Outlook 2007

Part of the Microsoft Office System, Microsoft Outlook (see Figure 9.1) is the most widely used Exchange client in small- and medium-sized networks. It provides personal and shared access to e-mail, calendars, contacts, tasks, RSS feeds, and public folders. Outlook 2007 can even act as an offline client for Windows SharePoint Services (WSS) content, including custom lists, document and photo libraries, and other types of SharePoint data.

What's New in Outlook 2007

Outlook 2007 received some sizeable usability improvements over the 2003 version. E-mail improvements include attachment preview inside the e-mail, color categories, the ability to delay message delivery, different internal and external Out-of-Office messages, Out-of-Office scheduling, and multiple signatures. E-mail can now be flagged as a task, and auto-account setup and RSS feed reader features have also been added.

The calendar has been improved to allow overlaying multiple calendars, calendar snap-shots, task integration showing tasks on the calendar under the day they are due, and calendar publishing.

Other improvements in Outlook 2007 include electronic business cards in the Contacts section, SMS, InfoPath and OneNote integration; two-way synchronization with Windows SharePoint Services (WSS) and search has been improved to search as you type and to save search folders.

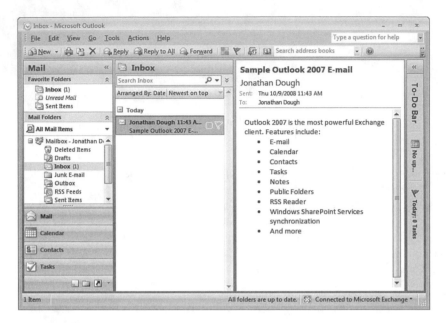

FIGURE 9.1   The main page of Outlook 2007 has a similar look and feel to Outlook 2003, but the subpages carry the new Outlook 2007 Ribbon interface.

Installing Outlook 2007

Unlike previous versions of Small Business Server, there is no desktop e-mail client software included in SBS 2008. This means that the Outlook 2007 program is not on the SBS 2008 DVD—a copy of Outlook must be purchased separately for each user. The reason for this change has nothing to do with SBS 2008 and everything to do with Exchange 2007. Exchange 2007 doesn't provide an Outlook 2007 Client Access License (CAL) with the Exchange 2007 CAL.

Microsoft Outlook 2007 can be purchased as either a stand-alone product or in a Microsoft Office bundle. It is available through Microsoft Volume Licensing (http://www.microsoft. com/licensing/default.mspx), retail channels, or from an OEM that pre-installs Office on a new PC when it's being built.

> **NOTE**
>
> Many Original Equipment Manufacturers (OEMs) sell computers with 60-day trials of Microsoft Office, which can later be converted to a "full" version. However, Microsoft Outlook 2007 comes bundled in all versions of Microsoft Office 2007 *except* for the Home and Student version. To compare Office versions and to determine which suite is best for you, visit the Microsoft Office Online web site for a side-by-side comparison grid (http://office.microsoft.com/en-us/products/FX101635841033.aspx).

Depending upon the number of workstations on the network, it may be faster to deploy Microsoft Office 2007 via Group Policy. For detailed instructions on using Group Policy to deploy Office 2007, visit the Microsoft TechNet web site (http://technet.microsoft.com/en-us/library/cc179214.aspx).

> **NOTE**
>
> Only Volume Licensing versions of Microsoft Office can be installed via Group Policy. OEM and Retail versions of Office 2007 do not support deployment via Group Policy.

Configuring Outlook 2007

Thanks to the new configuration features in Outlook 2007 and Exchange 2007, setting up e-mail for clients has never been easier. Once the computer has been joined to the domain and Outlook has been installed on the workstation, setting up the connection to the Exchange server is straightforward. There are two methods for Outlook configuration: automatic and manual.

Automatically Configuring Outlook 2007 Settings

Automatic Configuration of Outlook 2007 takes only a few moments, thus easing the administrative burden of setting up e-mail on workstations for new employees. To use Automatic Configuration, follow these steps:

> **NOTE**
>
> If the workstation is not on the same LAN as the SBS server, follow the manual configuration instructions.

1. Make sure Outlook is installed on the workstation and the PC is connected to the LAN; then start Microsoft Outlook. The Outlook 2007 Startup wizard will launch. Click Next.

2. On the E-mail Accounts screen, you are asked if you would like to configure an e-mail account. Check Yes and click Next.

3. The Auto Account Setup wizard detects the connection to the Exchange server, and then auto-fills the Your Name field (which is the display name of the user currently logged into the workstation, and cannot be changed) and enters the internal domain e-mail address of that user (see Figure 9.2); for example, Jonathan Dough and jon.dough@smallbizco.local. Verify that this information is correct, and click Next.

> **NOTE**
>
> If the Auto Account Setup wizard fails at Step 4, follow the Manually Configuring Outlook 2007 Settings instructions. You can also refer to "Troubleshooting Auto Account Setup" later in this chapter.

4. If the wizard completes successfully, the message "Your e-mail account is successfully configured to use Microsoft Exchange" is displayed. Click Finish.

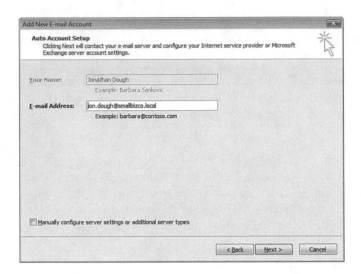

FIGURE 9.2   The Outlook 2007 Auto Account Setup wizard tries to detect the default Exchange server information based on the current user logged into the workstation. Alternately, there is a manual configuration option.

Manually Configuring Outlook 2007 Settings

If Outlook cannot establish a connection to the SBS server at the time the Auto Account Setup wizard is run, such as if the workstation is being configured remotely and no VPN is available, the wizard fails. The wizard instead prompts for the display name, e-mail address, and password of the user, but will still fail again if the Exchange server is not available.

To manually configure Outlook 2007, follow these steps:

1. Make sure Outlook is installed on the workstation; then start Microsoft Outlook.

2. The Outlook 2007 Startup wizard will launch. Click Next.

3. On the E-mail Accounts screen, you are asked if you would like to configure an e-mail account. Check Yes and click Next.

4. When the Auto Account Setup wizard fails to detect the connection to the Exchange server, click Manually Configure Server Settings or Additional Server Types (refer to Figure 9.2) and click Next.

5. On the Choose E-mail Service screen, choose Microsoft Exchange and click Next.

6. Enter the server name (for example, sbserver.smallbizco.local) and the user name (for example, jondough), as shown in Figure 9.3. Check the Use Cached Exchange Mode box, click Next, and then click Finish.

After manual configuration is complete, the wizard will try to open Outlook and connect to the SBS server, but it will fail and Outlook will close. This is normal behavior because the server isn't available to complete the setup process. However, once the connection between the workstation and the SBS server is established, Outlook will finish setup and begin to function normally.

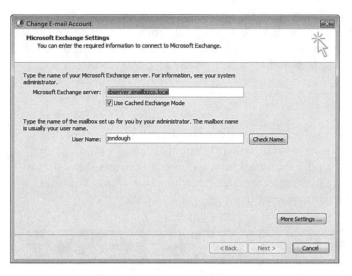

FIGURE 9.3   Users can manually configure Outlook 2007 by entering the server name and user name into the E-mail Account configuration screen.

Cached Exchange Mode

Cached Exchange Mode in Outlook provides access to employee mailbox information and public folders normally stored in Exchange or on SharePoint, even in the event of a network outage or if the Exchange server is unavailable. This is accomplished by storing a copy of the user's data from the Exchange server onto the local user's machine in an Offline Folder (OST) file. A copy of the address book is also stored locally as an Offline Address Book (OAB) file. The client's mailbox still resides on the Exchange server, but most of the traffic takes place between Outlook and the OST file, even when network conditions are normal.

Cached Exchange Mode is enabled by default in Outlook 2007 and Outlook 2003, but not when upgrading from older versions of Outlook. When Cached Exchange Mode is enabled, it automatically synchronizes the local OST file with the Exchange server. If you watch the lower-right corner of the Outlook status bar carefully, you can see it flash a message when synchronization occurs, followed by a message that says "All folders are up to date." The Offline Address Book file synchronization also happens automatically, but only once every 24 hours.

NOTE

By default, users have the ability to manually initiate synchronization of the OST file by clicking the Send/Receive button in Outlook, though it is rarely necessary. In fact, as the network administrator, you might want to disable manual and scheduled synchronization to minimize unnecessary traffic on the Exchange server, unless the user is also using POP3, IMAP, or HTML-based webmail accounts such as Hotmail, Gmail, or Yahoo!.

6

Likewise, a manual synchronization of the OAB file can be initiated by clicking on Tools, Send/Receive, and Download Address Book. For complete and detailed information on administering the OAB file in Outlook 2003 and 2007, including answers to over 30 common OAB questions, check out Microsoft KB article 841273 (http://support. microsoft.com/kb/841273).

Storing the OST and OAB files on the local machine does increase the amount of disk space Outlook consumes. But there are several trade-off benefits such as a reduction in network traffic and reduced load on the Exchange server. It also gives users the ability to continue to access their data if the Exchange server goes offline. This data is available, even if they disconnect from the network intentionally.

Best Practice—Keep OST Files Under 2GB and 5,000 Items for Best Performance with Cached Exchange Mode

Caching mailboxes that are either larger than 2GB in size or that contain more than 5,000 items in any one of the core folders (Calendar, Contacts, Inbox, or Sent Items) can negatively affect the performance of Outlook 2007 in Cached Exchange Mode on the workstation. Table 9.2 shows Microsoft's hardware recommendations for best Cached Exchange Mode performance.

TABLE 9.2   Memory and Disk Recommendations for Outlook 2007 Cached Exchange Mode Clients

Mailbox Size	Memory Size	Hard Disk Speed
1GB	1GB	5,400 RPM
2GB	1–2GB	7,200 RPM

To keep mailboxes under the 2GB recommended limit, users have the following options:

▶ Delete old e-mail that is no longer needed.

▶ Archive old e-mail to a local or networked PST file by opening Outlook and clicking on File, click Archive, and then follow the wizard.

▶ Add a custom Cached Exchange Mode filter to omit a folder from being cached on the local machine.

Custom Cached Exchange Mode Filters
Sometimes deleting old e-mail isn't an option, whether for corporate, legal, or employee compliance reasons. And archiving to PST does shrink the footprint in Exchange and Outlook, but that e-mail is no longer searchable, PST files are less secure than OST files, and remotely stored PST files that are left open all the time can become corrupt.

Another option is creating a "pseudo-archive" folder that isn't cached to the local OST folder. This is a handy way to keep the Outlook footprint small on the client, keep the data secure on the Exchange server, and still allow access to the old content by simply changing to Online mode and restarting Outlook.

Why would you need to do this? Think of an attorney who gets a large volume of e-mail with attachments on multiple cases. A case may contain Word documents, scans of faxes, photographs, and perhaps even voicemails sent by her VOIP phone system. She needs to be able to access e-mail regarding closed cases at a future date, but she doesn't want all of those old e-mails and attachments to push her laptop over the 2GB performance limit on their OST file.

Follow these steps to create an Outlook folder that is not cached locally:

1. Open Outlook 2007 and create a new subfolder into which users will manually drag the items they do not want cached locally; then drag the items into that folder you want removed from the local cache. (For example, create a folder named "Cases 2005–2007" and drag the old cases into it.)

2. Right-click the newly created folder; then left-click Properties.

3. In the Outlook Folder Properties window, click the Synchronization tab; then click the Filter button.

4. In the Filter window, click the More Choices tab.

5. Although there is no actual button to omit this folder from synchronization to the locally cached file, we can set a filter rule that will logically exclude all items in this folder. At the bottom of the More Choices tab, set "Size (kilobytes) less than 0." This will effectively filter out every item in this folder (because all items are inherently greater than 0 bytes).

6. Click OK to close the Filter window.

7. Back on the Folder Properties window, click the General tab; then click Clear Offline Items, and click OK.

This process allows the data in the archive folder to reside on the Exchange server and therefore to be accessed by Outlook Web Access 2007. However, the contents will only be available to Outlook when running in Online mode. The folder contents will also be available on a Windows Mobile device that has cached that folder.

Remember: Removing an item or folder from the Outlook OST cache doesn't change the size of the user's mailbox in the Exchange store; it only keeps the items from being stored on the local workstation.

NOTE

For more details on mailbox storage calculations, capacity planning, logs, and performance considerations, check out the Microsoft TechNet article "Mailbox Server Storage Design" (http://technet.microsoft.com/en-us/library/bb738147.aspx). Also, to configure hard limits for PST and OST files in Outlook 2007 and Outlook 2003 via the registry, see KB article 832925 (http://support.microsoft.com/kb/832925).

Laptop users who dock and undock their workstation, or often move between various wireless access points, find Cached Exchange Mode especially beneficial. While disconnected from the network, they can compose e-mail, look up contacts, and make schedule changes with no Internet or LAN access whatsoever. When they eventually reconnect to the network, the folders and contents can be synchronized with the Exchange server. Newly composed e-mail and calendar updates on the laptop are sent up to the Exchange server, and new messages, schedule changes, and other mailbox updates are brought down to the OST file on the local machine.

Configure Cached Exchange Mode in Outlook 2007 Via Group Policy

System administrators can control the settings of Cached Exchange Mode in Outlook 2007 via Group Policy using the Outlk12.adm. This template is a free download and is available as part of the Microsoft Office 2007 Resource Kit. For information on using Office policy templates with Group Policy and a download link, see KB article 924617 (http://support.microsoft.com/kb/924617). For instructions specific to configuring Cached Exchange Mode via Group Policy, see the detailed TechNet article in the Outlook 2007 deployment section (http://technet.microsoft.com/en-us/library/cc179175.aspx).

Cached Exchange Mode Settings

Cached Exchange Mode is enabled by default for Exchange accounts and has four settings. These modes can be adjusted by opening Outlook and then clicking the File menu and Cached Exchange Mode. Turning Cached Exchange Mode on or off completely requires a restart of Outlook, but users can switch between the four settings without needing to restart Outlook (see Figure 9.4).

The four Cached Exchange Mode settings are as follows:

▶ **Download Full Items**—Downloads header, body, and attachments at the same time. This setting works best when connected on a LAN or across a high-speed Internet connection.

▶ **Download Header and then Full Items**—Outlook downloads the headers first, and then starts to download the entire e-mail bodies and attachments in order. Clicking on a specific e-mail causes that message and any attachments to download immediately. This setting works best with lower bandwidth connections when users need to quickly check e-mail. For example, if a user is on a laptop at a Wi-Fi spot at an airport, they can use this setting to quickly grab all the new e-mail headers, and then click the attachment they've been waiting for (before they have to board their flight).

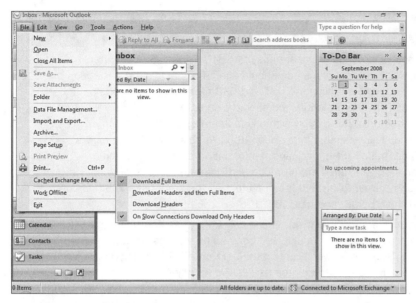

FIGURE 9.4   Users can easily switch between different Cached Exchange Modes without needing to restart Outlook 2007.

▶ **Download Headers**—Only downloads the headers, not the e-mail body. This setting works best in metered bandwidth conditions, when a user needs to keep their bandwidth usage to a minimum, such as when traveling abroad or on certain wireless data plans.

▶ **On Slow Connections Download Only Headers**—This setting can be enabled independent of the other three modes. This setting is useful for letting Outlook automatically detect a slow network connection, such as a dial-up connection, and then down-shift to only download the headers, preventing Outlook from saturating all available bandwidth across a slow connection, and the OAB will not be downloaded in this mode. A slow connection speed is defined as 128 KB or lower.

To disable Cached Exchange Mode in Outlook, click Tools, Account Settings, highlight the Exchange account and click Change, uncheck the Use Cached Exchange Mode box, click Next, click Finish, and restart Outlook. Cached Exchange Mode can be also disabled on the Exchange server by the network administrator via Group Policy.

NOTE

Some features such as new e-mail notification, un-cached public folder access, free/busy lookup, and delegate support work with Outlook in Cached Exchange Mode, but only when Outlook has a live network connection to the SBS server. If the network connection drops, these features cease to function until network connectivity is reestablished. A detailed explanation of the various synchronization modes and folder states available in Outlook is located in the "Troubleshooting Cached Exchange Mode" section found later in this chapter.

Best Practice—Computers Using Cached Exchange Mode Should Use NTFS Partitions or Bitlocker

Laptops and computers in public areas are easy targets for theft. So computers running Outlook in Cached Exchange Mode should use NTFS file system encryption or Bitlocker on the hard drive containing the OST and OAB files due to the potential for theft or misuse of sensitive information. You should also research the possible need for encryption on those drives to comply with any federal regulations if company files or e-mail include Personally Identifiable Information (PII) like social security numbers, Protected Health Information (PHI), or financial information such as credit card numbers. Bitlocker is only included in Enterprise and Ultimate editions of Windows Vista and in Windows Server 2008, but it can protect all the hard disks in a computer, or partitions larger than 1.5GB, and uses AES 128- or 256-bit encryption.

Encryption may seem like overkill and something only Enterprise corporations need to worry about, but a security solution is only as strong as its weakest link. Strong firewalls protecting your SBS server won't protect the data on a FAT32 partition in your salesman's laptop—especially if that laptop gets left at a coffee shop or stolen in an airport terminal. For more information on securing workstations and servers, see the TechNet Bitlocker site (http://technet.microsoft.com/en-us/windows/aa905065.aspx) and the TechNet Vista Security Guide web site (http://technet.microsoft.com/en-us/library/bb629420.aspx).

Outlook Anywhere

Outlook Anywhere (formerly called RPC over HTTP or Outlook via the Internet) enables users outside the network firewall to use Outlook 2007 or Outlook 2003 to remotely access their mailbox and public folders on the SBS 2008 as easily as users inside the corporate network.

Benefits of Outlook Anywhere include the following:

▶ Access the Exchange server remotely without the need for a Virtual Private Network (VPN).

▶ Uses port 443, so you don't need to open additional ports in the firewall.

▶ Uses the same SSL certificate for the other sites on the SBS 2008 server.

▶ Uses the same namespace as Outlook Web Access and Exchange ActiveSync, which eases deployment and support issues.

▶ Huge hardware and administrative cost savings over dial-up access.

▶ Supports Cached Exchange Mode (discussed earlier in this chapter), which improves performance and end-user experience—especially over slow Internet connections.

How Outlook Anywhere Works

Just like in previous version of SBS, instead of opening RPC ports on the server and exposing them to the Internet, Outlook Anywhere uses the Windows RPC over HTTP Proxy component to access the Exchange information from the Internet. This technology wraps remote procedure calls (RPCs) with an HTTP layer and sends them through port 443. Thus, traffic is allowed to traverse network firewalls without requiring RPC ports to be opened.

Configuring Outlook Anywhere

When users log into the Remote Web Workplace site, there is a link on the main page entitled "How Do I Use Outlook Anywhere?" This link launches a help page with the step-by-step instructions and detailed information about Outlook Anywhere.

To print out a copy of these instructions from inside the LAN, visit https://sites/remote/outlook.aspx. Or to access them from the WAN, visit https://remote.domain.com/remote/outlook.aspx. Both sites require valid RWW credentials to log in.

The phases for configuring Outlook Anywhere are as follows:

▶ Meet prerequisites for using Outlook Anywhere.

▶ Confirm that the SSL certificate is trusted on the client machine.

▶ Configure Outlook Anywhere on the workstation.

Meet Prerequisites for Using Outlook Anywhere

The following prerequisites must be met before attempting to configure Outlook Anywhere:

▶ **Client Operating System**—Windows XP SP1 with hotfix 331320, Windows XP SP2, Windows XP SP3, or Windows Vista.

▶ **Outlook 2003 or 2007**—The Outlook software must already be installed on the client machine.

▶ **The SBS 2008 server connected to the Internet**—You must have already purchased a domain name (for example, smallbizco.net), the SBS server must have either a self-issued or third-party certificate installed, and port 443 on your firewall should be forwarded to the internal IP address of your SBS server. These processes are accomplished by running the Connect to the Internet and the Setup Your Internet Address wizards on the Home tab in the Windows SBS Console.

▶ **A Record**—If you are manually controlling your own DNS records for your domain name and haven't already set up an "A" record, contact the company that controls your public DNS records (typically the company you purchased your domain name from) and have them set up an A record for you. This is not the same thing as an MX record (those are for e-mail). The A record should be formatted as "remote.domain.com" and point to the public IP address of your router. So, for example, if your domain is smallbizco.net, and your router's public IP address is

6

217.142.22.7, you would need to create your A record for remote.smallbizco.net and point it to 217.142.22.7. Important: In this example, remote.smallbizco.net is your Fully Qualified Domain Name (FQDN) for your SBS server.

Confirm That the SSL Certificate Is Trusted on the Client Machine

Many third-party certificates you purchase for your SBS server will be automatically trusted by client web browsers. However, if your certificate is not trusted by default, or if you are using a self-issued SSL certificate, users accessing your FQDN via a web browser will receive an error, as shown in Figure 9.5, unless they've previously trusted the certificate on their local machine.

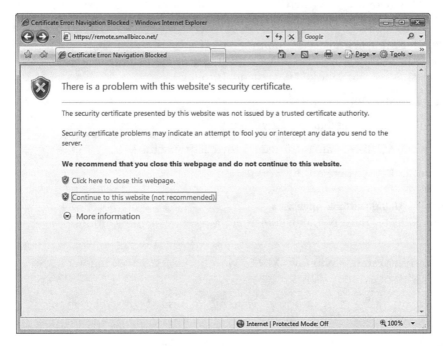

FIGURE 9.5   Internet Explorer 7 does not trust self-issued certificates, and prompts users in green letters to close the browser window.

SBS 2008 has a new feature that makes the installation of security certificates much easier. Computers that are connected to the network can browse to \\servername\public\downloads and download the Install Certificate Package.zip. This zip file contains the SSL certificate and the InstallCertificates.exe application. After extracting and running this application, the user is prompted to install the certificate on their computer or on a mobile device. Remote computers that do not have access to the LAN might have to manually install the SSL certificate.

To manually trust a self-issued certificate on a Vista workstation running Internet Explorer 7, take the following steps:

1. Right-click the Internet Explorer icon, and choose Run as Administrator. If User Account Control is enabled and the An Unidentified Program Wants to Access Your Computer prompt appears, click Allow.

2. Enter the FQDN of your SBS server, and hit Enter (for example, https://remote.smallbizco.net).

3. When prompted with the certificate warning (see Figure 9.5), click Continue to This Web Site (Not Recommended). If you do not receive this warning, the certificate is already trusted on this machine.

4. At the top of the screen, click the red Certificate Error icon, and choose View Certificates.

5. On the Certificate Properties page, click the Install Certificate button on the General tab.

6. When the Certificate Import Wizard begins, click the Next button.

7. On the Certificate Store page, the radio button for Automatically Select the Certificate Store Based on the Type of Certificate is already checked. Instead, click Place All Certificates in the Following Store and click the Browse button.

8. On the Select Certificate Store page, click the Show Physical Stores checkbox, expand Trusted Root Certification Authorities, click Local Computer, and click OK.

9. Back on the Certificate Store page, the Certificate store listed should be Trusted Root Certification Authorities\Local Computer (see Figure 9.6). Click Next, Finish, OK, and OK.

FIGURE 9.6   Instead of allowing automatic placement of the self-issued SSL certificate, manually place it in the local computer store after launching Internet Explorer using Run as Administrator.

10. Close IE7, re-open it normally, browse to the FQDN, and you should no longer get the certificate error.

If you are still getting a certificate error, you can also check the Certificates MMC snap-in:

1. On the Vista workstation, click Start; in the Search box, type MMC and click OK. (If UAC prompts you, click OK.) This will open the MMC console.

2. Next, add the Certificates snap-in. In the Console screen, click File, Add/Remove Snap-in..., click Certificates on the Available snap-ins pane, click Add, click the Computer Account radio button, click Next, click Finish, and click OK.

3. Finally, in the Console Root on the left, expand Certificates (Local Computer), Trusted Root Certification Authority, and Certificates. Scroll down in the center pane, and you should see the installed SSL certificate. If you see more than one SSL certificate bearing your FDQN, you can delete them from here and follow Steps 1–9 again.

Configure Outlook Anywhere on the Workstation

Follow these steps to configure Outlook Anywhere and a new Outlook profile:

> **NOTE**
>
> If you have an Outlook profile set up on a workstation that is already connected to the server on the LAN, and you just want to add Outlook Anywhere (for example, if this is a laptop that you want to take on the road), you can skip several steps in the following list. Just open Outlook, click Tools, Account Settings, highlight the Exchange account you want to modify, click Change, click the More Settings button, and then skip to Step 9 in the following list.

1. Click Start, click Control Panel, click Classic View, double-click the Mail icon, and then click the Show Profiles button.

2. To create a new profile, click Add, type a profile name (for example, OutlookAnywhere), and click OK.

3. When the Auto Account Setup wizard launches, enter the display name (for example, Jonathan Dough), enter the e-mail address (for example, jon.dough@small-bizco.net), type the password twice, and click Next.

4. When the Connect to domainname.com box comes up, type the username in the format of domain\username, type the password, and click OK. (If the wizard fails, go to Step 6.)

5. Once the Auto Account Setup wizard completes successfully, it will fill in your Exchange server information and configure Outlook Anywhere for you. Click Finish.

6. The wizard will try to locate the server settings using an encrypted connection. If that fails, it will try again with an unencrypted connection. If it fails again, the wizard will check the Manually Configure Server Settings box. Click Next.

7. On the Choose E-mail Service screen, click the Microsoft Exchange radio button; then click Next.

8. Enter the local name of the SBS server (for example, sbserver.smallbizco.local), check Use Cached Exchange Mode, type the user name (for example, jondough), and click More Settings. (Do not click the Check Name button.)

9. Click the Connection tab on the Outlook Anywhere section, check the Connect to Microsoft Exchange Using HTTP checkbox, and click the Exchange Proxy Settings button (see Figure 9.7).

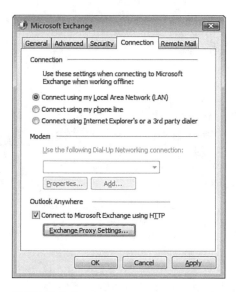

FIGURE 9.7   Outlook Anywhere functionality can be added to computers that already have Outlook installed and configured for LAN or VPN use.

10. On the Microsoft Exchange Proxy Settings screen, enter the necessary information, as shown in Figure 9.8.

FIGURE 9.8   The connection URL used for Cached Exchange Mode is the same one used for Remote Web Workplace. Don't forget to add "msstd:" in front of the proxy server URL.

11. Close the remaining windows (by clicking OK, OK, Next, and Finish).

12. Open Outlook 2007. If prompted, choose your new Outlook Profile and click OK. Enter your user name in the format domain\username (for example, smallbizco\jon-dough) and password; then click OK.

Outlook should now connect to the Exchange server and begin synchronizing to the local OST file.

Outlook Web Access 2007

Outlook Web Access (OWA) 2007 is a web-based Exchange client that enables users to access e-mail, calendar, contacts, tasks, SharePoint documents, and public folders using only a web browser. As stated previously in this chapter, Small Business Server 2008 no longer comes with Microsoft Office Outlook, so Outlook Web Access is the only e-mail client that comes in the box with SBS 2008.

Both OWA and Outlook are intentionally similar in function and design to minimize the learning curve for end users. However, there are important feature differences between Outlook and OWA that must be taken into consideration before deciding which tool to use as the primary Exchange client. For example, Outlook can cache information locally and function offline, which is ideal for laptop users who often frequently travel and have extended periods of time without Internet access. However, OWA requires a live network or Internet connection to the Exchange server. Another consideration is that Outlook requires installation on the client workstation and initial configuration, whereas OWA is active and configured as soon as the user account is created.

Clients may require a combination of Outlook and OWA to fit their business needs. OWA is an excellent choice for high- or low-bandwidth environments and allows multiple users access to their Exchange data without storing profiles on the local machine. But it's not as robust as Outlook and is unavailable when there is no network connectivity. So, the rule of thumb is to use Outlook 2007 for the knowledge worker who spends all day accessing Exchange data, and use OWA for the occasional user and shared computer user at the office, or for the knowledge worker who wants to check her e-mail and schedule from home.

Improvements in Outlook Web Access 2007

Outlook Web Access has been around for a while and was available in previous versions of SBS. The latest version of OWA, running on Exchange Server 2007 with Service Pack 1, incorporates numerous usability improvements over previous versions:

▶ Recover deleted items

▶ Calendar month view

▶ Add and edit personal distribution lists

▶ Ability to utilize custom forms and UI buttons

▶ Rules wizard

▶ Access to files inside the Companyweb SharePoint site

▶ Advanced Out-of-Office features

▶ Native ability to change network password through OWA

▶ Employees can wipe a lost Windows Mobile device through OWA

▶ Access to files on UNC shares

Using Outlook Web Access 2007

Outlook Web Access is installed by default in SBS 2008, and because it shared the same name space as Remote Web Workplace, it doesn't require a separate SSL certificate.

OWA can be accessed via several methods, as follows:

▶ **On the LAN**—https://sites/owa.

▶ **From the Internet**—https://remote.domain.com/owa.

▶ **Remote Web Workplace**—https://remote.domain.com.

▶ **Desktop Links Gadget**—Click the Check E-Mail link.

> **NOTE**
>
> When a Vista workstation is joined to the SBS 2008 domain using the Connect Wizard, the Desktop Links Gadget containing the OWA link is automatically imported into the gallery on the workstation. However, this gadget is not automatically installed on the sidebar. To manually add the gadget to the sidebar, click the + sign at the top of the Vista sidebar to open the gadget gallery and then double-click the Windows Small Business Sever Desktop Links gadget.

After bringing up the OWA login screen, users must enter their username in the domain\username format (for example, smallbizco\jondough), type their password, and pick which version of Outlook Web Access they want to use. There are three versions of OWA 2007, as follows:

▶ Outlook Web Access Light 2007

▶ Outlook Web Access Premium 2007

▶ Outlook Web Access Premium 2007 with S/MIME

Outlook Web Access Light 2007

Outlook Web Access Light is a simplified version of the OWA client, as you might expect from the name. The way to access the OWA Light version is to check the Use Outlook Web Access Light checkbox on the OWA page, or to access it with a web browser other than Internet Explorer.

The purpose for this lightweight Exchange client is to perform quickly and consistently in low-bandwidth or high-security scenarios and across a variety of web browsers (see Figure 9.9).

Because OWA Light runs in a single web browser window, it loads faster than OWA Premium. It's also useful in Mac and Unix environments, and it runs in IE, Firefox, Safari, Opera, Chrome, and other browsers.

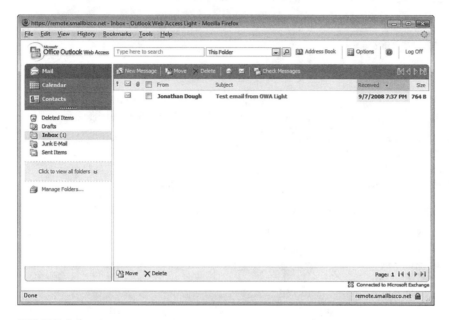

FIGURE 9.9   Outlook Web Access Light 2007 (shown in Mozilla Firefox) is a fast lightweight Exchange client that works on nearly any web browser.

However, OWA Light can't pop-up additional windows or dialog boxes, so it lacks features some users may consider a necessity, including tasks, spell checking, and the ability to mark messages as read or unread, and there is no new mail notification or reminders. To check for new mail, the user must manually refresh the browser window, typically by pressing F5 or by clicking on the Inbox link.

Outlook Web Access Premium 2007

OWA Premium 2007 is very powerful and has been greatly enhanced over previous versions. The feature set in Premium is much closer to what users are accustomed to in Outlook 2007, and the layout is nearly identical (see Figure 9.10). If users log into OWA and do not check the OWA Light option on the sign-in page, they will automatically be logged in with OWA Premium (unless they're using a browser other than Internet Explorer).

Some of the core improvements over previous versions include the following:

▶ Integrated reminders and new mail notifications

▶ Native password changes through OWA

▶ The ability to administer Windows Mobile devices

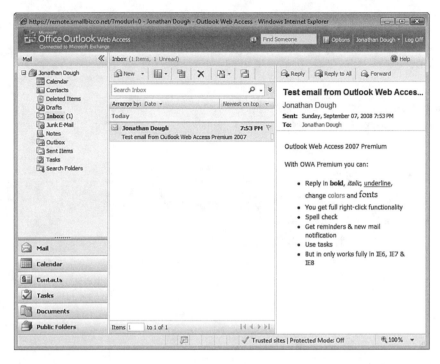

FIGURE 9.10   Outlook Web Access Premium 2007 (shown in Internet Explorer 7) is so similar to the full Outlook 2007 client, some people may not notice the difference at first glance.

Unfortunately, the ability to customize the OWA dictionary is still not an available feature from Microsoft, but there are third-party plug-ins that can add spell-check and other features to OWA.

Outlook Web Access Premium 2007 with S/MIME

S/MIME support for OWA was added in OWA 2003, and that functionality continues on with OWA 2007. S/MIME allows OWA to send and receive signed or encrypted e-mail. Signed messages offer proof of the authenticity of the sender, and encrypted messages can only be opened and read by the recipient. Not only are encrypted e-mails secure when in transit, they're also unreadable to administrators (who can traditionally give themselves permission to any mailbox) or other network users that have been given delegate rights.

Downloading and installing the S/MIME control on the user's workstation turns OWA Premium into OWA Premium with S/MIME. Once installed, the S/MIME control can be viewed or removed from the Add/Remove Programs Wizard in the Control Panel of Windows listed as "Microsoft Outlook Web Access S/MIME (2007)."

To install OWA Premium 2007 with S/MIME, perform the following steps:

1. Log in to OWA Premium from the user's workstation as normal.
2. Click Options at the top of the main page.
3. Click E-Mail Security on the Options page.

4. Click the Download the Outlook Web Access 2007 S/MIME Control link. The necessary ActiveX control, called the S/MIME control, can be downloaded and installed
   from the Options page in OWA Premium (see Figure 9.11).

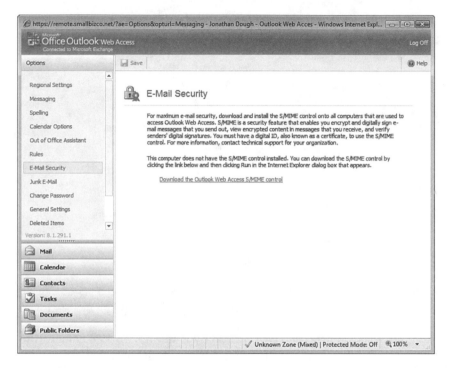

FIGURE 9.11   Outlook Web Access Premium 2007 with S/MIME is installed by downloading
and running the S/MIME control on the user's workstation.

5. When prompted to download the OWASMIME.MSI file, choose Run, and when the
   IE security warning pops up, choose Run again, accept the UAC prompt, and you're
   done.

After installing the S/MIME control, the E-Mail Security is changed to include three
options, as follows:

▶ Encrypt contents and attachments of all outgoing messages.

▶ Add a digital signature to all outgoing messages.

▶ Reinstall the Outlook Web Access S/MIME control.

By default, the first two options are unchecked. Do not check these options until you have
successfully installed an e-mail certificate on your workstation.

E-Mail Certificates in OWA and Outlook 2007

When most people think of certificates and e-mail, they typically remember the SSL certificate that clients have to install to get Outlook Anywhere or OWA to access remote.domain.com without an error. But e-mail certificates are different, and unique to each user. An e-mail certificate verifies you, as an individual, rather than a company or a server. In fact, at one time or another, you've probably already gotten an e-mail and noticed a little ribbon next to the person's name. These e-mail certificates can be attached to more than one e-mail address, but should only be used by one person. For example, you can set up your certificate to authenticate your home e-mail address and your business e-mail address, because you are the same person.

An e-mail certificate, used in conjunction with the S/MIME feature in OWA or Outlook, lets you sign your own e-mail to prove it came from you (that little "ribbon" next to your name). Your individual e-mail certificate can also be used to allow people to send encrypted e-mail that only you can open (your clients and colleagues save that little ribbon onto your contact card in their copy of Outlook).

For clarification, Table 9.3 is a breakdown of what is needed on each end of an e-mail transmission that uses e-mail certificates.

TABLE 9.3   Requirements on Each End of an S/MIME E-Mail Transaction

If Jonathan Wants To:	Jonathan Requires:	Sara Requires:
Digitally sign an e-mail and send it to Sara.	S/MIME installed and an e-mail certificate containing his private key installed.	Nothing.
Send an encrypted e-mail to Sara.	S/MIME installed and a copy of Sara's public key.	S/MIME installed and Sara's private key.
Receive an encrypted e-mail sent from Sara to him.	S/MIME installed and a copy of Jonathan's private key installed.	S/MIME installed and a copy of Jonathan's public key.
Receive a digitally signed e-mail from Sara.	Nothing.	S/MIME installed and Sara's private key.

Each e-mail certificate contains two keys: a private key (that is never shared) and a public key (that is shared with everyone). If that doesn't make sense, think instead that a public key is a special padlock that only you can open (with your private key). You can post this public key on your web site, on public key servers, or even include it in your signature line in normal e-mail. You freely distribute your public key far and wide. Likewise, your friends or colleagues give you their public keys (that can only be opened with their private keys). Once each party has the public key of the other person, they can begin to send encrypted e-mail back and forth.

9

NOTE

Many companies on the Internet provide personal e-mail certificates. Two of the most popular are Comodo (http://www.comodo.com) and Thawte (http://www.thawte.com). If you are interested in testing e-mail certificates, you may want to try one of the free online certificates. However, be aware that the free certificates Comodo provides cannot export their private key, therefore, they cannot be installed on more than one PC or on a Windows mobile device because you can't open or sign new e-mail without that private key. Also, most free certificates are not approved for business use.

Remote File Access in OWA 2007

By far, one of the coolest and most useful new features in Outlook Web Access 2007 is the ability to access files on the Companyweb site and on network shares. This new feature is available via the "Documents" button in OWA 2007, but it is not turned on by default. The network administrator has to enable this feature.

Enabling Remote File Access in OWA 2007

To enable Remote File Access, take the following steps:

1. Log into the SBS 2008 server with administrator credentials.

2. Click Start, All Programs, Microsoft Exchange Server 2007, Exchange Management Console.

3. Once you accept the UAC warning and the Exchange Management Console loads, expand Server Configuration and click Client Access.

4. On the Outlook Web Access tab at the bottom of the screen, right-click OWA (SBS Web Applications) and left-click Properties.

5. On the OWA (SBS Web Applications) Properties page, click the Allow button in the Allow list.

6. Type the name of the item you want to expose to the OWA Remote File Access; then click Add. (For example, SBS SharePoint Site: companyweb or NTFS network share: \\sbserver\contracts.)

7. Click OK twice; then close the Microsoft Exchange Server console.

To test your settings, log into OWA 2007 as a user with permissions to the items you just added to the Allow list and click the Documents button.

Best Practice—Train Users with the Microsoft OWA Training Videos

Outlook Web Access 2007 has been improved in so many ways, it is easy to overlook some of the key feature improvements. And once users have been trained on OWA, they may forget how to use some features over time. Fortunately, Microsoft has put together some excellent web-based training videos that can be used to bring IT pros or end users up to speed quickly. These videos are well worth the time investment for anyone who will use OWA 2007 on a regular basis. The videos can be viewed online at the following URL: http://www.microsoft.com/exchange/code/OWA/index.html.

ActiveSync

The market for mobile devices is steadily growing worldwide, and although capabilities and features vary widely by device, form factor, manufacturer, and country, most of these devices store a user's calendar and contacts. Many of the new phones on the market also store e-mail and tasks and can synchronize all that information with a central server. These devices are commonly referred to as smart phones.

All smart phones utilize some type of synchronization technology to handle the legwork of adding, deleting, updating, and archiving information. The necessary data is then transmitted and synchronized via a cellular network, a Wi-Fi connection, Bluetooth, or via a cradle or USB cable.

Different device and mobile operating system manufacturers use different brands of synchronization technology. Palm OS devices use Hotsync; Blackberry devices use Blackberry for Exchange or Blackberry Enterprise Server (BES). Windows Mobile Devices, iPhones, and a few Palms use ActiveSync.

Different Versions of ActiveSync

In an SBS 2008 network, there are three types of ActiveSync synchronization technologies available for Windows Mobile devices, as follows:

▶ **ActiveSync 4.5**—Installs on Windows XP or older workstations; synchronizes a connected mobile device through Outlook and XP using a USB cable, cradle, or Bluetooth. Can be downloaded from the following URL: http://www.microsoft.com/windowsmobile/en-us/help/synchronize/activesync45.mspx.

▶ **Windows Mobile Device Center 6.1 (WMDC)**—Installs on Windows Vista or newer workstations; synchronizes the mobile device through Outlook and Vista using a USB cable, cradle, or Bluetooth. Can be downloaded from the following URL: http://www.microsoft.com/windowsmobile/en-us/help/synchronize/device-center.mspx.

▶ **Exchange ActiveSync (EAS)**—Installs on the Exchange server, comes pre-installed on SBS 2008, synchronizes a wireless mobile device that is connected to a cellular or Wi-Fi network, and communicates directly with the Exchange server.

One of the key benefits of Exchange ActiveSync and synchronizing wirelessly is that users only need to plug in their device to recharge the batteries—no more cradling the device to get new e-mail or calendar updates. As long as they have some type of wireless signal (cellular signal with a data plan, Wi-Fi at a home, office, hotel, or airport) they can be in touch and synchronized with the office. Even if users don't have a cell signal, such as when traveling on an airplane, they can still compose e-mail offline and sync wirelessly when they land. Understandably, most mobile device users prefer Exchange ActiveSync over ActiveSync 4.5 or WMDC because of the ease of automatically updating their data from almost anywhere.

Exchange ActiveSync existed in SBS 2003, and has been enhanced in SBS 2008 to provide new and improved features, including the following:

▶ Support for rich HTML e-mail messages

▶ Follow-up flags

▶ Fast message retrieval option

▶ Meeting attendee information and global address list search

▶ Windows SharePoint Services and Windows file share document access

▶ Password reset and device password security policy settings

▶ Out-of-office support

▶ Self-service device management through Outlook Web Access

▶ Allowance for device synchronization by device ID

▶ Direct push

Windows Mobile Devices

Over the last several years, Windows Mobile devices have undergone a series of name changes. New phones and devices are released and retired every month, and it is common to have over 50 different Windows Mobile devices to choose from. Without a clear understanding of the features and capabilities of the various devices, it's easy for a user to purchase the wrong device. Fortunately, in spite of the name changes, the devices still fall into three categories, as shown in Table 9.4.

TABLE 9.4   The Three Categories of Mobile Devices

New Device Name	Old Device Name	Phone Capability	Touch Screen
Windows Mobile 6 Classic	Windows Mobile 5 Pocket PC	No	Yes
Windows Mobile 6 Standard	Windows Mobile 5 Smart Phone	Yes	No
Windows Mobile 6 Professional	Windows Mobile 5 Pocket PC Phone Editione	Yes	Yes

Windows Mobile Operating System Versions

Like the mobile device categories and names, the Windows Mobile Operating system itself has gone through many revisions. Older devices still work when cradled or connected via Bluetooth to Windows XP or Vista machines, but only Windows Mobile devices with an operating system number of Build 14847 or higher can talk directly to the Exchange 2007 server via ActiveSync. This is due to the security changes in the operating system. To check the OS build number of a Windows Mobile device, click Start, Settings, System, About. Table 9.5 contains a list of the last few Windows Mobile versions and their compatibility with Exchange Server 2007 and SBS 2008.

TABLE 9.5   Windows Mobile Compatibility with Exchange Server 2007 and SBS 2008

Windows Mobile Operating System	ActiveSync 4.5	Windows Mobile Device Center 6.1	Exchange 2007 ActiveSync
Windows Mobile 2003 and 2003 Second Edition	Yes	Yes	No
Windows Mobile 5 (before Build 14847)	Yes	Yes	No
Windows Mobile 5 with MSFP (14847 or higher)	Yes	Yes	Yes
Windows Mobile 6, 6.1, and higher	Yes	Yes	Yes

Configuring Windows Mobile to Use Exchange ActiveSync

The ease of reaching for the phone on your hip or in your purse and checking your e-mail has a broad appeal. Yet the configuration of the mobile device can be a lesson in frustration without proper planning and testing. And as any IT pro can attest, the first phone is always the hardest.

The key pieces to the mobility puzzle are the phone, the firewall, the URL, the credentials, and the certificate. If any one of those pieces is missing, you can't complete the puzzle. Once you've set up a few phones, however, it'll get to be as simple as opening your high school locker.

Best Practice—Download and Install the Windows Mobile 6.1 Device Emulator

The single most important tool any IT pro supporting Windows Mobile devices can possess is the Windows Mobile Device Emulator. This free stand-alone utility lets you run the Windows Mobile operating system on a Windows XP or Vista desktop operating system. It includes OS emulators of various screen sizes and configurations, so you can think of it as "Virtual Windows Mobile PC." Configurations can be paused and saved to disk just like a regular virtual PC.

Ideally, the emulator should be used to completely test the network configuration and certificate **before the client even purchases a Windows Mobile device**.

One of the reasons this tool is so valuable is that it's often difficult to determine if the synchronization failure is happening because of the certificate, because the cell phone company modified the OS on the phone, or even if the user's password has expired. Being able to completely set up and test a real Windows Mobile operating system in a matter of minutes, without spending a dime or even getting out of your chair, saves time, money, and frustration.

The Windows Mobile 6.1 emulator images are currently available in English, and can be downloaded at the following URL:

http://www.microsoft.com/downloads/details.aspx?FamilyId=3D6F581E-C093-4B15-AB0C-A2CE5BFFDB47&displaylang=en.

The older Windows Mobile 6.0 images are available in 24 languages, and can also be downloaded from the Microsoft Downloads site by searching for "Windows Mobile Device Emulator."

IMPORTANT: To connect your virtual Windows Mobile devices to the Internet, you'll also need a virtual network adapter. Microsoft used to offer this as a separate download, but now it's incorporated into Microsoft Virtual PC 2007 (another free download). Virtual PC 2007 can be downloaded here: http://www.microsoft.com/downloads/details.aspx?FamilyID=04d26402-3199-48a3-afa2-2dc0b40a73b6&DisplayLang=en.

For step-by-step instructions on configuring the emulator, refer to the Microsoft Exchange Team Blog post, "Installing and Running Windows Mobile Emulators" (http://msexchangeteam.com/archive/2007/09/17/447033.aspx).

To configure Windows Mobile 6.1 to synchronize with SBS 2008, complete the following steps:

1. **Get the certificate**—Obtain the SSL certificate for the SBS server. The easiest way is to navigate to \\server\public\downloads on the network and copy the certificate from the folder or extract it from the Install Certificate Package.zip file.

2. **Copy the certificate to the device**—Copy the SSL certificate onto the Windows Mobile device. This can be accomplished by using an SD flash memory card, or by connecting to the phone with ActiveSync 4.5 or WMDC and a USB cable.

3. **Install the certificate**—Once the certificate is on the phone, navigate to that location using File Explorer; then double-click the certificate. If the certificate is accepted, you will see the Certificate Installer message, "One or more certificates were installed successfully." Click OK. If an error is displayed, you will need to follow the instructions given at the time of the failure.

4. **Reset**—Perform a soft reset on the phone. If you can't find a reset button on the phone, you can just take out the battery and wait for 20–30 seconds. Put the battery back in and turn the phone back on.

5. **Confirm certificate installation**—On the phone, click Start, Settings, System tab, click Certificates, and then click the Intermediate tab. If the certificate was properly installed, it should show up in the same place as Figure 9.12. Click OK and "X" to close the windows and get back to the Home screen.

6. **Run auto configuration wizard**—Click Start, Programs, ActiveSync. Windows Mobile 6.1 will prompt you with "set up your device to sync with it" that will attempt to auto-detect your server settings based on your e-mail address. Enter the user's e-mail address and click Next (for example, jon.dough@smallbizco.net).

7. **Enter user's information**—Enter the username (for example, jondough), password, and domain (for example, smallbizco). Click Next. The wizard will attempt to connect to the server automatically. See Figure 9.13 for an example of the credentials.

8. **Enter server address**—If the Automatic Configuration cannot detect the server address, enter the fully qualified domain name of the SBS 2008 server when prompted and make sure the This Server Requires an Encrypted (SSL) Connection box is checked; then click Next (for example, remote.smallbizco.net).

FIGURE 9.12 It is important to verify that the SSL was successfully installed on the mobile phone before trying to complete the rest of the configuration.

FIGURE 9.13 It is not necessary to add the domain prefix to the user name when setting up ActiveSync on a Windows Mobile 6.1 device.

9. **Finish**—For the time being, leave Contacts, Calendar, E-mail, and Tasks alone and just click Finish. ActiveSync will now begin syncing with the Exchange server.

If everything is set up properly, synchronization will progress, and the green bar will move across the bottom of the screen.

Best Practice—Get Free Windows Mobile Training Online

One of the most challenging things about selling and supporting Windows Mobile devices is the learning curve. There are so many devices, cellular providers, connectivity methods, and support questions, it's difficult to know where to start to get up to speed. Oftentimes, people are forced to learn by trial and error.

Microsoft has put together a fabulous web site designed specifically for people who sell and support Windows Mobile devices. The site contains walk-through demos, PowerPoint slide decks, comparison charts, and online simulations and training. It is one of the best web sites for IT pros Microsoft has ever released, and it's constantly being updated with new material. Visit the following URL to sign up for access to the site: http://www.windowsmobiletraining.com.

iPhone

The original first-generation iPhone did not have the capability to synchronize over the air using Exchange ActiveSync. The only way to wirelessly sync was to enable IMAP over SSL. This workaround gave e-mail functionality, but that's only one piece of the puzzle.

In mid-2008, Apple announced the second-generation iPhone (the 3G) along with a firmware update, known as the iPhone 2.0 software. This new firmware worked for the 3G iPhones, as well as the first-generation iPhone and the iPod Touch devices. One of the much-anticipated new features added with the 2.0 update was Exchange ActiveSync support.

The 2.0 software was later updated to 2.1, which included primarily bug fixes, better battery life, and few usability improvements. To upgrade a 1.0 or 2.0 firmware iPhone to 2.1, users need to download iTunes 8 to their Windows PC or Mac and check for any available updates. iTunes can be downloaded at the following URL: http://www.apple.com/itunes/download/.

Best Practice—Download the iPhone and iPod Touch Enterprise Deployment Guide

iPhones have become very popular, especially with the introduction of the iPhone 2.1 software and Exchange connectivity. If you will be supporting iPhones or the iPod Touch on your SBS 2008 server, download the 60-page "iPhone and iPod Touch Enterprise Deployment Guide." This guide covers Exchange ActiveSync, certificates, system requirements, passwords, remote wipe, wireless support, and features of ActiveSync that aren't supported, the iPhone Configuration Utility, Cisco VPN configurations, and more. The guide can be downloaded at the following URL: http://manuals.info.apple.com/en_US/Enterprise_Deployment_Guide.pdf.

The iPhone can contain more than one POP e-mail account, but only supports one Exchange ActiveSync account.

CAUTION

After configuring an Exchange ActiveSync account on an iPhone, all existing contact and calendar information on the iPhone or iPod Touch will be automatically overwritten. iTunes will also no longer sync contacts and calendars with your desktop computer. However, you can still sync your iPhone or iPod Touch wirelessly with MobileMe services.

To set up an Exchange ActiveSync account on an iPhone running the 2.1 firmware, follow these steps:

1. On the iPhone, tap the Home button, then Settings, Mail, Contacts, and Calendars.
2. Select Add Account, and then choose Microsoft Exchange at the top of the list.
3. **E-mail (case-sensitive)**—Enter the e-mail address for the Exchange account.
   Example: jon.dough@smallbizco.net.
4. **Domain**—Enter the user's domain.
   Example: smallbizco.
5. **Username**—Enter the username. (A domain prefix is not needed on the 2.1 firmware.)
   Example: jondough.
6. **Password (case-sensitive)**—This is the same password used to check e-mail via OWA, not the password for the user's iTunes account.
7. **Description**—Enter a description for this account (optional).
   Example: SBS 2008 or SmallBizCo.
8. Select Next. If you get an Unable to Verify Certificate message, click Accept.
9. **Server**—Enter the FQDN of your server.
   Example: remote.smallbizco.net.
10. Select Next. The phone will try to create an SSL connection to the Exchange server. If you get an Unable to Verify Certificate message, click Accept. Depending on the settings of your Exchange server, you may be prompted to change your device pass-code or to enter a longer one.
11. After successfully connecting to the Exchange server, choose which types of data to synchronize by clicking ON or OFF next to Mail, Contacts, and Calendar. (The iPhone cannot sync tasks like a Windows Mobile phone.)
12. Select Save.

NOTE

By default, only the last three days of e-mail will sync with the iPhone Exchange account. To adjust the number of days of e-mail, click Settings, Mail, Contacts, Calendars, select the Exchange account you just created, and tap on Mail Days to sync.

6

Palm Devices

There is often quite a bit of confusion about synchronizing Palm devices with Exchange. This is largely because Palm devices can come with either a Windows Mobile operating system or a Palm operating system. In times past, you could simply look at the last letter of the model number and see the P for Palm or W for Windows Mobile, but that naming convention has changed.

The following are examples of Palm phones with Windows Mobile. These phones sync with ActiveSync, WMDC, or Exchange ActiveSync and use Outlook Mobile on the device:

▶ Treo 700w | wx

▶ Treo 750

▶ Treo 800w

▶ Treo Pro

The following are examples of Palm phones with Palm OS. These phones sync with Hotsync or Exchange ActiveSync and use VersaMail on the device:

▶ Centro

▶ Treo 650 and 680

▶ Treo 700p and 755p

> **NOTE**
>
> Some phones with the Palm operating system, like the Treo 650, 680, and 700p, need a software update to use Exchange ActiveSync. This update can be downloaded directly from Palm at the following URL: http://www.palm.com/us/software/eas_update/.

As with many mobile devices, the hardest part of configuring the phone is often getting the SSL certificate in the phone and getting it recognized properly. Palm phones running Windows Mobile can be configured by following the instructions "Configuring Windows Mobile to Use Exchange ActiveSync" found earlier in this chapter.

Palm phones that are running the Palm operating system should be configured using the Palm Desktop/Hotsync software, which can be downloaded directly from the Palm web site, and includes an in-depth troubleshooting guide at http://www.palm.com/us/support/palmdesktop.html.

Troubleshooting Exchange 2007 Client Connectivity

The clients for Exchange 2007 have improved in stability and ease of configuration, yet things don't always go smoothly. This section details some of the most common issues with Exchange clients.

Troubleshooting Auto Account Setup

Both Outlook 2007 SP1 and Windows Mobile 6.1 have a new feature called Auto Account Setup that tries to establish the proper e-mail configuration using only an e-mail address and a password. When setting up SBS 2008, the Setup Your Internet Address Wizard can fully configure the necessary server-side components (called the Autodiscover Service) if you purchase a new domain name from one of the approved registrars in the wizard. However, if you already own a domain name you may need to add an additional DNS entry for Auto Account Setup to work properly. Log into the server that controls your DNS records and verify (or create if necessary) a DNS entry in the Forward Lookup Zones as follows in this example:

- **Record Type**—Service Location (SRV)
- **Domain**—smallbizco.local
- **Service**—_autodiscover
- **Protocol**—_tcp
- **Priority**—0
- **Weight**—0
- **Port Number**—443
- **Host Offering This Service**—remote.smallbizco.net

For more information on troubleshooting the Autodiscover Service, see Microsoft KB 940881 (http://support.microsoft.com/kb/940881).

Troubleshooting Cached Exchange Mode

The following modes and notes visible in the lower-right corner of the Outlook status bar indicate in which mode Outlook is functioning and the status of the offline folders:

- **Disconnected**—This folder was last updated at (time). Status: There is no network connectivity with the Exchange server. Outlook will retry the connection every 15 minutes, or you can force the connection attempt manually by clicking on File and Connect to.
- **Trying to Connect**—This folder is trying to update. Status: Establishing connection with the Exchange server.
- **Connected**—All folders are up-to-date. Status: Cached Exchange Mode is enabled, and local OST and OAB folders are up-to-date.
- **Trying to Connect**—Status: Connection to the server is not active, and Outlook is continuously trying to reconnect to the Exchange server.
- **Online**—Status: Cached Exchanged Mode is disabled, and Outlook is communicating directly with the Exchange server.
- **Offline**—This folder was last updated at (time). Status: Cached Exchange Mode and Outlook will not try to automatically synchronize with the Exchange server.

6

> **TIP**
>
> While working in Offline mode, clicking the Send/Receive button on the Standard Outlook toolbar temporarily puts Outlook in Connected mode, manually synchronizes the folders, and then automatically returns Outlook to Offline mode. This also brings up an Outlook Send/Receive Progress dialog box with helpful synchronization and error information. Unfortunately, the box closes automatically after attempting synchronization, leaving you no time to view the window contents. But if you click the pushpin icon located in the lower-right corner of the window, this pins open the window even after synchronization is complete. You can also click the Send/Receive drop-down list, Send/Receive Settings, and Show Progress to bring up the last synchronization box if it has already closed.

A common tech support call comes from users who state that Outlook is running, but they haven't gotten any new e-mail in quite some time. Ask the user if the mode indicator on the Outlook status bar says Disconnected or Offline. If it does, have the user click the word Disconnected or Offline and uncheck the Work Offline selection. Outlook should then attempt to connect to the Exchange server to synchronize the folders.

If Work Offline is already unchecked, make sure that the user has network connectivity. If network connectivity is already established, verify that the user has valid credentials on the Exchange server. This can be done by having the user attempt to access OWA with Internet Explorer using his username and password. This simple test also ensures that the Exchange server is running and available.

Another area with valuable troubleshooting information is the SyncIssues folder located in the Folder List view in the Navigation Pane in Outlook. If Outlook is disconnected from the Exchange server, you should see two subfolders named Conflicts and Local Failures. If Outlook is connected to the Exchange server, you should also see a third folder called Server Failures. Look in these folders for possible synchronization errors.

Troubleshooting Exchange 2007 ActiveSync

By far, the single most common error on a Windows Mobile device usually pertains to the certificate. Sometimes the wrong one gets exported, it may be expired, the URL could change on the server, the certificate could have been regenerated when someone re-ran the Internet Connection wizard, or you could be missing an installed intermediate certificate (which often happens with GoDaddy.com certificates).

If there is an error when trying to sync, the progress bar will disappear and the message "Attention Required" will appear as a hyperlink. You can click the hyperlink for an error message, and then click View Support Code to see the actual error code. The most common ActiveSync error code is on a Windows Mobile device "0x80072F0D," which is caused by an invalid certificate.

To look up an on-going list of Exchange ActiveSync errors and solutions, check out the extensive troubleshooting list on the Pocket PC FAQ web site: http://www.pocketpcfaq. com/faqs/activesync/exchange_errors.php.

Summary

The days of answering e-mail from a single desktop computer between 9 a.m. and 5 p.m. have passed. Workers are more mobile than ever. They want and need access to their data using a variety of devices and connectivity methods to check their calendar, reply to e-mail, update their contacts, and keep on top of their tasks.

The blow of Outlook being removed from Exchange Server 2007 was slightly softened by a much-improved Outlook Web Access experience. Mobile devices are seeing rapid adoption in companies both large and small, and Windows Mobile 6.1 continues to be the leading mobile platform in Microsoft networks. IT pros need to be up to speed on installing and supporting a variety of Exchange clients.

Best Practice Summary

▶ **Keep OST Files Under 2GB and 5,000 Items for Best Performance with Cached Exchange Mode**—Caching mailboxes that are either larger than 2GB in size or that contain more than 5,000 items in any one of the core folders (Calendar, Contacts, Inbox, or Sent Items) can negatively affect the performance of Outlook 2007 in Cached Exchange Mode on the workstation.

▶ **Computers Using Cached Exchange Mode Should Use NTFS Partitions or Bitlocker**—Laptops and computers in public areas are easy targets for theft. So, computers running Outlook in Cached Exchange Mode should use NTFS file system encryption or Bitlocker on the hard drive containing the OST and OAB files due to the potential for theft or misuse of sensitive information.

▶ **Train Users with the Microsoft OWA Training Videos**—Outlook Web Access has been greatly improved. Get users up to speed quickly without investing additional resources.

▶ **Download and Install the Windows Mobile 6.1 Device Emulator**—Absolutely the single most important tool any IT pro supporting Windows Mobile devices can possess is the Windows Mobile Device Emulator. This free stand-alone utility lets you run the Windows Mobile operating system on a Windows XP or Vista desktop operating system.

▶ **Get Free Windows Mobile Training Online**—The second-best tool an IT pro supporting Windows Mobile can have. Constantly updated, and excellent content.

▶ **Download the iPhone and iPod Touch Enterprise Deployment Guide**—iPhones have become very popular. If you will be supporting iPhones or the iPod Touch on your SBS 2008 server, download the 60-page "iPhone and iPod Touch Enterprise Deployment Guide."

CHAPTER 10

Exchange Disaster Recovery

There are no prizes for realizing that e-mail has become ubiquitous. E-mail addresses can be found on everything from sweets wrappers to billboards. Not only has it essentially replaced the fax machine, its attachments are replacing mailed and couriered documents, from orders and contracts, to graphics, and multimedia. E-mail is also replacing telephone communications in areas such as enquiries, complaints, and the help desk.

It is no surprise, then, that Microsoft Exchange is part of the base platform of Small Business Server. Exchange provides huge benefits in terms of collaborative communication between staff, customers, and suppliers, locally via the network and remotely via the Internet, Outlook Web Access, and Outlook Anywhere. There is also huge growth in mail-enabled mobile devices such as iPhones, Smartphones, and PDAs directly synched to Microsoft Exchange via ActiveSync.

One missed order or complaint can be disastrous for a small or medium business. The messaging system is therefore both time sensitive and business critical.

All systems fail, and there is always a risk that at some time Microsoft Exchange will be unable to service e-mail. However, this need not be a show stopper. Both the Microsoft Exchange and the Small Business developer teams have provided many enhancements in Small Business Server 2008 and in Exchange Server 2007 to minimize the down-time and its impact on the business' users, suppliers, and customers.

With a full Windows Backup-generated backup, the server, users, mailboxes, and data can all be brought back online quickly. Using Microsoft Exchange Server's deleted mail and deleted mailbox retention, and recovery storage groups, users and administrators can recover items within minutes. Should the Exchange database be infected, corrupted, or lost for any reason, a database can be brought back online using a local replica. If the replica is affected by corruption somehow, a valid backup can be used to bring your Exchange mailbox database back to the last backup point. Because incremental backups are an integral part of SBS 2008, it's not unreasonable to take multiple scheduled backups a day to protect you against any significant data loss. These features dramatically increase uptime while simultaneously reducing recovery time.

Best Practice—Use a Layered Approach to Protection

The key to protecting Exchange on SBS 2008 is not so much in knowing what arcane techniques to use to recover data, but in proactively providing multiple layers of protection so that, in the event of a problem, there are a variety of obvious actions you can take to easily make the best of what might seem to be a dark situation.

Bear in mind that Murphy's Law holds true. If it can happen, it will happen; it's just a question of when. Providing that you are prepared when disaster strikes, it need not be the total disaster it first appears to be, so plan, implement, and practice—above all, practice. Keep in mind that a backup is only as good as the last time you actually restored it.

This chapter explains something about Microsoft Exchange databases, of the types of disasters that can occur, the tools used for backup and recovery, and how and when to use them.

It can't be emphasized strongly enough that you should not just read and follow these steps and methods after disaster has struck, but use them to plan, implement, and practice.

Understanding the Exchange Database Structure

Although Windows Server Backup retention settings and the recovery wizards take the tedium and risk out of complex, multi-faceted operations, it is important to understand what should be backed up, why it should be done, and the process by which it occurs. Without understanding these fundamentals, it is almost impossible to plan and implement an efficient disaster recovery program and resolve or work around the issues. Moreover, such knowledge lends a framework and context to the various processes, techniques, and tools used for data recovery.

This chapter concerns itself with the backup and restoration of Microsoft Exchange Data, not the SBS Server, Exchange Server, or its messaging components. Restoration of the Exchange Server application can be achieved through restoring a Full System Backup, a Disk Image, or a Recovery Re-install of the Exchange Server using the /M:RecoverServer switch.

The choice of backup media will no doubt be determined by the business' cost/benefit analysis together with the needs and the risk analysis. The media to be used, whether it is a hard disk, external USB drive, Network Attached Storage (NAS), or other, may affect the speed of backup and recovery, but it does not affect the basic method.

The following are the main elements of Microsoft Exchange relating to data backup:

▶ Exchange storage groups

▶ Extensible Storage Engine (ESE) databases and log files

▶ Circular logging

▶ The checkpoint file

▶ Transactions

Exchange Storage Groups

Because Small Business Server 2008 contains Exchange Server 2007 Standard Edition, it is limited to having five storage groups and five databases accessible by MAPI (Messaging Application Programming Interface) clients, such as Microsoft Outlook. Storage groups can hold up to five databases in them, and all the databases in a storage group share the same set of transaction logs.

Best Practice—Working with Multiple Storage Groups

It should be noted that even though up to five storage groups can be created, that does not mean that up to 25 databases can be created. The limit for databases is also five, so you could put each database in its own storage group, or you could put four mailbox databases in a single storage group. For both performance and the purpose of simplifying recovery, the best practice is to put each mailbox or public folder database in its own storage group. This is because each storage group uses the same set of transaction logs for all the databases within it, and recovery is simplified if each set of transaction logs corresponds to a single database. If two mailbox databases are in a single storage group, they share one set of logs and are backed up and restored together as a single unit.

Because the goal of creating multiple mailbox databases is to reduce recovery time, having multiple mailbox databases in a single storage group negates the recovery time benefit you would gain from splitting them up in the first place.

During the setup of SBS 2008, only two storage groups are created. Table 10.1 lists the two default storage groups.

These groups are created upon installation, as shown in Figure 10.1.

10

TABLE 10.1   SBS 2008 Exchange Storage Groups

Store	Description
First storage group	This storage group contains the mailbox database.
Second storage group	This store contains the public folder database, which is the repository for collaborative information shared by all Exchange users on the network.

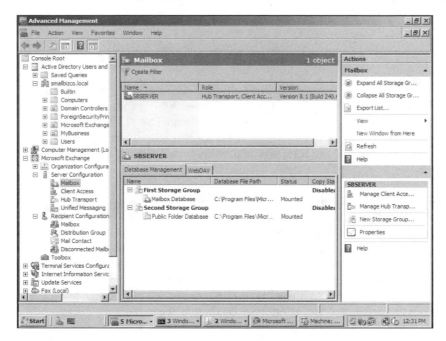

FIGURE 10.1   Small Business Server storage groups.

In addition, it is also possible to create what is known as a recovery storage group. Databases in this kind of storage group are not accessible by MAPI clients, but they are responsive to the Exchange API for the recovery of a mailbox store or its contents. Unfortunately, unlike in SBS 2003, it is not a simple matter to utilize a recovery storage group alongside the native Windows Backup that comes with SBS 2008. Later in the chapter we will look at the gymnastics involved to make that work. To most easily use a recovery storage group, it is necessary to run third-party software that includes the ability to restore directly to a recovery storage group.

In Microsoft Exchange 2007 Standard, each storage group can contain between one and five databases. As mentioned earlier, the total number of databases on the server cannot exceed five, due to version restrictions, so in addition to the two that are created by default, three more could be created. The databases themselves are Microsoft Extensible Storage Engine databases, single files with an .edb extension. The last version of Exchange included an additional file that used an .stm extension, and that file stored MIME attachments separately from the main database file. The database architecture changed in Exchange 2007, however, and now the MIME attachments are stored in the main .edb file.

NOTE

Because Windows Backup backs up and restores all the storage groups at once, use a single mailbox database and storage group as long as you can to make the recovery process less complicated. If you are using a separate third-party application for backups, you will probably be able to restore storage groups discretely and shouldn't worry then about working with more than one storage group for mailbox databases.

Extensible Storage Engine (ESE) Databases

Exchange Server 2007 uses ESE98, an Extensible Storage Engine (ESE), as its database engine. This was previously known as Joint Engine Technology (JET) Blue. The ESE is optimized for fast retrieval of data because this is the database's main function.

Properties of Extensible Storage Engine databases include the following:

▶ Transaction-based

▶ Relational

▶ Multi-user

▶ ISAM (Indexed Sequential Access Method) table management

▶ Fully Data Manipulation Language (DML) capable

▶ Fully Data Definition Language (DDL) capable

▶ Low-level Application Programming Interface (API) exposed

The ESE allows applications to store records, create indexes, and access those records in a variety of ways. You can find the location of the files that underlie the databases by mousing over the Database File Path field for each of the databases in the Exchange Management Console. Alternately, you can get properties on a database, and the properties sheet will show the file path. The default file path for the mailbox database is C:\Program Files\Microsoft\Exchange Server\Mailbox\First Storage Group. The default file path for the public folder database is C:\Program Files\Microsoft\Exchange Server\Mailbox\Second Storage Group.

The .edb File

The .edb database file contains folders, tables, messaging data, attachments, and metadata for MAPI messages and other items in the Exchange database.

By default, Small Business Server creates the files as `Mailbox Database.edb` and `Public Folder Database.edb` within their respective storage groups.

Best Practice—Plan Storage Carefully

Take into account the mail usage and retention practices of the business and plan to store your Exchange Data and Log files on disks or partitions with ample free space for additional copies of the databases and logs in a recovery or repair situation. The additional space required can be considerable, and free space of at least 120% of your projected maximum Exchange database size (`.edb` files plus `.logs` if hosted on the same partition) is recommended.

Furthermore, copying and moving data on the same partition is much faster than doing so between partitions, across the LAN, or to/from backup tape or external storage. Having ample room on the Exchange partition can dramatically reduce the time involved in recovery/restore operations of large Exchange databases.

Log Files

As Microsoft Exchange receives data, it simultaneously writes the information to a Transaction Log and to memory, until the load on the server allows for the data to be written to the database. If a database shuts down unexpectedly, uncommitted transactions can be restored by replaying the sequentially numbered transaction log files into the database.

There are a series of transaction logs for each storage group. The sequential file names prefix with an E00, E01, and so on, and each log file has a .log extension and contains an eight-digit number; the letter and first two characters identify the storage group that the log file belongs to. By default, each log file (except the temporary log currently being written to, such as E00tmp.log) is exactly 1 megabyte in size. When the temp file reaches 1 megabyte, it is saved as the next sequentially numbered transaction log.

Each storage group also maintains two reserve log files, E00res0001.jrs and E00res00002.jrs. These are created to reserve disk space. If the drive containing the log files runs out of disk space, these will be used so that the database can be closed down in a consistent state without data loss.

Figure 10.2 shows the transaction logs in their native habitat.

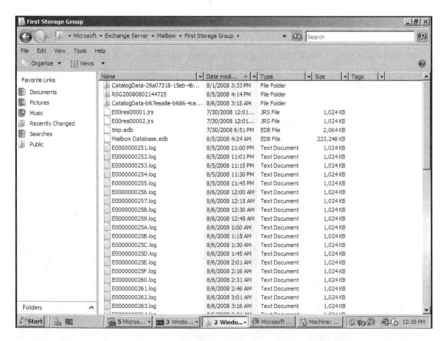

FIGURE 10.2   Transaction logs in the First Storage Group directory.

Circular Logging

Circular logging is turned on by default in Small Business Server 2008 installations to protect systems that have not configured an "Exchange-aware" backup, which deletes committed log files after a successful backup and prevents them from filling the hard drive partition. The SBS Backup Wizard disables circular logging upon completion.

Best Practice—Disable Circular Logging

You should configure an Exchange-aware backup as soon as it is practical after setup, ensuring that circular logging is disabled and a full System State backup run and verified. Immediately after disabling circular logging, a full backup of Exchange should be run to provide the base point for future backups.

Because you cannot recover Exchange 2008 data that is more recent than the last backup without a complete set of transaction logs, you should not have Circular Logging enabled in production environments. It is only there to protect administrators who for some reason have not configured an Exchange-aware backup from encountering a crash due to lack of disk space once the disk completely fills with logs.

Using Circular Logging in a Disk Space Crisis

Sometimes an administrator for one reason or another shuts off his or her backup, or by failing to provide any backup media for the server, lets it error out for a long period of time. In that situation, the transaction logs will steadily accumulate and will eventually use up all the space on the disk. Once the space is used up, the mailbox database dismounts and mail will be offline. At that point, since a backup can't be made because the database is offline, turning on circular logging and remounting the database causes all the committed logs to be deleted, giving you back the disk space you need. Before doing this, run a file-level backup of all the logs, just in case you end up needing them. And once you've remounted the database, it is vital to do an Exchange backup, because without the logs, the mailbox database is in a very vulnerable position.

To determine whether circular logging is enabled, check the properties of the storage group. Figure 10.3 shows the First Storage Group properties sheet.

Checkpoint File

A checkpoint file exists for each storage group. This file has a .chk extension with a prefix containing the letter and the two numbers that identify the storage group it belongs to and the logs to which it refers. This prefix is also the prefix of the related log files with the database identifier.

10

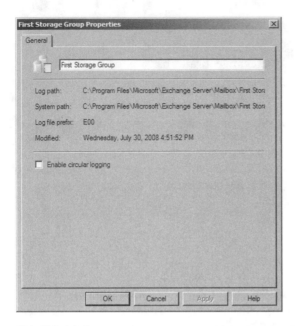

FIGURE 10.3   Once you've run the SBS Windows Backup wizard, circular logging will always be disabled.

The purpose of the checkpoint file is to track the progress of transaction logging and which logs have been committed to the database. Transaction log files accumulate over time, and this tracking dramatically reduces the amount of time taken during a recovery, as the logs only need to be rolled forward from the point indicated in the checkpoint file.

Transactions

Microsoft Exchange is transaction based. A *transaction* is defined as an inseparable set of database operations such as inserts, deletes, and updates, which must be executed either in their entirety or not at all.

A transaction should adhere to the following (ACID) properties:

- **Atomic**—The operation occurs in its entirety or not at all.

- **Consistent**—The database is left in a consistent state at all times.

- **Isolated**—Changes are not available while in an intermittent state.

- **Durable**—Once committed, transactions are preserved in the database even in the event of a system failure.

All data begins in memory and moves toward the database. The database engine only commits data to the database when it can verify that it has successfully committed that data from memory to the transaction log file on disk.

All data committed to the database is first written to a transaction log so that it can be properly rolled back if there is a problem writing the transaction to the database. Transaction logs are used so that critical information isn't stored in volatile memory (RAM) and so that RAM can be freed up to do other things. Transaction logs also track all information that has been written to the database since the last backup, so when you think about Exchange recovery, remember this formula, which is illustrated in Figure 10.4:

Last backup + all transaction logs created since last backup up to the point of failure = The point up to which a server can be recovered.

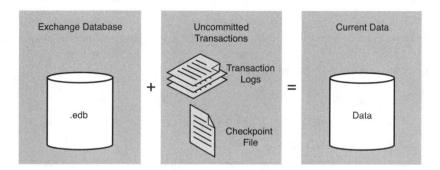

FIGURE 10.4   Exchange current data.

The following list outlines the steps that take place in the Exchange message transaction process:

1. The user sends a message.
2. MAPI calls the information store to tell it that the user is sending the message.
3. The information store starts a transaction in the database engine and makes the corresponding changes to the data.
4. The database engine records the transaction in memory by dirtying a new page in memory.
5. Simultaneously, the database engine secures the transaction in the transaction log file and creates a log record. When the database engine reaches the end of a transaction log file, it rolls over the file, creating a new log file in sequence.
6. The database engine writes the dirty page to the database file on disk.
7. The checkpoint file gets updated.

Understanding Exchange Backup Methods and Requirements

Now that you have a better idea how the Exchange databases are structured and how data flows through the Exchange processes, you are better able to understand the different backup methods used with Exchange and the requirements to back up the databases successfully. There are basically two types of Exchange backup: online backups and offline backups.

Online Backup

Regular online backups are made using Windows Backup while the Exchange 2008 services are running. SBS 2008 Windows Backup uses the Volume Shadow Copy Service (VSS) with a block-level backup. As will be discussed in Chapter 18, "Backup and Disaster Recovery," the first time Windows Backup runs using a particular set of backup media, a full backup is run. Thereafter, every backup is an incremental. If you are familiar with the way Shadow Copy worked on Windows Server 2003, you will have an idea of how Exchange backups function on SBS 2008. As part of the full SBS 2008 Windows Backup process, the Exchange 2007 VSS writers capture the Exchange 2007 Database in a way that can be restored to that particular point-in-time.

There are two types of online backups that can be run against an Exchange 2007 database. They are VSS snapshot backups and the legacy streaming backups using the streaming API. The native Windows Backup that is included in SBS 2008 uses VSS.

VSS Backup Process

This is the basic under-the-hood process for VSS backups:

1. The backup application requests a backup to be made.

2. The VSS requestor built into the backup application communicates with the VSS subsystem to order a shadow copy of the Exchange storage groups.

3. The VSS subsystem lets the Exchange VSS writer know that a snapshot backup is coming, and Exchange stops all writes and changes to the storage group, making both the databases and the transaction logs read-only. During the window of the snapshot backup, changes are held in a temporary file.

4. VSS queries the NTFS subsystem to create a snapshot of the volume that holds the storage group. The snapshot only takes a few seconds to complete. Once the snapshot is complete, orders are issued to allow Exchange to resume write access to the database and log files, and whatever information was being held in the temp file is then written to new log files.

5. Consistency of the snapshot is verified, and if successful, transaction logs are truncated; then the backup is considered complete.

Third-party applications can use streaming as their Exchange backup method. Streaming does not use a block-level snapshot of the database, but instead "streams" the contents of the database out to the backup application, which steadily writes the data to disk. This is what NTBackup does to back up Exchange, and was the standard Exchange backup method for SBS 2003.

TIP

How would you back up using NTBackup? By running NTBackup on another Windows 2003 server and remotely connecting to your SBS 2008 server. There is a registry entry that needs to be changed to allow for remote streaming backups, and it is listed in this article: http://technet.microsoft.com/en-us/library/aa998870.aspx. In addition to the registry key, the remote system you are running NTBackup from also needs to have the Exchange 2007 management tools installed. There's a 32-bit version of those tools, so the backup would not have to be run from a 64-bit server or workstation. When doing a remote restore from a backup that was made using this method, a repair of the database is typically necessary, so it's not the ideal solution. For restoring those backups, the best thing is to download a recovery version of NTBackup that Microsoft wrote to run on Windows 2008. That version does not allow you to run backups but does allow local restores of backups made via remote streaming backup, and is much less likely to cause you to have to follow up with a repair procedure. You can download that tool here: http://www.microsoft.com/downloads/details.aspx?familyid=7DA725E2-8B69-4C65-AFA3-2A53107D54A7

Streaming Backup Process

Backups made using the streaming APIs follow this process:

1. The backup agent establishes a connection to and communication with the Microsoft Exchange Information Store service (MSExchangeIS).

2. The checkpoint is frozen. New data continues to be written to the databases, but the checkpoint pointer is not updated until the backup ends.

3. The first log file that must be copied to the backup media is recorded in the database header in the "Current Full Backup" section.

4. The copying of the databases begins. Changes during the backup that cannot be reconstructed fully from the log files are not flushed to disk. Instead, an extra file page is created and attached to the end of the .edb file as a mini header containing information relating to the transaction log files required to recover the database.

5. Because log files cannot be backed up while open, the current temp log file is closed and sequenced regardless of its size immediately after copying the database files.

6. The transaction log files required to reliably restore the databases are now copied to the media. This includes all transaction log files from that flagged in the checkpoint file up to and including the file just closed.

7. Based on the Last Backup Date/Time information stored in the database headers together with the logs that were required, and the information in the checkpoint file, those transaction logs not required for a successful restore of the database are deleted from disk.

8. The "Previous Full Backup" section of the database header is updated with the Date/Time and Log Range of the backup just completed.

Offline Backup

Offline backups are file-level backups made while the Exchange 2007 services are shut down or the mailbox and public folder data stores dismounted. These backups could be made using a third-party application or by merely copying the data from the storage group folders using Explorer or the command-line.

It is highly recommended that you do not use offline backups except in special cases immediately prior to recovering databases. Their one advantage is this: Because they do not check data integrity during the backup process, they can be performed in cases where an online backup may fail due to data corruption. But that situation is very rare.

To ensure the integrity of the data and transactions including those in memory and as yet uncommitted to disk, you should use online backups.

Security Permissions

The user account that you are logged into must have the requisite permissions or rights assigned when trying to back up or restore Microsoft Exchange Data. Only those accounts with domain-level backup operator rights or administrator rights can back up Exchange 2007 databases. To restore Exchange 2007 backups, the account must have full Exchange administrator rights for the domain.

Table 10.2 lists the minimum account levels needed for backup and restore.

TABLE 10.2   Minimum Account Levels for Backup and Restore

Operation	Minimum Account Level
Exchange backups	Domain backup operator
Exchange restore operations	Full Exchange administrator
Windows backups	Local backup operator
Windows restore operations	Local administrator rights

Note that you can assign users domain backup operator permission without granting them full administrator rights. You can also use "Run As" to perform operations such as scheduled jobs in a security context other than that of the logged-on user.

Table 10.3 lists the group memberships and backup and restore privileges assigned to various security groups.

TABLE 10.3   Group Memberships and Backup and Restore Privileges

Group Membership	Backup Privileges
Local Administrators group	Members can back up most files and folders on the computer where the account is a member of the Local Administrators group. If the computer is an Exchange 2003 member server, you cannot back up Exchange database files unless you are also a member of the Backup Operator or Domain Administrator groups.
Domain Administrators group	Members can back up all files and folders on all computers in the domain.
Local Backup Operators group	Members can back up all files and folders on the computer where the account is a member of the Local Backup Operators group.
Domain Backup Operators group	Members can back up all files and folders on all computers in the domain.
Any other domain or local group	Members can back up all files and folders that the account owns. Members can back up files or folders for which the account has Read, Read and Execute, Modify, or Full Control permissions.

Configuring Deleted Item and Mailbox Retention

At the storage allocation for deleted files and e-mail screen, shown in Figure 10.5, you can configure the period of time Exchange will retain deleted e-mails and mailboxes before flushing them from the system. Users and administrators can then recover these items during the retention period directly from disk without recourse to the backup media.

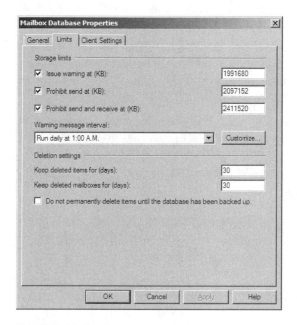

FIGURE 10.5   Setting retention limits.

Before setting the retention period, you should consider the following issues:

▶ The volume of e-mail.

▶ The size of the e-mail.

▶ The size of the database and logs on disk.

▶ The effect this will have on performance.

▶ The effect on the size and duration of the backup.

▶ The effect on the free space available on disk for a recovery or repair.

▶ The effect that this will have on the duration of a restore.

There's an equation you should think about when it comes to setting retention times: If you are willing to pay in storage, you can reap in stability. If you set longer deleted item retention times, you reduce the frequency with which you will have to recover mailboxes. On a non-SBS Exchange 2007 Server, the default deleted item retention time is 14 days, double what it was on Exchange 2003. The goal is to reduce the need for administrative intervention and let users restore their own files as needed.

10

On an SBS 2008 Server, the default deleted item retention time is 30 days. As you can imagine, this is because a small business with an SBS server usually has more storage per-user than larger enterprise organizations do, but less time to spend doing administration, so the less required involvement of admins, the better. The cost, of course, is that the mailbox database ends up running a bit heavier because it will always be carrying 30 days worth of deleted mail with it. As you can see, the lower the deleted item retention time, the less padding the database will have, and the longer the retention period, the larger you can expect the database to be.

If space is not an issue at all, and you would like the users of a particular SBS server to be able to restore items all the way back to 90 days, you could set deleted item retention to 90 days. If space starts to become a valuable commodity, you can reduce the retention time down to 14 days.

To configure the deleted item retention time, you need to use the Exchange Management Console and go into the Server\Mailbox area. From there, get properties on a mailbox database and go to the Limits tab. Valid values range from zero to 24,000!

Mailbox retention limits work hand-in-hand with the mailbox management processes. Normally, these processes fire off every night from 1 a.m. to 5 a.m. and, among other things, delete items from the deletion cache that have exceeded the retention period. So, if you have changed your retention time to a smaller period, the older messages will still be recoverable until the mailbox management processes have run, and at that point, the only way you will be able to restore those items is by restoring a backup and using a recovery storage group to extract the messages you need.

Note in Figure 10.5 the option to "not permanently delete items until the database has been backed up." This sounds like a good idea, but in practice sometimes it has led to cached deleted items being permanently deleted far ahead of the retention deadline, as the system considered it deletable once backed up. Because our goal with deleted item retention is to relieve administrative burden, it is best to leave that box unchecked.

Using Local Continuous Replication

One very cool new feature of Exchange 2007 is the ability to set up a separate, constantly updating copy of the mailbox database on a separate volume. The technology that enables this is called Local Continuous Replication. The goal behind this feature is to be able to get up and running quickly in case there is a corruption or disk crash that affects the production database. While it might normally take over an hour to restore a database from backup, switching over to the fully updated LCR copy of the database is a process that only takes a few minutes.

LCR works by having copies of the transaction logs that are being generated for the production database replicated to another volume, where the LCR process plays the contents of each log against the "passive" copy of the database, and by doing so, synchronizes it with the production database.

As you may have been able to guess by the way it uses transaction logs, LCR is not something that is set up on a per-mailbox basis, but is instead configured on a per-storage group basis.

To set up LCR, you want to have a separate volume available. That volume does not have to be mirrored necessarily and could technically be an eSATA or USB drive, but it should be on a different physical set of drives than your main mailbox database is on. This is because to get the most availability out of LCR, you want it to be able to cover your worst scenarios, and total loss of disk is a big one.

One important requirement for LCR is that the storage group that you set up for LCR can only have a single database in it. That's another reason for the best practice of only putting a single database in each storage group.

CAUTION

Before you get too excited about LCR, you should know that Microsoft never managed to get Windows Backup to play nice with LCR, so if you have LCR enabled, you will not be able to get a good backup of Exchange using Windows Backup. Only enable LCR if you have a third-party backup solution; otherwise you will break the backup and will not be able to restore Exchange mailbox databases from backups made using Windows Backup. If you attempt to back up Exchange with Windows Backup while LCR is enabled, your backup will succeed, but you will also see a failure in your logs saying that the Exchange application will not be available for recovery.

Enabling Local Continuous Replication

Once you have that volume available, you are ready to enable LCR using the following process:

Open the Exchange Management Console; in the Server\Mailbox section, select the first storage group, and in the Action pane, select Enable Local Continuous Replication. That begins a setup wizard to take you through the process.

The first page of the wizard verifies the storage group and mailbox database that will be affected by LCR. Simply click Next to move on.

The Set Paths page enables you to determine where the LCR system and log files will be kept (see Figure 10.6). Normally, this would be the same directory in which you intend to put the LCR database.

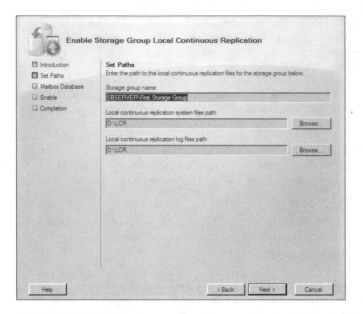

FIGURE 10.6   Selecting a target directory for the LCR logs to live.

On the next page of the wizard, the path to the actual LCR database is configured. In Figure 10.7, it's stored in the D: drive, but on your own server, that might not meet the separation criteria outlined previously.

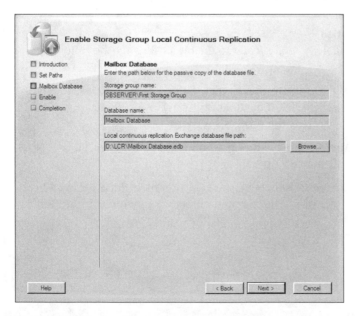

FIGURE 10.7   Selecting a target directory for the LCR replica database.

The last step of the wizard enables LCR on the storage group. Note that, once finished, it also shows you what PowerShell scripts were used to set up LCR behind the scenes: Enable-DatabaseCopy and Enable-StorageGroupCopy.

Once you've completed the wizard, look back at the Exchange Management Console, and you should see the copy status of the first storage group set to Healthy, once the initial replica seed has been created. For more details about the status of LCR, you can get properties on that storage group to check on log replication, as shown in Figure 10.8.

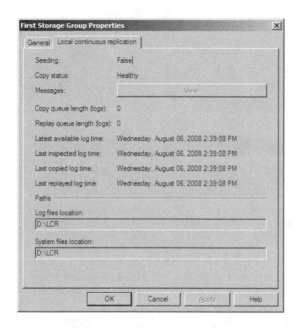

FIGURE 10.8   Displaying the status of the LCR database replica.

If you do an offline defragmentation of a mailbox database that is protected by LCR, LCR will fail and you will need to disable and re-enable LCR in order to bring the LCR copy back online. Alternately, you can use this cmdlet to reset the LCR database:

```
Update-StorageGroupCopy –Identity "First Storage Group"
```

Executing this command recreates the database copy. Naturally, it may take a bit of time to complete as it requires a full copy of the mailbox database to be copied over to the LCR location.

Failing Over to an LCR Database in a Disaster Situation

If there is an issue with the mailbox database in a storage group protected by LCR, and you want to make the LCR copy live, you need to run a PowerShell cmdlet to make that switch. Here is the path you would need to take:

1. In the Exchange Management Console, check to ensure that the affected mailbox database is dismounted. It should be, since that is why you are wanting to use the LCR database!

2. Open up an Exchange Management Shell window.

3. The next step is to tell Exchange 2007 that you will be bringing the LCR database into production. In that interface, use this command and specify the affected storage group:

   ```
   Restore-StorageGroupCopy -Identity "First Storage Group"
   ```

4. Now you need to move the LCR database and log files to the original production database directory. Use your favorite method for moving files, whether that's XCopy or Windows Explorer. You can either delete the production database and its logfiles before the move or put them into a subdirectory if disk space is not an issue.

5. Once the LCR copy has been moved to the production directory, you can mount the database, and the mailstores will be back online.

TIP

A quicker way of bringing the LCR database online is to use the –ReplaceLocations parameter when you run the Restore-StorageGroupCopy cmdlet. The command looks like this:

```
Restore-StorageGroupCopy -Identity "First Storage Group"
-ReplaceLocations:$true
```

That alters the database paths and makes your current LCR directory the production directory! Then you can immediately mount the database without having to copy files. The downside is that the volume on which you had your LCR copy might not be robust enough to accommodate the kind of disk access you will need to run Exchange in production, so you need to consider that before you use this option. The best thing would be to plan for this, and put your LCR database on a volume that will perform well enough for production.

Using Windows Backup

By default, the Configure Server Backup Wizard automatically configures and schedules Windows Backup to perform an initial full backup on each backup media that it encounters, followed by a system of incrementals. The backup includes the Exchange stores, local SQL databases, the Windows System State, and user data. Windows Backup is discussed in much greater detail in Chapter 18.

There is no need (and, in fact, no option) to select the Exchange stores and logs when configuring the Configure Server Backup Wizard. Exchange is not mentioned in the wizard, only the volumes that exist on your SBS 2008 server. Exchange is automatically included in the backup.

The Configure Server Backup Wizard configures a restorable backup set that includes System State, as well as your Microsoft Exchange data stores, and is the easiest and recommended way to back up Small Business Server.

You can run non-scheduled instances of Windows Backup if you need additional snapshots to work with, depending upon your plan and needs using either the graphic user interface in wizard or manual mode, or via the command line using wbadmin.

If you choose to use an alternate backup application instead of Windows Backup, it may be necessary to configure properties on the storage group and on the mailbox and public folder databases that the SBS Backup Wizard would normally configure automatically. These include the following:

▶ Circular logging

▶ "Do not permanently delete items and mailboxes until the store has been backed up"

Using Export-Mailbox

Although you cannot use the Exchange Management Console to back up data, you can use the Exchange Management Shell (EMC) to do so. The EMC is a PowerShell-driven command-line tool new to Exchange 2007 and Server 2008, and it gives an administrator many powerful new capabilities. The power of the EMC is built around the mini-scripts or "cmdlets" that can be run within it. Much more coverage of PowerShell and cmdlets useful for administering SBS 2008 will be provided in Chapter 20, "PowerShell."

Export-Mailbox is one of those useful cmdlets, and it enables you to export a mailbox to an Outlook .pst file or even into a target folder in another user's mailbox. It handles every type of mailbox object, including rules, views, tasks, items in the dumpster, and journal items, to name some of the more obscure ones. You can also use it to remove certain messages from a mailbox, effectively deleting them, which is useful when dealing with corrupted messages.

The only limitations are that you cannot run Export-Mailbox against a mailbox that is in a recovery storage group, and (here's the real gotcha) you can't export to .pst from the Exchange Management Console while it's on the server. Instead, you have to install the 32-bit version of the Exchange 2007 Management Tools on a separate 32-bit server or workstation, along with Outlook 2003 SP2 or higher, and then use the Exchange Management Console to do the job.

If you just want to export mail from one mailbox into a particular folder on another mailbox, you can do that from the Exchange Management Console running on the server, only exports to .pst have the weird requirements.

To utilize Export-Mailbox (taking what was mentioned previously into account), you must open up the Exchange Management Shell from the Programs menu. If you are on Vista or your SBS 2008 Server, you need to right-click the program icon and choose Run as Admin; otherwise, you won't have the rights you need for the export.

Assuming we are now running the EMC from a 32-bit client, in order to export data from William Dough's mailbox to a .pst file called Bill at the root of C:, you use the following command:

```
Export-mailbox -Identity bill.dough@smallbizco.net -PSTFolderPath C:\bill.pst
```

To export the contents of William Dough's mailbox to a folder called Bill in Sara's mailbox (which we can do on the SBS 2008 server), you use the following command:

```
Export-mailbox -Identity bill.dough@smallbizco.net -TargetMailbox
➥"sara dough" -TargetFolder Bill
```

To copy only sent messages created between Christmas and New Year's Eve of 2008 into a .pst, you use something like this:

```
Export-mailbox -Identity bill.dough@smallbizco.net -PSTFolderPath c:\billsent.pst
➥-IncludeFolders '\Sent Items' -StartDate "12/25/08" -EndDate "12/31/08"
```

You get the idea. For more information on how to use this cmdlet, see the article called "How to Export Mailbox Data" at http://technet.microsoft.com/en-us/library/bb266964(EXCHG.80).aspx.

Using ExMerge

The Exchange Server Mailbox Merge Wizard (ExMerge) is a powerful and mostly familiar tool used to extract and import information from and to Exchange Mailboxes using Outlook .pst files.

Since its creation in 1997 as a tool to remove Melissa Virus-infected messages, it has grown into a sophisticated multi-threaded application with considerable search and filtering capabilities on single or multiple mailboxes in a store.

ExMerge can extract and copy, move, or delete messages by selecting or excluding folders, by specific subject, by attachment name, or by date/time range.

It can be used in a one- or two-step process from a GUI interface or command line and supports logging and scripted calls to a configuration (.ini) file.

Best Practice—ExMerge

Download the latest version of ExMerge appropriate to the version of Exchange (you can find it at http://www.microsoft.com/downloads/details.aspx?familyid=429163ec-dcdf-47dc-96da-1c12d67327d5) and install it to the %Program Files%\Microsoft\Exchange Server\bin directory. Add the %Program Files%\Microsoft\Exchange Server\bin directory to the Systems Path variable so that ExMerge can locate required Exchange DLLs, and you can easily execute both it and other utilities such as ESEutil and ISinteg from the command line. Prepare yourself by reading the comprehensive manual. Add ExMerge to your toolkit and practice using it.

ExMerge supports Outlook Calendar, Contacts, Journal, Notes, Tasks, Views, and Folder rules.

Although ExMerge works with both the default storage groups and the recovery storage group, it cannot extract data from public folders nor can it handle all data and meta-data. Its search and filtering cannot find a string in a substring or an attachment to a message that is nested within another message.

ExMerge requires "Receive As" and "Send As" permission for the mailboxes in order to be able to import and export information. The logged-on user account must have Service Account Administrator permissions at the organization, site, and configuration levels of the Administrator program and have both permissions on the mailboxes.

ExMerge is ideally suited to creating "brick-level" backups and archives. It can write data to media such as internal or external HDD or NAS. It can also create incremental backups by using either of these functions:

▶ **Merge**—Copy only new messages and folders, skipping all messages and folders previously copied.

▶ **Replace**—Replace data only if the copy in the source store is more recent.

ExMerge uses a sophisticated process that helps recover all uncorrupted data even if individual mailbox folders contain corrupted messages. All messages in a mailbox folder are extracted collectively to minimize remote procedure call (RPC) traffic and time. On encountering an error, ExMerge automatically skips the message and then begins copying the messages that remain in the folder individually. After reaching the end of the folder, the tool then resumes copying messages collectively again until another error is encountered. This makes it an ideal recovery tool.

Another feature of ExMerge is that it is highly scriptable. You can create sophisticated .ini files (either manually or by saving your setting from the GUI), as seen in Figure 10.9. You can then script calls to the appropriate file for a variety of backup and disaster recovery operations.

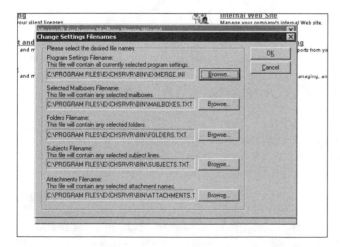

FIGURE 10.9   ExMerge Change Settings Filenames window.

Other Backup Solutions

Although not specifically necessary, there are other backup solutions to use with SBS and Microsoft Exchange. These vary in price, feature set, usability, and support for VSS and streaming backups. Many solutions can provide support for features that Windows Backup does not, such as backup to tape, backing up from another server, and direct single mailbox backup and restore. Microsoft's main offering for backing up Exchange on Windows 2008 Server is called Data Protection Manager, and it's an enterprise-ready system for backing up multiple servers. It's not usually a good solution for the small-to-midsized business space because it requires its own server and additional licensing, but it can be the right solution for some SBS shops, particularly if there are multiple servers to be backed up, including SQL servers.

Additionally, there are vendor and service provider solutions that include offsite backup to remote storage backup via broadband and snapshot or streaming backup to NAS or "Hot Spare" servers.

In evaluating backup software for Small Business Server and Microsoft Exchange 2007, you should consider the following:

▶ Price (cost/value benefit).

▶ Additional hardware requirements.

▶ Use of and support for MS Backup APIs (Exchange aware).

▶ Use of and support for Volume Shadow Copy Services (VSS aware).

▶ Support for the backup hardware/medium.

▶ The duration of the backup and restore scenarios and methods.

▶ Reliability and appropriateness of the solution.

▶ The degree of difficulty of use.

▶ Documentation.

▶ Vendor support and longevity in the market—Archived backups may be many years old.

Recovering Exchange Databases from Backup

The sole point of an Exchange backup is for the data to be restored to disk at some point in time and the data to be accessed via client applications. You should do this often to validate the integrity of your backup, practice your techniques, and fine tune and re-evaluate the process for timing to suitability.

Although backup technologies are getting more bullet-proof every year, historically a large percentage of backups fail to restore successfully. This can be for a variety of reasons, from devices that are no longer compatible with the archived backup to operator error that may be due to lack of training or practice.

Having a backup on media, and a backup log that states that the backup process verified the data transfer, is not enough. A backup operator should restore data from the media to the hard disk and verify it at least once a month and do a full disaster recovery restore and verify (possibly to a test server or the recovery storage group and a dummy "RestoreVerify" user) at least once a quarter. This is the only way to verify the disaster recovery plan and will highlight any issues with the media, the hardware, the operator, or the efficiency of the plan itself.

The aim here is to successfully restore the most current or archived data in the least time, with the minimum of disruption to the business and its ongoing services.

As part of your disaster recovery implementation plan, you should create a recovery checklist, similar to the following, that is appropriate to your own environment and plan.

Recovery checklist:

- ▶ Have the latest backup media available.

- ▶ Alert users and concerned parties about a planned outage.

- ▶ Use the Exchange Troubleshooter tool and dismount the mailbox and public folder stores that you are restoring.

- ▶ Determine the database and log file locations of the files to be restored (optional).

- ▶ Ensure that there is sufficient free space on the volume or volumes to be used.

- ▶ Offline copy the current database and log files to another location (optional).

- ▶ Make sure that the Microsoft Exchange Information Store service (MSExchangeIS) is running.

- ▶ Select the backup files that you want to restore from your backup media.

- ▶ Restore the selected files.

- ▶ Make sure that the restore process was successful.

- ▶ Mount the databases (stores).

- ▶ Advise users and concerned parties that messaging services have been resumed.

- ▶ Complete and sign off on the issue and process update in the server log book. (You do have a server log book and keep it current, don't you?)

This list is by no means definitive and needs to be tailored to your own processes.

In restoring Exchange, patience under pressure is a virtue and time is the key.

Events Requiring Exchange Recovery

There are many scenarios that may require the recovery of Exchange data:

▶ Catastrophic loss of the Small Business Server 2008 (Hardware/HDDs).

▶ Migration of the Small Business Server 2008 to new hardware.

▶ Loss of the Exchange 2008 Server (Exchange database and transaction log files are also lost).

▶ Loss of the Exchange 2008 Server (Exchange databases and transaction log files are intact).

▶ Lost database/storage group.

▶ Lost Exchange databases.

▶ Lost mailbox.

▶ Lost mail item (deleted mail).

▶ Corruption in the data stores.

Some events, such as lost e-mail or lost mailboxes, may be recovered almost instantly if Deleted Item Retention is turned on in Exchange and the recovery is attempted within the retention period. Otherwise, recovery will require restoration from backup media via one or more methods.

Your backup plan should take into account the possible types of disaster and the type of backup and schedule that is both cost effective and timely for the business. Your disaster recovery plan needs to incorporate a suitable range of recovery methods based on the recovery time that is best suited to each disaster and the business needs.

Recovery Process

As mentioned previously, Microsoft Exchange 2007 has features that reduce the time required to recover from disasters. In that context, two terms should be mentioned here:

▶ **Soft Recovery**—An uncontrolled shutdown of the Exchange 2007 Server databases can leave them in a State: Dirty Shutdown, as indicated by an entry in the headers. On remounting the databases, if Exchange finds them in this state, it will attempt a soft recovery by automatically playing back the relevant log files as indicated by the pointer in the checkpoint file. This ensures the Exchange databases operate in a consistent state.

▶ **Hard Recovery**—A hard recovery occurs after you restore a database from backup or use the ESEutil /cc option from the command line. Hard recovery replays the available logs into the database to bring it up to date, after which, on re-mounting, an additional soft recovery is also triggered.

Using the SBS Backup Wizard to Restore

The backup created by the Small Business Server Backup Wizard is a Full System State backup, including an "Exchange aware," online backup of Microsoft Exchange data stores and logs.

The backup can be restored either as part of the complete System Restore from Directory Services Restore Mode or from the Windows 2008 Server install prior to the Small Business Server and component server setup. In this event, the system is brought back online with Exchange operational and the data stores as they were at the time of the backup.

Windows Backup uses Application Programming Interface (API) calls to the Exchange VSS Writers to restore Exchange database files.

The process for restoring the Exchange databases using Windows Backup is fairly simple:

1. In the SBS Console, go to the Backup and Storage section and go to the Backup sub-tab. You see the status of your backup displayed there.

2. Next, click the Restore Server Data from Backup link in the Backup Tasks section of the Action pane. That brings up the Windows Backup interface, and you see a list of recent backups listed, among other things.

3. On the right side, you see a Recover link. Clicking it brings up the Recovery Wizard.

4. The Recovery Wizard asks whether you want to recover data from the local server or from a separate server. For your purposes, you will usually choose to recover from the local server.

5. The next screen enables you to choose what date you would like to roll the data back to and displays the different days on which backups ran and a drop-down menu displaying the times at which backups were done on a particular day. Select the date and time of the backup you would like to restore to the server.

> **NOTE**
>
> If you do not choose the latest backup, the transaction logs will not be used to bring your server back to the point at which it recently failed, so be careful in your choices. If you have the transaction logs since your last backup, you should be able to recover up to the point at which your mailbox database corrupted. If the disk on which your mailbox database and logs was located is no longer available, then the logs don't matter and your recovery will be back to the time of the backup that you choose.

6. The next screen asks whether you want to restore files and folders, applications, or an entire volume. For an Exchange database recovery, you want to select the Applications option.

7. Now it is time to select the application that will be recovered. On a default install of SBS 2008 Standard, there will only be two options, SharePoint and Exchange, but other applications might show up on this list. Select Exchange.

10

> **NOTE**
>
> If you have chosen to recover Exchange using your latest backup, this page of the Recovery Wizard will give you the option to not replay your transaction logs after the recovery. By default, this selection is unchecked, as the wizard assumes that you would want to restore mail up to the latest time possible. If you do not want to do a recovery up to the last minute, check the box, and your restore will only bring your server back to the point at which the backup you are restoring was made.

8. The decision of where you want to apply the restore comes next. By default, you would be applying the restore to the same server on which the restore was taken, and doing so will result in a live and online restored database. If you choose instead to redirect the restore to the file system, you will have a copy of the database from the time of the backup that you made, but it will not be mountable and will most likely need to be repaired before it can be mounted. That database could be attached to a recovery storage group for the purpose of mailbox recovery if you want. There is more information on that option later in this chapter.

9. The last screen of the Recovery Wizard does not ask for any decisions, but merely displays information about the VSS snapshots that will be restored.

When Windows Backup begins the restore process, the Exchange mailbox and public folder databases will be dismounted before the restore and then remounted after the restore completes. At this point, look at the Windows Backup console to see if there are any errors associated with the restore you just did. Log on to a mailbox using OWA and see what the message history for a mailbox looks like to see how far forward the recovery was able to roll.

> **NOTE**
>
> It's important to realize that Windows Backup restores all storage groups and the mailbox databases in them at once. If you have set up multiple storage groups, all of them are going to be restored, and if you don't redirect the restores, they will overwrite your production mailbox databases. Normally if you are just restoring from the most recent backup, this is not a problem because the logs will bring the databases up to the current time. But if you are restoring an older backup, you will lose mail in all the mailbox databases. When you want to restore only a single mailbox database, it's best to redirect the restore to a nonproduction directory and use eseutil to repair the database before mounting.

If you have clients running Outlook with Cached Exchange Mode turned on, even a restore that did not involve playing the transaction logs afterward may still result in a full recovery for those users, since the cached copy of their mail will be synced up to the server when they reconnect after a restore.

Using the Recovery Storage Group

The recovery storage group was designed to aid in speedy recovery of Exchange data with the minimum of down-time for the business/users by allowing the recovery of mailboxes while the Exchange server continues to service messaging requests. This also saved the need for a separate recovery server.

Recovery storage groups are not as simple to use in the context of SBS 2008 as they have been in the past. This is due to the fact that, unlike NTBackup on SBS 2003, Windows Backup cannot restore a mailbox database directly to a recovery storage group. Fortunately, there are ways to get around this issue, and you'll look at some of those techniques later on when we cover single-mailbox restores.

Individual or multiple mailboxes restored to the recovery storage group from a backup can be combined or merged with live mailboxes directly from the Exchange Management Console with a few clicks using the Exchange Troubleshooter Wizard. Using ExMerge and its advanced features can provide a more selective mailbox data restore.

There are, however, limitations, as follows:

▶ You cannot use the recovery storage group to recover public folders.

▶ You can only have a single recovery storage group on a server. Multiple mailbox databases can be restored to a single RSG, as long as they all came from the same original storage group.

▶ The recovery storage group uses three types of AD-based identifiers to match up mailboxes in the RSG with mailboxes in the production database. If the Exchange configuration in Active Directory has changed, databases re-created, or mailboxes have been deleted from the Active Directory, the association between the objects may have trouble being established for the recovery of data.

The three properties that can be used for linking a mailbox in the RSG are as follows:

  ▶ MsExchMailboxGUID

  ▶ Exchange legacy distinguished name

  ▶ Display name

▶ When you recover a database to the recovery storage group, its unique identifier (being its "distinguished name," the value for msExchOrigMDB in the Active Directory) must match that of the "distinguished name" of the database you will be restoring.

▶ To move the path to the database in the recovery storage group, you need to delete and re-create the group with the new name and path details.

The only functionality allowed for the recovery storage group is recovery. To this extent, the following functional differences are in place:

▶ Mail cannot be sent to or from a database in a recovery storage group. The only protocol available to it is MAPI.

10

▶ Active Directory accounts cannot be connected to user mailboxes in a recovery storage group, and new mailboxes cannot be created there.

▶ System and mailbox management policies including online maintenance and defragmentation are not applied to the recovery storage group.

▶ The databases cannot be set to mount automatically at startup of the information store service.

Best Practice—Recovery Storage Group

Do not leave a recovery storage group longer than necessary for the recovery operation. It takes up needless space, and can conflict with other operations. You can remove the recovery storage group using the Database Recovery Management console, but you have to manually delete the files in the RSG folder to reclaim the space used by the restored database.

NOTE

The next several sections walk you through some procedures that include using the Exchange Database Recovery Management Console and the Exchange Troubleshooter. For more coverage of those tools, read the "Recovery Tools" section later in this chapter.

Creating a Recovery Storage Group

The recovery storage group is easily created from the Exchange Management Console, as follows:

1. Go to the Exchange Management Console and open the toolbox in the left pane.
2. Open Database Recovery Management.
3. On the first screen, click Go To Welcome Screen.
4. Name the task something, enter the Exchange server name, and click Next.
5. On the next screen, after the server has gathered information, click the Create a Recovery Storage Group task.
6. The next step involves linking the new RSG to an existing storage group. To recover mail from your default mailbox database, choose First Storage Group from the list and click Next.
7. On the next screen, you have to choose file paths. If the drive that your mailbox database is on doesn't have enough room to mount an additional copy of your mailbox database, a new location will need to be chosen. It could be an external removable drive if it needed to be, although that would make the process slower. Once you've set the path, click Create Recovery Storage Group to generate the RSG.

When you create the RSG with the Create a Recovery Storage Group Wizard, the RSG is automatically populated with a recovery mailbox database that will be replaced by whatever database is restored from backup. Once the recovery storage group and its mailbox store exist, any streaming restore from backup of the Exchange databases to the "original location" will automatically be directed to the recovery storage group.

NOTE

Remember that Windows Backup cannot do a streaming restore, so much of this section only applies in the context of third-party products that are able to do that type of restore.

If you want to allow a normal restore to the production storage group itself while the recovery storage group exists, you can set a registry key to override the behavior:

`HKEY_LOCAL_MACHINE\System\CurrentControlSet\Services\MSExchangeIS\ParametersSystem`

Create a DWORD value called `Recovery SG Override`, and set its "Value Data" to 1. Remember to flip this value or delete the key when done to avoid future accidents.

Providing Dial Tone with a Recovery Storage Group

The ability to copy or merge from the recovery storage group to the default (first storage) group can provide a means of dramatically reducing the recovery down-time. The technique uses what is called a "Messaging Dial Tone Database."

In the event of a crash of the mailbox database, a new (clean) database is created and users are brought online immediately to provide "dial tone service." Although there is no access to historic data, the business is online and messaging can move forward.

Data can be restored to the recovery storage group from backup and/or repaired or recovered database and logs. The most important online mailboxes can then be progressively populated with the historic data in the recovery storage group. Although expeditious, the process can still take some considerable time, particularly if the mailboxes are large.

In a variation that inserts a brief down-time, but can dramatically reduce the rebuild time, the databases are switched.

When the data has been satisfactorily restored to the recovery storage group, both the mailbox store and the recovery storage group are dismounted. The databases are then swapped, placing the high-volume database back as the users live mailboxes and the low-volume database, which can be merged in minimal time, as the RSG database.

Having the two databases in the same partition helps decrease transfer times during the swap process.

Minimizing the amount of data being merged into the mailboxes also lessens the impact on other running server processes.

10

The steps for creating and using the "dial tone" messaging are the following:

1. Stop the databases in the default storage group.

2. Copy all transaction logs for the storage group to a safe location. These may be required if the original log files are purged when the databases are mounted.

3. Move or rename the .edb for the failed database (if it exists).

4. In Exchange System Manager, mount the failed database. The following warning appears:

   "At least one of this store's database files is missing. Mounting this store will force the creation of an empty database. Do not take this action if you intend to restore an earlier backup. Are you sure you want to continue?"

5. Select "Yes" and Exchange generates a new database. When you mount the datastore from which the files have been removed, Exchange Server 2007 creates blank database files. As users attempt to access their mailboxes, Exchange creates new mailboxes in the database, and the users are able to send and receive mail. The user objects retain their original Exchange attributes (including msExchMailboxGUID). Because the new mailboxes have the same GUID values as the old mailboxes, Task wizard or ExMerge can successfully transfer data between the recovery storage group database and the "dial tone" database.

6. Set up the recovery storage group using the procedure outlined earlier in this chapter.

7. Restore the original database or backup to the recovery storage group. If you are using Windows Backup and not a third-party product, you might need to repair and/or hard recover the database before you are ready for the swap and re-mount. That process is outlined in the "Recovering from a Dirty Shutdown State" section of this chapter.

8. Disconnect from both databases and swap the database files between the original storage group and the recovery storage group. This process is automated by a wizard in the Database Recovery Management tool called Swap Databases for Dial Tone Scenario.

9. After using the wizard to swap the "Dial Tone" database into the recovery storage group and the original database back to its original storage group, users can access their previous data (including rules, forms, and offline or cached mode .ost data files). However, until the merge from the RSG is done, they cannot access items in the "Dial Tone" database.

10. Using another wizard in the Database Recovery Management tool, you can merge data from the "Dial Tone" database that is mounted in the RSG back into the original database to bring the user mailboxes fully up-to-date.

11. The recovery storage group can then be dismounted, archived, and deleted along with the database it was holding.

For the process to be efficient, you should definitely practice the technique on a spare server or virtual machine.

Mailbox Recovery Using a Recovery Storage Group

Even though Windows Backup does not restore a backup directly to a recovery storage group, it is still fairly easy to restore a backup and then mount it in the RSG. Assuming that you've already created a recovery storage group using the steps outlined earlier in the chapter, let's now look at what it takes to get a historical backup mounted.

The first step is restoring a copy of the database to an alternate path. During the Windows Backup Restore Wizard, you are given the option to restore the database to the production directories or to redirect it to an alternate location. At that point, you should choose to recover the database to a new directory on the same volume as the RSG, assuming there is disk space.

Once the restore process has completed, you should have a new folder hierarchy in the folder you chose for the restore. It will look like the live hierarchy, following \Program Files\Microsoft\Exchange Server\Mailbox down to the storage groups that you restored.

Populating the Recovery Storage Group

Now that the RSG has been created, it is now time to copy the files from your redirected backup into the newly created RSG folder. This can be done either with Windows Explorer or from the command line. The following steps clarify the command-line method:

1. Open up an elevated command line by typing **CMD** in the search field and holding down Shift+Ctrl when hitting Enter. You see the UAC prompt, which lets you know that you are creating an admin-level command-line instance.

2. Browse to the directory that you redirected the database recovery to and navigate down into \Program Files\Microsoft\Exchange Server\Mailbox\First Storage Group. Once you are there, you see your logs (.log extensions) and your mailbox database (.edb extension).

3. Now, copy those files into the new RSG folder that was created in your production First Storage Group directory. Normally that would be a subfolder of C:\Program Files\Microsoft\Exchange Server\Mailbox\First Storage Group.

Once the files have been copied, the next step is to mount the RSG.

Go back to the Exchange Troubleshooter and choose the Mount or Dismount Databases in the Recovery Storage Group option. You will be able to select the RSG to mount and then attempt to mount it.

At this point, you are very likely to get an "Unable to Mount Database 80004005 error," and you will need to do some things to prepare the database for mounting. Because the database was restored to a file location and not restored to production using the Exchange VSS writers, the database is in a dirty shutdown state.

Recovering from a Dirty Shutdown State

At this point, you attempt to verify the logs and database using another task in the Troubleshooting Assistant.

Run the Verify Database and Transaction Log Files task and select the recovery storage group as the target. Click Next and then choose Analyze Selected Databases. You will most likely see that the state is Dirty Shutdown.

10

Performing a Soft Recovery

The next step, doing a soft recovery, is not critical and can be skipped, but it is a good idea to try it just in case the database can be fixed without a full repair because the repair process sometimes causes slight damage to the database by throwing away recent pages of data that can't be reconciled into a clean database state. The soft recovery works by attempting to replay the logs into the database in case not all the logs had been committed.

You will open an elevated command line and go to the Exchange Server\Bin directory on the server. At this point, you are going to use the ESEUTIL utility to attempt a recovery. This command uses the /r switch along with the /l, /s, and /d parameters, each of which should supply a file or folder path:

```
eseutil /r E00 /d "[full path to RSG]\mailbox database.edb" /l "[full path to RSG]"
➥/s "[full path to RSG]"
```

If this operation succeeds, use the GUI to attempt to mount the RSG database again.

Performing a Database Repair

If the database still fails to mount, which is common, the next step is to run a repair on the database using Repair Database task in the Database Recovery Management tool. The Repair task will actually run several operations using ESEUTIL and ISINTEG, as follows:

▶ Database repair

▶ Defragmentation

▶ Integrity check

After the processes run, the results will be reported to you. If this step completes successfully or with only an ISINTEG error, and running another Verify operation shows a clean shutdown, the next step is to mount the RSG using the link in the Database Recovery Management tool. If the repair did not succeed, the database should be restored from a different previous backup. Normally, a repair operation after a redirected restore will complete without errors.

Merging the Contents of the Recovery Storage Group Database

Once the RSG has been mounted, go to the Task Center console again; this time, choose Merge or Copy Mailbox contents.

The wizard asks you to pick the RSG mailbox. Select Gather Merge Information, and on the next screen, choose Perform Pre-Merge Tasks.

The wizard will itemize the mailboxes that it found in the RSG and enable you to select the mailboxes that you would like to merge back into the production mailbox database. Duplicate items are ignored.

Select the mailbox whose contents you would like to merge and exclude all others; then click Perform Merge Actions. Any mail present in the user's mailbox in the RSG that is not present in their production mailbox will be merged to the production mailbox.

If you desire a more granular merge operation and only want certain types of messages or only items created between certain dates, you will want to use ExMerge instead of the Merge or Copy wizard.

Using ExMerge to Restore

ExMerge is a powerful tool, not only for backing up Exchange Data to `.pst` files, but also merging `.pst` data into existing mailboxes. It can, however, only be used with mailboxes, and not public folders. In moving data to and from `.pst` files, it can lose some meta-data, and the process breaks Exchange's single storage, so the sum of the resultant data may be significantly greater than the original.

As shown in Figure 10.10, ExMerge allows for both single step, in which the backup to `.pst`, merge, and cleanup occur as a single transaction, and dual step, where you can either export (backup) to `.pst` or import/merge `.pst` files to mailboxes.

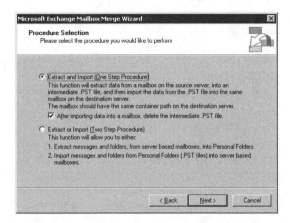

FIGURE 10.10 ExMerge step selection.

Although some of the functionality has been incorporated into the Database Recovery Management tool, ExMerge provides far greater control over data to be recovered.

With scripting, and the use of the `.ini` file (created by saving the options from the GUI), even greater functionality can be teased out of ExMerge, such as the ability to map disparately named mailboxes and `.pst` files. It cannot, however, create destination mailboxes on the server if they do not exist.

The data selection criteria provide the following options:

- ▶ **Data:**
  - ▶ User messages and folders.
  - ▶ All user data including messages, folders, calendars, contacts, tasks, journal items, and notes.
  - ▶ Associated folder messages.

10

▶ Some hidden data, such as folder rules and views.

▶ Folder permissions.

▶ Will overwrite the permissions on the target folder with those on the source.

▶ Items from dumpster.

▶ Will copy all deleted items still available for recovery.

▶ **Import Procedure:**

▶ Copy data into the target store.

▶ Will copy to target store regardless, and may result in duplicate messages.

▶ Merge data into the target store.

▶ Will only copy messages that do not exist on the target.

▶ Replace existing data on the target.

▶ Will overwrite messages on the target.

▶ Archive data to target store.

▶ Copy from source to target deleting the message on the source when the source is an exchange mailbox.

▶ **Folders:**

▶ Select to process or ignore selected folders and subfolders.

▶ **Dates:**

▶ Select a message date range for the operation based on the delivery or last modified time.

▶ **Message Details:**

▶ Filter on message subject and attachment name at the top level only.

▶ It includes options for substring and full string match ignoring case or for an Exact string match. The filter uses the following operation: (Date Criteria) AND (subj.1 OR subj.2 OR subj.n....) AND (att.1 OR att.2 OR att.n...).

Using Third-Party Solutions to Restore

Third-party software solutions might provide for restoration of either the whole of the Exchange database or individual mailboxes either directly or via the recovery storage group and the Backup APIs. Functionality varies based on vendor and price. You should carefully consider your requirements set before selecting a package and verify that not only the backup, but the restore functionality is suitable and timely.

Repairing a Damaged Exchange Database

Exchange 2007 is far more "self-healing" than previous versions; however, there are times when corruption occurs and you need to manually repair the databases offline. The truth is, 75% of the time that data corruption occurs, it's caused by issues with your disk subsystem. There are other possible reasons, like power outages, running out of disk space, and having your AV program steal logfiles, but if you have database corruption outside of those circumstances, look in your logs for disk errors, do a chkdisk, and keep an eye out for another episode of corruption.

Although repair is an option, it is always best to restore from a backup whenever possible. A repair may delete an unknown number of corrupted data pages and/or links in order to bring the database back to an operational state, and these may not be immediately obvious. Consider a repair as a last option.

If you restore from a backup, you ensure that you have a good, clean, stable, database that will start and run on your server. In almost every circumstance, it is faster and more reliable to restore from a backup than to perform a hard repair on the database.

Recovery Tools

When it is your job to bring a corrupted database back online, there are two categories of tools at your disposal: the wizard-driven tools in the Database Recovery Management console, and the command-line tools. In reality, the wizard-driven tools are just overlays that utilize the command-line tools (some of them are traditional Exchange tools, and others are PowerShell cmdlets) and give you more informative and contextual feedback than the command-line tools would if you were using them directly. When possible, it is best to use the wizard-driven recovery tools, but a familiarity with the command-line tools is a valuable asset when it comes to planning out a recovery path and interpreting errors you may see in the logs.

The Database Recovery Management Console

The Database Recovery Management console is a subset of the larger Exchange Troubleshooting Assistant collection of wizards. This console provides scripted access to some common operations that in the past were done exclusively with the command line. Because of the complexity of the command-line tools and because there was a lot of room for error and data loss using the tools manually, the collection of scripts in the Database Recovery Management console was created to streamline and stabilize data recovery operations. The console provides scripted wizards for the following tasks:

▶ Checking the space on the logging drive and moving the location of the logfiles. The logfiles are moved using the `Move-StorageGroupPath` PowerShell cmdlet.

▶ Displaying all events from the Application log that are related to Exchange database operations. This is the most efficient way to get up to speed on recent issues with an Exchange server, because the script knows which event numbers are relevant and consolidates them all into a single view.

10

▶ Check the database headers and log files to verify database health and identify particular issues. This is equivalent to running the `eseutil /mh` and `eseutil /mk` commands.

▶ Repair a corrupted database, defragment it, and then verify the organizational integrity of the database file. Under the hood, this is an `eseutil /p`, an `eseutil /d`, and an `isinteg fix`.

▶ Create, remove, mount, or dismount a recovery storage group. Behind the scenes, the `new-database`, `remove-database`, `mount-database`, and `dismount-database` PowerShell cmdlets are used.

▶ Copy or merge data from mailboxes on a recovery storage group into mailboxes on a production database. This script uses the `Export-Mailbox` cmdlet to move data between the databases.

▶ Prepare a database to be overwritten by an upcoming restore. This option is only used with a streaming backup/restore application. The `Set-MailboxDatabase` cmdlet is used to accomplish this task.

▶ Switch production and recovery storage group databases for a "dial tone" scenario.

If you are familiar with recovery options on Exchange 2000 or 2003, you will see that most of the basic bases have been covered by these scripts. Some administrators feel more comfortable using the traditional tools, but even experienced admins should try out these scripts as there are some pleasant surprises there, and far less room for mistakes.

Best Practice—Be Prepared

The Database Recovery Management console in the Exchange toolbox has most of the tools you will need to survive a disaster. Knowing what your options are when a crisis strikes is one of the most important things you can do ahead of time, so that you don't take any rash actions based on lack of information. True preparedness requires that you familiarize yourself with these tools ahead of time.

Because the preceding repair option uses the tools discussed next, repair is covered in the context of the command-line tools, even though the tools can be accessed more safely and indirectly via the scripts.

The Command-Line Tools

There are two traditional command-line tools to use when working on errors that can occur at the page, database, or application store level: ESEutil and ISinteg. ESEutil checks and fixes individual database tables, whereas ISinteg checks and fixes links between tables. Both utilities can be found in the Program Files\Microsoft\Exchange Server\Bin directory.

Repair (whether using ESEUTIL directly or via the Repair wizard) requires both considerable disk space (for the original, copy, temp, and restored database) and time.

Depending on the source and destination (for example, from tape to HDD, between disks, or within the same partition), transfer rates can be as slow as 3–6GB per hour. The repair process itself can run at approximately 4–6GB per hour and the ISinteg check at a similar 3–6GB per hour. If this is not run on separate hardware, the process can impact on the server's ability to service "Normal" operations.

It is worth warning here that ESEutil commands can be quite dangerous to the uninitiated.

ESEutil can be looked at from several aspects. The harmless /m options, such as /mh, provide an extensive read-out of information about the database. Those options that regularly occur as part of Exchange's own maintenance processes, such as the /cc command, ensure consistency. The more risky are those that make physical changes to the data, such as the /d Defragment option, which performs a special operation to compact the databases, and then the high-risk operations, such as a /p, which do a page-level repair.

The tools should not be used indiscriminately, and you should ensure that you have an offline copy of your databases and logs before running these commands. For example, you should consider an offline defragmentation only if you are moving an Exchange Server database or after a database repair. Performing offline defragmentation when it is not required could affect performance and stability. There is no need (yes, that's NO NEED) to do a periodic offline defragmentation because the online defragmentation process adequately defragments the database.

> **NOTE**
>
> Because offline defragmentation actually creates the new database, database files, and log file signatures, a new defragmented database file will have a different database signature. Because the databases and transaction logs point to each other based on signatures, all previous backups of this database are invalidated by the offline defragmentation. You should create new backups of Exchange Server 2007 databases immediately after offline defragmentation.

Overall, ESEutil is a rich tool that any operator involved in Exchange recovery processes needs to be familiar with. Table 10.4 shows some of the command-line options that are available for ESEUTIL on Exchange 2007, their function, and description.

TABLE 10.4   ESEutil Command-Line Options

Command	Function	Description
ESEutil /c	Restore	Performs a hard recovery after a database restore.
ESEutil /a	LLR Log Replay	Last Log Resilience log replay.
ESEutil /d	Defragment	Defragment the .edb database and overwrite.
ESEutil /d /p	Defragment	Defragment and leave new database in the temp folder.
ESEutil /g	Integrity	Verifies the integrity of a database.

10

TABLE 10.4   ESEutil Command-Line Options

Command	Function	Description
ESEutil /i	Bypass	Bypass database and streaming file mismatch error.
ESEutil /k	Checksum	Verifies the checksums of a database.
ESEutil /m	File Dump	Generates formatted output of various database file types.
ESEutil /mh	Verify	Verifies the state of an Exchange database.
ESEutil /mk	Checksum	Provides information about the checkpoint file.
ESEutil /ml	Integrity	Integrity check on log files.
ESEutil /mm	Metadata Dump	Database metadata dump.
ESEutil /p	Repair	Hard repair a corrupted store database—discard corrupt pages.
ESEutil /r	Recovery	Recovery repair Exchange 2007 log files.
ESEutil /y	Copy	Copies a database, streaming file, or log file.

After ESEutil has been run in a mode that affects the data, ISinteg should be run until it reports that there are zero errors.

NOTE

If ISinteg is run multiple times and does not correct the database corruption, you must use the ExMerge utility, which can skip individual corrupt messages, to extract data from the database to .pst files or another database.

ESEUTIL /R

ESEutil /r performs "Soft Recovery" to attempt to bring a single database into a consistent or "Clean Shutdown" state. This is a non-trivial operation to repair the database after a restore.

ESEutil takes the parameters /r [Base log file number. Usually E00] /i.

ESEUTIL /P

The /p option used on its own will discard corrupt pages while overwriting the database. There is no guarantee that the database will be useable if critical or sufficient pages are discarded, so there is real potential of losing the database altogether. If the operation was not run on a copy, it would be catastrophic.

The use of ESEutil /p should be considered an absolute last-resort measure only.

ESEutil /d /p, on the other hand, will have a different result. The /d tells ESEutil to defragment the designated database. The /p option used after the /d instructs ESEutil to leave the newly created defragmented database in the temporary work area, and not to overwrite the original database.

Note that the order of the command-line options is important!

ISINTEG

ISinteg is the tool that sees and treats the Exchange database as a relational database.

ISinteg scans the tables and B-trees that organize the ESE pages into their logical structures. It looks at the mailboxes, public folders, and other parts of the information store, checking for orphans, incorrect values, and broken references.

ISinteg builds an Exchange database, Refer.mdb, of reference counts. It then browses the tables, and compares the counts found to the counts in the reference database; if running with the -fix switch, these counts are updated to the values to those it considers correct.

What appears valid to ESEutil from a physical data point of view might not be valid from a logical database view. Because ISinteg focuses on the logical level, it can repair and recover data that ESEutil can't. Valid data that was unavailable because of a broken reference in the database may be made available again after ISinteg repairs the link.

ISinteg has two modes: the default Test mode, which runs the specified tests and reports the results, and the Fix mode, where ISinteg runs the specified tests and attempts to fix any errors. Table 10.5 shows some of the operator options.

TABLE 10.5   ISinteg Command-Line Switches

Command	Function	Description
ISinteg -test	Test(s)	Use with a variety of command lines.
ISinteg -test Alltests	All Tests	Run all tests.
ISinteg -fix	Fix	Fix any inconsistencies in your database.
ISinteg -s	Server	Specify server name.
ISinteg -l	Log	Log file name.
ISinteg -dump	Dump	Create a verbose dump file of store data.
ISinteg -verbose	Verbose Mode	Display a detailed report of issues discovered.

It is important to run ISinteg until it no longer reports any errors. Running the command once will not guarantee the information store is functioning properly. The process can take some time depending on the size of the information store and the power and resources of the computer on which it is run.

Troubleshooting Exchange Disaster Recovery Issues

The most important thing you can do to be successful at restoring Exchange is to have options available and not send yourself down a dead-end alley. Keep your options open. How do you do that? Have more than one backup available. If your mailbox store gets corrupt and goes offline, stop and do a file-backup or copy of the complete storage group folder before you start doing anything to the database. That way, if something goes wrong, you can just delete what's there, copy the original files back in, and try again a bit wiser.

Also remember that you are not alone. At any time of day or night, there are semi-bored Exchange admins in other parts of the world who are checking the newsgroups to see if anyone needs help with something. Many of those admins have done dozens of database and mailbox recoveries and can answer your questions on forums and newsgroups if you get stuck.

Gather any clues that are available regarding what the nature of the problem is. Well-written applications will display meaningful error messages when issues are encountered. Most applications will create log files of the running processes, including any issues encountered by the process. The location of these logs can sometimes be obscure, so you might need to look in the application properties, the application folder, the system folder, or even perform a search of the system. Sometimes doing a search of all files that have changed in the last 24 hours is enough to turn up a log file that would have been difficult to track down otherwise.

In some instances, the application itself enables you to specify the location of the log file, or require you to specifically initiate one with a sub-command such as –dump. It is good practice to know how to require the creation of these logs and where these files are located for the tools you will be using well before you need to do a disaster recovery under pressure.

Errors are usually also written to the System and Application event logs by the application, and the system will write events that it encountered as a result of the operation; you can view these in the Event Viewer. Bear in mind that system and hardware events may be equally relevant. Note should be taken of the exact error message and any references and/or error number.

If the resolution is not obvious, you can use the resources listed in Appendix A, "SBS 2008 Resources," to help track down the cause and resolution to the problem.

Summary

Exchange disaster recovery is not trivial. The impact of the disaster, the time taken to recover, and the degree of success of that recovery depends upon how well it has been planned for, how well the plan has been implemented, and how well the plan has been practiced prior to any actual disaster taking place.

Exchange disaster recovery is not "set and forget." Things change over time. The volume and reliance on messaging, the tolerance to outage, the tools available, the hardware available, and the operators available are all variable within the overall plan, which should be re-assessed on a regular basis.

Small Business Server 2008 with Microsoft Exchange contains sufficient and powerful tools for successful backup and restore of Exchange messaging data. Third-party tools are also available that may enhance or simplify some of the processes; however, at the very least, the Recovery Operator should be comfortably familiar with the included tools as situations may occur where the third-party tools may not be available.

With proper planning, implementation, and practice, the most catastrophic disaster can be recovered from.

Best Practice Summary

▶ **Data Storage**—Take into account the mail usage and retention practices of the business and plan to store your Exchange Data and Log files on disks or partitions with ample free space for additional copies of the databases and logs in a recovery or repair situation. The additional space required can be considerable, and free space of at least 120% of your projected maximum Exchange database size (.edb files plus .logs if hosted on the same partition) is recommended.

▶ **Storage Groups**—Do not create more than one mail database in a storage group. Instead, create a new storage group for each database. That way, you keep the transaction logs of each database separate and can deal with mailbox database issues one at a time and keep other mailboxes online if one database has issues.

▶ **Disable Circular Logging**—You should configure an Exchange-aware backup as soon as practical after setup, ensuring that circular logging is disabled and a full System State backup is run and verified. Immediately after disabling circular logging, a full backup of Exchange should be run to provide the base point for future backups.

▶ **Database Recovery Management**—This console in the Exchange toolbox has most of the tools you need to get through a recovery scenario without having to worry about typos or tricky command-line switches. Familiarize yourself with it ahead of time.

▶ **Copy/Move Data**—Copying and moving data on the same partition is much faster than doing so between partitions, across the LAN, or to/from backup tape or external storage. Having ample room on the Exchange partition can dramatically reduce the time involved in recovery/restore operations of large Exchange databases.

▶ **Recovery Storage Group**—Do not leave a recovery storage group longer than necessary for the recovery operation. It takes up needless space, and can conflict with other operations.

▶ **Layered Solutions**—Combining layers of protection will give you the most options when it comes to recovery: Use local continuous replication, extended message retention times, and regular backups to make outages shorter and data loss much less of a hassle.

10

PART 4

Managing Client Connectivity

IN THIS PART

Group Policy in SBS 2008

Those who have been managing networks for any length of time know of the challenges associated with trying to maintain a standard environment across multiple computers. With the ever-important need to keep anti-virus and anti-spyware tools up to date, keeping current on software and system updates, and even protecting users against their own curiosity, system administrators are constantly working to make sure software and settings are kept current on all the computers in the network. Fortunately, the implementation of Group Policy in Active Directory networks helps to automate many of these types of management processes.

Group Policy is a complex and powerful component of Active Directory, yet it should not be intimidating to system administrators. This chapter breaks down Group Policy into its elemental components, describes the default policies created by SBS during setup and configuration, and discusses troubleshooting steps to find and resolve Group Policy problems.

With the release of Vista and Windows Server 2008, Microsoft introduced a number of enhancements to Group Policy, and those enhancements have been included in SBS 2008. Group Policy for Vista alone includes over 700 new Group Policy settings. Entire books have been written about Group Policy, so the scope of this chapter as it relates to Group Policy is understandably limited. However, by going through this chapter, you gain a basic understanding of how Group Policy is used and the mechanics of reviewing and making basic changes to the Group Policy environment in SBS 2008.

How SBS 2008 Employs Group Policies

SBS 2008 builds upon the default policies included in all Windows AD domains by adding a set of policies specifically written for SBS 2008. Without these policies unique to SBS 2008 present and correctly configured you will not experience the "standard" behavior in your domain, on your workstations or for your users. It's important to understand what they do, how to protect them if you make customizations, how to reset them back to default condition if needed, and how to handle any custom policies you may want to use.

Even if you don't choose to study this chapter, you should take the time to review and first understand what SBS 2008 does with Group Policy so that you can at least recognize if and when you are having an issue that is either affecting or actually breaking Group Policy management behavior.

As an SBS administrator you should think of the collection of Group Policies you will manage as having relevance as:

▶ **A domain default policy**—A typical policy that every AD domain will include (with or without SBS involved)

▶ **An SBS 2008 standard policy**—A policy typically defined by the SBS product to apply some standard settings you find in any SBS environment

▶ **A custom policy you design**—Many administrators (or even an application vendor) may create a simple or complex policy with a unique purpose in mind

This chapter is intended to help you understand how to identify what policies you should consider as critical to normal domain behavior and normal SBS 2008 client and server operations. In addition, it will be helpful if you are considering simple customizations of your own, even if that is only to set something like a standard screen saver for you workstations. It may sound trivial, but you want to avoid making a major breakdown in standard policies while attempting to make a trivial change.

The following sections identify and briefly describe the standard Group Policy elements present in SBS 2008. These high-level descriptions of the various policies are intended to give you an idea of the settings used by SBS 2008. A detailed description of the actual polices is covered later in the chapter.

Default AD Policies

All Windows server 2008 Active Directory domains contain two Group Policy objects— Default Domain Policy and Default Domain Controllers Policy. These policies exist in SBS 2008 and have only very slight modifications from the standard server policies for SBS.

▶ **Default Domain Policy**—Contains default settings for password defaults, account security defaults, and trusted root certification authority defaults.

▶ **Default Domain Controllers Policy**—Contains settings related to security access to domain controllers, backing up and restoring data on domain controllers, and SMB signing settings.

User Folder Redirection

The Small Business Server Folder Redirection Policy object is created when folder redirection settings are enabled on the server, but does not exist at the time of the server installation. This policy indicates whether folder redirection from a workstation to the server is enabled, which folders are redirected, and which users have their folders redirected.

WSUS Implementation in SBS 2008

As with the traditional implementation of WSUS, the SBS 2008 implementation of WSUS manages much of its implementation through Group Policy. There are three GPOs for the SBS 2008 implementation of WSUS:

▶ **Update Services Client Computers Policy**—Enables Automatic Updates to download and install updates and schedules installation for 3 am.

▶ **Services Common Settings Policy**—Sets default options to be applied to both client computer and server computer groups, including setting the detection frequency and which server the computers should use as the update service location.

▶ **Update Services Server Computers Policy**—Enables Automatic Updates to download but not install updates on server computers.

Workstation Client-Specific Settings

Because most SBS 2008 networks contain a mixture of Windows XP and Windows Vista workstations, the server contains Group Policy Objects that apply to each platform, as well as other settings that are common across all platforms. There are four policies set for workstation-related settings:

▶ **Windows SBS Client Policy**—Contains basic firewall settings that apply to all Windows-based workstations joined to the domain, Security Center settings, and some Terminal Server settings.

▶ **Windows SBS Client–Windows Vista Policy**—Contains more granular firewall settings specifically for Windows Vista clients.

▶ **Windows SBS Client–Windows XP Policy**—Contains firewall settings specifically for Windows XP clients.

▶ **Windows SBS CSE Policy**—Contains settings to install SBS-specific client side extensions on connected workstations.

SBS 2008 User Account Settings

The Windows SBS User policy sets the home page and other important URLs in client workstation Internet Explorer settings. The home page is set to http://companyweb, and URLs for Outlook Web Access and Remote Web Workspace are added to the favorites list.

Overview of Group Policy

In a nutshell, Group Policy enables an administrator to apply settings to users and computers on the network in a managed and granular fashion. The items listed in Table 11.1 are examples of tasks that can be managed through Group Policy.

TABLE 11.1   Tasks That Can Be Managed Through Group Policy

Task	Description
Assign Scripts	Group Policy can designate different scripts (logon, logoff, startup, shutdown, and so on) to be run.
Redirect Folders	Group Policy can take standard system folders (My Documents, Application Settings, Desktop, and so on) and point them to locations on the network.
Manage Applications	Group Policy can assign applications for use by specific users or computers, install updates for applications, or remove unwanted applications.
Modify Registry Settings	Group Policy can set values for registry settings for users or computers.
Manage Removable Media	Group Policy can set parameters for if and how removable media is accessed on workstations.

As the preceding table implies, there are some Group Policy settings that apply to computers, and some that apply to users. Logon and logoff scripts only apply to users when they log on and off the network. Startup and shutdown scripts only apply to computers. This is only one way that Group Policy is broken down into logical parts. The next section discusses in more detail the different components that make up Group Policy.

Group Policy Settings

Group Policy settings are elements of the computer environment that are enforced on users and/or computers that participate in the Active Directory network. Each Group Policy Object (GPO) can contain computer settings and/or user settings, and those settings have three main sections: Software Settings, Windows Settings, and Administrative Templates. Each individual policy element is stored in one of these three areas in either the user or computer Policy Group.

Software Settings
Policy elements under this section relate to the installation, update, or removal of software on computers on the network. Software policies enabled in the Computer Configuration apply to all users who log on to the workstation affected by the policy. This is useful to make an application available to all users of a workstation. Software policies enabled in the User Configuration apply to the users identified in the Group Policy Object no matter

which workstation they use. If a user needs to have an application available to him or her wherever he or she logs in, you set the policy element in the User Configuration.

Windows Settings

Policy elements under this section relate to scripts, security settings, folder redirection, and many other settings. There is a significant difference in the settings between the Computer Configuration and User Configuration. Table 11.2 lists and describes some of the policy elements and whether they apply to users or computers.

TABLE 11.2   Group Policy Items for Windows Settings

Policy Element	Location	Description
Scripts	Computer Configuration	Startup and shutdown scripts for workstations
Scripts	User Configuration	Logon and logoff scripts for users
Account Policies	Computer Configuration	Password and account lockout settings
Folder Redirection	User Configuration	Alternate location settings for My Documents, Application Data, and other system folders
Internet Explorer Maintenance	User Configuration	Changes to IE defaults, including security zone, favorites, and user interface settings

Administrative Templates

Policy settings in this section generally apply to the environment in which the user or computer account operates. Settings applied through Administrative Templates are stored in the computer's registry: User Configuration settings are placed in the HKEY_CURRENT_USER (HKCU) hive, and Computer Configuration settings are placed in the HKEY_LOCAL_MACHINE (HKLM) hive. Settings in the Computer Configuration apply to all users who log on to the workstation, and settings in the User Configuration apply to the user no matter which workstation in the domain he or she uses.

Group Policy Preferences

Group Policy Preferences are new in Windows Server 2008 and SBS 2008. Unlike Group Policy Settings, which cannot be changed once applied, elements enabled by Group Policy Preferences can be modified by the user after application. Group Policy Preferences are available and enabled by default in Windows Server 2008, but a Client-Side Extension (CSE), which must be installed separately, is supported on Windows XP SP2 and later, Windows Vista, and Windows Server 2003 SP1 and later.

NOTE

For a full explanation of the differences between Group Policy Settings and Group Policy Preferences, and the extent to which Group Policy Preferences can be used, please refer to the Microsoft white paper, "An Overview of Group Policy Preferences," by Jerry Honeycutt. To take full advantage of Group Policy Preferences, you need to install the Client-Side Extensions, which can be downloaded from Microsoft at http://support.microsoft.com/kb/943729.

Group Policy Preferences extensions fall into two categories: Windows Settings and Control Panel Settings. The next sections provide more detail of the elements in each of these groups.

Windows Settings

Items in the Group Policy Preferences Windows Settings area generally apply to the operating system environment. System administrators who are well-versed in writing scripts to configure the OS environment might be pleasantly surprised to find that they can handle most, if not all, of those customizations through Group Policy Preferences.

Table 11.3 gives more detail about the different elements available in Group Policy Preferences Windows Settings.

TABLE 11.3   Group Policy Preferences Windows Settings

Element	Location	Description
Applications	User Configuration	Allows software vendors to add templates for preference settings for their applications.
Drive Maps	User Configuration	Allows standardized drive mappings without using logon scripts. Can be customized for security groups, location, machine type, and so on.
Environment	Computer and User Configuration	Manage system or user environment variables, such as system paths. Settings in Environment can be used by other Preferences elements to define application paths or other system variables.
Files	User Configuration	Add, delete, or modify files on the workstation. Can be used to push common files out to groups of workstations.
Folders	Computer and User Configuration	Add, delete, modify, or clean up folders on computers. Can be used to clean up Windows temp directories, such as temporary Internet files.

TABLE 11.3   Group Policy Preferences Windows Settings

Element	Location	Description
INI Files	Computer and User Configuration	Add, delete, or modify properties in .ini files.
Network Shares	Computer Configuration	Manage network shares on multiple computers.
Registry	Computer and User Configuration	Manage individual registry settings without using Administrative Templates. Configure individual registry items up to entire registry branches.
Shortcuts	Computer and User Configuration	Add, delete, and modify shortcuts on the desktop, in the Start menu, in the Quick Launch toolbar, and so on.

Control Panel Settings

Items in the Group Policy Preferences Control Panel Settings allow modifications to Control Panel objects through GPOs. Table 11.4 details the different Control Panel elements that can be controlled through Group Policy Preferences.

TABLE 11.4   Group Policy Preferences Control Panel Settings

Element	Location	Description
Data Sources	Computer and User Configuration	Manage data source settings for Open Database Connectivity (ODBC).
Devices	Computer and User Configuration	Manage removable media devices attached to computers. Does not prevent devices from being installed, but can disable them once they are present.
Folder Options	Computer and User Configuration	Provides management of folder view settings (show hidden files, display file extensions) and file type application mapping.
Internet Settings	User Configuration	Provides non-mandatory settings for Internet Explorer, such as home page, favorites, and other settings provided in the Control Panel options for IE.

TABLE 11.4   Group Policy Preferences Control Panel Settings

Element	Location	Description
Local Users and Groups	Computer and User Configuration	Manage local user and group settings, such as adding local users or controlling membership in local groups.
Network Options	Computer and User Configuration	Manage VPN and dial-up networking configurations by creating or modifying connection settings.
Power Options	Computer and User Configuration	Provides non-mandatory management of power settings (display sleep times, hard disk sleep times).
Printers	Computer and User Configuration	Create, delete, or update printer objects similar to managing drive mappings.
Regional Options	User Configuration	Manage regional options for date, time, currency, and so on.
Scheduled Tasks	Computer and User Configuration	Create, delete, and modify scheduled tasks.
Services	Computer Configuration	Manage services on the workstation by modifying their startup type, services action, log on as, and recovery settings.
Start Menu	User Configuration	Configure settings for the Start menu for both XP and Vista.

Working with the Group Policy Management Console

Given the changes Microsoft has implemented in Group Policy since the release of Windows Server 2003, it's not a huge surprise that the Group Policy Management Console (GPMC) has changed as well. Readers who are familiar with the Group Policy Management Console from the Server 2003 days will notice quite a few differences, but not so many that the new console will take time to relearn. SBS 2003 administrators will also notice another change—the Group Policy Management Console snap-in is no longer available in the Windows Server "Cougar" Console. It can be found in the standard Server Manager console and can be loaded manually from the command prompt as gpmc.msc. Note that you will receive a User Account Control (UAC) prompt when opening the GPMC.

Navigating the Group Policy Management Console

Figure 11.1 shows the Group Policy Management Console (GPMC) expanded to the
domain level so you can see all the policy objects present at the domain level.

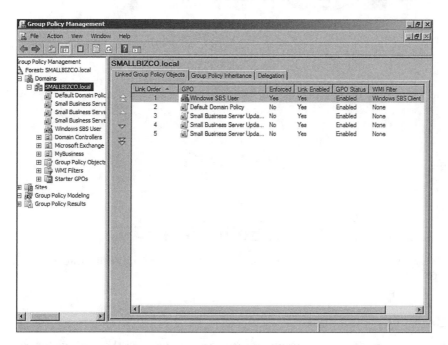

FIGURE 11.1   The Group Policy Management Console snap-in is listed with other snap-ins
under the Advanced Management section of the Server Management console.

From this view, many of the properties of the policy objects can be seen, including the
name of the GPO, whether the GPO is enabled or enforced, any WMI filters applied to the
GPO, and the order in which the policy objects are applied. As shown in the figure, the
first policy object processed, the Windows SBS User GPO, has the Windows SBS Client
filter set, meaning that only objects matching the criteria in that filter process the settings
in that GPO.

Figure 11.2 shows that you can browse the Active Directory OU structure to locate additional policies. In this case, the figure shows one additional GPO linked to the Domain
Controllers OU, three linked to the SBSComputers OU, and one linked to the SBSUsers OU.

In addition, navigating the browse tree to the Group Policy Objects folder, shown in
Figure 11.3, displays all the GPOs present in the Active Directory structure. Unfortunately,
in this view, you cannot immediately tell where in the AD structure the GPOs are tied.

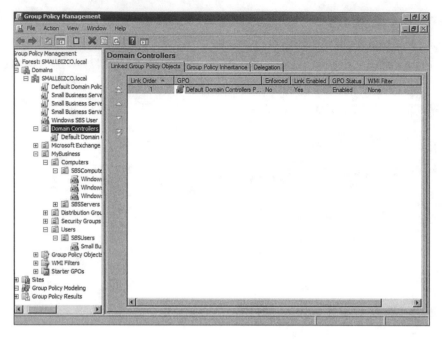

FIGURE 11.2   The browse tree in the left pane enables you to navigate the Active Directory structure to view GPO items.

Viewing Group Policy Settings

The Group Policy Management Console provides easy access to view all the settings for each GPO. Those who worked with Group Policy prior to the Windows Server 2003 series remember having to browse to an OU or domain (or suite) in Active Directory Users and Computers and selecting the correct options in the Group Policy tab under the object properties. The GPMC puts all the relevant settings of the GPO in one location for simple review. If you double-click on a GPO object listed in the GPO view shown previously in Figure 11.1, the GPMC displays the settings of the GPO, the details of which are described in the following sections.

Group Policy Scope

The initial view of the GPO in the GPMC is shown in Figure 11.4. The Scope tab is initially displayed, which describes the details of how and where the GPO is applied.

In the figure, the Windows SBS User GPO links to the domain, so its settings are applied to every user and computer in the domain. You can also quickly see that the GPO link is enabled and enforced. The figure also shows the Security Filtering applied to the object. Only Active Directory objects listed in the Security Filtering area have the settings from the GPO applied to them. This is yet another way applying settings can be controlled for a specific user or group. For more information about implementing Security Filtering, see the Microsoft Technet document "Security Filtering Using GPMC" at http://technet. microsoft.com/en-us/library/cc781988.aspx.

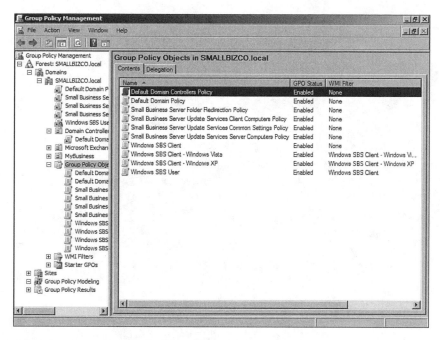

FIGURE 11.3 The Group Policy Objects folder displays all the GPOs that exist in Active Directory.

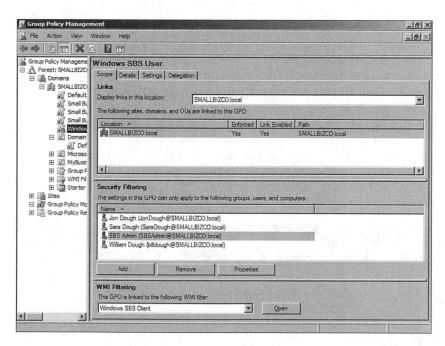

FIGURE 11.4 The Scope tab for each GPO indicates where the GPO is linked, what security filtering is applied, and what WMI filtering is applied, if any.

Group Policy Details

When you click on the Details tab, you see the view detailed in Figure 11.5.

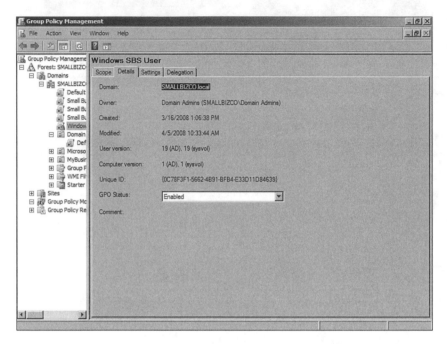

FIGURE 11.5   The Details tab gives technical information about the GPO.

In the Details tab, you can see where the GPO is linked (SmallBizCo.local), who owns the GPO (SMALLBIZCO\Domain Admins), when it was created and modified, the GUID for the object, and its enabled status. The versions for the user configuration and computer configuration are listed as well. In this example, the User version shows 19 for AD and 19 for sysvol. This indicates that the user configuration for this GPO has been modified 19 times following the original installation. The Computer version shows 1 for AD and sysvol, indicating that one set of modifications has been saved to this GPO since it was originally created. The Details tab also shows the globally unique identifier (GUID) for the GPO. This GUID identifies the specific folder in which the GPO files are stored in the SysVol folder (usually C:\WINDOWS\sysvol\sysvol*internaldomain*\policies).

> **NOTE**
>
> If you see different version numbers between AD and sysvol, then the GPO files stored on the SysVol share are out of sync with the GPO settings stored in Active Directory. You will not generally see this happen, however, unless an administrator has attempted to edit the GPO files in SysVol by hand.

Group Policy Settings

Clicking the Settings tab displays the view shown in Figure 11.6. This is the view most administrators use when reviewing Group Policy settings.

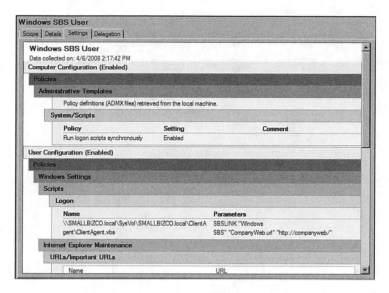

FIGURE 11.6   The Settings tab displays all the active settings in the selected GPO.

When you first select the Settings tab, the GPMC runs a report on the GPO settings in order to display them in the format shown in the figure. The settings are broken down into the group elements described in the "Group Policy Settings" section earlier in the chapter. In this figure, you can see that the Computer Configuration settings starts with settings in the Administrative Templates element, yet omits mention of the Software and Windows sections entirely. This means that there are no settings defined in this GPO for the Software or Windows settings elements. The path to the setting in the GPO is also listed, so the first element listed, Run Logon Script Synchronously, can be found by navigating the path Computer Configuration | Policies | Administrative Templates | System | Scripts to find the specific policy.

Figure 11.7 shows a better view of the settings included in the Windows SBS User GPO, specifically the Logon Scripts and Internet Explorer Maintenance settings configured by default.

Group Policy Delegation

The last tab in this view, the Delegation tab shown in Figure 11.8, lists the permissions on the GPO enabled for the listed security groups.

In the figure, the Domain Admins, Enterprise Admins, and SYSTEM objects have what amounts to full control over the selected GPO. The Authenticated Users and ENTERPRISE DOMAIN CONTROLLERS objects only have Read permissions on the GPO.

There are three levels of access that can be assigned to a GPO. Read allows an object to see the contents of the GPO and determine, based on the settings on the GPO, if the contents should be applied. Edit Settings allows an object to modify the policy settings within the GPO, but not to modify the permissions on the GPO or remove it from the domain. Edit

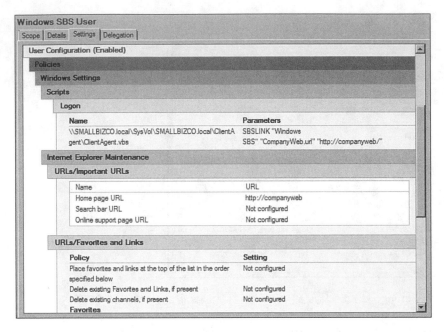

FIGURE 11.7   All the details for each policy setting defined are listed in this view.

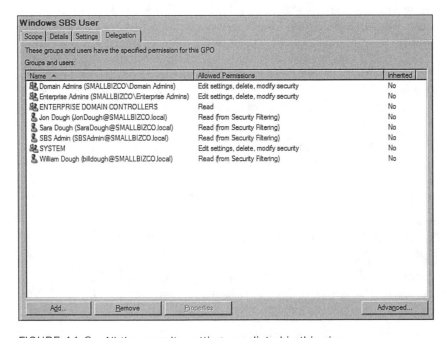

FIGURE 11.8   All the security settings are listed in this view.

Settings, Delete, Modify Security allows the object to perform all actions on the GPO, including removing the object from the domain.

Also seen in Figure 11.8, the SBS Admin account (as well as other accounts) have the Read (from Security Filtering) permission identified in the Allowed Permissions column. This indicates that those users have been assigned the Read permission by virtue of being included in the Security Filter on the object, as shown in Figure 11.4 previously.

Group Policy Scope and Order of Application

One of the most important features of Group Policy is that there can be more than one policy applied depending on the domain configuration. This aids in the management and planning of policy for the entire network, while affording a level of granularity not possible prior to Active Directory.

Each group of settings is bundled into a Group Policy Object (GPO). Each GPO exists as an Object in Active Directory and is linked to an Organizational Unit (OU) in AD. All objects contained in the OU will have the GPO applied when the object authenticates to Active Directory. For a user object, this is when the user logs into a Windows-based workstation with a domain account. For a Windows-based, domain-joined computer, this is when the computer boots and attaches to the domain. The GPO contains not only the computer and user policy settings but also contains the security settings and filters that determine if the policy gets applied to a specific user or computer.

There are specific rules that determine the order in which policy elements are applied: local, site, domain, and organizational unit (OU). The following list describes the function of each:

- **Local settings**—Each computer has a set of local policies that are applied at boot time before any other policies. Each computer contains only one local policy object.

- **Site settings**—Each Active Directory site can contain a set of policy objects. There can be multiple GPOs assigned at the site level. A default SBS installation has no site-level GPOs.

- **Domain settings**—Each domain object in Active Directory can contain another set of GPOs, which are processed after the site settings. A default SBS installation has multiple GPOs defined at the domain level. See the "Default SBS 2008 Group Policy Objects" section of the chapter for more information.

- **Organizational unit settings**—Organizational units can contain multiple sets of GPOs as well. GPOs associated with OUs are processed last.

In addition, there are three other aspects of Group Policy that control when and how policy is applied. These items are described below:

- **Enforcement**—When a GPO is set to Enforced, the settings contained in any subsequent GPOs processed cannot override the settings contained in the enforced object. This means that if a GPO linked to the site is marked as enforced, any settings it contains will be applied even if GPOs linked to an OU have conflicting settings.

▶ **Link Order precedence**—In a case when an OU has multiple GPOs linked to it, the GPOs have an order in which they are processed. When a new GPO is linked to an OU with existing GPOs linked, the new GPO will be added at the end of the list and will therefore be processed last.

▶ **Loopback processing**—Loopback processing is one of the more confusing aspects of Group Policy because it goes against the regular order of application. In general, the GPOs that apply to a user object are based on where the user object is located in Active Directory. With Loopback processing, the GPOs that apply to a user depend on where the computer object the user is logging into is located in AD. The best example for understanding Loopback processing is when a Terminal Server is present in the environment. When dealing with a Terminal Server, there may be settings that you want to have applied to all users who log in on the Terminal Server (such as removing the Shut Down button from the Start menu) that you would not want applied to the user when logging in on other workstations. Loopback processing operates in two modes when enabled—merge and replace. When merge mode is enabled, the Group Policy user settings for the Loopback object are merged with other GP settings that have already been applied to the user. When replace mode is enabled, any Group Policy user settings that may have been applied already are discarded and replaced with the user settings identified in the Loopback GPO. For more information about Group Policy Loopback processing, see MSKB 231287 (http://support.microsoft.com/kb/231287). For information about using Loopback processing to manage Terminal Servers, see MSKB 260370 (http://support.microsoft.com/kb/260370).

NOTE

Group Policy can only be applied to organizational units, not system containers. This is why the SBS wizards do not place user and computer objects into the Users and Computers containers. When users or computers are added manually in Active Directory and placed into these containers, the only GPOs that are applied are the Local, Site, and Domain GPOs. No further fine tuning of Group Policy can then take place.

If there are settings conflicts between multiple GPOs, the settings in the most recently applied GPO take precedence. Figure 11.9 shows the processing order of GPOs in the SBS 2008 environment. Note that the workstation processes policy along a different path than the user object.

Group Policy Filtering

Besides achieving some level of granularity in Group Policy assignment by assigning policies at different OU levels, you can also further control the application of Group Policy by

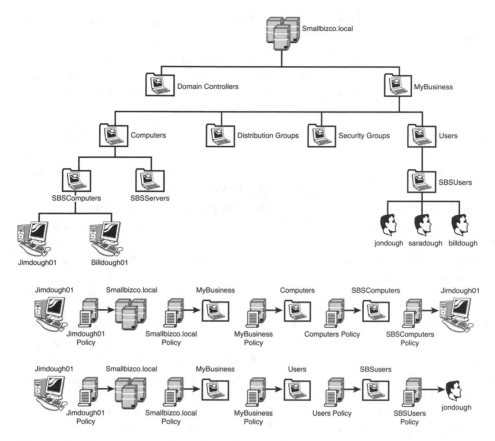

FIGURE 11.9   Group Policy processing order.

security group and WMI filters. In general, WMI filters add a level of granularity that is probably not needed in the SBS environment, but it's nice to know that it's available should you need it.

> **NOTE**
>
> WMI filtering of Group Policy is supported by Windows XP, 2003 and later versions of Windows including Vista and 2008. Windows 2000 workstations do not understand WMI filtering, and as a result do not process any policy objects that have a WMI filter attached.

Security filtering is another important aspect of restricting how Group Policy is applied. By default, a GPO can only be processed by an object that has been assigned permissions to access the object in the Security Filtering control in the GPMC, as shown in Figure 11.4

previously. This allows for multiple objects to be linked to an OU, yet not processed by all objects in that OU.

Suppose you want to create a GPO that maps a drive letter to a path on the server, but you want to have some users map the drive letter to one path and have other users map the same drive letter to a different path. The following actions could be taken to achieve this goal:

1. Create a GPO named GPO1 linked to the domain that maps drive H: to a path on the server (for example, *servername**group1*).

2. Create a GPO named GPO2 linked to the domain that maps drive H: to a different path on the server (for example, *servername**group2*).

3. Create two security groups on the server (Group1 and Group2), and give the members of group 1 access to *servername**group1* and members of group 2 access to *servername**group2*.

4. In the Security Filter window in GPMC, add the security group that has access to the path mapped in the GPO.

5. In the Security Filter window in GPMC, remove all other objects from the list.

This will have the net result that GPO1 can only be processed by members of Group1 and GPO2 can only be processed by members of Group2.

Additionally, Group Policy Preferences allow for filtering by security group, WMI, and on individual preference items through Item-level targeting. Item-level targeting is an incredibly powerful feature of Group Policy Preferences in that within a single GPO you can have multiple settings that apply to different objects. The previous example of having a mapped drive pointing to different locations depending on security group could be accomplished in a single GPO with Group Policy Preferences. For more information about Item-level targeting, see the Microsoft Technet document Preference Item-Level Targeting at http://technet.microsoft.com/en-us/library/cc733022.aspx.

Group Policy Inheritance

The term Group Policy Inheritance means that lower-level objects in Active Directory "inherit" any GPO settings that were applied by higher-level objects. This is essentially a restating of the Group Policy order of processing. If a lower-level GPO does not contain settings that override settings applied in a higher-level GPO, then the settings from the higher-level GPO are "inherited" by the lower-level containers. This does not mean that those settings are re-applied by the lower-level objects, just that the lower-level objects have not modified the settings from the upper objects. You can use a Block Inheritance setting at a specific OU to effectively erase any Group Policy settings that have been applied by higher-level objects. This would mean that only GPOs assigned to that OU and lower would apply to objects contained within that GPO. However, Block Inheritance should be used sparingly as it could lead to unexpected behavior and cause difficulty in troubleshooting Group Policy problems.

Overriding Group Policy Processing Order

There might be times when you want to have a domain-level policy apply, no matter what settings are applied at the OU level. To achieve this, you need to mark the policy object as "enforced." When a policy object is enforced, no subsequent policy settings can override settings contained in the enforced object.

For example, a system administrator has set a policy in a domain GPO that sets all user desktop backgrounds to be a specific image file. Another administrator creates an OU GPO that sets the desktop background to be a different image file. Because the OU policy processes after the domain policy, the image set in the OU policy is what will appear on the desktop of user objects within that OU. If the main administrator wants to have the domain GPO apply no matter what settings are changed in the OU GPO, the administrator can set the domain GPO as enforced. Then when the OU GPO is processed, if there are any conflicting settings between the OU GPO and the domain GPO, the settings in the domain GPO will still apply.

NOTE

Setting a GPO as enforced only applies to settings defined in that GPO. A subsequent policy object can change any policy items that are undefined in a GPO that has been set as enforced.

Working with Group Policy Modeling and Results

The Group Policy Modeling and Group Policy Results Reports can provide useful planning and troubleshooting information when implementing new Group Policy elements in the network. These reports offer two different looks into the way Group Policy impacts the network. The Modeling Report shows how Group Policy should be applied to a specific user and workstation combination, whereas the Results Report shows how Group Policy was actually applied to a user or workstation. You use Group Policy Modeling to test how a new or modified GPO would impact the production environment without actually making changes to the environment and potentially causing problems. You use Group Policy Results to see how Group Policy settings have been applied to a specific user and workstation to troubleshoot problems with an existing GPO implementation.

Both tools enable you to view the information in a report similar to the GPO settings screen seen in Figure 11.7. The next two sections detail how to generate the Modeling and Results Reports.

Creating the Modeling Report

Follow these steps to create a new Group Policy Modeling Report:

1. Open the Group Policy Management Console.

2. Right-click on Group Policy Modeling from the navigation tree and select Group Policy Modeling Wizard.

3. In the initial title page of the wizard, click Next.

4. Make sure that the internal domain listed in the Show Domain Controllers for This Domain field is correct, and then click Next.

5. In the User and Computer selection page, shown in Figure 11.10, select the user and computer you want to model. If you are looking for general behavior across the network, select the MyBusiness | Users | SBSUsers Organizational Unit (OU) for the user information, and the MyBusiness | Computers | SBSComputers OU for the computer information. Click Next to continue.

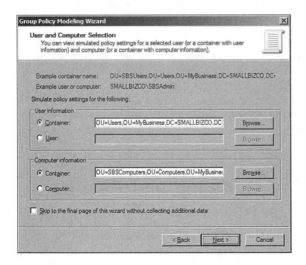

FIGURE 11.10   Select the global user and computer OUs in the wizard, or select a specific user and computer for the report.

NOTE

If you are not doing any WMI or security group processing with the GPO, click the Skip to the final page of this wizard without collecting additional data checkbox before clicking Next. This skips over the next several steps and takes you directly to the Summary Selections page in step 11.

---

6. In the Advanced Simulation Options page, you can check for slow network connection conditions (users connecting over a WAN link) or loopback processing options if needed. Generally, these will not be needed. Click Next to continue.

7. In the User Security Groups page, you can select a specific security group to include, if your GPO is being filtered by security group. Click Next to continue.

8. In the Computer Security Groups page, you can select a specific security group to include, if your GPO is being filtered by security group. Click Next to continue.

9. In the WMI Filters for Users page, select any WMI filters that apply to the GPO. Click Next to continue.

10. In the WMI Filters for Computers page, select any WMI filters that apply to the GPO. Click Next to continue.

11. Review the summary of selections, and then click Next to process the simulation.

12. Click Finish to close the wizard.

Now you have a report in the GPMC that you can review for the session. The Summary tab shows you the policy objects that should be applied to the user/computer combination specified in the wizard. Figure 11.11 shows the summary for this sample report, including the GPOs that were applied and denied.

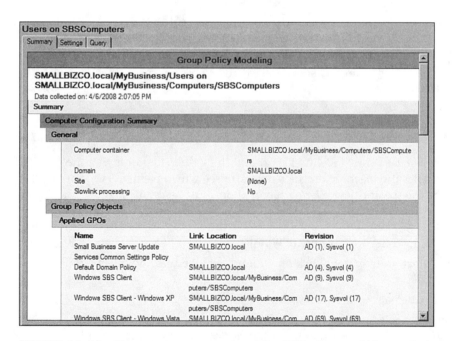

FIGURE 11.11   The report summary shows the GPOs that would be applied to a user and computer.

You can review the settings in the Settings tab, shown in Figure 11.12, to make sure that the settings for the specific environment you want to create are evident in the report. This view shows each element of policy that would be applied and which GPO the element came from.

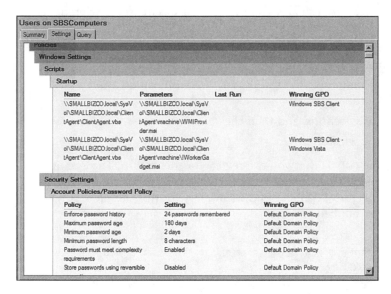

FIGURE 11.12   The settings summary shows the individual policy elements that would get applied in this scenario.

Creating the Results Report

The key difference between the Modeling Report and the Results Report is that the Results Report actually queries the machine on the network to see which elements were applied. To run this report, the specific device being reported on must be available on the network.

Follow these steps to create a Results Report:

1. Open the Group Policy Management Console.

2. From the navigation tree, right-click on Group Policy Results and select Group Policy Results Wizard.

3. In the initial title page of the wizard, click Next.

4. In the Computer Selection page of the wizard, click the Another Computer radio button, and then click Browse and select the workstation to run the report against. Click Next to continue.

5. In the User Selection page of the wizard, choose the specific user from the list of available users and click Next to continue.

> **NOTE**
>
> Only users who have ever logged into the workstation prior to running the report will be available in the User Selection page of the wizard.

6. Click Finish to close the wizard and view the report.

Like the Modeling Report, the Results Report shows the GPOs applied in the Summary tab and the actual policy elements applied in the Settings tab. Again, the difference in this report is that the GPOs and the elements shown are the actual settings that were applied to the user and workstation.

Default SBS 2008 Group Policy Objects

Undocumented changes to Group Policy Objects can cause a number of headaches for a server administrator. Changes to Group Policy can significantly alter the behavior of a workstation, and if it is not clear that a change was made to any GPO settings, the server administrator may go down the wrong road when troubleshooting any problems that arise from that. Given the number of policies created by default in SBS 2008, that pain can be significantly greater. This section of the chapter details the default settings of these objects at installation time to be used as a reference when troubleshooting Group Policy issues.

If a policy element is not explicitly defined, it is not listed in the table and its value in the Group Policy Management Editor (GPME) can be assumed to be "Not Defined." The terms *domainname* and *servername* listed in the tables refer to the internal NetBIOS domain name for the network and the internal NetBIOS name of the server. The term *FQDN* refers to the fully-qualified internal domain name for the network (that is, domain.local), and the term *publicFQDN* refers to the fully-qualified public DNS name for the server (that is, remote.domain.com).

> **Best Practice—Do Not Modify Default Domain Policies**
>
> Although you might be tempted to change the Default Domain Policy or the Default Domain Controllers Policy objects, do not make any modifications to these objects. Follow the example of the SBS development team and create new policy objects or modify the SBS policy objects if you need to add policy elements to the SBS network. If you make a change to one of the Default objects and find out that something has gone wrong on the network as a result, it is difficult to undo the changes made to those policy objects.
>
> The "Troubleshooting Group Policy" section later in the chapter discusses a method for defining, testing, and implementing Group Policy changes. Follow the guidelines there for correctly implementing Group Policy changes to the network.

Default Domain Controllers Policy

Table 11.5 contains the default settings for the Default Domain Controllers Policy.

TABLE 11.5   Default Domain Controllers Policy

Policy	Setting
Computer Configuration	
Policies| Windows Settings | Security Settings | Local Policies | User Rights Assignments	
Access this computer from the network	Everyone, BUILTIN\Administrators, NT AUTHORITY\Authenticated Users, NT AUTHORITY\ENTERPRISE DOMAIN CONTROLLERS, BUILTIN\Pre-Windows 2000 Compatible Access
Add workstations to the domain	NT AUTHORITY\Authenticated Users
Adjust memory quotas for a process	*domainname*\SQLServer2005MSFTEUser$*servername*$ SBSMonitoring, *domainname*\SQLServer2005MSSQLUser$*servername*$ MICROSOFT##SSEE, NT AUTHORITY\LOCAL SERVICE, NT AUTHORITY\NETWORK SERVICE, BUILTIN\Administrators, *domainname*\SQLServer2005MSSQLUser$*servername*$ SBSMonitoring
Allow log on locally	BUILTIN\Administrators, BUILTIN\Backup Operators, BUILTIN\Account Operators, BUILTIN\Server Operators, BUILTING\Print Operators
Back up files and directories	BUILTIN\Administrators, BUILTIN\Backup Operators, BUILTIN\Server Operators
Bypass traverse checking	*domainname*\SQLServer2005MSFTEUser$*servername*$ SBSMonitoring, *domainname*\SQLServer2005MSSQLUser$*servername*$ MICROSOFT##SSEE, Everyone, NT AUTHORITY\LOCAL SERVICE, NT AUTHORITY\NETWORK SERVICE, BUILTIN\Administrators, NT AUTHORITY\Authenticated Users, BUILTIN\Pre-Windows 2000 Compatible Access, *domainname*\SQLServer2005MSSQLUser$*servername*$ SBSMonitoring
Change the system time	NT AUTHORITY\LOCAL SERVICE, BUILTIN\Administrators, BUILTIN\Server Operators
Create a pagefile	BUILTIN\Administrators
Debug programs	BUILTIN\Administrators
Enable computer and user accounts to be trusted for delegation	BUILTIN\Administrators

TABLE 11.5   Default Domain Controllers Policy

Policy	Setting
Force shutdown from a remote system	BUILTIN\Administrators, BUILTIN\Server Operators
Generate security audits	NT AUTHORITY\LOCAL SERVICE, NT AUTHORITY\NETWORK SERVICE
Increase scheduling priority	BUILTIN\Administrators
Load and unload device drivers	BUILTIN\Administrators, BUILTIN\PRINT OPERATORS
Log on as a batch job	*domainname*\SQLServer2005MSFTEUser$*servername*$ SBSMONITORING, *domainname*\SQLServer2005MSSQLUser$*servername*$ SBSMONITORING, *domainname*\SQLServer2005MSSQLUser$*servername*$ MICROSOFT##SSEE, BUILTIN\Administrators, BUILTIN\Backup Operators, BUILTIN\Performance Log Users, BUILTIN\IIS_IUSRS
Manage auditing and security log	BUILTIN\Administrators, *domainname*\Exchange Servers
Modify firmware environment values	BUILTIN\Administrators
Profile single process	BUILTIN\Administrators
Profile system performance	BUILTIN\Administrators
Remove computer from docking station	BUILTIN\Administrators
Replace a process-level token	*domainname*\SQLServer2005MSFTEUser$*servername*$ SBSMONITORING, *domainname*\SQLServer2005MSSQLUser$*servername*$ MICROSOFT##SSEE, NT AUTHORITY\LOCAL SERVICE, NT AUTHORITY\NETWORK SERVICE, *domainname*\SQLServer2005MSSQLUser$*servername*$ SBSMONITORING
Restore files and directories	BUILTIN\Administrators, BUILTIN\Backup Operators, BUILTIN\Server Operators
Shut down the system	BUILTIN\Administrators, BUILTIN\Backup Operators, BUILTIN\Server Operators, BUILTIN\Print Operators
Take ownership of files and other objects	BUILTIN\Administrators

11

TABLE 11.5   Default Domain Controllers Policy

Policy	Setting
Policies| Windows Settings | Security Settings | Local Policies | Security Options	
Domain controller: LDAP server signing requirements	None
Domain member: Digitally encrypt or sign secure channel data (always)	Enabled
Microsoft network server: Digitally sign communications (always)	Enabled
Microsoft network server: Digitally sign communications (if client agrees)	Enabled
Network security: LAN Manager authentication level	Send NTLMv2 response only

Default Domain Policy

Table 11.6 contains the default settings for the Default Domain Policy.

TABLE 11.6   Default Domain Policy

Policy	Setting
Computer Configuration	
Policies | Windows Settings | Security Settings | Account Policies | Password Policy	
Enforce password history	24 passwords remembered
Maximum password age	180 days
Minimum password age	2 days
Minimum password length	8 characters
Password must meet complexity requirements	Enabled
Store passwords using reversible encryption	Disabled
Policies | Windows Settings | Security Settings | Account Policies | Account Lockout Policy	
Account lockout threshold	0 invalid logon attempts
Policies | Windows Settings | Security Settings | Account Policies | Kerberos Policy	
Enforce user logon restrictions	Enabled

TABLE 11.6   Default Domain Policy

Policy	Setting
Maximum lifetime for service ticket	600 minutes
Maximum lifetime for user ticket	10 hours
Maximum lifetime for user ticket renewal	7 days
Maximum tolerance for computer clock synchronization	5 minutes
Policies | Windows Settings | Security Settings | Local Policies | Security Options	
Network access: Allow anonymous SID/Name translation	Disabled
Network security: Do not store LAN Manager hash value on next password change	Enabled
Network security: Force logoff when logon hours expire	Disabled
Policies | Windows Settings | Security Settings | Public Key Policies | Trusted Root Certification Authorities	
Allow users to select new root certification authorities (CAs) to trust	Enabled
Client computers can trust the following certificate stores	Third-Party Root Certification Authorities and Enterprise Root Certification Authorities
To perform certificate-based authentication of users and computers, CAs must meet the following criteria	Registered in Active Directory only

Small Business Server Folder Redirection Policy

Table 11.7 contains the default settings for the Small Business Server Folder Redirection Policy.

TABLE 11.7   Small Business Server Folder Redirection Policy

Policy	Setting
User Configuration	
Policies | Windows Settings | Folder Redirection | Desktop	
Setting: Basic (Redirect everyone's folder to the same location)	Path: *servername*\RedirectedFolders\ %USERNAME%\Desktop
Grant user exclusive rights to Desktop	Enabled
Move the contents of Desktop to the new location	Enabled

TABLE 11.7   Small Business Server Folder Redirection Policy

Policy	Setting
Also apply redirection policy to Windows 2000, Windows 2000 server, Windows XP, and Windows Server 2003 operating systems	Enabled
Policy Removal Behavior	Restore contents
Policies | Windows Settings | Folder Redirection | Documents	
Setting: Basic (Redirect everyone's folder to the same location)	Path: *servername*\RedirectedFolders\ %USERNAME%\My Documents
Grant user exclusive rights to Documents	Enabled
Move the contents of Documents to the new location	Enabled
Also apply redirection policy to Windows 2000, Windows 2000 server, Windows XP, and Windows Server 2003 operating systems	Enabled
Policy Removal Behavior	Restore contents
Policies | Windows Settings | Folder Redirection | Music	
Setting	Follow the Documents folder
Policies | Windows Settings | Folder Redirection | Pictures	
Setting	Follow the Documents folder
Policies | Windows Settings | Folder Redirection | Videos	
Setting	Follow the Documents folder

Update Services Client Computers Policy

Table 11.8 contains the default settings for the Update Services Client Computers Policy.

TABLE 11.8   Update Services Client Computers Policy

Policy	Setting
Computer Configuration	
Policies | Administrative Templates | Windows Components | Windows Update	
Configure Automatic Updates	Enabled
Configure automatic updating	4—Auto download and schedule the install
The following settings are only required and applicable if 4 is selected.	
Scheduled install day	0—Every day
Scheduled install time	03:00

Update Services Common Settings Policy

Table 11.9 contains the default settings for the Update Services Common Settings Policy.

TABLE 11.9   Update Services Common Settings Policy

Policy	Setting
Computer Configuration	
Policies | Administrative Templates | Windows Components | Windows Update	
Allow Automatic Updates immediate installation	Enabled
Allow non-administrators to receive update notifications	Enabled
Automatic Updates detection frequency	Enabled
Check for updates at the following interval (hours)	1
Configure Automatic Updates	Enabled
Configure automatic updating	2—Notify for download and notify for install
Delay restart for scheduled installations	Enabled
Wait the following period before proceeding with a scheduled restart (minutes)	5
No auto-restart for scheduled automatic updates installations	Disabled
Re-prompt for restart with scheduled installations	Enabled
Wait the following period before prompting again with a scheduled restart (minutes)	10
Reschedule Automatic Updates scheduled installations	Enabled
Wait after system startup (minutes)	1
Specify intranet Microsoft update service location	Enabled
Set the intranet update service for detecting updates	http://*servername*:8530
Set the intranet statistics server	http://*servername*:8530

Update Services Server Computers Policy

Table 11.10 contains the default settings for the Update Services Server Computers Policy.

TABLE 11.10   Update Services Server Computers Policy

Policy	Setting
Computer Configuration	
Policies | Administrative Templates | Windows Components | Windows Update	
Configure Automatic Updates	Enabled
Configure automatic updating	3—Auto download and notify for installation

Windows SBS Client Policy

Table 11.11 contains the default settings for the Windows SBS Client Policy Group Policy.

TABLE 11.11   Windows SBS Client Policy

Policy	Setting
Computer Configuration	
Policies | Windows Settings | Security Settings | Windows Firewall with Advanced Security | Global Settings	
Policy Version	Not Configured
Disable stateful FTP	Not Configured
Disable stateful PPTP	Not Configured
IPsec exempt	Not Configured
IPsec through NAT	Not Configured
Preshared key encoding	Not Configured
SA idle time	Not Configured
Strong CRL check	Not Configured
Policies | Windows Settings | Security Settings | Windows Firewall with Advanced Security | Domain Profile Settings	
Firewall state	On
Inbound connections	Not Configured
Outbound connections	Not Configured
Apply local firewall rules	Not Configured
Apply local connection security rules	Not Configured
Display notifications	Not Configured

TABLE 11.11   Windows SBS Client Policy

Policy	Setting
Allow unicast responses	Not Configured
Log dropped packets	Not Configured
Log successful connections	Not Configured
Log file path	Not Configured
Log file maximum size (KB)	Not Configured
Policies | Administrative Templates | Network | Network Connections | Windows Firewall | Domain Profile	
Windows Firewall: Protect all network connections	Enabled
Policies | Administrative Templates | System | Remote Assistance	
Offer Remote Assistance	Enabled
Helpers	*domainname*\Domain Admins
Policies | Administrative Templates | Windows Components | Security Center	
Turn on Security Center (Domain PCs only)	Enabled
Policies | Administrative Templates | Windows Components | Terminal Services | Terminal Server | Connections	
Allow users to connect remotely using Terminal Services	Enabled
Policies | Administrative Templates | Windows Components | Terminal Services | Terminal Server | Security	
Require user authentication for remote connections by using Network Level Authentication	Disabled
Policies | Administrative Templates | Windows Small Business Server Group Policy Client Side Extensions	
Outlook recovery settings for mailbox folders	Enabled
The version number for Windows Small Business Server 2008	Enabled
Setting (The version number for Windows Small Business Server 2008)	6.0.5601

Windows SBS CSE Policy

Table 11.12 contains the default settings for the Windows SBS CSE Policy Group Policy object.

TABLE 11.12   Windows SBS CSE Policy

Policy	Setting
Computer Configuration	
Policies | Windows Settings | Scripts | Startup	
Name	*internaldomain*\SysVol*internaldomain*\ClientAgent\ ClientAgent.vbs
Parameters	*internaldomain*\SysVol*internaldomain*\ClientAgent\ machine\sbslogon.exe SBSCSE32
	internaldomain\SysVol*internaldomain*\ClientAgent\ machine\clientagentx86.msi X86
Name	*internaldomain*\SysVol*internaldomain*\ClientAgent\ ClientAgent.vbs
Parameters	*internaldomain*\SysVol*internaldomain*\ClientAgent\ machine\sbslogon.exe SBSCSE64
	internaldomain\SysVol*internaldomain*\ClientAgent\ machine\clientagentamd64.msi X64
Policies | Administrative Templates | System | Scripts	
Run startup scripts asynchronously	Disabled

Windows SBS Client—Windows Vista Policy

The Windows SBS Client–Windows Vista Policy Group Policy Object is large and complex. It is beyond the scope of this book to include the default contents of the policy in print. The contents of the policy can be found at the SBS 2008 Unleashed web site (http://www. informit.com/title/9780672329579) under the "Additional Resources" area.

Windows SBS Client—Windows XP Policy

Table 11.13 contains the default settings for the Windows SBS Client–Windows XP Policy Group Policy.

TABLE 11.13   Windows SBS Client—Windows XP Policy

Policy	Setting
Computer Configuration	
Policies | Administrative Templates | Network | Network Connections | Windows Firewall | Domain Profile	
Windows Firewall: Allow inbound file and printer sharing exception	Enabled
Allow unsolicited incoming messages from these IP addresses	Localsubnet

TABLE 11.13   Windows SBS Client—Windows XP Policy

Policy	Setting
Windows Firewall: Allow inbound remote administration exception	Enabled
Allow unsolicited incoming messages from these IP addresses	Localsubnet
Windows Firewall: Allow inbound Remote Desktop exceptions	Enabled
Allow unsolicited incoming messages from these IP addresses	Localsubnet
Windows Firewall: Allow local port exceptions	Enabled
Windows Firewall: Allow local program exceptions	Enabled
Windows Firewall: Define inbound port exceptions	Enabled
Define port exceptions:	135:TCP:Enabled:Offer Remote Assistance—Port
Windows Firewall: Define inbound program exceptions	Enabled
Define program exceptions:	%windir%\system32\sessmgr.exe:*: Enabled:Remote Assistance
	%windir%\PCHealth\HelpCtr\Binaries\Helps vc.exe:*:Enabled:Offer Remote Assistance
	%windir%\PCHealth\HelpCtr\Binaries\Helpc tr.exe:*:Enabled:Remote Assistance — Windows Messenger and Voice
Policies | Administrative Templates | Network | Network Connections | Windows Firewall | Standard Profile	
Windows Firewall: Allow local port exceptions	Enabled
Windows Firewall: Allow local program exceptions	Enabled
Windows Firewall: Protect all network connections	Enabled

Windows SBS User Policy

Table 11.14 contains the default settings for the Windows SBS User Policy Group Policy.

TABLE 11.14   Windows SBS User Policy

Policy	Setting
Policies | Windows Settings | Internet Explorer Maintenance | URLs | Important URLs	
Home page URL	http://companyweb
Search bar URL	Not configured
Online support page URL	Not configured
Policies | Windows Settings | Internet Explorer Maintenance | URLs | Favorites and Links	
Place favorites and links at the top of the list in the order specified below	Not configured
Delete existing Favorites and Links, if present	Not configured
Delete existing channels, if present	Not configured
Policies | Windows Settings | Internet Explorer Maintenance | URLs | Favorites and Links | Favorites	
Internal web site	http://companyweb
Remote Web Workplace	https://*publicFQDN*/Remote
Check E-mail	https://*publicFQDN*/OWA
Policies | Administrative Templates | Windows Components | Internet Explorer	
Prevent performance of First Run Customize settings	Enabled—Go directly to home page
Turn off Managing Phishing filter	Enabled—Automatic
Policies | AdministrativeTemplates | Windows Small Business Server Group Policy Client Side Extensions	
Add the external Remote Web Workplace web site to the local intranet zone.	Enabled
Setting	https://*publicFQDN*/

Creating and Modifying Group Policy Objects in SBS 2008

In order to tailor the network environment to suit each installation, especially with the new Group Policy Preferences features available, system administrators will probably be making more use of Group Policy than they had in the past. This section of the chapter covers ways to plan, test, and implement changes in Group Policy.

Best Practice—Create New or Modify Existing GPOs?

When planning to implement new functionality in the network via Group Policy, the question of whether to create a new GPO or to modify an existing GPO should be answered first. Here are a few things to consider when deciding how to implement a new policy:

▶ Do not modify the Default Domain Policy or the Default Domain Controllers policy objects. These policy objects are core to the proper function of the network and can cause significant problems if not modified properly. It is difficult to isolate individual changes to these policy objects for testing, and an incorrect setting in these objects could make the entire network unusable and difficult to recover.

▶ Start with a new GPO. It is far easier to test the functionality of new policy settings by creating a new GPO. The object can be enabled and disabled to test the impact of the settings, rather than modifying an existing object over and over to test proper operation of the settings. Plus, it is difficult to test new policy settings on a subset of the network when modifying an existing GPO.

▶ Always create a new policy with a small number of specific and related settings. Creating sets of simple policies used in combination is easier to manage and troubleshoot than one large policy with many unrelated settings.

▶ Incorporate into an existing GPO if necessary. If the policy changes have a number of elements being modified, or if the changes don't logically align with an existing GPO, keep the GPO as a separate object. If the settings are single settings that align with an existing object, modify the existing object after testing and remove the test object. The total number of GPOs that exist in a domain can add to the processing time during login, so don't get carried away with creating a new object for every individual setting.

▶ Back up before changing. Back up an existing object before modifying the object. This way, the original object can be restored easily if problems ensue following the changes.

▶ Document, document, document. If changes to existing GPOs are made, document what those changes are and when they were made so that someone troubleshooting after the fact can understand them.

Finally, before doing anything with Group Policy, make sure you have a backup of the existing environment so that you can recover the working environment should something go awry in your testing.

Planning the GPO

Before running headlong into a Group Policy change, stop and ask a few questions first:

▶ Does the policy change affect all users or computers on the network?

▶ If the policy is not universal in scope, will it impact a majority of users or computers on the network or will it impact only a small number?

▶ Is the policy change in line with existing policy objects?

▶ Does the policy change conflict with other policies that have been set by previously processed GPOs?

▶ Could the policy change be overridden by GPOs that are processed after it?

By asking a few simple questions, you can determine up front where the policy object needs to be placed and if the settings need a separate policy object or if they can be bundled in with another policy object.

Determining the GPO Location

A new GPO can be placed in several locations in Active Directory: at the site level (which is generally not used in the SBS environment), at the domain level, or at any of the OU levels created by the SBS setup. Alternately, you can create a new OU in Active Directory and associate the new GPO with that.

Here are a few guidelines for determining where to place the GPO:

▶ If the policy impacts only a subset of users on the network, place the GPO at an existing OU level or create a new OU.

▶ If the policy applies to a majority of users or computers across the network, create the GPO at the domain level and use WMI or security group filtering to allow only those accounts that need to process the GPO the ability to access it.

▶ If the policy applies at the domain level, consider making modifications to one of the existing SBS GPOs instead of creating a new one.

Determining the GPO Scope

In many cases, creating new policy elements in an SBS environment means creating or modifying GPOs at the domain level. There are a few issues that can impact how new policy elements are applied.

A default SBS installation already has several custom GPOs created at the domain level. Before you create or modify a GPO to contain your policy elements, review the existing GPOs to see if the policy elements you want to change are already defined. If the policy elements are present in an existing SBS GPO (not the Default Domain Policy or Default Domain Controllers Policy GPOs), it might make more sense to change the settings in that GPO than to create a new GPO and make sure the object is processed in the correct order at the domain level.

If you decide that creating a new GPO at the domain level is the best place to implement the policy changes, you need to determine the correct placement in the GPO processing order for the domain-level GPOs. If the new GPO contains settings that conflict with settings in the Default Domain Policy GPO, you need to make sure that the new GPO processes after the Default Domain Policy GPO has processed.

Another option to consider for making sure that your policy changes do not get overridden by another policy object is to make the settings on the GPO Enforced. If a policy is marked as Enforced, any subsequent policy objects with conflicting policy settings will not have their changes applied.

Testing the GPO

Before unleashing your policy changes on the network, you should test the policy settings to make sure that the changes do not adversely impact your normal network environment. There are several ways to create a test environment within your production network so that you can see the results of the policy changes without affecting all users or computers in the environment.

The remainder of this section walks you through the process of creating sample objects in your SBS environment to test the process and give you a real-world example of how to create and implement a GPO test on your network.

Create a Test OU

The first step to establishing a test environment is to create a Test OU in Active Directory. Follow these steps to create the Test OU:

1. Open Active Directory Users and Computers. Click Continue when the UAC prompt appears.
2. Expand the domain, then the MyBusiness OU.
3. Right-click on the MyBusiness OU and select New | Organizational Unit.
4. Enter **Test OU** in the Name field and click OK.
5. Close Active Directory Users and Computers.

Create a Test GPO

Next, you need a GPO associated with the Test OU. Follow these steps to create the GPO:

> **NOTE**
>
> This example uses Group Policy Preferences settings. To fully test this example in your own network, you need to install the Group Policy Preferences Client-Side Extensions on the workstations involved in the test.

1. Open the Group Policy Management Console.
2. Expand Forest | Domains | your internal domain | and MyBusiness. Select Test OU.
3. Right-click on Test OU and select Create a GPO in this domain, and link it here.
4. Enter the GPO name as **Test GPO** and click OK.

Now that the GPO exists, you need to edit the settings in the GPO. As an example, follow these steps to create an easily identifiable policy setting in the new GPO:

1. Right-click on Test GPO and select Edit.
2. Under User Configuration, Preferences, Windows Settings, right-click Drive Maps and select New, Mapped Drive (see Figure 11.13).
3. Select Replace from the Action drop-down menu.

4. In the Location field, type **servername\Usershares\%USERNAME%**, where *servername* is the name of the server.

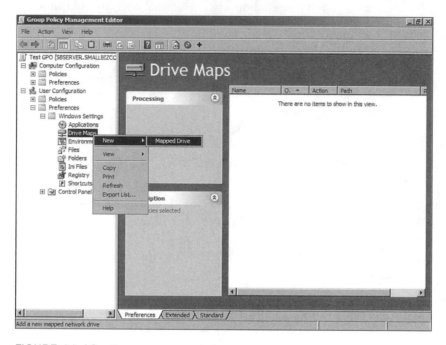

FIGURE 11.13   Create a new mapped drive element in Group Policy Preferences.

5. Under Drive Letter, select the Use radio button and select H from the drop-down menu (see Figure 11.14).

6. Click OK and close the Group Policy Management Editor.

Run a Group Policy Modeling Report

Now that the Test OU and Test GPO have been created and modified, you can run a Modeling Report to make sure the settings will get applied properly. Follow these steps to run the Group Policy Modeling Report and use the new Test OU for results.

1. Right-click on Group Policy Modeling in the Group Policy Management Console and select Group Policy Modeling Wizard. Click Next.

2. In the Domain Controller Selection page, click Next.

3. In the User and Computer Selection page, select a user and computer from the network, and then click Next. **Do not enable the checkbox next to Skip on the final page of this wizard without collecting additional data.**

4. In the Advanced Simulation Options page, click Next.

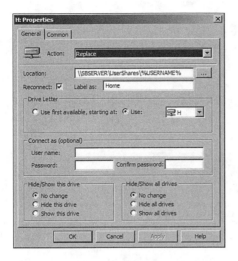

FIGURE 11.14   Specify an alternate Active Directory location to test the settings in the Test GPO.

5. In the Alternate Active Directory Paths page, click the Browse button next to User Location and browse to the Test OU created earlier. Enable the checkbox next to Skip to the final page of this wizard without collecting additional data, as shown in Figure 11.15. Click Next when complete.

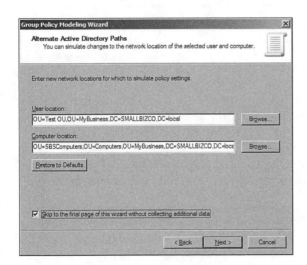

FIGURE 11.15   Specify an alternate Active Directory location to test the settings in the Test GPO.

6. In the Summary of Selections page, click Next.

7. Click Finish to close the wizard.

Now you can browse through the report and see in the Summary page that the Test GPO was applied under the User Configuration Summary section. You can also see in the settings page, as shown in Figure 11.16, that the drive mapping preference was enabled by the object Test GPO.

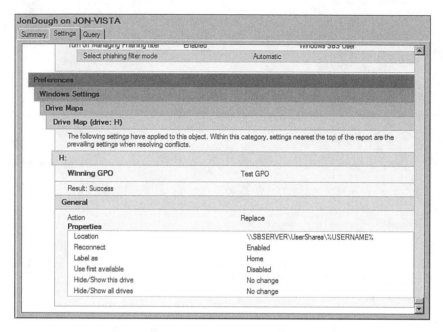

FIGURE 11.16   The winning GPO is listed in the Settings of the Group Policy Monitoring Report.

Run a Live Test

After you have verified that the policy settings are processed in the Modeling Report, you should now test the settings on a live box. There are two basic methods for doing this. The first is to move either the computer or user object for the accounts you want to test into the Test OU. The next time the computer reboots and the user logs in, it picks up the settings from the Test OU. The drawback of this method is that you have to remember to move the user or computer object back to its original location after you complete the test.

> **CAUTION**
>
> If you have a more complex Group Policy scheme that has GPOs applied at multiple OUs, you need to make sure that moving the user or computer object to the Test OU would not remove it from the processing path for the existing GPO structure. If that happens, you will not have a valid test result.

The other method for testing is to link the Test GPO to the OU or Domain object where it will reside in production and filter access to the Test GPO through security group settings.

This would involve creating a security group, possibly called GPO Testers, in Active Directory and giving only that group read access to the policy object. When you are ready to test, add the desired users or computers to that security group and reboot the workstation to have the Test GPO apply. Again, you need to remove the members of that security group once the GPO has been implemented successfully on the network.

No matter which method you choose, you should try to test with several user and computer accounts to make sure that there are no unexpected behaviors resulting from the changes you made to Group Policy.

Implementing the GPO

After you have fully tested the policy changes and are satisfied that you have not created any new problems on the network as a result, you can go ahead and implement the changes on the network. How you do this depends on how you created the test environment.

If you created a test policy object and linked it to a test OU, rename the GPO, unlink it from the test OU, and link it to the OU or Domain element where you want it to go. To link an existing policy object to an Active Directory object, follow these steps:

1. Locate the object where you want the GPO to apply in the Group Policy Management Console.
2. Right-click on the object and select Link an Existing GPO.
3. Select the GPO from the list and click OK.

If you linked the test GPO to the desired domain element and restricted access to it with security group or other filters, remove the filters.

Troubleshooting Group Policy

With a standard SBS setup, there are generally very few Group Policy issues to troubleshoot. Clients might encounter errors showing up in the event logs on servers and workstations, indicating that there were problems applying Group Policy settings. These errors, usually UserEnv 1030 and 1058 errors, actually indicate a communications problem between the workstation and the server or a misconfiguration of network settings, and not actually a problem with the Group Policies themselves.

Group Policy issues often appear as anything but Group Policy problems. The issues that appear depend largely on the types of changes that were made in Group Policy. In most cases, when Group Policy is applied and not fully tested, a policy change will have an impact on another aspect of the network. The only clue the system administrator has that Group Policy might be the culprit is that the problems started appearing around the time that a change was made in Group Policy.

Group Policy Testing Tools

This chapter has already covered the Group Policy Modeling and Group Policy Reporting Wizards, but they deserve mention yet again because of their importance in determining not only what *should* happen with Group Policy, but also what actually *does* happen.

Other tools that are useful in troubleshooting Group Policy problems are the command-line tools gpresult and gpupdate.

Using Group Policy Modeling and Results

Both the Modeling and Results Wizards are good first-step tools to aid in troubleshooting. If you suspect problems with Group Policy, try the following:

1. Run a Group Policy Modeling Report for a workstation or user who is experiencing a problem.

2. Review the report and make sure that the policy settings you are expecting to be there actually show up in the model.

3. Run a Group Policy Results Report against the same user and/or machine and compare the results to the Modeling Report. If the settings between the two reports do not match, drill down into where the differences appear and try to determine why the policy is not being applied in the same way.

Using gpresult and gpupdate

Another way to determine what policies have been applied on a workstation is through the gpresult command. This tool, which only runs in a command prompt, generates text data that matches the graphical output of the Group Policy Results Report. This tool is run directly on the workstation and can be used to collect results data when the Windows XP SP2 firewall blocks RPC requests from the server.

To get the most information out of gpresult, run gpresult /v at the command prompt and redirect the output to a text file. You see output from the command similar to the following listing:

```
Microsoft (R) Windows (R) Operating System Group Policy Result tool v2.0
Copyright (C) Microsoft Corp. 1981-2001


Created On



RSOP data for SMALLBIZCO\SBSAdmin on JON-VISTA : Logging Mode
-------------------------------------------------------------


OS Configuration:         Member Workstation
OS Version:               6.0.6001
Site Name:                N/A
Roaming Profile:          N/A
Local Profile:            C:\Users\SBSAdmin
Connected over a slow link?: No



USER SETTINGS
-------------
    CN=SBS Admin,OU=SBSUsers,OU=Users,OU=MyBusiness,DC=SMALLBIZCO,DC=local
```

```
Last time Group Policy was applied:
Group Policy was applied from:      SBSERVER.SMALLBIZCO.local
Group Policy slow link threshold:   500 kbps
Domain Name:                        SMALLBIZCO
Domain Type:                        Windows 2000


Applied Group Policy Objects
----------------------------
    Windows SBS User


The following GPOs were not applied because they were filtered out
------------------------------------------------------------------
    Default Domain Policy
        Filtering:  Not Applied (Empty)

    Small Business Server Folder Redirection Policy
        Filtering:  Denied (Security)

    Local Group Policy
        Filtering:  Not Applied (Empty)

    Small Business Server Update Services Client Computers Policy
        Filtering:  Denied (Security)

    Small Business Server Update Services Server Computers Policy
        Filtering:  Denied (Security)

    Small Business Server Update Services Common Settings Policy
        Filtering:  Not Applied (Empty)


The user is a part of the following security groups
---------------------------------------------------
    Domain Users
    Everyone
    Offer Remote Assistance Helpers
    BUILTIN\Users
    BUILTIN\Administrators
    NT AUTHORITY\INTERACTIVE
    NT AUTHORITY\Authenticated Users
    This Organization
    LOCAL
    Domain Admins
    Windows SBS Virtual Private Network Users
    Windows SBS SharePoint_OwnersGroup
    Windows SBS Link Users
    Exchange Public Folder Administrators
```

```
        Windows SBS Fax Users
        Exchange View-Only Administrators
        Exchange Organization Administrators
        Exchange Recipient Administrators
        Windows SBS Admin tools group
        Windows SBS Remote Web Workplace Users
        Denied RODC Password Replication Group
        High Mandatory Level


    The user has the following security privileges
    ----------------------------------------------



    Resultant Set Of Policies for User
    ----------------------------------


        Software Installations
        ----------------------
            N/A

        Logon Scripts
        -------------
            GPO: Windows SBS User
                Name:         \\SMALLBIZCO.local\SysVol\SMALLBIZCO.local
➥\ClientAgent\ClientAgent.vbs
                Parameters:   SBSLINK "Windows SBS" "CompanyWeb.url"
➥"http://companyweb/"
                LastExecuted: 5:50:44 PM


        Logoff Scripts
        --------------
        Public Key Policies
        -------------------
            N/A


        Administrative Templates
        ------------------------
            GPO: Windows SBS User
                KeyName:      Software\Policies\Microsoft
➥\Internet Explorer\PhishingFilter\Enabled
                Value:        2, 0, 0, 0
                State:        Enabled


            GPO: Windows SBS User
                KeyName:      Software\Policies\Microsoft
➥\Internet Explorer\Main\DisableFirstRunCustomize
```

```
        Value:         1, 0, 0, 0
        State:         Enabled

Folder Redirection
------------------
    N/A


Internet Explorer Browser User Interface
----------------------------------------
    GPO: Windows SBS User
        Large Animated Bitmap Name:      N/A
        Large Custom Logo Bitmap Name:   N/A
        Title BarText:                   N/A
        UserAgent Text:                  N/A
        Delete existing toolbar buttons: No


Internet Explorer Connection
----------------------------
    HTTP Proxy Server:   N/A
    Secure Proxy Server: N/A
    FTP Proxy Server:    N/A
    Gopher Proxy Server: N/A
    Socks Proxy Server:  N/A
    Auto Config Enable:  No
    Enable Proxy:        No
    Use same Proxy:      No


Internet Explorer URLs
----------------------
    GPO: Windows SBS User
        Home page URL:             http://companyweb
        Search page URL:           N/A
        Online support page URL:   N/A

    URL:                     https://remote.smallbizco.net/OWA
    Make Available Offline:  No

    URL:                     http://companyweb
    Make Available Offline:  No

    URL:                     https://remote.smallbizco.net/Remote
    Make Available Offline:  No

Internet Explorer Security
--------------------------
    Always Viewable Sites:   N/A
```

```
        Password Override Enabled: False

    GPO: Windows SBS User
        Import the current Content Ratings Settings:      No
        Import the current Security Zones Settings:       No
        Import current Authenticode Security Information: No
        Enable trusted publisher lockdown:                No


    Internet Explorer Programs
    -------------------------
        GPO: Windows SBS User
            Import the current Program Settings: No
```

As you can see from the listing, you get access to the same data that is present in the Group Policy Results Report. Some administrators find this output harder to work with, but it can always be generated at the workstation, especially when the Group Policy Results Wizard cannot contact the workstation to collect the data remotely.

The gpupdate command is another tool that can be used to troubleshoot Group Policy issues. The most common use of gpupdate in troubleshooting policy issues is to force policy to be reapplied on demand either at the server or a workstation. Normally, Group Policy is applied on a regularly scheduled basis at both the server and workstation level. When you are troubleshooting a Group Policy problem, you want to avoid any unnecessary delays when you can, and gpupdate can help cut down on those delays.

To force the server to immediately update changes made in GPOs across the entire network, run gpupdate /force from a command prompt on the server. This forces the server to process and apply all Group Policy Objects defined in Active Directory. When workstations are connected correctly to the domain, this also triggers an update to occur on the workstations as well.

If needed, gpupdate /force can be run on a workstation to ensure that it has pulled the latest policies from the server and applied them locally.

Backing Up and Restoring Group Policy

Before making any changes to Group Policy, you should use the tools in the Group Policy Management Console to back up the GPO first. You can also back up the entire set of GPOs on the server through the GPMC. In the Console, expand Forest, Domains, *domainname*, and right-click on the Group Policy Objects folder. One of the options from the pop-up menu is Back Up All. When you select this option, you can save all the GPO configurations to a single location on the server. This location should be a secure location so that normal users cannot access and/or modify the settings files. Alternatively, you can right-click on each individual GPO and select the Back Up option to save the settings for just that object. Ideally, you should do this immediately after setting up the server so that you have a set of default settings to recover should something happen to the Group Policy configuration.

Best Practice—Do Not Use `dcgpofix` to Recover from Group Policy Problems

You might have heard of the `dcgpofix` tool that some have used to try to recover from Group Policy issues. This tool should only be used on an SBS server as an absolute last resort. This tool restores the Default Domain Policy and Default Domain Controllers Policy objects to a point immediately following the promotion of the server to a domain controller. Because the SBS setup modifies these policies as part of the setup process, using this tool to recreate the default policy objects will not restore all the SBS customizations. Use this tool only when there is absolutely no other way to get control back on a server.

If you do have to run `dcgpofix` to regain access to a server, you need to find a way of restoring previous versions of the Default Domain Policy and Default Domain Controllers Policy objects. If you do run `dcgpofix` to recover access to your server, do not assume that it is safe to put that server back into production without further work.

Summary

Group Policy gives a network administrator incredible power over the settings on the network. With Group Policy, applications can be installed and removed from workstations, registry entries can be modified, scripts can be assigned and run, and folders can be redirected to alternate locations. The settings that control these network features are collected into Group Policy Objects that are linked to objects in Active Directory that determine how the policy will be applied. Policies are always applied in the same order: Local, Site, Domain, and OU. If multiple OUs are present between the user or computer object, policies linked to the OUs closest to the Domain object are processed first, and those linked closest to the user or computer objects are processed last. When different GPOs have conflicting settings, the settings from the last GPO processed are the ones that apply. GPOs can be filtered by WMI filters and security group filters to give greater granular control over where policy elements are applied. Troubleshooting Group Policy is most effectively done with the Group Policy Modeling and Results Wizards. The `gpresult` and `gpupdate` command-line tools can also be used to help diagnose Group Policy problems.

Best Practice Summary

▶ **Do Not Modify the Default Domain Policies**—Changes made to the default policies are difficult to test and undo if problems are encountered.

▶ **Create New or Modify Existing GPOs**—The complexity and scope of the Group Policy Object determines whether to create a new GPO or modify an existing one. If you want to add a single application exception to the Windows Firewall setting for the entire organization, it might make sense to modify one of the firewall-related existing GPOs. If you want to modify the environment for a subset of the organization, create a new GPO.

▶ **Do Not Use dcgpofix to Recover from Group Policy Problems**—dcgpofix should be used only as a last resort because it does not fix SBS-specific policies when it runs.

CHAPTER 12

User and Computer Management

If you are a consultant, managing users and computers is an area where you are not likely to spend much time, except during installations and migrations. If you are an employee within a small business, responsible for many of the day-to-day "IT" tasks, this chapter will be invaluable. In either case, user and computer management, if done properly, ensures that users have access to the tools and information they need in their daily work and, at the same time, secures the company's data from those who do not or should not have access.

> **Best Practice—Research, Analyze, Plan, and Verify**
>
> Taking the time to ask the questions about user access to data and computer resources before entering anything regarding users and computers means you'll get it right the first time. That makes everyone happy. After you've created user roles and user accounts, verify what you've set up with the appropriate level in the business before rolling it out.

Understanding the Role of User and Computer Management in SBS 2008

A thorough understanding of User and Computer roles is critical to properly deploying SBS 2008. It's important to think about the types of users (Standard, Administrator, or somewhere in between) you have in your environment, and then create the User Role templates. Then think about the types of users you have and create logical groups for users. Taking the time to preplan user roles and groups before creating your first user account saves critical time and ensures that users are not granted greater access to information than is absolutely required.

Failure to use the built-in set of tools included with Small Business Server and instead using the standard set of Active Directory tools will cause the following:

- ▶ Increased amount of time needed to set up users

- ▶ Users and computers not placed in the proper OU, and thus default Group Policies not applied

- ▶ Users not assigned to designated computer(s) as desired

NOTE

If you are a previous user of SBS 2003, the concept of using "the wizards" to perform day-to-day tasks, such as adding users and so on, is not new.

If you are new to SBS, it is important, prior to creating any users, that you become familiar with the tasks that can be performed on the SBS console and the concepts laid out in this chapter.

Understanding the Role of User Management in SBS 2008

User management in SBS 2008 should, whenever possible, be accomplished using the Windows SBS Console. Using the standard Active Directory Users and Computers tools to create new users and groups may result in unexpected behaviors.

User management in SBS 2008 focuses on three areas, as follows:

- ▶ Users

- ▶ User roles

- ▶ Groups

Additionally, the following topics regarding user management are addressed:

- ▶ User management security

- ▶ Modifying user account properties

- ▶ Modifying access to shared folders

- ▶ Modifying access to SBS web sites

- ▶ Modifying remote access

- ▶ Modifying user quotas

Each of these areas is explored in much greater detail later in the chapter.

Understanding the Role of Computer Management in SBS 2008

Like user management, managing client computers in the SBS 2008 domain should be done, whenever possible, using the Windows SBS Console. Using the standard domain computer management tools often results in something less than the desired outcome. Every effort is made to clarify which tasks should be done using the Windows SBS Console and which tasks should be accomplished using the standard computer management tools.

This chapter focuses on the following areas of computer management:

- Deploying client computers

- Assigning user access to a client computer

- Power management on client computers running Windows Vista

- Remote desktop and remote assistance configuration

- Renaming client computers

- Removing a client computer from the domain

Understanding the Default Settings of User and Computer Management

For most small businesses, the default settings for users and computers will meet your needs. You will save yourself (and your company or client) time and money by first reviewing the default settings for both users and computers available to you out of the box.

Understanding User Default Settings

In order to better understand user default settings, you need to have an understanding of user roles. A *user role* provides the ability to group together things such as group membership, SharePoint Services, disk quotas, e-mail distribution groups, and so on. Creating these predefined user roles and assigning users to those roles prevents having to manually assign each of those account properties.

CAUTION

It cannot be pointed out strongly enough that user accounts and the management of them should, whenever possible, be done using the tasks found on the Windows SBS Console.

Understanding Default User Roles

Out of the box, SBS 2008 has three user roles defined, as follows:

- **Standard User**—These users have access to shared folders, printers, faxes, e-mail, Remote Web Workplace, Companyweb, and the Internet. They cannot perform any management of either workstation (that is, install new software, printers, and so on) and might have difficulty using some software programs that require local administrator permissions.

NOTE

In SBS 2003, users were, by default, made members of the local administrators group on their primary workstation. This is not the case with SBS 2008. Depending on the business applications in use, it may be necessary to add the user to the local administrators group. This can be done via the SBS Console and is detailed later in the chapter.

▶ **Standard User with Administration Tools**—In addition to functionality of the Standard User outlined previously, users who are assigned this role have access to the Remote Web Workplace administrative links. Additionally, they will have access to the Desktop Gadgets link. When accessing one of the administrative links, the user will then be prompted to enter network administrator credentials.

▶ **Network Administrator**—A user assigned to the role of network administrator becomes a member of the Domain Administrators group and unrestricted access to domain resources.

You might find that the three pre-defined user roles may not meet the needs of certain groups of users, based on the needs of the business. In that case, you may need to add new user roles.

Adding User Roles

You can add new user roles in two ways: Add a new user role wizard or create a new user role based on an existing user account. To use the wizard, follow these steps:

1. Open the Windows SBS Console, as shown in Figure 12.1 (click Start, All Programs, Windows Small Business Server, Windows SBS Console).

2. On the navigation bar at the top of the Windows SBS Console, click the Users and Groups tab. Then, at the top of the lower-left pane, click the User Roles tab (see Figure 12.2).

3. In the task pane on the far right, click Add New User Role Task and follow the instructions to complete the wizard (see Figure 12.3).

To add a user role based on an existing user:

1. Open the Windows SBS Console (Start, All Programs, Windows Small Business Server, Windows SBS Console).

2. On the navigation bar at the top of the Windows SBS Console, click the Users and Groups tab. Then, toward the top of the lower-left pane, click the Users tab (see Figure 12.4).

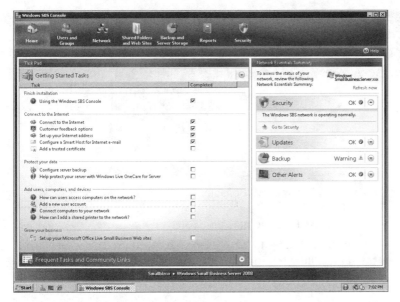

FIGURE 12.1   The Windows SBS Console.

FIGURE 12.2   The User Roles Console.

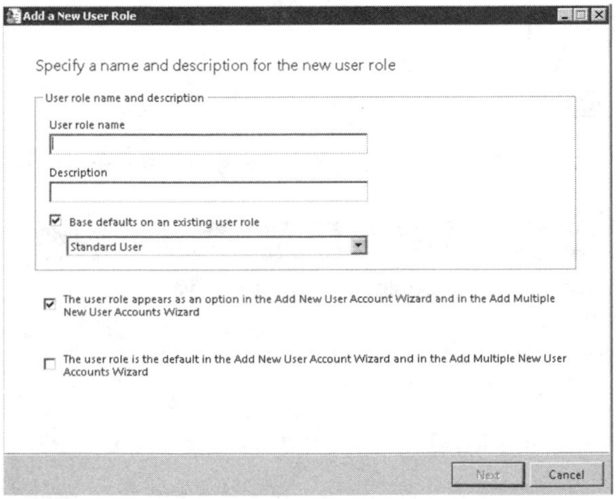

FIGURE 12.3   Adding a new user role task screen.

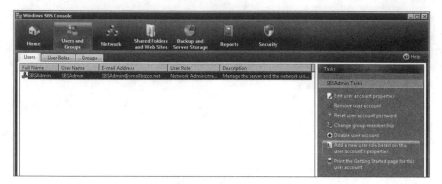

FIGURE 12.4   The Users tab on the Windows SBS Console.

3. Select the user's account to be used for the new user role.

4. In the task pane on the far right, click Add New User Role Based on This User Account's Properties task and follow the instructions to complete the wizard (see Figure 12.5).

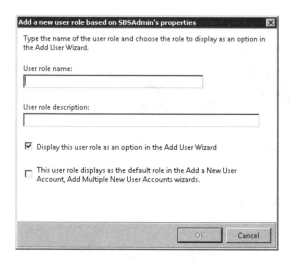

FIGURE 12.5   Add New User Role Based on This User Account's Properties task screen.

Best Practice—Choosing the Method for Connecting to the Network

After 10 years of answering questions regarding Small Business Server in a variety of community venues, this continues to be the one thing that people don't get. Use the SBS Console and Wizards! Somehow people seem to have a greater sense of being a "network administrator" if they use the more traditional tools.

Adding User Accounts

During the initial rollout of your Windows SBS Server, depending on the number of users in the organization, it might be more efficient to add several users who perform like duties at the same time. If there are a small number of users, or each user performs a significantly different function, it might be wiser to add each account separately.

To add a single user account, perform the following steps:

1. Open the Windows SBS Console (Start, All Programs, Windows Small Business Server, Windows SBS Console).

2. On the navigation bar at the top of the Windows SBS Console, click the Users and Groups tab. Then, in the lower-left pane, click the Users tab.

3. In the task pane on the far right, click Add User and follow the instructions to complete the wizard (see Figure 12.6).

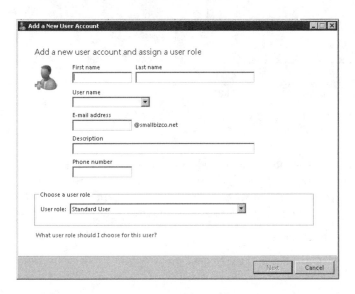

FIGURE 12.6   Add User Wizard screen.

To add multiple user accounts, follow these steps:

1. Open the Windows SBS Console.

2. On the navigation bar at the top of the Windows SBS Console, click the Users and Groups tab. Then, in the lower-left pane, click the Users tab.

3. In the task pane on the far right, click Add Multiple User Accounts and follow the instructions to complete the wizard (see Figure 12.7).

NOTE

Often situations occur where users have a requirement to access resources on the server, but for some reason, management does not want those users to have mailboxes. In SBS 2008, you simply leave the e-mail address blank when adding either single or multiple new users.

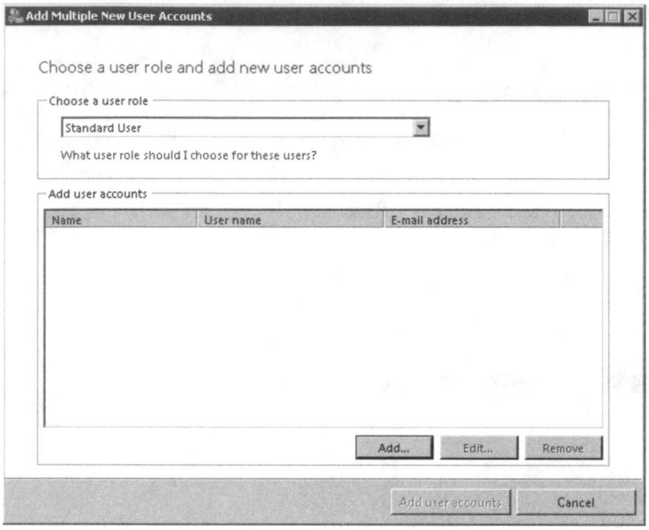

FIGURE 12.7   Add Multiple User Accounts Wizard screen.

User Management Security

Everyone has visited a workstation where the password was on a yellow sticky at the bottom of the computer monitor, or the user's password is a pet's or child's name. These are simple things that, in today's world of non-stop network intrusion attempts, cause the corruption, deletion, or theft of sensitive company data and resources.

At a minimum, the following areas must be addressed:

▶ User education

▶ Implementing strong passwords

▶ Change password policies

Educating Users on Security   Users need to understand that their network password should be guarded the same way they would guard credit card, debit card, and social security information. Following are some guidelines to share with users that should help in minimizing any unauthorized access to vital company information:

▶ Do not use all or any part of the user's account name.

▶ Do not use all or any part of either the user's real name or e-mail address.

▶ Do not use the name of a user's child, parent, spouse/partner, or friend.

▶ Do not use any word that can be found in the dictionary.

▶ Do not use an old password and just add numbers to it.

▶ Do not use your birthdate.

- ▶ Do not use your social security number or other identification number.

- ▶ Do not use any other easily obtained information, such as city of birth.

Implementing Strong Passwords   Out of the box, SBS 2008 implements strong passwords. The default password requirements for users of SBS 2008 are as follows:

- ▶ Minimum of eight characters.

- ▶ Must have at least one character from three of the following four categories:

  - ▶ English uppercase characters (A–Z).

  - ▶ English lowercase characters (a–z).

  - ▶ Base 10 digits (0–9).

  - ▶ Non-alphabetic special characters (that is, # @ & ! *).

- ▶ Maximum password age (in days) = 180 days.

- ▶ Number of passwords remembered = 24.

Most small business users and even small business owners will probably express considerable concern and probably resist any attempt to implement these requirements; however, taking the time to properly educate users and business owners concerning the risk they face by not implementing them can usually overcome the obstacles.

Change Password Policies   As previously mentioned, the out-of-the-box requirement to change passwords is twice a year (every 180 days). This is not acceptable from a security standpoint, nor is it clear why this is set as the default. In previous versions of Windows Small Business Server, the maximum password age was 42 days (about every six weeks).

So, what is the right setting? If you ask 100 different consultants, you'll probably get at least 50 different answers. Because hackers are always creating new tools to discover users' passwords, it is imperative to change passwords frequently enough that intruders will be thrown off, but not so often that users are adversely affected. Implementing a required password change of between 60 and 90 days should work well for most small businesses.

To change the password policies, follow these steps:

1. Open the Windows SBS Console (click Start, All Programs, Windows Small Business Server, Windows SBS Console).

2. On the navigation bar at the top of the Windows SBS Console, click the Users and Groups tab. Then, in the lower-left pane, click the Users tab.

3. In the task pane on the far right, click Change Password Policies task. Enter a new value for the Max Password Age (see Figure 12.8). You can also change the password length if desired (it is not recommended to shorten this, however). Click Apply and OK.

Users are required to change passwords at the next logon after making these changes.

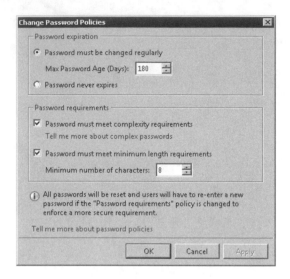

FIGURE 12.8   Change Password Policies Wizard screen.

Using the Network Administrator Account

Every user in the domain, even the network administrator, should have a standard user account for day-to-day use on the network. Only log on to the network with a network administrator-level account when absolutely required. Activities that require using a network administrator-level account are related to user and computer management (or other management) tasks on the server. Rather than logging on directly to the server, you can accomplish these by connecting to the server via remote desktop connections with a network administrator level account.

Understanding Default Computer Settings

As previously noted, it's important to examine the settings (such as Remote Desktop, or Remote Assistance) that are enabled (or disabled) by default, upon joining the first client computer to the domain. For most small businesses, the default settings are appropriate. If you don't understand the default settings for client computers in the domain, you might spend countless wasted hours creating new Group Policies or modifying other domain settings which are probably not necessary.

NOTE

Just as with SBS 2003, Windows XP Home and Windows Vista Home editions are not supported for deployment with SBS 2008. Windows XP Professional, Vista Business, and Vista Ultimate Editions are the only computer operating systems that are supported by the tools found in the SBS 2008 Console. Windows 2000 Professional and earlier operating systems, although no longer supported by Microsoft and the SBS 2008 console tools, might be joined to the domain manually; all support tasks have to be done using standard tools.

Preparing the Computer for Deployment

In previous versions of SBS, other than ensuring that the client computer had an operating system that was capable of joining an Active Directory domain, no other real checks were done.

New to SBS 2008 are a set of prerequisites that must be in place on the client computer prior to joining the domain using the Connect Wizard. These prerequisites, in addition to running Windows XP Professional or Vista Business Edition or higher, are as follows:

▶ Client for Microsoft Networks must be installed and enabled.

▶ .NET Framework 2.0 or higher must be installed.

▶ Remote Desktop Protocol 6.0 or higher is installed on Windows XP computers.

One of the following Internet browsers must be installed:

▶ Internet Explorer 6.0 or higher is installed on Windows XP computers.

▶ Internet Explorer 7.0 or higher is installed on Windows Vista computers.

▶ Firefox.

NOTE

Computers with the word "Home" in the operating system name cannot join the domain. Don't try to make it work.

To make this task easier, SBS 2008 introduces the Windows SBS Client Advisor. The utility should be run on each client computer prior to attempting to join it to the network. This utility can be copied from the server to a USB key and run on each computer.

To get the SBS Client Advisor, you need physical access to the server, as follows:

1. Insert a portable USB drive into any available USB port on the server. Wait until you receive the message that hardware is ready for use.

2. Start the Windows SBS Console (click Start, All Programs, Windows Small Business Server, Windows SBS Console).

3. On the main navigation bar at the top of the Windows SBS Console, click Network; then find and click the Computers tab.

4. To the right, find the Tasks pane and click Connect Computers to your Network task (see Figure 12.9).

5. Review the information on the first page of the Run Connect Computer Wizard page and click Next.

6. Select Copy the Wizard to portable media.

7. On the Specify a Location for the Connect Computer program page, click the Browse button and navigate to the drive letter of the portable USB drive you inserted in step 1. Click Next.

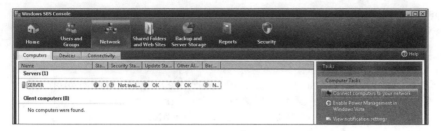

FIGURE 12.9   Windows SBS Console—Computers tab screen.

8. After the wizard completes, take the portable USB drive to each computer that will connect to the SBS network.

9. On the client computer, insert the portable USB drive. Navigate to the portable USB drive, find ClientAdvisor.exe, and double-click.

10. Complete the Client Advisor on each computer and take the steps necessary to meet the prerequisites.

Connecting the Computer to the Network

Connecting client computers to the SBS 2008 network and domain is a simple task and does not require either the computer consultant or network administrator credentials.

NOTE

In previous versions of SBS, it was necessary to create computer accounts in AD prior to joining the computer to the domain. This was typically done using the Server Console, which created the computer account in Active Directory.

Creating computer accounts in advance of connecting to the network is no longer required. However, it is advisable to create all user accounts prior to joining computers to the network. For users of SBS 2003, also take note of the new URL for connecting computers to the network shown later in this section.

Client computers can be joined in two different ways, as follows:

▶ Via web browser.

▶ Via portable USB drive (using the Connect Computer Wizard copied to the portable USB drive from the server earlier in this chapter).

Best Practice—Choosing the Method for Connecting to the Network

The truth is, both methods are essentially the same. You must have the client computer "connected" physically to the network in order for the wizard to work. If the computer you are joining to the network is in a remote location, you would at a minimum have to be connected to the SBS network by VPN. In such a case, launching the wizard from the portable USB drive might provide slightly faster results.

Customizing User and Computer Management

As pointed out in the previous sections, the default settings for users and computers meet most small businesses needs. If, however, after thoroughly reviewing the default settings for users or computers, you find they do not meet your specific requirements, the following sections assist you in making the necessary changes. You may also find it helpful to review Chapter 11, "Group Policy in SBS 2008."

Customizing User Settings

As mentioned earlier in this chapter, once users are set up, customization is not frequently required. In the following sections, we cover the most common and a few not-so-common customizations.

Modifying General User Information

It is not uncommon that users have events in their lives—such as marriage, divorce, and so on—that require a name change, e-mail change, or phone number change. The new SBS 2008 wizards have made this task much easier.

To modify general information about a user, follow these steps:

1. Open the Windows SBS Console (click Start, All Programs, Windows Small Business Server, Windows SBS Console).

2. On the navigation bar at the top of the Windows SBS Console, click the Users and Groups tab. Then, in the lower-left pane, click the Users tab.

3. In the left pane, select the user account you want to modify.

4. In the task pane on the far right, click Edit User Account Properties.

5. In the User Account properties page, click the General tab and then update any of the following information: first name, last name, user name, e-mail address, description, or phone number (see Figure 12.10).

6. Click Apply; then click OK.

Resetting User Passwords

To reset a user's password, perform the following:

1. Open the Windows SBS Console (click Start, All Programs, Windows Small Business Server, Windows SBS Console).

2. On the navigation bar at the top of the Windows SBS Console, click the Users and Groups tab. Then, in the lower-left pane, click the Users tab.

3. In the left pane, select the user account you want to modify.

4. In the task pane on the far right, click Reset User Account Password.

5. In the Reset User Account Password page, type the new password and then retype it to confirm.

6. Click Apply; then click OK.

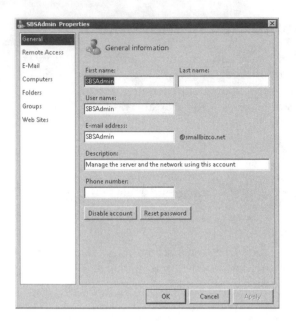

FIGURE 12.10   Modifying the General User Account Properties screen.

User Must Change Password at Next Logon

For some reason, this option was not included in the Reset User Account Password page. If you reset a user's password, but want him to change it again when he logs on to ensure a greater degree of security, then this must be changed using Active Directory Users and Computers. Navigate to My Business, Users, SBSUsers. Highlight the account, right-click it, and select Properties. Click the Account tab and, in the Account Options section, check the box labeled User Must Change Password at Next Logon.

Disabling (or Enabling) a User Account

There are circumstances when a user account must be disabled, which prevents the user from accessing any resources on the network. This also prevents e-mail from being delivered to the user's mailbox. This might include employees who are on leave of absence or who are suspended from working for some reason. See more on this at the end of this section.

To disable or enable a user account:

1. Open the Windows SBS Console (click Start, All Programs, Windows Small Business Server, Windows SBS Console).

2. On the navigation bar at the top of the Windows SBS Console, click the Users and Groups tab. Then, in the lower-left pane, click the Users tab.

3. In the left pane, select the user account you want to disable (or enable).

4. In the task pane on the far right, click Disable (Enable) User Account.

5. Click Apply; then click OK.

TIP

When should you disable and when should you remove a user? Even when a user has been terminated, it's probably still best to disable the account initially, rather than remove it. You can modify the user's properties (through standard tools) to have e-mail delivered to an alternate location. This, of course, will be a business-by-business decision.

Removing a User Account

To remove a user account:

1. Open the Windows SBS Console (click Start, All Programs, Windows Small Business Server, Windows SBS Console).

2. On the navigation bar at the top of the Windows SBS Console, click the Users and Groups tab. Then, in the lower-left pane, click the Users tab.

3. In the left pane, select the user account you want to remove.

4. In the task pane on the far right, click Remove User Account.

5. A warning message appears that contains two checkboxes (see Figure 12.11). If you want to keep the user's mailbox and user's shared folder, make sure to uncheck those boxes.

6. Click OK.

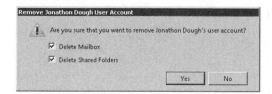

FIGURE 12.11   Removing a user account warning screen.

Modifying Access to Internal Shared Folders

By default, the group Everyone has access to all shared folders (Public, Redirected Folders, and UserShares). To modify access to these (or other shared folders that might have been created):

1. Open the Windows SBS Console (click Start, All Programs, Windows Small Business Server, Windows SBS Console).

2. On the navigation bar at the top of the Windows SBS Console, click the Shared Folders and Web Sites tab. Then, in the lower-left pane, click the Shared Folders tab (see Figure 12.12).

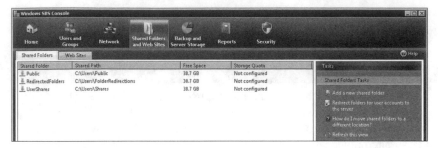

FIGURE 12.12   Windows SBS Console—Shared Folders tab.

3. In the left pane, select the shared folder for which you want to modify access.

4. In the far-right pane, click Change Folder Permissions.

5. In the Share Permissions page, click the Add or Remove button to make the neces-
    sary changes (see Figure 12.13).

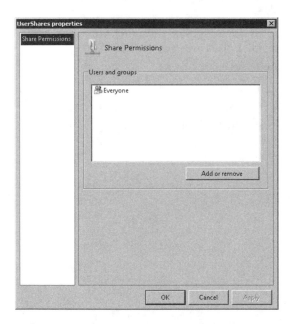

FIGURE 12.13   Shared Folders—Share Permissions screen.

Modifying Access to SBS Web Sites

The Windows SBS Console provides access to the three default web sites created during
installation: Remote Web Workplace (RWW), Outlook Web Access (OWA), and the Internal
Windows SharePoint Services 3.0 web site (Companyweb). By default, access to all three
sites is enabled for all levels of users. However, management might want to limit what
access some users or groups of users have to company data and e-mail outside the office.

To modify access to these (or other shared folders that might have been created):

1. Open the Windows SBS Console (click Start, All Programs, Windows Small Business Server, Windows SBS Console).

2. On the navigation bar at the top of the Windows SBS Console, click the Shared Folders and Web Sites tab. Then, in the lower-left pane, click the Web Sites tab (see Figure 12.14).

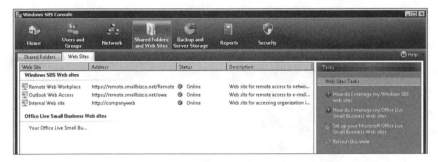

FIGURE 12.14   Windows SBS Console—Web Sites tab.

3. In the left pane, select the web site for which you want to modify access.

4. In the far-right pane, click Manage Permissions task.

5. Depending on the web site selected, the properties page may be slightly different but very self-explanatory, and help is available. See Figure 12.15 for Remote Web Workplace, Figure 12.16 for Outlook Web Access, and Figure 12.17 for Internal Web Site (Companyweb).

FIGURE 12.15   Manage Permissions—Remote Web Workplace.

FIGURE 12.16 Manage Permissions—Outlook Web Access.

FIGURE 12.17 Manage Permissions—Companyweb.

Modifying E-Mail Distribution and Security Group Access

As a business changes, new applications are deployed or user's responsibilities change; there might be a need to add, remove, or modify a group membership. This could be membership in an e-mail distribution group or a security group. The Windows SBS

Console provides access to both kinds of groups. From the console, you can add a new group, remove an existing group, change group membership, or edit the group properties.

To modify access to e-mail distribution groups or security groups:

1. Open the Windows SBS Console (click Start, All Programs, Windows Small Business Server, Windows SBS Console).

2. On the Navigation Bar at the top of the Windows SBS Console, click the Users and Groups tab. Then, in the lower-left pane, click the Groups tab (see Figure 12.18).

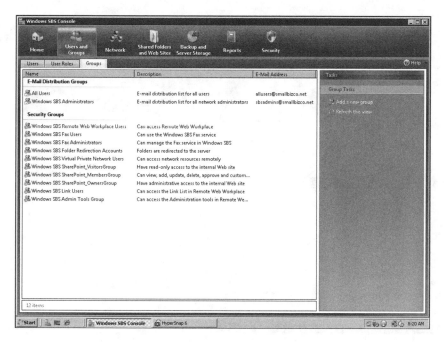

FIGURE 12.18   Windows SBS Console—Groups tab.

3. In the left pane, select the group you want to modify.

4. In the task pane on the far right, click the task for the action to be performed—Add a New Group (see Figure 12.19), Remove an Existing Group (see Figure 12.20), Change Group Membership (see Figure 12.21), or Edit the Group Properties (see Figure 12.22).

Modifying Remote Access Permissions

By default, users are granted remote access to their main desktop. Business owners may choose to limit a user's ability to access their desktop remotely. The following steps assist you in modifying remote access permissions.

1. Open the Windows SBS Console (click Start, All Programs, Windows Small Business Server, Windows SBS Console).

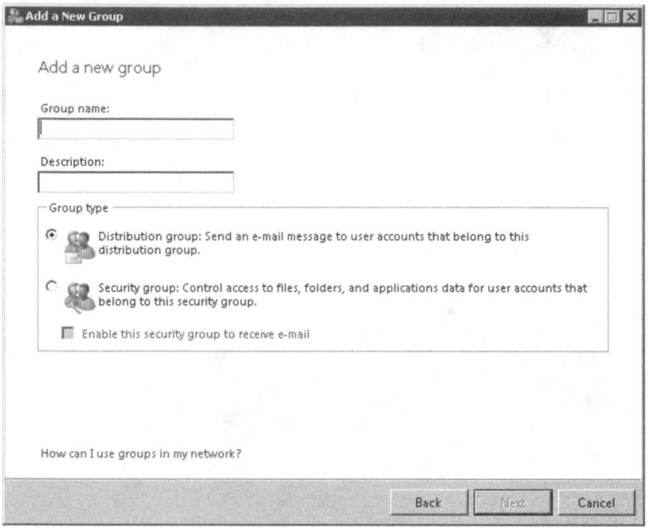

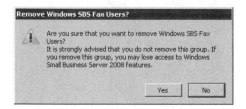

FIGURE 12.19   Add New Group task screen.

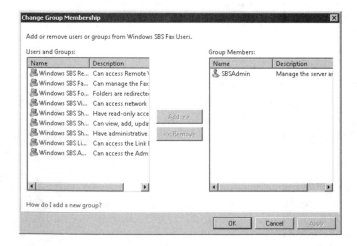

FIGURE 12.20   Remove Existing Group task screen.

FIGURE 12.21   Change Group Membership screen.

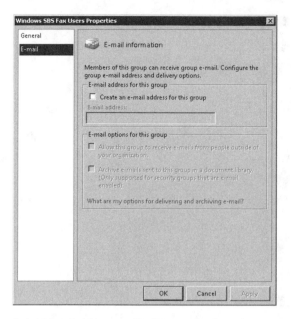

Windows SBS Fax Users Properties

General

E-mail

E-mail information

Members of this group can receive group e-mail. Configure the group e-mail address and delivery options.

E-mail address for this group

☐ Create an e-mail address for this group

E-mail address:

E-mail options for this group

☐ Allow this group to receive e-mails from people outside of your organization.

☐ Archive e-mails sent to this group in a document library. (Only supported for security groups that are e-mail enabled).

What are my options for delivering and archiving e-mail?

OK   Cancel   Apply

FIGURE 12.22   Edit Group Properties screen.

2. On the navigation bar at the top of the Windows SBS Console, click the Users and Groups tab. Then, in the lower-left pane, click the Users tab.

3. In the left pane, select the user account for which you want to modify remote access permissions.

4. In the task pane on the far right, click Edit User Account Properties.

5. On the User Account Properties page, click the Remote Access link in the left column.

6. Take the following actions as required (see Figure 12.23):

   ▶ Select (or clear) the User Can Access Remote Web Workplace checkbox to allow (or prohibit) the user access to the network via the RWW web site.

   ▶ Select (or clear) the User Can Access Virtual Private Network checkbox to allow (or prohibit) a VPN connection to the network for this user account.

Modifying Folder Redirection and Quotas

The SBS server should serve as the central repository for company-related information. Very few, if any, organizations take steps to back up any data stored on user workstations, and therefore, it is strongly recommended that folder redirection to the server be enabled for all users. By default, folder redirection to the server **is not** enabled for users.

To enable folder redirection and set storage quotas:

1. Open the Windows SBS Console (click Start, All Programs, Windows Small Business Server, Windows SBS Console).

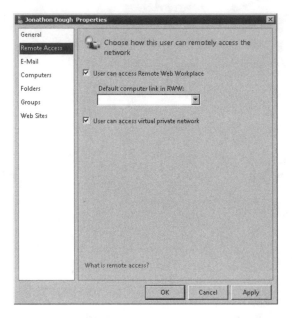

FIGURE 12.23   Configuring User Account Remote Access Permissions screen.

2. On the navigation bar at the top of the Windows SBS Console, click the Users and Groups tab. Then, in the lower-left pane, click the Users tab.

3. In the left pane, select the user account for which you want to modify remote access permissions.

4. In the task pane on the far right, click Edit User Account Properties.

5. On the User Account Properties page, click the Folders link in the left column.

6. Take the following actions as required (see Figure 12.24):

   ▶ Select (or clear) the Enforce Shared Folder Quota checkbox to set up (or remove) disk quotas for the selected user account. You may also reduce or increase the default quota size of 2GB (gigabytes).

   ▶ Select (or clear) the Enforce Folder Redirection to the Server checkbox to redirect (or stop redirecting) My Documents to be stored on the server. You may also reduce or increase the default quota size of 2GB (gigabytes).

7. Click Apply and then OK.

You can also change which folders are redirected to the server. By default, only the desktop and document folders are redirected when redirection is enabled using the steps previously outlined. You can also enable (or disable) redirection of Start menu items using the following steps:

1. Open the Windows SBS Console (click Start, All Programs, Windows Small Business Server, Windows SBS Console).

FIGURE 12.24   Shared folder quota and folder redirection screen.

2. On the navigation bar at the top of the Windows SBS Console, click the Users and Groups tab. Then, in the lower-left pane, click the Users tab.

3. In the task pane on the far right, click Redirect Folders for User Accounts to the Server.

4. A dialog box appears and allows you to select (or unselect) which folders are to be redirected.

You will also see a tab labeled User Accounts. You can click there to select (or deselect) multiple accounts for folder redirection.

Modifying E-Mail Quotas

By default, a quota of 2GB is enforced for all new user accounts. You should consider carefully prior to raising or removing this limit. Many small businesses make the mistake of using the e-mail system as a "filing cabinet" and keep attachments in user's mailboxes, rather than saving the attachment to a folder on the server that can be accessed by everyone needing access. Additionally, when a user's offline mailbox storage (.ost file) becomes larger than 2GB, performance declines significantly, even on well-powered workstations.

To modify e-mail quota enforcement and limits:

1. Open the Windows SBS Console (click Start, All Programs, Windows Small Business Server, Windows SBS Console).

2. On the navigation bar at the top of the Windows SBS Console, click the Users and Groups tab. Then, in the lower-left pane, click the Users tab.

3. In the left pane, select the user account for which you want to modify remote access permissions.

4. In the task pane on the far right, click Edit User Account Properties.

5. On the User Account Properties page, click the E-Mail link in the left column.

6. Select (or clear) the Enforce the Mailbox Quotas checkbox to set up (or remove) e-mail quotas for the selected user account (see Figure 12.25). You may also reduce or increase the default quota size of 2GB.

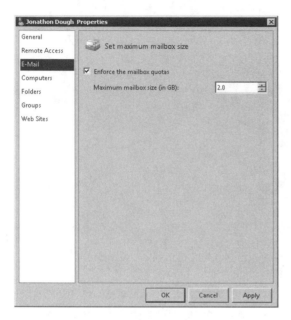

FIGURE 12.25   Individual Mailbox Quota screen.

Customizing Computer Management

As pointed out at the beginning of this chapter, after initial deployment there are minimal requirements for customization of the computers in the domain. However, should you find yourself in need of making modifications to computers, such as computer access, power management, or other features, the following sections assist you in making the necessary changes.

Modifying Access to Computers

It may be necessary for users to access multiple computers in the company, either as a standard user, or as a local administrator on computers, depending on the applications to be run and the availability of workstations. Optimally, all users should run with a least-privileged user (LUA) account. In other words, users should only have an account that gives them access to just what they need to do their job—no more, no less. Conversely, you might want to restrict a user to a single computer with only standard user permissions.

To allow a user account access to multiple computers:

1. Open the Windows SBS Console (click Start, All Programs, Windows Small Business Server, Windows SBS Console).

2. On the navigation bar at the top of the Windows SBS Console, click the Users and Groups tab. Then, in the lower-left pane, click the Users tab.

3. In the left pane, select the user account you want to modify.

4. In the task pane on the far right, click Edit User Account Properties.

5. On the User Account Properties page, click Computers (see Figure 12.26).

FIGURE 12.26   Windows SBS Console—Computers tab.

6. Click the computers to which you want to grant access, and then grant the user account the appropriate level of access from the drop-down of user roles. You can also grant (or revoke) remote access to the computer here.

To allow one or more user accounts access to a single computer:

1. Open the Windows SBS Console (click Start, All Programs, Windows Small Business Server, Windows SBS Console).

2. On the navigation bar at the top of the Windows SBS Console, click the Network tab. Then, in the lower-left pane, click the Computers tab.

3. In the left pane, select the computer you want to allow access to.

4. In the task pane on the far right, click Edit Computer Properties.

5. On the Computer Properties page, click User Access (see Figure 12.27).

6. Click each user account that you want to grant (or revoke) access to this computer. Then specify the access level as appropriate.

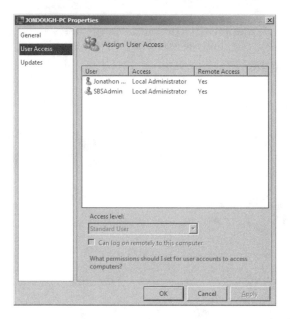

FIGURE 12.27   Computer Properties—User Access screen.

Power Management on Client Computers Running Windows Vista

The default installation of Windows SBS 2008 configures a Group Policy setting that disables power management for client computers running the Windows Vista operating system. This enables remote users to establish a remote desktop connection to the office computer.

The Windows Vista Power Options feature enables users to control how their computer uses and manages power. The default power management setting in Windows Vista turns off a client computer after one hour of inactivity. Although this feature can help some businesses reduce energy costs, when it is enabled, the feature prevents users from establishing remote desktop connections to their office computers.

To enable or disable power management on computers running Windows Vista:

1. Open the Windows SBS Console (click Start, All Programs, Windows Small Business Server, Windows SBS Console).

2. On the navigation bar at the top of the Windows SBS Console, click the Network tab. Then, in the lower-left pane, click the Computers tab.

3. In the task pane on the far right, click Enable (or Disable, as appropriate) Power Management in Windows Vista.

4. The warning box appears. The warning box informs the administrator to carefully consider whether power management should be enabled. The warning notifies the

administrator that if Power Management is on Vista-based computers, these computers might not be available for connection via RWW.

5. Click Yes or No.

If you enable power management in Windows Vista and find later that you want to disable power management, simply repeat the preceding steps.

Modify Computers to Allow (or Not Allow) Remote Desktop Connections

Earlier in the chapter, we discussed how to permit users to access Remote Web Workplace (RWW). Most commonly, users connect only to the primary computer that they use at work. In addition to the user having permission to use RWW, the computer they will be connecting to must also be properly configured.

On computers running Windows Vista Business Edition or higher, follow these steps:

1. Open the System Control Panel by clicking the Start button and then the Control Panel. Double-click the System icon to open the System Control Panel (see Figure 12.28).

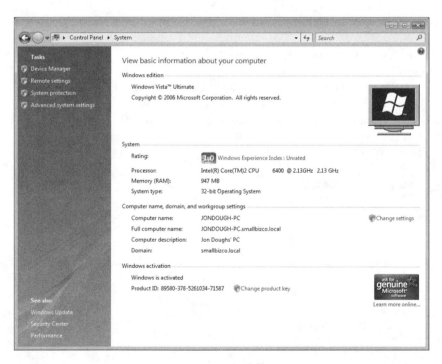

FIGURE 12.28   Vista System Control Panel screen.

2. In Tasks, click Remote Settings. The System Properties page appears (see Figure 12.29).

FIGURE 12.29   Vista System Properties—Remote tab.

3. In the Remote Desktop section, select (or deselect as appropriate) either Allow Connections from Computers Running Any Version of Remote Desktop or Allow Connections Only from Computers Running Remote Desktop with Network Level Authentication. Then click Select Users. The Remote Desktop Users dialog box appears (see Figure 12.30).

FIGURE 12.30   Remote Desktop Users dialog box screen.

4. Click Add. The Select Users or Groups dialog box appears. Type the user names of the users you want to grant permission to connect to this computer using Remote Desktop. Click the Check Names button (see Figure 12.31); you should see the user's full name appear in the box and be underlined, then click OK.

FIGURE 12.31   Vista Select Users or Groups dialog box screen.

5. Click OK to close the dialog box.

6. Click OK to close the System Properties page.

On computers running Windows XP Professional, follow these steps:

1. Open the System Control Panel by clicking the Start button and then clicking the Control Panel. Double-click the System icon to open the System Properties page.

2. Click the Remote tab (see Figure 12.32).

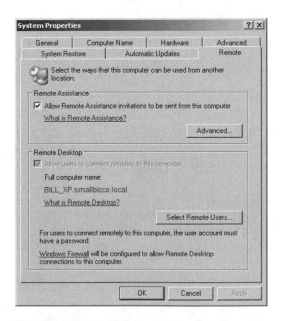

FIGURE 12.32   Windows XP System Properties—Remote tab.

3. In the Remote Desktop section, select Allow Users to Connect Remotely to This Computer; then click Select Remote Users. The Remote Desktop Users dialog box appears.

4. Click Add. The Select Users or Groups dialog box appears. Type the user names of the users to whom you want to grant permission to connect to this computer using Remote Desktop; then click OK.

5. Click OK to close the dialog box.

6. Click OK again to close the System Properties page.

TIP

You can use the same steps just listed to enable the ability to offer Remote Assistance to your users. The Enable Remote Assistance checkbox is located in the section just above Remote Desktop.

Offering Remote Assistance

To allow one or more user accounts access to a single computer:

1. Open the Windows SBS Console (click Start, All Programs, Windows Small Business Server, Windows SBS Console).

2. On the navigation bar at the top of the Windows SBS Console, click the Network tab. Then, in the lower-left pane, click the Computers tab.

3. In the left pane, select the computer for which you want to offer remote assistance.

4. In the task pane on the far right, click Offer Remote Assistance and follow the on-screen instructions (see Figure 12.33).

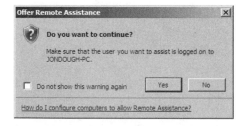

FIGURE 12.33   Windows SBS Console—Offer Remote Assistance task screen.

Renaming Client Computers

Small businesses use many methods of naming computers. The computer name may reflect the user or a function, so from time to time business owners or administrators might want to rename a computer to reflect the new user or its use in a different area. The following steps assist you in this task.

For computers running Windows Vista Business Edition or higher, follow these steps:

1. Open the System Control Panel by clicking the Start button and then the Control Panel. Double-click the System icon to open the System Control Panel.

2. In the computer name, domain, and workgroup settings, click Change Settings. If you are prompted for a password or confirmation, provide the information as needed.

3. Click the Computer Name tab; click Change.

4. In the Computer Name box, clear the old computer name and enter the new name (see Figure 12.34). Click OK.

FIGURE 12.34   Vista System Properties—Computer Name screen.

5. You are prompted to provide a user name and password for an account with the network administrator role.

6. Restart the computer.

For computers running Windows XP Professional, follow these steps:

1. Open the System Control Panel by clicking the Start button and then the Control Panel. Double-click the System icon to open the System Properties page.

2. Click the Computer Name tab; then click the Change button. The Computer Name Changes dialog box appears (see Figure 12.35).

3. In the Computer Name text box, clear the old computer name and enter the new name. Click OK.

4. You are prompted to provide a user name and password for an account with the network administrator role.

5. Restart the computer.

Removing a Client Computer from the Domain
All computers in the network eventually need replacing. Before adding a new computer to the domain with the same name, you must remove the existing computer from the domain. The following steps walk you through the process:

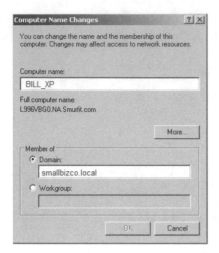

FIGURE 12.35   Windows XP Professional System Properties—Computer Name Changes
screen.

1. Open the Windows SBS Console (click Start, All Programs, Windows Small Business
   Server, Windows SBS Console).

2. On the navigation bar at the top of the Windows SBS Console, click the Network
   tab. Then, in the lower-left pane, click the Computers tab.

3. In the left pane, select the computer you want to remove from the network.

4. In the Tasks pane on the far right, click Remove *Computer* (where Computer is the
   name of the computer you selected to remove in the left pane).

Summary

With the exception of your initial rollout and setup, management of users and computers
should be an uncommon task to perform. Taking the time to ask the right questions about
user permissions and required access before creating users, user roles, and connecting
computers to the network means that users have access to the information they need to
perform the job for which they were hired; they find ways to use these resources to ultimately be more productive and efficient, rather than constantly complaining and looking
for ways to get around the new network.

Best Practice Summary

▶ **Use the Wizards/Console**—After 10 years of answering questions regarding Small
  Business Server in a variety of community venues, this continues to be the one thing
  that people don't get. Somehow they seem to have a greater sense of being a
  network administrator if they use the "old school" tools.

▶ **Research, Analyze, Plan, and Verify**—Taking the time to ask the questions about user access to data and computer resources prior to entering anything regarding users and computers means you'll get it right the first time. That makes everyone happy. After you've created user roles and user accounts, verify what you've set up with the appropriate level in the business, before rolling it out.

▶ **Choosing the Method for Connecting to the Network**—The truth is, both methods are essentially the same. You must have the client computer "connected" physically to the network in order for the wizard to work. If the computer you are joining to the network is in a remote location, you would at a minimum have to be connected to the SBS network by VPN. In such a case, launching the wizard from the portable USB drive might provide slightly faster results.

12

Macintosh Integration

It doesn't take a pop culture-savvy person to recognize the impact that Apple has had on the electronics marketplace over the last few years. Although Apple has historically been a major player in the creative and visual arts industries, more and more small businesses are beginning to take a serious look at Apple technology and the possibility of incorporating it into their work environments.

From the business owner who is passionate about his or her Macintosh to the specialized hardware that requires a Macintosh for proper operation, the range of reasons people want to incorporate the platform into their small business networks continues to increase. Small business IT consultants who are willing to learn the basics of Macintosh integration and support can benefit from doing so. Not only can the consultant open the doors into new client bases, but he or she can differentiate himself or herself from competitors by having this support offering.

Whether the integration of the Macintosh platform into an SBS 2008 network is something you dread or is a critical element in an upcoming implementation, this chapter provides the essential elements for a successful deployment.

Understanding the Role of Macintosh Integration in an SBS 2008 Network

Despite all the negative publicity to the contrary, the Macintosh and Windows platforms do integrate well enough that some small businesses are making the move to include more Macintosh-based workstations in their networks.

More than just iPods and iPhones, Macintosh workstations and laptops are providing more choices for the business decision maker when considering new or replacement systems for business employees. Coupled with an increase in software availability for the Mac platform, the virtualization capabilities of the Intel-based Macintoshes give end users significantly more options to consider when deciding on the best way to perform their day-to-day tasks.

That said, incorporating the Macintosh into an SBS 2008 network is not a trivial process. The support tools that a technician becomes familiar with in supporting SBS 2008 might not carry across to the Mac platform.

Integration of Apple hardware and software can vary greatly in complexity. Factors that can impact this include how sophisticated or entrenched the existing environment is, the inclusion of additional or new Apple technologies, or the use of multi-OS virtualization on the Mac. Although this chapter and this book in general cannot cover all possibilities, the remainder of the chapter covers the basic integration of Macintosh systems into an SBS 2008 network, which provides a solid foundation for more complex implementations in the future.

Software support on the Macintosh is not always on par with its Windows counterpart. To that end, this chapter covers the most common aspects of providing access to SBS 2008 resources from the Macintosh platform.

Native Tools

The bulk of the information in this chapter covers the built-in resources of both SBS 2008 and the Macintosh platform. The three main types of information that Macintosh workstations need in order to access from the SBS server—file shares, e-mail, and web resources—can be configured to work without any add-on tools or third-party products. This information borrows heavily from information contained in other chapters of this book, and when additional background may be needed for a particular topic, references to the appropriate chapter are identified.

Third-Party Tools

There are some cases where the native tools do not provide sufficient access to SBS 2008 resources, and in those cases where a third-party solution exists (at the time of printing), that solution is identified. Many of the third-party tools can have a hefty price tag associated with them, which is another reason the chapter focuses heavily on using the native tools.

The e-mail section of the chapter contains detailed information about Entourage, the Exchange-aware e-mail client that comes as part of Microsoft Office 2004 and Office 2008 for the Mac. Mac users who want to manage their contacts and calendar appointments through Exchange will want to look at Entourage for a more fully-featured solution to interacting with Exchange over the native Apple tools or even Outlook Web Access.

Finally, because of the additional capabilities of the recent Macintosh models based on Intel CPUs, there are several third-party tools worth mentioning that provide virtual machine options for running a Windows environment on the Macintosh. This is not a requirement for connecting a Mac to an SBS 2008 network, but it is an option to consider for additional flexibility and performance. The advanced topic of virtualization on the Mac comes at the end of the chapter.

Planning and Preparing the Network Environment

13

Before continuing to the setup instructions provided later in this chapter, please make note of the following items to ensure as successful an integration as possible. Overall, there are few Mac-specific constraints that can get in the way of a deployment. However, because there have been issues historically that did interfere with network communications, updates to those items follow in the next few sections.

Domain Naming Conventions

Historically, there had been a great deal of difficulty getting Macintosh workstations running early versions of Mac OS 10 properly connected to Windows-based networks that used the .local internal domain nomenclature. The best practices presented in *SBS 2003 Unleashed* included the recommendation that the internal domain name should be .lan or some other extension other than .local. This was thanks to the Rendezvous service that Apple introduced with Max OS 10.2. Rendezvous was a networking technology that allowed Rendezvous-enabled devices to self-discover their network surroundings. Apple accomplished this with a multicast DNS query that, unfortunately, used a .local internal DNS namespace for the queries. The way the queries were handled did not coexist well with traditional DNS networks using the .local namespace, and another factor of Macintosh/Windows incompatibility was born.

In Mac OS 10.4 and 10.5, the .local issue is no longer a problem. Apple modified the way the .local namespace was used with Rendezvous (now called Bonjour) so that it would be able to perform proper DNS lookups from a Windows DNS server. As long as the Macintosh is pointing to the SBS server for DNS, internal lookups will not present a problem with a .local internal namespace.

Active Directory Integration

Workstations running Mac OS 10 have been able to communicate with Active Directory since the initial release. Interaction with Active Directory has continued to improve with each release of Mac OS 10. System administrators can choose to join a Mac to Active Directory, or leave the Mac as a non-domain workstation.

Best Practice—Join Macintosh Workstations to Active Directory

Because Mac OS 10 does not fully integrate with Active Directory, many support professionals choose not to join the Mac to Active Directory; they instead rely on the Mac to handle saving the username and password for accessing network resources. However, there are many more advantages to joining a Mac to Active Directory than just single sign-on.

Even though Mac OS 10.5 and the latest updates to Mac OS 10.4 enable Mac users to save authentication information for network shares so that they are not prompted to enter their username and password every time they access a share from the server, IT professionals will still want to have their Mac users log in to the Mac using their AD credentials. Should a system administrator need to block a user from logging into the Macintosh, he or she can disable the user's AD account, which keeps the user from logging in while the Mac is on the internal network.

Server administrators can configure a profile path in a user's Active Directory account, and this automatically mounts the volume where the profile path is located and puts a shortcut to the user's folder on the server in the Dock automatically. For users who have a hard time locating their folder on the server, or forgetting to open the share before trying to save files to it, this feature can be a significant time saver for the user. This is achieved by configuring a "roaming profile" for the user in AD. On the Mac side, this has the effect described previously. If that particular user also uses PCs on the network, the user will be using a roaming profile on those PCs, and that may not be desired; taking advantage of this benefit on the Mac may not be in the best interest of the rest of the network.

As mentioned in the Active Directory sidebar earlier, best practice guidelines recommend configuring a desktop Macintosh in an SBS 2008 network to join the domain so that users can log in to the Mac with their Active Directory credentials and take advantage of the integration that Mac OS X has with Active Directory. Administrators might not want to join a Mac laptop to the domain if the user will be primarily out on the road. If a laptop user spends most of his or her time connected to the internal network, however, it is best to join the laptop to Active Directory and have the user log in with Active Directory credentials.

The steps to join a Mac to Active Directory are outlined in the "Connecting to Active Directory" section later in the chapter.

Account Username Conflicts

Special attention needs to be paid to network and user settings on the Macintosh prior to connecting the Macintosh to the SBS network. One of the biggest roadblocks to getting proper access to the SBS network occurs if the Active Directory username matches the username on the Macintosh. Even partial matches can cause problems. For example, if Jonathan Dough has the Active Directory username "jonathan," he will encounter problems logging in to AD if his Macintosh account name is "Jonathan" or "Jonathan Dough" or has the short name "jonathan." If the Macintosh is being set up after the Active Directory username is in place, it is easier to avoid possible name conflicts. So, if Jonathan's AD login is "jondough," make sure not to set up a local Macintosh account with the short name "jondough" or have "jondough" in the long name.

If the local account is in conflict with the AD username, the best practice would be to set up a new local account with a different name, transfer the information from the existing account to the new account, and then delete the original account from the Mac.

Operating System Notes

This chapter focuses on providing configuration information for Mac OS 10.4 and 10.5 in an SBS 2008 network. Some of the information presented in this chapter may apply to earlier versions of Mac OS as well, but the reader is encouraged to upgrade any Macs that will be integrating with an SBS 2008 network to Mac OS 10.4 or 10.5, if possible.

This chapter does not cover any configuration information for any versions of the Macintosh operating system prior to Mac OS 10. Mac OS 9 (also known as Classic in some earlier versions of Mac OS 10) is not supported on any Intel-based Macintosh systems, and Windows Server 2008 no longer includes File Services for Macintosh as an installable option. Classic Macs relied on the AppleTalk and AFP protocols to communicate with other computers on the network, and those protocols are not available or supported in the SBS 2008 environment. If support is needed for older Mac workstations running Mac OS 9 or earlier, third-party solutions exist that might allow connectivity of older Macs to the SBS network. Preparation for this book did not include testing of any of these third-party solutions, so no specific recommendations can be made.

Best Practice—Keep Mac OS Up to Date

SBS 2008 provides a way to manage and maintain security updates on Windows workstations through WSUS. Macintosh workstations have a mechanism to get updates as well, just not through WSUS.

Prior to doing any configuration changes to a Mac workstation, you should check for and install any updates from Apple. The easiest way to check for updates is to select the Software Update item from the Apple Menu. If updates are found, install them.

Software Update can also be configured to check for updates weekly, or another interval determined by the system administrator. In the Software Update preferences, enable the checkbox to Download important updates in the background. This notifies the user once the update has been downloaded and is ready for installation. In general, Mac users should be instructed to install updates when the notification that updates are available appears.

Preparing SBS 2008 Server

Out of the box, neither SBS 2008 or Mac OS X are ready for the two systems to talk with each other for file shares. To effectively allow Mac workstations to interact in the SBS 2008 environment, there are some changes that need to be made first on the SBS server itself. This is an essential requirement to enable Macintosh users to gain access to shared files on the server, as well as other network resources.

SBS 2008 as the Network DHCP Server

As is best practice for the SBS network, the SBS server needs to provide DHCP services to the network. Specific information about the DHCP configuration of the SBS network is covered in Chapter 4, "DNS, DHCP, and Active Directory Integration." As long as the SBS server is configured to provide the proper IP addresses for DNS, Macintosh network connectivity will not be a problem.

File Services for Macintosh Not Required

With Mac OS 10, Apple introduced support for the Server Message Block (SMB) protocol, meaning that Macs could directly access Windows file shares, rather than having to install File Services for Macintosh on the Windows server. Because File Services for Macintosh is no longer supported on Windows Server 2008, Mac users have to rely on SMB to access data on the SBS 2008 server.

SMB Signing Compatibility Requirements

At its core, SBS 2008 is a domain controller, acting as the root of the Active Directory forest for the network. By default, Microsoft enables encryption for SMB connections (often referred to as SMB signing) on servers that are domain controllers. The use of signed-SMB packets was first introduced as an additional security element for Active Directory communications. This is managed through the Default Domain Controllers Policy group policy object that is created during Active Directory installation.

Understanding SMB Signing

SMB signing refers to the process of encrypting and adding a validation signature to data packets used in the SMB communication process. SMB signing increases the security of SMB traffic by, for example, eliminating the possibility of a "man in the middle" attack between a workstation and a server.

Mac OS and other non-Windows operating systems cannot correctly interface with encrypted SMB connections. Although these systems can easily connect to shares on "regular" servers, they cannot connect to any domain controllers running the default SMB signing-enabled configuration.

Adding SMB Signing Support on the Macintosh

Mac OS X does not offer a native way to enable support for encrypted SMB communications. In cases where company policy or other regulations mandate SMB signing on the domain controller, third-party tools such as DAVE from Thursby Software (http://www.thursby.com/products/dave.html) add the ability to communicate with a Windows server via encrypted SMB connections. In many cases, however, the added expense of third-party software is not needed.

Turning Off SMB Signing

The workaround for this SMB signing issue is to disable the requirement to encrypt the SMB channel on the SBS 2008 server. These changes do not create a compatibility tradeoff for Windows-based workstations. Review the "Disabling SMB Signing" sidebar for background on the steps addressed in this section.

Disabling SMB Signing

The procedure detailed in this chapter for disabling SMB signing on the server only modifies half of the SMB signing process on the server. Group Policy provides two settings related to SMB signing. One setting mandates that all SMB connections must be encrypted. The other sets up an encrypted SMB connection if the workstation requests it. By default, domain-joined XP and Vista workstations request an encrypted SMB connection with the server. By leaving that setting enabled in group policy, when the XP or Vista workstations connect to the SMB shares on the server, they will do so over an encrypted connection. Thus, the GPO described in this chapter will not affect the way XP or Vista workstations connect to the server.

For more information about the way Group Policy works in the SBS 2008 environment, see Chapter 11, "Group Policy in SBS 2008."

Follow these steps to disable SMB signing on the SBS 2008 server:

1. From the Start menu, open the Group Policy Management console (type **gpmc.msc** in the search field and press Enter).
2. Click Continue in the User Account Control prompt.
3. Expand Forest, Domains, and select the internal domain.
4. Right-click on the internal domain name and select Create a GPO in This Domain, and Link It Here.
5. In the Name field, enter **SMB Signing Disabled** and click OK.
6. Right-click on SMB Signing Disabled and select Edit.
7. Expand Computer Configuration, Policies, Windows Settings, Security Settings, Local Policies and select Security Options.
8. Double-click Microsoft Network Client: Digitally Sign Communications (Always).
9. Enable the Define This Policy Setting checkbox and make sure the Disabled radio button is selected, and then click OK.
10. Double-click Microsoft Network Server: Digitally Sign Communications (Always).
11. Enable the Define This Policy Setting checkbox and make sure the Disabled radio button is selected, and then click OK.

12. Close the Group Policy Editor.

13. Right-click on SMB Signing Disabled and select Enforced. After making this change, the Group Policy Management Console should appear similar to Figure 13.1.

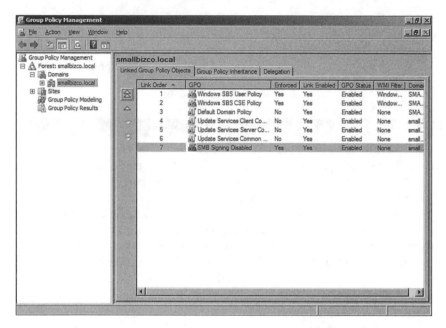

FIGURE 13.1   Confirming proper configuration of the SMB Signing Disabled GPO.

14. Close the Group Policy Management Console.

15. Open a command prompt and run `gpupdate /force`.

At this point, the Mac should be ready to connect to file shares on the server. You can confirm that the new policies have been enacted on the server by looking in the event logs for an SceCli 1202 event, indicating proper application of Group Policy on the server.

Connecting Macs to the SBS 2008 Network

Having resolved the SMB signing concerns, the next step to integration is ensuring that the Macintosh can communicate properly on the SBS 2008 network.

Configure DHCP Support on the Mac

Adopting the best practice of using the SBS 2008 server as the DHCP provider for the network, all Macintosh workstations should be configured as DHCP clients on the SBS 2008 network.

DNS, DHCP, and Active Directory

As discussed more thoroughly in Chapter 4, "DNS, DHCP, and Active Directrory Integration," proper DNS configuration is essential for an SBS 2008 network to function properly. To that end, all network devices in an SBS 2008 network need to point to the SBS 2008 server as the primary DNS server, since the DNS services running on the server handle all DNS requests for both internal and external name resolution. Mac users who might be familiar with setting their DNS settings to point to a public DNS server, or one provided by their ISP, encounter problems accessing internal network resources if they configure Macs on an SBS 2008 network that way. It is important, then, to let the Macintosh workstation get all of its network settings, including DNS, from the DHCP services running on the SBS 2008 server.

Configuring DHCP in Mac OS 10.4

Follow these steps to configure and confirm the network settings for a Macintosh running Mac OS 10.4:

1. From the Apple menu, select System Preferences.
2. From the Internet & Network group, click Network.
3. Double-click the active network interface (Built-in Ethernet or AirPort).
4. Ensure that the Configure IPv4 drop-down menu is set to Using DHCP.
5. The IP Address, Subnet Mask, and Router fields should have appropriate information based on the internal network configuration (see Figure 13.2).

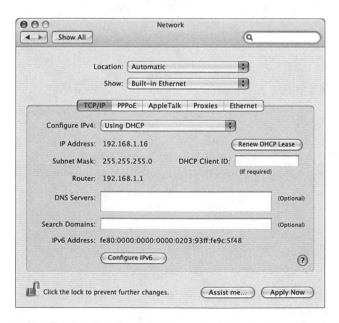

FIGURE 13.2   Proper TCP/IP configuration for Mac OS 10.4.

NOTE

Even though the Network control panel does not display the DNS server or the search domains, if that information is provided by the DHCP server, they are picked up by the Mac OS. Complete all the steps in this process to ensure proper DNS resolution.

6. If any changes were made, click Apply Now, and then close the System Preferences pane.

7. From Macintosh HD, Applications, Utilities, open the Terminal application.

8. At the command prompt, type ping servername (where *servername* is the NetBIOS name of the server) and press Enter.

9. Confirm that the servername fully resolves and the server responds to the ping (see Figure 13.3). Press Control-C to stop the ping process.

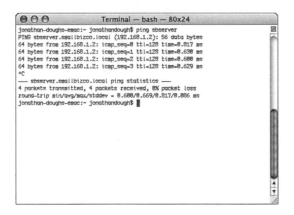

FIGURE 13.3   Using ping to test proper TCP/IP configuration.

10. Quit the Terminal application.

At this point, the Macintosh should be able to access all basic network resources. The "Accessing Files" section of the chapter contains instructions for testing proper network access.

Configuring Mac OS 10.5

Follow these steps to configure the network settings on a Macintosh running Mac OS 10.5:

1. From the Apple menu, select System Preferences.

2. From the Internet & Network group, click Network.

3. Select Using DHCP from the Configure drop-down menu.

4. If the Macintosh workstation receives a proper DHCP response from the SBS server, the settings for the default network connection should show the proper values for IP

address, subnet mask, default gateway, DNS server, and search domains should be
displayed in the settings window (see Figure 13.4).

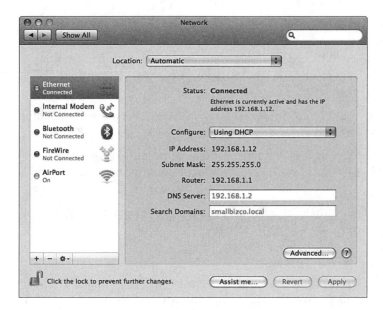

FIGURE 13.4   Confirming correct DHCP settings for the workstation.

5. If any changes were made, click Apply, then close System Preferences.

6. From Macintosh HD, Applications, Utilities, open the Terminal application.

7. At the command prompt, type **ping *servername***, where *servername* is the NetBIOS
   name (short name) of the SBS server, then press Enter.

8. Confirm that the servername fully resolves and the server responds to the ping (see
   Figure 13.5). Press Control-C to stop the ping process.

9. Quit the Terminal application.

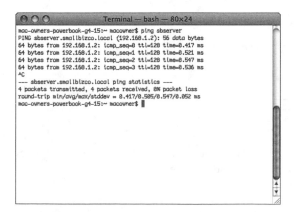

FIGURE 13.5   Using ping to test proper TCP/IP configuration.

The next section, "Accessing Files," provides instructions for testing access to network resources

Accessing Files

After the SBS 2008 server has had SMB signing disabled and the Macintosh workstations are configured to obtain DHCP addresses, you can test access from the Mac without making any configuration changes.

At this point, the Macintosh should be able to access all basic network resources, including surfing the Internet and accessing web services, such as Companyweb, on the SBS server.

The ability to centrally store and protect data is at the core of almost every SBS installation, and allowing Macintosh users to access this shared data is an important part of the integration process.

At this point, the Mac should be ready to connect to file shares on the server. Steps to test access to the shares are included in the next two sections of the chapter.

Configuring Mac OS 10.4

At this point, you can test access from the Mac without making any configuration changes. Follow these steps to open a share on the server from the Mac to confirm proper file access:

1. Bring the Finder to the foreground.

2. From the Go menu, select Connect to Server (or press Command-K).

3. In the Connect to Server window, type **smb://*servername*** in the Server Address field, where *servername* is the NetBIOS or DNS name of the server, and click Connect (see Figure 13.6).

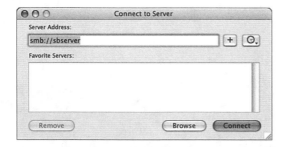

FIGURE 13.6   Entering the SMB path for the server.

4. In the SMB/CIFS File System Authentication window, enter the Active Directory username and password for the user, then click OK (see Figure 13.7).

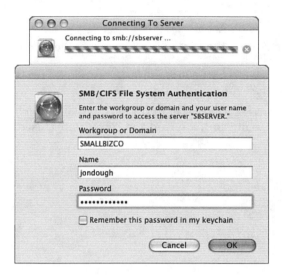

FIGURE 13.7   Entering Active Directory credentials.

5. Select the desired server share from the list and click OK to mount the share (see Figure 13.8).

FIGURE 13.8   Selecting the server share.

If you can complete all of these steps successfully, the Mac is ready to access files on the server. If an error occurs in Step 4, it is likely that SMB signing has not been properly disabled on the server.

Configuring Mac OS 10.5

Follow these steps to open a share on the server from the Mac to confirm proper file access:

1. Bring the Finder to the foreground.

2. From the Go menu, select Connect to Server (or press Command-K).

3. In the Connect to Server window, type **smb://servername** in the Server Address field, where *servername* is the NetBIOS or DNS name of the server, and click Connect (see Figure 13.9).

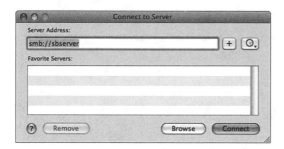

FIGURE 13.9   Entering the SMB path for the server.

4. In the authentication window, enter the Active Directory username and password for the user, then click OK (see Figure 13.10).

FIGURE 13.10   Entering Active Directory credentials.

5. Select the desired server share from the list and click OK to mount the share (see Figure 13.11).

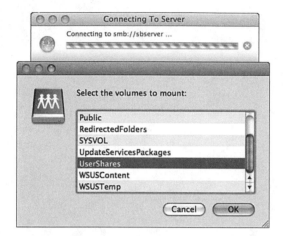

FIGURE 13.11   Selecting the server share.

If you can complete all of these steps successfully, the Mac is ready to access files on the server. If an error occurs in Step 4, it is likely that SMB signing has not been properly disabled on the server.

Connecting to Active Directory

As mentioned in the Active Directory sidebar earlier, best practice guidelines recommend configuring a desktop Macintosh in an SBS 2008 network to join the domain. The following sections provide instructions for configuring Active Directory access on Mac OS 10.4 and 10.5.

Configuring Mac OS 10.4

The Directory Access tool in Mac OS 10.4 enables users to configure default network settings to make it easier for the Mac to locate resources on the local network.

Configuring Directory Access

Follow these steps to configure Directory Access settings on the Macintosh:

1. Open the Macintosh HD icon from the desktop.
2. Open the Application folder, then the Utilities folder.
3. Open the Directory Access application.
4. Double-click on the SMB/CIFS entry under Services (you might need to click the lock to gain access to the settings; see Figure 13.12).

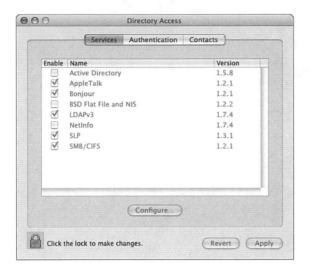

FIGURE 13.12   The Directory Access application contains settings for a number of networking tools.

5. In the Workgroup field, make sure the internal NetBIOS domain name is present.

6. In the WINS Server field, enter the IP address for the SBS server (see Figure 13.13) and click OK.

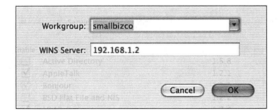

FIGURE 13.13   Configuring the workgroup settings in Directory Access.

At this point, the Macintosh is ready to participate in the local SBS 2008 network.

Connecting to Active Directory

As mentioned in the Active Directory sidebar earlier, best practice guidelines recommend configuring a desktop Macintosh in an SBS 2008 network to join the domain so that users can log in to the Mac with their Active Directory credentials and take advantage of the integration that Mac OS X has with Active Directory. Administrators might not want to join a Mac laptop to the domain if the user will be primarily out on the road. If a laptop user will be spending most of his or her time connected to the internal network, however, it is best to join the laptop to Active Directory and have the user log in with Active Directory credentials.

Follow these steps to join the Macintosh to Active Directory and log in with the user's AD credentials:

1. Open the Directory Access application from Macintosh HD, Applications, Utilities.

2. Double-click on the Active Directory item from the Services list (you might have to click the Lock and provide credentials to access the settings).

3. In the Active Directory Domain field, enter the internal domain name (that is, domain.local).

4. In the Computer ID field, enter a name for the Mac (changing the default name of the Mac to a shorter name is advised) and click the Show Advanced Options button (see Figure 13.14).

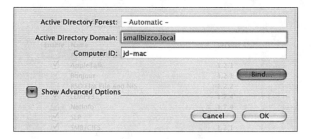

FIGURE 13.14   Setting the computer name for Active Directory.

5. Under the User Experience tab of the expanded window, ensure the Create Mobile Account at Login and Require Confirmation Before Creating a Mobile Account checkboxes are both enabled (see Figure 13.15).

6. Under the Administrative tab, enter the internal name for the SBS server in the Prefer This Domain Server field (see Figure 13.16).

7. Click Bind to start the process of joining the workstation to the domain.

8. Enter the username and password of a domain administrator account and click OK (see Figure 13.17).

> **NOTE**
>
> The default location for the computer object is the default Computers container in AD. You can modify the OU to be OU=SBSComputers,OU=Computers,OU=MyBusiness, DC=internaldomain,DC=local to place the Macintosh computer object into the same OU as the rest of the workstations on the network that have been joined using the Connect Computer wizard. Because the Macintosh is not affected by any group policy settings applied to this OU, this change is not necessary. The decision as to where to place the Macintosh computer objects in Active Directory is left up to the discretion of the administrator supporting the network.

9. Enter the username and password of the local user when prompted.

10. Once the binding process has completed, quit Directory Access.

FIGURE 13.15   Setting the mobile account settings in Directory Access.

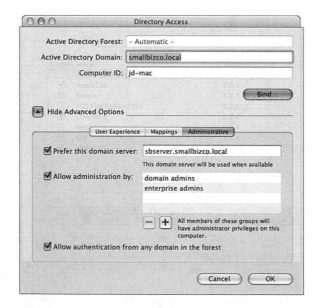

FIGURE 13.16   Setting the preferred domain server in Directory Access.

11. Open System Preferences from the Apple menu.

12. From the Personal items, click Security.

13. Enable the Disable Automatic Login checkbox and close System Preferences.

14. Log off the user account by selecting Log Off from the Apple menu.

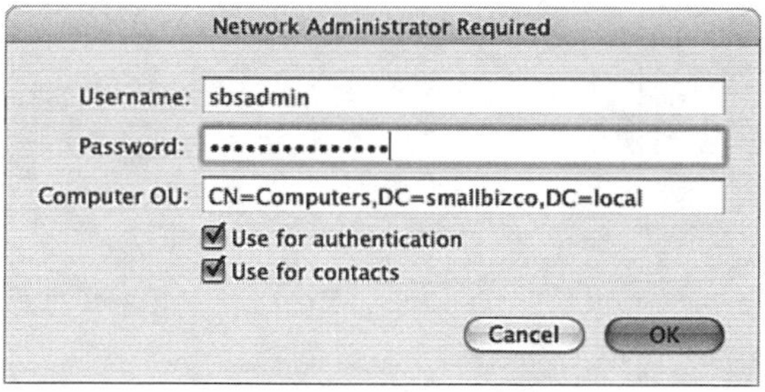

Network Administrator Required	
Username:	sbsadmin
Password:	••••••••••••••
Computer OU:	CN=Computers,DC=smallbizco,DC=local
	☑ Use for authentication
	☑ Use for contacts
	Cancel OK

FIGURE 13.17   Entering the domain administrator credentials.

13

15. In the Login window, you will see an icon for the local user, and an item for Other (see Figure 13.18).

FIGURE 13.18   Confirming proper configuration of Active Directory settings.

16. Click Other, and enter the domain username and password in the format domain-name\username (see Figure 13.19).

17. When prompted to create a portable home directory on this computer, click Yes (see Figure 13.20).

18. The Active Directory account will log in and a new user profile will be created on the Macintosh.

19. After the account has been created, log out of the domain account by selecting Log Out from the Apple menu.

20. The Login window now shows an icon for the domain account as well as for the local account (see Figure 13.21).

FIGURE 13.19   Entering the domain credentials for the first time.

FIGURE 13.20   Creating the mobile account settings.

21. Log in with the local account from the Login window.

22. Open System Preferences.

23. From the System items, select Accounts.

24. Click the lock and enter the local authentication information.

25. Select the mobile account from the Other Accounts area of the account pane.

26. Enable the Allow User to Administer This Computer checkbox (see Figure 13.22).

27. If desired, click the Picture tab and select an icon for the domain user account. When done, close System Preferences and log out of the local account.

Now the user can log in with his or her domain account.

Configuring Mac OS 10.5

The Directory Utility tool in Mac OS 10.5 enables administrators to join the Macintosh workstation to Active Directory. The process is handled differently in Mac OS 10.5, and as such the user interface is different as well.

FIGURE 13.21   Confirming proper creation of the domain account profile.

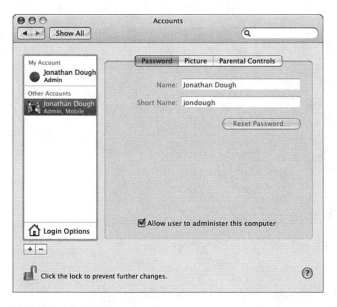

FIGURE 13.22   Configuring the domain account for local administrator access.

Follow these steps to join a Macintosh running Mac OS 10.5 to Active Directory and log in with the user's AD credentials:

1. Open the Directory Utility application from Macintosh HD, Applications, Utilities.

2. Click the padlock and enter the local Macintosh user credentials to unlock the settings.

3. Click the Show Advanced Settings button, then click the Services tab.

4. Double-click Active Directory.

5. In the Computer ID field, enter a name for the Mac (changing the default name of the Mac to a shorter name is advised) and expand the Show Advanced Options area.

6. Under the User Experience tab of the expanded window, ensure the Create Mobile Account at Login and Require Confirmation Before Creating a Mobile Account checkboxes are both enabled (see Figure 13.23).

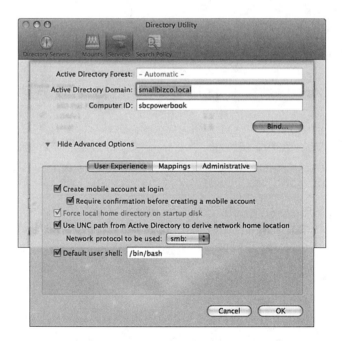

FIGURE 13.23   Setting the mobile account settings in Directory Access.

7. Under the Administrative tab, enable the Allow Administration By checkbox.

8. Enable the Prefer This Domain Server checkbox, and enter the internal name for the SBS server in the Prefer this domain server field (see Figure 13.24).

9. Click Bind to start the process of joining the workstation to the domain.

10. Enter the username and password of a domain administrator account and click OK (see Figure 13.25).

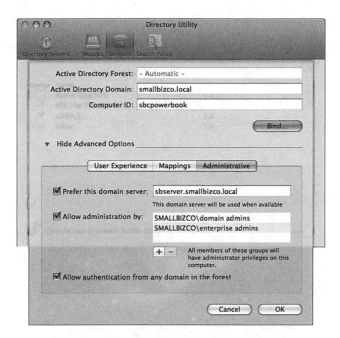

FIGURE 13.24   Setting the preferred domain server in Directory Access.

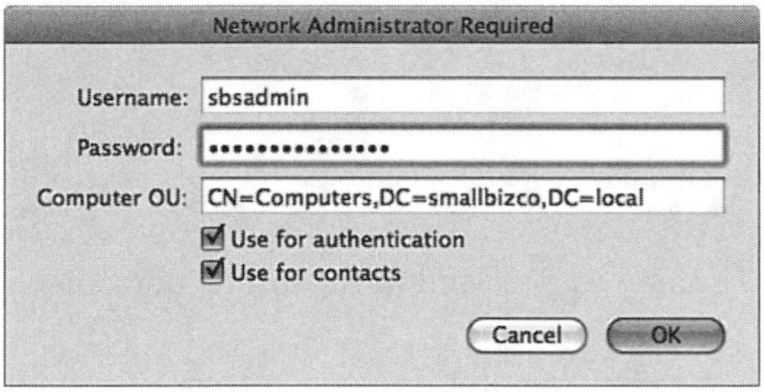

FIGURE 13.25   Entering the domain administrator credentials.

NOTE

The default location for the computer object is the default Computers container in AD. You can modify the OU to be OU=SBSComputers,OU=Computers,OU=MyBusiness, DC=internaldomain,DC=local to place the Macintosh computer object into the same OU as the rest of the workstations on the network that have been joined using the Connect Computer wizard. Because the Macintosh is not affected by any group policy settings applied to this OU, this change is not necessary. The decision as to where to place the Macintosh computer objects in Active Directory is left up to the discretion of the administrator supporting the network.

---

11. After the binding process has completed, quit Directory Utility.

12. Open System Preferences from the Apple menu.

13. From the Personal group, click Security.

14. Enable the Disable Automatic Login checkbox and close System Preferences.

15. Log off the user account by selecting Log Off from the Apple menu.

16. In the Login window, you see an icon for the local user, and an item for Other (see Figure 13.26).

FIGURE 13.26   Confirming proper configuration of Active Directory settings.

17. Click Other, and enter the domain username and password in the format domainname\username (see Figure 13.27).

18. When prompted to create a portable home directory on this computer, click Create New (see Figure 13.28).

19. The Active Directory account logs in and a new user profile is created on the Macintosh.

20. After the account has been created, log out of the domain account by selecting Log Out from the Apple menu.

21. The Login window now shows an icon for the domain account, as well as for the local account (see Figure 13.29).

22. Log in with the local account from the Login window.

23. Open System Preferences.

24. From the System group, select Accounts.

25. Click the lock and enter the local authentication information to unlock the settings.

26. Select the mobile account from the Other Accounts area of the account pane.

FIGURE 13.27   Entering the domain credentials for the first time.

FIGURE 13.28   Creating the mobile account settings.

FIGURE 13.29   Confirming proper creation of the domain account profile.

27. Enable the Allow User to Administer This Computer checkbox (see Figure 13.30).

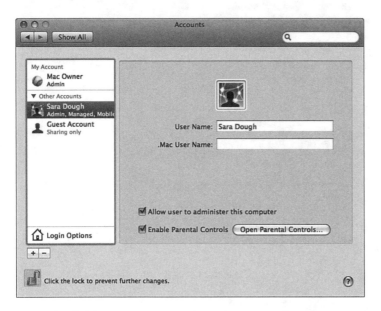

FIGURE 13.30   Configuring the domain account for local administrator access.

28. If desired, click the picture icon and select an icon for the domain user account. When done, close System Preferences and log out of the local account.

Now the user can log in with his or her domain account.

Accessing E-Mail

Next to shared file access, user access to e-mail is the most requested SBS resource from the Mac user. Unfortunately, there are not any native Macintosh tools that interface effectively with Exchange, so Mac users wanting to gain the full benefit of Exchange have to use Outlook Web Access or Entourage.

Many Macintosh users will be familiar with the Mac Mail or other third-party e-mail client interfaces and might want to try to use those tools to connect to Exchange. Although it is possible to configure Exchange 2007 to act as a POP3 or IMAP mail server, a discussion of setting up this type of access is beyond the scope of this book. There are blog posts and other how-to documents that detail the proper ways of configuring Exchange in SBS 2008 to allow POP3 and IMAP clients to connect, including iPhones and other hand-held mail-enabled devices.

Changes from SBS 2003—E-Mail Client Tools

As covered in Chapter 9, "Exchange 2007 Client Connectivity," Microsoft has changed the way they handle licensing e-mail client tools with Exchange 2007. In Exchange 2003, and thus in SBS 2003, the Exchange license included a license for an e-mail client, as well as the server mailbox license. That meant that every licensed user in the SBS 2003 network had a license to install and run Outlook 2003 or Entourage 2004 on their workstation.

Not so in Exchange 2007. Mac users wanting to use Entourage to connect to Exchange in SBS 2008 need to provide their own licensed copy of Entourage in order to access e-mail on the server. Entourage is included as part of Office 2008 and Office 2004, but is now subject to the license of the suite, not the license of the Exchange server. The bottom line is this: Every Mac user who wants to use Entourage to access his or her e-mail on SBS 2008 needs a valid licensed copy on each workstation he or she uses.

The remainder of this section of the chapter discusses configuration of Entourage for accessing e-mail. A discussion of Outlook Web Access from the Mac appears later in the chapter.

Preparing the SBS 2008 Network

By default, SBS 2008 is pre-configured for allowing e-mail connectivity from a Mac workstation using either Outlook Web Access or Entourage. As discussed in Chapters 5 and 6, the new standard in SBS 2008 is to use the public URL for all SBS web resources, even from the internal network. The same applies to Entourage. In previous versions of SBS, a special DNS configuration was needed to allow a traveling laptop running Entourage to connect to the e-mail server successfully, whether in the office or on the road. These changes are no longer needed with SBS 2008. As described in more detail in the following section, Entourage uses the public DNS name for the server as configured in the Set up your Internet address wizard.

Preparing the Macintosh for Entourage Connectivity

Although Microsoft released Office 2008 in January of 2008, there are still a number of users continuing to run Office 2004. To address those users, this chapter includes information for configuring Entourage 2004 as well as Entourage 2008 to connect to the SBS 2008 server. The configuration of Entourage 2004 is the same whether the Mac is running Mac OS 10.4 or Mac OS 10.5.

Entourage uses WebDAV to communicate with the Exchange server, and as such will be accessing the WebDAV services over SSL. Entourage does not recognize the self-signed SSL certificate that SBS 2008 creates during initial setup. There are two ways to avoid certificate warnings in Entourage: install a third-party SSL certificate in IIS (more information about third-party SSL certificates can be found in Chapter 5, "Internet Information Services 7.0"), or install the self-signed SSL certificate from the SBS 2008 server in the Macintosh certificate store. The next two sections provide instructions for installing the certificate on Mac OS 10.4 and Mac OS 10.5.

13

Installing a Self-Signed SSL Certificate in Mac OS 10.4

Follow these instructions to install the SBS 2008 self-signed SSL certificate into the Mac OS 10.4 certificate store:

1. Bring the Finder to the foreground, and from the Go menu, select Connect to Server (or press Command-K).
2. In the Server Address field, enter `smb://servername/Public.`
3. In the Downloads folder, open the Certificate Distribution Package folder.
4. Double-click on the SBSCertificate.cer file.
5. After the Keychain Access application opens, from the Add Certificates window, select the X509Anchors keychain (see Figure 13.31).

FIGURE 13.31   Selecting the proper Mac OS 10.4 keychain to store the self-signed certificate.

6. Enter the username and password of the logged-in user and click OK.
7. Close Keychain Access.

Installing a Self-Signed SSL Certificate in Mac OS 10.5

Follow these instructions to install the SBS 2008 self-signed SSL certificate into the Mac OS 10.5 certificate store:

1. Bring the Finder to the foreground, and from the Go menu, select Connect to Server (or press Command-K).
2. In the Server Address field, enter `smb://servername/Public.`
3. In the Downloads folder, open the Certificate Distribution Package folder.
4. Double-click on the SBSCertificate.cer file.
5. After the Keychain Access application opens, from the Add Certificates window, select the login keychain (see Figure 13.32).
6. When Keychain Access asks about trusting the certificates from the SBS Root CA, click Always Trust (see Figure 13.33).
7. Enter the username and password of the logged-in user and click OK.
8. Close Keychain Access.

FIGURE 13.32   Selecting the proper Mac OS 10.5 keychain to store the self-signed certificate.

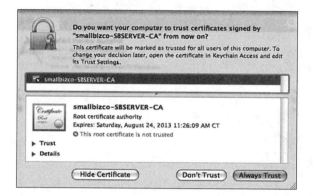

FIGURE 13.33   Trusting the SCS Root CA certificate chain.

Configuring Entourage 2004

When opening Entourage 2004 for the first time, Entourage detects that no mail profiles exist on the Mac, and it initiates the startup wizard. You can choose to go through the wizard to configure Entourage, or you can use the manual configuration method. This section details the manual configuration method.

Follow these instructions to manually configure Entourage 2004 to connect to the SBS 2008 server:

1. Open Macintosh HD, Applications.
2. Run the Microsoft AutoUpdate application and click Check for Updates.
3. If any updates are found, install the updates. Repeat this process until Microsoft AutoUpdate reports that no more updates are available.
4. Launch Entourage from the Applications, Microsoft Office 2004 folder.
5. If the startup wizard launches, cancel the wizard.
6. From the Tools menu, select Accounts.
7. From the Accounts window, click the Exchange tab, then click New.

8. Click the Configure account manually button.

9. Enter a name for the account in the Account Name field (for example, "Exchange" or the name of the server or company could be used as the account name).

10. Enter the user's name and e-mail address in the appropriate fields.

11. Enter the user's AD account information in the Account ID, Domain, and Password fields.

12. In the Exchange Server field, enter the public DNS name for the server in the format `remote.domain.com/exchange/user@domain.com`, where `user@domain.com` is the e-mail address of the user for the Entourage profile. An example is shown in Figure 13.34.

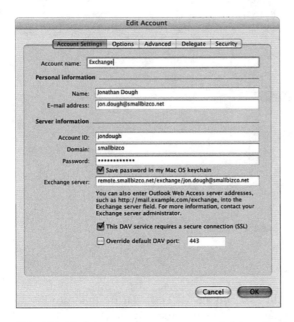

FIGURE 13.34   Entering mail server information in Entourage 2004.

13. Enable the This DAV Service Requires a Secure Connection (SSL) checkbox (see Figure 13.34).

14. Select the Advanced tab.

15. In the Public Folders Server field, enter the public DNS name for the server in the format `remote.domain.com/public`. An example is shown in Figure 13.35.

16. Enable the This DAV Service Requires a Secure Connection (SSL) checkbox and click OK (see Figure 13.35).

17. Close the Accounts window.

Entourage now connects to the Exchange server and downloads any messages that exist for that user. The user will want to minimize the Folders on the My Computer node to allow the folders from the Exchange profile to display more prominently.

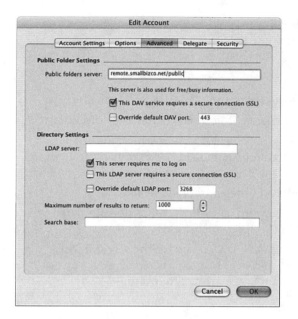

FIGURE 13.35   Entering advanced mail server information in Entourage 2004.

Entourage and Endless URLs

You might have noticed that the information that has to be entered into the Exchange server fields in the Entourage configuration is not exactly intuitive. Entourage 2004 was built specifically for Exchange 2003 and was hard-coded to use the /exchange virtual directory. So even though Outlook Web Access has a URL of remote.domain.com/owa, Entourage 2004 must use the /exchange path in order to communicate.

In addition, the path to the mailbox for the user must be included as part of the config-uration. This is documented in KB931350 (http://support.microsoft.com/kb/931350) but still does not completely explain why. The bottom line is that Entourage 2004 (and Entourage 2008 as well) do not communicate with Exchange using MAPI, but rely on WebDAV and as such must have these unusual configurations on both programs to communicate correctly.

Configuring Entourage 2008

Follow these instructions to manually configure Entourage 2008 to connect to the SBS 2008 server:

1. Open Macintosh HD, Library, Application Support, Microsoft, MAU2.0.

2. Run the Microsoft AutoUpdate application and click Check for Updates.

3. If any updates are found, install the updates. Repeat this process until Microsoft AutoUpdate reports that no more updates are available.

4. Launch Entourage from the Applications, Microsoft Office 2008 folder.

5. If the Entourage Setup Assistant starts, close it.

6. From the Tools menu, select Accounts.

7. From the Accounts window, click New.

8. In the Account Setup Assistant window, click Configure Account Manually.

9. In the New Account window, select Exchange from the Account Type drop-down menu. Then click OK.

10. Enter a name for the account in the Account Name field (for example, the account could be named "Exchange" or "SBS 2008").

11. Enter the user's name and e-mail address in the appropriate fields.

12. Enter the user's domain login name, password, and the NetBIOS domain name (that is, domain instead of domain.local) in the appropriate fields.

13. In the Exchange server field, enter the public DNS name for the server in the format `remote.domain.com/exchange/user@domain.com`, where `user@domain.com` is the e-mail address of the user for the Entourage profile. An example is shown in Figure 13.36.

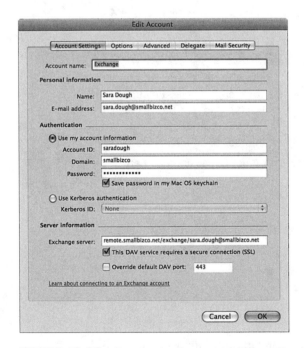

FIGURE 13.36   Entering basic account information in Entourage 2008.

14. Enable the This DAV Service Requires a Secure Connection (SSL) checkbox (see Figure 13.36 for a summary of the settings thus far).

15. Click the Advanced tab.

16. In the Public Folders Server field, enter the public DNS name for the server in the format `remote.domain.com/public`. An example is shown in Figure 13.37.

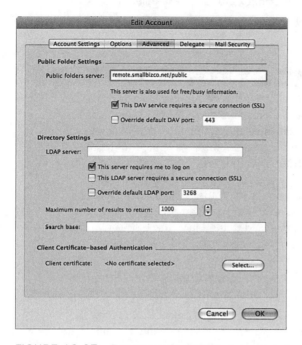

FIGURE 13.37   Entering advanced mail server information in Entourage 2008.

17. Enable the This DAV Service Requires a Secure Connection (SSL) checkbox (see Figure 13.37).

18. Once you confirm the settings are correct, click OK.

19. Close the Accounts window and return to the main Entourage screen.

Entourage now connects to Exchange and builds the local profile.

Accessing SBS 2008 Web Resources

SBS 2008 contains a number of web-based services, as discussed in Chapters 5, 6, and 7. Macintosh workstations can access many of these web services, but not all the features are available in the Mac environment. This section of the chapter covers the main web resources that Mac users will access and identifies the limitations of each service.

> **NOTE**
>
> Apple bundles the Safari web browser with the Mac OS, so it is available by default on all Macintosh workstations. Apple released Safari version 3.0 along with the release of Mac OS 10.5. Safari 3.0 is included with Leopard and is available as an update to older OS versions. Information in this chapter is based on the latest build of Safari 3.0.

Many Mac users also download and run the Firefox web browser, as it can be more compatible with some web technologies than Safari is. In cases where the interface is significantly different between the Safari and Firefox browsers, examples of both browsers are included. If there is no significant difference in the interface or interaction between the two browsers, examples from either browser may be included.

Best Practice—Dealing with Self-Signed Certificates

Safari and Firefox deal with self-signed certificates in different manners, and this can impact how Mac users access SBS 2008 web services from off-site. Safari uses the Mac OS certificate store to verify a certificate's validity, whereas Firefox maintains its own separate certificate store. To eliminate any Safari warnings related to the default self-signed SSL certificates provided by SBS 2008, the SBS 2008 cert should be installed in the OS certificate store using the instructions in the "Preparing the Macintosh for Entourage Connectivity" section earlier in the chapter. If the Mac is a truly remote machine that will never be connected to the internal network to get the certificate file off the server, the file can be copied to the Mac via a USB key, or from the Web if the certificate has been placed in the SharePoint site, as described in Chapter 5, "Internet Information Services 7.0."

To eliminate any certificate warnings in Firefox, simply follow the instructions Firefox provides to accept the certificate permanently in the initial certificate warning dialog.

If the system administrator runs the Internet Address Management Wizard after the certificates have been installed in either Firefox or Mac OS, the updated certificates will need to be installed.

The best solution for the certificate issue, however, is to purchase and install a third-party SSL certificate on the SBS 2008 server. The process for this is detailed in Chapter 5.

Companyweb

Both the Safari and Firefox browsers can access the Companyweb site on the SBS 2008 server. For Macintosh workstations on the internal network, the site can be accessed as http://companyweb in the browser address bar. Both Safari and Firefox prompt for user authentication to access companyweb, as neither Safari or Firefox can pass along login credentials from the currently logged-on user on request by the web site.

Once logged in to Companyweb, Mac users can access most of the default functions built into the SBS configuration. There is one significant difference between accessing Companyweb in IE on Windows and in Safari or Firefox on a Mac. When working with documents in the document libraries, individual files can be edited, but the user must first download the file to the Mac, edit and save the file locally, then upload back to the library. The ability to launch the application to edit the file directly from the library is only supported in Internet Explorer 6.0 or later for Windows. In addition, only Office applications for Windows can access files in the Sharepoint libraries directly from within the application. Office 2004 and Office 2008 for Mac do not have this feature.

When connecting from outside the network, Macs must access the Companyweb site using the https://remote.domain.com:987 URL just like PCs. There is no difference in functionality when accessing the site remotely, but overall performance will likely be slower than when connecting to Companyweb locally.

Outlook Web Access

Mac users can access their e-mail through the web using the Outlook Web Access (OWA) interface. As with previous versions of Exchange, however, the Macintosh can only access OWA using the reduced-functionality interface, called Outlook Web Access Light in Exchange 2007 terminology. The good news is that Exchange 2007 has significantly improved the functionality of the reduced-access interface to OWA. Interacting with mail, calendar, and contact items in OWA from the Mac provides access to most of the features in those areas. Access to Journal, Notes, and Tasks is still very limited. More information about the full feature set of OWA is covered in Chapter 9.

Remote Web Workplace

As discussed in Chapter 6, "Remote Web Workplace and Other Remote Access Solutions," there are significant improvements and changes to the Remote Web Workplace (RWW) interface in SBS 2008. As with SBS 2003, Mac users can log into the RWW interface and access the basic features of RWW, including access to OWA, access to Companyweb, and viewing links that have been placed in the interface by the system administrator. Mac users still cannot take advantage of the Connect to a Computer feature of RWW, and an internal Mac cannot be controlled by this feature, either.

Two of the new features added to RWW can be used by Mac users, however. One is the Change Password interface, and the other is the Access Files interface. Both of these features work in the same way from the Mac as they do from Windows systems. More details about all the updated Remote Web Workplace services are covered in Chapter 6.

Troubleshooting

Although this chapter has tried to cover the basics of Macintosh connectivity in a default SBS 2008 installation, there may be circumstances that interfere with expected operations. This section of the chapter covers some common troubleshooting tips and tools to help resolve connectivity issues.

Network Connectivity

In a properly-configured SBS 2008 network, setting the Mac to get its network settings from DHCP should be sufficient to allow the workstation to communicate with the remainder of the network. If the Mac is not getting a proper DHCP configuration (that is, getting a 169.254 APIPA address), you can assign a static IP to the Mac temporarily to test basic network connectivity. If you set a static IP, however, you also need to manually set the DNS server settings, and for testing purposes, the DNS settings should still point to the SBS 2008 server as the primary DNS server. This process differs slightly in Mac OS 10.4 and 10.5, so both scenarios are covered as examples.

Setting a Static IP in Mac OS 10.4

Follow these steps to set up a static IP in Mac OS 10.4:

1. From the Apple menu, select System Preferences.

2. From the Internet & Network group, select Network.

3. Double-click on the active network connection (usually Built-in Ethernet or AirPort).

4. From the Configure IPv4 drop-down menu, select Manually.

5. Enter an IP address, subnet mask, and router IP based on the local network settings.

6. Enter the IP address for the SBS server in the DNS Servers field, or enter the IP of a known-good DNS server.

7. Click Apply Now to save the settings.

After confirming proper network configuration and communication, reset the Macintosh network configuration to pick up its IP configuration from DHCP.

Setting a Static IP in Mac OS 10.5

Follow these steps to set up a static IP in Mac OS 10.5:

1. From the Apple menu, select System Preferences.

2. From the Internet & Network group, select Network.

3. Select the active network interface (usually Ethernet or AirPort).

4. From the Configure drop-down menu, select Manually.

5. Enter an IP address, subnet mask, and router IP based on the local network settings.

6. Enter the IP address for the SBS server in the DNS Server field, or enter the IP address of a known-good DNS server.

7. Click Apply to save the settings.

After confirming proper network configuration and communication, reset the Macintosh network configuration to pick up its IP configuration from DHCP.

Testing the Network with Command-Line Tools

Instructions for using the ping command-line tool to test network connectivity were given earlier in the chapter. In a properly-configured SBS 2008 network, pinging the SBS server by name is sufficient to test proper DNS resolution and communication with the server by ping. If the DNS lookup fails, or if the network is not set up correctly, this single test may not be sufficient to tell if the Mac is properly configured.

Two network tools, ping and nslookups, can be used in the Terminal application to test network connectivity. Terminal can be opened from the Macintosh HD, Applications, Utilities folder.

The following are some general guidelines for testing proper connectivity using ping:

▶ Ping the IP address of the SBS server.

▶ Ping the IP address of the gateway/firewall.

▶ Ping the IP address of an external DNS server (you can get this information from the ISP or use one of the global DNS servers: 4.2.2.1, 4.2.2.2, 4.2.2.3, or 4.2.2.4).

▶ Ping the SBS server by fully-qualified domain name (FQDN)—that is, sbserver.domain.local.

▶ Ping the SBS server by short name (that is, if the internal FQDN of the server is sbserver.domain.local, ping sbserver).

If the Macintosh can ping by IP but not by name, use nslookup in the Terminal application to troubleshoot where the problem may be.

Enter nslookup by typing `nslookup` and pressing Enter in the Terminal application. At the nslookup prompt, type the short name of the server (that is, sbserver) and press Enter. You should get a response similar to the following:

```
Server:        192.168.1.2
Address:       192.168.1.2#53

Name:          sbserver.SMALLBIZCO.local
Address:       192.168.1.2
```

The IP address following Server in the preceding listing should be the IP address of the SBS server. If not, the Mac is pointing to the wrong location for DNS, and the IP address listed will indicate which DNS server is being used. To test against the SBS DNS server, type `server 192.168.1.2` and press Enter at the nslookup prompt, substituting the proper IP address for the SBS server if `192.168.1.2` is not the IP address of the server. Then you can enter the short name of the SBS server at the prompt to see if the Mac is able to make a DNS request against the updated DNS server.

If the Mac is not able to communicate with the DNS server, you may see a response similar to the following in nslookup:

```
;; connection timed out; no servers could be reached
```

This response simply means that the Mac did not receive a response from the query it sent to the currently-selected DNS server.

If you have split DNS setup, you can use nslookup to verify that the internal workstation is receiving the proper IP address for the public name of the server. Follow these steps to check for proper Split DNS configuration:

1. In the Terminal application, type **nslookup** and press Enter.

2. At the nslookup prompt, type **serverw.x.y.z** and press Enter, where *w.x.y.z* is the address of a public DNS server.

3. Type the public DNS name for your connection (that is, remote.domain.com) and press Enter. The DNS response should give the public IP address for your network connection.

4. Type **serverw.x.y.z** and press Enter, where *w.x.y.z* is the internal IP address of your SBS server.

5. Type the public DNS name for your connection and press Enter. The DNS response should give the internal IP address of the SBS server. If the same public IP address is returned, then Split DNS is not properly set up on the SBS server.

6. Type **exit** and press Enter to close out of nslookup.

File Share Access

The most common issues related to access to the SBS file shares from a Mac generally belong to one of two problems. Either the domain credentials were not properly entered, or SMB encryption is still enabled on the server. When a Mac is joined to Active Directory and the user is able to log in with his or her domain credentials, the issue is almost certainly that SMB signing is blocking the connection.

In Mac OS 10.5, attempts to access shares on the server generally fail with the error, "You do not have permission to access this server." In Mac OS 10.4, the failure to connect generally gives the error, "Could not connect to the server because the name or password is not correct," or a constant prompting of the username and password, even if the user is logged in with his or her domain credentials.

To verify that the Mac can connect to an SMB share, create a share from a Windows XP or Vista workstation that is open to all users (the share can be read-only, but should be set to allow everyone to access the share). Then connect to the share from the Mac using smb://*workstationname,* where *workstationname* is the name of the workstation that has the share (you may want to ensure that you can resolve workstationname by pinging the name first). If the Mac can connect to the workstation share, but not the server share, then either the SMB Signing Disabled GPO has not been properly created or enabled, or another policy is overriding the settings in the policy. Refer to Chapter 11, "Group Policy in SBS 2008," for information on how to troubleshoot group policy problems.

E-Mail Access

Troubleshooting access problems in Entourage is fairly straightforward. Most of the time, access issues in Entourage have to do with the way the server information is configured in the account settings. To verify that the correct server information has been entered into Entourage, follow these steps:

1. In Entourage, open Accounts from the Tools menu.

2. Double-click on the Exchange mail profile.

3. Copy the information from the Exchange Server field.

4. Open Safari or Firefox.

5. In the address bar of the web browser, enter **https://remote.domain.com/owa**, where remote.domain.com is the information copied from the Entourage account profile.

6. If the Outlook Web Access login screen does not come up in the web browser, the incorrect server name has been entered into Entourage.

As discussed earlier in the chapter, if the SBS 2008 server is using the default, self-signed SSL certificates and that certificate has not been installed into the Mac certificate store,

Entourage generates the certificate warning error. If the SSL certificate on the server is modified after the certificate is installed on the Mac, Entourage starts generating certificate warnings, because the certificate stored on the Mac does not match the certificate presented by the server.

Windows Support on the Macintosh

A common challenge Macintosh users face when using the Mac in a business environment is software incompatibility. Not all programs that run on Windows have versions that run on the Mac, or the Mac version of the program is not fully compatible with its Windows counterpart. One specific example is web-based applications that are built on ActiveX technology, which includes some of the SBS web components as well. There is no support for ActiveX components on the Mac, so when a person who prefers to use the Mac platform needs to use one of these tools, there is usually a difficult decision to make: either run two workstations to get access to the tools on both platforms, or abandon the use of the Mac as a workstation and use only a Windows workstation.

With the release of Macintosh systems running on Intel architecture, however, a new option is available for users finding themselves needing to run tools unique to each platform. The following sections describe two methods for being able to run the Windows operating system on Macintosh hardware. These Windows environments are not limited or crippled environments and can fully participate as Windows workstations in an SBS 2008 network. If users are covered by User CALs in the SBS 2008 network, no additional licenses are needed for either of these solutions.

Although there are additional costs associated with running Windows on a Mac, as explained in each of the following sections, the additional cost to enable Windows support might be significantly less than running and maintaining two distinct workstations to allow access to platform-specific tools. This gives business owners and IT professionals additional options for enhancing employee productivity in these cases.

Boot Camp

Apple's Boot Camp software (http://www.apple.com/macosx/features/bootcamp.html) was available as a Beta tool for Mac OS 10.4 (Tiger) and is included with Mac OS 10.5 (Leopard). Boot Camp enables the end user to install and run Windows operating systems directly on the Macintosh hard drive. Boot Camp is a dual-boot tool, meaning that you can have either the Mac OS environment or the Windows environment running, but not both at the same time. Additionally, the Macintosh hard drive must be repartitioned to create a place for the Windows operating system to be installed. However, all Windows software runs in the Boot Camp environment, and if the end user needs to run software that has significant graphics requirements, running that application under Boot Camp provides the best graphics response.

Although the Boot Camp software is free, users need a properly-licensed Windows operating system and Windows software to run under boot camp.

Parallels Desktop for Mac and VMWare Fusion

Parallels Desktop for Mac (http://www.parallels.com/en/products/desktop/) and VMWare Fusion (http://www.vmware.com/products/fusion/) are two virtualization products available for Intel-based Macintosh workstations that allow a Windows environment to be loaded on the Mac, and both the Macintosh and the Windows environments are available at the same time. As both environments run virtually, performance on the Windows side is not as good as under Boot Camp, but the performance is still good enough for most needs, as long as the Macintosh environment is configured properly. Best practice recommendations for running Parallels or Fusion is to have at least 2GB of RAM in the Mac (1GB for the Mac and up to 1GB for the Windows environment) and a large hard drive to store not only the Mac OS and software but the virtual hard disk file for the Windows environment.

Both Parallels and Fusion virtualize the video environment as well as the underlying hardware, so graphics-intensive applications may not perform as well under the virtual installations as they would under Boot Camp.

Both Parallels and Fusion have a modest cost associated with them, but neither include a license for the Windows operating system. As with Boot Camp, a properly-licensed Windows operating system is needed, and Windows Vista licensing has some restrictions to being run in a virtual environment that would apply to Parallels and Fusion installations, but not to Boot Camp installations. Refer to the End User Licensing Agreement for the various versions of Vista to determine what restrictions may apply to running Vista in a virtual environment.

Summary

This chapter covered the basics of connecting a Macintosh workstation into an SBS 2008 network. Although the information provided is complete, it by no means represents the entirety of Macintosh support. But the small business consultant who chooses to add Mac support to his or her repertoire should have enough information from this chapter to be able to successfully integrate the Macintosh platform into an SBS 2008 network and troubleshoot basic connectivity issues that might arise.

Best Practice Summary

▶ **Keep Mac OS Up to Date**—Configure Software Update in Mac OS to check for updates on a regular basis and to download important updates in the background, which reduces the time needed to install the updates when users are prompted to install.

▶ **Join Macintosh Workstations to Active Directory**—Macintosh users benefit from having their Macs joined to Active Directory because they can take advantage of single sign-on, not having to enter credentials to access server shares, and administrators can disable user access to a Mac by disabling the user's AD account.

▶ **Dealing with Self-Signed Certificates**—The default self-signed SSL certificates provided with SBS 2008 need to be installed in the Mac OS certificate store to ensure proper operation of Safari and Entourage. Firefox maintains its own certificate store, and the SBS cert should be added in there as well. Third-party SSL certificates should be installed in SBS to avoid certificate issues with Macintosh tools.

13

Additional Servers

As feature rich as SBS 2008 is in its own right, the addition of further servers to the network is a necessity for many environments. These additional servers can take on many roles and can be running a multitude of operating systems. The decision to add a server to a network needs to be made with careful consideration of what its purpose is—if this purpose requires a separate server or can be added to an existing server; the ability to manage and maintain this server on an ongoing basis; how the server will be backed up and how it will be recovered in the event of failure. This chapter specifically addresses the addition of Windows Server 2008-based servers to the SBS 2008 network, where these servers can fulfill several common scenarios likely to be encountered.

> **NOTE**
>
> For the purpose of clarity, this chapter may refer to a server other than the SBS 2008 server as the "second server;" however, in reality, there is no reason why an additional server cannot be the third, fourth, or fifth server on the network—it all depends on the specific requirements of your network environment as to how many servers you have. Any reference to the term "second server," therefore, can also be read as "additional server."

Understanding the Role of Additional Servers in an SBS 2008 Network

Prior to the implementation of any server on a network, the role it is going to serve on the network needs to be determined. In addition, there is the question of how the server is going to be licensed, which can be almost as time-consuming as the installation of the operating system!

This section provides an overview of some of the licensing models available from Microsoft for SBS based networks together with a summary of the most common roles the second server might fulfill on the network.

Licensing for Additional Servers

Any discussion on adding servers to a network needs to include some coverage of licensing. A server on the network needs to have a valid operating system license if it's going to legally exist, although this license can be supplied under any one of several license options from Microsoft, and not all licenses necessarily need to be the same. Although complete coverage of Microsoft's licensing programs is beyond the scope of this book, the following list identifies the most relevant license programs for the typical SBS 2008 network:

- ▶ OEM

- ▶ Retail

- ▶ Microsoft Open License Program (MOLP)

- ▶ Microsoft Open Value Licensing (MOVL)

Determining the correct licensing program for your environment can be as simple, or as complex, as you want it to be. There are factors that need to be considered when making a choice and certainly no "one size fits all" solution exists.

OEM licenses are typically the lowest-cost license to purchase but come with limitations in terms of being able to reassign the license to another piece of hardware (unless you purchase Software Assurance for the license within 90 days of the original license purchase). The OEM license can only be purchased with new system components (the complexity starts when you start to consider what constitutes a "system component") and requires an OEM license sticker be attached to the associated hardware. If you lose the OEM license sticker then you have effectively lost the license and therefore the right to use the software.

Retail licenses (also known as Full Package Product (FPP) or boxed product) can be purchased independently of any hardware and typically constitute a very low proportion of SBS license sales. There is no license sticker; however, you do get a certificate that must be stored as evidence of your right to use the software. The software license can be reassigned to another system in the event of hardware failure or retirement. If you lose the license certificate, you have effectively lost the license and therefore the right to use the software.

MOLP and MOVL license agreements are electronically tracked licenses—there is no sticker or piece of paper to keep. The key differences between these license agreements are the following:

▶ MOLP license agreements are effective for two years; MOVL license agreements are effective for three years. (This does not mean the licenses themselves expire.)

▶ MOLP license agreements require the license cost to be paid in full with the license purchase; MOVL license agreements are typically paid in three annual installments (but can be completely paid up-front if the client desires).

▶ MOVL license agreements include Software Assurance; MOLP licenses can be purchased with or without Software Assurance.

From Microsoft's perspective, MOLP or MOVL licenses are the best choice because they provide Microsoft with the maximum visibility of who their end users are—the licenses are electronically tracked through the Microsoft licensing portal at https://eopen.microsoft.com. From a business's perspective, these licenses are easy to manage and track as there is no physical license that needs to be stored and no OEM sticker that needs to be applied to a computer.

This summary should not be used to make any final decision about which licensing program is right for your environment. Information on which license program is best should be sought from your trusted Microsoft partner or by visiting the Microsoft License Advisor page at http://www.microsoft.com/licensing/mlahome.mspx. Information on all Microsoft volume license programs can be found at http://www.microsoft.com/licensing/default.mspx.

14

> **NOTE**
>
> An overview of SBS 2008 licensing can be found at http://www.microsoft.com/windowsserver/essential/sbs/prodinfo/licensing-overview.mspx.

Premium Server License

The Premium Edition of SBS 2008 includes a second Windows Server 2008 Standard server license. This is a full Windows Server 2008 Standard license governed by the rights of the license agreement under which the server license is supplied (OEM, retail, MOLP, MOVL).

Additional License Purchase

Apart from obtaining a second server license by purchasing SBS 2008 Premium, you can also purchase separate Windows Server 2008 licenses under any of Microsoft's licensing programs. There is no functional difference between the second server license provided with SBS 2008 Premium or a separately purchased server license.

Scenarios for Additional Servers

The role given to the second server on the network really depends on the particular needs of the business environment into which the server is being deployed. Factors that can affect the server role include the number of sites across which the network operates, business applications in use, the number of users on the network, requirement for availability of some network resources, and the hardware onto which the server operating system is installed.

Best Practice—Get Your Server Hardware Right

Consider carefully the role of the second server on your network and make sure the hardware is adequate for the task.

For example, if you are planning on using the server for supporting a SQL database, you should strongly consider using SCSI or SAS disks in an appropriate RAID configuration in order to provide optimal performance and reliability; SATA disks are more appropriate for desktop use and should ideally not be used in a server. In addition, use a hardware RAID controller with battery-backed cache, which not only provides better performance, but also protects any data that has not yet been written to the disk array in the event of a power failure.

Terminal servers should have plenty of RAM and enough disk space to accommodate not only the programs the users will be accessing, but also user profiles, which can grow quite large over time if not properly managed.

If the decision comes down to a faster CPU vs. more RAM, go with more RAM, as this will result in less paging of data to the disk subsystem and therefore improved performance. Sacrificing RAM for a faster CPU is going to be like an Olympic swimming champion practicing in a bathtub—they simply won't have enough room to perform optimally.

Buy the best hardware you can afford, with more than the minimum specifications you need, in order to ensure you start out with the best chance of a successful server implementation.

Some of the scenarios call for the server to be dedicated to the task to which it is being assigned, where others allow the server to be multi-functional. This ties in with the new Windows Server 2008 concepts of server *roles* and server *features*.

NOTE

Windows Server 2008 configuration is very much focused around roles and features. Roles define the primary function, purpose, or use of the server, such as Active Directory Domain Controller, Terminal Services server, web server, virtualization (Hyper-V) server, print server, or firewall. Features are more often supportive or additive functions to the roles, but can be standalone too, and include being a backup server, Telnet client or server, Group Policy management server, SMTP server, or WINS server. Visit http://technet2.microsoft.com/windowsserver2008/en/servermanager/default.mspx to learn more about Windows Server 2008 roles.

Additional Domain Controller for Branch Office

For networks where there is more than a single location, the additional server can be installed as a domain controller (DC) for a remote site. The domain controller role allows the server to authenticate user login requests, check permissions to network objects, facilitate user password changes, and so on. Having an additional domain controller at a site where users are remote to the main SBS 2008 server can improve WAN performance, and it enables users logging into the network to successfully authenticate in the event of a WAN link failure between the sites.

Windows Server 2008 includes the ability for a domain controller to be deployed in a read-only configuration, also called a Read-Only Domain Controller (RODC). The RODC is just like a global catalog server in Active Directory, which can be deployed at a remote site to enable users at this site a better network authentication response time, as well as act as a resource against which users can look up objects in Active Directory. The key difference, however, is as the name implies—the domain controller is read only. Although changes cannot be written to it, it can forward change requests to a non-read-only domain controller. The RODC also maintains a read-only copy of the SYSVOL share.

The RODC is an ideal solution for several reasons, including the following:

▶ Environments where the remote site is connected to the main network by a slow WAN link

▶ Environments where the domain controller is not as physically secure as it could be if located at the main site

▶ Situations where a required application needs to run on a domain controller and the staff maintaining this application need to be restricted from making any changes to the Active Directory configuration

You can read more about planning and deploying RODCs at http://go.microsoft.com/fwlink/?LinkID=122172.

Terminal Server

Windows Server 2008 Terminal Services enables users to run Windows-based programs, or a full Windows desktop, which can access LAN-connected resources, from a multitude of devices and locations.

Many readers are familiar with Microsoft Terminal Services technology and how it can be used to benefit an organization's operations. Windows Server 2008 builds on the functionality available in Windows Server 2003 Terminal Services, giving both users and administrators greater functionality, performance and security.

Terminal Services is a Windows Server role and is best implemented as the sole task of a Windows server.

More detailed and in-depth information regarding Microsoft's Windows Server 2008 Terminal Services technology can be found at http://go.microsoft.com/fwlink/?LinkId=48555.

SQL/LOB Server

Another function for the second server is to support a line of business (LOB) application or database. In the case of SBS 2008 Premium, where a license for Microsoft SQL 2008 Standard is included, this can be installed onto the second server in order to host a business database, thereby freeing up the SBS 2008 server to look after the network.

The process for setting up the second server to host the LOB is dependent on the particular requirements of the database or application itself, and the application vendor should be consulted for their system requirements before committing to a hardware purchase.

Virtual Server Host/Hyper-V

Virtualization is one of the hottest topics around for multiple reasons, including the fact that it offers the following: better overall utilization from your server hardware investment; lower power consumption, less physical space consumed, and less heat emissions due to fewer physical servers; easier management of multiple servers; simplified backup and disaster recovery; and more efficiency in building and using development and test environments.

Windows Server 2008 now includes out-of-the-box virtualization support through the use of Microsoft's new Hyper-V product. Hyper-V provides the ability to install, host, and manage multiple operating system instances on a single server chassis in a virtualized environment.

Misconceptions About Using Additional Servers

For some years, there has been a myth circulated about SBS-based networks and domain controllers—the myth is that there can only be a single domain controller on the network, which is the SBS server itself.

This is simply not true.

Although SBS-based networks do have some specific limitations by design, this does not include limiting the number of domain controllers on the network. In fact, there is nothing to prevent you from having dozens of domain controllers on the network if this is something you really want to achieve (within licensing limitations, of course).

The actual limitations of an SBS network include the following:

▶ You cannot have more than one SBS server in the same domain.

▶ The SBS domain cannot establish trusts with other domains.

▶ Parent and/or child domains are not supported.

▶ The SBS domain must be the root domain of the Active Directory forest.

▶ The SBS server must own all the domain and forest Flexible Single Master Operations (FSMO) roles.

So with this in mind, rest assured that your second (and third, fourth, and so on) server can indeed be a domain controller on an SBS 2008 network.

Implementing Additional Servers

Although Windows Server 2008 has a simpler setup process than previous Windows Server operating systems, this does not negate the need for proper planning before inserting the setup DVD into the server and hitting the power button.

Understanding the role the server is going to play on the network is the beginning of the planning process. Other areas to consider include network connectivity and performance (both LAN and WAN based), power quality and reliability, and the physical environment in which the server will be operating. From this you can determine the correct hardware and software licenses to purchase. Only then are you ready to start setting up your server.

Taking care to get the basics right at the start of the server deployment process means you have a much better result when the server goes into production.

Common Implementation Tasks

Let's assume you have successfully installed Windows Server 2008 onto the server hardware and are ready to add this server to the SBS 2008 domain.

> **NOTE**
>
> Microsoft provides comprehensive installation information, including troubleshooting assistance, in the Windows Server 2008 Technical Library on TechNet. Point your browser to http://technet2.microsoft.com/windowsserver2008 and select the link for "Installing and Upgrading to Windows Server 2008."
>
> The latest release notes for Windows Server 2008 are available at http://go.microsoft.com/fwlink/?LinkID=99299.

Once you have completed the operating system installation, you should be presented with a screen similar to Figure 14.1.

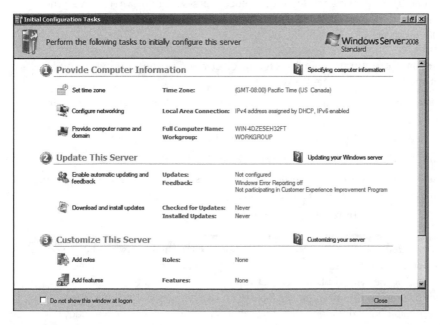

FIGURE 14.1   Initial Windows Server 2008 screen.

Setting the Correct Time Zone

Change the server time zone to match the time zone of the SBS 2008 server (assuming it has been correctly set) by following these steps:

1. Select the Set Time Zone link.

2. Click the Change Time Zone button.

3. Select the appropriate time zone from the drop-down box and click the OK button.

4. Ensure the date and time are also correct and, if necessary, change by selecting the Change Date and Time button.

5. Click OK to return to the Initial Configuration Tasks screen.

IP Address Assignment

A server should always have a static IP address on the network. This address can either be manually entered into the network configuration settings for the network card or can be assigned to the server as a DHCP reservation from the SBS 2008 server. Both methods are generally acceptable; however, it is generally best practice to manually set the IP details for the server to avoid potential connectivity problems if the DHCP service becomes unavailable for an extended period of time.

The process for setting a static address for the server is very similar to that used for Windows Server 2003 and Windows 2000 Server, as follows:

TIP

Although IPv6 is the default protocol for Windows Server 2008, if you do not have plans to use this in your network, it should be disabled from the protocol stack. This can be easily done by unchecking the Internet Protocol Version 6 item when viewing the properties of the network connection after item 2. IPv6 is covered in more detail in Chapter 19, "IPv6 Overview."

---

1. From the Initial Configuration Tasks screen, select the Configure networking link. This opens the Network Connections screen.

2. Right-click the network adapter for the server and select Properties from the drop-down menu.

3. Select Internet Protocol Version 4 (TCP/IPv4) and then click Properties.

4. Enter the appropriate IP address, subnet mask, and gateway addresses.

5. The DNS server address entered should be the address of the SBS 2008 server; for this example, it is 192.168.16.2 (see Figure 14.2).

6. Click the OK and Close buttons to save your changes.

Best Practice—IP Addressing for the SBS Network

Ask 10 people for their best IP addressing methodology, and chances are you'll get 10 different answers. For the typical SBS 2008 network, you won't need to get too fancy. First, you need to consider the environment into which the servers are going to be installed—what equipment exists, and therefore what static addresses have already been allocated?

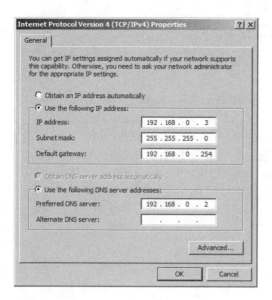

FIGURE 14.2 IP address, subnet mask, gateway, and DNS server entries.

In most cases, the following guidelines have served well for the typical SBS network:

▶ Give the servers on the network a low IP host address; for example, 192.168.16.2, 192.168.16.3, up to 192.168.16.10.

▶ Assign printers and other resource devices an address starting from 192.168.16.20.

▶ Assign client computers addresses between 192.168.16.50 and 192.168.16.150. This gives more than enough addresses for an SBS network. These addresses should be assigned by the DHCP Server service on the SBS 2008 server.

▶ Assign routers, firewalls, and wireless access devices a high IP address. The main Internet router can be 192.168.16.254 and then move backwards for other access devices.

Where a static address is being assigned to a device, try to set the IP address on the device itself and configure a reservation on the DHCP server so conflicts will be avoided.

These are, of course, only guidelines, but have proven to work well for keeping servers, network resources, client machines, and access devices in separate address ranges with ample headroom for growth.

Remember to document the static IP addresses and the devices/servers to which they are assigned.

Server Name

It is also a good idea to change the server name at this stage, to match the name it will have on the domain. Changing the server name is a very simple process, but it requires a restart of the server:

1. In the Initial Configuration Tasks screen, select the Provide computer name and domain link.
2. The System Properties dialog box is displayed. Click the Change button.
3. Enter the server name in the top text box; spaces and special characters are not permitted for the name, so use letters and numbers only. If you enter an invalid name, you receive the warning shown in Figure 14.3.

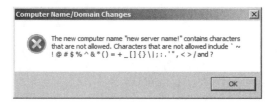

FIGURE 14.3   Invalid computer name warning.

4. Click the OK button to save the new server name. You are prompted to restart the server for the changes to apply.
5. Click OK and then Close, and restart the server.

TIP

Another way to change the server name is to use the netdom command prompt utility. The syntax for this is as follows:

```
netdom renamecomputer %computername% /newname:<NewComputerName>
```

where <NewComputerName> is the new name for the server. If you append the /Reboot switch, the server is also automatically restarted after 30 seconds. Note that the command prompt needs to be set to "run as administrator."

Joining the SBS 2008 Domain

Now that your server has the correct time zone, IP address, and name, it can be added to the SBS 2008 domain.

In SBS 2003, the process for adding a server to the network was relatively similar to adding client computers to the domain—a server computer account was created, and the server was then added to the domain using the Connect Computer Wizard. With SBS 2008, you no longer use this wizard for servers.

If you try to add the server to the domain using the http://connect site, you receive the error message shown in Figure 14.4.

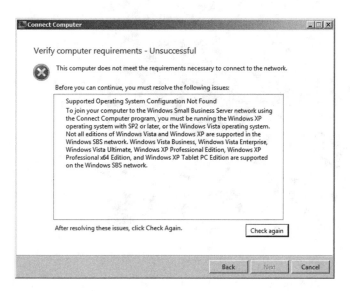

FIGURE 14.4   Operating System warning message.

Complete the following steps to correctly join your server to the SBS 2008 domain:

1. From the Server Manager screen, click the Change System Properties link.

2. In the System Properties dialog box, select the Change button.

3. In the Computer Name/Domain Changes dialog box, select the radio button next to Domain and enter the domain name into the text box; then click OK.

4. Enter the domain administrator username and password into the Windows Security dialog box and click OK.

5. When the server has been added to the domain, you receive a welcome to the domain notification. Click OK.

6. You are prompted that the server needs to be restarted to complete the process. Click OK.

7. Click the Close button and then the Restart Now button to restart the server.

After the server has restarted and you login, make sure you change from the local server account to the domain account. The initial login screen will look like the one shown in Figure 14.5.

FIGURE 14.5   Initial login screen.

Click the Switch User button to see the screen shown in Figure 14.6.

FIGURE 14.6   Change username login screen.

Select Other User to see the screen shown in Figure 14.7.

User name

Password

Log on to: SMALLBIZCO
How do I log on to another domain?

Switch User

Windows Server 2008
Standard

FIGURE 14.7   SBS 2008 domain login screen.

You see that you are being prompted to log into the domain. Enter the administrator username and password and click the login arrow, or press the Enter key to complete the login process.

The Server Manager console is displayed with the Full Computer Name showing that the server has been successfully joined to the domain (see Figure 14.8).

You can also verify that the server has been successfully added to the domain by referring to the Network tab on the SBS Console (see Figure 14.9).

Figure 14.8 shows the main screen from which server roles and features are installed.

CAUTION

When a server is added to the SBS 2008 domain, it initially appears under the Client Computers section of the SBS management console. This is because the server object is placed in the SBSComputers OU by default. Leaving the server in this OU means the group policies applicable to PCs on the network are applied to it, rather than the server group policies.

Move the server into the SBSServers OU by performing the following: Open Active Directory Users & Computers (or clicking Start, Run, typing dsa.msc and clicking OK); browse to MyBusiness\Computers\SBSComputers; locate and right-click the server object and select Move; expand the presented domain tree to MyBusiness\Computers

OU and select the SBSServers OU. Then click the OK button. Close Active Directory Users & Computers.

Refresh the Computers tab in the SBS Management Console to see the server object has moved into the Servers section.

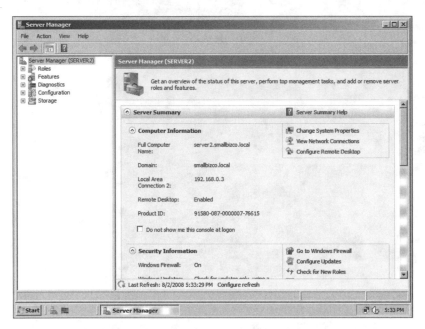

FIGURE 14.8   Server Manager console on second server.

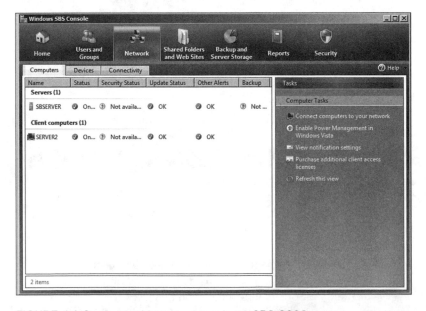

FIGURE 14.9   Server Manager console on SBS 2008.

Additional Domain Controller Configuration

One of the roles the second server can fill is that of an additional domain controller for either the main office or a remote office. To configure the second server as an additional domain controller, follow these steps:

1. From the Server Manager console shown in Figure 14.8, scroll down to view the Roles Summary section.

2. Click the Add Roles link.

3. Click Next at the Before You Begin page after you have read the initial text (you can skip this page in the future by selecting the Skip This Page by Default checkbox). This text simply introduces the Add Roles Wizard and reminds you to ensure the domain administrator account has a strong password (which is enforced by default by SBS 2008); network settings have been configured and the server has been updated from Windows Update.

4. Select the checkbox for Active Directory Domain Services; then click Next to see the screen shown in Figure 14.10.

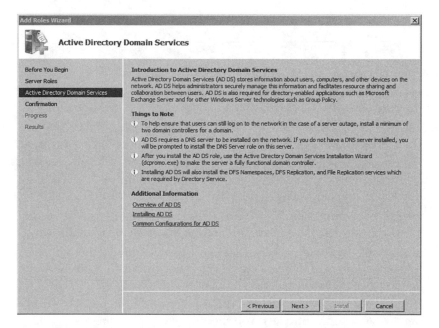

FIGURE 14.10   Active Directory Domain Services Installation Wizard.

5. Read the text shown, as seen in Figure 14.10. Note that you will be required to install DNS Server onto the domain controller as part of the process. You can also click on links under Additional Information to review further information related to the task being undertaken.

6. Click the Next button and note the informational messages presented, which advise that the server might need to be restarted after the wizard has run (although it won't)

and that you still need to run the dcpromo utility to make the server a fully functional domain controller, as shown in Figure 14.11. Click the Install button to continue.

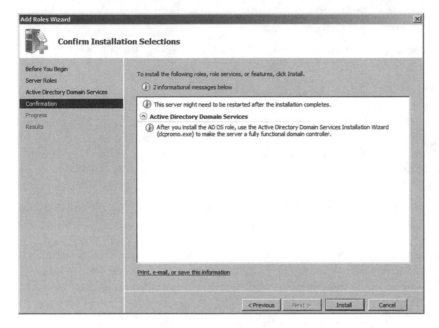

FIGURE 14.11   Confirm installation selections.

7. Once the installation process has completed, you will find the server is not yet a domain controller—it has only had the role binaries added to it (see Figure 14.12). You need to run the dcpromo utility to perform the actual promotion of the server to be a domain controller. This can be done from a command prompt or from the final informational screen that appears after running the Server Roles Wizard.

8. Clicking on the link to run the dcpromo wizard closes the informational screen and starts the Active Directory Domain Services Installation Wizard (see Figure 14.13).

9. For the typical SBS 2008 network, the Advanced Mode Installation checkbox should not be selected. Further information about advanced mode installation can be found by selecting the Advanced Mode Installation link below the checkbox.

10. The next screen provides a warning related to the security of communication with Windows Server 2008 domain controllers. You should take a few moments to read this if you have any operating systems older than Vista SP1 present on the network, as well as operating systems that act as SMB clients (including Linux distributions). Further information regarding this can be read at http://go.microsoft.com/fwlink/?LinkId=104751. Click the Next button to continue.

11. Select the default setting of adding a domain controller to an existing domain. Click Next.

12. You will be presented with a dialog box confirming the forest credentials to use for the domain controller promotion process. Click Next.

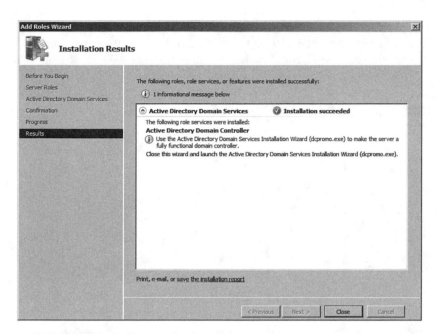

FIGURE 14.12   Installation Results screen.

FIGURE 14.13   Active Directory Domain Services Installation Wizard.

13. Because SBS networks allow only a single domain per forest, the next dialog box has no options other than to go back, continue, or cancel. It simply shows you the domain for this domain controller. Click Next.

14. Similarly for the Select a Site dialog box, you are simply shown the Default-First-Site-Name site with no additional options. Click Next to continue the promotion process.

15. You can now specify additional domain controller options, specifically if this will be a read-only domain controller (RODC) (see Figure 14.14). Refer to the earlier section in this chapter, "Additional Domain Controller for Branch Office," for more information on RODCs.

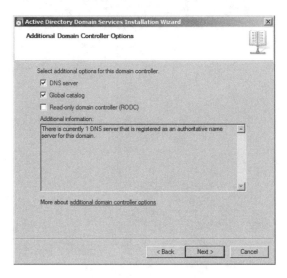

FIGURE 14.14   Additional domain controller options.

16. If, as part of your planning, you have determined this domain controller needs to be an RODC, select the checkbox for the RODC option. Click Next to continue.

17. If you select the option to have this server set up as an RODC, you will be asked to specify a user or group to whom you can delegate server management. This user or group (it should be a security group to which you add users) will have local administrative rights over the server in the event the server is unable to contact a writable Windows Server 2008 domain controller.

    Note that this group will therefore be able to login locally on the server and, if they want, demote the server from being a domain controller. Leaving this text box blank means that only domain administrators will have rights to manage this server. This would be the typical selection for an SBS 2008-based network. Click Next to continue.

18. You are next prompted to specify the location for the Active Directory database, log files, and sysvol. Accept the defaults for most SBS-based networks, which will be the same locations these files are found on the SBS 2008 server itself. Click Next.

19. Enter the Directory Services Restore Mode (DSRM) password. This is the password you enter if starting the server in DSRM, which is available by pressing the F8 key as the server first boots. This mode is typically used to restore a backup of Active Directory in the event of database corruption. This password does not need to be the same as the domain administrator account password but should be guarded as closely as that password and will need to meet the password policy that is in effect

on the SBS 2008 server. Click Next after entering the password twice and noting it down for future reference.

20. Read the summary provided in the next box to ensure you have entered the correct information. You can also export the settings to an answer file, which can be useful for documentation purposes. Passwords are not exported to this file, though, so don't discard the passwords noted earlier. Click Next, and the domain controller wizard will start the DC setup process including, if necessary, the installation of DNS.

21. When the promotion process has completed, you are presented with a dialog box indicating that Active Directory Domain Services is now installed on the computer. Simply click the Finish button and then Restart Now to restart the server as a domain controller.

Moving the Domain Controller

In instances where the second domain controller is to be located at a remote site, the IP address of the server needs to be changed to one in the subnet for this site.

These deployments would typically use a VPN connection between the sites managed by either the hardware routers for each site or some software-based firewall/VPN solution. See Figure 14.15 for an example network.

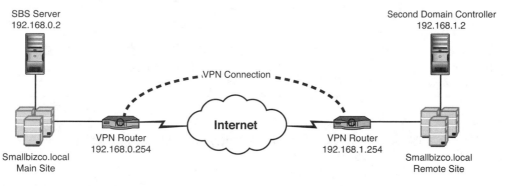

FIGURE 14.15   Example network.

Assuming the VPN connection is operational, the change to the second server is simply changing the IP address and gateway address. The DNS server address on the server should stay set to the SBS 2008 server address.

The IP address change is best performed as the last step before shutting down and relocating the server. This is to allow the server to start correctly, being able to communicate with the SBS 2008 server as services start.

If this server is going to be a DHCP server to the client machines on the remote network, it should provide its address as their DNS server (see the following section).

Installing and Setting Up DHCP Services

The SBS 2008 server will be providing DHCP services to the main office; however, this is not suitable for remote sites. The additional domain controller can be configured to provide DHCP-assigned addresses to the client computers at the remote site by installing the DHCP Server role and creating the appropriate DHCP scope.

Before installing the DHCP Server role, you need to know the DHCP scope details that will be configured as part of the service setup process. Using the example network shown previously, Table 14.1 provides the information needed for the installation wizard.

TABLE 14.1   DHCP Server Information

Item	Example Information
DHCP Server IP address and subnet mask	192.168.1.2, 255.255.255.0
Parent domain	Smallbizco.local
DNS server IPv4 address	192.168.1.2
Alternate DNS server IPv4 address	Not required
WINS	Not required
Scope name	Site 2 IP addresses
Starting IP address	192.168.1.50
Ending IP address	192.168.1.100
Subnet mask	255.255.255.0
Default gateway	192.168.1.254
Subnet type	Wired (default lease time of six days)
Activate scope	Yes

Note that the WINS service is not installed by default on the SBS 2008 server and is not required for most networks today.

TIP

Ensure the router at the site is not providing DHCP services. Many routers have the DHCP server service running by default, which could assign inappropriate IP addresses and DNS addresses to the client machines. Having incorrect DNS server addresses can create network performance problems, particularly with regard to resolving internal network resources.

Once you have determined the DHCP scope information for the remote site, install the DHCP role onto the domain controller, as follows:

1. Open the Server Manager console.
2. Click on the Roles branch on the left side of the console.

3. Click on the Add Roles link on the right side of the console to start the Add Roles Wizard.

4. If the Before You Begin page appears, click Next to move to the Select Server Roles screen.

5. Select the DHCP Server role by clicking the checkbox next to its name and clicking Next.

6. Read the introduction screen; then click Next.

7. The Network Connection Bindings screen enables you to confirm the network connection to which the DHCP service will be bound. Where the server has only one network card, there will only be a single connection shown. Click Next.

8. Enter the IP address of the DNS server the clients use to resolve network resources (see Figure 14.16). This should be the IP address of the domain controller at the remote site. Click Next.

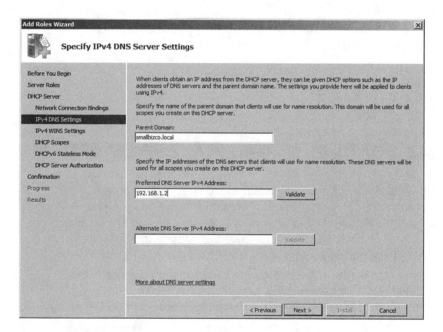

FIGURE 14.16   IPv4 DNS server settings.

9. If you are not using the WINS service on your network, leave the WINS Server Settings option at its default of not required; otherwise, enter the IP address of the WINS server on your network and then click Next.

10. Click the Add button and enter the information prepared earlier regarding the DHCP scope as per Table 14.1 (see Figure 14.17). When the information has been entered, click the OK button and then click Next.

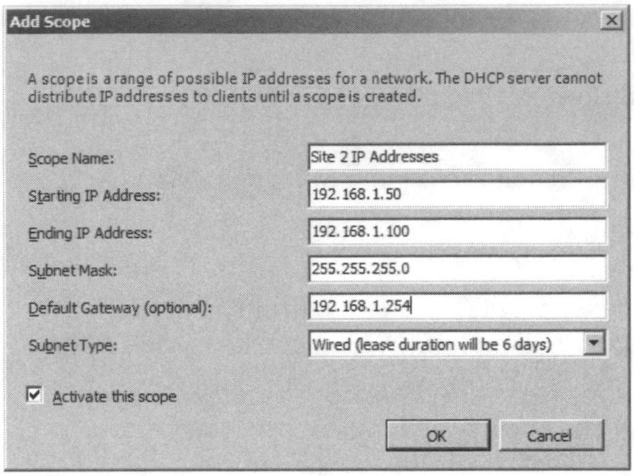

FIGURE 14.17   New scope settings.

11. If you are not using IPv6, select the Disable DHCPv6 option for the DHCPv6 Stateless Mode option; then click Next.

12. Authorize the DHCP Server service on the domain using the credentials supplied, which will be the domain administrator account with which you are currently logged in. If you do not authorize the DHCP Server, the DHCP Server service will not be able to start. Click Next.

NOTE

The Windows Server 2008 DHCP Server service is integrated with Active Directory in order to ensure it starts only if authorized to do so. As the DHCP Server service starts, it sends a DHCPInform message, which requests information about the root Active Directory from other DHCP Servers on the network. A DHCPAck message is then sent back to this server by other DHCP Servers on the domain, informing the DHCP Server where to locate the Active Directory root domain.

The DHCP Server then queries the Active Directory to ensure that its address is listed as an authorized DHCP Server; if its address is found in the list, the DHCP Server service will start. If it does not find its address in the list, the service will shut down.

In an Active Directory domain, all DHCP Servers must be either domain controllers or member servers before they can be authorized to provide DHCP Server services to the computers on the network.

In the case where the DHCP Server is also a domain controller, it simply refers to its copy of the list of authorized DHCP Servers.

---

13. Confirm the DHCP Server service setup summary and, if correct, click the Install button to start the installation process.

14. On completion of the installation process, the wizard presents a completion dialog box. Simply click the Close button to exit the wizard.

If the DHCP Server service has installed and started successfully, the server is ready to assign IP addresses to the computers on the network. Any existing computers with addresses assigned by the router (if previously providing addresses) should have their IP address released and then renewed in order to be assigned an address by the Windows Server.

Active Directory Replication Schedule

By default, Active Directory replication is set to occur once per hour between domain controllers. This schedule should be adequate for most implementations but can most certainly be changed to be either more or less frequent.

To change the replication of AD information, open the Active Directory Sites and Services branch under Roles in the Server Manager console, from either domain controller (unless the second server is an RODC, in which case you can only do this from the SBS 2008 server). Continue to expand the console and select the NTDS Settings node under the secondary domain controller to see something similar to Figure 14.18.

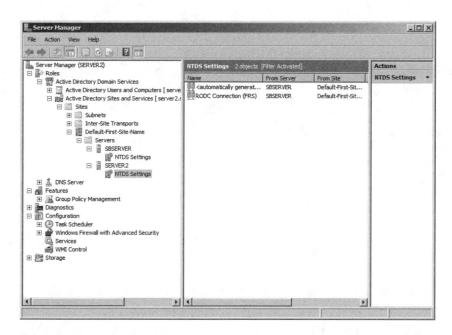

FIGURE 14.18   NTDS settings.

Right-click the RODC Connection (FRS) in the middle pane and select Properties (see Figure 14.19).

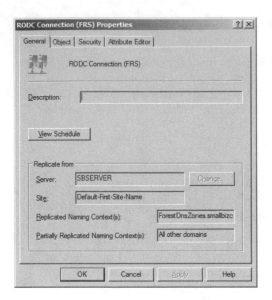

FIGURE 14.19   RODC Connection (FRS) properties.

Select the View Schedule button to view the replication schedule (see Figure 14.20).

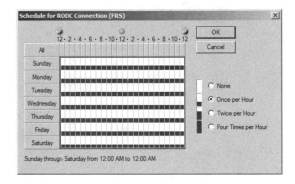

FIGURE 14.20   RODC connection schedule.

The dialog box indicates the days of the week, together with every half-hour increment throughout each day.

By default, the entire week is selected; however, you can change this to select only particular days and times by dragging the mouse over a rectangle of days and times you want to change. Alternatively, you can select individual times.

Change the replication schedule for the selected time(s) by choosing from the radio buttons on the right side of the dialog box: none, once per hour, twice per hour, or four times per hour.

> **CAUTION**
>
> Take into account the speed of the connection between your sites where the domain controllers are located. Replicating too often, during busier business hours, over a slow link could cause performance problems for other tasks relying on the link.

Click the OK button twice to save your changes.

Manual Active Directory Replication

You can also perform a manual replication of the Active Directory from the RODC, as follows:

1. Open the Active Directory Sites and Services branch under Roles in the Server Manager console of the RODC.
2. Right-click on NTDS Settings on the left side under the SBS 2008 server.
3. Left-click on the Replicate configuration from the selected DC menu item to initiate a replication process.

This process is useful when you may have turned off replication between the sites during the work day but want to perform an update (for example, due to a user password being reset or group membership changes) without waiting for the next scheduled synchronization.

Terminal Server Configuration

As noted earlier, if you are intending the second server to be a Terminal Services server for network users, this should be selected as the only role for the server.

Terminal Services (TS) is different from Remote Desktop on the SBS 2008 server. Remote Desktop is limited to two concurrent connections, whereas TS allows virtually any number depending on licensing and hardware specifications. Typically, though, it allows up to around 40 users per server. TS licensing does not need to be installed for Remote Desktop connections.

Installing Terminal Services

Perform the following steps to install Terminal Services onto the second server:

1. Open the Server Manager console and click on the Roles branch on the left.
2. Click the Add Roles link on the righthand side.
3. Click Next at the Before You Begin screen.
4. Select the checkbox next to Terminal Services in the Select Server Roles screen; then click Next.
5. Click Next on the Introduction to Terminal Services screen.
6. Select Terminal Server from the list of Role Services; then click Next.

7. Read the information provided about applications on the server—if you have already installed applications for use by users, they need to be removed prior to completing the installation of the Terminal Services role. If you have already installed, for example, Microsoft Office, you need to cancel the wizard, remove Office, and then re-run the role installation wizard. Click Next.

8. Select whether or not you want to require Network Level Authentication; then click Next.

Network Level Authentication

Network Level Authentication (NLA) is a new authentication method where user credentials are requested and processed prior to the full remote desktop screen being displayed to the user. This provides greater security overall, together with reducing the processing load on the Terminal Services server during the initial authentication process.

NLA requires the server to be at least Windows Server 2008 and the client to be running an operating system that supports the Credential Security Support Provider (CSSP) protocol, such as Windows Vista.

9. If you have not yet determined your TS Licensing mode, select the Configure Later option; then click Next. (See the following section for more information on Terminal Services licensing.)

10. Select the user group(s) allowed to access the Terminal Services server; then click Next.

11. Review the installation selections presented; then click the Install button to install Terminal Services onto the server.

12. Upon completion of the installation process, you must restart the server. When the server has restarted, and you have logged into the server, the setup wizard finalizes the Terminal Services installation process.

Understanding TS Licensing

In order to use Terminal Services (TS) on your network, you need to have a TS licensing server set up and configured. The licensing server is used to install, issue, and manage device and user Terminal Services licenses.

Running in Grace Mode

If you're not ready to set up your TS licenses when your server is being deployed, don't panic. Microsoft understands that when given the choice between rolling out a new server or setting up a licensing service, the server is the much more exciting choice.

With this in mind, the terminal server will operate properly without TS licensing set up for a grace period of 120 days. You can monitor the number of grace period days you have left when logging into the server with a local administrator account—a message will appear in the lower-right corner of the screen to advise the number of days you have remaining before the grace period expires. After this time, if no TS licensing server has been set up, the TS server will not accept any further connections to it.

Prior to the grace period expiring, you need to have set up the TS licensing service (ideally on the SBS 2008 server), purchased the appropriate number of licenses, and entered the license details into the TS License Manager console (see link in Figure 14.21).

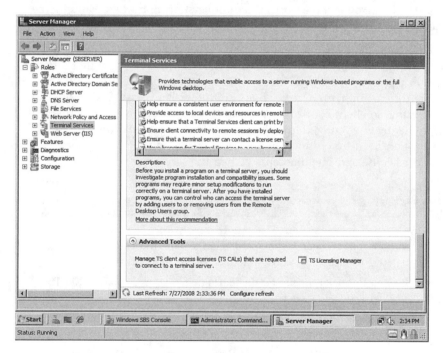

FIGURE 14.21   TS Licensing Manager under Advanced Tools.

The grace period ends when either the number of grace period days is exceeded or a permanent TS CAL is issued by the TS licensing server to a client connecting to the TS server.

Since the introduction of Windows Server 2003, the ability to have licenses based on users or devices accessing the TS server has been available. Typically, one type of license is used for the server—a license is issued for each named user that logs in, or for each client device that is used to access the TS server. This is called "Per User" and "Per Device" licensing mode, respectively.

When Per Device licensing is used, and a client device connects to the TS for the first time, a temporary license is issued to the device by the TS licensing server. Where this is a Windows-based device, an entry is made into the registry for this license—this is in addition to the temporary license information stored on the TS licensing server. If this device should connect to the TS a second time, the temporary license is converted to a permanent TS Per Device license.

The registry key for the license is HKEY_LOCAL_MACHINE\SOFTWARE\Microsoft\MSLicensing\Store\LICENSExxx, where "xxx" is a number starting from 000 and incrementing by 1, depending on the number of TS servers this device has connected to.

Per User CALs are handled somewhat differently than Per Device CALs. The Per User CAL gives a single user the right to connect to a domain-joined TS from an unlimited number of devices. Note that the user should only access the server from one device at a time in order to remain licensing compliant. Another point to note is Per User CALs are not enforced by TS licensing, so client connections can be made with the server regardless of the number of Per User licenses entered into the licensing management console. This means your organization needs to ensure it has purchased sufficient licenses in order to avoid violation of the license agreement accepted when the server was installed.

Best Practice—Tracking User TS CALs

Make sure you have enough licenses by tracking them properly. This can be done using a simple spreadsheet that records your license purchases against the users accessing the TS, or you can use the TS Licensing Manager tool to generate reports.

This tool can only be used to track licenses for domain-joined Windows Server 2008 TS servers using the Per User licensing model.

The TS Licensing Manager tool reads the Per User CAL information stored in Active Directory against each user account and presents this in the generated report.

The TS Licensing Manager tool can be found under Administrative Tools/Terminal Services on the TS licensing server.

Identifying the right license for your environment can be as complex or as simple as you make it. For most SBS environments, user-based licenses are the best option to choose because they give users the flexibility to access the TS from any computer on the LAN, a thin client device, from a notebook computer, a Windows Mobile device, or a computer at the user's home (for example).

Device-based licenses are ideal for environments where there are typically more users than devices accessing the server—for example, a factory where there are multiple shifts of workers sharing computers. If there were three shifts of 30 workers and only 30 computers, and users do not need to access the TS from outside the workplace, it makes good economic sense to use Per Device licenses such that only 30 need to be purchased instead of 90 user CALs.

Keep in mind the TS Licensing mode is either Device or User; you should not try to use both types of licenses on the same server.

More detailed information about Terminal Services licensing can be found on the Microsoft TechNet web site at http://go.microsoft.com/fwlink/?LinkID=85873

Installing and Configuring TS Licensing

TS licensing is a server role service that is best installed onto the SBS 2008 server. This role should be deployed after the TS server itself has been set up and installed on the network and is running in the licensing grace period.

By default, the Terminal Services role is installed onto the SBS 2008 server, so adding the TS Licensing role service is done from within the Terminal Services branch of the Server Manager console.

Install TS licensing by following these steps after you have determined the type of TS CALs you are going to use:

1. Open the Windows Server 2008 Server Manager tool by clicking Start, Administrative Tools, Server Manager or clicking Start and typing ServerManager.msc and hitting Enter.
2. In the left pane, click Roles and then select Terminal Services.
3. In the right pane, scroll down to the Role Services section and click the Add Role Services link.
4. Select the TS Licensing checkbox; then click Next.
5. Accept the default setting for TS Licensing Discovery Scope; then click Next.
6. Click Install to complete the installation.
7. Click Close when the installation process has completed.

Now that TS licensing is installed, scroll to the bottom of the Terminal Services management console to Advanced Tools and select TS Licensing Manager (see Figure 14.21).

Prior to using the TS Licensing console, the license server must be activated with the Microsoft Clearing House, which installs a digital certificate onto the server that validates the server ownership and identity. Once this certificate is installed, the server will accept the installation of TS licenses.

NOTE

If you do not activate the TS licensing server, the server will issue temporary Per Device CALs, which are valid for only 90 days, or temporary Per User CALs.

Terminal Services RemoteApp

Terminal Services RemoteApp (TS RemoteApp) is a part of the Terminal Services role that enables you to make applications, or a complete desktop, hosted by the TS easily deployed across a network.

TS RemoteApp enables you to create .RDP files that can be supplied pre-configured to users, which they simply double-click to access the application or desktop. You also can distribute a .MSI file using group policy, which installs a link onto the desktop of the user's computer, and into the Start menu if desired, such that it looks like a locally installed application!

This process can reduce complexity and confusion for users in instances where they lose track of where they are actually running an application—on their local desktop or on a remote server. Programs accessed through TS RemoteApp can look and operate like a locally running application; they can be minimized and allow cut and paste between other applications, and their windows can be resized.

This can be especially useful when deploying a new version of an application, and you want to perform testing parallel to an existing program installed on the users' computers, or a different terminal server.

TIP

TS RemoteApp requires the client computers to be running RDC 6.1, which is included in Windows Server 2008, Windows Vista with SP1, and Windows XP with SP3.

Let's assume you have a new application installed on the TS, called WordPad, which you want to make available to users without their needing to access a full desktop on the server. Perform the following steps to make this application available through TS RemoteApp:

1. Open the Server Manager console on the TS server.
2. Expand the Roles branch on the left side; then expand the Terminal Services role and click on the TS RemoteApp Manager link, as shown in Figure 14.22.
3. Click the Add RemoteApp Programs in the top-right corner of the Server Manager console.
4. Click the Next button to show the list of registered applications on the server. If the actual application you want to add is not listed, click the Browse button; otherwise, select the checkbox next to the application you want to make available (see Figure 14.23).

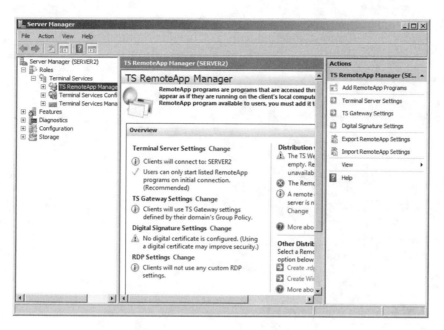

FIGURE 14.22   TS RemoteApp Manager console.

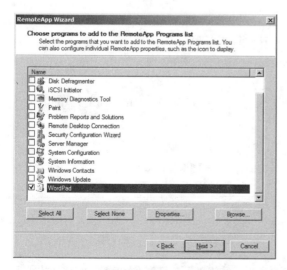

FIGURE 14.23   RemoteApp Wizard application selection.

5. If you click the Properties button, you are able to verify the path to the application executable, the alias of the program, whether or not the user can pass command-line

arguments to the application (including any particular command-line arguments you want to enforce), and also change the icon, as shown in Figure 14.24.

FIGURE 14.24   RemoteApp properties.

6. Click Next and then Finish to complete the RemoteApp Wizard.

The application will now appear under the RemoteApp Programs section in the Server Manager console, as shown in Figure 14.25.

You are now able to create either a .RDP file or a .MSI file, or both, which can be deployed to client computers on the network.

To create a .RDP file, perform the following steps:

1. Select the RemoteApp program, as shown in Figure 14.25, and then select the Create .rdp File link in the righthand side of the Server Manager console.

2. Click the Next button to specify the location for the .RDP to be placed. By default, this location is C:\Program Files\Packaged Programs. Click Next and then Finish to create the file.

> **NOTE**
>
> This dialog box also enables you to make additional changes, including the server or server farm name, TCP port, whether server authentication is required together with TS Gateway, and whether or not the file will be signed by a digital certificate.
>
> Refer to http://go.microsoft.com/fwlink/?LinkId=85872 for more information on TS Gateway.

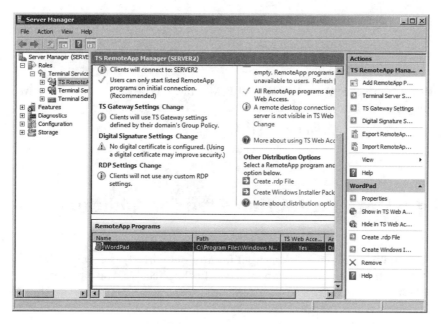

FIGURE 14.25   RemoteApp Programs listing.

3. When the wizard completes, the folder with the .RDP file is opened in Windows Explorer. You can now copy this file to a client computer and use it to access the TS RemoteApp application.

Similarly, you can create the .MSI file, which has the added advantage of creating shortcuts to the application in the user's Start menu, as well as on the desktop, if desired:

1. Select the RemoteApp program, as shown previously in Figure 14.25, and then select the Create Windows Installer Package link in the righthand side of the Server Manager console.

2. Click the Next button to specify the location for the .MSI to be placed. By default, this location is C:\Program Files\Packaged Programs. Click Next.

3. Select where you want the shortcut icons to appear on the client computer. By default, the Start menu is selected where the icon will appear in a group called Remote Programs. You can also select to have filename extensions on the client computer associated with this RemoteApp program. Click Next and then Finish to create the .MSI file.

NOTE

Client-side extension redirection enables you to associate files locally accessed on the client computer with the RemoteApp program being published to the computers.

So, for example, if you were publishing WordPad, which uses files with the filename extension .RTF, any file on the client that is opened and has this filename extension will be opened on the TS instead of on the client machine itself.

The users are not prompted to accept the TS taking over the file extensions for this program.

4. Once the wizard completes, the folder with the .MSI file will be opened in Windows Explorer. This can now be deployed to the computers on the network

If you decide to make changes to the .RDP or .MSI file, you can simply re-run the wizard and recreate the file.

Developing a Data Protection Plan for Additional Servers

A functional backup and recovery plan is essential for any network. This section discusses the process for installing the Windows Server Backup feature, running manual backups, and configuring scheduled backups for the server. Further information related to backups can be found in Chapter 18, "Backup and Disaster Recovery."

Installing Backup Services

Windows Server 2008 employs new technology for performing and managing backups. Gone is the old NTBackup utility! Windows Server 2008's backup feature is a powerful tool that performs fast image-based volume backups, which can be used for the simple and rapid recovery of files, folders, and even the complete server.

Windows Server 2008's backup feature is not installed by default. To install backup, which also requires the PowerShell feature, perform the following steps:

1. Open the Server Manager console.
2. Select the Features branch on the left side.
3. On the right side of the console, click the Add Features link.
4. From the Features list, select the checkbox next to Windows PowerShell.
5. Click the + next to Windows Server Backup Features item and select the Windows Server Backup and Command-Line Tools options.
6. Click the Next button and then the Install button.
7. When the installation process has completed, click the Close button.

To access the backup interface, expand the Storage branch in the Server Manager console and select Windows Server Backup. (If you have previously selected Windows Server

Backup before installing the feature, you need to close and reopen the Server Manager console to view the backup interface.)

Running a Manual Backup

It's a good idea to take a backup of your server prior to making any significant changes to its configuration. Windows Server Backup makes this backup process extremely simple.

Assuming there is a backup disk shared from the SBServer called "backups," a manual backup can be run using the following process:

1. Open the Server Manager console and expand the Storage branch.
2. Select the Windows Server Backup branch.
3. On the right side of the console, click the Backup Once link, which will open the Backup Once Wizard.
4. If this is the first time a backup has been run, the Different Options radio button will be selected. If a backup has been previously scheduled, you will have the option to use the same settings as the scheduled backup job. Click the Next button.
5. Select the Full Server option to back up all server volumes; then click Next.
6. Select to backup to a Remote shared folder; then click Next.
7. Type the UNC path to the backup disk (in this example, \\SBServer\backups); then click Next.
8. Select the VSS backup option appropriate for your environment—the text below the options provides more information, and the help link at the bottom of the dialog box provides further detail. If you are not using any other backup product on the server, select the lower option, VSS full backup, and then click Next.
9. Click the Backup button to start the backup process.

A backup status box will appear to show the backup progress. You can either watch the backup proceed or click the Close button to let the backup continue in the background.

The backup process creates a VHD file on the backup device as part of the initial backup job setup and will alert you if there is insufficient space available, so there is no need for you to monitor the backup job simply to ensure it completes before running out of space.

Scheduling Regular Backups

Your server protection plan needs to include a regular backup process to ensure you can recover the server in the event of a disaster, whether this is a loss of files or data, disk failure, fire or flood, or some other fault that renders the server unusable on the network.

This then begs the question: "How often should I perform a backup?" The general rule of thumb is the server should be backed up a minimum of once per day; however, if you are in an environment where many transactions are being performed on a daily basis, more frequent backups should be considered, particularly for the data.

Windows Server 2008 backup enables you to schedule frequent backups of your server's data volume through the day with minimal performance impact on the network users; these backups are both very fast and take up only a small amount of storage space on the backup device. Due to backup's ability to take snapshots of only the data that has changed since the last backup, each incremental backup will be as small as the amount of data that has changed.

This shows the importance of getting your server disk layout correct from the very beginning, where the data is ideally held on a separate volume and can therefore be backed up and recovered separately to the operating system and server-based applications.

Let's assume you have a volume E: on which all user data is stored, and you want to create a scheduled backup of this data to the backup disk for the server. Perform the following steps:

CAUTION

Windows Server 2008 backup requires a separate, dedicated disk for running scheduled backups. This disk can be an external USB or FireWire disk. You cannot use a share from another server—the backup disk needs to be local to the server itself.

---

1. Open the Server Manager console and expand the Storage branch.
2. Select the Windows Server Backup branch.
3. On the right side of the console, click the Backup Schedule link, which will open the Backup Schedule Wizard.
4. Click the Next button on the Getting Started screen.
5. Select the Custom option to back up selected server volumes; then click Next.
6. Ensure the data disk is selected and deselect any other volumes you do not want to include in this backup schedule. Note that you cannot exclude the operating system itself from these backups. Click Next.
7. Specify the time(s) of day you want to perform a backup. By default, 9 p.m. is selected for a once-per-day backup. However, you can select the More Than Once a Day option and specify any number of backup times as are appropriate by selecting the time in the left column and then clicking the Add button. Click Next to continue.
8. If this is the first time you have scheduled a backup, you will not see any disks listed as available. Click the Show All Available Disks button to list the disks the server sees as available for accepting backups (see Figure 14.26).
9. Select the disk to which you want to back up by clicking in the checkbox next to it; then click OK (see Figure 14.27).
10. The disk you have chosen to be available for backups will now show in the list. Select it by clicking in the checkbox next to the disk; then click Next.

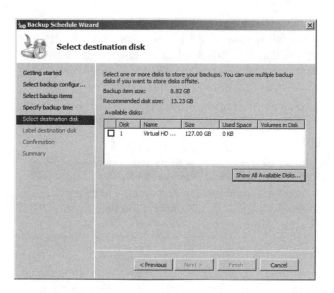

FIGURE 14.26   Select destination disk.

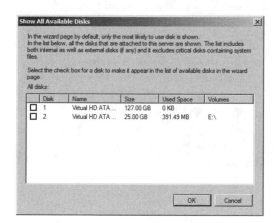

FIGURE 14.27   Show All Available Disks.

CAUTION

The first time you select a disk to accept Windows Server 2008 backups, you will receive a warning that advises that the disk will being formatted prior to being used as a backup disk. If there is anything of importance on the disk, you should remove it prior to continuing. In addition, the disk will no longer appear in Windows Explorer because it will be dedicated for backups only.

11. Note the Windows Server Backup label that will be applied to this disk by the backup process. The disk label is a combination of the server name, date and time of the backup wizard being run, and the disk ID. This label should be noted on the disk itself to allow for easy identification in the event it is needed for server/data recovery. Click Next.

12. Confirm the backup schedule summary information provided by the wizard and, if it looks correct, click Finish to save the backup schedule, or click Previous to go back and make the appropriate changes.

CAUTION

As soon as you click the Finish button, the backup disk will be formatted and prepared for use. So, if you have yet to copy off any data from this disk, now is the time to do so. Once you click the Finish button, it's too late.

13. You will be presented with a summary screen, which advises when the first scheduled backup will take place. Click the Close button to return to the Server Manager console.

You can use the same Backup Schedule link on the right of the Windows Server Backup console to make modifications to the backup schedule, or set up additional backup schedules.

You can also see the backup process scheduled from within the Task Scheduler utility, which is available under Administrative Tools. Expand the Task Scheduler Library, Microsoft, Windows and select Backup, as shown in Figure 14.28.

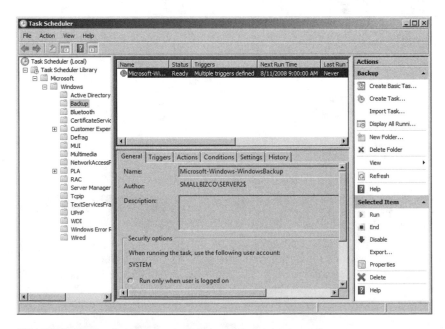

FIGURE 14.28   Scheduled Windows backup job.

Summary

Many businesses today find they need to have more than just a single server installed on the network to fulfill the business's requirements. The actual process of setting up a server and connecting it to a network can be a simple enough task; however, performing this task in such a way as to ensure a reliable, robust, manageable, and expandable network takes more than sheer good luck. Careful planning and preparation needs to be undertaken to assess the actual role of the server on the network both now and into the future. This needs to be combined with an understanding of the most appropriate licenses and hardware to purchase together with the development of a sound backup and recovery strategy.

Best Practice Summary

▶ **Licensing**—Determine the best license purchasing program for your organization by consulting with your trusted Microsoft partner or use the tools and resources provided by Microsoft. Settling for what appears to be the cheapest option can cause problems when you need additional flexibility.

▶ **Hardware**—Ensure you purchase quality hardware that is appropriate to the task for which the server is being set up and ensure all hardware components are certified for use with Windows Server 2008 (www.windowsservercatalog.com).

▶ **Environment**—Consider the environment into which the server is going to be deployed, paying particular attention to the WAN connection speed to other sites, physical security, and quality of power available to the server. Endeavor to provide the best of these as possible for the server.

▶ **IP Addressing**—Ensure you plan and document your IP addressing scheme for the network and configure IP address reservations for devices and hosts that have static addresses configured on them.

▶ **AD Replication Schedule**—When configuring your AD replication schedule, remember to consider the speed of the link between sites and the impact the replication traffic might have on the users' ability to perform their normal work tasks.

▶ **TS Licensing**—Determine the correct TS licensing for your environment (user or device) and configure the server for this licensing model before making it available for users to log into.

▶ **Tracking TS User CALs**—Use the tools provided with the operating system for reporting on TS User CAL usage or consider creating a simple spreadsheet to track license usage to ensure you remain compliant.

▶ **Backups**—Ensure you have a tested and proven backup process in place before deploying a server into a production environment. Make sure you regularly test your backups and store your backup media offsite.

14

CHAPTER 15

Managing Workstations Through Group Policy

When you have a Windows domain with Active Directory, it is a very powerful management tool at your immediate disposal. The addition of Group Policy to a network means that the administrator can control many mundane tasks. Group Policy with the combination of Vista and Windows Server 2008 is more powerful than ever. For some deployments, you will want to deploy settings, preferences; for others, you will want to lock down USB ports. But whatever level of control that is deployed, don't overlook this key tool.

The biggest changes under the hood for Group Policy include the use of ADMX files, categories of policy changes, and network awareness that makes connections over slow links more efficient.

New in Windows Server 2008 and Vista is a format for registry-based policy settings. This new format is a standards-based, XML file format called ADMX. This replaces the ADM format that was used in prior Group Policy versions. In the use of the Group Policy Management Console and the Group Policy Object Editor, there is no notice of any change in format. Group Policy looks like Group Policy. Editing these ADMX-based policies needs to be performed on a Windows Server 2008 or Windows Vista workstation; ADMX-based policies cannot be edited on a Windows 2003 or Windows XP workstation. When Vista was introduced into the SBS 2003 network, it was a bit awkward to edit policies if the administrator did not have access to a Vista workstation also. With SBS 2008, you can now use the Domain Controller Group Policy Management Console itself to edit and deploy Group Policy settings.

Unique to SBS 2008 is the handling of Vista Power settings. Because Vista workstations need to be powered up to run the Remote Web Workplace feature, a balance needs to be made between power needs and usability.

Changes to the Vista firewall group policy include enhanced areas in wired and wireless policy, remote assistance, print management, and especially Windows Firewall and IPsec. The specific updates and changes that impact a Vista workstation on an SBS 2008 network are covered in more detail in Chapter 11, "Group Policy in SBS 2008."

New and expanded policies for Vista include those in Table 15.1.

TABLE 15.1   New or Expanded Group Policies Settings in Vista

Group Policy Category	Description	Location of Group Policy Setting
Antivirus	Manages attachments	User Configuration\Administrative Templates\Windows Components\Attachment Manager
Background Intelligent Transfer Service	Configures the new BITS Neighbor Casting feature to facilitate peer to peer transfer within a domain	Computer Configuration\Administrative Templates\Network\Background Intelligent Transfer Service
Client Help	Determines if your users access external (untrusted) help content	Computer Configuration\Administrative Templates\Online Assistance User Configuration\Administrative Templates\Online Assistance
Deployed Printer Connections	Deploys printer connections. Used in a locked down environment	Computer Configuration\Windows Settings\Deployed Printers User Configuration\Windows Settings\Deployed Printers
Device Installation	Allows or denies a device installation (think USB categories)	Computer Configuration\Administrative Templates\System\Device Installation
Disk Failure Diagnostic	Controls the level of information displayed by disk failure diagnostics	Computer Configuration\Administrative Templates\System\Troubleshooting and Diagnostics\Disk Diagnostic
DVD Video Burning	Customizes the video disc authoring experience	Computer Configuration\Administrative Templates\Windows Components\Import Video User Configuration\Administrative Templates\Windows Components\Import Video

TABLE 15.1   New or Expanded Group Policies Settings in Vista

Group Policy Category	Description	Location of Group Policy Setting
Enterprise Quality of Service	Alleviates network congestion issues	Computer Configuration\Windows Settings\Policy-based QoS
Hybrid Hard Disk	Configures the hybrid hard disk to allow for non-volatile cache management	Computer Configuration\Administrative Templates\System\Disk NV Cache
Internet Explorer 7	Replaces and expands the settings for IE Maintenance	Computer Configuration\Administrative Templates\Windows Components\Internet Explorer User Configuration\Administrative Templates\Windows Components\Internet Explorer
Networking: Quarantine	Manages: Health Registration Authority Internet Authentication Service Network Access Protection	Computer Configuration\Windows Settings\Security Settings\Network Access Protection
Networking: Wired, Wireless	Applies a standard architecture for centrally managing media types	Computer Configuration\Windows Settings\Security Settings\Wired Network (IEEE 802.11) Policies Computer Configuration\Windows Settings\Security Settings\Wireless Network (IEEE 802.11) Policies
Power Options	Configures power options in the control panel	Computer Configuration\Administrative Templates\System\Power Management
Removable Storage	Allows Administrators to protect corporate data that can be read from and written to removable storage devices	Computer Configuration\Administrative Templates\System\Removable Storage Access User Configuration\Administrative Templates\System\Removable Storage Access

15

TABLE 15.1   New or Expanded Group Policies Settings in Vista

Group Policy Category	Description	Location of Group Policy Setting
Security Protection	Management of Windows Firewall and IPsec technologies	Computer Configuration\Windows Settings\Security Settings\Windows Firewall with Advanced Security
Shell Application Management	Manages access to toolbar, taskbar, start menu and icons	User Configuration\Administrative Templates\Start Menu and Taskbar
Shell First Experience, Logon and Privileges	Configures the logon experience to include roaming user profiles, redirected folders and logon dialog screens	User Configuration\Administrative Templates\Windows Components\
Shell Sharing, Sync and Roaming	Customizes: Autorun for different devices and media Creation and removal of partnerships Sync schedule and behavior Creation and access to workspaces	User Configuration\Administrative Templates\Windows Components\
Shell Visuals	Configures the display to include: AERO glass display New screen saver behavior Search and views	User Configuration\Administrative Templates\Windows Components\
Tablet PC	Configures Tablet PC to include: Tablet PC desktop features Tablet Ink Watson and personalization Input panel features Tablet PC Touch input	Computer Configuration\Administrative Templates\Windows Components\ Input Personalization Pen Training TabletPC\Tablet PC Input Panel TabletPC\Touch Input User Configuration\Administrative Templates\Windows Components\ Input Personalization Pen Training TabletPC\Tablet PC Input Panel TabletPC\Touch Input

TABLE 15.1   New or Expanded Group Policies Settings in Vista

Group Policy Category	Description	Location of Group Policy Setting
Terminal Services	Configures features and ease of use Allows or prevents redirection of supported devices to the remote computer in the Terminal Services session Requires the use of Transport Layer Security (TLS) 1.0 or native RDP encryption, or negotiate a security method Requires the use of a specific type of encryption level (FIPS Compliant, High, Client Compatible or Low)	Computer Configuration\Administrative Templates\Windows Components\Terminal Services User Configuration\Administrative Templates\Windows Components\Terminal Services
Troubleshooting and Diagnostics	Controls the diagnostic level from automatically detecting and fixing problems to indicating resolutions for: Application issues Leak Detection Resource Allocation	Computer Configuration\Administrative Templates\System\Troubleshooting and Diagnostics
User Account Protection	Configures the user account properties for: Determine the behavior for the elevation prompt Elevate the user account during application installs Identify the least privileged user accounts Virtualize file and registry write failures to per user locations	Computer Configuration\Windows Settings\Security Settings\Local Policies\Security Options

15

TABLE 15.1   New or Expanded Group Policies Settings in Vista

Group Policy Category	Description	Location of Group Policy Setting
Windows Error Reporting	Disables Windows Feedback only for Windows or all components. By default feedback is enabled for all Windows Components	Computer Configuration\Administrative Templates\Windows Components\Windows Error Reporting User Configuration\Administrative Templates\Windows Components\Administrative Templates\Windows Error Reporting

Windows Vista has greatly increased the amount of control and settings you can manage in a network. Whereas Windows XP and Windows 2000 also allow group policy controls to be applied, Vista greatly enhances key areas like USB device control.

Best Practice—Group Policy

After building an SBS 2008 server, always ensure that you add group policies and don't edit existing ones (as much as possible). When you do add your own, clearly define the security groups and policies you are adding so that you can easily define your policies as compared to the default settings.

Download the Group Policy spreadsheet from http://www.microsoft.com/downloads/details.aspx?familyid=2043B94E-66CD-4B91-9E0F-68363245C495&displaylang=en and review the settings that are possible. Taking the time to plan your Group Policy deployment will help you to be more efficient in your deployments. Build the policies, ensuring that they are enforced, and do not impact the running network as you plan them.

Many readers looking at a technical resource like this book often do not read it cover to cover, and so you might have forgotten or not read the foundations of Group Policy that the server sets up as well as the default policies that the SBS 2008 server has preconfigured. Therefore, we recommend that you re-read Chapter 11, which provides the foundations of the server view of Group Policy, before continuing on in this chapter.

To refresh, the six pre-built polices that are deployed on every SBS 2008 server are: Default Domain Policy, Update Services Client Computer Policy, Update Services Common Settings Policy, Update Services Server Computer Policy, Windows SBS CSE Policy, and Windows SBS User Policy. As was mentioned in Chapter 11, when adding any Group Policy to the server, always add a new policy rather than editing an existing one. This ensures that you always have the base policies that the server shipped with as a reference point, in addition to ensuring that the base functions of the network are not impacted by the additions.

Windows Small Business Server 2008 also has some new tricks up its sleeve. On your workstations, you'll see Windows Small Business Server 2008 Client Agent. This is a Group Policy client extension to ensure that client computers are configured with the proper SBS settings. With this extension, if the machine is under the SBSComputers Organizational Unit, it gets SBS 2008 applied settings.

Editing and Adding to Default Policies and Settings

If you've read the book out of order and haven't yet read Chapter 11 on Group Policy, now's the time to go back and read that chapter first. Now that you have the foundation, this chapter points out some areas that can be edited, added to, and changed in the Group Policy Management console to better control the workstations.

Organizational Units

When dealing with Windows Small Business Server 2008, there are standard Organizational Units (OU) that, even for the experienced Group Policy administrator, may be confusing at first. SBS uses a standard OU that is called MyBusiness. Underneath the MyBusiness OU is the category of Computers that, in turn, has the OU of SBS Computers (see Figure 15.1). Under Users, there is the OU of SBSUsers. The MyBusiness OU should stay intact. Create new OUs as needed, but leave these key OUs as is. The Add User Wizard in particular needs this OU to be left as is.

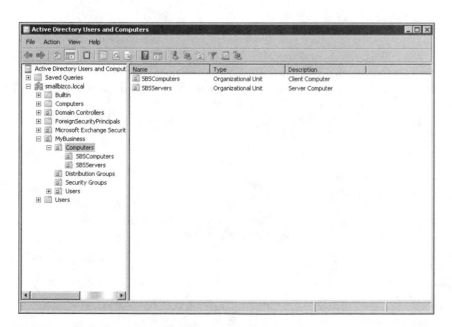

FIGURE 15.1   Default Organizational Units in SBS 2008.

Security Groups

Windows Small Business Server 2008 sets up eleven security groups (see Figure 15.2). Some of these groups impact a single type of function of the server (for example, faxing), whereas others facilitate security roles in SharePoint.

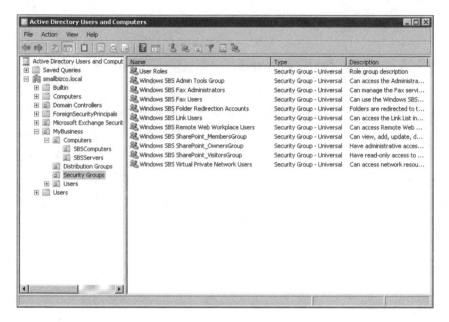

FIGURE 15.2   Default security groups in SBS 2008.

Starting with User roles, SBS adds several special security groups, which are listed in Table 15.2. When building Group Policies, configure them to apply to Security Groups rather than specific users. This makes tracking turnover of roles easier and ensures that it's easier to understand why a specific person in a firm has the Policies applied to him or her. Feel free to add to this list of SBS 2008 Security Groups with a custom group for the needs of the network but leave these standard groups intact.

TABLE 15.2   SBS 2008 Security Groups

Security Group	Duties
Windows SBS Admin Tools Group	Can access the Administration tools in Remote Web Workplace.
Windows SBS Fax Administrator	Can manage the fax service in Windows SBS.
Windows SBS Fax Users	Can use the Windows SBS fax service.
Windows SBS Folder Redirection Accounts	Folders are redirected to the server.

TABLE 15.2   SBS 2008 Security Groups

Security Group	Duties
Windows SBS Link Users	Can access the Link List in Remote Web Workplace.
Windows SBS Remote Web Workplace Users	Can access Remote Web Workplace.
Windows SBS SharePoint_MembersGroup	Can view, add, update, delete, approve, and customize the content on the internal web site.
Windows SBS SharePoint_OwnersGroup	Have administrative access to the internal web site.
Windows SBS SharePoint_VisitorsGroup	Have read-only access to the internal web site.
Windows SBS Virtual Private Network Users	Can access network resources remotely.

Default Policies

Take the time to go back and review Chapter 11 to understand the default policies that ship with every SBS 2008 server (see Figure 15.3). To launch the Group Policy Management Console that is installed on SBS 2008, click Start, All Programs, Administrative Tools, Group Policy Management.

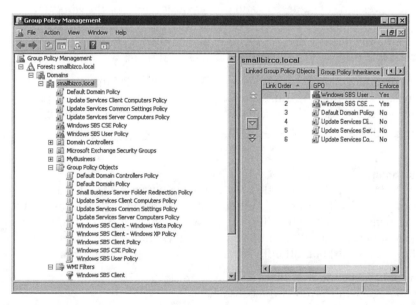

FIGURE 15.3   Default policies in SBS 2008.

The default policies that are included in Windows Small Business Server 2008 control many facets of the network. Beginning at the top, they are as follows:

▶ Default Domain Policy

▶ Update Services Client Computers Policy

▶ Update Services Common Settings Policy

▶ Update Services Server Computers Policy

▶ Windows SBS CSE Policy

▶ Windows SBS User Policy

Under Domain Controllers, there is one policy: Default Domain Controllers Policy.

Under the MyBusiness Organizational Unit, there are three specific SBS Group policies that directly impact the workstations, as follows:

▶ Windows SBS Client—Windows Vista

▶ Windows SBS Client—Windows XP

▶ Windows SBS Client Policy

Under the Users, there is one specific policy: Small Business Server Folder Redirection.

Each policy setting has a specific purpose in an SBS 2008 network. They control Update settings, Computer settings, and Users and also ensure that Firewall settings are configured for basic networking.

Whereas the best practice guidelines recommend that you start a new policy when building a Group Policy for the server, when you need to add port exclusion rule for the workstations that require specific port access to the server, it's acceptable to use the Specific Workstation Group Policies that configure the basic firewall settings and edit them as needed. Leave these basic policies intact and add your own Group Policies as you need them.

There are specific Group Policy settings on the server that have specific impact to the end users and workstations. Some of these settings are located in the Default Domain policy, some are specific SBS policies. These were covered in Chapter 11, but there are specific recommendations for impact on client workstations that need to be reviewed by the administrator.

Password Policy Adjustment

Included in the default domain policy are basic policies for the network. One important policy is the password policy for the network. Authenticated users on the domain will have this policy applied to them. If you want to adjust the password policy in SBS 2008, this is the setting you need to adjust to set a different password policy. The recommendation is to not disable this policy completely, but rather to adjust it to the needs of your firm.

1. To build a new policy, click Start, All Programs, Administrative Tools, and then click Group Policy Management to launch the console.

2. Click and expand the forest and view the domains and policies listed.

3. Right-click the domain name and click Create a GPO in This Domain and Link It Here.

4. Name the new GPO in the window that launches and call it Password Policy. Click OK.

5. After the new GPO has built a link in the Management Console, go back and right-click the Password Policy GPO and click Edit.

6. Expand the Computer Configuration, Policies, Windows Settings, Security Settings and look for Account Policies.

7. Expand Account Policies and click Password Policy to expand the settings.

8. Determine the new password policy settings you want to enforce.

Although Group Policy best practices always stress building a new policy rather than editing an existing one, the Password Policy is arguably one setting that, because the SBS server has already preconfigured it, you can't get in too much trouble editing the values already there. This is one Group Policy where it may be less risky to edit the policy already in place rather than build a potentially conflicting policy.

Choosing Password Policies   From the start, the SBS 2008 server enforces a password policy for the entire firm (see Figure 15.4). When logging in for the first time, you might be surprised that you are required to choose a complex password. Any user set up on a workstation is also prompted to choose a good password.

```
Enforce password history        24 passwords remembered
Maximum password age     180 days
Minimum password age     2 days
Minimum password length         8 characters
Password must meet complexity requirements    Enabled
Store passwords using reversible encryption   Disabled
```

The policy enforces that 24 passwords are remembered so that a user can't reuse the same password. Users are reminded to change their password every 180 days. Minimum password age setting ensures that the password history can be enforced. Thus, this value cannot be zero. Minimum password length sets the required complexity setting. Because this is the default setting, all passwords you enter must meet this requirement. The setting to set complexity ensures that you must meet specific requirements. These requirements dictate that passwords:

▶ Not contain significant portions of the user's account name or full name.

▶ Be at least six characters in length.

▶ Contain characters from three of the following four categories:

  ▶ English uppercase characters (A through Z).

  ▶ English lowercase characters (a through z).

  ▶ Base 10 digits (0 through 9).

  ▶ Non-alphabetic characters (for example, !, $, #, %).

15

The final setting should never be changed. If enabled, it would effectively store passwords in plain text on the network. It is used only if you have an application that requires it.

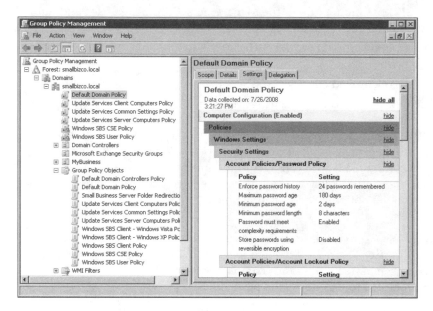

FIGURE 15.4   Password Policy settings in SBS 2008.

If you determine that one of the settings is too much for the firm, or perhaps too little, add the value you want to apply. For example, if you want to enforce a minimum password length of 14 characters, double-click Minimum Password Length Properties, ensure that Define This Policy Setting box is checked and change the character box to 14.

TIP

For some firms, you might want to adjust and lengthen both the minimum password length and the maximum password age. The longer the passphrase, the less often you need to change the passphrase. A passphrase of 14 characters or more automatically ensures that Lanman hash values (a password hash that can be easily cracked on the inside of your network) are not saved on your network.

Account Lockout Policies   Account lockout is an often-debated topic. In large enterprises, the cost of dealing with account lockouts can be high. In a smaller firm, account lockout can be manageable. In an SBS 2008 network, the following settings are enabled for Account Lockout:

```
Account lockout duration                    10 minutes
Account lockout threshold                   10 invalid logon attempts
Reset account lockout counter after         10 minutes
```

If an account is locked out, you see evidence in the event log. In an SBS network, most of the lockouts are due to managerial staff being unable to handle some of the basics in logging in.

Kerberos Policies Kerberos is the default authentication service in a Windows network. The policies in the next section set the basic settings for this authentication:

```
Enforce user logon restrictions                          Enabled
Maximum lifetime for service ticket             600 minutes
Maximum lifetime for user ticket                     10 hours
Maximum lifetime for user ticket renewal        7 days
Maximum tolerance for computer clock synchronization  5 minutes
```

User logon restrictions ensures that each session request is validated against the Kerberos v5 Key distribution system. User ticket settings are then set in the policy. The final setting is one that has tripped up many an administrator. If the workstation's time clock is not within plus or minus five minutes to the network's time clock, the workstation will not be able to log onto the network. As a troubleshooting step when having issues with a computer joining a domain, always check this time differential and ensure that it is no more or less than five minutes from the clock on the domain controller. Do not change this policy to allow for greater workstation/server clock time difference. Check the workstation and ensure that it is set to sync its time from the server rather than resetting this value. Normally the workstation syncs to the server's time automatically, but if there are issues, enter a w32tm command at the workstation.

Network Security The Network Security policy has one of the largest changes in the SBS 2008 network. From the initial outset, Windows Server 2008 has LAN Manager hash values disabled. This impacts Windows 98 and Windows 2000 systems attempting to access the domain, as well as older legacy devices for some printers and scanning devices. Force logoff when logon hours expire is disabled as a default policy in Windows Small Business Server 2008: You might find that you need to disable this setting to work with legacy devices. Understand, however, that this will decrease the security of your network by ensuring that hash values are stored on the network. An internal attacker can download any number of free password-cracking tools, such as Cain and Able, to easily read and crack the password of any user on the network.

```
Network security: Do not store LAN Manager hash value on next password change Enabled
Network security: Force logoff when logon hours expire          Disabled
```

Public Key Policies/Encrypting File System In a default Windows Server 2008 system, the administrator, by default, has the ability to recover files when encrypted by EFS. Because SBS 2008, by default, disables the built-in administrator account, you need to be aware of this and plan your EFS recovery strategy accordingly:

```
Certificates
Issued To       Issued By      Expiration Date         Intended Purposes
Administrator   Administrator  5/15/2011 5:30:57 PM    File Recovery
```

Public Key Policies/Trusted Root Certification Authorities   New to SBS 2008 is the use of certificates to provide additional certificate-based authentication. For example, if you use self-signed certificates, you must add the certificate bundle to a remote machine to be able to connect to the desktop remotely. This setting uses Group Policy to set the workstations to trust the certificates in the Active Directory domain:

```
Allow users to select new root certification authorities (CAs) to trust
Enabled
Client computers can trust the following certificate stores
Third-Party Root Certification Authorities and Enterprise Root Certification
Authorities
To perform certificate-based authentication of users and computers, CAs must meet the
following criteria                            Registered in Active Directory only
```

Local Policies/Security Options

The next section is one that you might need to adjust depending on the client's computers that you connect to the network, as well as scanners and other devices. This section includes requirements for digital signing that might impact scanners and Macintosh computers being attached to the domain, as well as Windows 2000 and Windows 98 workstations being able to connect to the domain.

Domain Controller Policy Setting

```
Domain controller: LDAP server signing requirements None
```

You would enable this setting if you wanted additional security for your Exchange server. It is unnecessary for an SBS 2008 network.

Domain Member Policy Setting

```
Domain member: Digitally encrypt or sign secure channel data (always) Enabled
```

This setting requires that channel data between the domain controller and a domain member is signed.

Microsoft Network Server Policy Setting

```
Microsoft network server: Digitally sign communications (always)      Enabled
Microsoft network server: Digitally sign communications (if client agrees)
          Enabled
```

For this setting, you might need to disable Digitally Sign Communications (Always) in order to support Macintosh systems, as well as attach scanners to your domain if they are not able to support such signing protocols.

Network Security Policy Setting

```
Network security: LAN Manager authentication level Send NTLMv2 response only
```

This setting ensures that the client computers that can support NTLMv2 (XP and Vista) will use only that protocol, but the domain controller can accept connections from Windows 98 and 2000 machines.

Group Policy Impact on Workstations

With the exception of one policy, all the remaining pre-setup Group Policy settings on a Windows Small Business Server 2008 server directly impact the client workstations. Use these settings as guidance for devising your own policies, but in general it's recommended to not adjust these default policies other than to enable or disable them if you deem they are not relevant for your network. This section calls out a few settings that you may wish to adjust.

Update Services Client Computer Policy

Although the Group Policy settings for Windows Update Services are included as a Group Policy setting, this is not the normal place where they are adjusted. Do not edit these values here; rather go to the Windows SBS Console, then go to the Security tab and then to the Update tab in the console. On the right side in the Tasks pane, click Change the Software Update Settings. In this Software Update Settings Wizard, change the Server and Client Update Behavior as well as the schedule. As you make changes in this wizard, they impact the Group Policy settings on the server. The default values are as shown in Figure 15.5.

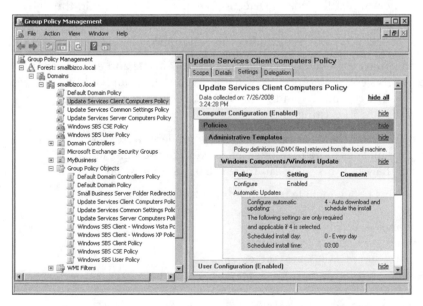

FIGURE 15.5   Update Services Client Computer policy in SBS 2008.

These settings set updates to be automatic and with a scheduled install at 3 a.m. every morning. By default, SBS 2008 approves definitions, security updates, and service packs.

Update Services Common Settings Policy

Certain settings are not exposed in the wizard for configuration. These settings, which are controlled by Group Policy, have a direct impact on the workstations. One such setting that might need to be edited and adjusted is the Check in for Updates at the Following Interval (Hours) value that is set at one hour. For firms with underpowered workstations, it's best to either add a new policy that sets this to once a day for those specific workstations, or edit this globally for the network to be less.

If you want to add a new policy that overrides the existing policy, perform the following steps:

1. Click Start, All Programs, Administrative Tools, Group Policy Management to launch the console.
2. Click and expand the forest and view the domains and policies listed.
3. Right-click the domain name and select Create a GPO in This Domain and Link It Here.
4. Name the new GPO in the window that launches and call it WSUS Check In. Click OK.
5. After the new GPO has built a link in the Management Console, go back and right-click the WSUS Check in GPO and click Edit.
6. Expand the Computer Configuration, Policies, Administrative Templates, Windows Components. Look for the Windows Update section.
7. Expand to find the Automatic Updates Detection Frequency Properties in the right side pane.
8. Configure it to be Enabled, with a maximum interval (hours) of 22. Click OK.

Alternatively you can launch the Group Policy Management Console and edit the specific setting in the Update Services Common Settings that is set for 1 hour and adjust it to 22 hours (see Figure 15.6). The complexity and scope of the GPO determines whether to create a new GPO or modify an existing one.

Setting this value to be greater than one hour ensures that underpowered workstations don't poll the server for updates more than once a day. Most of the time, updates do not come out sooner than that, and this value can therefore be adjusted safely.

The default values for this policy include the following:

```
Windows Components/Windows Update
Policy Setting Comment
Allow Automatic Updates immediate installation Enabled
This allows for automatic updates to immediately be installed at the set 3 a.m
install time.
Allow non-administrators to receive update notifications Enabled
This setting allows non administrators to receive update notifications.
```

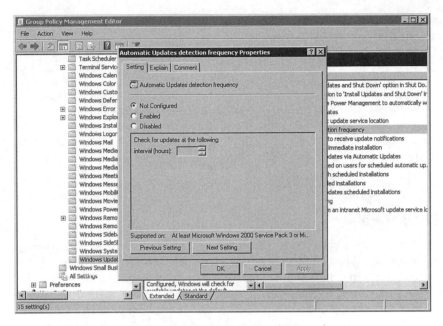

FIGURE 15.6   Setting the automatic updates detection frequency.

```
Automatic Updates detection frequency Enabled
Check for updates at the following interval (hours): 1
```

This is also the section that sets the restart requirement:

```
Delay Restart for scheduled installations Enabled
Wait the following period before
proceeding with a scheduled
restart (minutes): 5
```

If you want to have workstations not demand a restart after five minutes, you can adjust this setting here. Keep in mind that it is highly recommended that you do not adjust this setting. Installing patches that require a reboot and then not rebooting the system puts the workstations and servers at risk of being unpatched and leaving the systems in an unstable state:

```
No auto-restart with logged on users for scheduled automatic updates installations
Disabled
```

This setting ensures that if there is a user on the workstation, the system will not auto restart. If you leave the patching window to be 3 a.m., it's highly unlikely that you will have someone logged in during that timeframe who will be impacted. If, however, you reschedule the install to a time when users might be in the workstation, you might want to adjust this:

```
Re-prompt for restart with scheduled installations        Enabled
```

When a workstation has been deployed a scheduled patch, this setting enables the prompting of a restart in the lower-right window:

```
Wait the following period before
prompting again with a scheduled
restart (minutes): 10
```

If the restart is delayed, the next scheduled restart will be 10 minutes later. If the user selects to be reminded in 4 hours, this policy setting overrides that to only allow 10 minutes. If you want to allow your users to delay longer than 10 minutes, adjust this setting accordingly.

Windows SBS User Policy

The next Group Policy setting is one that you might want to edit. It sets forth Internet Explorer URLs. For example, if you want to reset the home page URL to be something other than http://companyweb, this is the section to edit in order to adjust the setting. The default settings, as illustrated in Figure 15.7, are as follows:

```
Windows Settings
Internet Explorer Maintenance
URLs/Important URLs
Name URL
Home page URL http://companyweb
Search bar URL Not configured
Online support page URL Not configured
```

By opening up this policy and editing the home page or the Search box URL, you can easily push these settings down to all workstations. If you do not want Companyweb to be the default home page, you can edit that group policy setting there. To do so, right-click that particular policy, click Edit, and then drill down to the Windows Settings, Internet Explorer maintenance and edit the home page URL to be what you want for the entire firm.

If you want a standard set of favorites in IE, this is also the place to edit this setting. Consider the additional customizations you might want to deploy in this section.

In this section, you can edit and customize favorites and other IE shortcuts. To edit this section, right-click and edit the policy. Drill down to User Configuration, Policies, Windows settings, Internet Explorer Maintenance. From here, you can adjust several items.

The item that you'll most likely want to edit and customize for your firm is the setting URLs. Under Favorites and Links, this policy setting has three settings preset by SBS 2008 (see Figure 15.8):

```
Check E-mail = https://remote.smallbizco.net/OWA
Remote Web Workplace = https://remote.smallbizco.net/remote
Internal Web site = http://companyweb
```

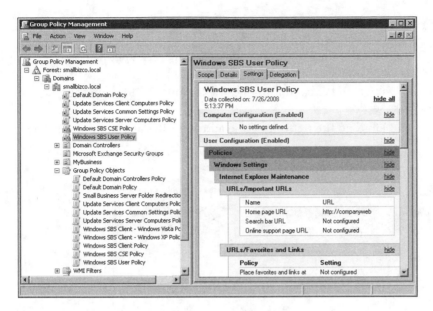

FIGURE 15.7   Windows SBS User policy in SBS 2008.

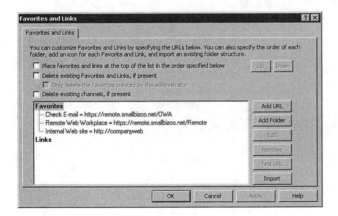

FIGURE 15.8   Customizing URLs for IE Favorites.

If you want to add a new policy that overrides the existing policy, perform the following steps:

1. Click Start, All Programs, Administrative Tools, Group Policy Management to launch the console.

2. Click and expand the forest and view the domains and policies listed.

3. Right-click the domain name and click Create a GPO in This Domain and Link It Here.

4. Name the new GPO in the window that launches and call it IE Favorites. Click OK.

5. After the new GPO has built a link in the Management Console, go back and right-click the IE Favorites GPO and select Edit.

6. Expand the User Configuration, Policies, Windows Settings, Internet Explorer Maintenance.

7. Look for the URL section and expand it to find the Important URLs and the Favorites and Links section.

8. Click Favorites and Links on the right side pane and add URLs as you need. Click OK.

To edit or add to this, merely click Add URL and add the web site address you'd like to push out to all workstations (see Figure 15.9).

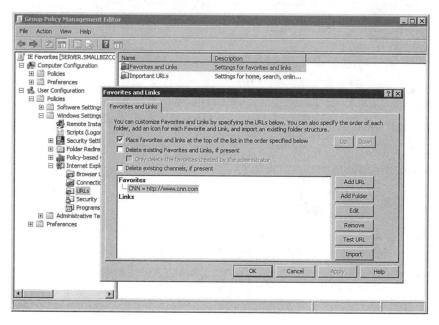

FIGURE 15.9   Editing URLs and adding custom entries.

You can add and edit URLs, and each of these web sites will be pushed to all domain workstations.

Group Policy per Workstations

The next section of specific Group Policy settings are primarily setting the firewall policies for XP and Vista. Vista, in particular, has preset firewall policies to ensure that the workstations are able to connect to the server and network appropriately.

Typical adjustments you probably need to make are to add port exclusions for antivirus software inside your network. You notice that these policies are set to filter and apply to only certain workstations. For example, the Vista policy filter applies only to the Vista workstation.

The two firewall policies set up on the SBS 2008 network are specifically designed to only apply to separate types of workstations. The first policy only works on Vista and the second only works on Windows XP Service Pack 2 and later. This is due to WMI filters. The server has three filters:

▶ **Windows SBS Client**—WMI filter looking for a workstation product and which applies to the Windows SBS CSE Policy and the Windows SBS User Policy

```
select * from Win32_OperatingSystem Where ProductType!=2
```

▶ **Windows SBS Client—Windows Vista Policy**—WMI filter looking for versions of the operating system greater than 6.0.6000

```
select * from Win32_OperatingSystem Where Version>='6.0.6000'
```

▶ **Windows SBS Client—Windows XP Policy**—WMI filter looking for versions of the operating system that are greater than 5.1.2600, less than 6.0.6000 and the Service Pack version of 2 or higher.

```
select * from Win32_OperatingSystem Where Version>='5.1.2600' and
➥'6.0.6000'>Version and ServicePackMajorVersion>=2
```

You can be even more selective in your WMI filter composition and build custom WMI filters to target specific operating systems.

CAUTION

You might need to experiment a bit with various WMI filters. Unfortunately, Microsoft does not provide an all inclusive listing of the various values.

After you build that filter, you later on link the filter to the GPO you build to give granular control over the application of the policy. Thus, this policy that you are building impacts only Vista workstations. The query ensures that the group policy is only looking at Vista/Windows 2008 era machines (that is, Version>6.0) and only at workstation-level machines (that is, ProductType=1).

Windows SBS Client—Windows Vista Policy

The Vista firewall with Advanced Security is located under Computer Configuration, Windows Settings, Security Settings, Windows Firewall with Advanced Security (see Figure 15.10).

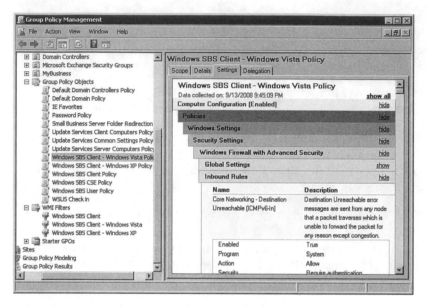

FIGURE 15.10   Group Policy for Windows firewall.

There are some basic rules of Vista firewall policy that should be understood. First, there are three actions for all connections that match a rule that you have designed:

▶ Allow the connection.

▶ Only allow a connection that is secured through the use of IPsec.

▶ Explicitly block the connection.

When firewall rules are applied from the server on the workstations, the order in which the workstations check for the rules is as follows:

▶ Authenticated bypass

▶ Block connection

▶ Allow connection

▶ Default profile behavior

Thus, if you have set a firewall rule to block a protocol or a port, while unknowingly at the same time setting a rule to allow the same protocol or port, the block will win. The key point to remember is that the more specific the rule you make, the less likely it is to be matched. The goal is to ensure that only those connections to which you want to connect are able to do so, and nothing else. Thus, it is better to set a program allowance rather than a port allowance.

The rules can be set for Programs, Ports, Predefined (well-known services and programs already defined), and Custom. The rules can be set to allow a computer to send or receive traffic from programs, system services, computers, or users.

The policies prebuilt in the Windows Small Business Server 2008 use five basic predefined firewall rules: Core Networking, File and Printer Sharing, Remote Assistance, Remote Desktop, and Windows Management Instrumentation. You may determine that you need additional rules for Remote Administration or Windows Media Player to better configure the needs for your firm. As an example, you probably will want to review the settings for the Key Management Service Rule group if you deploy a KMS server inside of your Windows 2008 network. When building a firewall policy, always start with a new group policy and do not edit or adjust the default domain or domain controller policies.

Default Vista Firewall Policies

If you installed Windows Server 2008 as a domain controller in a normal network and enabled the firewalls on the workstations, the workstations would have a difficult time connecting to the server because firewall polices would not be enabled. If you had to set up connectivity manually, the policies you need to enable make up Core Networking, File and Printer Sharing, Remote Assistance, Remote Desktop, and Windows Management Instrumentation. These rules provide basic connectivity and generally do not need to be edited or adjusted (see Figure 15.11).

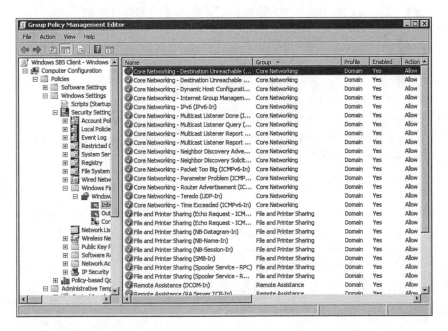

FIGURE 15.11   Advanced firewall rules.

Note that outbound rules are in place only if you enable the outbound filtering. Otherwise, all traffic from the workstations will route outbound as needed.

To add a new port exclusion (for example, for anti-virus), you need to adjust the port settings for both Windows Vista and Windows XP. To adjust for Vista, edit the Windows Vista Policy by performing the following steps:

CAUTION

Sometimes you might deem that editing a default Group Policy is appropriate and thus do not build a new rule. Adding an additional port exclusion to the existing Windows Vista Firewall Policy is an acceptable way, given that adding a port exclusion is easy to document. For the purposes of this chapter, adding a port exception is shown, along with adding a new policy setting so that the addition of this new rule can be tracked separately.

To add a new Firewall rule that impacts both Windows Vista and Windows XP sp2 workstations, perform the following steps:

1. Click Start, All Programs, Administrative Tools, Group Policy Management to launch the console.

2. Click and expand the forest and view the domains and policies listed.

3. Right-click the domain name and select Create a GPO in This Domain and Link It Here.

4. Name the new GPO in the window that launches and call it Antivirus Firewall Exclusion. Click OK.

5. After the new GPO has built a link in the Management Console, go back and right-click the IE Favorites GPO and click Edit.

6. Expand the Computer Configuration, Policies, Windows Settings, Security Settings.

7. Expand the Windows Firewall with Advanced Security and select Windows Firewall with Advanced Security – LDAP://CN={GUID}.

8. On the right side, scroll down to View and Create Firewall Rules and click Inbound Rules.

9. In the resulting open pane, right click and choose New Rule to start the New Rule Wizard.

10. In the first pane of the wizard, indicate what type of rule you would like to create. Options for rules include the following:

    ▶ **Program**—Rule that controls connections for a program.

    ▶ **Port**—Rule that controls connections for a TCP or UDP port.

    ▶ **Predefined**—Rule that controls connections for a Windows experience.

    ▶ **Custom**—Custom rule that doesn't fit in any of the above.

    For this example, choose Port and click Next.

11. In the Protocol and Ports screen, indicate if the rule applies to TCP or UDP by choosing the proper button.

12. In the Protocol and Ports screen, indicate if the rule applies to all local ports or to specific local ports. For the example, choose TCP in the top radio button.

13. Chose specific local ports in the bottom radio button section and enter the port number 9876 (just a sample port value). Click Next.

14. In the next action screen, choose from the following options:

   ▶ Allow the Connection.

   ▶ Allow the Connection if It Is Secure.

   ▶ Block the Connection.

   In this example, we'll choose Allow the Connection and click Next.

15. In the next Profile screen choose when the rule applies:

   ▶ **Domain**—Applies when a computer is connected to the corporate domain.

   ▶ **Private**—Applies when a computer is connected to a private network location.

   ▶ **Public**—Applies when a computer is connected to a public network location.

   In the example, ensure the Domain box is checked and all other boxes of Private and Public are unchecked and click Next.

16. Name the inbound rule a descriptive name, enter a description in the description box, and click Finish.

The resulting rule applies to any authenticated user, irrespective of operating system. If you wanted to have it only apply to Vista, you can click the Scope tab in the Group Policy Management console and in the WMI Filtering section, choose the WMI filter option of Windows SBS Client—Windows Vista.

Windows SBS Client—Windows XP Policy

The next group policy impacts only the Windows XP clients and is the master firewall rule set for these workstations. Just like with the Vista Workstations, the policy is masked to impact only the XP workstations by a filter:

```
Namespace: root\CIMV2
Select * from WIN32_OperatingSystem where ServicePackMajorVersion>=2
➥and Version='5.1.2600'
```

On Vista workstations, the Network Location Awareness service is set to Automatic; for Windows XP, the default for this service is set to manual. For dependable use of the Windows XP firewall inside a network, it's recommended to set the Network Location Awareness service to automatic as well. For Windows XP, the options to control are obviously more limited, as the Windows XP firewall is more limited in its functions.

As in the previous discussion, you might find that when you deploy software on a network that has a client application that needs to communicate to the software on the server, you may need to add a port exception.

To do so, browse to the Windows SBS Client—Windows XP Policy setting, and expand Computer Configuration, Policies, Administrative Templates, Network, Network Connections, Windows Firewall, and then Domain Profile. Expand the Domain Profile and open Define inbound port exception properties. Click Show Contents, and you see that you can now add additional ports as needed for your environment.

Windows SBS Client Policy

This final Organization Unit Group Policy sets the default settings for all workstations. This policy contains several settings that impact all workstations in the network.

It enables the following settings:

- ▶ The firewalls on all workstations.

- ▶ The Windows Firewall: Protect all network connections setting.

- ▶ Remote Assistance inside the network. It also authorizes domain administrators to remotely control the computer.

- ▶ The Security Center on domain PCs so that the network can track the status of the firewall and anti-virus.

- ▶ The Allow Users to Connect Remotely Using Terminal Services option.

- ▶ Specific settings for Windows Small Business Server Group Policy Client Side Extensions.

In addition to enabling these settings, it also disables the setting that allows for remote connections using Network Level Authentication. This enables RDP connections from any version of the client software.

If you decide that you can increase the security posture of the network, use this section to edit and enable rather than disable the setting that allows for remote connections using Network Level Authentication. You will need the RDP v6 client installed on all workstations connecting remotely to the SBS network after this setting is enabled.

Small Business Server Folder Redirection

One Group Policy setting you maight want to edit for the needs of the firm is the Folder Redirection policy. The default settings on the server are to move the My Documents folder to the path on the server: \\SERVER\RedirectedFolders\%USERNAME%\Desktop. In addition, Music, Pictures and Videos folders are also redirected.

If you deem that these folders should not be copied to the server (such as the 8 GB iTunes repository on the boss's computer), edit the Group Policy settings as follows:

CAUTION

In this instance, due to the low impact on the network, the editing of the existing policy is being advocated over the addition of a policy. Use judgment when editing versus adding new policies.

---

1. Click Start, All Programs, Administrative Tools, Group Policy Management to launch the console.

2. Click and expand the forest and view the domains and policies listed.

3. Right-click the Small Business Server Folder Redirection Policy and select Edit.

4. Drill down to User Configuration, Policies, Windows Settings, Folder Redirection and then to the items you wish to edit, such as Music.

5. Right-click the name of the folder for which you want to edit the redirection and select Properties.

6. In the Properties tab, edit the behavior of the folder redirection, as seen in Figure 15.12.

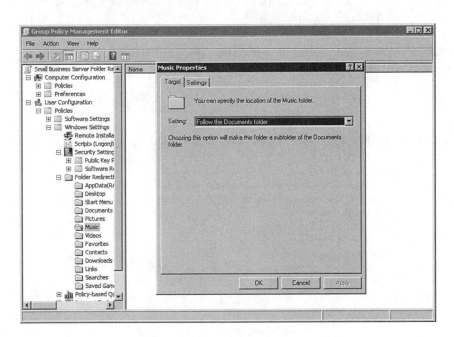

FIGURE 15.12   Folder redirection policy.

The settings for music, pictures, and folders have been set to follow the policy for the Documents folder redirection. In the Vista operating system, you have the ability to redirect music separately from the other folders. In Windows XP you do not. Thus, the default for the server is to redirect all such folders if you enable the user folder redirection on the Windows SBS Console, Users, and Groups tabs in the task section.

Deploying Software

Now comes the fun part of group policy: using it to deploy software. In Windows Small Business Server 2003, there was a built-in deployment tool that did a basic deployment. It placed the shortcut for the software on the desktop, and then the end user would be instructed to deploy the software from the shortcut and install it manually. In SBS 2008, standard group policy deployment can be used to deploy the software to workstations.

First, begin by creating a network share underneath the Users folder. Ensure it is shared out with the user group Everyone having read rights. Share it such as \\Server\Office2007 and copy the Office 2007 CD to that share location.

Find the Standard.WW folder, which contains the `.msi` you will use for the Group Policy Object deployment, as shown in Figure 15.13. In our example, Standard is the Office 2007 standard suite that was purchased under Open License. If the product you are deploying is the Office 2007 Enterprise version, the folder to look for is Enterprise.WW. If the version you are deploying is Office Professional Plus 2007, the folder to edit the `config.xml` file is ProPlus.WW. The Office product folders can be found at http://technet. microsoft.com/en-us/library/cc179070.aspx.

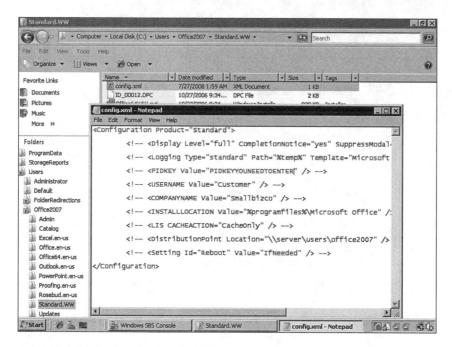

FIGURE 15.13   Configuring the XML.

Edit the `config.xml` file in that location for your needs, as discussed in the following para-graphs. You need to edit the customer name, location of deployment, and the install point.

Review the `config.xml` options on the Office 2007 resource page—
http://technet2.microsoft.com/Office/en-us/library/e16af71c-fed4-40da-a886-95e596c3999e1033.mspx?mfr=true.

The default `config.xml` looks like this:

```
<Configuration Product="Standard">
```

```
<!-- <Display Level="full" CompletionNotice="yes" SuppressModal="no"
➥AcceptEula="no" /> -->

<!-- <Logging Type="standard" Path="%temp%" Template="Microsoft Office Standard
➥Setup(*).txt" /> -->

<!-- <PIDKEY Value="Insertyourvaluehere" /> -->
<!-- <USERNAME Value="Customer" /> -->

<!-- <COMPANYNAME Value="MyCompany" /> -->

<!-- <INSTALLLOCATION Value="%programfiles%\Microsoft Office" /> -->

<!-- <LIS CACHEACTION="CacheOnly" /> -->

<!-- <SOURCELIST Value="\\server1\share\Office12;\\server2\share\Office12" /> -->

<!-- <DistributionPoint Location="\\server\share\Office12" /> -->

<!-- <OptionState Id="OptionID" State="absent" Children="force" /> -->

<!-- <Setting Id="Reboot" Value="IfNeeded" /> -->

<!-- <Command Path="msiexec.exe" Args="/i \\server\share\my.msi" QuietArg="/q"
➥ChainPosition="after" Execute="install" /> -->
</Configuration>
```

For testing, the config.xml file ends up looking like this:

```
<Configuration Product="Standard">
 <!-- <Display Level="full" CompletionNotice="yes" SuppressModal="no"
➥AcceptEula="no" /> -->

<!-- <Logging Type="standard" Path="%temp%" Template="Microsoft Office Standard
➥Setup(*).txt" /> -->
```

The top section remains as is with no changes:

```
 <!-- <PIDKEY Value="Insertyourvalue" /> -->
```

Enter the product identification key:

```
 <!-- <USERNAME Value="Customer" /> -->
```

Enter the customer name:

```
<!-- <COMPANYNAME Value="MyCompany" /> -->
```

Enter your company name:

```
<!-- <INSTALLLOCATION Value="%programfiles%\Microsoft Office" /> -->
```

Enter the location that you wish Office to be installed to:

```
<!-- <LIS CACHEACTION="CacheOnly" /> -->
<!-- <DistributionPoint Location="\\server\Office2007" /> -->
```

Enter the specific shared folder value:

```
 <!-- <Setting Id="Reboot" Value="IfNeeded" /> -->
</Configuration>
```

Now build a Group Policy Object on the SBS 2008 Server:

1. Click Start, All Programs, Administrative Tools, Group Policy Management to launch the console.
2. Click and expand the forest and view the domains and policies listed.
3. Click the domain name, right-click Create, and Link a GPO Here. Name it Office 2007.
4. Right-click the GPE named Office 2007 and select Edit.
5. Click to expand the item entitled Computer Configuration, then Policies, Software Settings, and Software Installation.
6. Right-click Software Installation, click New, and then click Package.
7. Now browse to the StandardWW folder and click the `StandardWW.msi` on the \\Server\Office_2007 share that was built previously. (Please note that you will need to do this all over again if you need to deploy 64-bit applications.)
8. You might be warned that you are deploying from a location that may not be seen by the clients; click OK, click Assigned, and then click OK again. The Microsoft Office Standard 2007 package now shows up in the right pane of your software installation.
9. Right-click that package and select Properties.
10. Click the Deployment tab and check Uninstall This Application When It Falls Out of the Scope of Management. Click OK.

The resulting Group Policy looks like Figure 15.14.

In an SBS 2008 network, you have a computer machine-based Organizational Unit called Domain Computers. If you are licensed to deploy Office 2007 to all the computers in that OU, you can use this OU to deploy out the Office 2007 software package. Otherwise, you might need to set up a special OU to deploy the Office 2007 software to only those workstations and users that have rights to the software package. Right-click this Organizational Unit, choose Link an Existing GPO, and choose the Office 2007 Group Policy you made earlier.

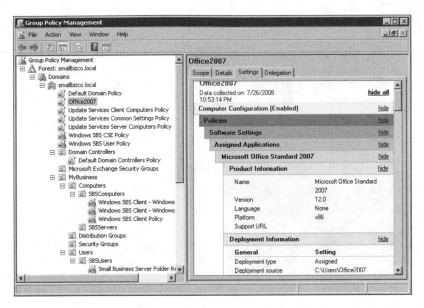

FIGURE 15.14   Office 2007 deployment policy.

You can also specifically deploy Office 2007 to specific computers. Confirm that the Office 2007 GPO is linked and in the Security filtering pane, perform the following steps:

1. Click Authenticated Users, and click Remove.

2. Click Add, Object Type, Domain Computers (or the specific OU of computers that you want this applied to), and click OK.

3. Test the group policy by going to a workstation, and at a command prompt, type gpupdate /force. GPupdate /force is the command that makes the server force down the Group Policy faster to workstations and the network rather than having to wait 90 minutes for the Group Policy to propagate. After you reboot, Office will begin to install.

Controlling the Workstations

Vista workstations offer a multitude of policy settings to better control the workstations. From USB drives to even whitelisting software, the number of ways to secure and protect a workstation is huge. But with every decision to lock something down comes the balance of the need to ensure that the business can continue to work efficiently. For small firms, there is always a balance between using the tools of a large enterprise on a small scale if the means to do so is efficient. If you only need to take an action against one workstation, perhaps Group Policy isn't appropriate.

Adjusting Permissions Using Group Policy

In Vista, the move to restrict user rights and rely less on Administrator rights means that some third-party software needs elevation before it can be launched. For some firms, the resulting UAC prompt can be a nuisance. If it is, the answer is to place in Group Policy those permissions adjustments needed for that application.

Begin first by building a security group that includes the members of the firm that have this application deployed.

There are two ways to build a security group. The first is the "old-fashioned way."

1. Click Start, All Programs, Administrative Tools.

2. Click Active Directory Users and Computers. (If a UAC prompt appears, allow it to continue.)

3. Expand the domain name, the MyBusiness Organizational Unit, and then Security Groups (see Figure 15.15).

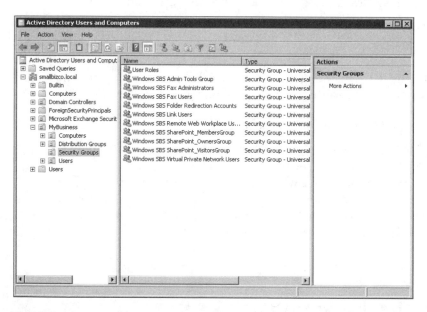

FIGURE 15.15   Active Directory Users and Computers.

4. Right-click the Security Group tab, click New, and then Organizational Unit, and follow the wizard to build a security group for the users of this application.

Alternatively, you can use SBS 2008's Security Group Wizard:

1. Click the Windows SBS Console

2. Click the User and Groups tab.

3. Click the Groups tab, and on the righthand side in the Group tasks, click Add New Group. This opens the Add a New Group Wizard (see Figure 15.16).

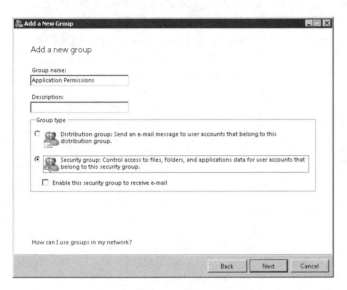

FIGURE 15.16   Adding a new security group.

4. Click Next and name the security group something identifying, such as Application Permissions (preferably use a description that tells you immediately which application this security group is built for). Then follow the wizard, setting up Sara Dough to be a member in this group (see Figure 15.17). Click Finish.

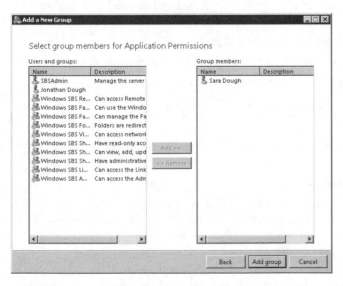

FIGURE 15.17   Adding a user to a security group.

15

5. Now, launch the Group Policy Management console. GPMC is located in the Administrative tools as well. Right-click the domain name and click Create a GPO in this domain and link it here. Again, name the group policy something descriptive and click OK. Go back to the group policy you just set up and click Edit.

6. Click Computer Configuration, Policies, Windows Settings, Security Settings, File System.

7. Click Add File and type **c:\Program Files\SoftwareVendorName** and click OK (see Figure 15.18). The system automatically flips it to %Program File%\ SoftwareVendorName.

FIGURE 15.18   Adding a file location in Group Policy.

You then receive a permissions screen that you can use to select the security group you previously chose. You can do this by clicking Advanced in the User window and then Find Now.

8. Choose the security group that was built and click OK.

9. Adjust the permissions to give the security group members full control.

10. Approve the permission propagation to the folders (see Figure 15.19).

To add similar keys for registry values, use the Registry section to open up the permissions on the specific vendor's registry keys:

1. Click Computer Configuration, Policies, Windows Settings, Security Settings, Registry System.

2. Right-click and then click Add Key.

3. Choose Machine, which is the equivalent of HKLocal Machine. Add the location of the registry key (see Figure 15.20). For example, if the registry key you need to open is HKLocal Machine\Software\Vendorname, add that string to the location.

4. Click OK, and then choose the security group to which you need to apply permissions.

After you have built this group, develop a Group Policy.

FIGURE 15.19   Adjusting permissions.

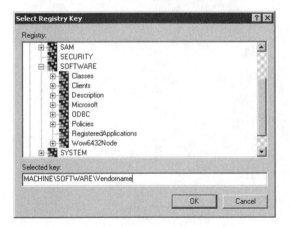

FIGURE 15.20   Adding registry entries.

Typically, to get a contentious application that is not built for a non-administrator to behave properly, most of the time all you need to do is to open up the registry keys to have full access. To do so, identify those registry settings and program file locations that need to be given additional permissions. Typically, these locations are Program Files\program name and HKey Local Machine. Once you've identified these values, define them in your group policy.

Using Group Policy in the Vista Era

There are a few new Group Policy settings unique to Vista and Server 2008. Some of these are obvious, such as settings to adjust and control User Account Control. Some are related to USB and other removable devices.

User Account Control

For User Account Control, one Group Policy setting that is recommended is to allow UAC to elevate in a Remote Access session. If you want to use remote assistance and not have to ask the person on the other side of the support session to click Approve the UAC prompt, by setting this value, the Remote Assistance session acts similar to the Windows XP remote assistance experience. To set this, edit this value as shown in Figure 15.21:

User Account Control: Allow UIAccess applications to prompt for elevation without ➥using the secure desktop.

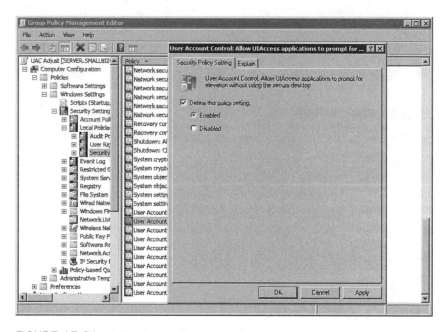

FIGURE 15.21   Adjusting UAC.

This security setting controls whether User Interface Accessibility (UIAccess or UIA) programs can automatically disable the secure desktop for elevation prompts being used by a standard user.

1. Click Start, All Programs, Administrative Tools, Group Policy Management to launch the console.

2. Click and expand the forest and view the domains and policies listed.

3. Click the domain name, right-click Create, and Link a GPO Here. Name it UAC Adjust.

4. Right-click the GPE named UAC Adjust, and select Edit.

5. Click to expand the item entitled Computer Configuration, then Policies, Windows Settings, Security Settings, and then click Local Policies.

6. Click Security Options. Scroll to the bottom and find the User Account Control: Allow UIAccess Applications to Prompt for Elevation Without Using the Secure Desktop.

7. Click the box to define the policy setting and click Enable. Click OK.

If you enable this setting, UIA programs, including Windows Remote Assistance, can automatically disable the secure desktop for elevation prompts. Unless you have also disabled elevation prompts, the prompts will appear on the interactive user's desktop instead of the secure desktop.

Mapping Network Drives

As discussed in Chapter 11, the new Group Policy Preferences are included in Windows Server 2008. To deploy these preference items to the workstations, you first need to ensure that all the workstations include the following updates to have the preference items on the desktops ready to go.

The following Group Policy Client Side extensions are supported on Windows XP, Vista, and Windows Server 2003:

▶ Group Policy Preference Client Side Extensions for Windows Vista (KB943729)

▶ Group Policy Preference Client Side Extensions for Windows Vista x64 Edition (KB943729)

▶ Group Policy Preference Client Side Extensions for Windows Server 2003 (KB943729)

▶ Group Policy Preference Client Side Extensions for Windows Server 2003 x64 Edition (KB943729)

▶ Group Policy Preference Client Side Extensions for Windows XP (KB943729)

▶ Group Policy Preference Client Side Extensions for Windows XP x64 Edition (KB943729)

After you have the extensions installed on the workstations, deploy the preferences, such as mapping of drives. To set the preference of a mapped drive, perform the following steps:

1. Click Start, All Programs, Administrative Tools, Group Policy Management to launch the console.

2. Click and expand the forest and view the domains and policies listed.

3. Right-click the domain name and select Create a GPO in This Domain, and Link It Here.

4. Name the New GPO in the window that launches and call it Map Drives. Click OK.

5. After the new GPO has built a link in the Management Console, go back and right-click the Map Drives GPO and select Edit.

6. In the editor navigational pane, click User Configuration to open it. Then click to expand the Preferences folder, and then expand the Windows Settings folder.

7. Find the Drive Maps node; right-click it and select New, Mapped Drive.

8. In the New Drive Properties dialog box, select an action for Group Policy to perform. In this example, choose Create.

9. Enter drive map settings for Group Policy to configure, including the drive letter preference, as shown in Figure 15.22. Click OK to complete the drive mapping.

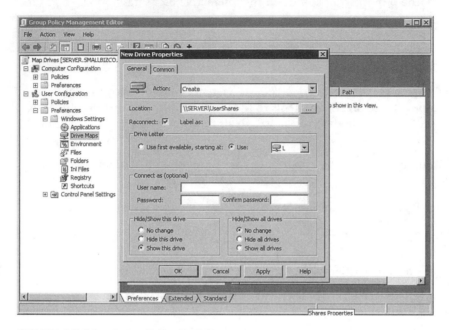

FIGURE 15.22   Group Policy Preferences.

Controlling USB Devices

New with Vista is the capability to use Group Policy to control USB and other removable media. You can prevent all such devices from being installed in a network, or you can allow only approved devices to be installed. Conversely, you can set the network to prevent users from installing devices that are on a blacklisted list. Finally, you can set certain types of removable media devices to restrict reading from or writing to CD and DVD burners, floppy disk drives, external hard drives and portable devices. To do all this, follow these steps:

1. Determine the device identification string to identify the specific USB device for which you want to set a policy.

2. Plug the USB device into the computer.

3. In the Search box within the Start menu type `mmc  devmgmt.msc` and press Enter.

4. Find the device listed for which you want to build a policy.

5. Double-click the device to open up the USB device properties window.

6. Click the Details tab, then the Property list and find the Hardware IDs listing.

7. Under Value, note the string information there and copy the value.

8. In the same Property list, click Compatible IDs. Under the Value, copy the string information there, as shown in Figure 15.23.

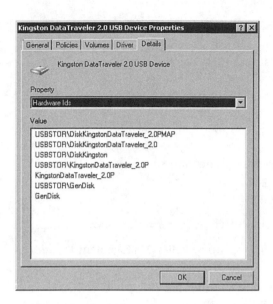

FIGURE 15.23   Determining USB Hardware ID.

If you are building this policy from a workstation or server, you need to remove the USB device using the Devmgmt MMC to place the system back into the proper state for purposes of building a group policy. If the driver has been installed on a system previously, the policy will not work as you intend it to. In this case, perform the following steps:

1. Enter **devmgmt.msc** into the Search box on the Start menu.
2. Right-click the entry for the USB device and select Uninstall.
3. In the confirm device removal window that pops up, click OK.

Decide first if you wish to block the removable devices at the computer level so that no matter what user connects to it, the device will be blocked. Conversely, you can also choose to build a policy at the user level that only applies to the users and groups in Active Directory.

To block all devices, perform the following steps:

1. Click Start, All Programs, Administrative Tools, Group Policy Management to launch the console.
2. Click and expand the forest and view the domains and policies listed.
3. Right-click the domain name and select Create a GPO in This Domain, and Link It Here.
4. Name the New GPO in the window that launches and call it Block USB. Click OK.
5. After the new GPO has built a link in the Management Console, go back and right-click the Block USB GPO and select Edit.
6. In the editor navigational pane, click Computer Configuration to open it.

7. Click Policies, Administrative Templates, System, Device Installation, and then open Device Installation Restrictions.

8. On the right side, choose Prevent Installation of Devices Not Described by Other Policy Settings, and click Properties.

9. In the settings tab, click Enabled. Click OK.

If you want administrators to have the right to override this setting, perform the following steps:

1. In the Group Policy Editor, right-click Allow Administrators to Override Device Installation Policy and select Properties.

2. In the settings tab, click Enabled. Click OK.

To create a Group Policy that allows for authorized devices, perform the following steps:

1. Click Start, All Programs, Administrative Tools, Group Policy Management to launch the console.

2. Click and expand the forest and view the domains and policies listed.

3. Right-click the domain name and select Create a GPO in This Domain, and Link It Here.

4. Name the new GPO in the window that launches and call it Block USB. Click OK.

5. After the new GPO has built a link in the Management Console, go back and right-click the Block USB GPO and select Edit.

6. In the editor navigational pane, click Computer Configuration to open it.

7. Click Policies, Administrative Templates, System, Device Installation, and then open Device Installation Restrictions.

8. On the right side, right-click Allow Installations of Devices That Match Any of These Device IDs and select Properties.

9. In the settings tab, click Enabled.

10. Click Show to view the list of allowed devices.

11. Click Add to open the Add Item dialog box.

12. Enter the device ID (the first hardware ID) for the USB device you want to allow. Click OK twice to close the open dialog boxes.

The resulting policy should look like the results in Figure 15.24.

To apply policies based on computer, perform the following steps:

1. Click Start, All Programs, Administrative Tools, Group Policy Management to launch the console.

2. Click and expand the forest and view the domains and policies listed.

3. Right-click the domain name and select Create a GPO in This Domain, and Link It Here.

4. Name the new GPO in the window that launches and call it Block USB Policy Computers. Click OK.

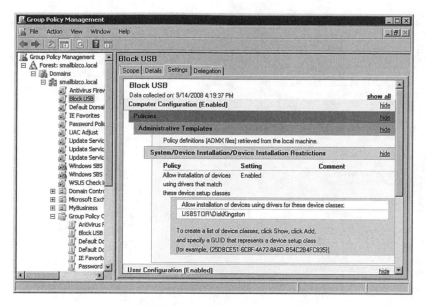

FIGURE 15.24   Setting policy to USB devices to allow.

15

5. After the new GPO has built a link in the Management Console, go back and right-click the Block USB Policy Computers GPO and select Edit.

6. Expand the Computer Configuration, Policies, Administrative Template, System, and click Removable Storage Access. Setting the policies in this section controls the USB on all computers that match the policy.

To build a policy that applies to users, perform the following steps:

1. Click Start, All Programs, Administrative Tools, Group Policy Management to launch the console.

2. Click and expand the forest and view the domains and policies listed.

3. Right-click the domain name and select Create a GPO in This Domain, and Link It Here.

4. Name the new GPO in the window that launches and call it Block USB Policy Users. Click OK.

5. After the new GPO has built a link in the Management Console, go back and right-click the Block USB Policy Users GPO and select Edit.

6. Expand the User Configuration, Policies, Administrative Templates, System, and click Removable Storage Access.

Using this location to build your USB policy allows you to build a policy based on user credentials, as shown in Figure 15.25.

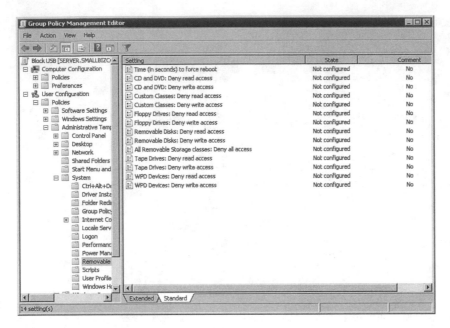

FIGURE 15.25   Setting policy for USB devices per user.

Choose the location of the policy based on the needs of the firm. If users log into many workstations, choose computer based settings. If users log into only a few workstations, choose user settings.

Troubleshooting

Just as in Chapter 11, your best troubleshooting technique is to use the Group Policy Modeling and Reports to review the settings you have made. If you ensure that you document your non- or low-impacting edits to the existing policies and place any major policy changes as new policies, then you can ensure that you can track what changes you have made and disable any new policies that you have built that are not working as they should.

Summary

Group Policy is a very powerful tool and typically underutilized in a Small Business setting. Deploying software is just one task it can do to make your deployments easier. Take the time to add the power and flexibility to your network. Use it to redirect files, set permissions for applications, block removable devices, deploy applications, and even block rogue applications if you want to take the time to do so. Many small firms rely too much on verbal policies to enforce security and don't implement technology policies as well.

Best Practice Summary

▶ **Do Not Modify the Default Domain Policies**—Changes made to the default policies are difficult to test and undo if problems are encountered.

▶ **Create New or Modify Existing GPOs**—The complexity and scope of the Group Policy Object determines whether to create a new GPO or modify an existing one. If you want to add a single application exception to the Windows Firewall setting for the entire organization, it might make sense to modify one of the firewall-related existing GPOs. If you want to modify the environment for a subset of the organization, create a new GPO.

▶ **Use Group Policy to Enforce the Security Policies of the Firm**—Use Group Policy to efficiently and effectively enforce the policies of the firm.

15

PART 5

Managing Security and System Health

IN THIS PART

CHAPTER 16

Monitoring and Reporting

One of the more visible areas of change on the SBS 2008 server is the area of Monitoring and Reporting. The monitoring reports include information about the workstations. In addition, you can develop custom reports based on selected items. In some respects, the reports are much improved over SBS 2003 as they now report automatically on the status of the workstations for Security; however, in other respects, they do not allow for the flexibility that SBS 2003 allowed in its reports.

To give a bit of history, SBS 2003 based its reporting module on HealthMon, a Windows 2000 era monitoring program. In the SBS 2008 era, a redesign of the monitoring program brings a different console and a different manner of adjusting and adding to it. You can either view the reports online or have them e-mailed to an e-mail account or a mobile phone. HealthMon is a deprecated platform, however, and thus a redesign was needed. In making this change, there has been a change in the monitoring information provided.

The monitoring e-mails of SBS 2003 include some information that is no longer tracked in the SBS 2008 monitoring system. Such information includes disk drive space and hardware specifications of the server, as well as CPU usage. Some could argue this is a step back from the reports that SBS 2003 provided. For these items, a third-party monitoring tool may need to be used, as the native monitoring reports do not include this. SBS 2008, however, does monitor the firewall and antivirus status of workstations and has the capability to add custom alerts easier than SBS 2003 did, in addition to a better presentation of information to the receiver of the alerts.

Understanding the Role of Monitoring and Reporting in SBS 2008

Monitoring is the foundation of many roles in a Small Business Network. For the consultant, it's a means to review the daily operations and health of the network. It can monitor the status of patching, as well as events in the event log. There are several places where the server gives you an overview of the network health, as well as the daily e-mail that SBS owners and consultants are used to.

New in SBS 2008 is the integration of OneCare server antivirus and Forefront Exchange antivirus into the health and monitoring functions. In addition, the Windows Small Business Server 2008 can keep track of the antivirus and firewall status of not only the SBS 2008, but also Vista and XP SP2.

However, there are limitations that you need to be aware of in reporting of SBS 2008. You might want to augment the existing monitoring and reporting with additional built-in reporting mechanisms that are in other parts of the Small Business Server. These augmentations include using the built-in reporting modules of Windows Software Update Services and the File Reporting System modules.

Built-in Monitoring Versus External Monitoring

The native monitoring that is included in Windows Small Business Server 2008 might be adequate for standalone operation of the server but is lacking for more managed networks. Thus, for many servers under managed services, the consultant would be better served using third-party monitoring tools rather than relying on the native monitoring. The individual reports are not suited for rolling up into a reporting console. Even standalone servers might consider either augmenting reporting or looking to third-party solutions when the reporting does not adequately monitor the status of the network. Many vendors provide third-party monitoring solutions such as Microsoft's own System Center Essentials, and other third-party solutions such as Kaseya (a managed services tool), Level Platforms (a managed services tool), EventSentry.com (a monitoring tool), N-able (remote monitoring and reporting), Hound Dog (remote monitoring and reporting), and Spiceworks (monitoring and community), among many others.

Consider adding third-party monitoring to the Windows Small Business Server 2008. Third-party monitoring typically can better integrate into consultant tools and provide the ability to provide additional proactive service. A differentiation of services found in the SBS 2008's built-in monitoring and that of many third-party services is found in Table 16.1.

TABLE 16.1   Included Monitoring Versus Value Added

Built-in Monitoring	Third-Party Monitoring
Monitors for security, antivirus, and firewall.	Monitors for security, antivirus, firewall.
Sends out alerts approximately every 30 minutes.	Sends alerts as necessary.
Cannot be tuned to turn off alerts; the alert item must be fixed	Alerts can be tuned.
Does not natively monitor for unexpected shutdowns.	Typically sends out alerts for start-up events.
Can be customized.	Can be customized.
Can't be accumulated into a roll-up report.	Typically accumulated into a roll-up report.
May be able to be included in consultant billing applications.	Typically able to be included in consultant billing applications.

Understanding the Default Settings of Monitoring and Reporting

The main SBS Console gives you the high-level view of the overall health of the network. On the main SBS Console, a Network Essentials Summary gives you an overview of four major areas: Security, Updates, Backup, and Other Alerts. Now, you would think that Security and Updates are the same items, but they are actually very different. The main reporting console can be seen in Figure 16.1.

16

FIGURE 16.1   The main reporting overview.

Security

The first section on the upper-right side of the SBS Console gives the consultant the first overview of the server's health and well-being. The first area that is monitored is Security. The monitoring of Security polls the Security Center settings for each Vista and XP sp2 or higher workstation and reports on Antivirus being installed, if it is up to date and if the client firewall is enabled. Expanding the tab gives you the high-level overview of the category. If the network is in good health in that area, the color for that section is green. If the network is of concern, there is a yellow warning; finally, if the network has critical issues that you need to review, the item is red. Clicking Go To Security immediately jumps to that section of the console so that you can take action on that item.

Updates

The Update reporting module gives you the high-level view of security and software updates in your network. If you need to take action on a security or software update, this area of the console is red. Clicking the Go to Updates takes you to the area of the server that you need to review to take action on these updates. If you have changed the settings of the WSUS console so that the Windows Small Business Server 2008 cannot control the Windows Software Update Services Server, this area will be gray.

Backup

The Backup reporting module informs you of the status of the disk-based backup module. If you have not set up the server for backing up, this module is yellow in color. If the server has backed up successfully, the area is green in color. If the server has had a problem backing up, the area is red in color.

Other Alerts

This "catch all" category includes system event logs and other alerts from the system. It may be alerts that the consultant needs to ignore or determines are of no consequence. Sometimes normal rebooting of the server might place events in this section that you can safely ignore.

Notification Settings

A second area that provides the network administration with information regarding the server is the Notification section. This area sends e-mail alerts when the server's services are not functioning or when there is a malfunction in certain areas of the server. You can send this to a recipient inside the firm or outside. However, it goes without saying that if e-mail is one of the impacted services, the e-mail notification will not be received. To set up notifications, go to the Network tab in the SBS console and ensure that you are in the Computers tab of this section. On the right side in the Tasks section, click View Notification Settings, as shown in Figure 16.2.

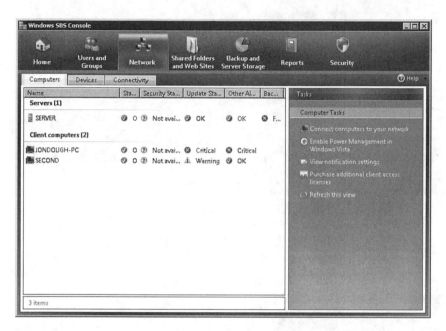

FIGURE 16.2   View notification settings.

Setting Up the Default Monitoring Reports

There are two main areas for setting up the monitoring and reporting features. The first section that you can customize to your liking is in the Computers section of the SBS console. In this section, you can edit what notifications and alerts you wish to receive. On the Network tab, and then on the Computers tab, is the View Notification Settings task. This task enables you to customize three areas of alerts.

The first area is the Services monitoring. Each service that should be set to be automatically started is set to be monitored. If the service does not turn on, you will be alerted. Figure 16.3 shows the services that will be monitored. To get to this section, on the Network tab of the SBS console, click View Notifications Settings in the task pane. A pane launches that gives you the various notification options including Services, Performance Counters, and Event Log Errors and enables you to set up e-mail address forwarding.

The next section that allows adjustment is Performance Counters. In this section, the only item that is tracked is Percent Free Disk space. This area is a bit lightweight in scope; you would hope that additional items, such as hardware issues, can be added to this list by external vendors that can hook into the SBS Console through the use of APIs. Figure 16.4 documents the performance counter that is tracked by SBS 2008.

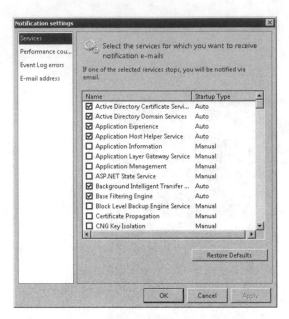

FIGURE 16.3   Services alerting.

FIGURE 16.4   Performance counters.

Event Log errors include specific items unique to the Windows Small Business Server 2008 platform. Table 16.2 lists the specific events that the notification section tracks.

TABLE 16.2   Notification Events

Checked	Event Notification
Yes	A FSMO role is out of compliance, and it cannot be corrected.
Yes	A router port is not open.
Yes	An application is blocked by the Windows firewall.
Yes	An error occurred in Active Directory Domain Services.
Yes	An external trust is not permitted and cannot be fixed.
Yes	Cannot detect Internet connection.
Yes	Domain controller licensing error.
Yes	Domain Name Status Alert.
Yes	Domain provider authentication error.
Yes	External DHCP server found.
Yes	Forefront Security for Exchange Server Engine Updates (Event 7004).
Yes	Forefront Security for Exchange Server Engine Updates (Event 7007).
No	Forefront Security License—Expiring (Event 2057).
Yes	Forest trust licensing error.
Yes	FSMO roles licensing error.
Yes	Leaf certificate expiring.
Yes	Licensing error for the additional server check.
Yes	Licensing error for the additional server number check.
Yes	Network router not found.
Yes	OneCare Event 10010.
Yes	OneCare Free Trial Expiration.
Yes	OneCare Grace Period.
Yes	OneCare Paid Subscription Expiration.
Yes	Root certificate expiring.
Yes	The additional server does not comply with the license policy.
Yes	The domain is deleted from the forest trust list.
Yes	The external check for licensing has failed.
Yes	The FSMO role does not comply with the license policy.
Yes	The licensing component cannot load the server policies on to this server.
Yes	The Licensing Enforcement service cannot load the external checks for licensing.
Yes	The number of additional servers does not comply with license policy.
Yes	The number of user accounts and computers in the domain might exceed the maximum allowed.
Yes	The server did not pass the external checks for licensing.
Yes	The server has a trust with an external forest that is not permitted.
Yes	The server must shut down; your environment does not comply with the licensing policy.

The interesting item to note in that list is the number of licensing compliance items that are included in the notifications checking. Because licensing compliance was removed from the product, monitoring many of these items is now unnecessary, as can be seen in Figure 16.5.

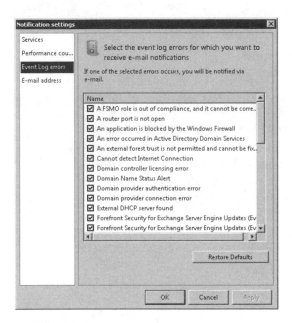

FIGURE 16.5   Event log errors.

The notifications can be sent to a local e-mail address, as well as external addresses. It's as easy as entering multiple addresses with a semi-colon in between, as can be seen in Figure 16.6.

The Daily Report

The second phase of monitoring and reporting is the area that you are probably most used to: the daily report. To find this next monitoring section, click the Reports tab of the Windows SBS console. There are two preconfigured reports: Summary Network Report and Detailed Network Report, as shown in Figure 16.7. In addition to these two reports, you can build your own reports.

FIGURE 16.6   E-mail notifications.

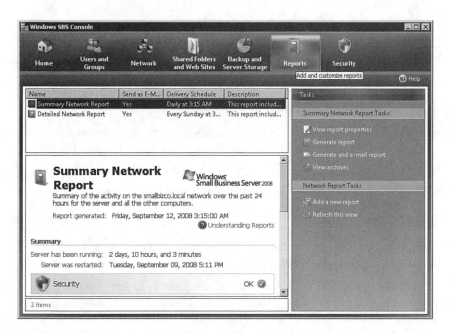

FIGURE 16.7   Summary Network Report.

The Summary Network Report just gives a high-level overview of the major areas that you want to monitor. To review what this report showcases, go to the Reports tab on the

Windows SBS Console and then click Summary Network Report. On the right side of the Tasks pane, click View Report Properties and review the settings, as shown in the settings for Figure 16.8.

FIGURE 16.8   Summary settings.

In this e-mail is the recap of items that make up the following categories:

▶ **A summary of the status of Security**—This section tracks antivirus status on the workstations and the server, spam settings for the Internet Message Filter, Forefront Security settings for the Exchange Server, and if the firewall is enabled on all workstations.

▶ **Updates settings tracks the installation of the updates on the network**—This includes critical updates, definition updates, security patches, service packs, and update rollups.

▶ **Backup settings that report on the backup status of the server**—This tracks the backup schedule and reports on its completion.

▶ **Other alerts that track miscellaneous events on the server**—Other events that occur in the event logs of the server are summarized. These alerts include the exact error messages for backup failures, task scheduler events, any issues you might have with Forefront engine file updates and other issues that throw off an error message in the application event logs.

▶ **E-mail usage and mailbox sizes are tracked and monitored.**

▶ **Server event log issues.**

You can review the summary report on the server itself, as shown in Figure 16.9, or you can generate and e-mail the report.

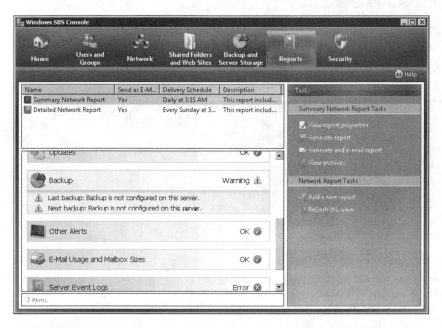

FIGURE 16.9   Summary report.

The default settings for this report can be edited by clicking View Report Properties. The first section you can change is the title of the e-mail report. The default value for this is Summary Network Report, but this can be customized to be the name of the server for purposes of tracking. The content for the Summary report is only the first category of Summary. For the e-mail options in the next section, Windows SBS administrators are checked by default, but you can add additional external addresses in this section. The schedule for this daily e-mail can be set as needed. Finally the last section of Archives can be used to review the generation of this report.

The Weekly Report

The second report, the Detailed Network Report, goes into the issues and monitoring in greater detail. In fact one could argue (and strongly) that this report should be edited to be sent out daily. This is easy to do in the Report Properties pane. Click View Report Properties on the right side and edit the e-mail schedule of the report. The default schedule is to e-mail this report every week, but you might want to turn off the summary reports and make the weekly reports into daily reports, as seen in Figure 16.10.

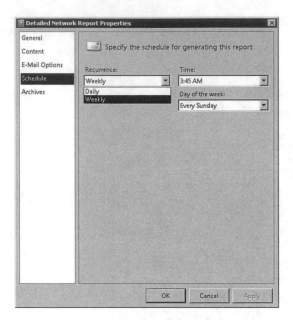

FIGURE 16.10   Editing the e-mail schedule.

Unlike the summary report, this report gives more details of the events seen on the server and the network in the prior 24 hours. For each category of events, there is the ability to click details and expand down to the details of the errors listed, as shown in Figure 16.11. The major difference between the summary report in Figure 16.7 and the detailed report in Figure 16.11 is that, in the detailed report, you can click on the detail button and see the exact alerts that are included in the report. Thus this is why the detailed report is ultimately more flexible than the summary report and of more value on a regular basis. It's therefore recommended to change this report and receive it daily.

In many cases, the details for each listed error may not be explained clearly enough, though there can be a detailed analysis in some cases. Therefore, it's recommended that you review third-party error-tracking sites like http://www.eventid.net and http://www.myeventlog.com.

The detailed report settings are similar to the summary report. Click the detailed report and then View report properties to edit and view the settings. The first tab, General, is the area where you can edit and customize the name of the report. The content section is where you select the content. For the detail network report, all the content radio buttons are selected. These content radio buttons select the sections that are included in the detailed report. The top section is the Summary section that recaps the events. Below that are the detailed sections of Security, Updates, Backup, Other Alerts, E-mail Usage, and Server Event Logs, which are all selectable in the report. The next section, e-mail options,

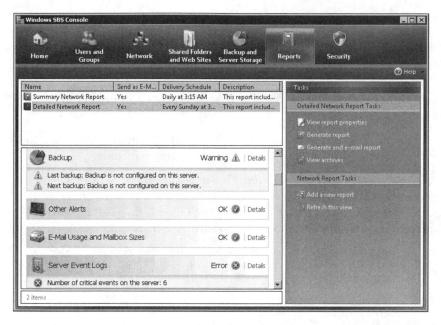

FIGURE 16.11   Detail section of the report.

enables you to add external e-mail addresses in addition to the Windows SBS administrators that are already included. The default setting for schedule of the e-mail is once a week, but many administrators prefer that the detailed e-mail report get sent once a day. Finally, the archives tab enables you to review the past reports.

Best Practice—Daily Reports

The daily report tends to not be detailed enough for the needs of most administrators; thus, set up the Detailed Network Reports to be sent daily instead. These Detailed Network Reports include the specific wording of the events that triggered the alerts; thus, the administrator will not need to log onto the server to review the alerts. If the Summary Network Report is sent as the daily report, the administrator will not be able to quickly review the alerts from the network because the details are not included in the report. In many cases, the alerts sent by the server are informational in nature and do not need immediate attention or can be dealt with at a later time.

Customizing Monitoring and Reporting

Once you have configured the default monitoring so that it is set up to meet your needs, it is time to customize the monitoring to the needs of the network. There are several ways to customize the reports and information included.

Setting Up Your Own Report

Creating a new report is easy to do in the Reporting console. In the Windows SBS Console, on the navigation bar, click Reports. In the Tasks pane, click Add a new report. In this New Report Properties screen, set up the preferences for each tab, as follows:

> ▶ In the General tab, type a name for the new report. Type a short description for the report.

> ▶ On the Content tab, select the checkbox for each type of information you want to include, or clear the checkbox for any item you don't want to include.

> ▶ In the E-mail Options tab, set up the options to e-mail the report. Set the schedule for the e-mail and select the internal recipients for the e-mail. If you want to send it to an external recipient, set the e-mail address in the Other E-mail Address section. For more addresses, use semi-colons to separate multiple e-mail addresses.

The E-Mail option tab predefines the users on the network and allows customization of external notifications to an outside consultant, which can be seen in Figure 16.12.

FIGURE 16.12   Detail section of the report.

TIP

Leave the existing report as is and build new reports to better customize the need for detailed monitoring. Ensure that the e-mail address for sending the reports is properly configured and test the configuration before beginning the custom event process. Leaving the original default reports as is allows you to use these as template guidelines for customizing your own reports.

Creating Custom Alerts and Notifications

In reviewing the monitoring and reporting events that are tracked by the server, there are certainly events that you'd like to add to be reviewed. Fortunately, the Windows Small Business Server 2008 team has released a Software Development document known as an SDK that details this process. This document is located at http://msdn.microsoft.com/en-us/library/cc721719.aspx.

Best Practice—Custom Alerts

Setting up custom alerts is one of the most important tasks in setting up the server. Ensuring that key server events are sent properly is one of the most important steps in ensuring a healthy server. Review the SBS 2008 SDK to better understand how you can customize the reports for specific events that occur in the event log on the servers.

After downloading the SDK document, begin by thinking of an alert you would like to add to the notification. In this example, you add a notification for when the server has shut down unexpectedly because any unscheduled restart of the server is something that you should investigate. You also demonstrate how to set up an e-mail notification through the event log so that you know when such an event occurs.

Assigning a GUID

First, you need to assign a GUID (Globally Unique Identifier) to the alert. Follow these steps to generate a new GUID:

1. Click Start, All Programs, and expand Windows PowerShell 1.0; then click on Windows PowerShell.

2. In the command prompt window for Windows PowerShell, type the following:

   ```
   [System.Guid]::NewGuid().ToString()
   ```

3. Record the GUID that is returned. You will need it later. Figure 16.13 shows that the GUID returned for this example was 196f6d6c-ae1c-4982-8757-1f5b94f4a538.

```
Windows PowerShell
Windows PowerShell
Copyright (C) 2006 Microsoft Corporation. All rights reserved.

PS C:\Users\SBSAdmin> [System.Guid]::NewGuid().ToString()
196f6d6c-ae1c-4982-8757-1f5b94f4a538
PS C:\Users\SBSAdmin> _
```

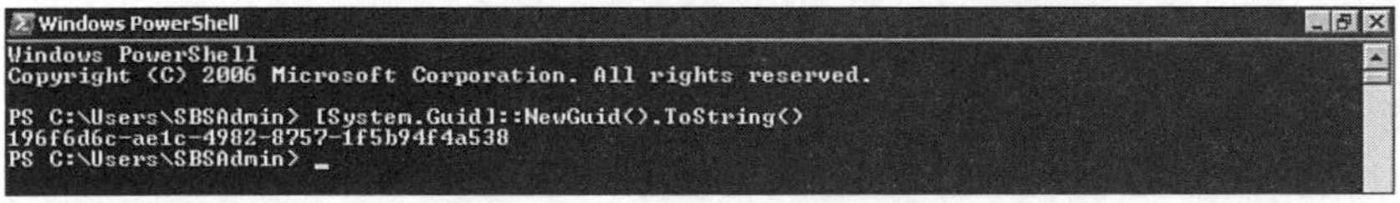

FIGURE 16.13   Determining a random GUID.

TIP

For an easier way to generate a GUID, you can use the GUIDGEN web site at http://www.guidgen.com/ to generate a unique GUID.

Finding Alert Items in the Event Viewer

Now, use the Event Viewer and find those items for which a custom event needs to be set up:

1. Click Start, All Programs, Administrative Tools; then click Event Viewer.

2. Access the Event Log. Most of the events to track will be in System or Security logs.

3. For this example, select the event with an ID of 6008, as follows:

```
Log Name:       System
Source:         EventLog
Date:           8/1/2008 3:56:48 PM
Event ID:       6008
Task Category:  None
Level:          Error
Keywords:       Classic
User:           N/A
Computer:       SBSERVER.smallbizco.local
Description:
```

The previous system shutdown at 4:33:42 PM was unexpected.

4. Now click the Details tab, select the Friendly view, and then expand System.

5. Look for the information for provider name and channel, as shown in Figure 16.14. In this example, the provider name is EventLog and the channel is System.

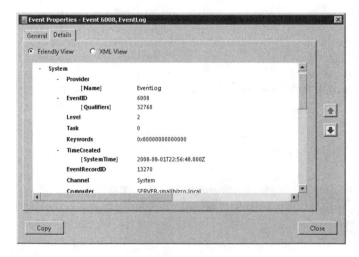

FIGURE 16.14   Recording provider name and channel.

Defining the Alert in a Custom XML File

Next, an .xml file needs to be created that contains the elements and attributes to represent the custom alert. The custom alert provides event information to the reports and e-mail notifications in the Windows SBS Console.

To make a custom alert, open Notepad and, using the formatting example, add the following XML data to the new file to define the ID, name, and application for the custom alert. Using the previous GUID generation step using either PowerShell or www.guidgen.com, the custom-generated GUID is placed behind the `<AlertDefinition ID="Custom Guid"` to assign a guide to the alert. Then, the next settings are setting forth the title and source:

```
<?xml version="1.0" encoding="utf-8" ?>
<AlertDefinitions>
  <AlertDefinition ID="896e6561-b29d-42b5-b349-a87460c8556f"
                   Default="1"
                   Title="Unexpected Shut down"
                   Source="Server">
```

In the example, the line `AlertDefinition` has been assigned the unique GUID you generate for each custom alert. Please note that you need to generate one for each custom alert you define.

`<AlertDefinition ID="896e6561-b29d-42b5-b349-a87460c8556f"` represents this custom generated line.

`Default="1"` indicates that this alert will be default enabled.

`Title="Unexpected Shut Down"` indicates the title of the event in the monitoring.

`Source="Server"` indicates the application that will be monitored.

Table 16.3 lists the attributes that are used with an AlertDefinition Element.

TABLE 16.3   Attributes Used with Alert Defintions

Attribute	Description
ID	Defines the GUID that uniquely identifies the custom alert. Use the GUID that you obtained earlier in this document.
Default	Defines whether the custom alert is enabled and whether it is included in the list of alerts that are restored when Restore Defaults is clicked in the Notifications Settings dialog box.
Title	Defines the name that is displayed for the alert in the Windows SBS Console.
Source	Defines the application that the alert is monitoring.

The Parameters Element is added to the AlertDefinition element to define the event parameters for the custom alert. The custom alert uses the parameters to obtain the appropriate event from the specified event log. Add the following XML data to the file to specify the event parameters for the custom alert and add this to the bottom of the previous XML code section:

```
<Parameters>
  <Path>System</Path>
  <Provider>EventLog</Provider>
  <SetEventID>6008</SetEventID>
  <ClearEventID>    </ClearEventID>
</Parameters>
```

Table 16.4 lists the elements that are used to define the event parameters.

TABLE 16.4   Event Parameters

Element	Description
Path Element	Specifies the name of the event log where the event will be recorded. The value that is used for this element is the Channel value that you obtained earlier in this document.
Provider Element	Specifies the name of the provider that wrote the event to the event log. The value that is used for this element is the Provider Name value that you obtained earlier in this document.
SetEventID Element	Specifies the ID number of the event that triggers the alert.
ClearEventID Element	This is an optional element that specifies the ID number of the event that clears the alert. If this element is not defined, the alert will be cleared after 30 minutes. If this element is defined, the alert will not be automatically cleared after the timeout period; it will only be cleared if the specified event occurs. In the example, there is no clear event, so this cannot be included in the xml file. In another example, event ID 5024 is used, which is the event that is logged when the Windows Firewall service is started.

To end the XML code, place the ending arguments at the last of your code:

```
  </AlertDefinition>
</AlertDefinitions>
```

Save the .xml file and name it a descriptive name so that you can know what you are monitoring. It will have to be saved in some other folder, such as the Documents folder, and then moved into position, as discussed in the next section.

The final alert code looks like the following:

```
<?xml version="1.0" encoding="utf-8" ?>
<AlertDefinitions>
  <AlertDefinition ID="38C4B89D-6A30-41EA-8FCC-C485AAD3C01C" Default="1"
➥Title="Custom Windows Firewall Add-in" Source="Windows Firewall Service">
    <Parameters>
   <Path>Security</Path>
      <Provider>Microsoft-Windows-Security-Auditing</Provider>
      <SetEventID>5025</SetEventID>
      <ClearEventID>5024</ClearEventID>
    </Parameters>
  </AlertDefinition>
</AlertDefinitions>
```

Deploying the Custom Alert

Place the .xml file that was previously created in the directory where the Windows SBS Console can locate it, and then verify that the custom alert is functioning correctly.

Copy the .xml file that was created earlier in this document to the %programfiles%\Windows Small Business Server\Data\Monitoring\ExternalAlerts directory on the computer that is running the Windows SBS 2008 operating system. Double-click the file to ensure that the custom .xml file appears in Internet Explorer as a valid XML file and does not record an error.

Finally, to have the monitoring take effect, restart the Window SBS Manager Service. Click Start, All Programs, Administrative Tools, Services. Find and right-click the Windows SBS Manager Service; then select restart. Restarting the manager service triggers the alert.

There may be a 30-minute delay until the alert is displayed or the notification is sent.

To view the new alert, click the Network tab, click the Computers tab, click the server, and then click the View computer alerts task, as shown in Figure 16.15.

You can also see information about alerts by generating a report.

Additional custom events that should be added to the server include the following:

▶ Unexpected reboot:

```
<?xml version="1.0" encoding="utf-8" ?>
<AlertDefinitions>
  <AlertDefinition ID="d96f3b40-e786-406c-bbc5-23a081569dd5" Default="1"
➥Title="Unexpected Reboot" Source="USER32">
    <Parameters>
   <Path>System</Path>
      <Provider>USER32</Provider>
      <SetEventID>1076</SetEventID>
    </Parameters>
  </AlertDefinition>
</AlertDefinitions>
```

▶ Disk error:

```xml
<?xml version="1.0" encoding="utf-8" ?>
<AlertDefinitions>
  <AlertDefinition ID="674dd41c-aec7-4025-8601-aef90c18e595" Default="1"
➥Title="DiskError" Source="Disc">
    <Parameters>
  <Path>System</Path>
      <Provider>Disk</Provider>
      <SetEventID>11</SetEventID>
      </Parameters>
  </AlertDefinition>
</AlertDefinitions>
```

▶ Prediction of disk error:

```xml
<?xml version="1.0" encoding="utf-8" ?>
<AlertDefinitions>
  <AlertDefinition ID="499ed578-f7b4-46da-a097-8ed39760b9ea" Default="1"
➥Title="DiskErrorPrediction" Source="Disc">
    <Parameters>
  <Path>System</Path>
      <Provider>Disk</Provider>
      <SetEventID>52</SetEventID>
      </Parameters>
  </AlertDefinition>
</AlertDefinitions>
```

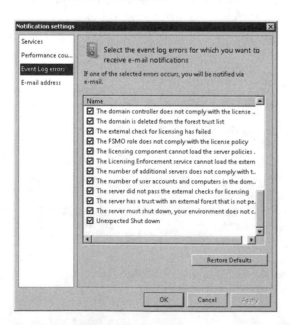

FIGURE 16.15   Custom alerts.

> **TIP**
>
> This is just an example of the types of events that need to be monitored. Think of those key elements that should be tracked and build custom event tracking to assist in keeping the server and network healthy. Add custom alerts for key items in your network.

Sample Event for OneCare

Many times the best way to develop a custom event is to review an existing event that is predefined on the server. A sample custom event for OneCare is already included in the Windows Small Business Server 2008. From reviewing this alert for OneCare, you can get a feel for additional syntax used:

```xml
<?xml version="1.0" encoding="utf-8" ?>
- <AlertDefinitions>
- <_locDefinition>
  <_locDefault _loc="locNone" />
  <_locTag _locAttrData="Title">AlertDefinition</_locTag>
  <_locTag _locAttrData="Source">AlertDefinition</_locTag>
  </_locDefinition>
- <AlertDefinition ID="38C4B89D-6A30-41EA-8FCC-C485AAD3C01C" Default="1"
➥Title="OneCare Free Trial Expiration" Source="OneCare">
- <Parameters>
  <Path>Windows OneCare</Path>
  <Provider>WinSS</Provider>
  <SetEventID>10001</SetEventID>
  <ClearEventID />
  </Parameters>
  </AlertDefinition>
- <AlertDefinition ID="2C90F74A-BCCF-41D7-ABA8-532755BB37E8" Default="1"
➥Title="OneCare Grace Period" Source="OneCare">
- <Parameters>
  <Path>Windows OneCare</Path>
  <Provider>WinSS</Provider>
  <SetEventID>10003</SetEventID>
  <ClearEventID>10002</ClearEventID>
  </Parameters>
  </AlertDefinition>
- <AlertDefinition ID="0074573C-62A7-44B4-B73D-1C8B73ECCFA2" Default="1"
➥Title="OneCare Paid Subscription Expiration" Source="OneCare">
- <Parameters>
  <Path>Windows OneCare</Path>
  <Provider>WinSS</Provider>
  <SetEventID>10004</SetEventID>
  <ClearEventID>10002</ClearEventID>
```

```
  </Parameters>
  </AlertDefinition>
- <AlertDefinition ID="A23C27F2-C758-4A01-B16D-FFB0C18E0330" Default="1"
➥Title="OneCare Event 10010" Source="OneCare">
- <Parameters>
  <Path>Windows OneCare</Path>
  <Provider>WinSS</Provider>
  <SetEventID>10010</SetEventID>
  <ClearEventID>10011</ClearEventID>
  </Parameters>
  </AlertDefinition>
  </AlertDefinitions>
```

These alerts do not fire off immediately, so you might need to wait up to 30 minutes before the alert will be sent. Community-built alerts will be added to the community codeplex site located at http://www.codeplex.com/sbs. The authors encourage SBS administrators and consultants to share the custom alerts you build to this community code-sharing location.

Developing a Data Protection Plan for Monitoring and Reporting

Depending on which version of Windows Small Business Server 2008 you have installed, your options for backing up the Monitoring database are defined as either basic or advanced. Basic merely relies on the built-in Windows Small Business Server backup tools; Advanced includes using the SQL backup commands to prepare special backups of the database.

Special Backups of the Database

For the SBS 2008 standard server, the SQL 2005 Management Studio Express tool is included with the server. This tool provides the ability to do an immediate backup, and other maintenance tasks.

Thus, it is very important that you perform an image-based backup of the server in the Standard version of Windows Small Business Server 2008 that is performed by the built in backup of Windows Server 2008. If you need to make a special backup of the SQL database, right-click start, All Products, SQL Server 2005, and then click the icon for the SQL 2005 Management Studio Express tool and select Run as Administrator. Connect to the SBSMonitoring instance on the SQL server in the SQL 2005 Management Studio Express, as seen in Figure 16.16.

To back up the database, perform the following steps:

1. Launch the SQL Server Management studio application by right-clicking its icon and selecting Run as Administrator.

2. Ensure the Connect to Server window is SERVER\SBSMONITORING and click Connect.

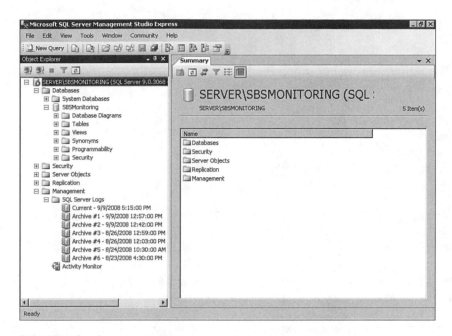

FIGURE 16.16   SQL 2005 Management Studio Express.

3. Expand databases and click on the database called SBSMONITORING.

4. Right-click the name of the SBSMonitoring SQL instance and select Tasks, Backup.

5. Ensure that the database you are backing up is SBSMonitoring and then choose Disk or Tape as appropriate.

6. If you choose disk, click Add to choose a filename.

7. Add the filename of your choice and click OK. Then click OK again to begin the backup.

The backup is executed, and following its completion, you'll receive a message that indicates the backup was successful.

Scheduling a Backup

Due to the fact that SBSMonitoring uses the SQL 2005 express database to store the information, it does not natively have a backup maintenance tab that other SQL databases based on the larger SQL servers include. You can, however, set up a task to back up the server:

1. Enter the following code into Notepad and save it in a location on the server such as shared folder on the server as `backup.sql`:

```
DECLARE @name VARCHAR(50) — database name
DECLARE @path VARCHAR(256) — path for backup files
DECLARE @fileName VARCHAR(256) — filename for backup
```

```
DECLARE @fileDate VARCHAR(20)  — used for file name

SET @path = 'C:\Backup\'

SELECT @fileDate = CONVERT(VARCHAR(20),GETDATE(),112)

DECLARE db_cursor CURSOR FOR
SELECT name
FROM master.dbo.sysdatabases
WHERE name NOT IN ('master','model','msdb','tempdb')

OPEN db_cursor
FETCH NEXT FROM db_cursor INTO @name

WHILE @@FETCH_STATUS = 0
BEGIN
        SET @fileName = @path + @name + '_' + @fileDate + '.BAK'
        BACKUP DATABASE @name TO DISK = @fileName

        FETCH NEXT FROM db_cursor INTO @name
END

CLOSE db_cursor

DEALLOCATE db_cursor
```

2. Next, to test that the process will work, go to a command line using administrator privileges and type the following:

```
sqlcmd -S .\SBSmonitoring -E -i "c:\backup\backup.sql"
```

The SQL databases should be backed up to c:\backup.

3. Place the following phrase into a batch file:

```
sqlcmd -S .\SBSmonitoring -E -i "c:\backup\backup.sql" into a batch file.
```

Now you need to schedule a task to make use of all this:

1. Click Start, All Programs, Accessories, System Tools, Task Manager.
2. Click Create Task.
3. Name the new task SQL Backup.
4. Select the option to run whether the user is logged in or not.
5. Select the option to run with highest privileges.
6. Select the trigger tab and click New.
7. Set a schedule time you want the backup to occur.
8. Click the Actions tab and click New.
9. Click Start a Program.
10. Choose the backup batch file you created earlier.

11. Click OK and provide the appropriate administrator credentials to ensure this task has rights of the administrator in order to run.

Although the normal Windows Small Business Server backup gives you a sufficient backup, for any administrator who wants to provide themselves with more backup and recovery options, these Advanced backup tasks provide that flexibility.

Shrinking a Database

Sometimes databases grow too large. Generally the server is set to delete items and shrink on a regular basis. Note that shrinking the database is typically not needed and these steps should be followed only if the monitoring database is massively large and into the giga-bytes in space. On a small datafile, the size will be only shrunk in small amounts (less than 2%). On larger datafiles, the size should be more significant.

To shrink a database that has grown too large, perform the following steps:

1. Launch the SQL Server Management studio application by right-clicking its icon and selecting Run as Administrator.

2. Ensure the Connect to Server window is SERVER\SBSMONITORING and click Connect.

3. Expand databases and click the database called SBSMONITORING.

4. Right-click the name of the SBSMonitoring SQL instance and select Tasks, Shrink Database.

Additional Reporting Capabilities

In addition to the notifications and monitoring e-mails, there are native reporting tools built into the software that is part of the SBS 2008 suite that can be leveraged to provide reporting capabilities. Keep in mind that these additional reporting abilities are not true monitoring and reporting features for SBS 2008. They are not integrated into the monitoring console; however, they can assist in providing some missing information from the built-in monitoring and reporting tools.

> **CAUTION**
>
> Although these reports may assist in filling in some of the gaps of the native SBS 2008 monitoring tools, they are also large and unwieldy to review on a regular basis. Thus, it may be necessary to run these reports for a day or two, determine which ones add value, and then go back in and disable all the reports that merely take up space in your inbox.

WSUS Reports

The Windows Software Update Services console provides two separate reports that assist in augmenting the reporting from the SBS 2008 box itself. The first report that you can generate is the reporting of synchronization of patches, and the second is a report of patch status in the network.

To prepare an e-mail of the patch synchronization status, launch the WSUS mmc console. Click Start, All Programs, Administrative Tools, Microsoft Windows Software Update Services. Then, launch the management console. Click Options from the navigation pane on the left and then select E-mail Notifications (see Figure 16.17).

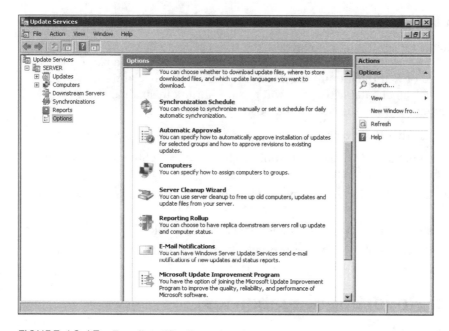

FIGURE 16.17   E-mail notifications.

In the E-Mail Notifications dialog that appears, enter the e-mail address you want to use for notification of synchronization. Then, enter in the e-mail address you want to use for the status reports (see Figure 16.18).

Next, set up the mail server information and the necessary authentication in order for the server to be able to relay messages out to the mail server. The WSUS notifications need to use an account to relay e-mail out, thus you need to enter in an appropriate username and password to provide credentials to the mail server. This allows the notification to be sent.

Best Practice—Authenticator User

Set up a user on the network that is an "authenticator user" that has standard rights, but also the ability to provide authentication for such needs. Once you have set up this user, test the settings to ensure that they can be used for e-mail authentication but do not have domain administrator rights. Using a standard user to provide authentication to the mail server ensures that domain administrator credentials are not saved on the server. Limit the use of domain credentials stored on the server.

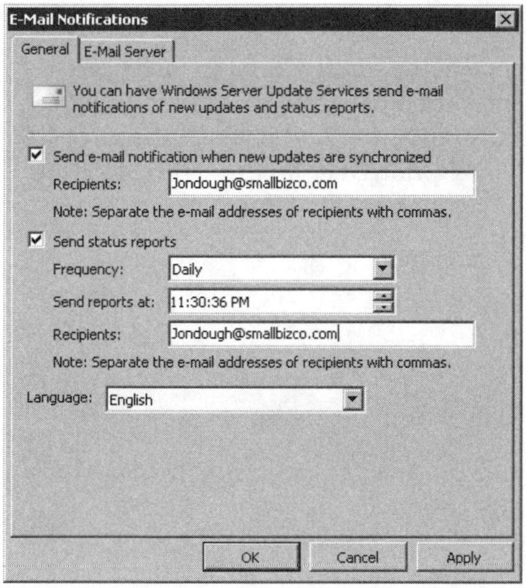

FIGURE 16.18   Setting up the options.

Ensure that you have tested the e-mail settings and can receive a test e-mail before closing out of this screen (see Figure 16.19).

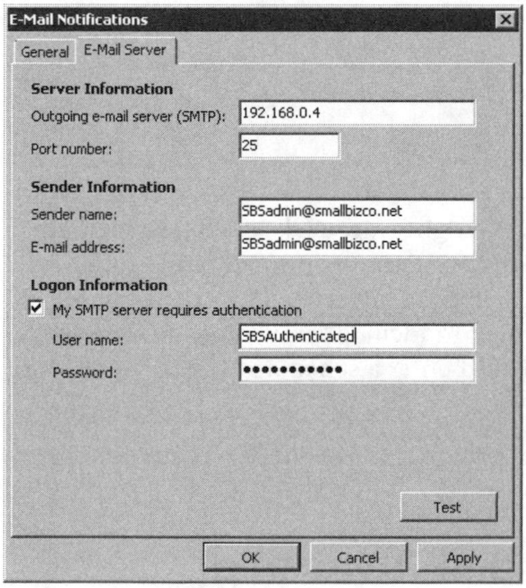

16

FIGURE 16.19   Setting up authenticated e-mail.

FSRM Reports

File Server Resource Manager may sound like a fancy name for disk quotas, but it can also be a source of additional information needed to monitor a network. To add reporting to the FSRM features, click Start, All Programs, Administrative Tools, File Server Resource Manager. On the righthand side of the console, click Options. Set up the settings for the mail server as needed (see Figure 16.20).

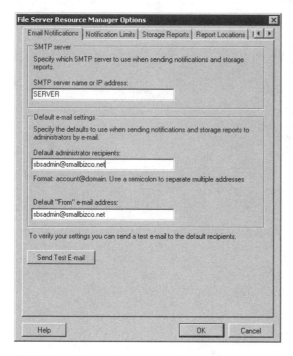

FIGURE 16.20   Setting up e-mail options in FSRM.

Now, click Storage Reports Management and, on the right side, click Schedule a New Task. On the Settings tab, click the Add button to add a drive to be monitored (see Figure 16.21). In this example, it is the main C: drive. Click the Delivery tab, click the box to add an e-mail and add addresses accordingly. (Remember to include semi-colons in between each e-mail address.) Then click the Schedule tab and enter a scheduled task time for this report to be generated.

At the scheduled time, you receive an e-mail that not only tracks the server storage use, but also gives you file growth indications of your server.

Troubleshooting Monitoring and Reporting

Most of the time, Monitoring and Reporting functions as needed. However, sometimes you might need to repair the installation of the Monitoring and Reporting elements. Due to the image-based installation of SBS 2008, this is done using the additional repair media

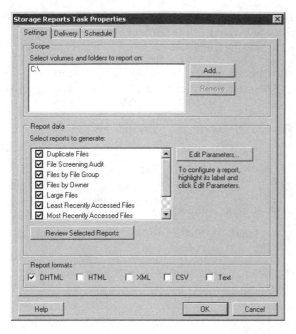

FIGURE 16.21   Setting up options in FSRM monitoring.

that is provided with SBS 2008. Referred to as the partner repair disk, to reinstall the console components, merely place that DVD into the drive tray, go to Start, Control Panel, and then go to the Program and Features applet in the control panel, choose Windows Small Business Server 2008, browse to the SBS.msi file on the CDROM, and reinstall the console, as seen in Figure 16.22.

FIGURE 16.22   Reinstalling the console.

If an alert was expected and it didn't get e-mailed, review the e-mail settings of the server, as the server might have an e-mail issue rather than a monitoring issue. Open up the Alert notification section and review the settings of default monitored events. An event may have inadvertently become unchecked. If there is an alert that is working on one server but not on the other, consider copying the working XML file to the non-working one. The service Windows SBS Monitor should be running on the server. The program files that should be reviewed to ensure they are intact are located in the folder C:\Program Files\Windows Small Business Server\Bin\DataCollectorSvc.exe.

The XML file format can be easily checked by browsing to c:\Program Files\Windows Small Business Server\Data\Monitoring and comparing the files to a working server. The following files should be in that subdirectory:

▶ **ClientDataCollectionRules.xml**—This file scans the workstations for antivirus, firewall, and other security rules.

▶ **SBSAlertDefinitions.xml**—This is the XML file for the default alerts that come preconfigured on the server.

▶ **SBSDataCollectionRules.xml**—A small placeholder file for WMITestCollection.

▶ **ServerDataCollectionRules.xml**—A small file that monitors for free drive space on the drives.

In this folder are additional folders named ExternalAlerts, Images, and Transformer. Underneath the Transformer folder should be additional report templates and XML configuration files. These include the following:

▶ **AlertEvent.html**—Basic formatting template.

▶ **AlertEventText.xml**—XML format template for alerting for events.

▶ **AlertFreeSpace.html**—Basic formatting template for free space issues.

▶ **AlertFreeSpaceText.xml**—XML format template for space issues.

▶ **AlertFSE.html**—Basic formatting template for Forefront license expiration.

▶ **AlertFSELicense.html**—Basic formatting template for Forefront.

▶ **AlertFSELicense2.html**—Basic formatting template for Forefront.

▶ **AlertFSCLicense2Text.xml**—Alert regarding the upcoming expiration of Forefront.

▶ **AlertFSCLicenseText.xml**—Alert regarding expiration of Forefront.

▶ **AlertFSCText.xml**—Alert regarding updating issues.

▶ **AlertLicensingEvent.html**—Basic formatting template.

▶ **AlertLicensingEventText.xml**—Alert regarding licensing (note that it appears that these alerts no longer are enforced).

▶ **AlertServices.html**—Basic formatting template.

▶ **AlertServicesText.xml**—Alert regarding stopped services.

▶ **ReportStandardHTMLTransformer.html**—Basic format for the reports.

Last but not least, ensure that the SBSMonitoring SQL instance is enabled and running and that the SBSMonitor service is running. If these are not functioning, the monitoring will be impacted as well.

Another way to generate a notification of an event from the log file that you want to track is to find the event in the Event viewer, and on the right pane of the Event Viewer, click Attach Task. Click Start, All Programs, Administrative Tools, Event Viewer. Find the event you want to track in the Windows logs of Application, Security, or System. Click the specific event you want to receive e-mail notifications for. On the right side of the Event Viewer, click Attach Task. On the first tab of the Create Basic Task Wizard, customize the name of the event if you wish. Click Next. The next part of the wizard is predefined to select the Event Log, the Source, and the Event ID. Click Next.

In the next part of the wizard, choose Send an E-Mail and click Next. Set up the e-mail address to which you want to send an e-mail and then set up the SMTP server. In the sample included earlier in the chapter, you found Event 6008, which indicates an unexpected shut down of the server.

You need to enter a "from" that is an authenticated user on the system. Enter the "to" as any recipient you wish to send the alert to, along with the appropriate subject line and text for the event. Click Next to continue.

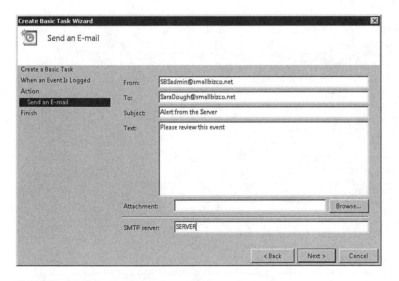

FIGURE 16.23   Setting up alerts from Event Viewer.

Review the settings you have chosen and click Open the Properties Dialog for This Task When I Click Finish. Now adjust the user settings for certain tasks, such as configuring it to run without the user logging in. When selecting this option, consider that this means that credentials need to be saved on the server. Although this presents its own security issues, the need to be alerted of unusual and unplanned events means this is a risk many will accept as reasonable in this circumstance.

Best Practices Analyzer

When monitoring a server using the native monitoring and reporting tools, don't overlook the Windows Small Business Server 2008 Best Practices tool (see Figure 16.24). The SBS 2008 Best Practices Analyzer is available for download from the Microsoft download site and can be installed and run on the server. Using this tool on a regular and scheduled basis ensures that you are able to proactively monitor the health and condition of the server. It runs a predefined checking of rules against the server to ensure that the server is set up appropriately. The rule sets are updated on a regular basis and, after the tool is installed on the server, it automatically checks for updates before you run the tool each time.

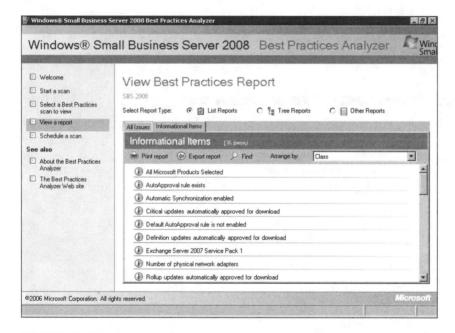

FIGURE 16.24   Best Practices Analyzer.

Using this tool, you can even schedule it to run itself on a regular basis. To do so and, optionally, specify the output to a file name, perform the following steps:

1. Click Start, Administrative Tools, Task Scheduler.

2. Click Action and then Create Task. Customize the name of the task, such as "SBSBPA," and then select the administrative user to run the task as. This gives the task the ability to run without the server being fully logged in.

3. Select Run Whether User Is Logged On or Not and then click Run With Highest Privileges.

4. Next, click the Actions tab and click the New button.

5. Click Start a Program and specify c:\program files (x86)\sbsbpa\bpacmd.exe (the default location). To the command, add the additional arguments that allow it to be placed in a file location. To do this, add arguments: -dat "bpaout.xml". Ensure that you have entered Start in c:\program files (x86)\sbsbpa (notice no quotes for this one) and finally click OK.

6. When you complete setting up the task, you need to specify the user's password when prompted.

7. To test that the command works, right-click the scheduled task in the task scheduler to run the task to verify it works. You should see the bpaout files created in the c:\program files (x86)\sbsbpa directory.

Third-Party Monitoring Solutions

Should you decide that you would like to consolidate reporting amongst many SBS 2008 servers, or other disparate ones, a third party monitoring solution is perhaps a wise investment. There are various tools in the managed services offerings that will allow such a rollup possibility. None of these solutions are without cost and more importantly none are without impact to the resources on the server and may need to be on a member server in order to not take resources from the Small Business Server itself. When setting up Small Business Server 2008 the investment in either a third party management tool or customizing the monitoring is a mandatory step. Do not overlook the importance of this step. Failure to monitor and watch for unexpected reboots, hardware issues and other key elements of the server may be very costly to a small firm. Thus take the time to investigate and install the monitoring tool that is right for the needs of the firm.

You might want the monitoring to combine all the servers and the workstations of all the networks you support into one roll-up report like the one used by managed service providers. Or you might want monitoring to be complete for each specific network and provide additional features such as community resources and solution sharing.

Select a monitoring solution based on the needs of the servers you control.

Summary

Monitoring a server is one of the most proactive things you can do. Customize and consider third-party solutions to proactively monitor the health of the server. Many issues can be proactively caught and fixed long before it causes undue hardship to a network. From alerting you to predictive disk failures, to alerting you when the server reboots or the backup fails, monitoring provides a network administrator with the capability to manage the network and provide the needed security and stability that a small firm needs. Tailor the reporting and monitoring to alert you to those key items that identify the health of the network. A backup failure is a critical event to be tracked and investigated. An unexpected reboot of the server should be reviewed. Follow up on these events to ensure that the firm is not impacted by these issues.

16

Best Practice Summary

▶ **Daily Reports**—Edit the Detailed Network Report to be sent daily. This report provides more detail and is a more useful monitoring report.

▶ **Custom Alerts**—Build custom alerts to track unexpected shutdowns and backup failures. Customizing those key items that need to be tracked will help you keep the server healthy and protected.

▶ **Authenticator User**—Build a special user account to use in various consoles to provide e-mail authentication. Do not use the Domain Administrator account and save it in consoles.

CHAPTER 17

Managing Server and Workstation Security

A lot has changed in security since the release of the previous version of SBS. During the intervening five years, Microsoft took some time off to revamp their development process to make "secure by default" the standard and eliminate the buffer overflow. SBS 2003 was built with Remote Access Server (RRAS) and the premium version had Internet Security and Acceleration Server (ISA). In SBS 2008, Microsoft takes a different approach to security. The individual components of SBS are in their secure by default state, but the only included firewall is the Windows firewall, and it isn't really designed to handle all of the server security needs of SBS 2008. For the first time, the security of SBS 2008 will be dependent upon your choice of external firewall.

In this chapter, we'll look at the default security settings in SBS 2008 and how you modify those for your environment, and mention along the way things to consider when making your external firewall purchase.

The Benefits and Pitfalls of a Single Integrated Server

SBS 2008 is a fantastic bargain for the small business. It's powerful, too. When a small business is ready to move from a workstation-only environment (known as peer-to-peer) to a server environment, the obvious choice is Small Business Server (SBS). A standard Windows server nets the small business little more than a new filing cabinet, whereas SBS opens up a whole new world of high-tech computing to rival the largest enterprise.

Integrating Windows 2008, IIS 7, SharePoint Services 3.0, Exchange 2007, plus the unique SBS features—fax server, health monitoring, and Remote Web Workplace—in a single box is unquestionably a boon to the small business. But in order to make all of these servers function together on a single piece of hardware, SBS walks the fine line between function and security. In some areas, different security choices have been made in order to provide functionality. Choosing security is always like walking a line. The difficult part is choosing where to place the line you're going to walk.

The owner or consultant assigned a Small Business Server needs to be aware of what the security settings are in SBS so they can be certain that it meets the requirements and desire for security of the business and the regulations to which it is subject.

Covering the Basics

The basics of network security are the same for SBS 2008 as they are for any network environment. Best practices for physical, file, share, and password security have grown and changed over the years, but only incrementally. If you are already familiar with how to set security for files and shares and set a password policy in Windows server, then you will already understand how to do this in SBS 2008. However, there are some handy time-saving tools available in SBS 2008 that you will want to learn how to use.

Physical Security

The need for physical security has been present since someone tripped over the power cord on the first server and brought down the network. The reason for physical security hasn't changed either. If people can lay their hands on the server, they can do damage to it. Only trusted knowledgeable staff should have physical access to the server. A server and all the networking components that go with it, like a router to the Internet, switches, punch panel, and so on, should all be behind a locked door. If your office doesn't have a room appropriate for a server, you will need to purchase a locking server cabinet into which all of the previously mentioned components of your network can be installed.

Never think that server theft or damage won't happen to you. Ask around the office and among your peers, and you will be told the sad tale of a stolen or destroyed server. Unfortunately, it is common. Fortunately, protecting yourself against this disaster is not difficult.

In addition to being physically secure, computer equipment needs to be kept cool. The room you choose needs to be well ventilated and probably air conditioned. It should be kept in the 65–75 F degree range.

Default Shares

Upon installation of SBS 2008, there are three shared folders: Public, RedirectedFolders, and UserShares. An additional folder is created for each user in the UserShares folder. Table 17.1 shows the default permissions and security settings for each shared folder and subfolder.

TABLE 17.1   Default Shares and Permissions

Share Name and Location	Share Permission	Security	Purpose
Public C:\Users\Public	Everyone	Everyone—Read, Read & execute, List folder contents. Creator Owner—All Special Permissions. Batch, Interactive, and Service applied to Subfolders and Files Only—All special permissions except Full Control, Change permissions, and Take ownership. Batch, Interactive, and Service applied to this folder only— Special permissions of Traverse folder, List folder, Read attributes, Read extended attributes, Create files, Create folders/Write data, Create folders/append data, Read permissions. System, Administrators—Full control.	Location for users to store files to be shared with everyone in the company.
RedirectedFolders C:\Users\FolderRedirections	Everyone	System, Domain Administrators— Full control. Domain Users—Special Permissions: Allow Traverse Folder, List Folder, Read attributes, Read extended attributes, Read.	This folder will contain sub-folders for individual users' redirected folders, including Desktop, Documents, and Start Menu.
UserShares C:\Users\Shares	Everyone	System—Full Control. Domain Users—Special Permissions: Allow Traverse Folder, List Folder, Read attributes, Read extended attributes, Read.	This folder holds individual user folders.

17

TABLE 17.1   Default Shares and Permissions

Share Name and Location	Share Permission	Security	Purpose
Individual User Folder C:\Users\Shares\jond ough	Not Shared	Jonathon Dough—Full Control. Administrators, System—Full control (inherited).	This folder is where individual users will store their private files.

Passwords

A good password policy is important to securing all network resources. In previous versions of SBS, administrators were left with the choice of implementing password policies, whereas in SBS 2008, a password policy is enabled by default.

The default password policy for the domain is defined in Group Policy. Specifically, the password policy is contained within the Default Domain Policy (see Table 17.2).

TABLE 17.2   Default Domain Policy, Password Policy

Policy	Setting
Enforce password history	24 passwords remembered
Maximum password age	180 days
Minimum password age	2 days
Minimum password length	8 characters
Password must meet complexity requirements	Enabled
Store passwords using reversible encryption	Disabled
Account lockout threshold	0 invalid logon attempts

This table shows the default settings for the password policy section of the Default Domain policy. The policy indicates that the password must meet complexity requirements. By this, it means that the password must contain at least three of the following four types of characters: numbers, uppercase letters, lowercase letters, or symbols. In total, the default password policy says that a password must be unique to the previous 24 passwords you have used. It must be at least eight characters long, with those characters having at least three of four required character types. The user must change his or her password twice per year.

The account lockout threshold policy is also significant. The setting of zero invalid logon attempts means that an account in the domain will never be locked out. A would-be intruder can try, try, and try a thousand times, and the account will never be locked. Each business should review the default domain password and account lockout policy to determine if it is sufficiently secure for their needs.

Although SBS 2008 has taken a giant step forward in enforcement of password policies, many businesses will need to make changes to the password policy. A typical business may want to enforce a password change every 90 days and require that a user account become locked out after five attempts.

To make this change, open the Group Policy Management MMC. Expand Forest, Domains, smallbizco.local, and then Group Policy Objects. Right-click Default Domain Policy and select Edit to open the Group Policy Management Editor. As shown in Figure 17.1, expand Computer Configuration, Policies, Windows Settings, Security Settings, Account Policies, and select Password Policy to edit the password policy.

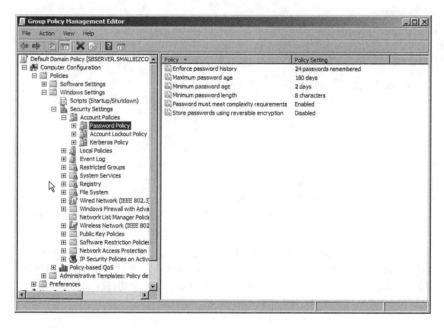

FIGURE 17.1   Use Group Policy Management Editor to edit the password and account lockout policies.

To change how often users are required to change their password, right-click on Maximum Password Age and choose Properties. In the Password Will Expire In: box, change 180 to 90 and press OK.

To change the account lockout threshold policy so that logon will be denied after five failed attempts, in the lefthand pane, select Account Lockout Policy, and in the right pane, right-click on Account Lockout Threshold and choose Properties. In the Invalid Logon Attempts box, change 0 to 5 and click OK. A box will now pop up, suggesting other settings for your account lockout policy. As shown in Figure 17.2, these are Account Lockout Duration 30 Minutes and Reset Account Lockout Counter after 30 Minutes. Click OK to accept these suggestions.

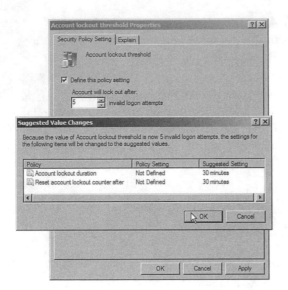

FIGURE 17.2   When you set an account lockout policy, you will be offered suggestions for other policy additions.

You have now set the password policy and account lockout policy for more restrictive settings. This change to group policy will take effect on the next scheduled group policy refresh. If you would like them to take effect immediately, open a command prompt, type **gpupdate /force**, and press Enter. This immediately pushes a group policy update to all computers.

The password policy can also be changed through the SBS Console. Making the change in the Console also edits the group policy. To change the password policy, move to the Users and Group navigation tab. In the Tasks pane, click Change Password Policies to open the Change Password Policies window. Here you have the ability to change the frequency of password expiration and change the password requirements.

Shared Folders

The Public folder brings back a concept from SBS 2000. In SBS 2000, a default shared folder was created called Company. All users had access to this folder by default. SBS 2008 resurrects this concept with the Public folder. By default, there are several folders created under Public: Public Documents, Public Downloads, Public Music, Public Pictures, and Public Videos. These folders are only present as sample subfolders. Your organization needs to create the subfolders that it requires. All are given the Everyone permission.

Pre-Windows 2003, the group everyone was granted anonymous logon. This meant that literally everyone in the world had access to a folder with Everyone in the permissions list. But with the release of Windows 2003, Microsoft changed the group Everyone and removed the anonymous access. This effectively changed the group Everyone, to mean everyone that has authenticated to your server, not everyone in the world.

If you have been in the IT industry long enough, the group Everyone probably still sends chills down your spine. If so, you may want to change permissions on the Public folder from Everyone to Domain Users or Authenticated Users.

Even if you have decided to change the permission level of the Public folder, this does not resolve the perception problem that a folder called Public may present to the user. The end user can be forgiven for not understanding the difference between "Public" meaning the general public and "Public" meaning everyone in the company.

Because the Public folder is a throwback to the SBS 2000 Company folder, a solution to end user confusion would be to create a Company folder and direct users to save their company data in this folder. Individual subfolders within the Company folder can then be further secured to allow access to only specific individuals or groups within the company. Let's look at how this is done.

Creating a Share Using the Add a New Shared Folder Wizard

One of the new wizards in SBS 2008 is called Add a New Shared Folder. This isn't one of those shining moments of brilliance that some of the SBS wizards have become famous for; it's not one of those that will save you hours of time. It is, however, thorough.

Best Practice—Naming Convention for New Folders

Notice that when we create a new folder, we do not follow the naming convention set forth by Microsoft, of Windows SBS <foldername>. This is intentional.

As a best practice, we want to separate out the default items in SBS from the ones that we have created. This will help with support later in the life of the server. In doing this, by simple glance we know that we created the shared folder Company, and that it is not one of the default folders.

Follow these steps to complete to add a new shared folder:

1. Move to the Shared Folders and Web Sites main navigation tab and click the Add a New Shared Folder link in the Tasks pane. The Provision a Shared Folder wizard will open.

2. Click the Browse button next to the Location box to select a location for your Company folder.

3. In the Browse for Folder window, either select an existing folder or press the Make New Folder button and, when finished specifying the location, click OK. Your selected location should be visible in the Location box.

4. Click Next. The wizard now asks whether you want to change NTFS permissions. For this exercise, leave the radio button on No, Do Not Change NTFS Permissions.

5. Click Next. The correct Share protocol is selected on the Share Protocols page.

6. Click Next. Type a description for this folder that indicates what users should save to it.

7. Click Next. On the SMB Permissions section, select Users and Groups Have Custom Share Permissions. Click the Permissions button. Click the Add button in the Permissions for Company pop-up window. Type the name of the group you created earlier, SmallBizCo Employees, and click Check Names. Then click OK. Check the Full Control box to give SmallBizCo Employees permission to use this folder. Highlight the Everyone group and click the Remove button. Then click OK.

8. We are now back at the wizard. Press Next to advance to the Quota Policy page. For the purpose of this exercise, we will not set a quota.

9. Click Next. You have now advanced to the File Screen Policy page. For this example, we will not specify a File Screen. File Screen Policies are discussed later in this chapter.

10. Click Next on the DFS Namespace Publishing screen.

11. Click Next. Review the settings for errors and click Create. When the folder has been created, click Close. The new Company folder will now be listed on the Shared Folders tab of the Windows SBS Console.

Now that we have created a folder called Company, for organizational and security purposes, we want to create subfolders.

1. Press Start, Computer and double-click the drive letter in which you created your Company folder.

2. Double-click the Company folder. Right-click in the white space in the right pane and choose New to create a new folder.

3. Name this folder Accounting. Repeat the adding of folders two more times to create a Documents folder and a Photos folder. Each of those folders inherits the permissions of the Company folder.

Although we've configured all users to be able to access files and folders in the Company folder, we want to restrict the Accounting folder to only members of that department. Minimize this Window and go back to the Windows SBS Console; create a security group called SmallBizCo Accounting and place the members of your accounting department into this security group. In the description of the group, be sure to indicate what this group is used for.

In the example, the SmallBizCo Accounting security group has the description People with Access to Accounting Data.

1. Right-click the Accounting folder and choose Properties. Move to the Security tab and click the Edit button. After you have done that, come back to the Accounting folder, right-click it, and select Properties.

2. Click the Advanced button and, on the Advanced Security Setting windows, click the Edit button.

3. Uncheck the Include Inheritable Permissions from This Object's Parent. In the Windows Security pop-up, select Copy. This keeps the permissions on the folder until we are ready to change them, while giving us the ability to edit the permissions. Click OK twice.

4. You are now back on the Security tab; click the Edit button. The top box on this page shows the default security settings for this folder. We want to modify those so that only our Accounting Security group has access to the folder.

5. Click the Add button. Then type the name of the accounting security group, SmallBizCo Accounting. Click Check Names and then click OK.

6. Check the Full Control Allow box. Highlight the other groups and individuals that may have access to this folder, and click Remove until the SmallBizCo Accounting group is the only one left with permission to the folder (see Figure 17.3).

7. Click OK. Click OK one more time to finish.

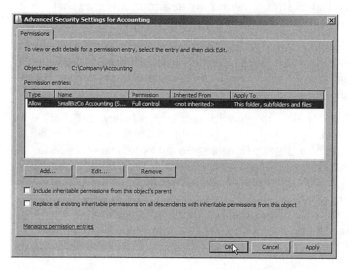

FIGURE 17.3   When making a new folder, copy existing permissions; then remove the ones that aren't required.

In this exercise, we have created a new folder called Company and sub-folders within. We then further secured the Accounting folder to restrict access to only the accounting department.

Creating a Share Without Using the Wizard

To create a share without using the wizard, press Start, Computer. Double-click the drive on which you would like to create the share. Right-click anywhere in the white space of the right pane and select New, Folder. Name this folder SmallBizCo.

Right-click the SmallBizCo folder and choose Share. This opens the File Sharing dialog box. Click the down arrow, select people or groups to add, and then click Share. For our example, choose the Everyone group and click Add. Select Everyone in the list, click the down arrow in the Permission Level column, and select Co-Owner. Click Share. When the share has been created, click Done. You will return to the folder directory list.

We have just created a share and allowed everyone access to it. Sub-folders and permissions for those can be created as in the previous section.

Folder Redirection

Folder redirection is a common security feature that administrators enable. Try as we might to train users to save all important corporate data to the server, it doesn't always happen. Users like the convenience of storing files in their Documents folder, or even on the desktop. The occurrence seems to be increasing as more and more users have laptop computers rather than fixed desktop computers. Mobility makes it difficult to always store data on the server, and so administrators struggle with how to capture the data that has been stored in common locations on the computer.

In folder redirection, user-specific folders are redirected to the server for backup. There's nothing like an angry user who just lost the contents of his or her Documents folder, or a failed hard drive on an office computer, to remind you of the need to capture data inadvertently saved to the local computer.

Like password policy, folder redirection is controlled through Group Policy and enabled by default. The SBS Console allows editing of the Folder Redirection Group Policy. To view or change the folder redirection settings in the SBS Console, move to the Share Folders and Web Sites navigation tab. In the Tasks pane, select Redirect Folders for User Accounts to the Server; the Folder Redirection Properties box will open. By default, Desktop and Documents are selected. There are two other options not selected that include the Start menu and Favorites. Move to the User Accounts menu item. Next to each name is a checkbox. For each user, the box must be checked to indicate that you want to enable folder redirection for this user. Check the box for any user you want to enable folder redirection and press OK.

There are a couple of things to know about folder redirection. The folders that are being redirected are components of the user's profile. The user profile is held on the PC they log in to. A user profile is made up of many folders, as shown in Figure 17.4. In the Group Policy for folder direction, each of these folders can be selected for folder redirection. If the administrator would like to also redirect any of these additional folders, the Group Policy needs to be edited directly. It should also be noted that a local cached copy of the folder is retained on the local computer so a traveling laptop will not be without its files when it leaves the office.

To edit the Small Business Server Folder Redirection policy, open the Group Policy Management MMC, expand Forest, Domains, smallbizco.local, Group Policy Objects, and select the Small Business Server Folder Redirection policy. In the right pane on the Scope tab, notice how this policy is applied. As can be seen in Figure 17.5, it is linked to the SBSUsers group, but it is filtered by members of the Windows SBS folder Redirection Accounts group. This means that while the policy is applied to the SBSUsers group, it is only in effect for members of the security group Windows SBS Folder Redirection Accounts. In the SBS Console, when you check the box to indicate which users will have folder direction enabled, what happens behind the scene is that the user is added to the Windows SBS Folder Redirection Accounts group.

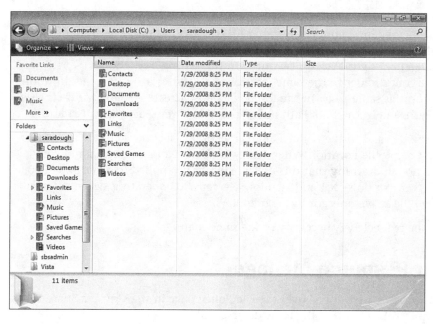

FIGURE 17.4   A user profile is made up of several folders, only three of which are available for folder redirection in the SBS Console.

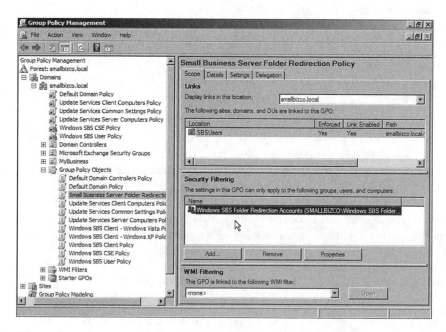

FIGURE 17.5   The Folder Redirection policy is enabled only for members of the Windows SBS Folder Redirection Accounts group. The policy uses security filtering to accomplish this.

A common request from users who move from one computer to another, whether because of job change or replacement computer, is to have their Favorites move with them. Using Group Policy, we can also select to have the user's Favorites folder redirected to the server. Under Folder Redirection, right-click on Favorites. In the Setting box, choose Basic–Redirect everyone's folder to the same location. This causes a Target folder location section to appear on this same page. In the top box, choose Create a Folder for Each User Under the Root Path, and in the Root Path box, type **sbserver****Redirectedfolders.**

Move to the Setting tab, and in the Policy Removal section, select the Redirect the Folder Back to the Local Userprofile Location When Policy Is Removed radio button and click OK. You receive a pop-up warning that this policy will not be applied to Windows 2000, Windows 2000 Server, Windows XP, and Windows Server 2003 operating systems. Press OK. This policy will be active only for Vista computers.

Other folders can be redirected as necessary in the same manner.

File Server Resource Manager

You probably noticed that we skipped over the File Policy page in the Create a Share Using the Wizard example. This is because the topic deserves full coverage. The source of the File Policy page of the Shared Folder wizard is the File Server Resource Manager (FSRM). Introduced in Windows 2003 R2, it is a powerful tool that enables the administrator to control what type of files are to be stored in which folder, set quotas, identify duplicate files, identify large files, and run regularly scheduled reports on the data management settings you have chosen. Data management has always been a serious problem in all networks. In FSRM, there is now a tool that enables you to gain control over this problem and make it more efficient for all users to find and store data.

How does this relate to server security? Because we store and secure data by folder, unless data is saved to the correct folder, we cannot be certain that the correct security restrictions have been applied. Managing data storage is a significant part of securing the data on your server.

Let's look at how this tool can be used to keep our server organized. To open FSRM, press Start, Administrative Tools, File Server Resource Manager. Expand the File Screening Management and select File Screens (see Figure 17.6). In the Action pane, click the Create File Screen link to open the Create File Screen window. Click the Browse button, and browse to the Company\Documents folder that you created earlier. In the middle of the page, you are presented with the choice of Derive Properties from This File Screen Template (Recommended) or Define Custom File Screen Properties. Press the arrow on the drop-down box to view the existing file screen templates. SmallBizCo only wants documents to be stored in the Company\Documents folder, so choose the Define Custom File Screen Properties radio button and click the Custom Properties button.

For this example, we use Active Screening to prevent users from saving anything but Office files into this folder. To do this, make sure that the Active Screening radio button is selected; then choose the file types to block, being careful to avoid selecting Office files.

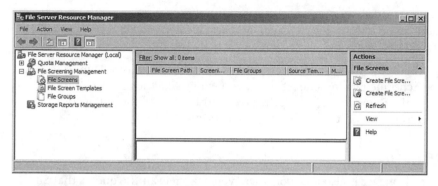

FIGURE 17.6   The Folder Redirection policy is enabled only for members of the Windows SBS Folder Redirection Accounts group. The policy uses security filtering to accomplish this.

We will also leave Text files and Temporary files unchecked so that users have the flexibility necessary for document storage. If you would like to see the definition of a file group in FSRM, highlight that group and click the Edit button. If you would like to create your own files group, click the Create button.

The remaining tabs on the File Screen Properties windows are optional settings that will alert the administrator in various ways when a user has attempted to save the wrong type of file into the folder. When you have finished, click OK to create the file screen. Then click Create. You are now presented with an opportunity to save this file screen as a template for later use on other folders. Choose whether to do so or not, and then click OK. If you do choose to create a template, be very descriptive so that it is obvious to anyone what the template does.

Best Practice—Create a File Screen for Each Shared Document Storage Folder

By creating a file screen for each shared document folder on the server, the administrator can finally prevent storage resources from being mismanaged. It may seem in the age of cheap abundant storage that what is stored where would be less of an issue than in the past, but exactly the opposite. A user will instead have the tendency to store unimportant, repetitive and sometimes even personal data. It's become too easy for users to plug in a camera and download all of the pictures or a music device and do the same.

By creating a file screen for each share, the IT manager finally has the tool necessary to help the business owner enforce good data habits.

Storage Reports Management

Storage Reports Manager is every administrator's dream. Here you can configure reports to run on a schedule to provide you with information on the files stored within folders on the server. Do we have duplicate files stored? Are the file screens that we set up sufficient? Is anyone storing very large files, and if so, where? Is our sensitive data stored in secured locations? If you have loaded your server with data from a previous server, it's likely that your data could use an organizational overhaul, and Storage Reports Manager is just the tool to use.

To create a report that locates duplicate files, uncheck all the boxes except Duplicate Files. Then move to the Schedule tab and choose when you would like the report to run and how frequently. On the Delivery tab, check the box Send Reports to the Following Administrators to have the report e-mailed to you each time it runs.

Quota Management

File Server Resource Manager is also the tool where you can view all the quotas that SBS sets up by default and modify them. You can also create your own quotas as necessary. The quota options are much more advanced than they were in SBS 2003. In SBS 2003, quotas were only applied to a volume, but in SBS 2003 R2 and forward, they are applied per folder and per user, making them much more powerful and functional. Additionally, quota usage can be reported for active monitoring of the server resources.

Expand Quota Management and select Quotas. In the center pane, you will see a list of folders that have quotas applied along with summary information on the % Used, Limit, and Quota type. Clicking an item in the center pane causes the bottom of the center pane to populate with more details about the quota status, including available space on the drive in which the folder is located.

To edit a quota select a folder, right-click it, and choose edit quota properties. In the example, you use Users\Shares\jondough. Notice that user jondough has a default space limit of 2GB on the users\shares folder. It is a hard quota, which means he will be not allowed to exceed 2GB of file storage in that folder. A warning is set up at 85% of quota. Both the administrator and Jon will be e-mailed when he is within 85% of reaching his quota. An event will also be written to the event log. This is the default quota configuration for all users in the domain.

The administrator could also create a soft quota. A soft quota is created when you choose to only warn and not prevent the user from working when the quota is exceeded.

Using Quota Management, you can configure custom quotas for each folder based on user or security group. Additional FSRM reports can report on quota usage.

Best Practice—Move Shared Folders off the OS Drive

You will notice that SBS 2008 installs everything to the C: drive by default. For security and performance reasons, as a best practice, shared drives should be moved to another drive on your server.

Consult Chapter 3, "Installing and Configuring SBS 2008," for instructions on how to perform this important task.

Default Security Groups

Security groups are the bundling together of groups of users with the same security needs. Using security groups makes the consistent application of security much easier to manage. Security groups are found in the Windows SBS Console under the Users and Groups main navigation tab. There are 10 security groups set up in SBS 2008, by default. The name of each starts with the words Windows SBS. This will help you keep track of which security groups are the default groups.

In managing a secure environment, it is important to know where you are starting from and to track how far you have moved from the starting point. For your reference, Table 17.3 is a list of the default security groups and their membership.

TABLE 17.3   Default Security Groups and Membership

Security Group	Members
Windows SBS Remote Web Workplace Users	Server Admin and any additional administrators. Any users created using the Add Users wizard.
Windows SBS Fax Users	Server Admin and any additional administrators. Any users created using the Add Users wizard.
Windows SBS Fax Administrators	Server Admin and any additional administrators.
Windows SBS Folder Redirection Accounts	Empty.
Windows SBS Virtual Private Network Users	Server Admin and any additional administrators.
Windows SBS SharePoint_VisitorsGroup	Empty.
Windows SBS SharePoint_MembersGroup	Any users created using the Add Users wizard.
Windows SBS SharePoint_OwnersGroup	Server Admin and any additional administrators.
Windows SBS Link Users	Server Admin and any additional administrators. Any users created using the Add Users wizard.
Windows SBS Admin Tools Group	Server Admin and any additional administrators.

17

Best Practice—Naming Convention for Security Groups

The default security groups all begin with the words Windows SBS, as in Windows SBS Fax Users. As you create additional security groups, you should not use this same naming convention. Rather, invent your own to indicate that these are custom security groups that you have created. For example, SmallBizCo Accounting Files would be an appropriate name for the security group for users that have access to the firms' accounting files.

In the Windows SBS Console on the Users and Groups main navigation tab, move to the Groups sub-navigation tab and press the Add a New Group link in the Tasks pane. This launches the Add a New Group wizard. Click Next. As Figure 17.7 shows, you type in a group name and description, and select the Security Group radio button. Pause here for a moment to notice a new feature in SBS 2008—the ability to e-mail enable a security group. Just under the Security Group description, there is a checkbox to Enable This Security Group to Receive E-Mail.

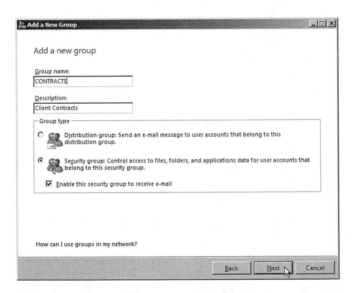

FIGURE 17.7   Adding a new security group.

This begs the question, why would you want to e-mail enable a security group? The answer is you would do so for archival purposes. When you create a distribution group, e-mail is sent to each member. When you e-mail enable a security group, e-mail is sent to each member and an archive copy is deposited into a SharePoint document library. In this manner, you can create a single group and use it to provide permission to access secure network folders, distribute e-mail, and archive those messages. The archived messages are stored in the sub-site called Archived E-Mails. Each e-mail-enabled security group that you've chosen to archive will have a document library in this sub-site. Permission for this library is pre-set to Contribute, which gives members of the security group view, add, update, and delete capability. This permission level can be edited to suit the specific archiving needs of the group. For more information about SharePoint, see Chapter 7, "SharePoint and Companyweb."

Continuing with the security group creation process, click Next. In the next window, you select the members for this group. Select each member that you want to add from the list on the left and press Add. When finished selecting group members, press Add Group. Press Finish on the final page.

User Roles

In SBS 2008, a new template is available called user roles. User roles enable you to define group memberships, remote access permission, disk and e-mail quotas, sharepoint group membership, and local address. When you assign a user to a role, he or she automatically gets the settings and permissions assigned to that role. User roles are a concept unique to SBS 2008. More powerful than Active Directory templates, a user role encompasses settings across several different security groups at once.

There are three user roles created by default in SBS 2008: Standard User, Standard User with Administration Tools, and Network Administrator. These roles can be edited. However, editing the default roles is not recommended. Rather than editing the permissions assigned by these roles, it is more appropriate to create roles that work for your company and assign users to those roles. The default roles and the permissions assigned to each are shown in Table 17.4.

TABLE 17.4   Default User Roles and Assigned Permissions

User Role	Permissions
Standard User	Access to Shared Folders, Printers, Faxes, E-mail, OWA, RWW, SharePoint, and the Internet. Member of Windows SBS Fax Users, Windowss SBS Link Users, Windows SBS Remote Web Workplace Users, and Windows SBS SharePoint_MembershipGroup security groups.

TABLE 17.4   Default User Roles and Assigned Permissions

User Role	Permissions
Standard User with Administrator Tools	Permissions of Standard User plus can view the Administration links in RWW and the Desktop gadget links. However, they must know the networking administration username and password to use any of the links. Member of Windows SBS Admin Tools, Windows SBS Administrators, Windows SBS Fax Users, Windows SBS Link Users, Windows SBS Remote Web Workplace Users, and Windows SBS SharePoint_MembersGroup groups.
Network Administrator	Unrestricted system access. Member of Domain Admins, Enterprise Admin, Schema Admins, Windows SBS Admin Tools Group, Windows SBS Administrators, Windows SBS Fax Administrators, Windows SBS Fax Users, Windows SBS Link Users, Windows SBS Remote Web Workplace User, Windows SBS SharePoint_OwnersGroup, and Windows SBS Virtual Private Network Users groups.

Creating and Editing User Roles

To create a new role, on the Users and Groups main navigation tab, in the User Roles sub-tab, on the Tasks pane, click Add a New User Role. In this example, we'll create a user role called Restricted Users as seen in Figure 17.8. Restricted User is the role at SmallBizCo that only needs limited access to network resources to do their job.

In the User Role Name box, type `Restricted User`. In the Description box, type a description for the group as Limited Use of Network Resources. Make sure the box for the user role appears as an option in the Add New User Account wizard and in the Add Multiple New User Accounts wizard, and click Next.

On the Choose User Role Permissions (Group Membership) page and throughout this wizard, you will see the permissions that are set for the standard user. By removing group membership and unchecking boxes, you are able to easily create the restricted user role. On this page, highlight Windows SBS Fax Users and click the Remove button. Do the same for Windows SBS Remote Web Workplace Users and Windows SBS Link Users. On the next page, uncheck the Outlook Web Access box. In the Enforce mailbox quota section, reduce the mailbox quota size to the minimum 1GB; then click Next. Because we have removed membership from remote access security groups, on the Choose Remote Access for This User Role page, both remote access options should be unchecked. Click Next. On this page, set the quota to the minimum allowed, 1GB, and check the Enable Folder Redirection to the Server box. Set the user folder redirection quota to the minimum allowed 1GB. Click Add User Role; then click Finish.

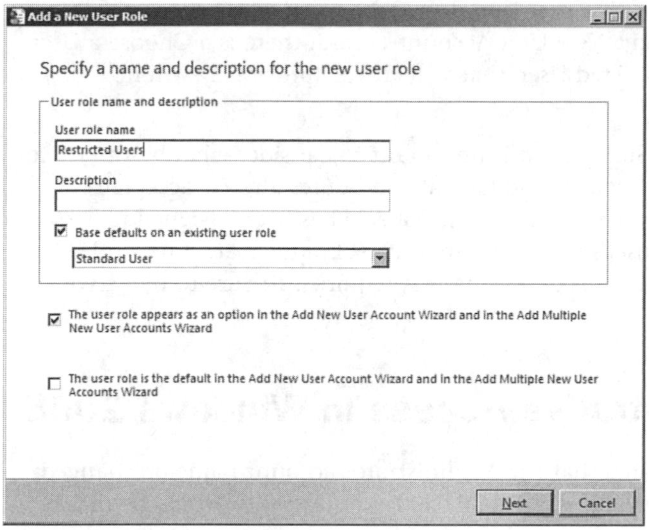

FIGURE 17.8   Creating a new user role.

A role can be applied to a user in one of two ways. You can assign a role to an existing user or to groups of users, or you also have an opportunity to assign a user to a role while adding a new user.

If a user already exists on your network, and you would like to apply a role to that user, move to the Users sub tab; on the Tasks pane, select Change User Role for User Accounts. This opens the Change a User Role wizard.

> **CAUTION**
>
> Unlike when you assign an Active Directory user a user role, re-applying a user role will overwrite any existing group memberships that do not conform to the role.

Continuing with the example, select Restricted User, choose the Replace User Permissions or Settings radio button, and click Next. This replaces the user's current permissions and settings to match the role to which you are assigning them. Next, select the users to whom you want to apply this role. Click the Add button to add them to the right column and, when finished, click Change User Role. Click Finish. On the Users tab under the User Role column, you now see the users associated with the new role.

> **NOTE**
>
> An individual user's permissions can be altered after a role has been applied. It is possible for a user to be listed as having the Standard User role applied but have additional permissions.

The other way to associate a role with a user is to do so when you add a new user. At the bottom of the first page of the Add a New User Account wizard, there is a Choose a User Role drop-down list. The role, Restricted User, that you created previously will now be available for selection.

Because this is a new concept for SBS 2008, it is important to consider what best practice should be for this feature. For this, you should look at procedures already accepted for other types of active directory templates. That is, once a role has been assigned to a user, you should not directly edit that user's settings; rather, you should create a new role, assign the user to that role, and then make the changes required. Be sure to name your custom roles intuitively.

Changes to Administrative Access in Windows 2008

For years, best practices have dictated that the Administrator account name be changed. This was recommended so that the all-powerful SID 500 Administrator would be more difficult to locate. As always happens with security by obscurity measures, it was only difficult for the bad guys to obtain the name of the SID 500 account for a matter of seconds. In SBS 2003, changing the name of the Administrator account also caused problems with service pack installation. All of that has changed with the introduction of Windows 2008 and Microsoft's secure by default initiative.

In SBS 2008, the Administrator account is disabled by default. During installation, you are prompted to create an administrative-level account. This is to comply with the new Windows 2008 best practice of disabling the Administrator account. In addition, all accounts have User Account Control (UAC) enabled, even members of the administrator security groups (with the exception of the Administrator account).

> **NOTE**
>
> By default, the disabled Administrator account does not have a password and therefore cannot log in to the server even once the account is enabled. In order to log in to the server as the Administrator, you need to select Change Password from the log on menu and set a password. After setting this password, you will be able to log in.

UAC—User Account Control

UAC has certainly gained a lot of press since its introduction with Windows Vista. Some administrators appreciate the greater security that results, while others find it an annoyance in their day-to-day administration tasks. Truth be told, UAC is both a tremendous security feature of Windows 2008 and an annoyance, but the annoyance is minor when compared with the additional level of security UAC brings to the server.

What Does UAC Do?

There are several components of UAC. The one that most administrators are familiar with is Admin Approval Mode (AAM) or the box you have to click when you try to launch an application that requires administrative access. This prompt happens because an administrator now gets two security tokens. One token is for non-administrative tasks, and the other token is for administrative tasks. Things like system state changes, firewall, security policies, drivers, and software installations all require a higher level of access because they affect not just the administrator's personal use of the server, but either everyone's use of the server or the core networking function of the server. When the administrator launches into one of these tasks, they are asked to positively confirm that they want to use their administrator access token and affect the server core or all users with their actions.

You will notice that when AAM launches, it launches within a secure desktop—that is, everything else is grayed out. Everything else becomes background and cannot reach the prompt. This is another security feature of UAC, called Secure Desktop. Should a malware application attempt to make an administrator-level change to the server, the secure desktop will launch and the AAM prompt will appear on the screen, but the malware will not be able to reach it without the assistance of a person at the keyboard.

UAC also performs other protective functions on the server. You may be familiar with Application Virtualization features of UAC. Application virtualization allows non-UAC-compliant applications (those that need to write to protected areas of the operating system) to run on Windows 2008. This feature creates a virtual copy of the operating system folders for the non-compliant application to write to, thereby protecting the operating system from any changes that the application makes. However, in SBS 2008, this compatibility feature is not present. This is because SBS 2008 is running Windows 2008 64-bit edition in the background to accommodate Exchange 2007, and Windows 2008 64-bit edition does not contain this application compatibility feature. Why mention a feature that SBS doesn't have? Because you are running a 64-bit operating system, all the applications that you install will need to be UAC compliant. That is, the applications are going to have to only write data into allowed areas and do not have access to protected areas of the operating system.

Internet Explorer 7's (IE) Protected Mode is also an extension of UAC. Protected Mode is a required feature for safe browsing in the era of malware drive-by downloads. Applications on the server run with low privilege but IE runs with even fewer privileges than other applications. With protected mode on, which is the default with UAC enabled, malware is unable to infect the server because IE itself is running with so few privileges.

Auditing UAC

One of the on-going challenges for SBS environments is that often there is more than one person logging in as administrator and making changes to the system. Auditing UAC prompts can help you track which tools were used to make changes on your system and at what time. It won't tell you who was actually standing at the keyboard when the change was made, but it will help you narrow down the possibilities or help to jog someone's memory as to what they did at the server.

Auditing privilege use tells you when a process with elevated permissions was created or launched. When this happens, an event is written to the security event log. There are several items for which the audit policy, although triggered, does not write an event log entry. These were intentionally left out so as not to fill the log with a bunch of noise. One

17

of these is Backup of Files and Directories and Restore of Files and Directories. You can imagine how the log would fill if the backup triggered an event log for every file it touched!

To enable auditing, it is necessary to edit the local security policy. To edit the policy, click Start, Run. In the Open box, type secpol.msc and click OK to open the Local Security Policy editor. Expand Local Policies and click once on Audit Policy. In the righthand pane, double-click Audit privilege use. Check the Success box and click OK. As shown in Figure 17.9, Audit privilege use is the only policy that is audited. The security log will now show events for the category Sensitive Privilege Use each time the administrator elevates privilege on the server.

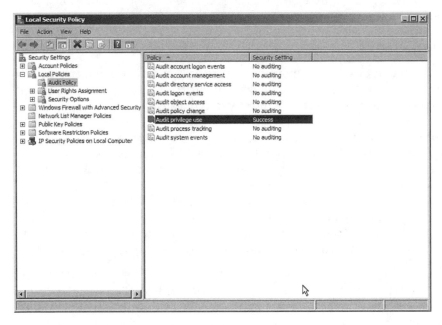

FIGURE 17.9   Auditing UAC privilege use will provide information about when and what changes were made to the server.

Changing UAC Behavior

UAC's behavior can be changed. The choices are On, Off, or Elevate Without Prompting. Up until now, we've been discussing On. On is the default and provides many benefits to server health and security, as we have shown. Because of the significant benefits and the intention of Microsoft to be secure by default, we will not discuss Off. It is self explanatory and not recommended. However, Elevate Without Prompting is an interesting option and may be appropriate in some circumstances.

Changing UAC behavior requires that you edit the local security policy. To edit the local security policy, click Start, Run, type secpol.msc, and click OK. Expand Local Policies and select Security Options. In the righthand pane, scroll down to the bottom of the page and double-click User Account Control: Behavior of the Elevation Prompt for Administrators in Admin Approval Mode. On the Local Security Setting tab, click the drop-down box to view the options, as shown in Figure 17.10. Prompt for Consent is the default. If you were to choose Elevate Without Prompting and click OK, the UAC prompt would no longer appear. However, the benefits of UAC, with the exception of one, would remain.

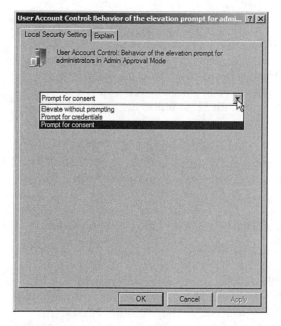

FIGURE 17.10   One of the UAC behaviors is Elevate Without Prompting, but it may not be the best option.

The setting Elevate Without Prompting is a temptation for most administrators. We don't want to be bothered to consent for everything we do, because obviously we are administrators. However, we need to remember that with Elevate Without Prompting, we have lost the secure desktop. Recall that the secure desktop is when the background grays out and only the consent prompt can be selected. Applications such as malware running on the server are unable to reach the secure desktop and elevate the privilege. By enabling Elevate Without Prompting, you will have opened the door for applications to elevate permissions on the server without your knowledge. Therefore, the option to Elevate Without Prompting should be used sparingly, if at all.

17

CAUTION

When performing significant changes to a server over multiple different console applications, it may become tiresome to continue to OK the consent of elevation prompts. Many administrators will turn off the prompt, intending to later turn it back on when they have completed the configuration. This leaves the chance open that you may forget to turn on the prompting level back to the default of Prompt for Consent, thus leaving open the possibility that another less-skilled administrator or worse, malware, could elevate privilege on the server and do damage.

Firewall Protection

The Windows Firewall is a new feature in Windows Server 2008, and it's turned on by default. The Advanced Security portion of the name of this firewall refers to the improvement in technology, enabling it to control both inbound and outbound access, and that IPSec policy management has been combined into its feature set.

It's a host-based firewall and should not be relied upon or confused with an edge firewall. A host-based firewall only controls access to and from itself, whereas an edge firewall protects access to and from the entire network. Every network should have both.

Windows Firewall with Advanced Security

The Windows Firewall controls both inbound and outbound access to and from the server. To view and configure the firewall, click Start, Administrative Tools, Windows Firewall with Advanced Security. Figure 17.11 shows the default configuration of the firewall, which the Windows Firewall service controls. This service must be running at all times. Applications running on Windows 2008 need to be aware of the Windows Firewall in order to configure the correct access settings. If your application is not, then you will need to configure the firewall manually.

If you look only at the overview page of the GUI, you can be forgiven for assuming that All Inbound traffic is denied and All Outbound traffic is allowed because that is what it says. Or does it? What it actually says is "Inbound connections that do not match a rule are blocked," and "Outbound connections that do not match a rule are allowed." As you will see, this is an important distinction.

There are two choices for configuring the firewall: You can use the GUI or you can use the command line.

To access the command-line configuration at the command prompt, type **netsh advfirewall** and press Enter. This displays your options for configuring the firewall via the command line. For example, to see all of the inbound rules configured in the firewall, type **netsh advfirewall firewall show rule name=all dir=in** and press Enter. This

FIGURE 17.11   Advanced Firewall configuration is easier to manage through the GUI.

produces a very long scrolling list of the default incoming rules. As you've seen, the commands are long and complex, and the output can also be long and complex, so for the purposes of the book, we will use the GUI interface.

There are 155 Inbound rules, 59 Outbound rules, and 3 profiles active in the firewall, by default. The three profiles represent different sets of rules that are applied based on the network that the server is attached to. Because the server doesn't move from network to network, the active profile should always be domain. The other two profiles will not be used. There are so many rules because for each service on the server, responds to requests made by that service must be allowed to communicate back to the server and, in SBS, there's a lot going on.

To view the Inbound rules using the GUI, click Inbound Rules. To view the Outbound rules, click Outbound Rules. To edit a rule, double-click it. To disable a rule, right-click it and choose Disable Rule, or in the Actions pane, click Disable Rule.

Windows Firewall with Advanced Security applies rules to the policy in a specific order. We'll use Inbound rule in the example, but the same concept applies for Outbound rules as well. Because you are operating under the Domain Profile, you know that inbound connections that do not match a rule are blocked. You also know that you have 155 inbound rules. You'll also notice that the rules are not numbered.

17

The firewall rules are, however, applied in a specific order. The order is as follows:

▶ Authenticated bypass rules (rules that override blocking rules)

▶ Block

▶ Allow

▶ Profile setting

Within each, the rules are further ordered by most specific to least specific, so rules that allow a specific destination are processed before those that allow any destination.

Enable Logging

In the left pane, click Monitoring. The firewall monitoring isn't very interesting. For the most part, it tells you whether or not the firewall is on and what general settings are configured. There are a couple of things, however, that should jump out to the security concerned administrator. Under General Settings, Display a Notification When a Program Is Blocked is set to No. This means there will be no notice when the firewall has blocked a connection. Under Logging settings, Log Dropped Packets and Log Successful Connection are also set to No. Together this means that there will be no notification when the firewall has blocked a connection and no log either. This makes troubleshooting connection issues difficult, if not impossible.

To change these settings, in the GUI, click on Windows Firewall with Advanced Security at the top of the left pane; then click Properties in the Action menu. On the Domain Profile tab in the Settings section, click Customize. In the Firewall Settings section, in Display a Notification, select Yes (default) from the drop-down list and then click OK.

Back on the Domain Profile tab, in the Logging section, click Customize. Decide whether you want to move the location of the firewall log and, if so, click Browse and select that location. Set the size of the log file in the Size limit box. Keep in mind that when the log fills, older entries are overwritten. The Windows Firewall only keeps a single log file per profile, so you need to ensure that this file is large enough to capture enough data for troubleshooting. In the Log Dropped Packets and Log Successful Connections boxes, select Yes from the drop-down list. Your settings should look similar to those in Figure 17.12. Click OK. Then click OK again to close and save the configuration changes.

The profiles that we just looked at define the Windows Firewall. But what about Advanced Security? Advanced Security refers to the firewall's IPSec capabilities. In conjunction with Group Policy, domain isolation can be configured to greatly enhance the security of your network. Configuring domain isolation is beyond the scope of this book; however, in Appendix A, "SBS 2008 Resources," you will find links to more information about using Windows Firewall with Advanced Security to configure domain isolation using Connection Security Rules.

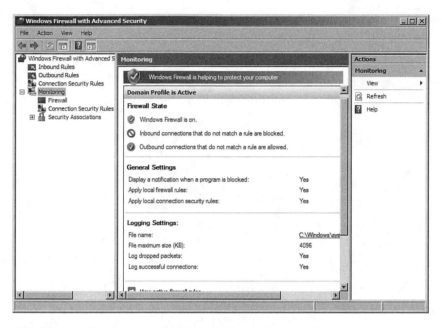

FIGURE 17.12   Enable firewall logging for ease of troubleshooting.

Configuring Rules

Rules can be configured in two ways. A rule can be defined by application or by specific protocols and ports. The recommended method is by application, and there is a big security advantage when creating rules this way. When you create a rule by application, when the application is running, the firewall will open the ports and allow the protocols necessary for the application, and when it is not running, it will dynamically close them. This can only be used on inbound connections if the application uses Windows Sockets to create port assignments. If the application does not, you will need to determine which ports the program uses and add those ports to the rule. When you create a rule defined only by port and protocol, that port will remain open at all times. Windows Firewall with Advanced Security is a modern intelligent firewall, and you should therefore not poke pinholes but rather create rules based on application and take advantage of the enhanced security that dynamic opening and closing of ports provides.

Follow these steps to create a new rule:

1. Click New Rule in the Actions pane to launch the New Inbound Rule wizard. Program is the default rule type. Click Next.

2. Click Browse to select the application for which you need to allow inbound connections; then click Next.

3. Verify that Allow the Connection should be selected and click Next.

4. Because this is a domain controller, the rule need only be applied to the Domain. Uncheck Private and Public, as in Figure 17.13; then click Next.

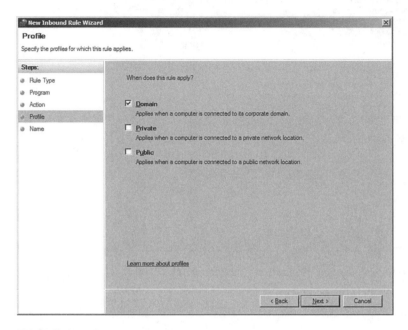

FIGURE 17.13　When creating a new firewall rule you need to choose in which profile the rule will be active.

5. On the last page of the wizard, specify a name for the rule you just created. Be sure to provide a short descriptive name and add any description you will find helpful; then click Finish.

The new rule will be listed in the Inbound Rules list and will be enabled. The firewall will now dynamically open the necessary ports and allow the protocols required by the application you have defined while it is actively running on the server.

If you have an application that runs as a service, the rule creation is exactly the same as the preceding. However, if the application service runs under the svchost, as many do, you will need to specify it by SID so as not to allow every application running under svchost access to the same permission. To do this, after you have created the rule, right-click it and select Properties. Move to the Program and Services tab, and in the Services section, click the Settings button. To specify the service, select the Apply to This Service radio button and select the service in the list box as shown in Figure 17.14. If the service is not listed, select the Apply to Service with Service Short Name radio button and type the name of the service in the box. Click OK twice to save the configuration.

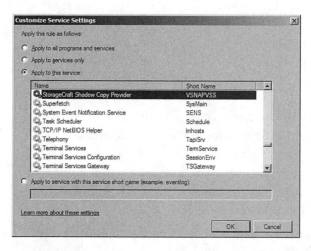

FIGURE 17.14   Select the service to which this rule applies.

Best Practice—Narrowly Define Firewall Rules

A firewall is only as good as the rules you have configured. When you find that you have an application that does not use Windows Sockets and requires that you manually specify ports and protocols in your rule, it is best to make that rule as specific as possible so that other applications or malware are not able to use those ports. Always-open ports are an invitation to hackers.

Windows Firewall in XP and Vista

The Windows Firewall has changed dramatically from XP to Vista. The Windows Firewall in Vista is identical to that described previously for SBS 2008. It is an application-aware firewall that monitors and filters traffic both incoming and outgoing. While in Windows XP, the firewall protection is inbound only.

Firewall policy for domain-joined computers is controlled through Group Policy. Because of the varied capabilities of each firewall, XP and Vista have separate policies. These are the Window SBS Client—Windows Vista Policy and the Windows SBS Client—Windows XP Policy. Once joined to the domain, the computer administrator no longer has control over firewall settings because group policy has taken over. To view the firewall settings in the Group Policy Management MMC, select the policy, and move to the Settings tab. Once the report has generated, you can view the firewall settings.

The policy can be edited, and as with the server firewall, the default settings are extensive. However, logging is not enabled. To enable logging of firewall-dropped packets, the policy needs to be edited.

To edit the policy, follow these steps:

1. Right-click the policy and click Properties.

2. In the Group Policy Management Editor, expand Computer Configuration, Windows Settings, and then right-click Windows Firewall with Advanced Security and choose Properties.

3. On the Domain Profile page, click the Customize button in the Logging section.

4. In the Customize Logging Settings for the Domain Profile window, uncheck both Not Configured boxes.

5. Next, in the Log Dropped Packets box and in the Log Successful Connections box, select Yes and click OK.

6. Click OK once more to close the dialog box.

Upon the next group policy refresh, firewall logging will begin on the Vista computers. Follow the same procedure to enable logging on XP computers using the Windows SBS Client—Windows XP Policy.

With domain-joined desktop computers, we are only concerned with the domain profile as the others will never be used. If you are configuring this policy for domain-joined mobile computers, repeat the process to enable logging for other profiles by selecting Logging from each Profile tab.

Edge Firewall

Before you deploy your SBS 2008 server, you need to purchase and configure an edge firewall. An edge firewall protects not only the server but the entire network. The purchase of that device should be carefully considered. You will want to consider all of the services, applications, and volume of traffic, both inbound and outbound, that you are expecting and compare those against the capabilities and performance benchmarks of the firewall you choose. It is best not to skimp on this purchase. Your edge firewall is your first line of defense against intruders.

Ports and Firewall Discovery

SBS 2008 has Internet Gateway Device Discovery and Control features built-in. That's a mouthful for saying that the server has the ability to configure some firewalls. If your firewall supports UPnP or Web Services for Devices, during configuration of the server, your firewall will be automatically configured with open ports for Small Business Server. Table 17.5 lists the required ports and their function.

TABLE 17.5   Required Ports and Their Function

Incoming Port	Purpose	Auto-Configured?
25	SMTP E-mail	Yes
987	SharePoint	Yes
80	IIS and Windows Remote Management	Yes

TABLE 17.5   Required Ports and Their Function

Incoming Port	Purpose	Auto-Configured?
1723	VPN	No
443	OWA, Outlook Anywhere	Yes

There is widespread concern about the use of UPnP for gateway devices. Business-grade firewalls do not support auto-configuration. In fact, a good indication of whether you are purchasing a business grade or home firewall device is the presence of UPnP support. If the device supports it, it is designed for home use.

UPnP was developed in 2001. Its purpose is to make things just work, and it was designed for home networks. In the case of a home network, it is assumed that the data is not critical and there is no administrator with the knowledge to configure a firewall appropriately. UPnP was developed prior to Internet security awareness. If it is enabled on your firewall, any application, whether friend or foe, is able to configure it regardless of whether you want it to or not. Microsoft has responded to this security concern by developing a new more secure protocol called Web Services for Devices. This protocol can configure your firewall automatically but first requires authentication to the device. Requiring a username and password for this auto-configuration increases the security of your network. Unfortunately, few manufacturers have added this feature to their devices. SBS 2008 supports both UPnP and WSD device configuration. The Connect to the Internet wizard attempts to use both on your edge device. However, because of the insecure nature of UPnP, it is recommended that if your firewall device supports it, you disable this feature. Otherwise, you may someday find that ports have been opened, allowing unauthorized access to your network. A network administrator should configure your firewall.

As we have seen in the Windows host firewall, a modern firewall should concern itself with more than just open ports. It should be aware of the services and applications running on your server and act to protect related incoming and outgoing traffic while dynamically opening and closing ports on the fly.

The Case for Controlling Outbound Access

Many businesses today are not controlling outbound access. In many cases, this is simply because the current gateway device doesn't support it. However, many of today's devices are able to not only control outbound access but log it as well. The best control of outbound access uses Active Directory to authenticate the user's permission for the outbound connection. For example, is the user allowed to send Instant Messages? Is the user allowed to access the Internet? Is the user allowed to send attachments or upload data to another location? Is the user allowed to use personal e-mail accounts? Which applications are allowed to access the Internet? Exchange, Office, Anti-Virus? Malware, printers, viruses?

Controlling outbound access to the Internet is a function of business policy and the feature set of your selected gateway firewall. It is, therefore, beyond the scope of this book. However, the topic should be taken very seriously. Many businesses are finding that it isn't the "bad guys" on the Internet that cause their business problems, but internal users losing productivity from inappropriate Internet access or data leaking from their network to their former employee's next employer. In addition, being a good citizen of the Internet is also being legally enforced by several states that have passed laws requiring you to pay businesses for damage caused by virus or malware sent from your network. If you didn't take precautions to prevent such outbound access, you could find yourself paying to repair and recover someone else's data.

Controlling outbound access is well within reach of modern firewall devices and should be carefully configured to protect the small business.

OneCare for Server

Small Business Server 2008 comes with a trial version of OneCare designed specifically for SBS called OneCare for Server. During installation, you had the choice of whether to install this feature or not. If you did install it, you need to activate your trial and configure the software.

After installation of your server, you will notice that on the home page of the SBS Console, the status of Security is Critical. Expanding this for details tells you that there are one or more alert conditions, and you should move to the Security tab. When you move to the Security sub-navigation tab, you notice that virus protection for e-mail has a status of Warning and the server virus and spyware protection status is Critical. This is because you have yet to configure One Care for Server and Forefront Security for Exchange.

Configuration of Forefront Security for Exchange is covered in Chapter 8, "Exchange Management," and will not be discussed here.

To configure Windows Live OneCare for Server in the Tasks pane, click the Open Windows Live OneCare for Server link. This opens the OneCare Getting Started wizard, as shown in Figure 17.15.

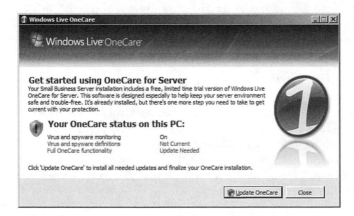

FIGURE 17.15   Getting started with OneCare for Server.

To get started with OneCare, click Update OneCare to be guided through the process. On the first page, you are warned that OneCare will be configured to allow Microsoft to make changes on your server. There is a link to the features summary that you should click and read through before continuing. This link takes you to the features page for OneCare for PCs. Although the feature list is somewhat different and not yet documented for OneCare for Server, you can get a pretty good idea of what type of access you are granting to Microsoft. They will configure the host firewall to allow anti-virus and anti-malware engine updates, they will allow application updates, and so on. When ready, click Next. When you are ready to accept the term of use, select the radio button and click Next. OneCare will now download and install updates. When complete, press Finish.

Upon completion, the Windows Live OneCare configuration window opens. The trial period is 120 days. To continue beyond the first 120 days, you need to subscribe to the service by clicking the Subscribe button.

Configuring OneCare

Now that OneCare has been activated, there are several additional steps that need to be taken to configure it. You will notice that there are three major categories of service on this page (see Figure 17.16).

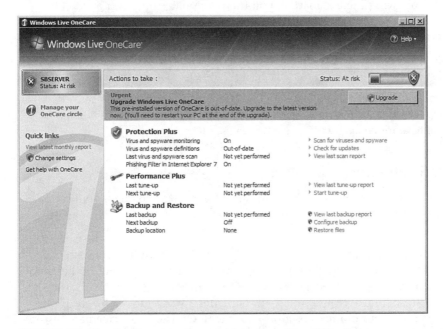

FIGURE 17.16   OneCare has three major categories of function.

NOTE

You might have noticed the Manage Your OneCare Circle link in Figure 17.16. A major concept in OneCare is the circle. When you configure a new computer for protection under OneCare, it becomes part of the circle. The manager of your circle will be the SBS server; it is known as the hub. Each circle can contain up to 25 computers.

The services shown here are the following:

▸ **Protection Plus**—Protection Plus is the OneCare component that keeps the antivirus and antispyware definitions up to date. It also runs scheduled scans, attempting to clean anything it finds.

The first action you should take to configure Protection Plus is to Check for Updates. To do this, click the Check for Updates link. OneCare will download the latest definitions.

▸ **Performance Plus**—Performance Plus is the OneCare component that maintains the disks in your server. It regularly defragments the drives and deletes unneeded files. It also cleans your registry of orphan entries.

▸ **Backup and Restore**—The backup and restore feature of OneCare is designed to work cooperatively with OneCare on the PCs. It centralizes the management of backup for each workstation and centrally locates the backup files for each PC to an external drive attached to the server. In order for the SBS server to centrally manage and store the backup files for your PCs, you need to purchase and install OneCare on each PC. Following the installation, you then designate the server as the hub computer. The backup feature of OneCare does not back up the server. It only manages the workstation backup, provided licenses are purchased for the workstations.

> **NOTE**
>
> If you install OneCare on the workstations, the OneCare firewall settings will take over from SBS Group Policy. Should you need to make a change to the workstation firewall settings you will have to manually configure each workstation.

Additional Online Features

OneCare is a subscription-based service. In addition to the server and client applications, there are additional features that are available when you log into the OneCare web site with your account.

To access the additional OneCare features, you need a Windows Live ID; if you do not already have one, there is an option during the sign in process to create one. To begin to use the Online services, click the Manage Your OneCare Circle button; then click the Sign In to Get the Most from Your Free Trial link. This launches a wizard to walk you through the process of activating your online subscription services. On the final screen are instructions for completing the OneCare installation on the PCs in your company. You should print these instructions, as they are not offered elsewhere.

You may have noticed the OneCare icon in the system tray. It is the M&M-looking icon with the numeral 1 in the middle. This icon changes colors to give you a quick status check on the system health. A green icon means that all is well: Everything is up to date, the server is tuned up, and the backup succeeded. A yellow icon means that almost everything is OK, but OneCare does need you to complete an action. The action could be downloading an update, running a tune-up, or checking the backup. When the icon is red, OneCare has determined that your server may be at risk. OneCare considers risk to be a failed update of the antivirus software, or when your host-based firewall is turned off. When the icon is not green, double-clicking it launches OneCare and shows you which items need attention. Clicking on each item brings up instructions or wizards to help you resolve the issue.

CAUTION

Once you have completed the online activation of OneCare, the Manage Your OneCare Circle screen will have new options. These are Add a PC to Your OneCare Circle and Rename This PC.

Under no circumstances should you ever click on the Rename This PC link. Many features of SBS 2008 are dependent on the name of the server. Changing the name of your SBS server results in PCs not being able to locate shared resources, such as file shares, printers, and internal web sites. The SBS server should never be renamed.

Each of the features of OneCare can be configured to meet the needs of your network. Clicking the Change Settings link within OneCare opens the Windows Live OneCare Settings configuration pages. There are four tabs. Three of those correspond to the major areas of OneCare, while the fourth addresses logging.

On the Tune-up tab, you are able to schedule the disk defragment. The default setting is once every four weeks, on Monday at 1:00 a.m. You need to adjust this schedule so that it does not interfere with the backup of your server. You do not want the defragment procedure and backup to be running at the same time, nor to overlap. The amount of time that the defragment takes to complete varies depending on the size of your hard drive, the size of the individual files stored on the drive, the speed of those drives, and the total amount of free space. You should be sure to keep 20% of the drive space free at all times for defragmenting to complete successfully. To estimate the amount of time to allocate for defragment you should run a defragment manually. As your hard drive fills or if the server has had a particularly busy month, you need to increase the estimated amount of time for the process to complete.

To run a baseline defragment, press Start, Accessories, System Tools, Disk Defragmenter. When you open this tool, it begins to analyze the disks on your server. You have to wait a few moments for this to complete, as seen in Figure 17.17. When it is complete, click the Defragment Now... button. Keep track of how long the defragment process takes, and use this figure when setting your scheduled tasks. You likely have other tasks on the server that can cause conflicts, included antivirus scanning, deletion of temporary files, defragment, exchange database maintenance, and backup. You will need to go through the procedure for each of these items, estimate the time to complete, and create the task schedules accordingly in each application.

17

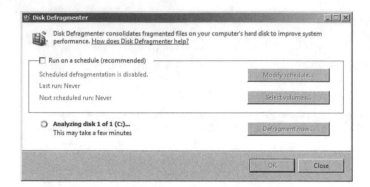

FIGURE 17.17 Taking a baseline defragment of your drives enables you to properly schedule the task to avoid conflicts with backup and other tasks.

Move to the Backup tab in OneCare settings and click Configure Backup. An important message pops up, alerting you to the function of OneCare backup (see Figure 17.18). OneCare backup is designed to back up your PCs, not your server. If you have purchased OneCare for your PCs, click Next. The wizard walks you through specifying which external hard drive device you want to store the PC backup files to; otherwise, press Cancel.

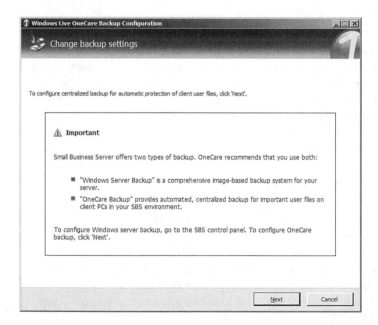

FIGURE 17.18 OneCare for Server manages and reports on client backup; it does not back up the server itself.

Move to the Viruses and Spyware tab. The default settings on this page are for virus and spyware monitoring to be On, and the Also Look for Virus-Like Behavior box is also checked. Scheduled scans occur daily at 11:00 p.m. The Take Automatic Actions Against Software Rated Moderate box also is checked. As with the defragment process, notice how long the antivirus scan takes to complete, and adjust the start time for this procedure so that it does not interfere with another process. Each maintenance task requires an exclusive time window.

Click the Quarantine button to open the Windows Live OneCare Quarantined Files window. This is where you go to view, delete, or restore files that OneCare has quarantined. Cleaning of quarantined files and folders should be done regularly to prevent the quarantine from growing too large.

Click the Exclusions button. This screen is where you will configure files or folders that you do not want the antivirus engine to scan. Many database applications require exclusions, as do some other applications. Exclusions for the applications included with SBS have been pre-populated into the exclusions list. The complete list of exclusions is

    C:\Program files (x86)\Microsoft Forefront Security\Exchange Server\Data

    C:\Program files (x86)\Microsoft Windows OneCare Live\database\

    C:\Program files\Microsoft\Exchange Server\Mailbox\First Storage Group

    C:\Program files\Microsoft\Exchange Server\Mailbox\First Storage Group\Mailbox Data

    C:\Program files\Microsoft\Exchange Server\Mailbox\Second Storage Group

    C:\Program files\Microsoft\Exchange Server\Mailbox\Second Storage Group\Public Folders

    C:\ProgramData\Application Data\Microsoft\Search\Data\Applications\Windows\tmp.edb

    C:\ProgramData\Application Data\Microsoft\Search\Data\Applications\Windows\

To add an exclusion, click the Add File or Add Folder button as appropriate and browse to the file or folder you do not want scanned. You should configure the file and folder exclusions according to manufacturer recommendations for your application.

Move to the Logging tab. This tab includes only one setting, The Display Monthly Report Automatically check box, which is checked by default. This causes OneCare to generate and save a report each month. The Create Support Log button is a tool designed to assist Microsoft support, but you should go ahead and press it anyway. It generates an HTML file with the settings and log information. It is a good troubleshooting tool for any administrator to quickly see all the current settings and view the OneCare application log in one handy page. If you manage multiple SBS 2008 servers, this information may also be useful.

Windows Software Update Services

SBS 2008 and the client workstations connected to it will receive updates, security patches, and service packs through Windows Software Update Services 3.0 with SP1 (WSUS). WSUS comes pre-configured with recommended settings for the server and workstations. WSUS is managed through the Security tab of the SBS Console or the WSUS MMC.

Managing WSUS

WSUS will primarily be managed through the SBS Console. It can be found on the Security tab, on the Updates sub-navigation tab. In the upper-center pane, you will see a summary indicating the status of each category of update.

The first status item is Update with Microsoft Software Licensing Terms that are pending approval. Items listed here have a EULA that must be accepted before deployment. To accept the EULA and deploy the update, highlight it and then press the Deploy Update link in the Tasks pane. Press OK, to acknowledge that the update will be deployed. The Software Licensing Terms EULA will now appear; after reviewing, click the I Accept button. This accepts the EULA for all computers in the network. Click OK to acknowledge the deployment schedule.

Updates with Errors and Optional Updates are handled in a similar manner. When an update appears under one of these categories, click the corresponding link in the Tasks pane to address the issue.

Changing Settings

As you can see in Figure 17.19, the SBS update services doesn't like change. If you change settings in WSUS, the SBS Console will not be able to report properly, and you will lose the ability to manage WSUS through the SBS Console. This, however, does not mean that WSUS isn't working. It just means that you will need to instead manage WSUS through its native MMC.

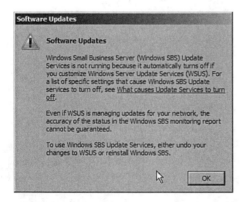

FIGURE 17.19   SBS Update services don't like it when you change the settings. If you do, you will need to manage updates through WSUS MMC.

There are certain changes that cause the SBS update services console integration to stop working. These are

▶ Unchecking any default classifications.

▶ The list of products is not set to all products.

▶ Revisions to updates are not automatically approved.

▶ Updates are not automatically declined when a new revision causes them to expire.

▶ You tell it to use Group Policy to assign computers to groups instead of the update services console.

▶ You choose to synchronize manually.

▶ Windows Update service is stopped.

The items that can be changed are found in the SBS Console in the Updates sub-navigation tab. In the Tasks pane, click the Change the Software Update Settings link to open the Software Update Settings window. From this screen, you can change the Server Update settings, the Client Update settings, the time when updates are automatically applied to computers, and the list of computers that you want to include in automatic updates.

There are a couple of key changes from SBS 2003 R2. On the Schedules menu item, the Server is scheduled to download the updates and then notify the administrator that the updates are ready to be installed. This is a much-needed change over SBS 2003 R2 defaults, which were to automatically install the updates. Figure 17.20 shows the configuration page where you notice that the workstations and server are configured to automatically update. Workstations will automatically install all updates and service packs, while the server will download, ready updates and alert the administrator that they are ready. Service packs will not be automatically approved for the server.

FIGURE 17.20 The server is configured to download and notify when updates are ready to be installed.

Another welcome addition is the ability to exclude certain computers from receiving updates. Generally speaking, it is best practice to keep all computers up to date, but if you have that one computer with very specific requirements or sensitivity to change, you are able to exclude it from automatic updating. Counterintuitively, you must first allow the computer that you want to exclude to be discovered through the normal process. Then once it has registered with WSUS, you can exclude it. Move to Included Computers, highlight the computer you want to exclude, and click the Remove button. When successfully excluded, your computer list will look similar to that in Figure 17.21.

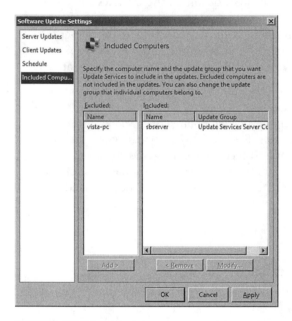

FIGURE 17.21   Administrators are able to choose which computers to exclude from automatic updates.

Maintaining WSUS Health

WSUS information is maintained as a Windows database, and as such, it does require maintenance for optimal function. The maintenance functions are not exposed in the SBS Console; you will need to use the native WSUS MMC to perform maintenance. The MMC is available at Start, Administrative Tools, Microsoft Windows Server update Services 3.0 SP1. This opens the Update Services MMC.

To perform database maintenance, in the left pane, select Options; then in the center pane, select Server Cleanup wizard. As seen in Figure 17.22, you have several choices for items to clean.

The choices listed are self explanatory and well described. For database maintenance purposes, you should run this wizard every couple of months. As new updates are released and your computers are updated, the number of unused, not needed, superseded, expired,

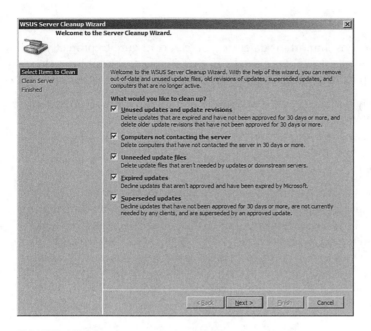

FIGURE 17.22   The WSUS Server Cleanup wizard should be run on a regular basis to maintain the WSUS database in a healthy state.

and revised updates will grow quite large. This makes your WSUS database ever more inefficient. Be aware that running this maintenance process is time consuming. You should plan that cleaning the database could take as long as eight hours or more and will take considerable server resources. Frequent running of this maintenance task reduces the impact upon your server.

Microsoft also recommends that you re-index the database monthly. Reindexing is done by running the sqlcmd utility against the WsusDbMaintenance.sql script. To use this script, you should run the following command:

```
sqlcmd -S np:\\.\pipe\MSSQL$MICROSOFT##SSEE\sql\query –i <scriptLocation>\
➥WsusDBMaintenance.sql
```

where *<scriptLocation>* is the directory where you have copied the WsusDBMaintenance script. The WsusDBMaintenance script can be copied from the Microsoft Technet article page at this URL:
http://www.microsoft.com/technet/scriptcenter/scripts/sus/server/ susvvb01.mspx?mfr=true.

Expanding the Definition of Security

Security should not be thought of as just firewall definitions and anti-virus. Security comes in many forms. In this section we'll take a high level look at security in other areas of the server.

Backup

Backup is arguably one of the most important defenses you can configure to protect your data. This book contains an excellent chapter on Backup that the reader should not skip over (see Chapter 18, "Backup and Disaster Recovery").

SBS 2008 Backup is completely re-written and based upon Windows Backup. From a security point of view, the transition from tape to disk-based backup is significant. In the world of tape, a non-admin user was typically put in charge of changing the tape nightly. This person was usually a member of the general office staff or the business owner. He or she then took home the tape for safekeeping in case of disaster at the office.

In the new world of disk-based backup, many consultants and business owners have been lured by the low cost of USB and eSata drives and are now using these to store the nightly backup. However, most aren't buying enough drives to replicate the two weeks of backup copies they had under the old tape system. Previously, most servers were protected by at least 10 tapes, providing two work-weeks worth of backup options. By contrast, it seems that most are now only using one, two, or three backup drives. Even if each drive contains multiple backups, that's still a lot of eggs in one basket. Stop to consider how quickly your nightly backup is being overwritten and whether or not you are secure in that timeframe.

> **CAUTION**
>
> Anytime you have to provide direct physical logon access to the server to a member of the company, take it as a sign that something is not right with the solution you've chosen.

The choice of USB or eSata drives as a backup solution should not be taken lightly. Providing direct access to the server console for the purpose of unplugging and plugging in drives is simply bad security practice. A person should be able to swap the backup media without needing to acquire access to the server to do so. Several manufacturers provide media bays, much like tape drives, that allow for the hot swapping of your disk-based backup media without user interaction required on the server itself. The consultant or business owner should seriously consider one of these systems to prevent accidental or malicious destructive acts on the server.

Group Policy

This book contains an excellent chapter on Group Policy (see Chapter 11, "Group Policy in SBS 2008"). Group Policy is a powerful tool that can be used by the administrator to enforce security policies on the server. These policies can be edited to suit your environment.

One of the policies that you might want to edit is the Default Domain Policy. The Default Domain Policy contains the password policy for the entire network. The default policy settings are set to only require a password change every 180 days. A more secure environment would change passwords every 45, 60, or 90 days. Experience with enforcing passwords changes is that the end user will complain at first, but soon changing their password becomes just part of the job they do, and the habit is adopted as standard practice.

Also found in the Default Domain Policy are the Account Lockout Policies. By default, 10 invalid attempts at logging in will cause the account to be locked for 10 minutes. Ten minutes is generally enough to cause an automated attack to give up and look elsewhere for easier prey. But 10 invalid login attempts seems like a lot of tries before the account is locked. This is one policy you might want to consider tightening up by reducing the number of invalid login attempts before an account is locked.

In the Windows SBS Client Policy, a setting that you might want to consider whether it is appropriate for your environment is Terminal Server/Connections. This policy enables users to remote connect to the PC using Terminal Services. In most businesses, the administrator should limit remote access to PCs to only those that require it. By changing this setting to Not Configured, Terminal Services use the Remote Desktop setting on the PC to determine whether access is allowed.

For a secure environment, the default policies should be reviewed for appropriateness for the business. Administrators looking to make changes to the policies should follow the guidance found in Chapter 11.

Remote Access to Network Resources

Remote Access to Network Resources is the hottest topic in small business. The increased cost of commuting, coupled with the ease of obtaining high-speed Internet access, has made working from almost anywhere a reality. SBS 2008 supports remote access to network resources through many different means. However, each remote access point of entry that the administrator allows is a compromise between security and productivity.

The SBS server can be accessed remotely by both users and administrators in various ways. Remote access to SharePoint, Outlook Web Access, Outlook Anywhere, Remote Web Workplace, Terminal Services, VPN, and mobile phones is all enabled. New mobile phones present much more of a security challenge than they did previously. Today, they can have direct access to files and folders on your network! All the methods of remote access are greatly enhanced over SBS 2003 and provide easier access and arguably more potential for security problems.

There are several chapters in this book that cover remote access to SBS 2008. Each should be read with an eye to whether the default permissions are acceptable to your company.

> **NOTE**
>
> One of the major changes to server access is the elimination of the encouragement for small business owners to host their public web site on the SBS server. Big kudos to Microsoft for not encouraging that travesty this time around. Anytime you invite the world to visit your server and browse around, it's a bad idea.

Summary

Security is the most undervalued administrative task until a problem occurs. At that point it is immediately assumed that security was your number one priority during your tenure as administrator. There are many components of SBS 2008 that can help protect data.

In this chapter we reviewed user roles, file and share security, quotas, file screening, OneCare, the Windows host firewall, UAC, group policy and WSUS. The default settings were also documented.

Best Practice Summary

▶ **Separate Out the Default Items in SBS from the Ones That You Create**—This will help with support later in the life of the server. In doing this, by simple glance we know that we created the security group SmallBizCo Employees, and that it is not one of the default folders.

▶ **Create a File Screen for Each Shared Document Folder**—By creating a file screen for each shared document folder on the server, the administrator can finally prevent storage resources from being mismanaged. By creating a file screen for each share, the IT manager finally has the tool necessary to help the business owner enforce good data habits.

▶ **Move Shared Drives**—You will notice that SBS 2008 installs everything to the C: drive by default. For security and performance reasons, as a best practice, shared drives should be moved to another drive on your server.

▶ **Make Firewall Rules Specific**—When you find that you have an application that does not use Windows Sockets and requires that you manually specify ports and protocols in your firewall rules, it is best to make that rule as specific as possible so that other applications or malware are not able to use those ports. Always-open ports are an invitation to hackers.

Backup and Disaster Recovery

All businesses, whether small or large, need to perform regular backups of their computer systems and business data, and routinely test those backups.

Unfortunately, many businesses have no backup procedures in place or perform a backup only when there's a known threat, such as an approaching hurricane. The consequence of not implementing a backup plan is only realized when it is too late: When you need to recover lost data, restore a down server, or recover from a catastrophic disaster.

Backing up your data should be as routine as locking your office at night. In both cases, you are being proactive, not reactive, in safeguarding the business assets of the company.

Backup and recovery processes need to be viewed within the broader context of business continuity planning and disaster recovery. Rotating backups offsite is good, but if no one has been trained on verifying that those backups are readable, then those backups are not very useful.

SBS 2008 provides new, easy-to-use backup and recovery tools that offer comprehensive data protection from unexpected events, such as the following:

▶ Disasters (fire or theft)

▶ System failures (power outage, disk crash)

▶ Data loss (user error, virus attack)

These are events that can lead to a partial or total loss of critical company data. Businesses must plan and anticipate such events and situations. A backup of company data files, for example, is of little use if the backup itself has been destroyed or stolen.

A risk assessment of data protection and recovery options might identify the need for new solutions. Although any type of backup is better than no backup, implementing multiple backup solutions may be deemed necessary to address your business continuity plans. With today's high-speed Internet connections, complementing a local backup of data with online remote backups is now feasible.

What's New with SBS 2008 Backup and Recovery

Technology continues to make advancements that seem mind-boggling at times, and that is certainly true in the area of storage and backup devices. When SBS 2003 was first released, 18GB hard disk drives were commonplace, and tape devices were the desired method for backing up data.

Today, we have disk drives with a storage capacity of 1TB or more, and external hard drives replacing tape as the preferred media for backups. Unlike tape, which is slow because it must be accessed serially, external disk backup devices offer both the speed and capacity to keep up with today's storage demands.

The backup and data protection features in SBS 2008 are based on the new Windows Server Backup utility that is implemented across the entire Windows Server 2008 platform.

> **NOTE**
>
> SBS 2008 enhances the Windows Server Backup platform with additional wizards, built-in support for backing up both Exchange and SharePoint, and a new user interface within the Windows SBS Console.

Backups are no longer file-based, but block-level based (also referred to as incremental snapshots), which provides for faster backups and easier recovery of business data.

This section covers many of the new features and changes to the Windows Server Backup (WSB) in SBS 2008.

New Backup Technology

NTBackup, the backup utility that has been part of Windows since the days of Windows NT 3.5, is finally gone.

SBS 2008 uses Windows Server Backup, which is a robust new data protection utility that has been designed from the ground up to address the backup and recovery needs of small business customers; it offers the following:

▶ **Faster backups**—Most backups are completed in minutes, not hours.

▶ **Reduced cost**—External USB and Firewire drives offer increased data storage capacity at a lower cost than tape media.

▶ **Improved recovery**—Bare metal recovery of the server, and files, folders, and volumes can be restored from a previous point in time.

▶ **Easier management**—SBS wizards designed to simplify managing backups and backup disk media.

Windows Server Backup is not intended to be a feature-for-feature replacement of NTBackup, nor can it be used to recover data from a backup created with NTBackup.

NOTE

A special version of NTBackup is available for the Windows Server 2008 platform that can recover data from backups created using NTBackup.

This version of NTBackup is designed for reading backups only, and cannot be used to create new backups. To download this special version of NTBackup, go to http://go.microsoft.com/fwlink/?LinkId=82917.

Underneath Windows Server Backup

When using Windows Server Backup, it might be helpful to consider that every backup is *incremental* from a storage point of view, but *full* from a restore point of view.

During a backup, only those blocks that have changed since the last backup are stored. The previous version of the block along with version-tracking metadata information is moved to another location. During a restore, the recovery logic looks at the metadata, picks up the correct blocks based on the version, adds up the blocks, and restores the file. Here's an example of how it works:

1. We have a file on a volume that is made up of four blocks of data (ABCD). On the first backup (full), all four blocks are copied to the backup destination drive:

   ABCD (Source), ABCD (Destination)

2. Next, let's say that data inside block B changes (which we will designate as B'). So, the file is AB'CD. During the next backup, only block B' will be copied to the destination disk, and block B (and its metadata information) will be saved in a separate location:

   B' (Source), AB'CD (Destination)

   B (+Metadata for version info)

3. Then let's say that block B is changed again (B"), so the file is AB"CD. During the next scheduled backup, block B" is copied to the destination drive, and the B' block and metadata is moved and saved.

   B" (Source), AB"CD (Destination)

   B' (+Metadata)

   B (+Metadata)

On the backup disk, the full version is always the most recent version (for performance reasons), while previous versions are moved to a different location with metadata to link it to the backup version. A restore of a particular backup version follows the same logic and goes through the same steps, but in reverse order.

Design Considerations

Windows Server Backup has several design considerations that are consistent across all Windows 2008 Server platforms, including SBS 2008. These design features are listed in Table 18.1.

TABLE 18.1   Windows Server Backup Design Considerations

Feature	Description
No tape backup support	Windows Server Backup does not support backing up to tape. Windows 2008 Server does support tape storage drivers, and use of a third-party software backup solution is required to backup to tape. Uses TB style.
No NTBackup support	Windows Server Backup cannot be used to recover backups created with NTBackup. Microsoft has released an NTBackup Restore Utility for Windows Server 2008 to recover data from backups created with NTBackup. See http://go.microsoft.com/fwlink/?LinkId=82917.
External USB or Firewire disks only for scheduled backups	Only external disk drives are supported in order to encourage backup disk rotation and taking backups offsite.
Only NTFS-formatted volumes can be backed up	FAT32 volumes will not appear in the list of available source drives to be backed up.
Volume-level backup	Windows Server Backup does not support backing up of individual files or folders.
Backing up to network-shared folders, optical drives, or internal local disk volumes	Storing backups to other disk devices can be performed via the Backup Once wizard in Windows Server Backup or by the backup WBAdmin command-line tool.

Improved Backup

Windows Server Backup uses Volume Shadow Copy Service (VSS) and block-level backup technology to efficiently back up files, folders, volumes, and applications. VSS functionality ensures that open files and data from VSS-aware applications, such as Microsoft Exchange and SQL Servers, are properly backed up and protected.

Block-level backup speeds up backups by copying only those blocks that have changed since the last backup. After the initial full backup to a backup device, regularly scheduled incremental backups should only take several minutes to complete.

Easier Scheduling

The SBS 2008 Configure Server Backup Wizard is used to configure and set up a recurring daily backup schedule. By default, backups are set to occur twice daily, at 5 p.m. and 11 p.m. However, backups can be scheduled more frequently, even every hour or every 30 minutes!

System volumes are automatically included in all scheduled backups to ensure protection against disasters. Backups can be saved to multiple disks in a rotation, enabling you to rotate backup devices to and from an offsite location.

Dedicated Backup Devices

The SBS Configure Backup Wizard requires the use of dedicated external disk drives directly attached to the server (USB or Firewire) for scheduled daily backups.

This is to encourage customers to take backup drives offsite for safety, and designed with the goal of making the backup process easier to set up and easier to manage for the small business.

CAUTION

External disk drives selected as backup devices with the SBS Backup wizard will be reformatted and relabeled. Previous data on those drives will be lost.

Once a drive is designated as a backup device, it will no longer show up on the SBS Console as an available drive. It is recommended to configure more than one backup drive, so that one is always attached while the other is taken offsite.

The Windows Server Backup console supports backing up to either external or internal hard drives, optical media (DVD), or network shares.

Exchange/SharePoint Backup and Recovery

SBS 2008 will backup and restore both Exchange stores and SharePoint databases. Exchange transaction log files will be truncated if the backup successfully completes.

The VSS-based Exchange plug-in for Windows Server Backup is included in SBS 2008.

NOTE

Although SBS 2008 already fully supports Exchange backup out of the box, you may read that other versions of Windows Server 2008 are not Exchange-aware and currently cannot back up Exchange 2007.

Microsoft has announced their intent to release an Exchange plug-in for Windows Server Backup that will be available for these other versions of Windows Server 2008.

18

Easier Recovery

The SBS 2008 Recovery wizard can be used to recover specific files, folders, volumes, or VSS-aware applications such as Exchange and SharePoint. Simply choose the desired backup period and select the items to be restored.

Windows Server Backup supports bare-metal restores using the Windows Recovery Environment (WRE), which is included on the SBS 2008 installation DVD.

No Built-in Client Backup

The initial release of SBS 2008 does not provide client PC backup functionality, such as the one built into the Windows Home Server product. Microsoft might consider adding this feature to a future version of SBS 2008.

User data files should be stored or redirected to the server, and backed up from there. Also, there is no built-in functionality for automatically backing up member servers from SBS 2008. Member servers should be backed up on their own.

Understanding Backup Issues

A backup plan is one part of a larger business continuity and disaster recovery strategy. Consideration of business needs and statutory requirements, for example, should be addressed prior to server installation and implementation. Disaster recovery planning can be a complex undertaking, and the analysis of risk versus cost may indicate the need for more than one type of backup solution or schedule.

Backups are generally viewed as insurance against data corruption or human error that results in the loss of critical data or e-mails. There is a business value associated with loss of data or loss of productivity of employees. In addition to the monetary value (cost to replace software, operating system, data), the overall impact to the business if information is lost or destroyed must not be ignored or marginalized.

File Recovery

It is important to have more than one solution to a problem. This is true for data recovery. In addition to performing daily backups, SBS 2008 offers three user-level recovery solutions that can be made available to SBS users from their desktops.

Shadow Copy Restore

The Volume Shadow Copy Service (VSS) feature in SBS 2008 stores copies of files and folders on a volume at specific intervals to the local server hard drive. Administrators and end users with proper permission can browse and retrieve previous versions of files directly from their desktop without having to restore from a backup device. The size of the shadow copy file can be managed by administrators, and can be enabled or disabled on each volume.

Exchange Deleted Item Retention

The Exchange Deleted Item Retention feature provides users with the capability to recover recently deleted e-mails directly from Outlook. The default retention period in SBS 2003 was 7 days, but has been increased to 14 days for SBS 2008.

SharePoint Recycle Bin

A new feature in SharePoint 3.0 for SBS 2008 is the Recycle Bin, which is actually a two-level recycle bin. If a SharePoint document is accidentally deleted, the user can restore it from the Recycle Bin. Removing the deleted item from the user's Recycle Bin moves it to the Site Collection Recycle Bin, where a server administrator can recover the document, if necessary.

> **NOTE**
>
> For all three file recovery solutions, keep in mind that as the retention period or recovery area is increased, more disk storage will be required on the server, and this will directly impact the storage capacity requirement of your backup media.

Shadow Copy, Exchange Deleted Item Retention, and SharePoint Recycle Bin should be considered as a first line of protection against users deleting an important file or e-mail. They are not a substitute for regularly scheduled backups that are an insurance against physical disk loss, damage, disasters, or corruption due to application error or malware attacks.

Archiving

It may be necessary to keep permanent or long-term copies of data for legal, financial, historic, or auditing purposes. Compliance with legislation, such as HIPAA, Sarbanes-Oxley, and Gramm-Leach-Bliley in the United States, may dictate the need to add an archiving strategy to your backup plans.

Beyond speed and convenience, consideration must be made for the type of media and devices used for long-term archival storage. Will the device, drivers, and software be available when the business needs to recover the archived data? A vault full of backups is useless if there is no way to access them.

Use of tape backup might be the better solution in cases where archiving requirements demand a rotation of backup media to be retained for one to ten years. Consider using Windows Server Backup for daily backups and a third-party tape solution for archival/tape rotation requirements in such cases.

System Recovery

For many small businesses, the SBS platform is an ideal entry into a server-based solution. The ability to run a variety of services (mail, application, Internet, printer, fax) and centralize business data on a single hardware platform is very appealing.

18

Because SBS 2008 does not support clustering or trusts, it can also become a single point of failure for all those services and data. When the server is down, users are left unproductive. Without access to e-mail, Internet, and line-of-business applications, communications with clients and vendors are disrupted. Should an outage continue for some considerable time, the harm done may be irreparable and may even be a terminal event for the business.

Restoring an SBS server to new hardware in the past was difficult at best, especially if the new hardware was significantly different than the original. With SBS 2008, a bare-metal restore of the server is not only possible, but easily performed.

Hardware and Media

The choice of backup hardware and media has changed significantly in the years since the release of SBS 2003. Back then, tape drives were the preferred medium for backing up the server. Purchasing decisions compared the features/benefits of DAT vs. DLT, and single tape loader vs. auto tape loader.

With SBS 2008, we enter a world of storage media with terminology such as USB, Firewire, SATA, eSATA, and storage solutions such as DAS (Direct Access Storage), NAS (Network Access Storage), and SAN (Storage Area Network).

Consideration of the reliability, portability, and expandability of each potential solution is critical in designing a backup and recovery strategy.

The Backup Plan

There are too many true stories of businesses that faithfully made backups of their data on a regular basis only to discover that when the time came to retrieve data from a backup, all of their backups were either unreadable, incomplete, or completely blank.

A detailed backup plan must be developed and documented, and then routinely tested and reviewed. Such a plan should include random testing of backup media on a regular basis. Backup and offsite logs should be reviewed, and training of users responsible for performing backup and recovery functions (and their backup counterpart) should be performed and documented.

Best Practice—Developing a Backup Plan

Create a written backup and recovery plan that contains step by step instructions that are easy to follow. The plan should be reviewed and updated annually, and a copy of the plan should be kept offsite.

All employees should be made aware of the plan and understand their responsibilities. Make sure that more than one person is trained and responsible for each identified task. If the office manager usually takes the Friday backup offsite but they are on vacation this week, who is responsible for doing this task?

Test your backups with a random recovery of files at least once a month, and a full recovery of your server to a separate drive or server on a quarterly or semi-annual basis. Not only does this verify that your backups are working, but you are reinforcing the training of the employees to perform their tasks.

Site and Security

Securing your system goes beyond implementing strong passwords for users. Care and consideration must be given to the location of your server(s) and where you store your backups, and the security surrounding them.

There are many businesses where their server and communication equipment are located in an unlocked, converted closet that happens to be right next to a lounge or restroom. Anyone could walk in, grab a USB backup disk, and walk out. Keep in mind that in many cases, such backups might contain the entire intellectual property of the business.

Access to the server and backup equipment must be controlled and restricted. Consider a combination lock on the door. Pay careful attention to the temperature of the room or area where your server and data equipment is located.

Take the case of fire prevention. Many businesses store their backup disks and tapes in a fireproof safe purchased at a local retail store. This might seem like a reasonable place to store them. But in the case of a real fire, where temperatures can rise to 1,200 degrees or more, the inside temperature of a fireproof safe may quickly rise to 350 degrees.

However, most backup disk drives and tapes are only warranted for reliability in a temperature range under 125 degrees. There are fireproof safes that will keep the inside temperature below 125 degrees, but such safes cost several thousand dollars.

The off-site location you use to store your backup devices should meet the same scrutiny and requirements. With today's technology and Internet speeds, you should consider remote online backup services as an adjunct to the SBS 2008 backup solution.

Backup Schedule

There have been many books and articles written on the merits of tape rotation methods, most based on either the Grandfather-Father-Son process or the Tower of Hanoi process. And if you still incorporate a tape backup methodology, such tape rotations are invaluable.

With image-based, block-level backups, we need to adjust how we view and plan our backup rotation.

Because we are only backing up blocks that have changed, each backup disk device might contain backup versions of the server stretching back to several days or weeks. The actual number of versions on each backup device will depend on (a) how frequently the backups occur each day, (b) the storage capacity of the backup device, and (c) the amount of data that is actually changed or modified between backups.

Monitoring your backup device for a week will give you a good indication of how much data you can expect each backup device to hold.

Assume we run two backups a day, and we calculate that each backup disk can easily hold a week's worth of changes. If you rotate between two backup disks, you have a two-week window for recovering a missing or deleted file. By simply adding in two additional backup disk devices, you now expand your protection window to four weeks.

However, this does not address the fact that some data is only changed monthly, quarterly, or annually. If you have a requirement to retrieve a file from that far back, some form of a Grandfather-Father-Son backup rotation is required.

For example, you might decide to use four backup disks in rotation for your daily backups. Then, at the end of each month, you purchase an additional backup disk, perform a one-time backup of your entire server, label it with the month and year, and store that device offsite. At the end of a year, you will have twelve monthly backup disks offsite, plus your four daily disks.

Using the SBS Backup Tools

SBS 2008 provides a variety of tools and interfaces for performing backup and restore operations and manage backup media. These options are listed in Table 18.2.

TABLE 18.2   SBS Backup Tools

Tool	Description
Windows SBS Console—Backup and Server Storage Section	The Backup and Server Storage section of the Windows SBS Console offers an easy to use Configure Server Backup wizard for configuring and managing your server backup schedule.
Windows Server Backup	The Windows Server Backup console provides access to the standard Windows Server 2008 backup and recovery tasks and wizards, such as the Recovery wizard and the Backup Once wizard.
WBADMIN command-line tool	WBADMIN is used to perform backup and restore operations from a command prompt. Create custom backup scripts with WBADMIN and the Powershell cmdlets for Windows Server Backup.

Windows Recovery Environment (WRE)	The Windows Recovery Environment is located on the SBS 2008 boot DVD and contains the Windows Complete PC Restore tool that is used to perform a bare-metal restore of an SBS server.

Windows SBS Console

Windows SBS 2008 includes the Windows SBS Console for managing and configuring your SBS 2008 network (see Figure 18.1).

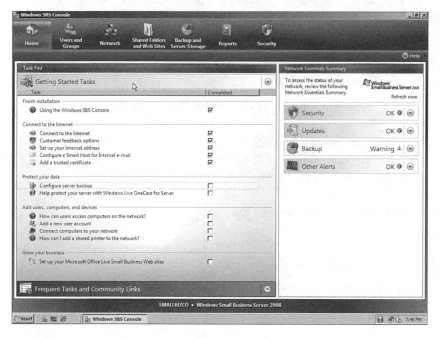

FIGURE 18.1   Windows SBS Console.

From the Getting Started Tasks pane on the left, you will use the Configure Server Backup link to help you initially assign backup media and schedule daily backups of the SBS server.

From the Backup and Server Storage tab along the top, you can access tasks and wizards to manage your backup storage and perform backup and recovery operations.

Configure Server Backup

The Configure Server Backup wizard in SBS 2008 is used to set up and schedule server backups. The wizard consists of three steps, as follows:

1. Select the backup destination(s).

2. Select the volume(s) to be backed up.

3. Select the backup schedule.

Before starting the Backup wizard, be sure to have at least one external (USB or Firewire) disk device attached to your server that will be dedicated for backups:

Best Practice—Offsite Backups

We recommend that two or more external disk devices (USB or Firewire) be used for the scheduled daily backups so that you can establish a practice of rotating your backups to an offsite location. A risk analysis of your business data needs will identify whether a daily or weekly offsite rotation is best for your company.

The storage capacity for each backup device should be at least 2.5 times greater than the amount of data that will be backed up to allow for future growth in data storage requirements.

1. Go to the Home tab in the Windows SBS Console.

2. Under Getting Started Tasks, click the Configure Server Backup link.

3. Review the information in the Change Server Backup page to make sure you have the information needed to schedule a backup, and click Next.

4. In the Specify the Backup Destination page, a list of available external disk drives to be used for backup purposes is displayed (see Figure 18.2).

   Select the drives to be dedicated for backup use, and click Next.

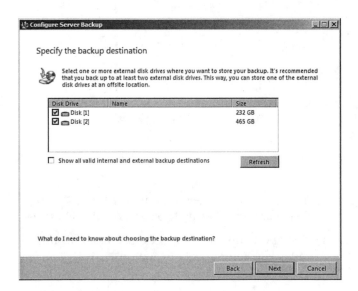

FIGURE 18.2   Specify the backup destination.

> **NOTE**
>
> Additional external disk devices can be assigned to the backup pool at any time. Use of multiple backup devices is encouraged, not only for offsite rotation, but as a preventive measure in case of a failure with a backup disk.

5. In the Label the Destination Drives page, enter a unique name for each backup device selected, and click Next.

> **NOTE**
>
> Be sure to place a physical label on the backup device and record the unique name assigned to the device. A good practice would be to also record the date this disk was first used as a backup device.

6. In the Select Drives to Backup page, a list of all internal hard drives that can be backed up is displayed. Uncheck any drives that you do not want to back up, and click Next (see Figure 18.3).

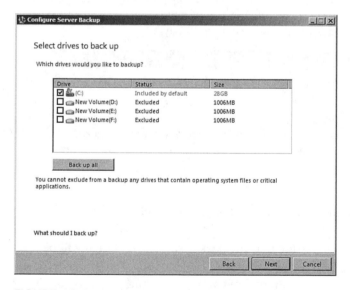

FIGURE 18.3   Select drives to back up.

The system drive (typically, drive C) must be backed up. Other drives that hold business critical information (such as Exchange, SharePoint, SQL databases, user's shared, or redirected folders) must also be backed up.

7. In the Specify the Backup Schedule page, select how often a backup should occur, and click Next (see Figure 18.4).

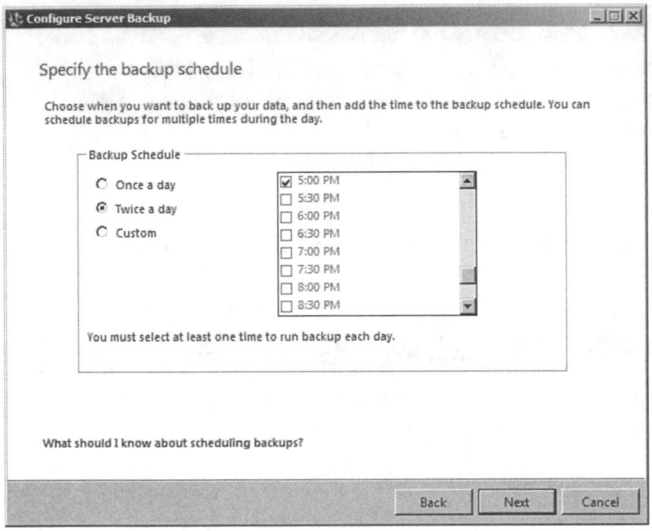

FIGURE 18.4   Specify the backup schedule.

By default, the wizard schedules backups to occur twice a day, at 5 p.m. and 11 p.m. The Once a Day option schedules the backup to run at 11 p.m. The backup schedule can be customized to meet your specific business requirements. The Custom option enables you to select when backups should occur every day.

NOTE

Windows Server Backup will complete quickly (in minutes as opposed to hours) and does not significantly impact server performance.

More frequent backups can be scheduled (up to every 30 minutes, if necessary). Be aware that increasing the number of daily backups might require the use of backup disks with larger storage capacity in order to retain the appropriate number of days of backups per your business continuity plan.

8. In the Confirm Backup Details page, verify that your backup plan is correct, and click Next.

9. A warning message appears, indicating that the backup device(s) selected will be formatted. Click Yes to proceed.

10. When the backup device(s) have been formatted and labeled, the Server Backup Configured page will display. Click Finish to end the wizard.

Add or Remove Backup Destinations

Use this task to assign or remove an external storage drive as a dedicated backup storage device by SBS 2008 (see Figure 18.5):

1. From the Backup and Server Storage tab, click the Add or Remove Backup Destinations task link, and click Add or Remove Drives.

FIGURE 18.5   Select backup destinations.

2. Click the adjacent checkbox next to the drive to be added or removed. If adding a drive, the drive will be reformatted and relabeled.

Add or Remove Backup Items

Use this task to include or exclude specific disk drives from being backed up by the scheduled backup operation (see Figure 18.6):

1. From the Backup and Server Storage tab, click the Add or Remove Backup Items task link.

2. Click the adjacent checkbox next to the disk drives to be added or removed from the backup schedule, or click the Back Up All button to select all drives, and then click OK.

Change Backup Schedule

Use this task to adjust the backup schedule (see Figure 18.7):

1. From the Backup and Server Storage tab, click the Change Backup Schedule task link.

2. Select the appropriate backup option: once a day, twice a day, or custom.

3. Select the appropriate checkboxes by each time of day that you want your backup to run. Clear the checkbox for any time that you do not want it to run, and click OK.

Pause/Resume Backup Schedule

Use this task to pause (or resume) the scheduled backup:

1. From the Backup and Server Storage tab, click the Pause Backup Schedule task link.

2. Click Yes to pause your currently scheduled backup.

18

FIGURE 18.6   Select drives to be backed up.

FIGURE 18.7   Specify backup schedule.

> **NOTE**
>
> You cannot pause a backup that is currently in progress.

3. Once the backup has been paused, the link on the Backup and Server Storage page will change to read: Resume backup schedule.

View Backup History

Use this task to view your backup history (see Figure 18.8):

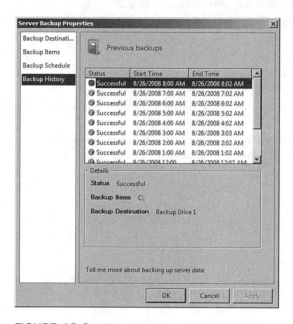

FIGURE 18.8   View log of previous backups.

1. From the Backup and Server Storage tab, click the View Backup History task link.

2. To view details for a backup, click the backup to select it.

Backup Now

After configuring a daily backup schedule for your SBS 2008 server, use this task to perform an incremental backup of your server at any time from the SBS Console.

> **Removing External USB Disk Drives**
>
> "How do I properly disconnect an external USB backup drive from the SBS 2008 server?" is an often-asked question.

We are familiar with the Safely Remove Hardware icon on our Windows workstations when we plug in a USB device, and so we might expect that we need to use it here before removing a backup drive. But this would require the person responsible for removing the backup disk to login to the SBS console!

The Windows Server Backup in SBS 2008 is designed so that the USB backup drives can be safely unplugged without the need to access the Safely Remove Hardware icon *as long as a backup is not actively using that drive*.

This can be handled with a proper backup schedule. For example, you have backups occurring every two hours between 6am and 6pm, and your operator needs to swap USB backup drives between 3pm and 5pm. In the backup schedule, uncheck the 4pm backup, and you now have a "window of opportunity" from approximately 2:30pm to 6pm to remove and replace the USB backup drive.

If you prefer that the user click the "Safely Remove Hardware" icon, the following steps will set up a User Role and User Account that would allow the user to login to the Server without any domain admin credentials, but have access to the Windows Server Backup console and the Safely Remove Hardware for disk rotation.

1. From the SBS 2008 Console, create a new User Role, label it "SBS Backup Operators," and choose Network Administrator as the base default.

2. Click the ADD button, remove all security group memberships from the right hand column, and then add Backup Operator from the left column so that this is the only group membership.

3. Be sure to uncheck OWA, RWW, and VPN options in the next several screens, and then create the role.

4. Use the Add User wizard to create a new user, and choose the SBS Backup Operators user group for this user.

Consider running such a backup just prior to installing an upgrade or hot-fix to a software application suite or the operating system:

1. From the Backup and Server Storage tab, first click the server object listed in the left pane; then click the Backup Now task link.

2. Click OK on the Backup Now dialog that appears to begin the backup using the same settings and options as the scheduled backup task.

Disable Backup

Use this task to completely disable the server from running the currently scheduled backup:

1. From the Backup and Server Storage tab, click the Disable Backup task link.

2. Click Yes on the Backup and Restore dialog to confirm disabling the scheduled backup task.

Restore Server Data from Backup

This task is covered in detail later in this chapter, in the section, "Disaster Recovery with SBS Backup Tools."

Windows Server Backup

Windows Server Backup is the new backup and recovery system that is part of the Windows Server 2008 platform, which includes SBS 2008.

SBS 2008 also comes with the Windows SBS Console and the Backup and Server Storage module. This is an SBS-designed front-end to Windows Server Backup and offers an easy-to-use user interface and wizards for performing many of the routine backup and recovery tasks.

Thus, you might see some similar or equivalent backup and recovery tasks in both consoles. For example, when you click the Recover Server Data Backup task link from the Windows SBS Console, it actually starts up the Windows Server Backup console.

To access Windows Server Backup, click Start, Administrative Tools, Windows Server Backup.

The Windows Server Backup console, shown in Figure 18.9, offers you a quick snapshot view of your backup operations, including a viewable log of recent backup and recovery activities, and details of current and scheduled backup tasks.

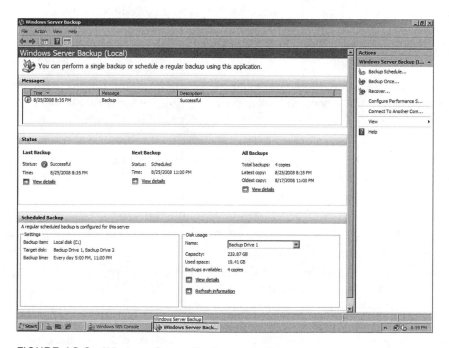

FIGURE 18.9   Windows Server Backup console.

In this section, we specifically look at two unique tasks that are found in Windows Server Backup, but are not accessible from the Windows SBS Console:

▶ Perform a custom one-time backup.

▶ Configure backup performance setting.

Backup Once Wizard

The Backup Once wizard is used to perform one-time backups to supplement your automatic backups. This backup is different than the Backup Now option found in the Windows SBS Console in two ways, as follows:

1. The Backup Once wizard enables you to direct your backup to an internal hard drive, an optical drive, a separate USB external drive, or to a network shared folder, whereas the Backup Now option only backs up to the designated backup devices.

2. The Backup Once wizard enables you to select which volume(s) you want to back up, whereas the Backup Now option always backs up the same volumes that are designated in the scheduled backup process.

Reasons for using the Backup Once wizard might be to create an end-of-year backup for archival purposes, or a full backup to be sent offsite due to an approaching hurricane.

1. From the Windows Server Backup console, click the Backup Once link from the Action pane on the right side of the screen.

2. In the Backup Options page, select what type of backup to create. You have two choices:

   ▶ **Same options**—This will perform an immediate backup using the same options and parameters that the scheduled backup uses, and functions exactly like the on-demand quick backup. If this option is selected, proceed to step 7 (Confirmation screen).

   ▶ **Different options**—This provides the ability to select which volumes should be backed up and where the backup should be stored.

3. If you selected the Different options, the Select Backup Configuration page displays. You can select to back up the Full Server (recommended) or choose the Custom option, which enables you to exclude some volumes from this backup.

   After making your selection, click Next.

4. If the Custom option is selected, in the Select Backup Items screen page, select which volume(s) should be backed up, and click Next (see Figure 18.10).

5. In the Select Destination Type page, select the type of backup destination you want to use to store the backup image to be created, and click Next. You have two options: Local Drives or Remote Shared Folder. Use Local Drives to direct a backup to an optical DVD drive or to another hard drive.

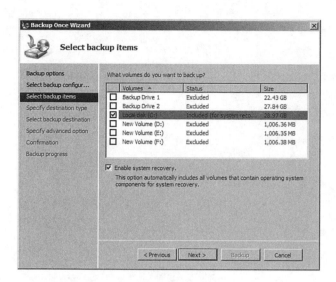

FIGURE 18.10   Select items to be backed up.

If Local Drives is selected, the Select Backup Destination page displays (see Figure 18.11). Click the drop-down backup destination field and select a drive from the list of available drives, and click Next.

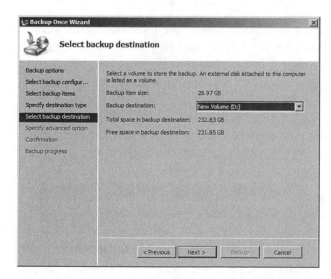

FIGURE 18.11   Select local backup destination.

If Remote shared folder is selected, the Specify remote folder page displays (see Figure 18.12). Enter the full UNC path name of the shared folder where the backup is to be stored (for example: \\ServerName\FolderName).

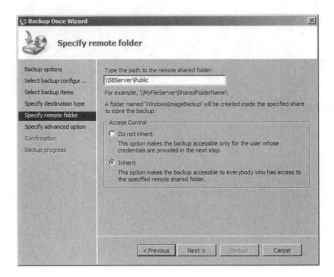

FIGURE 18.12   Specify remote folder.

The Access Control field is set to Inherit by default, and should normally not need to be changed. Click Next to proceed.

> **NOTE**
>
> If you want to restrict access to a single user, click the Do Not Inherit option for the Access Control field, and then enter the username and password credentials of the user on the next screen.

6. From the Specify Advanced Option page, choose what type of VSS backup you want to create: VSS Copy Backup (default) or VSS Full Backup, and click Next.

> **CAUTION**
>
> Unless otherwise required, leave this option set to the default selection (VSS Copy Backup).
>
> The VSS Full Backup option is designed to truncate the log files for applications such as Exchange. If you are using a third-party backup application, you should not use VSS Full Backup because it will delete the logs at the end of the backup. If the third-party application relies on those logs to take incremental backups, it would take full backups all the time.

7. In the Confirmation page, review your selection, and click Backup to start the back-up. Click Close once the backup is completed.

Configure Performance Settings

The Windows Server Backup console contains a screen for adjusting the performance of server backups.

Start up Windows Server Backup; then click the Configure Performance Settings link from the Action pane on the right. This opens the Optimize Backup Performance window (see Figure 18.13).

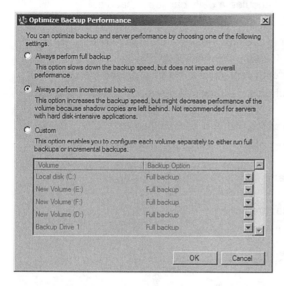

FIGURE 18.13   Optimize backup performance.

This screen enables you to select whether to always do full or incremental backups, or to specify full or incremental backups for each disk volume separately.

For SBS 2008, these settings should not normally need to be changed.

WBADMIN Command-Line

The WBADMIN command-line interface contains a set of commands for performing backup, restore, and query operations. In order to use WBADMIN, it must be started from an elevated command prompt. (Right-click Command Prompt from within the Start menu and select Run as Administrator.)

> **NOTE**
>
> WBADMIN commands can also be used in a batch file or scheduled as a recurring task from Windows Task Scheduler.
>
> For an example of scheduling a WBADMIN task, see http://technet.microsoft.com/en-us/library/cc732850.aspx

18

Table 18.3 includes a full list of all the WBADMIN commands available. Visit
http://technet.microsoft.com/en-us/library/cc754015.aspx to view the full syntax of each
command and parameters available.

TABLE 18.3   WBADMIN Commands

Command	Description
Wbadmin enable backup	Configures and enables a daily backup schedule.
Wbadmin disable backup	Disables your daily backups.
Wbadmin start backup	Runs a one-time backup. If used with no parameters, uses the settings from the daily backup schedule.
Wbadmin stop job	Stops the currently running backup or recovery operation.
Wbadmin get versions	Lists details of backups recoverable from the local computer or, if another location is specified, from another computer.
Wbadmin get items	Lists the items included in a specific backup.
Wbadmin start recovery	Runs a recovery of the volumes, applications, files, or folders specified.
Wbadmin get status	Shows the status of the currently running backup or recovery operation.
Wbadmin get disks	Lists disks that are currently online.
Wbadmin start systemstaterecovery	Runs a system state recovery.
Wbadmin start systemstatebackup	Runs a system state backup.
Wbadmin delete systemstatebackup	Deletes one or more system state backups.
Wbadmin start sysrecovery	Runs a recovery of the full system (at least all the volumes that contain the operating system's state). This command is only available if you are using the Windows Recovery Environment.
Wbadmin restore catalog	Recovers a backup catalog from a specified storage location in the case where the backup catalog on the local computer has been corrupted.
Wbadmin delete catalog	Deletes the backup catalog on the local computer. Use this command only if the backup catalog on this computer is corrupted, and you have no backups stored at another location that you can use to restore the catalog.

One example of using Wbadmin is to create a System State backup of the server. Because
SBS 2008 creates image backups, the need for a backup of the System State is not as critical
as in the past, but knowing how to prepare such a backup is still important.

The command to create a System State backup looks like this:

```
wbadmin start systemstatebackup –backuptarget:E: -quiet
```

where E is the local hard drive where the backup catalog will be stored and -quiet is the parameter used to not ask for confirmation.

> **NOTE**
>
> Don't be surprised when the System State backup takes a long time (up to one hour) to complete, or that the size of the resulting backup is 6-8GB, or larger. The reason for this is that included in the System State backup is a full set of core Windows 2008 OS files.

Windows Recovery Environment

The SBS 2008 DVD includes the Windows Recovery Environment (WRE), which is a set of tools to help diagnose and recover from serious errors that might prevent your server from booting successfully.

Later in this chapter, in the section labeled, "Disaster Recovery with SBS Backup Tools," we discuss how to use the Windows Recovery Environment to perform a full "bare-metal" restore of the SBS server from backup.

Backing Up SBS 2008 Premium Second Server

The Premium edition of SBS 2008 includes a copy of Windows Server 2008 Standard for use on a second, member server. This second server may be used, for example, as a line-of-business application server running SQL 2008. However, there are two issues that must be addressed, as follows:

▶ Windows Server Backup is not automatically installed on this second server.

▶ The Windows SBS Console on SBS 2008 server does not automatically back up this second server.

Installing Windows Server Backup on the Second Server

The following steps should be performed from the console of the second server:

1. Click Start, Server Manager.

2. In the Server Manager, click Features in the left pane and then click Add Features in the right pane.

3. Expand Windows Server Backup Features, and select the checkbox for Windows Server Backup. (The command-line tools are not required.)

4. Click Add Required Features, and then click Next.

5. Click Install from the Confirmation page.

After the installation is finished you can access Windows Server Backup by clicking Start, Administrative Tools, Windows Server backup.

Backing Up the Second Server

After installing Windows Server Backup, you must decide how you want to back up this second server. Two choices you might consider are as follows:

1. Use a separate set of external USB/Firewire drives and back up this second server separately from the SBS 2008 server.

2. If your SBS 2008 server has available space on an additional volume, create a network shared folder on that volume, and then configure Windows Backup Server on the second server to back up to that network shared folder. Then configure the SBS 2008 backup to include that volume in its daily backup.

Disaster Recovery with SBS Backup Tools

Creating, implementing, and testing a backup and recovery plan is a vital part of a larger disaster recovery (DR) plan for any business. A complete DR plan must address and identify critical business issues, in addition to the technical issues of recovering servers and data.

From a backup and recovery point of view, it is important that clear step-by-step instructions for recovering files, an application, or the entire server are part of your disaster recovery plan.

Backups must be regularly tested (at least monthly) by restoring some or all of the data to verify that created backups are both readable and usable. The Recovery Wizard in SBS 2008 is used to restore both data files and applications (Exchange and SharePoint).

On a more infrequent basis, a full "bare-metal" restore of a backup to a test server should be performed. The Windows Recovery Environment that ships on the SBS 2008 boot DVD is used to perform a full restore.

Best Practice—Document, Document, Document!

Besides creating and testing a backup and recovery plan, there are many other pieces of information that you should collect, review and document as part of an overall business continuity plan, such as:

▶ Maintain an itemized inventory of all hardware and software (including serial numbers and replacement cost). This inventory should be reviewed and updated quarterly and a copy stored offsite with your backup plans.

▶ Review your business insurance coverage against this inventory list to make sure that it covers the replacement cost of all your assets.

▶ Prepare a list of emergency contacts of your providers—insurance, phone, Internet, building maintenance, hardware, and software—and keep a copy with your backup plans.

▶ Contact your hardware and software vendors to find out what they might provide in the case of a disaster or emergency (replacement hardware, software, and so on).

The key to a successful plan is to "document, document, document"!

Document your plans.

Document whenever you test your plans.

Document that employees have been trained.

Document that backups taken offsite have been returned.

Document when problems occur and how they were resolved.

Document changes to your system.

Recovery Wizard

The Recovery Wizard is used to recover files, folders, applications, or an entire volume from a backup device. To access the Recovery Wizard:

1. Click the Backup and Server Storage tab of the Windows SBS Console.

2. In the Backup task pane on the right, click Restore server data from backup. This opens up the Windows Server Backup console.

3. From the Action pane on the right side of the screen, click Recover to start the Recovery Wizard (see Figure 18.14).

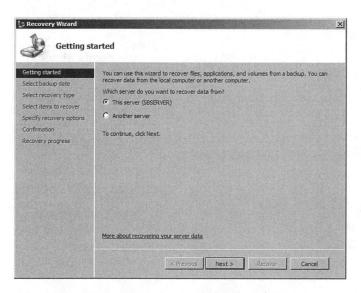

FIGURE 18.14   Recovery Wizard's Getting Started screen.

NOTE

Backup destinations may include assigned external USB/Firewire drives, other internal drives, optical DVD drives, or network-shared folders. The following examples assume you are recovering from one of the designated SBS backup drives.

Recover Files or Folder

The Recovery Wizard allows you to recover files or folders from any prior backup, and to restore those files either to their original location or to a different location. If the files being restored already exist, you can choose to rename the existing file or overwrite it.

1. In the Recovery Wizard's Getting Started page, leave the option set to This Server, and click Next.

2. The wizard scans the backup history log, and displays the Select Backup Date page. The most recent completed backup is selected by default.

   If you need to restore a file or folder from a prior point in time, use the Calendar to locate the desired backup to use. After selecting the appropriate backup to restore, click Next.

3. In the Select Recovery Type page, the Files and Folders option is selected by default. Click Next to continue.

4. In the Select Items to Recover page that displays, drill down to locate the file(s) or folder(s) that you want to recover. When all items to be restored have been selected, click Next.

5. In the Specify Recovery Options page shown in Figure 18.15, you have the chance to change what happens during the recovery process:

   ▶ **Recovery destination**—You can select to restore files and folders to a location other than their original location.

   ▶ **Files/folders already exist**—During the recovery process, you can decide what to do if any of the files/folders being recovered already exist in the recovery destination.

   ▶ **Security settings**—You can select whether or not to restore the security settings for each recovered file/folder.

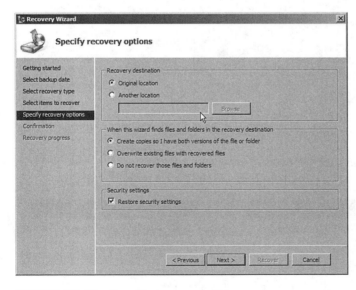

FIGURE 18.15   Specify recovery options.

The default options work just fine in most cases. If so, click Next to continue.

6. Review the Confirmation page, and if all is correct, click Recover to proceed. When the recovery operation is finished, click Close.

Recover Applications (Exchange/SharePoint)

SBS 2008 makes restoring the Exchange or SharePoint databases a simple task because Windows Server Backup is a VSS-based backup: Keep in mind that these are full data restores, meaning that you cannot restore just a single mailbox from Exchange or restore a particular document or folder from SharePoint.

> **NOTE**
>
> When restoring either Exchange or SharePoint, SBS 2008 will automatically dismount/mount the Exchange stores and stop/start any required services for you.

1. In the Recovery Wizard's Getting Started page, leave the option set to This Server, and click Next.

2. In the Select Backup Date page, click Next to recover from the most recent backup.

3. In the Select Recovery Type page, click the Applications option, and click Next.

4. In the Select Application screen, select which application (Exchange or SharePoint) you want to recover, and click Next (see Figure 18.16).

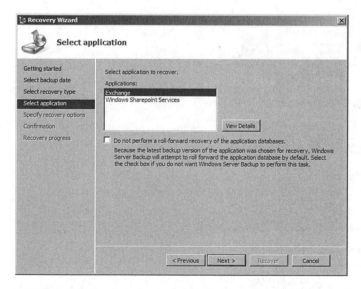

FIGURE 18.16   Select application to be recovered.

5. In the Specify Recovery Options page, you might select to restore the application to the original location (default) or to another location. Click Next to restore to the original location.

6. Review the Confirmation page, and if all is correct, click Recover to proceed. When the recovery operation is finished, click Close.

Recover a Volume

Recovering an entire volume might be required if an entire drive or data on the volume has been compromised or corrupted. Unlike recovering files, folders, or applications, you cannot restore a volume to its original location. It must always be directed to a different volume:

1. In the Recovery Wizard's Getting Started page, leave the option set to This Server, and click Next.

2. In the Select Backup Date page, click Next to recover from the most recent backup.

3. In the Select Recovery Type page, click Volumes and click Next.

4. In the Select Volumes page, shown in Figure 18.17, you can select from a list of volume(s) that might be restored (source volume), and specify the volume you would like to recover to (destination volume). Click Next to continue.

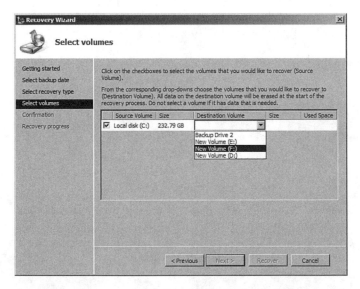

FIGURE 18.17   Specify where to restore the application.

5. After specifying your source and destination volumes, a warning message displays, warning that any data on the destination volume will be lost when you perform the recovery. Click Yes to proceed, or No to return to the previous step.

6. Review the Confirmation page, and if all is correct, click Recover to proceed. When the recovery operation is finished, click Close.

Full (Bare-Metal) Restore

Restoring a complete server is a far less complicated task with SBS 2008 than with previous versions of SBS or Windows Server products.

In the past, any discussion of a full system restore would require installing the core operating system files, and then any service pack files or other patches, before you could restore the data from backup tape using NTBackup.

Restoring a complete SBS 2008 server from backup, on the other hand, can be accomplished with just the SBS 2008 installation/boot DVD and your external backup disk, at a minimum.

NOTE

The term "bare-metal" refers to a computer that does not have an operating system loaded on it. That is, it is nothing but "bare metal"—no files, no data, no operating system.

A bare-metal restore refers to the process of restoring data to an empty ("bare metal") disk drive. Bare-metal recovery of an SBS 2008 server is now possible because of the imaging backup techniques used.

Prior to starting a full recovery of a server, be sure the following items are available:

▶ SBS 2008 boot DVD.

▶ Your USB backup disk device.

▶ If your server is configured with hardware disk controllers, you might need to obtain the appropriate .inf driver file from your hardware vendor for the disk subsystem. Store the .inf file onto a USB disk drive or thumb drive.

NOTE

Be sure to keep a copy of your current disk drivers offsite, along with your offsite backup disks and disaster recovery manual.

We are now ready to begin a full recovery of a server:

1. Boot up the server using the SBS 2008 boot DVD and get to the Install Windows page.
2. Confirm the Language, Time & Currency, and Keyboard or Input Method, and click Next.
3. Click Repair Your Computer (lower-left corner).

CAUTION

Do *not* click the Install Now link.

18

4. In the System Recovery Options page, confirm that your disk drives are listed. If not, you need to load the appropriate drivers for your disk subsystem, as follows:

   a. Plug in the USB drive that contains the appropriate .inf file.

   b. Click the Load Drivers link.

   c. A message window "Insert the installation media for the device" displays. Click OK to continue.

   d. Browse to your USB drive, locate your driver's .inf file, and click Open.

   e. A message window to confirm drivers to be loaded displays. Click the Add Drivers... link. A progress window displays while the driver is installed.

5. On the next screen, select the operating system (Windows Server 2008) to repair, and click Next.

6. In the Choose a Recovery Tool page, select option 1 (Windows Complete PC Restore).

7. In the Restore Your Entire Computer from a Backup page, confirm that the correct backup disk was found, and click Next.

8. In the Choose How to Restore the Backup page, click the Format and Repartition Disks option. When you do this, the Exclude Disks option is enabled.

9. Click the Exclude Disks link and select which disk drives should be excluded, and click OK. An Advanced button is available to override some options, but the defaults are acceptable as is.

10. Confirm information and click Finish to proceed.

11. A message window displays to confirm that you want to format the selected drives and restore the backup. Click OK to proceed.

Troubleshooting Backup Issues

As much as we might want it to be otherwise, scheduled backups may fail from time to time for various reasons. That is why it is so important to do random tests of your backups, and execute a test recovery of your server on a scheduled basis.

> **CAUTION**
>
> SBS 2008 does not have a way to send out an e-mail alert if the scheduled SBS back-up fails or does not complete successfully. The Windows SBS Console home page will flag a backup failure with a large red X.

In any troubleshooting scenario, it is always helpful to narrow down the scope of the failure in order to isolate and resolve the problem. This is true for diagnosing backup failures and errors.

Here are several places to begin troubleshooting backup or restore issues:

1. Collect information on the situation by reviewing event logs, the SBS Console, and the Windows Server Backup console.

2. Check the physical backup device and cable connection. A backup device with no power or with a disconnected USB/Firewire cable can be easily fixed!

3. Attempt a recovery of a single file from the backup device. If the recovery process cannot find the backup device, or has problems recovering the specified file, the backup device might need to be reformatted or replaced.

4. Attempt a manual backup to both the current backup device and to a second backup device. If either fails, this may indicate an issue with a specific backup device.

5. Rerun the Configure Backup Server and see if any errors are reported.

6. Check the Microsoft SBS newsgroups for any recently reported problems with the backup process.

7. If using a third-party backup solution, check the vendor's support web site.

8. A reboot of the SBS server, as a last resort, may clear up an issue with locked files or conflicts with running processes.

Although this is not an exhaustive list, hopefully it provides a starting point for diagnosing a failure with the backup process. As with most troubleshooting situations, resolving such problems is one part luck, one part experience, and one part magic!

Summary

A sure-fire recipe for failure is to not plan for one. Problems occur when you least expect them. Systems will go down at the worst time, such as when you are on vacation, or a critical business deadline is at hand.

A well thought-out backup and recovery plan needs to be tested, practiced, and revised on a regular basis. When a business cannot quickly recover from a disaster or system failure, the odds are good that they will be out of business completely within a year.

There are a variety of backup solutions, and the type of backup selected depends on many factors. That is why a risk analysis of a business and its data is so important. Operating without e-mail for several days is one thing. But losing recently entered contracts and invoices, or not being able to review current shipping inventory, is a death blow.

A properly backed-up server may be of help if a disk drive crashes or a user deletes an important file. But such good efforts go out the window if your office is vandalized, and your server and all your backup devices are stolen, as you did not implement keeping some backups offsite.

A disaster does not need to turn into a catastrophe.

Best Practice Summary

▶ **Developing a Backup Plan**—Create a written backup and recovery plan that contains step by step instructions, and keep a copy of this plan offsite. Make sure that more than one person is trained and responsible for each task. Test your backups on a regular basis.

▶ **Offsite Backups**—Use two or more external disk devices for your daily backups and implement an offsite rotation schedule of your backup devices.

▶ **Document, Document, Document!**—Keep an up-to-date inventory of your hardware and software for business insurance purposes. Compile a list of emergency contacts, and establish an emergency recovery plan with each of your vendors. Document everything—document your plans, document that you tested your plans, document that your employees are trained, document when things go wrong and document how they were resolved.

PART 6

Beyond SBS 2008

IN THIS PART

CHAPTER 19

IPv6 Overview

If you've been an IT professional long enough, you'll remember IPX/SPX and the transition to TCP/IP. Despite significant advantages in performance, flexibility, and security, some IT pros stuck their heads in the sand and didn't move their networks off of IPX/SPX until the operating system left them no other choice. It took years for the final holdouts to give in. The same thing is happening with the move from IPv4 to IPv6. This time around, it will be the ISPs that deliver the news that you have to change your network protocol.

In the old days, there were plenty of IPv4 addresses to go around, and desktops were issued public IP addresses; your router was responsible for making sure that internal traffic remained inside. The private ranges of 192.168.x.x, 10.x.x.x, and 172.16.x.x were largely ignored until an IP address shortage occurred. When that happened, ISPs started rationing public IP addresses, and NAT was invented. When private ranges became the new standard, most networks had to be renumbered, which helped make DHCP a networking standard. Rationing and the move to private IP addressing postponed the implementation of IPv6, but rationing can only take us so far, and the switch to IPv6 is inevitable. It's now likely that during the lifetime of your SBS 2008 server, you will make the switch to IPv6.

The transition from IPv4 to IPv6 will be led by China and India. In the initial distribution of IP addressing blocks, those countries were issued fewer of the total available. However, today they are using IP addresses at a rate far beyond capacity; as of this writing, they have already started issuing IPv6 addresses. The worldwide adoption of mobility, VOIP, peer-to-peer applications, and need for QoS make the transition inevitable.

The transition to IPv6 has a steep learning curve and will take a number of years for everyone to fully convert. Experts expect that IPv4 will be out of use in 5–7 years. But more importantly, the supply of new IPv4 addresses is expected to run out in 2010. At that time, your ISP will hand you an IPv6 address. Because you are reading this book, you already have IPv6 on your network—now is the time to begin to transition so you won't be one of those in 2010, staring at the IPv6 address given to you by your ISP and wondering what to do.

There are several reasons that IT pros are unprepared for IPv6: apathy, belief that improvement in technology negates the need to change, general dislike of change, and IPv6 addresses being hexadecimal. The latter is probably the biggest impediment to change. There's just no getting around the fact that hexadecimal numbers are difficult to read.

Difficult to read or not, IPv6 is the preferred protocol of Vista and Windows 2008. They are designed for their most efficient operation using IPv6. This chapter will not be a full primer on learning IPv6; rather, we discuss basic addressing considerations and an example of how IPv6 can be used to add productivity and remote collaboration opportunities. Microsoft also provides excellent resources for learning on http://www.technet.com.

Changing Technology

This change is kind of like when the world went from the telegraph to the telephone. If you stayed with the telegraph, eventually your conversations would go like this:

tap tap tap tap

HELLO

tap tap tap tap

Hello?

tap tap tap tap

Hello? WHO *IS* THIS?

tap tap

<click>

Introducing IPv6

Besides the obvious difference of the hexadecimal address, there are a number of other changes and additions from IPv4 to IPv6. This section helps you get to know IPv6 in more detail.

New Features

IPv6 is packed with new features. Some of the more interesting ones revolve around the efficiency of the new protocol and the benefits that it holds for new technologies like VOIP and peer-to-peer applications, as follows:

- ▶ **More efficient header**—Six fields have been removed and one added. The overall header size is much smaller, resulting in faster processing of packets.

- ▶ **Large address space**—By allowing jumbograms up to 32GBs in size, IPv6 takes better advantage of broadband availability.

- ▶ **Smaller routing tables**—Routers don't have to store as much routing information in their tables; more information about routes is contained in the address scheme itself.

- ▶ **QoS and IPSec included in header**—In demand by VOIP and government, these features are included in the header.

- ▶ **Neighbor Discovery protocol**—Enables the automatic configuration of networks based on proximity, vastly simplifying mobile use and ad-hoc networking.

Why Do I Need IPv6?

The need for IPv6 most likely won't be driven by the need of the IT staff or the business owner; rather, this is a change to the way the Internet communicates. On your local network, the benefits of IPv6 will be felt in faster download and file access times, fewer dropped or garbled VOIP communications, and improved ease of mobile networking. Once IPv6 takes hold, we'll see an immediate rise in demand for IP addresses from equipment not yet connected to the Internet.

But by far the biggest benefit of IPv6 is going to be felt in the user experience of effortlessly joining the network as they move from place to place. From an IT perspective, we'll know the magic behind the scenes is ad-hoc networking and the self-discovery features of IPv6. From an end-user perspective, suddenly things just got a lot easier for them. They will no longer have to stop and think about how to set up their computer to join a hotspot, conference room network, home network, or customer network, or how to get back into the office network.

How Do I Read IPv6?

Each IP address is made up of eight 16-bit chunks, and then converted to hex. If a section is all zeros, it can be replaced with :: as a shorthand. Any number of consecutive zeros is contained in the :: shorthand. Although the shorthand makes it easier to read, the reality of using IPv6 is that unlike IPv4, with complex subnetting and DHCP in practice, the need for reading an IPv6 address will not be as common. Most of the time, you simply release and renew your IP address in order to join the network that you've entered.

Table 19.1 lists the IPv6 addresses for the DNS root servers. Notice that rather than a subnet mask, only the prefix length is given. In IPv6, there are no subnet masks.

TABLE 19.1   IPv6 Addresses for Internet Root Servers

Authority	IPv6 Address
A.ROOT-SERVERS.NET	2001:503:ba3e::2:30/48
F.ROOT-SERVERS.NET	2001:500:2f::f/48

19

TABLE 19.1   IPv6 Addresses for Internet Root Servers

Authority	IPv6 Address
H.ROOT-SERVERS.NET	2001:500:1::803f:235/48
J.ROOT-SERVERS.NET	2001:503:c27::2:30/48
K.ROOT-SERVERS.NET	2001:7fd::1/32
M.ROOT-SERVERS.NET	2001:dc3::35/32

An IPv6 address is made up of three parts: Global Prefix, Subnet, and InterfaceID. When your ISP issues you an IPv6 address, they provide the Global Prefix; the rest is up to you to define.

Using our SBS 2008 server as an example, we notice that the IPv6 address is a link local address of fe80::7732:2308:83EA:229F/10. The Global Prefix is fe80:0:0:0. The Subnet is 0, and the InterfaceID is 7732:2308:83ea:229f. /10 is the prefix length.

IPv6 addresses come in four single (or unicast) address types and two multicast types: IPv6 unicast addresses can be global unicast (single address making the device unique in all the world), link local (small private networks), unique local (single address making the device unique on your WAN), and special (loop-back addresses).

IPv6 multicast addresses can be either routable multicast or anycast. Multicast is broadcast to members of the same group, and it is routable; however, your router will not forward the multicast unless it knows that there are members outside of the router to forward to. This prevents broadcast storms. Anycast addresses are single IPv6 addresses that have been assigned to multiple nodes. This allows for load balancing and failover of devices.

As in IPv4, certain address groups are reserved for specific purposes. Table 19.2 lists the network prefix and its allocation.

TABLE 19.2   IPv6 Allocations

IPv6 Prefix	Allocation
0000::/8	Reserved by IETF
2000::/3	Global unicast and anycast
FC00::/7	Unique local unicast
FE80::/10	Link local unicast
FF00::/8	Multicast

Saying Goodbye to DHCP

The difficulty of reading an IPv6 address becomes largely irrelevant when you realize that a DHCP server is not necessary on an IPv6 network. Probably one of the most difficult transitions for the current generation of IT administrators is saying goodbye to the DHCP server. How do network devices get IP addressing? In a pure IPv6 environment, a device queries a router to determine the prefix of the local network it has entered. It then assigns itself an IP address based on the information it has obtained from the router. Both static IP addresses and DHCP become a thing of the past.

In this manner, when a new PC enters the network, it is automatically configured for the local network, even if it is a visitor. As computer users become more mobile, the problem of configuring your computer for the local network on which they are present at the moment goes away, and the user can start to work immediately.

Creating IPv6 DNS Entries

Although you don't need to configure DHCP for IPv6, you do need to create DNS entries. Fortunately for IT administrators, creating an IPv6 DNS entry isn't very different from creating an IPv4 DNS entry—only the names have changed; the procedure itself has not.

In an IPv4 DNS environment, a host record is called an A record. In an IPv6 DNS environment, a host record is called an AAAA record. The only difference between the two record types is the IP address itself.

To create a new host AAAA record, do the following from within DNS Manager:

1. Right-click on the forwarding zone, smallbizco.net, and choose New Host (A or AAAA...).
2. The New Host configuration box appears. In the Name box, type **mysalesapp.** In the IP Address box, type the IP address of the web site. Press Add Host.
3. Click OK on the confirmation message. Click Done.
4. Test the name resolution by opening a browser window and typing the web site address.

Using IPv6

Simply talking about how IPv6 is going to work is not enough to develop an understanding of the impact that IPv6 will have. The following sections provide a practical example of using IPv6 that is available right now.

IPv6 in Action—Windows Meeting Space

In case you haven't heard, there is an application in Vista that requires IPv6; it's called Windows Meeting Space. Windows Meeting Space enables you to set up ad-hoc networks with up to 10 computers for the purpose of holding a meeting or collaborating on a document. It has powerful tools for sharing documents, desktop, or even making a presentation. Using IPv6, the computers in your ad-hoc network can be near or far. If you want to see IPv6 in action, look no further than your desktop.

Besides being able to provide several IP addresses for every powered-on device on the planet, one of the major purposes of IPv6 is to enable networking to automatically take place from anywhere. Windows Meeting Space showcases this feature of IPv6.

19

By default, your Vista PC has IPv6 enabled. For the purpose of this exercise, leave the default settings in place. Follow these steps to create a new Windows Meeting Space:

1. From the Start menu, select All Programs; then select Windows Meeting Space.
2. Click Yes; continue setting up Windows Meeting Space in the dialog box that opens.

You are now presented with the set-up wizard for People Near Me. People Near Me is the friendly name that Microsoft has chosen for ad-hoc networking. Using IPv6, people near you are not those physically near you (although they may be), but rather near you on your subnet. If your subnet can cross the boundary of your router, and your router knows that some members of your subnet are currently outside the local LAN, people near you might actually be physically located in other offices. This is the power of globally routable IP addresses in IPv6. The setup of People Near Me is done once. After you have People Near Me configured on your computer, this step is not necessary for future meetings or ad-hoc networking.

Before People Near Me configuration begins, you are asked to Allow People Near Me to configure Vista's host firewall. Click Yes and continue configuring Windows Meeting Space. People Near Me will open.

On the People Near Me window, you are presented with some very important choices in the Allow Invitations From drop-down menu box. Figure 19.1 shows this dialog box and its options of Anyone, Trusted Contact, and No One. On this screen, you are also asked whether you want to be automatically signed into People Near Me or not. If not, uncheck the box.

FIGURE 19.1   Choosing the security type for People Near Me is a very important first step in creating an ad-hoc network.

Before you can make the appropriate invitation selection, you need to know what People Near Me is and what Trusted Contacts are, as follows:

▶ People Near Me is a service that enables ad-hoc networking by identifying people nearby who are allowing ad-hoc connections. It enables those people to send you invitations to Windows Meeting Space and other IPv6-enabled applications. You can only be invited to use applications that are installed on your computer, and you have to be signed into the People Near Me service in order to receive the invitation.

▶ A Trusted Contact is someone, listed in Windows contacts, who has sent you his or her contact information in an e-mail message or given you the information on a disk or another type of removable media. A trusted contact's information always includes a certificate. To see your list of Trusted Contacts, open Windows Contacts.

Notice that in Windows Contacts, there is a contact entry for the currently logged-on user. To send this contact information to someone, right-click your personal contact (the contact with your name on it), and then click Copy. Open a new e-mail message and paste or drop the contact into it. If you see a message asking whether to convert the contact attachment to vCard, click No. The contact can also be sent as an attachment. The contact will have a file extension of .contact.

For the purposes of this example, choose Anyone in the People Near Me configuration window and press OK. A new icon appears in the System Tray to indicate that you are signed into People Near Me, and the Windows Meeting Space application opens.

At this point, ad-hoc networking has begun, and IPv6 is attempting to locate other devices in its subnet. The three peer networking services have also been started. Figure 19.2 shows that these services are now started.

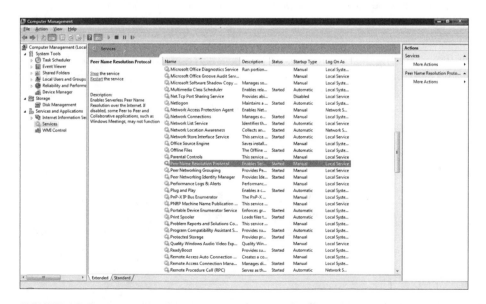

FIGURE 19.2   Peer networking services are set to manual and will not be started until you sign into People Near Me.

Figure 19.3 is the Windows Meeting Space configuration screen. You need to enter a name and password for your meeting; then press the green button to start a new meeting. Once a meeting has been started, anyone running People Near Me will be allowed to join the meeting and will see that a meeting is available to join when they open Windows Meeting Space.

FIGURE 19.3   Name the meeting, set a password, and press the green button to begin the meeting.

Running Windows Meeting Space gives you a glimpse into the future with IPv6. Now that you have People Near Me configured, anytime you are logged into the service and near other computers, you will be automatically networked with them. Ultimately, as ad-hoc networking becomes the norm, your ability to move within and between networks will happen smoothly and effortlessly.

Troubleshooting IPv6

Troubleshooting IPv6 is much like troubleshooting IPv4. The cast of characters is basically the same, as is the knowledge to interpret the results. In most cases, only the command has changed. There are also network resources available that can help you learn to troubleshoot IPv6.

Troubleshooting Utilities

The following utilities should be familiar, but they do have some changes to make them work as expected on an IPv6 network.

Ping

Ping is a utility that has never gone out of style. In SBS 2008, the ping command works in the same way it always has; however, it is now capable of pinging IPv6 addresses as well. To ping an IPv6 address, use the -6 switch:

```
C:\Users\sbsadmin>ping -6 fe80::5efe:157.59.138.63%2
Pinging fe80::5efe:157.59.138.63%2 with 32 bytes of data:
Reply from fe80::5efe:157.59.138.63%2: time<1ms
Reply from fe80::5efe:157.59.138.63%2: time<1ms
Reply from fe80::5efe:157.59.138.63%2: time<1ms
Reply from fe80::5efe:157.59.138.63%2: time<1ms

Ping statistics for fe80::5efe:157.59.138.63%2:
    Packets: Sent = 4, Received = 4, Lost = 0 (0% loss),
Approximate round trip times in milli-seconds:
```

Ipconfig

Ipconfig continues to be a useful troubleshooting tool. Just like ping, the command is the same, only there are new switches to apply, as follows:

▶ `Ipconfig /all` lists all IP configuring present on the system, including IPv6 addresses.

▶ `Ipconfig /release6` releases your IPv6 address.

▶ `Ipconfig /renew6` renews your IPv6 address.

Because we will not be using DHCP for IPv6, release and renew take on slightly different meanings. If you find that you have moved into a new network, but your workstation or mobile device is configured with the IPv6 addresses from another network, you use the /release and /renew commands to tell the system to query the router for the local addresses on the LAN.

Tracert

Trace Route has been updated to handle IPv6 addressing. There are new switches exclusively for IPv6, as follows:

▶ `Tracert -R` traces the round-trip route.

▶ `Tracert -S srcaddr` specifies the source address to use in the trace.

▶ `Tracert -6` forces tracert to use IPv6 addressing only.

Learning Path

The following resources help you get more information about IPv6 and how to troubleshoot IPv6 networks:

▶ Microsoft IPv6 TechNet page containing resources of all sorts from webcast to whitepapers: http://technet.microsoft.com/en-us/network/bb530961.aspx.

19

▶ Network World eight-minute audio primer: http://www.networkworld.com/primers/ipv6main.html.

▶ Cisco IPv6 Primer for Physical Security professionals: http://www.cisco.com/en/US/prod/collateral/vpndevc/ps6918/ps9145/ps9152/prod_white_paper0900aecd8073c232.pdf.

Summary

IPv6 is coming. In the lifetime of your SBS 2008 server, the change to IPv6 will happen. This chapter introduced the concept of IPv6, provided an example of how IPv6 can be used in your network today, and suggested a learning path. IPv6 will enable much easier mobile networking, eliminate the shortage of IP addresses, and enable clearer VOIP communication, but first administrators need to get comfortable with the coming change.

Best Practice Summary

▶ Although many IT administrators are reluctant to change and perhaps are intimidated by hexadecimal addressing, the reality is that the need to read IPv6 addresses is much less necessary than in IPv4. The fact that devices are self-addressing, and we no longer need DHCP, further reduces the complexity.

▶ The future is coming, and IPv6 will soon become dominant.

▶ IPv6 is the default protocol for Vista and Windows 2008. The transition of the Internet from IPv4 to IPv6 has begun. Experience the networking efficiency improvements by allowing your Vista and Windows 2008 computers to use IPv6.

▶ Try using Windows Meeting Space. Going through the exercise of configuring and using People Near Me will give you the feel for IPv6 in practice.

▶ When troubleshooting IPv4, take a moment to look at your favorite commands to see if there are any switches that have been added for IPv6 compatibility.

▶ Start learning IPv6 now. There are many excellent resources available.

PowerShell

Call it PowerShell or call it by its beta name of Monad, and neither one gives you a really good idea of what "it" is. "It" is a new command line and scripting language specifically designed for the Windows IT environment.

Still unsure of what that is? Think in terms of those basic rudimentary batch files that you've probably written in your career in information technology. Now think in terms of having a batch file that is powerful enough to configure user permissions in Exchange, move folders from one partition to another, and be used and called upon to augment Monitoring.

Who Needs PowerShell

For those of you SBS administrators who do not consider scripting your strong point, don't assume that PowerShell is not for you. Chances are that a wizard or a GUI that you use on a daily basis is built on the backbone of PowerShell. Furthermore, the version of PowerShell that you will be examining is version 1.0, though there is already a version 2.0 built. Arguably, in this version of SBS 2008, and even Windows Server 2008, there will not be an absolute requirement that you, personally, suddenly learn the nuances of cmdlets (pronunced "commandlets") and functions. You might, however, find that an application calls PowerShell behind the scenes or that a feature in SBS 2008 leverages PowerShell to provide additional features. Just don't be intimidated by the words, the verbs, the cmdlets, and the discussions about PowerShell. Although it is a command language built for administrators, Microsoft understands that PowerShell must be leveragable by developers to provide administrators with features and information they need.

Why PowerShell?

Windows Management Instrumentation (WMI) is a set of additional information or extensions. They augment the Windows Driver Model and provide the capability for the operating system to obtain information and notification. However, WMI fails in one way: It fails to showcase to third party developers the advantage of writing their own provider or agent to the operating system. Most developers rely on the WMI providers that are built by Microsoft.

With that in mind, the developers of Windows PowerShell wanted to develop a platform that provided the administrator the capability to script with .NET framework features but at the same time was open enough to encourage developers to use it to call upon it in various interfaces.

The best example of this meeting of the minds between administrators and developers is in the Exchange Management Console. As you use the troubleshooting tools built into the console, you can see references to PowerShell.

The most obvious use of PowerShell is in the Exchange Troubleshooting Assistant built into the console. To give you a more concrete view of how PowerShell is behind the scenes—and you don't even have to know it to use it—begin by launching the Exchange Management Console.

How PowerShell Is Used

To get an idea of how PowerShell is used under the hood without your even realizing it, let's take a look at one part of the Exchange Management Console that makes it obvious. In doing so, you'll understand how PowerShell is utilized.

1. Click Start, All Programs, Microsoft Exchange Server 2007.
2. Click Exchange Management Console.
3. Click Toolbox.
4. Underneath Mail Flow Tools, choose Message Tracking.
5. In the bottom of the Message Tracking Parameters window, shown in Figure 20.1, is a section called Exchange Management Shell Command, which is what we're going to examine.

In that bottom section is the PowerShell equivalent of what the graphical user interface is doing. The following command shown does exactly the same thing as checking the graphical box for receive, entering a start date, and then entering an end date:

```
get-messagetrackinglog -EventID "RECEIVE" -Start "8/24/2008 11:17:00 AM"
➥-End "8/24/2008 11:27:00  AM"
```

Let's examine the components of this command:

▶ `get-messagetrackinglog` is the Exchange PowerShell command that invokes the tracking log searching.

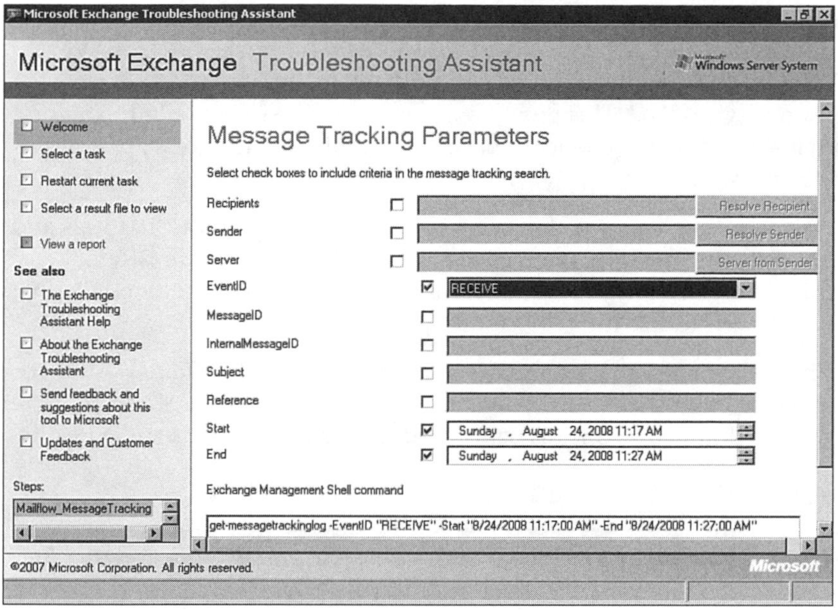

FIGURE 20.1   Shared Folders and Web Sites view.

▶ -EventID identifies the tracking event you are looking for.

▶ "RECEIVE" is the transaction type being tracked.

▶ -Start identifies the start of the timeframe you want to track.

▶ -End identifies the end of the timeframe you want to track.

On a single server, all you need is the graphical interface to perform functions. The same is true if you're using five servers. But if you do the same repetitive task over and over again, you might want to build your own repository of PowerShell commands and shortcuts.

Don't be intimidated by PowerShell. This is only the first version and already vendors are building graphical helpers; prebuilt script repositories are online; and a community of PowerShell-ers is out there to help support it. Although PowerShell certainly has more capabilities in large enterprises because of the economies of scale, and the Windows Small Business Server 2008 and Exchange 2007 development teams have done a great job wrapping graphical user interfaces around PowerShell, that doesn't mean you should not look for places where PowerShell creeps out under the covers and showcases its structure and use.

PowerShell Under the Hood

Historically, one of the areas of Windows management that needed improvement was enhancement of the command line. PowerShell was built on the Portable Operating System (POSIX) shell defined in IEEE Specification 1003.2. From that base, the decision was made to ensure that the structure of Windows data types was included as a supported category. The next decision made was to build on the .NET object model. .NET is a key component of Windows 2008 and is integrated in IIS 7.0, which is covered in Chapter 5, "Internet Information Services 7.0." This provides a means for developers, administrators, and—more important—third-party vendors to have a scriptable way to access applications built on the .NET Framework.

The ending result is a scripting language that can hook into Windows .NET platforms and infrastructure. What does that mean to the typical SBS consultant and administrator? As was showcased earlier, it means that you will be using PowerShell under the hood of SBS 2008 and probably not even realize it.

By default, PowerShell is installed and set for allowing scripts to run. In addition—due to SBS 2008's heavy reliance on Exchange 2007, which in turn relies on PowerShell— although you might not think PowerShell is being used, under the hood it's embedded in the product.

NOTE

Small Business Server 2003 and now 2008 are known for their wizards. So why is there a PowerShell chapter in a Small Business Server book? There is, as I'm sure you've figured out, a reason that PowerShell is featured here. Exchange 2007 in particular uses PowerShell and has a command shell that can be used in administering Exchange. Small Business Server 2008 uses PowerShell in its move folder wizards to move the storage location of folders from the original install location to a final destination. It's also used in the Configure Server Backup Wizard. PowerShell is utilized by custom XML files to enhance and extend the monitoring e-mail built into SBS. It's also used to enhance the spam filtering in Exchange 2007 on the SBS server. The bottom line is this: PowerShell is under the hood in many of the parts of Small Business Server 2008 and can be used by the administrator to perform tasks if you want to. Just remember that with the wizards included in SBS 2008, you don't have to feel that it's mandatory to administer the server.

PowerShell Basics

Unlike other platforms that have to install PowerShell to use it, due to Windows Small Business Server 2008's dependency on Exchange 2007, PowerShell is already installed. This brings up an interesting scenario, however: Because SBS 2008 ships with PowerShell, you cannot and should not upgrade to betas or other bleeding-edge builds of PowerShell. Although other PowerShell books tell you to download PowerShell, in SBS 2008 it's merely a matter of finding PowerShell on your system and launching it. There are two versions native to the Server platform. First up is the Exchange 2007 PowerShell command line, and second is the PowerShell that is included in Windows Server 2008. Internet Information Services 7 has also released a PowerShell module that can be downloaded from their community site at http://www.iis.net. Future releases will include more graphical versions of PowerShell so that it can be more easily used in implementations around the world. Although the typical SBS administrator might not see a need for PowerShell in a single deployment situation, in a setting where you have several Small Business Server networks as you are a consultant, you will probably find that building a script that you can reuse over and over again will serve you better in the long run for those tasks that you find that you are doing repeatedly.

Begin by clicking Start, Administration and then look for the PowerShell icon. Because PowerShell is needed by Small Business Server 2008, there is no need to go into the Feature Wizard in Server Management in order to add PowerShell. If you want to add PowerShell to a member server, however, you need to manually add the PowerShell feature.

So What Exactly Is a Shell?

Calling PowerShell a computer language tends to intimidate many people. But calling PowerShell a shell-scripting environment doesn't exactly describe it well either. We are all familiar with the command line. At a c: prompt, type **dir** and press Enter. We've used command line and not a single bit of a graphical user interface to get the information we need. The graphical user interface has been the foundational strong point in Windows, and the command line its weakest. Windows has an operating system kernel at its core. The programs that surround that kernel are typically called "shells."

When Windows 2008 was designed, there was a focus on several features. Amazingly enough for a company that built its reputation on graphical user interface, one of the focuses of Windows Server 2008 was command line and fewer services. Thus, Server Core, a base operating system with no graphical shell, and PowerShell, a command-line scripting language, were made a priority.

If you have an aversion to the command line, never fear. Future versions of PowerShell will include a more graphical interface because of the need to include support for other languages.

Using PowerShell

For some consultants and Small Business Server owners, the use of PowerShell is varied. You probably use it on a regular basis and not even know it, because its focus is both for the administrator audience and the developer audience.

For others, you use PowerShell through the use of third-party products and scripting web sites. Some of the resources for getting started include the following:

- ▶ **PowerShell location on Microsoft with links to the download**—http:// www.microsoft. com/windowsserver2003/technologies/management/powershell/ default.mspx. On this site you can download PowerShell and review additional resources.

- ▶ **TechNet Scripting with PowerShell**—http://www.microsoft.com/technet/ scriptcenter/hubs/msh.mspx. The TechNet site has over 500 PowerShell scripts preconfigured for your use.

- ▶ **PowerShell virtual labs**— http://msevents.microsoft.com/CUI/WebCastEventDetails.aspx?EventID=1032314395 &EventCategory=3. This site allows you to view various online labs on PowerShell.

20

▶ **PowerShell team blog**—http://blogs.msdn.com/PowerShell/. This is the team blog for the Windows PowerShell team; new information and releases are on this blog site.

▶ **Free PowerShell book for server administration**—http://blogs.technet.com/ chitpro-de/ archive/2008/02/28/free-windows-powershell-workbook-server- administration. aspx. This free book and workshops are great resources for envisioning server functions that can be automated in PowerShell.

▶ **PowerShell Scriptomatic tool**—http://www.microsoft.com/downloads/details. aspx?familyid=d87daf50-e487-4b0b-995c-f36a2855016e&displaylang=en. Scriptomatic is a helper tool that makes it easier to build scripts. They have released a specific helper tool for PowerShell.

Getting Started

One of the best ways to get started understanding PowerShell is not on your server at all but on your workstation. Use a test workstation, rather than a production server, to get a feel for the basics of PowerShell.

Download the current version of PowerShell from http://www.microsoft.com/powershell and open it up to see what it can do. You'll notice that when you go to Programs, Windows PowerShell and start the PowerShell icon, a command-line window opens up. Type **dir** and press Enter. You see output similar to the following:

```
PS C:\Users\JonDough
Directory: Microsoft.PowerShell.Core\FileSystem::C:\Users\JonDough


Mode              LastWriteTime                    Length      Name
d-r--             4/24/2008         9:56 AM                    Contacts
d-r--             5/18/2008         11:13AM                    Desktop
d-r--             5/26/2008         12:56AM                    Documents
d-r--             4/24/2008         9:56 AM                    Downloads
d-r--             4/24/2008         9:56 AM                    Favorites
d-r--             4/24/2008         9:56 AM                    Links
d-r--             4/24/2008         9:56 AM                    Music
d-r--             4/24/2008         9:56 AM                    Pictures
d-r--             4/24/2008         9:56 AM                    Saved Games
d-r--             4/24/2008         9:56 AM                    Searches
d----             4/24/2008         9:56 AM                    Tracing
d-r--             4/24/2008         9:56 AM                    Videos
```

As you can see, the dir command in PowerShell is similar to the dir command in the normal command shell. dir brings up a directory of the computer you are working on. What makes PowerShell different from a conventional command-line utility is its ability to use the .NET object model as the base. The .NET model brings self-describing data sets to the table. Self-describing data sets are data structures that make it obvious to the viewer of the script of what their intent is.

Commands

Every language has its own set of buzzwords, and PowerShell is no different. Basic commands in PowerShell start with a command, add a parameter, and add arguments.

Cmdlets

One of the first phrases you'll hear from the PowerShell community is "cmdlets," which are the first category of commands in PowerShell. It's the combination of the words "command" and "let." Specifically, this is implemented by a .NET class that is derived from the Cmdlet base class in the PowerShell Software Developers Kit (SDK). A class is a representation of a type of object, an object being a computer, a user or another identified item. A class is like a blueprint that describes the object in question.

TIP

If you really want to immerse yourself in a PowerShell education, download the PowerShell SDK, which is included in the Windows and Vista Software Developers Toolkit. Install only the parts you need at this web site: http://msdn.microsoft.com/en-us/library/cc136042(VS.85).aspx. You only need Win32 documentation, Win32Samples, and .NET development tools.

Cmdlets have a specific manner in which they are put together; there is a verb and a noun. Think of it in terms of an action command.

As a sample of a cmdlet, type the following into the PowerShell command screen:

```
get-help copy-item
```

Get-help is an action command that gets the detailed help file information for the cmdlet copy-item:

```
NAME
    Copy-Item

SYNOPSIS
    Copies an item from one location to another within a namespace.


SYNTAX
    Copy-Item [-path] <string[]> [[-destination] <string>] [-container] [-recurse]
➥[-force] [-include <string[]>] [-exclude <string[]>] [-filter <string>]
➥[-passThru] [-credential <PSCredential>] [-whatIf] [-confirm] [<CommonParameters>]

    Copy-Item [-literalPath] <string[]> [[-destination] <string>] [-container]
➥[-recurse] [-force] [-include <string[]>] [-exclude <string[]>] [-filter <string>]
➥[-passThru] [-credential <PSCredential>] [-whatIf] [-confirm] [<CommonParameters>]
```

20

DETAILED DESCRIPTION
     Copies an item from one location to another in a namespace. Copy-Item does not
➡delete the items being copied. The particular items that the cmdlet can copy depend
➡on the Windows PowerShell providers available. For example, when used with the
➡FileSystem provider, it can copy files and directories and when used with the
➡Registry provider, it can copy registry keys and entries.

RELATED LINKS
     Clear-Item
     Get-Item
     Invoke-Item
     Move-Item
     Set-Item
     New-Item
     Remove-Item
     Rename-Item
     about_namespace

REMARKS
     For more information, type: "get-help Copy-Item -detailed".
     For technical information, type: "get-help Copy-Item -full".

Functions

Functions are the next type of command. Functions are user-defined code—that is, they
are a PowerShell script that lives in memory while the interpreter program is running. A
script command is PowerShell code. A typical example of a function is a file with a .ps1
file extension. Think of functions as the DOS equivalent of batch files. With one or two
keystrokes, you can call a series of commands.

A function contains certain elements. There is a scope and a parameter list that is part of
the function:

```
function ¦ filter
        [<scope_type>:]<name>
        { param(<param_list>) <script_block> }
```

In the sample function file, the following script looks for small files of less than 100k in
size and returns a listing of those files found on the system that meet the criteria:

```
        function small_files
        {
            Get-ChildItem c:\ ¦ where { $_.length -lt 100
            -and !$_.PSIsContainer}
        }
```

In the future, we can then call the function whenever it's needed by referring to small_files in our scripting.

Native Commands

Finally, there are native commands. *Native commands* are executables that the operating system can execute. A native command is one that is not PowerShell specific. For example, if you build a PowerShell script to open up a Word document, that is a native command in the operating system:

```
PS C:\Users\JonDough\Documents\File.docx
```

Entering that command and hitting Enter launches the Word document file.docx and opens it up in Word.

Aliases

If you intend to use a certain set of commands over and over again and don't want to type in the full PowerShell command, you can use Alias to build a shortcut or abbreviation.

New-Alias is the command that you can use to build a small shortcut name for a long cmdlet that you may forget. Type **new-alias** and place a word to be your new placeholder for a cmdlet and press Enter. PowerShell asks you to provide a cmdlet that it now associates with the abbreviated command name until you close the session.

```
PS C:\Users\SBSAdmin> new-alias short
cmdlet new-alias at command pipeline position 1
Supply values for the following parameters:
Value:
```

If you want to use the same shortcuts in another session, create a PSConfiguration folder in your Windows PowerShell profile folder. To find your PowerShell profile location, type in the following:

Get-Variable profile ¦ Format-List

From that command you get back the information of where your profile is stored:

```
Name        : PROFILE
Description :
Value       :
➥C:\Users\SBSAdmin\Documents\WindowsPowerShell\Microsoft.PowerShell_profile.ps1
Options     : None
Attributes  : {}
```

In this folder, create a file named Microsoft.PowerShell_profile.ps1 and save your alias shortcuts in that file. When you restart your next PowerShell session the next time it saves these alias commands.

Execution Settings

When looking at what PowerShell can do, you need to review the security settings that allow executables to run. There are four settings that you can set, as follows:

▶ **Restricted**—No scripts can run. This is the default setting when installed on a system, and it limits what you can do with PowerShell. If you want to begin to use PowerShell, you need to avoid using this setting.

▶ **AllSigned**—Ps1 and Ps1xml files must be signed. This requires that you either have a code-signing certificate or other PKI infrastructure that allows for code signing. This may work for a firm that has a strong security policy but for most day-to-day administration it is hard to enforce.

▶ **RemoteSigned**—Ps1 and Ps1xml files from the Internet must be signed or unblocked and flagged as local. If you've ever downloaded a file from the web and had to change the security of the file to get it to install, you've seen the impact of files received from the Internet.

▶ **Unrestricted**—No digital signatures are required, and all scripts can be executed. This is the least secure setting and should be avoided except in lab settings. Unrestricted allows any script from any source to run in your environment.

It's not recommended that you run your PowerShell environment as unrestricted because that opens your system up for untrusted scripts to be run and lowers the security boundaries of your network. For the purpose of the following example, adjust the environment to Unrestricted. The way to do this is merely at a command prompt to change the policy. The command is Set-ExecutionPolicy. The values for this policy are Restricted, AllSigned, RemoteSigned, and Unrestricted. To set this value, you need to run the PowerShell as an administrator. Ensure that when you browse to the PowerShell shortcut, you right-click and choose Run as Administrator.

TIP

Small Business Server 2008 sets the execution setting as RemoteSigned by default. This enables you to run scripts local on the server but restricts scripts from the Internet to be untrusted.

Basic PowerShell Example

This section walks through setting up a basic PowerShell environment on any workstation. Follow these steps to set up the PowerShell environment:

1. Download PowerShell from http://www.microsoft.com/powershell.
2. Launch the PowerShell by right-clicking on the icon in the program list and selecting Run as Administrator.
3. Type **Get-ExecutionPolicy** and press Enter. You see that the computer is still set to the default of Restricted.

4. Set the policy to RemoteSigned, which is the same policy as the SBS 2008 server. Type **Set-ExecutionPolicy RemoteSigned** and press Enter.

At the end of these steps, the operating environment matches the default scripting settings for SBS 2008. In a true PowerShell environment, one should choose the proper level of security that is wise. For SBS 2008, the setting is to allow local PowerShell scripts, but scripts from a remote location are required to be signed. What this means is that when you receive a script from the Internet or from a web site, there are two ways to adjust the setting so that it is seen as a local script.

When you receive a script from the Internet, the script follows the Internet setting of zones. It is flagged as being from the Internet as the flag on the file is a value of 3. Values of 3 or 4 are considered "untrusted" when the flag is 3 or higher. Table 20.1 shows the values for the Internet zones.

TABLE 20.1   Internet Zone Values

Zone Name	Value
NoZone	−1
MyComputer	0
Intranet	1
Trusted	2
Internet	3
Untrusted	4

If you attempt to run this script without adjusting it, you get an error message indicating that the ps1 (PowerShell script) is not digitally signed and the script will not execute on the system. To adjust this, you can open up the zone identifier in notepad by typing **file.ps1:Zone.Identifer** and changing the ZoneID-3 to ZoneID-2. Quite frankly, an easier way is to right-click on the downloaded script and click "unblock," which flags the file as being safe.

Best Practice—Closely Examine Scripts from Third-Party Sites

Only use scripts from third-party sites that have been examined for content. It's important to understand what the script does before deploying it in a production server setting. Set up test networks and practice understanding and writing PowerShell scripts. Keep these scripts on a USB flash drive, SharePoint site, or other resource. Finally, keep the SBS 2008 server scripting setting configured to block remote scripts. This keeps an adequate level of safety when you are in a server-scripting environment.

If the server environment requires that PowerShell scripts are signed, consider using the self-signed certificate environment to deploy scripts. Additional information on how to set

20

up a signing policy can be found at http://www.hanselman.com/blog/
SigningPowerShellScripts.aspx.

Windows PowerShell Script

As an administrator, and specifically as a Small Business Server consultant and administrator, most of the time you will probably start with PowerShell repositories of scripts and build favorites from there. Let's take a sample PowerShell script from the script repository: http://www.microsoft.com/technet/scriptcenter/scripts/msh/default.mspx?mfr=true.

The PowerShell script chosen for this example prepares a list of hotfixes on a server or workstation. To get this script:

1. Go to http://www.microsoft.com/technet/scriptcenter/scripts/msh/
   default.mspx?mfr=true.
2. Scroll down to the section called Service Packs and Hotfixes.
3. Choose the script called List Installed Hot Fixes.

The script is as follows:

```
$strComputer = "."

$colItems = get-wmiobject -class "Win32_QuickFixEngineering" -namespace
➥"root\CIMV2" `
-computername $strComputer

foreach ($objItem in $colItems) {
      write-host "Caption: " $objItem.Caption
      write-host "CS Name: " $objItem.CSName
      write-host "Description: " $objItem.Description
      write-host "Fix Comments: " $objItem.FixComments
      write-host "HotFix ID: " $objItem.HotFixID
      write-host "InstallationDate: " $objItem.InstallDate
      write-host "Installed By: " $objItem.InstalledBy
      write-host "Installed On: " $objItem.InstalledOn
      write-host "Name: " $objItem.Name
      write-host "Service Pack In Effect: " $objItem.ServicePackInEffect
      write-host "Status: " $objItem.Status
      write-host
}
```

There are several ways to run this script on a system. The first way is to copy and paste the script straight into the PowerScript command line. Highlight the script from the site, and in the PowerShell window, click on the PowerShell icon at the top of the window, click on edit, and then click on paste. Alternatively, you can save the file to a .ps1 format and call the file from there.

Let's examine what each line does:

```
$strComputer = "."
```

This line tells the script to look at the local computer:

```
$colItems = get-wmiobject -class "Win32_QuickFixEngineering" -namespace
➥"root\CIMV2" `
```

This line tells the script to look for the object items that are labeled quickfixengineering. These are patches that were applied to the system:

```
-computername $strComputer

foreach ($objItem in $colItems) {
     write-host "Caption: " $objItem.Caption
     write-host "CS Name: " $objItem.CSName
     write-host "Description: " $objItem.Description
     write-host "Fix Comments: " $objItem.FixComments
     write-host "HotFix ID: " $objItem.HotFixID
     write-host "InstallationDate: " $objItem.InstallDate
     write-host "Installed By: " $objItem.InstalledBy
     write-host "Installed On: " $objItem.InstalledOn
     write-host "Name: " $objItem.Name
     write-host "Service Pack In Effect: " $objItem.ServicePackInEffect
     write-host "Status: " $objItem.Status
     write-host
}
```

This section states that for each item found, list the name, hotfix ID, service pack in effect, and so on. This script then writes to the screen the list of hotfixes and security patches applied to the system (see Figure 20.2). To write this same information to a text file, port it out to a file. The script to export out the results to a text file and ¦ out-File textname.txt to the PowerShell script is shown here:

```
$strComputer = "."

$colItems = get-wmiobject -class "Win32_QuickFixEngineering"
➥-namespace "root\CIMV2" `
-computername $strComputer ¦ out-File textname.txt


foreach ($objItem in $colItems) {
     write-host "Caption: " $objItem.Caption
     write-host "CS Name: " $objItem.CSName
     write-host "Description: " $objItem.Description
     write-host "Fix Comments: " $objItem.FixComments
     write-host "HotFix ID: " $objItem.HotFixID
     write-host "InstallationDate: " $objItem.InstallDate
     write-host "Installed By: " $objItem.InstalledBy
     write-host "Installed On: " $objItem.InstalledOn
     write-host "Name: " $objItem.Name
     write-host "Service Pack In Effect: " $objItem.ServicePackInEffect
```

20

```
        write-host "Status: " $objItem.Status
        write-host
}
```

This places the results in a text file.

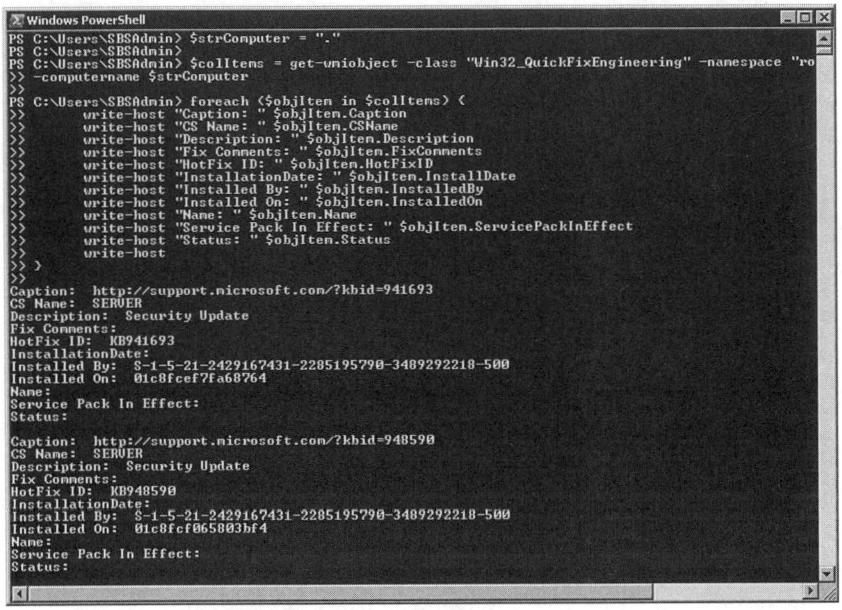

FIGURE 20.2   Output from the Windows PowerShell example script.

Exchange PowerShell Script

Now let's give some samples of where you most see PowerShell in action in Exchange 2007. In our sample, we're going to set Exchange 2007 so that it allows POP connections to it and also allows plain text logins.

We need to first set the POP service to be turned on with the following commands:

```
Set-service msExchangePOP3 –startuptype automatic
Start-service -service msExchangePOP3
```
Next, we need to set the server to allow for plain text login:

```
Set-POPSettings -LoginType PlainTextLogin
```

The commands set the login type to plain text.

We then need to restart the POP service with the following command:

```
Restart-Service -service msExchangePOP3
```

Note that in our example, we can run some of the commands from the native PowerShell 1.0 command line, but the Exchange PowerShell command mode is under the Exchange 2007 administration setting. Although we can set the services start mode from the normal

PowerShell command line, we cannot do specific Exchange commands like Set-POPSettings without being at the Exchange PowerShell administration.

In our example, some of the PowerShell commands can be done in the Windows PowerShell window, and some have to be done in the Exchange PowerShell console. If you are merely starting and stopping server services, this can be done in the normal Windows PowerShell window. Commands that are unique to Exchange, however, must be done in the Exchange PowerShell command window.

Launch the PowerShell command window by finding the Windows PowerShell underneath Program files on the server. Right-click and select Run As Administrator.

At the resulting PowerShell command prompt, type the following:

```
Set-service msExchangePOP3 -startuptype automatic
```

The response is a PowerShell command prompt. The next command turns on the service:

```
Start-service -service msExchangePOP3
```

Again, the response is a PowerShell command prompt. For the next command that enables the POP service on Exchange 2007, you have to use the Exchange Management PowerShell command window and not the Windows PowerShell command window, as shown in Figure 20.3.

FIGURE 20.3   Windows PowerShell versus Exchange PowerShell.

To perform Exchange commands, launch the Exchange PowerShell console:

1. Click Start, All Programs, Microsoft Exchange Server 2007.

2. Right-click the Exchange Management Shell icon and select Run as Administrator.

3. In the resulting command window, type in **Set-POPSettings -LoginType PlainTextLogin.**

After the command is entered, the Exchange PowerShell administration window responds with another prompt. This sets the POP service to allow plain-text logging into the service.

The final command stops and restarts the service on the server:

```
Restart-Service -service msExchangePOP3
```

The PowerShell commands set the service to automatic and start the service. Then, the Exchange PowerShell commands set the service to allow less-secure protocols and stop and restart the service.

It's important to keep in mind that all the commands discussed in this section could also be done within a graphical shell. You can manually go to the Services and adjust the POP service (not to be confused with SBS 2008's POP connector software) to be automatic and to then start it. You can also drill into the Exchange Console and adjust the POP settings to allow plain text and then go back to the Services and click on restart the services. However, think of the time spent in clicking around the Graphical interface versus the amount of time at the command line. Obviously, some tasks in PowerShell take you longer to look up than if you clicked around the Graphical shell, but there are probably some commands that are found that can be done in PowerShell faster than if done in the GUI.

Take, for example, the command that gives you an overview of the ActiveSync settings in Exchange. In the Exchange PowerShell command window, type the command **Get-ActiveSyncMailboxPolicy.** Get is the command to the system, and ActiveSyncMailboxPolicy lists the policies on the server set by the SBS 2008 system. As you scroll down the resulting window, review and understand the settings that have been set on the server:

```
[PS] C:\Windows\System32>Get-ActiveSyncMailboxPolicy
AllowNonProvisionableDevices               : True
AlphanumericDevicePasswordRequired         : False
AttachmentsEnabled                         : True
DeviceEncryptionEnabled                    : False
RequireStorageCardEncryption               : False
DevicePasswordEnabled                      : True
PasswordRecoveryEnabled                    : False
DevicePolicyRefreshInterval                : unlimited
AllowSimpleDevicePassword                  : True
MaxAttachmentSize                          : unlimited
WSSAccessEnabled                           : True
UNCAccessEnabled                           : True
MinDevicePasswordLength                    : 4
MaxInactivityTimeDeviceLock                : 00:05:00
MaxDevicePasswordFailedAttempts            : 10
DevicePasswordExpiration                   : unlimited
```

```
DevicePasswordHistory                          : 0
IsDefaultPolicy                                : True
AllowStorageCard                               : True
AllowCamera                                    : True
RequireDeviceEncryption                        : False
AllowUnsignedApplications                      : True
AllowUnsignedInstallationPackages              : True
AllowWiFi                                      : True
AllowTextMessaging                             : True
AllowPOPIMAPEmail                              : True
AllowIrDA                                      : True
RequireManualSyncWhenRoaming                   : False
AllowDesktopSync                               : True
AllowHTMLEmail                                 : True
RequireSignedSMIMEMessages                     : False
RequireEncryptedSMIMEMessages                  : False
AllowSMIMESoftCerts                            : Truc
AllowBrowser                                   : True
AllowConsumerEmail                             : True
AllowRemoteDesktop                             : True
AllowInternetSharing                           : True
AllowBluetooth                                 : Allow
MaxCalendarAgeFilter                           : All
MaxEmailAgeFilter                              : All
RequireSignedSMIMEAlgorithm                    : SHA1
RequireEncryptionSMIMEAlgorithm                : TripleDES
AllowSMIMEEncryptionAlgorithmNegotiation       : AllowAnyAlgorithmNegotiation
MinDevicePasswordComplexCharacters             : 3
MaxEmailBodyTruncationSize                     : unlimited
MaxEmailHTMLBodyTruncationSize                 : unlimited
UnapprovedInROMApplicationList                 : {}
ApprovedApplicationList                        : {}
AllowExternalDeviceManagement                  : False
MailboxPolicyFlags                             : 0
AdminDisplayName                               :
ExchangeVersion                                : 0.1 (8.0.535.0)
Name                          : Windows SBS Mobile Mailbox Policy SB
                                SERVER
DistinguishedName             : CN=Windows SBS Mobile Mailbox Policy
                                SBSERVER,CN=Mobile Mailbox Policies
                                ,CN=First Organization,CN=Microsoft
                                Exchange,CN=Services,CN=Configuration
                                ,DC=SMALLBIZCO,DC=local
Identity                      : Windows SBS Mobile Mailbox Policy SB
                                SERVER
Guid                          : 5cc6df12-808e-4ce6-b773-c260ca074b6f
```

```
ObjectCategory              : SMALLBIZCO.local/Configuration/Schem
                                   a/ms-Exch-Mobile-Mailbox-Policy
ObjectClass                 : {top, msExchRecipientTemplate, msExc
                                   hMobileMailboxPolicy}
WhenChanged                 : 5/15/2008 6:00:21 PM
WhenCreated                 : 5/15/2008 5:46:25  PM
OriginatingServer           : SBSERVER.SMALLBIZCO.local
IsValid                     : True
```

Could all of those settings be reviewed in the graphical user interface? Yes they could, but it would take much longer to go into each setting and review the settings. The Exchange PowerShell commands can even be added to the PowerShell script window so that only one PowerShell location is used.

TIP

There are actually two PowerShell command windows: One is a 32-bit window, and the other a 64-bit window. Due to the fact that Exchange 2007 is a 64-bit system, the Exchange PowerShell commands can be added to the 64-bit window, but not the 32-bit window.

Launch the 64-bit version of the PowerShell window and type the following instruction:

```
Add-PSSnapin -name Microsoft.Exchange.Management.PowerShell.Admin
```

The Exchange PowerShell commands can now be entered in the normal Windows-based PowerShell window so that two PowerShell environments are no longer needed.

The Power of PowerShell

It's important to stress the basics of PowerShell so that you can understand what PowerShell can do. In both the normal PowerShell command and the Exchange PowerShell command, the commands detailed in the following sections can be typed in to get your bearings on what PowerShell can do. Keith Hill's excellent foundational blog post spells it out in a series of basic commands: http://keithhill.spaces.live.com/blog/cns!5A8D2641E0963A97!788.entry.

get-command

The get-command gives the basics of what cmdlets are available. In both the PowerShell and in the Exchange PowerShell, type the following:

```
get-command
```

This gives you a listing of the commands you are able to do in each environment. In normal PowerShell, it's mainly Windows commands; in Exchange, the commands include provisioning and managing e-mail and mailboxes.

For example, typing get-excommand in the Exchange PowerShell window brings up the following Exchange PowerShell commands:

```
CommandType      Name
----------       ----
Cmdlet           Add-ADPermission
Cmdlet           Add-AvailabilityAddressSpace
Cmdlet           Add-ContentFilterPhrase
Cmdlet           Add-DistributionGroupMember
Cmdlet           Add-ExchangeAdministrator
Cmdlet           Add-IPAllowListEntry
Cmdlet           Add-IPAllowListProvider
Cmdlet           Add-IPBlockListEntry
Cmdlet           Add-IPBlockListProvider
Cmdlet           Add-MailboxPermission
Cmdlet           Add-PublicFolderAdministration
Cmdlet           Add-PublicFolderClientPermission
Cmdlet           Clean-MailboxDatabase
Cmdlet           Clear-ActiveSyncDevice
Cmdlet           Connect-Mailbox
Cmdlet           Copy-UMCustomPrompt
Cmdlet           Disable-AntispamUpdates
Cmdlet           Disable-ContinuousReplication
Cmdlet           Disable-DistributionGroup
Cmdlet           Disable-JournalRule
Cmdlet           Disable-Mailbox
Cmdlet           Disable-MailContact
Cmdlet           Disable-MailPublicFolder
Cmdlet           Disable-MailUser
Cmdlet           Disable-OutlookAnywhere
Cmdlet           Disable-ServiceEmailChannel
Cmdlet           Disable-StorageGroupCopy
Cmdlet           Disable-TransportAgent
Cmdlet           Disable-TransportRule
Cmdlet           Disable-UMAutoAttendant
Cmdlet           Disable-UMIPGateway
Cmdlet           Disable-UMMailbox
Cmdlet           Disable-UMServer
Cmdlet           Dismount-Database
Cmdlet           Enable-AntispamUpdates
Cmdlet           Enable-ContinuousReplication
Cmdlet           Enable-DatabaseCopy
Cmdlet           Enable-DistributionGroup
Cmdlet           Enable-ExchangeCertificate
Cmdlet           Enable-JournalRule
Cmdlet           Enable-Mailbox
```

```
Cmdlet          Enable-MailContact
Cmdlet          Enable-MailPublicFolder
Cmdlet          Enable-MailUser
Cmdlet          Enable-OutlookAnywhere
Cmdlet          Enable-ServiceEmailChannel
Cmdlet          Enable-StorageGroupCopy
Cmdlet          Enable-TransportAgent
Cmdlet          Enable-TransportRule
Cmdlet          Enable-UMAutoAttendant
Cmdlet          Enable-UMIPGateway
Cmdlet          Enable-UMMailbox
Cmdlet          Enable-UMServer
Cmdlet          Export-ActiveSyncLog
Cmdlet          Export-AutoDiscoverConfig
Cmdlet          Export-ExchangeCertificate
Cmdlet          Export-Mailbox
Cmdlet          Export-Message
Cmdlet          Export-TransportRuleCollection
Cmdlet          Get-AcceptedDomain
Cmdlet          Get-ActiveSyncDeviceStatistics
Cmdlet          Get-ActiveSyncMailboxPolicy
Cmdlet          Get-ActiveSyncVirtualDirectory
Cmdlet          Get-AddressList
Cmdlet          Get-ADPermission
Cmdlet          Get-ADSite
Cmdlet          Get-AdSiteLink
Cmdlet          Get-AgentLog
Cmdlet          Get-AntispamUpdates
Cmdlet          Get-AutodiscoverVirtualDirectory
Cmdlet          Get-AvailabilityAddressSpace
Cmdlet          Get-AvailabilityConfig
Cmdlet          Get-CASMailbox
Cmdlet          Get-ClientAccessServer
Cmdlet          Get-ClusteredMailboxServerSt...
Cmdlet          Get-Contact
Cmdlet          Get-ContentFilterConfig
Cmdlet          Get-ContentFilterPhrase
Cmdlet          Get-DetailsTemplate
Cmdlet          Get-DistributionGroup
Cmdlet          Get-DistributionGroupMember
Cmdlet          Get-DynamicDistributionGroup
Cmdlet          Get-EdgeSubscription
Cmdlet          Get-EmailAddressPolicy
Cmdlet          Get-EventLogLevel
Cmdlet          Get-ExchangeAdministrator
Cmdlet          Get-ExchangeCertificate
```

Cmdlet	Get-ExchangeServer
Cmdlet	Get-ForeignConnector
Cmdlet	Get-GlobalAddressList
Cmdlet	Get-Group
Cmdlet	Get-ImapSettings
Cmdlet	Get-IPAllowListConfig
Cmdlet	Get-IPAllowListEntry
Cmdlet	Get-IPAllowListProvider
Cmdlet	Get-IPAllowListProvidersConfig
Cmdlet	Get-IPBlockListConfig
Cmdlet	Get-IPBlockListEntry
Cmdlet	Get-IPBlockListProvider
Cmdlet	Get-IPBlockListProvidersConfig
Cmdlet	Get-JournalRule
Cmdlet	Get-LogonStatistics
Cmdlet	Get-Mailbox
Cmdlet	Get-MailboxCalendarSettings
Cmdlet	Get-MailboxDatabase
Cmdlet	Get-MailboxFolderStatistics
Cmdlet	Get-MailboxPermission
Cmdlet	Get-MailboxServer
Cmdlet	Get-MailboxStatistics
Cmdlet	Get-MailContact
Cmdlet	Get-MailPublicFolder
Cmdlet	Get-MailUser
Cmdlet	Get-ManagedContentSettings
Cmdlet	Get-ManagedFolder
Cmdlet	Get-ManagedFolderMailboxPolicy
Cmdlet	Get-Message
Cmdlet	Get-MessageClassification
Cmdlet	Get-MessageTrackingLog
Cmdlet	Get-NetworkConnectionInfo
Cmdlet	Get-OabVirtualDirectory
Cmdlet	Get-OfflineAddressBook
Cmdlet	Get-OrganizationConfig
Cmdlet	Get-OutlookAnywhere
Cmdlet	Get-OutlookProvider
Cmdlet	Get-OwaVirtualDirectory
Cmdlet	Get-PopSettings
Cmdlet	Get-PublicFolder
Cmdlet	Get-PublicFolderAdministration
Cmdlet	Get-PublicFolderClientPermission
Cmdlet	Get-PublicFolderDatabase
Cmdlet	Get-PublicFolderStatistics
Cmdlet	Get-Queue
Cmdlet	Get-ReceiveConnector

20

```
Cmdlet          Get-Recipient
Cmdlet          Get-RecipientFilterConfig
Cmdlet          Get-RemoteDomain
Cmdlet          Get-ResourceConfig
Cmdlet          Get-RoutingGroupConnector
Cmdlet          Get-SendConnector
Cmdlet          Get-SenderFilterConfig
Cmdlet          Get-SenderIdConfig
Cmdlet          Get-SenderReputationConfig
Cmdlet          Get-StorageGroup
Cmdlet          Get-StorageGroupCopyStatus
Cmdlet          Get-SystemMessage
Cmdlet          Get-TransportAgent
Cmdlet          Get-TransportConfig
Cmdlet          Get-TransportPipeline
Cmdlet          Get-TransportRule
Cmdlet          Get-TransportRuleAction
Cmdlet          Get-TransportRulePredicate
Cmdlet          Get-TransportServer
Cmdlet          Get-UMActiveCalls
Cmdlet          Get-UMAutoAttendant
Cmdlet          Get-UMDialPlan
Cmdlet          Get-UMHuntGroup
Cmdlet          Get-UMIPGateway
Cmdlet          Get-UMMailbox
Cmdlet          Get-UMMailboxPIN
Cmdlet          Get-UMMailboxPolicy
Cmdlet          Get-UmServer
Cmdlet          Get-UMVirtualDirectory
Cmdlet          Get-User
Cmdlet          Get-WebServicesVirtualDirectory
Cmdlet          Get-X400AuthoritativeDomain
Cmdlet          Import-ExchangeCertificate
Cmdlet          Import-Mailbox
Cmdlet          Import-TransportRuleCollection
Cmdlet          Install-TransportAgent
Cmdlet          Mount-Database
Cmdlet          Move-AddressList
Cmdlet          Move-ClusteredMailboxServer
Cmdlet          Move-DatabasePath
Cmdlet          Move-Mailbox
Cmdlet          Move-OfflineAddressBook
Cmdlet          Move-StorageGroupPath
Cmdlet          New-AcceptedDomain
Cmdlet          New-ActiveSyncMailboxPolicy
Cmdlet          New-ActiveSyncVirtualDirectory
```

Cmdlet	New-AddressList
Cmdlet	New-AutodiscoverVirtualDirectory
Cmdlet	New-DistributionGroup
Cmdlet	New-DynamicDistributionGroup
Cmdlet	New-EdgeSubscription
Cmdlet	New-EmailAddressPolicy
Cmdlet	New-ExchangeCertificate
Cmdlet	New-ForeignConnector
Cmdlet	New-GlobalAddressList
Cmdlet	New-JournalRule
Cmdlet	New-Mailbox
Cmdlet	New-MailboxDatabase
Cmdlet	New-MailContact
Cmdlet	New-MailUser
Cmdlet	New-ManagedContentSettings
Cmdlet	New-ManagedFolder
Cmdlet	New-ManagedFolderMailboxPolicy
Cmdlet	New-MessageClassification
Cmdlet	New-OabVirtualDirectory
Cmdlet	New-OfflineAddressBook
Cmdlet	New-OutlookProvider
Cmdlet	New-OwaVirtualDirectory
Cmdlet	New-PublicFolder
Cmdlet	New-PublicFolderDatabase
Cmdlet	New-ReceiveConnector
Cmdlet	New-RemoteDomain
Cmdlet	New-RoutingGroupConnector
Cmdlet	New-SendConnector
Cmdlet	New-StorageGroup
Cmdlet	New-SystemMessage
Cmdlet	New-TransportRule
Cmdlet	New-UMAutoAttendant
Cmdlet	New-UMDialPlan
Cmdlet	New-UMHuntGroup
Cmdlet	New-UMIPGateway
Cmdlet	New-UMMailboxPolicy
Cmdlet	New-UMVirtualDirectory
Cmdlet	New-WebServicesVirtualDirectory
Cmdlet	New-X400AuthoritativeDomain
Cmdlet	Remove-AcceptedDomain
Cmdlet	Remove-ActiveSyncDevice
Cmdlet	Remove-ActiveSyncMailboxPolicy
Cmdlet	Remove-ActiveSyncVirtualDire...
Cmdlet	Remove-AddressList
Cmdlet	Remove-ADPermission
Cmdlet	Remove-AutodiscoverVirtualDirectory

20

```
Cmdlet          Remove-AvailabilityAddressSpace
Cmdlet          Remove-ContentFilterPhrase
Cmdlet          Remove-DistributionGroup
Cmdlet          Remove-DistributionGroupMember
Cmdlet          Remove-DynamicDistributionGroup
Cmdlet          Remove-EdgeSubscription
Cmdlet          Remove-EmailAddressPolicy
Cmdlet          Remove-ExchangeAdministrator
Cmdlet          Remove-ExchangeCertificate
Cmdlet          Remove-ForeignConnector
Cmdlet          Remove-GlobalAddressList
Cmdlet          Remove-IPAllowListEntry
Cmdlet          Remove-IPAllowListProvider
Cmdlet          Remove-IPBlockListEntry
Cmdlet          Remove-IPBlockListProvider
Cmdlet          Remove-JournalRule
Cmdlet          Remove-Mailbox
Cmdlet          Remove-MailboxDatabase
Cmdlet          Remove-MailboxPermission
Cmdlet          Remove-MailContact
Cmdlet          Remove-MailUser
Cmdlet          Remove-ManagedContentSettings
Cmdlet          Remove-ManagedFolder
Cmdlet          Remove-ManagedFolderMailboxPolicy
Cmdlet          Remove-Message
Cmdlet          Remove-MessageClassification
Cmdlet          Remove-OabVirtualDirectory
Cmdlet          Remove-OfflineAddressBook
Cmdlet          Remove-OutlookProvider
Cmdlet          Remove-OwaVirtualDirectory
Cmdlet          Remove-PublicFolder
Cmdlet          Remove-PublicFolderAdministrator
Cmdlet          Remove-PublicFolderClientPermissions
Cmdlet          Remove-PublicFolderDatabase
Cmdlet          Remove-ReceiveConnector
Cmdlet          Remove-RemoteDomain
Cmdlet          Remove-RoutingGroupConnector
Cmdlet          Remove-SendConnector
Cmdlet          Remove-StorageGroup
Cmdlet          Remove-SystemMessage
Cmdlet          Remove-TransportRule
Cmdlet          Remove-UMAutoAttendant
Cmdlet          Remove-UMDialPlan
Cmdlet          Remove-UMHuntGroup
Cmdlet          Remove-UMIPGateway
Cmdlet          Remove-UMMailboxPolicy
```

Cmdlet	Remove-UMVirtualDirectory
Cmdlet	Remove-WebServicesVirtualDirectory
Cmdlet	Remove-X400AuthoritativeDomain
Cmdlet	Restore-DetailsTemplate
Cmdlet	Restore-Mailbox
Cmdlet	Restore-StorageGroupCopy
Cmdlet	Resume-Message
Cmdlet	Resume-PublicFolderReplication
Cmdlet	Resume-Queue
Cmdlet	Resume-StorageGroupCopy
Cmdlet	Retry-Queue
Cmdlet	Set-AcceptedDomain
Cmdlet	Set-ActiveSyncMailboxPolicy
Cmdlet	Set-ActiveSyncVirtualDirectory
Cmdlet	Set-AddressList
Cmdlet	Set-ADSite
Cmdlet	Set-AdSiteLink
Cmdlet	Set-AutodiscoverVirtualDirectory
Cmdlet	Set-AvailabilityConfig
Cmdlet	Set-CASMailbox
Cmdlet	Set-ClientAccessServer
Cmdlet	Set-Contact
Cmdlet	Set-ContentFilterConfig
Cmdlet	Set-DetailsTemplate
Cmdlet	Set-DistributionGroup
Cmdlet	Set-DynamicDistributionGroup
Cmdlet	Set-EmailAddressPolicy
Cmdlet	Set-EventLogLevel
Cmdlet	Set-ExchangeServer
Cmdlet	Set-ForeignConnector
Cmdlet	Set-GlobalAddressList
Cmdlet	Set-Group
Cmdlet	Set-ImapSettings
Cmdlet	Set-IPAllowListConfig
Cmdlet	Set-IPAllowListProvider
Cmdlet	Set-IPAllowListProvidersConfig
Cmdlet	Set-IPBlockListConfig
Cmdlet	Set-IPBlockListProvider
Cmdlet	Set-IPBlockListProvidersConfig
Cmdlet	Set-JournalRule
Cmdlet	Set-Mailbox
Cmdlet	Set-MailboxCalendarSettings
Cmdlet	Set-MailboxDatabase
Cmdlet	Set-MailboxServer
Cmdlet	Set-MailContact
Cmdlet	Set-MailPublicFolder

Cmdlet   Set-MailUser
Cmdlet   Set-ManagedContentSettings
Cmdlet   Set-ManagedFolder
Cmdlet   Set-ManagedFolderMailboxPolicy
Cmdlet   Set-MessageClassification
Cmdlet   Set-OabVirtualDirectory
Cmdlet   Set-OfflineAddressBook
Cmdlet   Set-OrganizationConfig
Cmdlet   Set-OutlookAnywhere
Cmdlet   Set-OutlookProvider
Cmdlet   Set-OwaVirtualDirectory
Cmdlet   Set-PopSettings
Cmdlet   Set-PublicFolder
Cmdlet   Set-PublicFolderDatabase
Cmdlet   Set-ReceiveConnector
Cmdlet   Set-RecipientFilterConfig
Cmdlet   Set-RemoteDomain
Cmdlet   Set-ResourceConfig
Cmdlet   Set-RoutingGroupConnector
Cmdlet   Set-SendConnector
Cmdlet   Set-SenderFilterConfig
Cmdlet   Set-SenderIdConfig
Cmdlet   Set-SenderReputationConfig
Cmdlet   Set-StorageGroup
Cmdlet   Set-SystemMessage
Cmdlet   Set-TransportAgent
Cmdlet   Set-TransportConfig
Cmdlet   Set-TransportRule
Cmdlet   Set-TransportServer
Cmdlet   Set-UMAutoAttendant
Cmdlet   Set-UMDialPlan
Cmdlet   Set-UMIPGateway
Cmdlet   Set-UMMailbox
Cmdlet   Set-UMMailboxPIN
Cmdlet   Set-UMMailboxPolicy
Cmdlet   Set-UmServer
Cmdlet   Set-UMVirtualDirectory
Cmdlet   Set-User
Cmdlet   Set-WebServicesVirtualDirectory
Cmdlet   Set-X400AuthoritativeDomain
Cmdlet   Start-ClusteredMailboxServer
Cmdlet   Start-EdgeSynchronization
Cmdlet   Start-ManagedFolderAssistant
Cmdlet   Stop-ClusteredMailboxServer
Cmdlet   Stop-ManagedFolderAssistant
Cmdlet   Suspend-Message

Cmdlet	Suspend-PublicFolderReplication
Cmdlet	Suspend-Queue
Cmdlet	Suspend-StorageGroupCopy
Cmdlet	Test-ActiveSyncConnectivity
Cmdlet	Test-EdgeSynchronization
Cmdlet	Test-ExchangeSearch
Cmdlet	Test-ImapConnectivity
Cmdlet	Test-IPAllowListProvider
Cmdlet	Test-IPBlockListProvider
Cmdlet	Test-Mailflow
Cmdlet	Test-MAPIConnectivity
Cmdlet	Test-OutlookWebServices
Cmdlet	Test-OwaConnectivity
Cmdlet	Test-PopConnectivity
Cmdlet	Test-ReplicationHealth
Cmdlet	Test-SenderId
Cmdlet	Test-ServiceHealth
Cmdlet	Test-SystemHealth
Cmdlet	Test-UMConnectivity
Cmdlet	Test-WebServicesConnectivity
Cmdlet	Uninstall-TransportAgent
Cmdlet	Update-AddressList
Cmdlet	Update-EmailAddressPolicy
Cmdlet	Update-FileDistributionService
Cmdlet	Update-GlobalAddressList
Cmdlet	Update-OfflineAddressBook
Cmdlet	Update-PublicFolder
Cmdlet	Update-PublicFolderHierarchy
Cmdlet	Update-Recipient
Cmdlet	Update-SafeList
Cmdlet	Update-StorageGroupCopy ..

In reviewing that list of possible commands, you can see the scope of all of the possible commands you can run with the Exchange PowerShell cmdlets. And if you need to perform the same tasks regularly, it is more efficient to perform these tasks with Exchange PowerShell scripts rather than a graphical interface.

TIP

PowerShell can be used for quick analysis of a system. Here's a sample script on how much free space is left on a drive. From a PowerShell window, type the following:

```
$DiskDrive = GWMI -CL Win32_LogicalDisk ¦

Where {$_.DeviceId -Eq "C:"}
$DriveSpace = ($DiskDrive.FreeSpace /1GB)
```

20

```
Write-Host Available Free Disk Space = $DriveSpace GB
```

This script, which was created by Don Hite at MyITforum, shows how much free space is on the drive. You can combine this with a text command and an e-mail command and have the report e-mailed to you on a regular basis.

Now let's look at the Windows-based cmdlets. Again, in the Windows PowerShell command window, type get-command and review the cmdlets that are available:

```
CommandType       Name
-----------       ----
Cmdlet            Add-Content
Cmdlet            Add-History
Cmdlet            Add-Member
Cmdlet            Add-PSSnapin
Cmdlet            Clear-Content
Cmdlet            Clear-Item
Cmdlet            Clear-ItemProperty
Cmdlet            Clear-Variable
Cmdlet            Compare-Object
Cmdlet            ConvertFrom-SecureString
Cmdlet            Convert-Path
Cmdlet            ConvertTo-Html
Cmdlet            ConvertTo-SecureString
Cmdlet            Copy-Item
Cmdlet            Copy-ItemProperty
Cmdlet            Export-Alias
Cmdlet            Export-Clixml
Cmdlet            Export-Console
Cmdlet            Export-Csv
Cmdlet            ForEach-Object
Cmdlet            Format-Custom
Cmdlet            Format-List
Cmdlet            Format-Table
Cmdlet            Format-Wide
Cmdlet            Get-Acl
Cmdlet            Get-Alias
Cmdlet            Get-AuthenticodeSignature
Cmdlet            Get-ChildItem
Cmdlet            Get-Command
Cmdlet            Get-Content
Cmdlet            Get-Credential
Cmdlet            Get-Culture
Cmdlet            Get-Date
Cmdlet            Get-EventLog
Cmdlet            Get-ExecutionPolicy
```

Cmdlet	Get-Help
Cmdlet	Get-History
Cmdlet	Get-Host
Cmdlet	Get-Item
Cmdlet	Get-ItemProperty
Cmdlet	Get-Location
Cmdlet	Get-Member
Cmdlet	Get-PfxCertificate
Cmdlet	Get-Process
Cmdlet	Get-PSDrive
Cmdlet	Get-PSProvider
Cmdlet	Get-PSSnapin
Cmdlet	Get-Service
Cmdlet	Get-TraceSource
Cmdlet	Get-UICulture
Cmdlet	Get-Unique
Cmdlet	Get-Variable
Cmdlet	Get-WmiObject
Cmdlet	Group-Object
Cmdlet	Import-Alias
Cmdlet	Import-Clixml
Cmdlet	Import-Csv
Cmdlet	Invoke-Expression
Cmdlet	Invoke-History
Cmdlet	Invoke-Item
Cmdlet	Join-Path
Cmdlet	Measure-Command
Cmdlet	Measure-Object
Cmdlet	Move-Item
Cmdlet	Move-ItemProperty
Cmdlet	New-Alias
Cmdlet	New-Item
Cmdlet	New-ItemProperty
Cmdlet	New-Object
Cmdlet	New-PSDrive
Cmdlet	New-Service
Cmdlet	New-TimeSpan
Cmdlet	New-Variable
Cmdlet	Out-Default
Cmdlet	Out-File
Cmdlet	Out-Host
Cmdlet	Out-Null
Cmdlet	Out-Printer
Cmdlet	Out-String

```
Cmdlet           Pop-Location
Cmdlet           Push-Location
Cmdlet           Read-Host
Cmdlet           Remove-Item
Cmdlet           Remove-ItemProperty
Cmdlet           Remove-PSDrive
Cmdlet           Remove-PSSnapin
Cmdlet           Remove-Variable
Cmdlet           Rename-Item
Cmdlet           Rename-ItemProperty
Cmdlet           Resolve-Path
Cmdlet           Restart-Service
Cmdlet           Resume-Service
Cmdlet           Select-Object
Cmdlet           Select-String
Cmdlet           Set-Acl
Cmdlet           Set-Alias
Cmdlet           Set-AuthenticodeSignature
Cmdlet           Set-Content
Cmdlet           Set-Date
Cmdlet           Set-ExecutionPolicy
Cmdlet           Set-Item
Cmdlet           Set-ItemProperty
Cmdlet           Set-Location
Cmdlet           Set-PSDebug
Cmdlet           Set-Service
Cmdlet           Set-TraceSource
Cmdlet           Set-Variable
Cmdlet           Sort-Object
Cmdlet           Split-Path
Cmdlet           Start-Service
Cmdlet           Start-Sleep
Cmdlet           Start-Transcript
Cmdlet           Stop-Process
Cmdlet           Stop-Service
Cmdlet           Stop-Transcript
Cmdlet           Suspend-Service
Cmdlet           Tee-Object
Cmdlet           Test-Path
Cmdlet           Trace-Command
Cmdlet           Update-FormatData
Cmdlet           Update-TypeData
Cmdlet           Where-Object
Cmdlet           Write-Debug
```

```
Cmdlet          Write-Error
Cmdlet          Write-Host
Cmdlet          Write-Output
Cmdlet          Write-Progress
Cmdlet          Write-Verbose
Cmdlet          Write-Warning
```

Get-help

One strong point of PowerShell is the built-in help that is already included in the scripting language. One of the ways you can get help with the language, in addition to tapping into the strong PowerShell community, is the help file itself. To access the available help, type the following:

```
Get-help
```

This provides a listing of what each cmdlet does and the function it provides. The help file is quite extensive, and you can even type Get-help cmdlet name to get specific help for that particular cmdlet. For example, typing the following:

```
Get-help set-acl
```

Gives you this output:

```
NAME
    Set-Acl

SYNOPSIS
    Changes the security descriptor of a specified resource, such as a file or a
➥registry key.



SYNTAX
    Set-Acl [-path] <string[]> [-aclObject] <ObjectSecurity> [-filter <string>] [-
➥include <string[]>] [-exclude <string  []>] [-passThru] [-whatIf] [-confirm]
➥[<CommonParameters>]



DETAILED DESCRIPTION
    The Set-Acl cmdlet changes the security descriptor of a specified resource,
➥such as a file or a registry key, to match the values in a security descriptor
➥that you supply.

    To use Set-Acl, use the Path parameter to identify the resource whose security
➥descriptor you want to change, and use the AclObject parameter to supply a security
➥descriptor that has the values you want to apply. Set-Acl uses the value of the
```

20

➥AclObject parameter as a model and changes the values in the resource's security
➥descriptor to match the values in the AclObject parameter.

RELATED LINKS
    Get-Acl
    about_namespace

REMARKS
    For more information, type: "get-help Set-Acl -detailed".
    For technical information, type: "get-help Set-Acl -full".

get-member

The command get-member helps identify those objects or items that can be referred to in
the language. To see a list of possible objects, type the following:

Get-command ¦get-member

Name	Member Type	Definition
Equals	Method	`System.Boolean Equals(Object obj)
GetHashCode	Method	System.Int32 GetHashCode()
GetType	Method	System.Type GetType()
get_CommandType	Method	System.Management.Automation.CommandTypes
get_CommandType()		
get_Definition	Method	System.String get_Definition()
get_HelpFile	Method	System.String get_HelpFile()
get_ImplementingType	Method	System.Type get_ImplementingType()
get_Name	Method	System.String get_Name()
get_Noun	Method	System.String get_Noun()
get_ParameterSets	Method	
System.Collections.ObjectModel.ReadOnlyCollection`1[[System.Management.Automatio...		
get_PSSnapIn	Method	System.Management.Automation.PSSnapInInfo
get_PSSnapIn()		
get_Verb	Method	System.String get_Verb()
ToString	Method	System.String ToString()
CommandType	Property	System.Management.Automation.CommandTypes
CommandType {get;}		
Definition	Property	System.String Definition {get;}
HelpFile	Property	System.String HelpFile {get;}
ImplementingType	Property	System.Type ImplementingType {get;}
Name	Property	System.String Name {get;}
Noun	Property	System.String Noun {get;}
ParameterSets	Property	

```
System.Collections.ObjectModel.ReadOnlyCollection`1[[System.Management.Automatio...
PSSnapIn              Property       System.Management.Automation.PSSnapInInfo
PSSnapIn {get;}
Verb                  Property       System.String Verb {get;}
DLL                   ScriptProperty System.Object DLL
 {get=$this.ImplementingType.Assembly.Location;}
```

Get-PSDrive

The last basic command to try out identifies the drive locations. Get-PSDrive identifies
those physical drive and registry locations for which you can devise scripts:

Name	Provider	Root	CurrentLocation
A	FileSystem	A:\	
Alias	Alias		
C	FileSystem	C:\	Users\SBSAdmin
cert	Certificate	\	
D	FileSystem	D:\	
Env	Environment		
Function	Function		
HKCU	Registry	HKEY_CURRENT_USER	
HKLM	Registry	HKEY_LOCAL_MACHINE	
Variable	Variable		

Any of these values can be called upon when writing PowerShell scripts.

PowerShell Resources

Merely typing get-command in each specific PowerShell window provides you with a list of
potential commands for each shell's management functions. get-command in the
PowerShell window gets you the list of cmdlets that work in Windows. get-command in the
Exchange Powershell window gives you the cmdlets that work in Exchange. As you peruse
the listing of commands, think of ways that you could use these functions in your deployments. If you enable the pop connector on each server you deploy, consider using the
earlier scripts that enable the service. If you want to compare patch levels on the 20 SBS
2008 servers you administrate, consider obtaining the patch file status for each via
PowerShell so that you can compare the patch levels side by side with each output.

Don't fear that PowerShell is beyond the reach and needs of the typical SBS administrator
or consultant. The PowerShell community has built add-ons and GUIs to help those who
are script challenged. PowerGUI, available from PowerGui.org, can control both Windows
and Exchange PowerShell commands and is just one possible site that can aid those who
are fearful of scripting (see Figure 20.4).

20

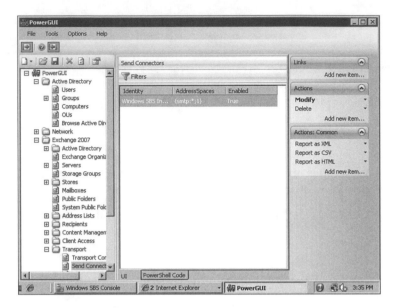

FIGURE 20.4   Community resources like PowerGUI.

Although you will find that you probably will utilize PowerShell in Exchange tasks, even mundane commands such as IPconfig /all can be turned into PowerShell commands. In the following sample we've used PowerShell to filter the results of Ipconfig /all to show only the Internet Protocol Version 4 results and to mask the Internet Protocol Version 6 results.

Ipconfig /all in PowerShell

Ipconfig/all is one of the best troubleshooting tools, but in the Windows 2008 era, it includes some IPv6 entries that can be confusing. Entering the following command in PowerShell eliminates the IPv6 information and limits the information to only the IPv4 data:

```
$lines= ipconfig /all; foreach ($line in $lines) { if ($line -notmatch
".*:.*:.*") { write-host $line }}
```

The output looks like this:

```
Windows PowerShell
Copyright (C) 2006 Microsoft Corporation. All rights reserved.

PS C:\Users\SBSAdmin> $lines= ipconfig /all; foreach ($line in $lines) { if
($line -notmatch ".*:.*:.*") { write-host $line }}

Windows IP Configuration
```

```
Host Name . . . . . . . . . . . . : SBSERVER
Primary Dns Suffix  . . . . . . . : SMALLBIZCO.local
Node Type . . . . . . . . . . . . : Hybrid
IP Routing Enabled. . . . . . . . : No
WINS Proxy Enabled. . . . . . . . : No
DNS Suffix Search List. . . . . . : SMALLBIZCO.local

Ethernet adapter Local Area Connection:

    Connection-specific DNS Suffix  . :
    Description . . . . . . . . . . . : Intel(R) PRO/1000 MT Network Connection
    Physical Address. . . . . . . . . : 00-0C-29-90-CB-84
    DHCP Enabled. . . . . . . . . . . : No
    Autoconfiguration Enabled . . . . : Yes
    IPv4 Address. . . . . . . . . . . : 192.168.0.3(Preferred)
    Subnet Mask . . . . . . . . . . . : 255.255.255.0
    Default Gateway . . . . . . . . . : 192.168.0.200
                                        192.168.0.3
    NetBIOS over Tcpip. . . . . . . . : Enabled

Tunnel adapter Local Area Connection* 8:

    Media State . . . . . . . . . . . : Media disconnected
    Connection-specific DNS Suffix  . :
    Description . . . . . . . . : isatap.{10FDC7AF-F1DD-4772-979C-11387E4F1461}
    Physical Address. . . . . . . . . : 00-00-00-00-00-00-00-E0
    DHCP Enabled. . . . . . . . . . . : No
    Autoconfiguration Enabled . . . . : Yes
PS C:\Users\SBSAdmin>
```

There are many resources and books for the PowerShell community, and some of the best resources are found all over the Internet. To give you an idea of what community resources are at your disposal, some of them can be found in Appendix A, "SBS 2008 Resources."

Summary

Small Business Server 2008 has PowerShell built in under the hood. Even the SBS 2008 administrator can rely on scripts and commands in PowerShell to do day-to-day administrative tasks faster than using the Graphical User Interface. On a daily basis, SBS 2008 uses PowerShell natively to perform daily tasks.

Take the time to look around the various PowerShell communities and in particular the scripting communities. Scripting can make your deployments more dependable and automated, so don't overlook PowerShell as an additional tool.

20

Best Practice Summary

▶ **Closely Examine Scripts from Third-Party Sites**—When getting scripts from the Internet, only use scripts from trusted sites. Test the script before use and keep the default PowerShell security settings on the server.

CHAPTER 21

Advanced Installation Options

Even though the new setup model for Windows Server 2008 is more restrictive than previous server versions, the SBS development team developed some mechanisms for the installation process to be customized. The driving force behind this is the SBS 2003 to SBS 2008 migration story, because the default setup process has no options for installing into an existing domain, for example.

To facilitate migrations, the SBS setup process makes use of an answer file, and when that answer file is detected, the SBS portion of setup changes behavior to accommodate the differences needed for migration. The tool can be used to accomplish other setup customizations, not just migration. This chapter covers ways to use the setup answer file to customize an SBS 2008 installation.

Understanding the Answer File

Those who have experienced customizing Windows Server 2008 installations will be familiar with the basic idea behind the answer file. The file itself is a text file, but uses XML formatting to convey the information the setup process needs to either customize the installation or complete the installation without manual intervention. The answer file used by the SBS 2008 setup accomplishes both of these objectives.

Answer File Generator

To generate the answer file, use the Answer File Generator tool from the SBS 2008 installation DVD. The file

SBSAfg.exe is located in the \Tools folder on the DVD. The tool can be run on any Windows-based PC that has the .Net 2.0 framework installed.

As seen in Figure 21.1, the first option that must be selected in the Answer File Tool is whether the answer file will be used for a new installation or a migration from an existing server. Depending on which of these options is selected, the Answer File Tool enables the user to enter certain pieces of information.

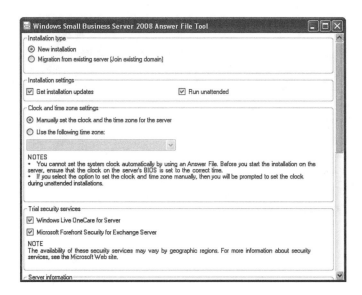

FIGURE 21.1   Answer File Tool Migration settings.

The two checkboxes in the Installation Settings section govern how the setup process will behave once it switches into Migration Setup. If the Get Installation Updates checkbox is enabled, SBS setup attempts to connect to the Internet and download any updated setup components that have been published following the initial release of SBS 2008. If the Run Unattended checkbox is enabled, the setup process skips over the sections where information is collected, assuming that the information needed for those sections has been provided in the answer file.

The clock and time zone settings section controls how time is set on the new server. When the Manually Set the Clock and the Time Zone for the Server radio button is selected, you are prompted during setup to open the Date and Time control panel to configure the time and time zone as necessary. If you select the Use the Following Time Zone radio button, you can select the correct local time zone and that time zone will be configured for the server during setup. However, setup will not adjust the actual time on the server, so the correct time needs to be configured in BIOS on the new server before starting setup.

The Trial Security Services section allows you to opt out of installing either or both Forefront Security for Exchange or OneCare for Server. If the checkboxes are enabled, the software is installed as part of setup. If the checkboxes are disabled, the software is not to be installed during initial setup.

Figure 21.2 shows the options available when the New Installation radio button is selected. The fields in the Server Information section specify default values for the new server. The Server Name field is the NetBIOS name of the server, the Internal Domain Name field is the NetBIOS name of the domain (that is, SMALLBIZCO) and the Full DNS Name field is the fully qualified internal domain name (that is, smallbizco.local). If you attempt to enter a single-label domain or other incorrectly-formatted DNS name, the tool displays an error symbol above the field informing you that the DNS name is formatted incorrectly. If you want to use an internal domain using a top level domain (TLD) other than .local, this is where you can enter it.

FIGURE 21.2   Answer File Tool New Installation settings.

You can use the fields in the Network Administrator Account section to specify the information needed to create the new administrator account on the server during setup. As mentioned in Chapter 3, "Installing and Configuring SBS 2008," the default administrator account that gets created with Active Directory is disabled by default, and this account is the one that will be used to manage the server.

The fields in the Company Information section are common in both new installation and migration modes. These fields are optional, but the Country/Region item should be selected even if no other information is completed in this section.

CAUTION

Be very careful about entering any information in the Certificate Authority Name field. This information is used to build the certificate authority with settings other than default. There can be serious problems if incorrect information is entered into this field. In general, this field can be left alone, and probably should be left alone. For additional information regarding this field and the problems that can be caused by entering incorrect information in it, see the Official SBS Blog (http://blogs.technet.com/sbs/archive/2008/08/27/the-sbs-2008-answer-file-and-the-certificate-authority-name.aspx).

Figure 21.3 shows the options available when the Migration from Existing Server (Join Existing Domain) radio button is selected. As mentioned previously, the Company Information section is common to both installation types. The Source (Existing) Server Information section contains settings that identify the source server and tells the setup process how to communicate with the existing server to connect to the existing Active Directory network.

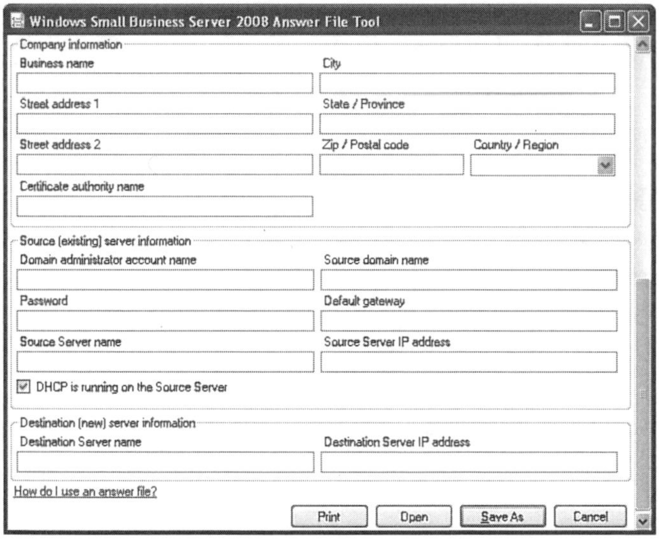

FIGURE 21.3   Answer File Tool Migration Settings.

The Destination (New) Server Information section contains fields to provide the name and the IP address for the new server. This information is needed so the new server can establish network connectivity and communicate with the existing server.

After selecting the installation type, all other elements in the Answer File Tool are optional. If none of the information is provided, the setup process either skips over the sections where that information is entered, or it prompts for missing information that is required for setup.

In a sense, selecting New Installation and turning off the Run Unattended checkbox is enough to put setup into "advanced mode," where the installer is able to enter customized information needed for the installation. The same is not necessarily true for the migration process, where accurate information about the source servers is needed prior to starting the installation.

Clicking on the Save As button in the Answer File Tool prompts the user for the location to save the XML file. By default, the tool tries to save the file as SBSAnswerFile.xml, as that is the filename that the SBS 2008 setup will look for to determine if it needs to go into migration mode or continue in default setup mode. Once the file has been saved, it can be copied to the removable media that will be used during installation.

Answer File Format

The information written to the answer file is different depending on which installation option is selected. Table 21.1 identifies which elements are present in the SBS 2008 Setup Answer File and provides a brief description of how the element is used.

TABLE 21.1   Answer File Format

Property	Description	New Install	Migration
Global			
JoinDomain (Boolean)	Specifies if the setup is new or a migration; `true` means migration, and `false` means new setup.	✓	✓
UpdateSetup (Boolean)	Specifies if updates should be downloaded before continuing setup.	✓	✓
ApplyUpdates (Boolean)	Specifies if updates should be applied after downloading.	✓	✓
Unattend (Boolean)	Specifies if setup should run without user intervention.	✓	✓
ManuallySetClockandTime-Zone (Boolean)	Specifies if the clock and time zone settings should be prompted during install.	✓	✓
TimeZoneID (string)	Contains the text code for the installation time zone.	✓	✓
RequireInstallFSE (Boolean)	Specifies if Firefront Security for Exchange trial software should be installed during setup.	✓	✓

TABLE 21.1   Answer File Format

Property	Description	New Install	Migration
Global			
InstallOneCare (Boolean)	Specifies if OneCare for server trial software should be installed during setup.	✓	✓
BusinessName (string)	Contains the name of the business.	✓	✓
Address (string)	Contains the address for the business.	✓	✓
Address2 (string)	Contains a second line of address information if needed.	✓	✓
City (string)	Contains the name of the city.	✓	✓
State (string)	Contains the name of the state.	✓	✓
Zip (string)	Contains the zip code.	✓	✓
Country (integer)	Contains a numeric value for country.	✓	✓
CANameOverride (string)	Contains the name of the certificate authority.	✓	✓
JoinDomainServer (string)	Identifies the name of the existing server.		✓
JoinDomainName (string)	Identifies the fully-qualified domain name of the existing AD network.		✓
JoinDomainPlainText-Password (string)	Identifies the password for the user account to be used for migration.		✓
JoinDomainUser (string)	Identifies the logon name of the account to be used for migration.		✓
JoinDomainDHCPOnSource (Boolean)	Identifies if DHCP is running on the existing server.		✓
JoinDomainGatewayIP (binary)	Identifies the IP address of the gateway.		✓
JoinDomainSourceIP (binary)	Identifies the IP address of the existing server.		✓

TABLE 21.1   Answer File Format

Property	Description	New Install	Migration
Global			
MachineName (string)	Specifies the name of the new server.	✓	✓
JoinDomainDestinationIP (binary)	Identifies the IP address of the new server.		✓
DomainNetbiosName (string)	Identifies the NetBIOS domain name for the new network.	✓	
NewDomainDnsName (string)	Identifies the fully-qualified internal domain name for the new network.	✓	
PlainTextPassword (string)	Specifies the password for the new admin account to be created during setup.	✓	
UseIpOverride (Boolean)	Specifies whether the answer file contains IP information for setup.	✓	
ServerIpOverride (string)	Contains the IP address for the server.	✓	
ServerGatewayOverride (string)	Contains the IP address for the default gateway.	✓	
UserData			
FirstName (string)	Specifies the first name of the new admin account.	✓	
LastName (string)	Specifies the last name of the new admin account.	✓	
LogonName (string)	Specifies the logon name for the new admin account.	✓	
CommonName (string)	Specifies the display name for the new admin account.	✓	

As seen in the table, the XML file is divided into two sections, one named Global and the other named UserData. The UserData section only contains information related to the creation of the new admin account. There are other elements in the XML file not listed in the table, but those elements either have no impact on the setup process or are placeholders for other processes.

Installing SBS 2008 with a Custom Internal Domain Name

In all likelihood, the most common customization that will be requested by IT profession-als will be the ability to change the internal domain name to have an extension other than `.local`, which is configured by default. As described in Chapter 3, there are no mechanisms in the default configuration process to change the domain name from `domain.local` to `domain.anythingelse`, but the answer file setup enables you to specify the desired internal domain name. This section of the chapter details how to start an SBS 2008 installation using an internal domain of `domain.lan`.

Changes from SBS 2003—Domain-Naming Limitations

During installation, the SBS 2003 Integrated Setup prompted the user to enter the full internal domain name information prior to installing and configuring Active Directory on the server. The setup routine presented a default internal domain name based on the company name that was entered earlier in setup. So, if a business name of Small Business Company was entered, the default internal domain name was `smallbusinesscompany.local`. That default internal domain could be fully modified at that point, and the installer could enter just about anything into that field to be used as an internal domain.

But this process led to confusion and problems in the hands of inexperienced installers. It was too easy to enter a single-label domain name (that is, `domain` instead of `domain.local`), which can cause all kinds of domain networking problems. Installers could also use public top-level domains (TLDs) for their internal name spaces, which can cause communications problems with public DNS resources (see Chapter 4, "DNS, DHCP, and Active Directory Integration," for a discussion on the potential problems with split DNS zones).

So, the SBS 2008 product development team opted to streamline the internal domain-naming process to give inexperienced installers a better chance of success by limiting the internal domain-naming options during installation. The proposed internal domain is still based on the company name entered during the process, but only the NetBIOS ver-sion of the name can be edited. In all cases, the fully-qualified domain name will be the NetBIOS domain name plus the `.local` extension. Only through the use of the answer file can an installer modify the internal domain to be something other than `.local`.

Prepare the Answer File

Follow these steps to prepare the answer file to use the desired internal domain name:

1. Open the Answer File Tool (\Tools\SBSAfg.exe on the installation DVD).
2. Make sure the New Installation radio button is selected.
3. Make sure the Run Unattended checkbox is selected.

4. If you want to set the time and time zone on the server manually during setup, leave the Manually Set the Clock and the Time Zone for the Server radio button selected. Otherwise, select Use the Following Time Zone radio button and choose the time zone from the drop-down list.

5. In the Server Information section, enter the server name, internal domain name, and full DNS name information in the appropriate fields.

6. In the Network Administrator Account section, complete the first name, last name, administrator user name, and administrator password fields. See Figure 21.4 for an example.

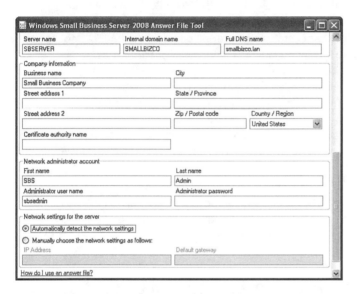

FIGURE 21.4   Answer File tool with custom internal DNS settings.

7. Save the information to SBSAnswerFile.xml.

Now you can copy the answer file to the removable media you will use for installation.

Perform the Installation

The installation process using the answer file to customize the internal DNS name is almost identical to the traditional installation process. Rather than repeat the entire setup process here, please refer back to Chapter 3 for the installation steps. You need to perform additional steps in the process, and those steps are outlined as follows:

▶ Insert the removable media (floppy disk, USB key, and so on) into the server after the first reboot of setup at the Windows 2008 installation splash screen, where you can click "Install Now." Make sure the media has time to recognize before clicking Install Now.

▶ Pay attention to the installation steps once the install process has rebooted again and you get to the Continue Installation screen. Because the answer file has specified an "unattended installation," the install process skips several sections and goes straight to Expanding and Installing Files.

The remainder of setup will complete normally, but now you will have a new server with a customized internal domain name.

Best Practice—Entering Fully-Customized Setup Mode

Although the example in this section provides a way to specify a customized internal domain name through the use of the answer file, some IT professionals may not want to go through and create fully-customized answer files for each new install they perform. For those individuals, there is a way to accomplish this with a minimum of effort.

Instead of creating an answer file that contains the internal domain information, use the SBS Answer File Generator to create a generic "empty" answer file that can be used on every install. To do this, open the Answer File Tool, make sure New Installation is selected, then turn off the Run Unattended checkbox and save the answer file without entering any other information. When the SBS 2008 setup encounters this answer file, all the fields in setup that can be customized will be "unlocked," and the installer can go through the installation process specifying the desired information. Alternately, you can create a zero byte file named SBSAnswerFile.xml on the removable media to achieve the same effect.

Note that this method does not completely open up the installation process. In reality, the only additional functionality unlocked with this method is the internal domain name. Still, for those who want to be able to enter a custom internal domain during the setup process, this generic answer file gives them the ability to do just that.

Installing SBS 2008 into an Existing Active Directory Domain

One specialized type of installation supported by the SBS 2008 installation process is the ability to install into an existing Active Directory domain. Technically, this is a migration as far as the setup tools are concerned, but this specific situation is not covered in the Migration whitepaper provided by Microsoft, which focuses specifically on migrating from an existing SBS 2003 network. In fact, several of the tools provided by the SBS team to make the migration process easier only work with an SBS server and not a standard Windows 2003 (or Windows 2008) server. To give an example of how the answer file can be used in a migration scenario, the remainder of this chapter covers the process of installing SBS 2008 into an existing Windows 2003 Active Directory domain. The process in this section is modeled directly off the "Migrate to Windows Small Business Server 2008 from Windows Small Business Server 2003" whitepaper (http://technet.microsoft.com/en-us/library/cc546034.aspx).

Best Practice—Perform Migration in a Virtual Environment First

Whether performing a full SBS 2003 to SBS 2008 migration using the Microsoft method, using the swing migration process, or using the following process to install SBS 2008 into an existing non-SBS Active Directory network, you should go through the entire migration process in a virtual environment before attempting a production migration. Because every source server is different, every migration will have different aspects to it, and running through the migration in a virtual environment first will help you identify those items that could cause problems during the live migration.

Because the migration process is a complex process, everyone should do several practice migrations in a lab environment before attempting a real migration on a production system, just to get the feel for how the migration process works. But even after you have done several live migrations, you should still plan to make at least one pass of each migration through a virtual environment to ensure you don't get caught by surprise when performing the migration on your production systems.

Prepare the Existing Server

There are a number of changes that must be made to the existing network before SBS 2008 can successfully install into the domain. Complete the steps in the following sections to ensure that the source network is fully prepared for the SBS 2008 installation.

NOTE

This section of the chapter covers the specific example of an existing Windows 2003 server that does not have an Exchange server present in the network. The process of working with an existing Exchange environment is complex and beyond the scope of this book. For more involved SBS 2008 migrations, refer to the Microsoft whitepaper (http://technet.microsoft.com/en-us/library/cc546034.aspx) or make use of third-party documentation and services such as the swing migration process at http://www.sbsmigration.com.

Back Up the Existing Server

Although this may seem obvious, backing up the source server is absolutely essential to be able to back out of migration should something go awry during the process. Create a full backup of the source server at this point, and make special effort to create a system state backup with your backup software of choice. If your backup software does not offer a system state backup, or if you want a separate system state backup for redundancy, follow these steps to use the ntbackup tool to create a working system state backup before continuing:

1. Open ntbackup on the source server (Start, Run, ntbackup, or Start, All Programs, Accessories, System Tools, Backup).

2. If ntbackup opens in Wizard mode, click the Advanced Mode link in the opening page.

3. Click the Backup tab.

4. In the selection screen, click System State.

5. In the Backup File Destination drop-down menu, select File.

6. Click Browse and select a location for the backup file. (About 1GB of free space will be needed for each system state backup.)

7. Click Start Backup; then click Start Backup again.

8. When the backup completes, close ntbackup.

NOTE

Consider running additional system state backups after each change that is made to Active Directory or to the server itself prior to the start of the SBS 2008 installation. This gives you a state to recover to if any of the migration preparation steps cause problems.

Update the Existing Server

The source server needs to be completely up to date with security patches and have a few additional tools installed that may not already be on the server. Follow these steps to get the server up to date and ready to start the migration:

1. Install the Support Tools on the source server (run \Support\Tools\SUPTOOLS.MSI from the Windows 2003 installation CD).

2. Install the .Net 2.0 Framework on the server.

3. Install the latest service packs and security patches on the existing server.

4. Continue to check for and install updates from Microsoft Update until no other updates are offered.

Configure the Network Layout

The SBS 2008 migration process expects that both servers have a single network card and rely on an external firewall device to separate the internal network from the Internet. Although using the source server as a router device is common in SBS 2003 installations, it may not be very common in networks with only a standard Windows 2003 server. However, if the source server does have two network cards and those cards are on different IP address networks to route traffic between the networks, the source server will need to be reconfigured to have a single NIC. For additional information, please refer to the Microsoft migration whitepaper.

Best Practice—Create a New Domain Administrator Account

The Microsoft migration whitepaper makes a passing mention of creating a new administrator account in a note of one of the steps, but this process is actually a fairly significant part of the source server preparation. Because the SBS 2008 setup process wants to disable the default administrator account, you should create another administrator-equivalent account and use that during the migration, leaving the SBS 2008 setup to disable the Administrator account as part of the process. Follow these steps to quickly create a new administrative account:

1. Open Active Directory Users and Computers (Start, Run, `dsa.msc`, or Start, Administrative Tools, Active Directory Users & Computers).

2. Expand the Users container and locate the Administrator account.

3. Double-click the Administrator account and click the Member Of tab.

4. Make sure that the Administrator account belongs to the following groups: Enterprise Admins, Schema Admins, Domain Admins.

5. Close the properties for the Administrator account.

6. Right-click the Administrator account and select Copy (see Figure 21.5).

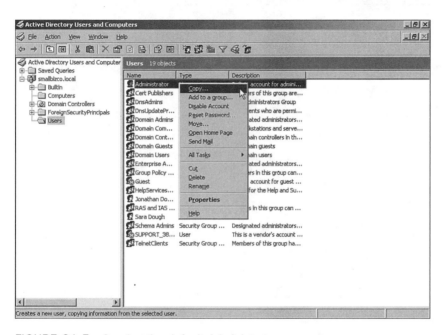

FIGURE 21.5   Copying the default Administrator account.

7. Enter the name information for the user and click Next.

8. Enter the password and uncheck the User Must Change Password on Next Login checkbox; then click Next.

9. Review the information and click Finish.

Raise the Functional Level of the Forest and Domain

The next phase in the process is to prepare Active Directory to accept the SBS 2008 server into the network. The updates to the Active Directory schema must be in place before a Windows Server 2008 server can become a domain controller. Follow these steps to prepare Active Directory on the existing server:

1. Open Active Directory Domains and Trusts from Start, Administrative Tools.

2. Right-click the domain and click Raise Domain Functional Level (see Figure 21.6).

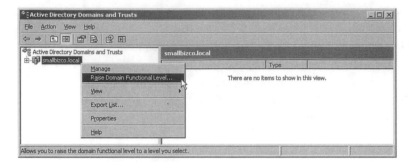

FIGURE 21.6   Raising the domain functional level in Active Directory Domains and Trusts.

3. Select Windows Server 2003 from the drop-down list; then click Raise (see Figure 21.7).

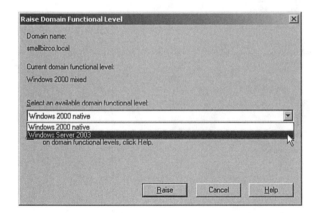

FIGURE 21.7   Selecting the correct functional level.

4. Click OK in the warning dialog box that appears.
5. When the operation completes, click OK.
6. Right-click Active Directory Domains and Trusts; then select Raise Forest Functional Level (see Figure 21.8).
7. Select Windows Server 2003 from the drop-down menu; then click Raise.
8. Click OK in the warning dialog box.
9. When the operation completes, click OK.

Verify Proper Network and Domain Operations

This section enables you to verify the overall health of the network configuration on the server. If you are not familiar with the netdiag and dcdiag tools referenced here, you can find additional information about them on the Microsoft Technet site. Netdiag is documented at http://technet.microsoft.com/en-us/library/cc783438.aspx. Dcdiag is docu-

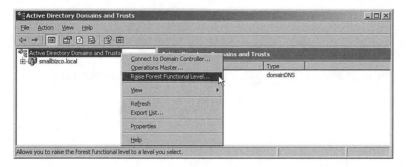

FIGURE 21.8   Raising the forest functional level in Active Directory Domains and Trusts.

mented at http://technet.microsoft.com/en-us/library/cc773199.aspx. Follow these steps to confirm that the network for the source server is operating properly:

1. Open a command prompt on the source server.

2. Change into the `C:\Program Files\Support Tools` directory. This directory does not exist if you did not install the Support Tools package mentioned previously in this chapter.

3. Run `netdiag /v > filename.txt`, where *filename.txt* is the name of an output file you review in the next step.

4. Open *filename.txt* in Notepad and take steps to correct any error conditions that are reported in the output.

5. Run `dcdiag /v > filename.txt`, where *filename.txt* is the name of an output file you review in the next step.

6. Open *filename.txt* in Notepad and take steps to correct any error conditions that are reported in the output.

Configure the Server to Synchronize Time With NTP

To ensure that both servers can synchronize Active Directory information during the migration, their clocks need to be in sync. Completing the following steps ensures that both servers are using the same time source for synchronization during setup:

1. Open a command prompt on the source server.

2. Type **w32tm /config /syncfromflags:domhier /reliable:no /update** and press Enter.

3. Type **net stop w32time** and press Enter.

4. Type **net start w32time** and press Enter.

5. Close the command prompt.

Update the Active Directory Schema

Once the network is in good shape and the domain components have been updated, the next step is to update the Active Directory schema to include the elements introduced with

Windows 2008. Without this schema upgrade, the SBS 2008 install will not be properly able to add the new server to the existing domain. Follow these steps to update the schema:

1. Insert the SBS 2008 installation DVD in the existing server.

2. Open a command prompt and navigate to the \Tools\ADPREP directory on the SBS 2008 DVD.

3. Run adprep /forestprep at the command prompt. When prompted, type C and press Enter.

4. After the process completes, which will take several minutes, run adprep /domain-prep at the command prompt.

5. Close the command prompt after the process completes.

Create the Answer File

The last step before installing SBS 2008 on the new server is to create the answer file. This process can be run on the existing server or on any other computer that has the .Net 2.0 Framework installed and can access the type of removable media that will be used to make the answer file available to the SBS 2008 installation server:

1. Open the \Tools folder on the SBS 2008 installation DVD.

2. Run SBSAfg.exe.

3. Select the Migrate from Existing Server radio button.

4. Turn off the Get Installation Updates checkbox.

5. Make sure the Run Unattended checkbox is enabled.

6. If you want to specify the time zone automatically, select the Use the Following Time Zone radio button and choose the correct time zone from the drop-down list.

7. Enable or disable the Forefront Security for Exchange and Windows Live OneCare for Server checkboxes as desired.

8. Complete the fields in the Company Information section.

9. In the Source (Existing) Server Information section, enter the logon name of the new account you created on the source server in the Domain Administrator Account Name field.

10. Enter the password for the new account in the Password field.

11. Enter the NetBIOS name of the source server in the Source Server Name field.

12. Enter the fully qualified internal domain name in the Source Domain Name field.

13. Enter the IP address of the default gateway on the network in the Default Gateway field.

14. Enter the IP address of the source server in the Source Server IP Address field.

15. If DHCP is running on the source server, make sure the DHCP Is Running on the Source Server checkbox is enabled.

16. Enter the name for the new server in the Destination Server Name field.

17. Enter the IP address for the new server in the Destination Server IP Address field.

18. Review the settings to confirm they are correct (see Figure 21.9 as an example).

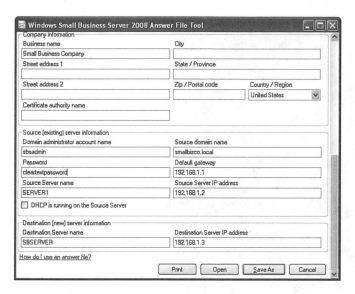

FIGURE 21.9   Answer File Tool with migration settings entered.

19. Click Save As and save the file.

20. Close the SBS Answer File Generator tool.

If you did not save the file directly to the removable media that will be used during the SBS 2008 installation, copy the file to that media now.

Install SBS 2008 in Migration Mode

As with the previous section on installing SBS 2008 with a custom domain name, the actual process involves only a couple of modifications to the standard installation. So, rather than detailing the entire setup process again in this chapter, this section points out the differences in the setup procedure as it relates to this process.

Follow these steps to install SBS 2008 on the new server in migration mode:

1. Boot the new server with the SBS 2008 DVD in the drive.

2. Confirm the language and regional settings and click Next.

3. Insert the removable media with the answer file into the server.

4. In the Windows Server 2008 window, click Install Now.

5. Continue with the installation process as outlined in Chapter 3.

6. After the server restarts, the server will go straight into the Expanding and Installing Files process instead of bringing up the Continue Installation page. If you see the Continue Installation page, setup was not able to detect the answer file correctly, and you need to start the process again by booting the new server from the SBS 2008 installation DVD.

7. When the installation completes, you see the Installation Finished window, shown in Figure 21.10.

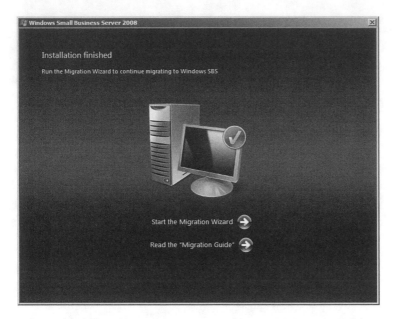

FIGURE 21.10   The Installation Finished window displays at the end of migration setup.

8. Click the Start the Migration Wizard button in the Installation Finished window to open the Windows SBS Console and complete the setup process.

At this point, you are ready to continue with configuring the new server, transferring data from the old server to the new server, and transitioning the old server into its new role.

> **NOTE**
>
> When the Windows SBS Console opens, you will see a Migrate to Windows SBS link. This link launches the Migration Wizard. However, the Migration Wizard only works when the old server is SBS 2003. If you launch the Migration Wizard, the wizard generates an error, indicating that the wizard cannot run unless the source server was SBS 2003.

Configuring the New Server

Now that SBS 2008 has been installed on the new server, it needs to be configured for proper operation. Many of the tasks needed for configuration are the same as in Chapter 3, but there are some differences when installing into an existing Active Directory domain. The remainder of this section covers the various configuration tasks needed as part of the customized setup. Where appropriate, tasks that are not significantly different will be referred back to other areas in the book that cover the task in detail.

Follow these steps to complete the configuration of the new server:

1. Move data storage locations on the server. This process is covered in Chapter 3, and should be done before any other tasks in this list. The Move Data Wizards are located in the Backup and Server Storage tab of the Windows SBS Console.

2. Connect to the Internet by running the Connect to the Internet Wizard from the Home tab of the Windows SBS Console.

NOTE

It may seem a bit odd that you still have to run the Connect to the Internet Wizard, given that you had to provide IP addressing information in the answer file for setup. The migration setup uses that IP information to establish the network connection between the two servers during setup so that a proper Active Directory connection between the two servers can be established. However, at the end of installation, the network settings for the SBS server are still not optimized for normal operation. For instance, the NIC in the SBS 2008 box lists the old server as the primary DNS server. Running the Connect to the Internet Wizard corrects the DNS server settings among other network configuration changes.

3. Run the Set Up Your Internet Address Wizard from the Windows SBS Console. If your firewall supports UPnP, this wizard makes the necessary changes for inbound traffic to arrive at the SBS 2008 server. If your firewall does not support UPnP, you need to manually configure the firewall at this point to redirect the proper ports. At a minimum, you need to configure ports 25, 443, and 987 to point to the SBS 2008 server, especially if any of these ports were opened to the old server.

4. Remove any login scripts that may have been in place on the old server. Because SBS 2008 uses a combination of group policy objects and its own login scripts to manage the network environment, any login scripts that might have been in place with the old server should be removed. Follow these steps to look for and clean up any existing login scripts:

   a. On the source server, open Start, Run and go to `\\localhost\sysvol\`*domainname*`\scripts`, where *domainname* is the fully qualified internal domain name for the network (that is, domain.local).

   b. Copy any scripts that might exist in this folder to another folder on the source server.

   c. If there are any scripts, delete them from the scripts folder after you have copied them elsewhere on the server.

5. Remove any custom group policies that might have been created on the old server. Old Group Policy Objects may interfere with some of the settings configured automatically by SBS 2008 and should be removed. The following steps outline how to locate custom group policy objects on the original server, make a backup of the settings, and remove the objects:

a. On the old server, open Start, Run and enter **gpmc.msc** to open the Group Policy Management Console. If the Group Policy Management Console is not installed on the old server, you can download it from http://www.microsoft. com/windowsserver2003/gpmc/default.mspx and install it on the server.

b. In the navigation tree, select the Group Policy Objects folder under Forest, Domains, *internaldomain*, as shown in Figure 21.11. The figure also shows all the default GPOs that SBS 2008 creates by default. If you see any objects that are not in the figure, those are custom objects and need to be removed.

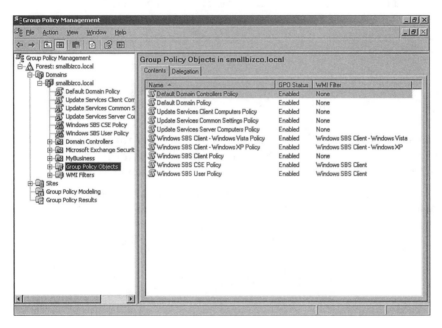

FIGURE 21.11   The Group Policy Objects node contains all the GPOs that exist on the domain.

c. For each custom GPO, double-click the GPO; then select the Settings tab. This will show all the settings for that object.

d. Right-click within the Settings window and select either Print or Save Report to make a human-readable backup of the object.

e. Right-click the object name in the navigation tree and select Back Up; then follow the instructions to make a backup copy of the object.

f. Right-click the object name in the navigation tree and select Delete to remove the object from the domain.

CAUTION

Do not delete either the Default Domain Policy or the Default Domain Controllers Policy from this list. Refer to Chapter 11, "Group Policy in SBS 2008," for information about those policies and their importance. If you have any questions about whether a policy showing in the list is an SBS 2008 policy or not, compare the policy list against a known good install of SBS 2008.

6. Remove any WMI filters that may have been created on the old server. Follow these steps to identify and remove old WMI filters:

   a. In the Group Policy Management Console, select WMI filters from the navigation tree, as shown in Figure 21.12.

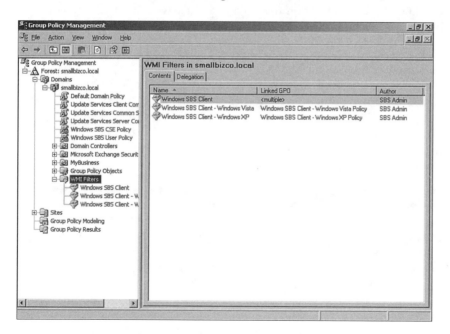

FIGURE 21.12   The WMI Filters node contains all the WMI filters that exist on the domain.

   b. Identify any WMI filter objects that were not created by the new SBS administrator account you created before the migration.

   c. Right-click any old WMI filters and select Delete to remove them.

7. Run the Fix My Network Wizard from the Network tab under Connectivity. This will build the missing companyweb record in DNS that is not created during this type of installation.

The server is now ready for normal operation, and you can begin the process of moving data from the old server.

Moving Data and Settings from the Old Server

The level of complexity for moving data from the old server to the SBS 2008 server depends on how much data exists on the old server and whether any applications are running on the old server that need to move as well. If you are planning to keep the old server running after installing SBS 2008, you may be able to minimize some of the effort needed to migrate information to the new server. If you are planning to retire the old server, you need to move all the data, applications, and settings to prevent loss of functionality.

This chapter cannot cover the entire scope of moving applications from the old server to the new. Given that the process has been based on a single Windows 2003 server, the following section covers moving data from shared folders on the old server to the SBS 2008 server and ensuring that the existing users and groups on the old server display properly in the SBS 2008 tools. Information for moving applications and their related data (that is, line-of-business applications with installed databases, and so on) is left up to the vendor for guidance.

Managing Users and Security Groups

The process of installing SBS 2008 into an existing Active Directory network preserves existing user accounts, security groups, and computer objects, saving the effort of recreating all these objects if a standard installation were done on the server. But even though the Active Directory information is shared between the two servers at this point, the SBS administration tools cannot fully see all the objects in Active Directory, so these objects need to be modified so that they can be properly managed with the new tools.

Viewing Active Directory Objects in the Windows SBS Console

When you go into the Users and Groups tab of the Windows SBS Console at this point in the migration process, you see that no users are listed under the Users sub-navigation tab. The objects still exist in Active Directory, but they are not visible within the tools. This is because the tools are written to look for a specific property on the Active Directory objects to determine if those objects were "created" by SBS 2008 tools or not. In SBS 2003, if accounts were created by other processes, say an anti-virus software generated accounts used to manage portions of the distribution of the software, those accounts appeared in the Server Management console. With SBS 2008, the development team wanted to have the Windows SBS Console only display objects that were created using SBS tools.

To achieve this, the SBS setup modifies the Active Directory schema to add a few attributes to certain Active Directory objects. The attribute that governs if user and group objects are visible in the Windows SBS Console is the msSBSCreationState attribute. All existing user and group objects that were present when SBS setup extended the AD schema have these attributes, but their value is "not set." When a new object is created by the SBS tools, the msSBSCreationState attribute value is set to "Created." Any user or group objects that are added to Active Directory by standard processes (that is, not using the SBS wizards) will not have this attribute set, so those objects will not appear in the Windows SBS Console.

Setting the msSBSCreationState attribute is done differently for user and group objects. Making the necessary changes to user objects can be done through a wizard, but changing the attribute for group objects must be done directly on the object through native tools. For that reason, you may choose to update the user objects using the wizard (strongly recommended) and then either ignore the group settings, or create new groups in the Windows SBS Console to replace the existing groups.

Follow these steps to change the user attributes so existing user objects will appear in the Windows SBS Console. The settings for the new domain administrator account will be changed first, and then the settings for the remaining users:

1. In the Windows SBS Console, select the Users and Groups main navigation tab; then select the Users sub-navigation tab.

2. Under User Tasks in the right pane, click the Change User Role for User Accounts link.

3. In the Select New User Role page, select the Network Administrator role from the Role Name list.

4. Select the Add User Permissions or Settings radio button; then click Next.

5. In the Select User Accounts page, enable the Display All User Accounts in the Active Directory checkbox and wait for the user objects to populate the list.

6. Select the network administrator account you created earlier in the chapter and click Add. If there are any other accounts to which you want to grant full network administrator rights, select those users and click Add (see Figure 21.13).

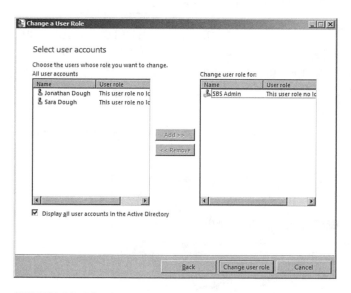

FIGURE 21.13   Select the new network administrator account to grant network administrator rights.

7. When all users have been added, click Change User Role.

8. Once the process completes, click Finish.

9. Open the Change a User Role Wizard again.

10. In the Select New User Role page, select the Standard User or Standard User with Administration Links role.

11. Select the Add User Permissions or Settings radio button; then click Next.

12. In the Select User Accounts page, enable the Display All User Accounts in the Active Directory checkbox and wait for the user objects to populate the list.

13. Select all the user objects you want to have the selected role and click Add.

14. After all the accounts have been selected, click Change User Role.

15. When the process completes, click Finish.

When you refresh the view in the Windows SBS Console, you now see all the user objects that you selected during the Change a User Role Wizard.

To enable visibility of groups, you need to use the ADSIEdit tool. Follow these steps to make the group objects visible to the Windows SBS Console:

CAUTION

ADSIEdit (Active Directory Service Interfaces Editor) is to Active Directory what regedit is to the Windows Registry. If you are not careful in using this tool, you can do significant and potentially permanent damage to Active Directory. As with regedit, make a backup of the system before making any changes to Active Directory.

1. From the Start menu, select Administrative Tools; then select ADSI Edit. If ADSI Edit is not available in the menu, type `adsiedit.msc` in the Search field and press Enter.

2. In the User Account Control prompt, click Continue.

3. From the Actions menu, select Connect to.

4. Click OK to accept the defaults.

5. Navigate to the Users container in Active Directory (see Figure 21.14) and locate the group to modify.

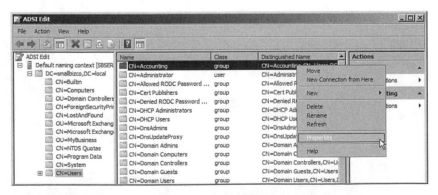

FIGURE 21.14 Locate the correct group object to edit.

6. Right-click the group object and select Properties.

7. Scroll through the list of attributes to find `msSBSCreationState` and click Edit (see Figure 21.15).

8. In the String Attribute Editor window, enter Created as the value (see Figure 21.16). Make sure to capitalize the first letter. Click OK to save changes.

9. Scroll through the list of attributes to find groupType and click Edit.

10. For a security group, change the value to `-2147483640` (see Figure 21.17). For a distribution group, change the value to 8.

11. Click OK to save changes to the object.

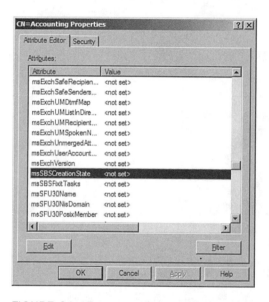

FIGURE 21.15   Locate the `mSSBSCreationState` attribute.

FIGURE 21.16   Change the msSBSCreationState value.

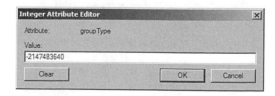

FIGURE 21.17   Change the groupType value for a security group.

Once you have modified all the groups you want to have visible, you will be able to see the groups listed in the Groups sub-navigation tab of Users and Groups.

Moving Data Shares

Moving shared data from the old server to the SBS 2008 server is the final process that is covered in this chapter. As mentioned earlier, more advanced steps for dealing with installed applications or databases are best handled by the vendor providing those applications and are beyond the scope of this book.

Follow these steps to move shared folders and data from the old server:

1. From the source server, open a command prompt (Start, Run, cmd).

2. At the command prompt, type **net share** and press Enter.

3. Review the output to identify shared data folders. Figure 21.18 shows a sample output with one shared folder, named "data." The other shares listed are system shares and do not need to be moved.

FIGURE 21.18   Review the net share output to identify the shared data folders.

4. Open the properties for each shared folder (in this case, open the properties of the C:\data folder).

5. Go to both the Sharing and Security tabs in the folder properties and make note of the permissions in each tab.

6. On the SBS 2008 server, create a new shared folder using the Add New Shared Folder Wizard, which is described in Chapter 17, "Managing Server and Workstation Security."

7. When creating the new shared folder, enter the NTFS and Share permissions as noted from the original folder.

8. After the share has been created, copy the data from the source share to the destination share.

NOTE

If there are a number of nested folders with varying levels of permissions in the source share, you could use the xcopy command with the /O (letter O not zero) flag to copy over the owner and permission settings from the source path. For example, if the source path were on SERVER01 in a share named Data, you could run the following xcopy command to copy the entire folder structure and security information:

```
xcopy \\SERVER01\data /E /O
```

---

9. Once the data has been copied from the old server to the SBS server, remove the shares from the old server.

At this point, you may continue to deal with the remaining information on the old server and refer back to the processes outlined in Chapter 3 regarding the setup of the SBS 2008 to address any steps that have not been included here.

Reconfigure the Old Server

Once the SBS server has been configured and all the data and settings have been moved from the original server, you can take the next steps with the original server. Unlike migrating from an existing SBS 2003 server, there is not a requirement that the original server be removed from the network. The next steps you take with the old server depend entirely on what you plan to do with the box. You may choose to leave the old server running as-is as a secondary domain controller; you could demote the server back to member server status, but leave it running on the network; or you could choose to remove the server from the network altogether. The next three sections outline the steps necessary for each of these options.

Update DNS

Regardless of what you plan to do with the old server, you need to modify the DNS settings on the server so that it will function properly with Active Directory on the SBS 2008 server (whether it will remain a domain controller or will be removed from Active Directory). Follow these steps to change the DNS settings on the old server:

1. Open the properties for the network card.
2. Select Internet Protocol (TCP/IP) and click Properties.
3. Under Use the Following DNS Server Addresses, change the IP address in the first field to be the IP address of the SBS 2008 server.
4. If you keep the old server as a domain controller, add the IP address of the old server into the second DNS server field.
5. Click OK then click Close to close out of the network card properties.

If you plan to leave the server as a domain controller, you are finished. Otherwise, continue with the steps in the next section.

Demote the Old Server to a Member Server

Whether you intend to use the old server as a member server or remove it from the network, you need to demote the server to remove its domain controller status. Follow these steps to demote the old server:

1. From a command prompt or from Start, Run, enter **dcpromo** and press Enter.

2. Click Next.

3. If you receive a warning about the server being a global catalog, press OK to clear the warning.

4. Make sure the This Server Is the Last Domain Controller in the Domain checkbox is disabled; then click Next.

5. Enter a new administrator password. This is the password that will be used if the server needs to be booted into safe mode. You can use the same password that you created for the new network administrator account if you choose.

6. Click Next; then click Finish when the process completes. The server will restart at this point.

If you will be using the server as a member server, you are finished. Otherwise, continue with the steps in the next section.

Remove the Old Server

If you plan to completely remove the old server from the domain, you need to do a little cleanup on the network. Follow these steps to completely remove the server from the domain:

1. On the old server, right-click My Computer and select Properties.

2. Select the Computer Name tab and click Change.

3. In the Member of section, select the Workgroup radio button.

4. Enter a name in the Workgroup field; then click OK.

5. Enter the credentials for a domain administrator account and click OK.

6. Once the server has been removed from the domain, it prompts for a restart. You can either restart the server, or simply power it off at this point.

7. On the SBS 2008 server, open the Active Directory Users and Computers console from Start, Administrative tools, or using `dsa.msc`.

8. Locate the old server in Active Directory by navigating to domain, MyBusiness, Computers, SBSComputers.

9. Right-click the server and select Delete, as shown in Figure 21.19. Click Yes to remove the object.

10. If you are presented with a Confirm Subtree Deletion dialog box, click Yes.

11. Open the DNS Management console from Start, Administrative Tools or using `dnsmgmt.msc`.

12. In the User Account Control prompt, click Continue.

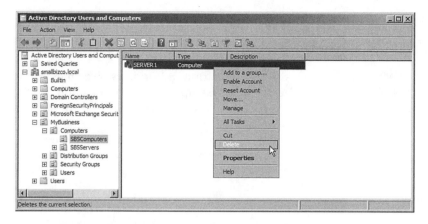

FIGURE 21.19   Removing the old server from Active Directory.

13. Locate the DNS record for the old server under Forward Lookup Zones, *internaldomainname*.

14. Double-click on the Name Server record with the old server name.

15. Select the record for the old server and click Remove (see Figure 21.20).

16. Click Apply, then click OK.

17. Look for any other records that might have pointed to the old server and either remove them or point them to the new server.

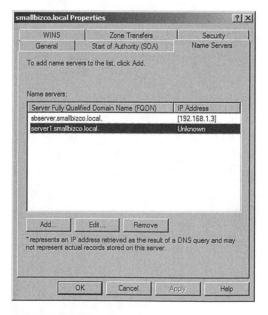

FIGURE 21.20   Removing the orphaned Name Server record.

Installing Forefront Security for Exchange and Windows Live OneCare for Server Manually

If you have set up SBS 2008 but chose to skip the installation of Windows Live OneCare for Server or Forefront Security for Exchange during the setup, you can go back and install the trial versions at a later time. The installers for these products are located on the second DVD in the install set. This section covers how to install the trial versions of Windows Live OneCare for Server and Forefront Security for Exchange from the SBS installation media.

Forefront Security for Exchange

The trial installer for Forefront Security for Exchange (FSE) is in the \CMPNENTS\FSS folder on the second installation DVD. To install the trial version, follow these steps:

1. From \CMPNENTS\FSS, double-click setup.exe.

2. In the User Account Control prompt, click Continue.

3. When presented with the trial license agreement, click Yes to accept the agreement and continue the installation.

4. Enter the user name and company name in the next page and click Next.

5. Select the Local Installation radio button and click Next.

6. Select the Full Installation radio button and click Next.

7. Select the Use Microsoft update When I Check for Updates (Recommended) radio button and click Next.

8. Select the Secure mode radio button and click Next.

9. Select up to five of the antivirus engines listed, or accept the five random preselected engines and click Next (see Figure 21.21).

10. In the Engine Updates Required page, click Next.

11. In the Proxy Server page, enter proxy server information if needed (probably will not be needed) and click Next.

12. In the Choose Destination Location page, click Browse to choose a different installation location, or accept the default installation path and click Next.

13. In the Select Program Folder page, accept the defaults and click Next.

14. In the Start Copying Files page, click Next.

15. In the Restart Exchange Transport Services page, click Next.

16. In the Recycling Exchange Transport Services page, wait until the message All Services Started appears, then click Next.

17. Click Finish to complete the installation.

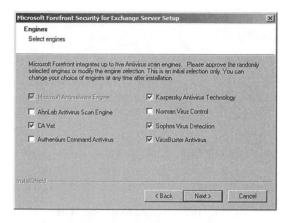

FIGURE 21.21   Select the antivirus engines for Forefront to use.

Following installation, a hotfix needs to be installed. From the same folder where you ran setup.exe, right-click on resetclientsid.exe and select Run as Administrator. After you click Continue in the User Account Control prompt, the hotfix installs, but there is no user interaction or indication that the installation completed successfully.

The last piece to the Forefront Security for Exchange installation is to apply the SBS-specific configuration for FSE. Follow these steps to complete the configuration:

1. From the Start menu, right-click Command Prompt and select Run as Administrator.

2. Change the directory to C:\Program Files (x86)\Microsoft Forefront Security\Exchange Server.

3. Type **FSCStarter.exe tlscfn C:\Program Files\Windows Small Business Server\Data\SBSForefrontTemplate.fdb** and press Enter. There will be no indication of success or failure.

4. Open the FSE Administative Console from Start, All Programs, Microsoft Forefront Server Security, Exchange Server, Forefront Server Security Administration.

5. Click Continue in the User Access Control prompt.

6. Select the SBS server from the drop-down list (it should be the only server listed) and click OK.

7. In the License Notice window, click OK.

8. Under the Settings tab, click General Options.

9. Scroll down to the Scanning section and adjust the following settings:

   a. Enable the Scan Doc Files as Containers—Manual checkbox.

   b. Enable the Scan Doc Files as Containers—Transport checkbox.

   c. Enable the Scan Doc Files as Containers—Realtime checkbox.

   d. Enable the Scan on Scanner Update (affects performance) checkbox.

    e. Change the Transport Process Count to 2.

    f. Change the Realtime Process Count to 2.

10. Under the Background Scanning section, disable the Enable Background Scan if 'Scan on Scanner Update' Enabled checkbox.

11. Click Save in the bottom right corner of the Forefront Server Security Administrator window.

12. Click Operate, and then click Schedule Job.

13. Check that the VSAPI Background Scan Job is enabled and scheduled to run at 4 am daily.

14. Close Forefront Server Security Administration.

You can confirm proper operation of FSE by looking on the Security tab of the Windows SBS Console. You will see an entry for Virus Protection for E-Mail provided by Forefront Security for Exchange Server.

Windows Live OneCare for Server

The installer for Windows Live OneCare for Server is located on the second installation DVD in the \CMPNENTS\ONECARE folder. The installer file is OCSetup.exe, but you must run the installer with several flags to get the full 120-day trial period. If you simply double-click the OCSetup.exe file, OneCare for Server will install, but you will only get ten days for the evaluation. Follow these steps to install Windows Live OneCare for Server with the full 120-day evaluation period:

1. Open a command prompt.

2. Change into the \CMPNENTS\ONECARE directory on the installation DVD.

3. Type **OCSetup /OEM /b /SBSOneCareServer /vendor /MicrosoftSBS** and press Enter. Make sure you match the case in the command.

4. The installation will proceed as shown in Figure 21.22.

5. When the OneCare installer completes, close the command prompt and restart the server.

NOTE

You can also download a 120-day trial of Windows Live OneCare for Server from http://onecare.lice.com/standard/en-us/server/install_server.htm.

After the server restarts, you can confirm that Windows Live OneCare for Server installed correctly by looking at the Windows SBS Console. In the Security tab, you will see an entry for Server virus and spyware protection with the source Windows Live OneCare for Server.

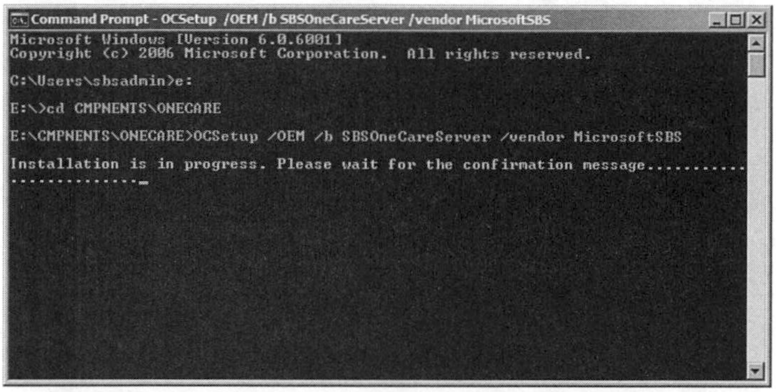

FIGURE 21.22   Windows Live OneCare for Server setup process.

Summary

This chapter provided insight into the installation answer file that can be used to customize an SBS 2008 installation. The answer file is needed for performing migrations from SBS 2003 networks, installations of SBS 2008 into non-SBS 2003 networks, and changing the .local internal domain name requirement. Although these examples cover many of the installation options for SBS 2008, there are many other installation scenarios that could not be covered here. Keep an eye on the SBS 2008 documentation site and the *Windows Small Business Server 2008 Unleashed* book site for updates for other installation scenarios.

Best Practice Summary

▶ **Entering Fully-Customized Setup Mode**—Use an "empty" answer file to trigger setup to go into customized setup mode. This same empty file can be used on every server install to streamline the customized installation process.

▶ **Perform Migration in a Virtual Environment First**—Because the migration process is so complex, testing each migration in a virtual environment prior to performing the migration on the live systems will help identify issues that could cause problems and allow you to identify solutions in advance.

▶ **Create a New Domain Administrator Account**—Before migrating from an existing Active Directory network to SBS 2008, create a new administrative account so that the SBS 2008 setup process can disable the default Administrator account as part of the setup process.

APPENDIX A

SBS 2008 Resources

The following is a list of online resources for materials presented in the book.

Microsoft Community Resources

These resources are hosted and/or developed by Microsoft.

SBS 2008 Technical Documentation

▶ **Microsoft Windows Small Business Server TechCenter**—
http://technet.microsoft.com/en-us/library/cc527559.aspx

▶ **Downloadable documentation for Small Business Server 2008**—
http://technet.microsoft.com/en-us/library/cc707659.aspx

Web Sites and RSS Feeds

▶ **Microsoft Windows Essential Server Solutions family**—
http://www.microsoft.com/windowsserver/essential/default.mspx

▶ **Microsoft Windows Small Business Server 2008**—
http://www.microsoft.com/windowsserver/essential/sbs/default.mspx

▶ **Windows Small Business Server 2003 recent KBs**—
http://support.microsoft.com/common/rss.aspx?rssid=3208&ln=en-us

- ▶ **Windows Server 2008 recent KBs—**
  http://support.microsoft.com/common/rss.aspx?rssid=12925&ln=en-us

- ▶ **Complete Microsoft Product RSS feeds—**
  http://support.microsoft.com/selectindex/?target=rss

- ▶ **Microsoft Small Business community—**
  http://www.mssmallbiz.com/

Newsgroups

- ▶ **SBS 2008 public newsgroup—**
  microsoft.connect.windows.server.sbs08; https://connect.microsoft.com/sbs08/
  community/discussion/richui/default.aspx

- ▶ **SBS 2008 private partner newsgroup (for Microsoft partners, password needed for access)—**
  microsoft.private.directaccess.smallbizserver

Web Logs (Blogs)

- ▶ **Windows Small Business Server documentation—**
  http://blogs.msdn.com/sbsdocsteam/

- ▶ **The Official SBS support blog—**
  http://blogs.technet.com/sbs/

Small Business Community Resources

The following non-Microsoft resources pertain to the small business market as a whole.

Web Sites/Blogs

- ▶ **SmallBizServer.net—**
  http://www.smallbizserver.net

- ▶ **Amy Babinchak [Forefront MVP]—**
  http://securesmb.harborcomputerservices.net

- ▶ **Tim Barrett [SBS MVP]—**
  http://www.nogeekleftbehind.com/

- ▶ **Susan Bradley [SBS MVP]—**
  http://www.sbsdiva.com/

- ▶ **Dean Calvert [SBS MVP]—**
  http://msmvps.com/calvert/

▶ **Sean Daniel—**
http://seanda.blogspot.com/

▶ **Dana Epp [Security MVP]—**
http://silverstr.ufies.org/blog/

▶ **Eriq Oliver Neale [SBS MVP]—**
http://simultaneouspancakes.com/Lessons/
http://msmvps.com/blogs/OnQ/

▶ **Daniel Petri—**
http://www.petri.co.il

▶ **Windows IT Pro magazine—**
http://www.windowsitpro.com/

▶ **Third Tier—**
http://www.thirdtier.net

Mailing Lists

▶ **SBS2k Yahoo group, Microsoft SBS 4.5, 2000, 2003, and 2008 support—**
http://groups.yahoo.com/group/sbs2k
Sbs2k@yahoogroups.com

▶ **SmallBizIT Yahoo group, Small Business IT consultants—**
http://groups.yahoo.com/group/smallbizIT
smallbizit@yahoogroups.com

▶ **SMBManagedServices Yahoo group, Small Business IT consultants—**
http://groups.yahoo.com/group/SMBManagedServices
SMBManagedServices@yahoogroups.com

▶ **SBS group leads Yahoo group, international SBS IT professional groups, leader's group—**
http://groups.yahoo.com/group/newSBSgroups
SBSgroupLEADS@yahoogroups.com

▶ **MSSmallbiz—**
http://groups.yahoo.com/group/mssmallbiz/
mssmallbiz@yahoogroups.com

Exchange Resources

▶ **Technical resources for Exchange Server—**
http://technet.microsoft.com/en-us/exchange/default.aspx

▶ **You Had Me at EHLO, the Exchange team blog—**
http://msexchangeteam.com/

▶ **MSExchange.org—**Microsoft Exchange Server resource site:
http://www.msexchange.org/

▶ **Exchange 2007—**Mailbox Server Storage Design:
http://technet.microsoft.com/en-us/library/bb738147.aspx

▶ **Slipstick—**Exchange and Outlook resource site:
http://www.slipstick.com

▶ **Test Exchange Connectivity—**
http://www.testexchangeconnectivity.com

Macintosh Resources

Web Pages and RSS Feeds

▶ **MacWindows:Integrating Macintosh and Windows—**
http://www.macwindows.com/

▶ **MacFixIt:Troubleshooting solutions for the Macintosh—**
http://www.macfixit.com/

▶ **Macintosh news network—**
http://macnn.com

▶ **Apple discussion forums—**
http://discussions.info.apple.com/

▶ **MacInTouch home page—**
http://www.macintouch.com/

▶ **Mac OS X hints—**
http://www.macosxhints.com/

▶ **MacForumz—**
http://www.macforumz.com/

Newsgroups

▶ **Microsoft Entourage newsgroup—**microsoft.public.mac.office.entourage:
http://www.microsoft.com/communities/newsgroups/en-us/
default.aspx?dg=microsoft.public.mac.office.entourage

▶ **Microsoft Remote Desktop Client for Macintosh newsgroup—**
microsoft.public.mac.rdc:
http://www.microsoft.com/communities/newsgroups/en-us/
default.aspx?dg=microsoft.public.mac.rdc

▶ **Microsoft newsgroup for other Mac products—**
microsoft.public.mac.otherproducts:
http://www.microsoft.com/communities/newsgroups/en-us/
default.aspx?dg=microsoft.public.mac.otherproducts

▶ **Other Macintosh-related Newsgroups—**
alt.mac
comp.sys.mac.
Microsoft.public.mac.general

Mailing Lists

▶ **MacUserGroup Yahoo group—**
http://tech.groups.yahoo.com/group/MacUserGroup/

▶ **AllMacs Yahoo group—**
http://groups.yahoo.com/group/allmacs/

iPhone Resources

▶ **iPhone and iPod Touch Enterprise Deployment Guide—**
http://manuals.info.apple.com/en_US/Enterprise_Deployment_Guide.pdf

▶ **How to Configure iPhone to Connect with Exchange—**
http://simultaneouspancakes.com/Lessons/2008/07/12/connecting-iphone-20-to-an-
exchange-server/

Outlook Resources

▶ **Managing Outlook Anywhere—**
http://technet.microsoft.com/en-us/library/bb123513(EXCHG.80).aspx

▶ **Comparison grid of Microsoft Office 2007 versions—**
http://office.microsoft.com/en-us/products/FX101635841033.aspx

▶ **Administering the offline address book in Outlook 2003 and Outlook 2007—**
http://support.microsoft.com/kb/841273

▶ **How to configure the size limit for both (.pst) and (.ost) files in Outlook 2007
and in Outlook 2003—**
http://support.microsoft.com/kb/832925

▶ **Troubleshooting Autodiscover Service—**
http://support.microsoft.com/kb/940881

Outlook Web Access Resources

▶ **Managing Outlook Web Access—**
http://technet.microsoft.com/en-us/library/aa996373(EXCHG.80).aspx

▶ **Outlook Web Access Training Videos—**
http://www.microsoft.com/exchange/code/OWA/index.html

ActiveSync/PocketPC Resources

▸ **Managing Exchange ActiveSync—**
http://technet.microsoft.com/en-us/library/bb124396(EXCHG.80).aspx

▸ **Test Exchange Connectivity—**
http://www.testexchangeconnectivity.com

▸ **Download ActiveSync 4.5—**
http://www.microsoft.com/windowsmobile/en-us/help/synchronize/activesync45.mspx

▸ **Download Windows Mobile Device Center—**
http://www.microsoft.com/windowsmobile/en-us/help/synchronize/device-center.mspx

▸ **Download Windows Mobile 5.0 with MSFP Device Emulator—**
http://www.microsoft.com/downloads/details.aspx?familyid=c62d54a5-183a-4a1e-a7e2-cc500ed1f19a&displaylang=en

▸ **Download Windows Mobile 6.0 Device Emulator—**
http://www.microsoft.com/DownLoads/details.aspx?familyid=38C46AA8-1DD7-426F-A913-4F370A65A582&displaylang=en

▸ **Download Windows Mobile 6.1 Device Emulator—**
http://www.microsoft.com/downloads/details.aspx?FamilyId=3D6F581E-C093-4B15-AB0C-A2CE5BFFDB47&displaylang=en

▸ **Installing and Running Windows Mobile Emulators—**
http://msexchangeteam.com/archive/2007/09/17/447033.aspx

▸ **Windows Mobile Training—**
http://www.windowsmobiletraining.com

▸ **Exchange ActiveSync Update for Palm Treo Phones—**
http://www.palm.com/us/software/eas_update/

SBS Monitoring and Reporting Resources

▸ **SBS 2008 Code Plex site—**
http://www.codeplex.com/sbs

▸ **SBS 2008 Reporting Plugins—**
http://sbsdeveloper.com/Plugins/SamplePlugins.htm

▸ **Windows Small Business Server 2008 SDK—**
http://msdn.microsoft.com/en-us/library/cc721712.aspx

Group Policy Resources

▸ **Group Policy—Microsoft—**Contains webcasts, whitepapers, and links about using/configuring Group Policy. See http://technet.microsoft.com/en-us/windowsserver/grouppolicy/default.aspx

▶ **Managing terminal servers using Group Policy**—Provides in-depth information and suggestions for locking down terminal servers using group policy. See http://www.microsoft.com/windowsserver2003/techinfo/overview/lockdown.mspx

▶ **Client-side extension downloads**— http://support.microsoft.com/kb/943729

▶ **Security filtering using GPMC**— http://technet.microsoft.com/en-us/library/cc781988.aspx

▶ **Group policy loopback processing**— http://support.microsoft.com/kb/231287

▶ **Using loopback processing to manage terminal servers**— http://support.microsoft.com/kb/260370

▶ **Group policy preference item-level targeting**— http://technet.microsoft.com/en-us/library/cc733022.aspx

▶ **Use Group Policy Software Installation to deploy the 2007 Office system**— http://technet.microsoft.com/en-us/library/cc179214.aspx

▶ **How administrators can use Office policy templates together with the Group Policy settings of Windows**— http://support.microsoft.com/kb/924617

▶ **Configure Cached Exchange Mode Group Policy settings in Outlook 2007**— http://technet.microsoft.com/en-us/library/cc179175.aspx

PowerShell Resources

Web Resources

▶ **Microsoft Script Center**— http://www.microsoft.com/technet/scriptcenter/default.mspx

▶ **TechNet Magazine PowerShell Resources**— http://technet.microsoft.com/en-us/magazine/cc135908.aspx

▶ **Keith Hill's PowerShell Blog: Four Key Cmdlets**— http://keithhill.spaces.live.com/blog/cns!5A8D2641E0963A97!788.entry

▶ **PowerShell Community Resource**— http://www.powershellcommunity.org

▶ **PowerShell Central Resource**— http://www.powershellcentral.com

▶ **Microsoft PowerShell Guide on Codeplex**— http://www.codeplex.com/PsObject/Wiki/View.aspx?title=PSH%20Community%20Guide&referringTitle=Home

- ▶ **Quest Active Directory Cmdlets**—
  http://www.quest.com/activeroles-server/arms.aspx

- ▶ **SpecOps Command PowerShell Group Policy Tool**—
  http://www.specopssoft.com/powershell/

- ▶ **PowerShell Scriptomatic**—
  http://www.microsoft.com/downloads/details.aspx?FamilyID=d87daf50-e487-4b0b-995c-f36a2855016e&DisplayLang=en

Books

- ▶ *PowerShell Unleashed* by Tyson Kopczynski—
  http://www.informit.com/store/product.aspx?isbn=0672329530

- ▶ *Windows PowerShell in Action* by Bruce Payette—
  http://www.manning.com/payette/

- ▶ *Windows PowerShell Cookbook* by Lee Holmes—
  http://oreilly.com/catalog/9780596528492/

- ▶ *Windows PowerShell TFM* by Don Jones and Jeffery Hicks—
  http://www.sapienpress.com/powershell2.asp

RRAS, VPN, and Network Security Resources

- ▶ **Discussion of GRE Protocol 47**—
  http://support.microsoft.com/kb/241251

- ▶ **Description of options in RDP Session file**—
  http://support.microsoft.com/kb/885187

- ▶ **Discussion of methods for programmatically creating RDP session files**—
  http://blogs.msdn.com/powershell/archive/2008/09/14/rdp-file-generation-use-of-here-strings.aspx

- ▶ **AuthAnvil Two-Factor Authentication**—
  http://www.authanvil.com

Terminal Server Resources

- ▶ **Windows Server Terminal Services home**—
  http://technet.microsoft.com/en-us/windowsserver/terminal-services/default.aspx

- ▶ **Terminal Services step-by-step guides**—
  http://technet.microsoft.com/en-us/library/cc770702.aspx

- ▶ **Remote Desktop Protocol Resources**—
  http://en.wikipedia.org/wiki/Remote_Desktop_Protocol

▶ Remote Desktop Client for the Macintosh—
http://www.microsoft.com/mac/products/remote-desktop/default.mspx

Workstation Security Resources

▶ BitLocker Drive Encryption—
http://technet.microsoft.com/en-us/windows/aa905065.aspx

▶ Download Microsoft Virtual PC 2007—
http://www.microsoft.com/downloads/details.aspx?FamilyID=04d26402-3199-48a3-afa2-2dc0b40a73b6&DisplayLang=en

Anti-Virus/Anti-Malware Tools

Free Online Scanning Tools

▶ F-Secure online scanner—
http://support.f-secure.com/enu/home/ols.shtml

▶ Authentium Command on Demand—
http://www.commandondemand.com/

▶ WindowsSecurity.com trojan scanner—
http://www.windowsecurity.com/trojanscan/

▶ TrendMicro HouseCall—
http://housecall.trendmicro.com/

▶ Symantec Security Check—
http://security.symantec.com/

▶ Windows Live OneCare safety scanner—
http://onecare.live.com/site/en-US/default.htm

Free Anti-Virus Programs (Includes Evaluation Versions and Cleanup Tools for Specific Outbreaks)

▶ Malwarebytes Anti-Malware—
http://www.malwarebytes.org/mbam.php

▶ Malwarebytes RogueRemover Free—
http://www.malwarebytes.org/rogueremover.php

▶ Sophos evaluation version—
http://www.sophos.com/products/small-business/eval.html

▶ AntiVir Personal Edition Classic—
http://www.free-av.com/antivirus/allinonen.html

▶ AVG Anti-Virus Free Edition—
http://free.avg.com.

▶ F-Prot Anti-Virus for Windows trial version—
http://www.f-prot.com/download/corporate/trial/

734 A SBS 2008 Resources
734   A   SBS 2008 Resources

▶ NOD32 trial version—
http://www.eset.com/download/index.php

▶ McAfee Stinger—
http://vil.nai.com/vil/stinger/

▶ Trend Micro Sysclean—
http://www.trendmicro.com/download/dcs.asp

Security Response Toolkit

▶ NetCat—
http://netcat.sourceforge.net/
http://www.securityfocus.com/tools/139

▶ Sysinternals AccessEnum—
http://technet.microsoft.com/en-us/sysinternals/bb897332.aspx

▶ Sysinternals AutoRuns—
http://technet.microsoft.com/en-us/sysinternals/bb963902.aspx

▶ Sysinternals Contig—
http://technet.microsoft.com/en-us/sysinternals/bb897428.aspx

▶ Sysinternals DiskView—
http://technet.microsoft.com/en-us/sysinternals/bb896650.aspx

▶ Sysinternals FileMon—
http://technet.microsoft.com/en-us/sysinternals/bb896642.aspx

▶ Sysinternals ListDLLs—
http://technet.microsoft.com/en-us/sysinternals/bb896656.aspx.

▶ Sysinternals Page Defrag—
http://technet.microsoft.com/en-us/sysinternals/bb897426.aspx

▶ Sysinternals ProcessExplorer—
http://technet.microsoft.com/en-us/sysinternals/bb896653.aspx

▶ Sysinternals PS Tools—
http://technet.microsoft.com/en-us/sysinternals/bb896649.aspx

▶ Sysinternals RegMon—
http://technet.microsoft.com/en-us/sysinternals/bb896652.aspx

▶ Sysinternals Rootkit Revealer—
http://technet.microsoft.com/en-us/sysinternals/bb897445.aspx

▶ Sysinternals Sdelete—
http://technet.microsoft.com/en-us/sysinternals/bb897443.aspx

▶ Sysinternals ShareEnum—
http://technet.microsoft.com/en-us/sysinternals/bb897442.aspx

- ▶ **Sysinternals Sync—**
  http://technet.microsoft.com/en-us/sysinternals/bb897438.aspx

- ▶ **Sysinternals TCPView—**
  http://technet.microsoft.com/en-us/sysinternals/bb897437.aspx

- ▶ **Heysoft LADS—**
  http://www.heysoft.de/Frames/f_sw_la_en.htm

- ▶ **myNetWatchman SecCheck—**
  http://www.mynetwatchman.com/tools/sc/

- ▶ **Inetcat.org NBTScan—**
  http://www.inetcat.org/software/nbtscan.html

- ▶ **FoundStone BinText—**
  http://www.foundstone.com/index.htm?subnav=resources/navigation.htm&subcontent=/resources/freetools.htm

- ▶ **WinPcap—**
  http://www.winpcap.org/install/default.htm

- ▶ **WinDump—**
  http://www.winpcap.org/windump/

- ▶ **Wireshark Installer—**
  http://www.wireshark.org/download.html

- ▶ **Nmap—**
  http://www.insecure.org/nmap/

- ▶ **Tigerteam.se SBD (encrypted netcat)—**
  http://tigerteam.se/dl/sbd/

- ▶ **BlackIce PC Protection—**
  http://www.digitalriver.com/dr/v2/ec_dynamic.main?SP=1&PN=10&sid=26412

- ▶ **CPU-Z—**
  http://www.cpuid.com/cpuz.php

- ▶ **ISCAlert—**
  http://www.labreatechnologies.com/

Security and Patching Resources

- ▶ **Windows Vista Security Guide—**
  http://technet.microsoft.com/en-us/library/bb629420.aspx

General Security Information

- ▶ **Microsoft security advisories—**
  http://www.microsoft.com/technet/security/advisory/default.mspx

▶ **MSRC blog**—
http://blogs.technet.com/msrc/

▶ **Full disclosure**—
https://lists.grok.org.uk/mailman/listinfo/full-disclosure

▶ **Daily Dave**—
https://lists.immunitysec.com/mailman/listinfo/dailydave

▶ **Metasploit RSS feed**—
http://www.metasploit.com/

▶ **OSVDB mailing list**—
http://www.osvdb.org/mailing-lists.php

▶ **Ntbugtraq**—
http://www.ntbugtraq.com/

▶ **SecuriTeam**—
http://www.securiteam.com/mailinglist.html

▶ **SecurityFocus mailing lists**—
http://www.securityfocus.com/archive

WSUS Resources

▶ **Technet Update Management TechCenter**—
http://technet.microsoft.com/en-us/updatemanagement/default.aspx

▶ **WSUS listserver**—
http://www.patchmanagement.org

▶ **WSUS community forum**—
http://www.wsus.info/default.asp

▶ **WSUS wiki**—
http://www.wsuswiki.com/

▶ **WSUS download**—
http://www.microsoft.com/windowsserversystem/updateservices/default.mspx

▶ **WSUS blog**—
http://blogs.technet.com/wsus/

▶ **WSUS MVP blog**—
http://msmvps.com/athif/

Index

Symbols

A

M

X–Z

UNLEASHED

Unleashed takes you beyond the basics, providing an exhaustive, technically sophisticated reference for professionals who need to exploit a technology to its fullest potential. It's the best resource for practical advice from the experts, and the most in-depth coverage of the latest technologies.

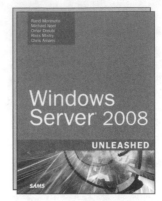

Windows Server 2008 Unleashed
ISBN-13: 978-0-672-32930-2

OTHER UNLEASHED TITLES

ASP.NET 3.5 Unleashed
ISBN-13: 978-0-672-33011-7

C# 3.0 Unleashed
ISBN-13: 978-0-672-32981-4

LINQ Unleashed
ISBN-13: 978-0-672-32983-8

Microsoft Dynamics CRM 4.0 Unleashed
ISBN-13: 978-0-672-32970-8

Microsoft Exchange Server 2007 Unleashed
ISBN-13: 978-0-672-32920-3

Microsoft Expression Blend Unleashed
ISBN-13: 978-0-672-32931-9

Microsoft ISA Server 2006 Unleashed
ISBN-13: 978-0-672-32919-7

Microsoft Office Project Server 2007 Unleashed
ISBN-13: 978-0-672-32921-0

Microsoft SharePoint 2007 Development Unleashed
ISBN-13: 978-0-672-32903-6

Microsoft SQL Server 2005 Unleashed
ISBN-13: 978-0-672-32824-4

Microsoft Visual Studio 2008 Unleashed
ISBN-13: 978-0-672-32972-2

Microsoft XNA Unleashed
ISBN-13: 978-0-672-32964-7

Silverlight 2 Unleashed
ISBN-13: 978-0-672-33014-8

VBScript, WMI, and ADSI Unleashed
ISBN-13: 978-0-321-50171-4

Windows Communication Foundation Unleashed
ISBN-13: 978-0-672-32948-7

Windows PowerShell Unleashed
ISBN-13: 978-0-672-32953-1

Windows Presentation Foundation Unleashed
ISBN-13: 978-0-672-32891-6

Windows Server 2008 Hyper-V Unleashed
ISBN-13: 978-0-672-33028-5

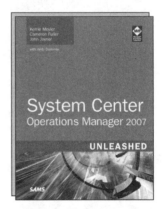

System Center Operations Manager 2007 Unleashed
ISBN-13: 978-0-672-32955-5

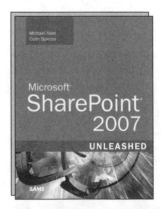

Microsoft SharePoint 2007 Unleashed
ISBN-13: 978-0-672-32947-0

SAMS

informit.com/sams

SAMS

REGISTER

THIS PRODUCT

informit.com/register

Register the Addison-Wesley, Exam Cram, Prentice Hall, Que, and Sams products you own to unlock great benefits.

To begin the registration process, simply go to **informit.com/register** to sign in or create an account. You will then be prompted to enter the 10- or 13-digit ISBN that appears on the back cover of your product.

Registering your products can unlock the following benefits:

- Access to supplemental content, including bonus chapters, source code, or project files.
- A coupon to be used on your next purchase.

Registration benefits vary by product. Benefits will be listed on your Account page under Registered Products.

About InformIT — **THE TRUSTED TECHNOLOGY LEARNING SOURCE**

INFORMIT IS HOME TO THE LEADING TECHNOLOGY PUBLISHING IMPRINTS Addison-Wesley Professional, Cisco Press, Exam Cram, IBM Press, Prentice Hall Professional, Que, and Sams. Here you will gain access to quality and trusted content and resources from the authors, creators, innovators, and leaders of technology. Whether you're looking for a book on a new technology, a helpful article, timely newsletters, or access to the Safari Books Online digital library, InformIT has a solution for you.

informIT.com

THE TRUSTED TECHNOLOGY LEARNING SOURCE

Addison-Wesley | Cisco Press | Exam Cram
IBM Press | Que | Prentice Hall | Sams

SAFARI BOOKS ONLINE

LearnIT at InformIT

Go Beyond the Book

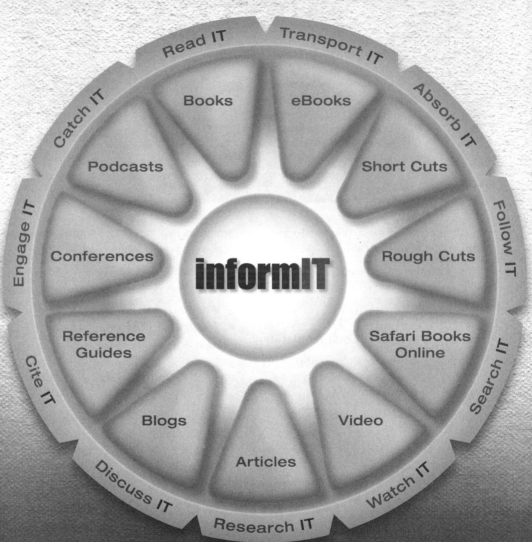

Read IT — Books

Transport IT — eBooks

Absorb IT — Short Cuts

Catch IT — Podcasts

informIT

Follow IT — Rough Cuts

Engage IT — Conferences

Search IT — Safari Books Online

Cite IT — Reference Guides

Discuss IT — Blogs

Research IT — Articles

Watch IT — Video

11 WAYS TO LEARN IT at www.informIT.com/learn

The digital network for the publishing imprints of Pearson Education

 Addison Wesley   Cisco Press   EXAM/CRAM   IBM Press.   que   PRENTICE HALL   SAM

Try Safari Books Online FREE

Get online access to 5,000+ Books and Videos

FREE TRIAL—GET STARTED TODAY!
www.informit.com/safaritrial

Find trusted answers, fast

Only Safari lets you search across thousands of best-selling books from the top technology publishers, including Addison-Wesley Professional, Cisco Press, O'Reilly, Prentice Hall, Que, and Sams.

Master the latest tools and techniques

In addition to gaining access to an incredible inventory of technical books, Safari's extensive collection of video tutorials lets you learn from the leading video training experts.

WAIT, THERE'S MORE!

Keep your competitive edge

With Rough Cuts, get access to the developing manuscript and be among the first to learn the newest technologies.

Stay current with emerging technologies

Short Cuts and Quick Reference Sheets are short, concise, focused content created to get you up-to-speed quickly on new and cutting-edge technologies.

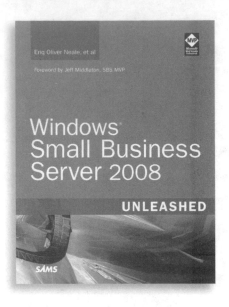

FREE Online Edition

Your purchase of **Windows Small Business Server 2008 Unleashed** includes access to a free online edition for 45 days through the Safari Books Online subscription service. Nearly every Sams book is available online through Safari Books Online, along with more than 5,000 other technical books and videos from publishers such as Addison-Wesley Professional, Cisco Press, Exam Cram, IBM Press, O'Reilly, Prentice Hall, and Que.

SAFARI BOOKS ONLINE allows you to search for a specific answer, cut and paste code, download chapters, and stay current with emerging technologies.

Activate your FREE Online Edition at www.informit.com/safarifree

> **STEP 1:** Enter the coupon code: UHZVGCB.

> **STEP 2:** New Safari users, complete the brief registration form.
> Safari subscribers, just log in.

If you have difficulty registering on Safari or accessing the online edition, please e-mail customer-service@safaribooksonline.com